FILM

AN INTER-NATIONAL HISTORY OF THE MEDIUM

FILM

AN INTER-NATIONAL HISTORY OF THE MEDIUM

By Robert Sklar

Harry N. Abrams, Inc., Publishers

CONTENTS

Shooting The Battle of Paris *(1929) on Paramount's Astoria, N.Y., back lot*

Luis Buñuel and Sergei Eisenstein in Hollywood

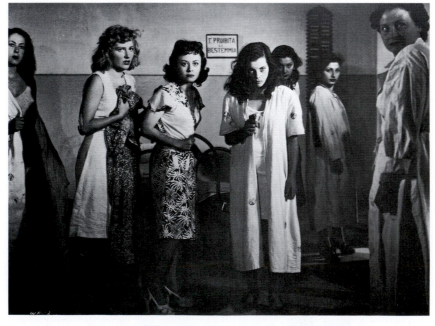

Senza pietà (Without Pity, 1948), *directed by Alberto Lattuada*

Lo sceicco bianco (The White Sheik, *1952), directed by Federico Fellini*

Der Himmel über Berlin (Wings of Desire, 1987), directed by Wim Wenders

Director Spike Lee making She's Gotta Have It *(1986)*

Pages 2–3: Ruth Roland (under umbrella)
directs a garden scene for her Pathé serial
The Adventures of Ruth *(1919–20).*
Below: 2001: A Space Odyssey *(1968),*
directed by Stanley Kubrick

Library of Congress Cataloging-in-Publication Data
  Sklar, Robert.
    Film: an international history of the medium/Robert Sklar.
       p. cm.
    Includes bibliographical references, filmography, and index
    ISBN 0–8109–3321–7
    1. Motion pictures—History   I. Title.
  PN1993.5.A1S55   1993
  791.43'09—dc20   93–12279
                                                                    CIP

Editor: Beverly Fazio
Designer: Robert McKee
Picture Editor: John K. Crowley

Preface and Acknowledgments

Cinema is a medium that refuses boundaries. Filmmakers move between countries; films combine genres; film practices overstep the limits of terms such as documentary, fiction, avant-garde. A history of cinema differs from a dictionary or an encyclopedia in its capacity to make connections, rather than impose categories. The interrelations of the film medium at every level—from craft, artistry, and textual citation to financing, distribution, and exhibition—shape the organization and argument of this book.

Given restrictions of space, how many films make an appropriate number to include in a history of the medium? After attending the inaugural Cannes Film Festival in 1946, French critic and film theorist André Bazin offered this observation: "Out of two or three thousand full-length films produced in the world every year, there are perhaps only about fifteen whose titles are worth remembering, a half dozen that are worthy of mention in the future histories of cinema."

In this book, somewhat more than eleven hundred specific films are mentioned, almost twice as many (extrapolating over cinema's first century) as Bazin deemed worthy. But the criteria for inclusion here are broader than his were at that moment. Bazin was looking for masterpieces. A history of cinema recognizes such great works of art, but also tells a different story: of the medium's manifold levels of pleasure and function, derived from elements such as technology, genre, craft, and performance, and even from its role in political propaganda.

Even so, more than eleven hundred films do not exhaust the list of titles for which strong cases could be made. Many worthy works have had to be excluded, and every reader may recall a favorite film whose title or director does not appear in the text. Some of my own favorites are missing.

Some notes on technicalities:

Film histories vary as to their method of assigning a date to a film; some use year of production, some the year of first public screening (say, at a festival), some the official release date. Julie Dash's *Daughters of the Dust*, for example, was photographed in 1989, edited and completed in 1990, screened at festivals in 1991, and released in 1992. In this book, films are dated according to the year of release in the country of origin (thus *Daughters of the Dust* is dated 1992); occasionally production dates are added to note a gap of years between production and release.

On first mention, film titles are given in the original language, with the English-language release title, if any, in parentheses. In those instances where there is no English-language release title, or when the English title varies greatly from the original, a direct translation is provided in quotation marks.

Illustrations of specific films are either drawn from publicity stills or are frame enlargements. Readers should be aware that publicity stills generally are not actual scenes from films as recorded by motion picture cameras; rather, they are photographs taken by still cameras before, during, or after a motion picture shot. This difference accounts for the frequent discrepancy in angle or movement that may be noted between a publicity still and the shot as it appears in the film.

A history of film depends, to alter a familiar phrase, on the kindness of scholars. In nearly every decade since the cinema emerged, writers have contributed invaluable research or per-

It Happened One Night (1934), *directed by Frank Capra*

sonal observations to our knowledge of the medium. A glance at the Selected Bibliography will suggest how the pace of scholarship has accelerated, and its breadth has expanded, in recent years. This book owes its primary debt to all the historians of cinema, past and present. Perhaps among its readers will be a few who discover here opportunities to develop and revise the always incomplete project of cinema's history.

I want to acknowledge more specifically the remarkable endeavors in film scholarship and screenings by the Italian film organizations Le Giornate del Cinema Muto, in conducting the annual silent film retrospective in Pordenone, and Mostra Internazionale del Nuovo Cinema, organizer of annual festivals in Pesaro and elsewhere, that have influenced and aided film historians from many countries. Among Italian film scholars at these organizations and others, I thank especially Gian Piero Brunetta, Lorenzo Codelli, Giuliana Muscio, and Vito Zagarrio for their support and encouragement.

For innumerable courtesies and assistance in introducing me to Chinese cinema, I thank Professor Cheng Jihua of Beijing, China,

and Chen Mei, of the China Film Association, currently at the Margaret Herrick Library of the Academy of Motion Picture Arts and Sciences, Beverly Hills, California.

My approach to film history and historiography has been developed in mutual exploration with students and colleagues of the Department of Cinema Studies, Tisch School of the Arts, New York University. Ann Harris, Cathy Holter, and their staffs at the department's George Amberg Film Study Center supported this project in many ways. I also received invaluable assistance from Charles Silver and Nancy Barnes of the Film Study Center, Department of Film, and from Mary Corliss and Terry Geeskin of the Film Stills Archive, The Museum of Modern Art, New York. My graduate assistant, Peter Sacks, compiled the Filmography and carried out other important research tasks for the book. Others whom I thank for providing aid and support include Akira Shimizu, General Secretary, Japan Film Library Council, Tokyo; Dr. Kyoko Hirano of Japan Society, New York; Steve Ricci, Bob Gitt, and Eric Aijala of the Film and Television Archive, University of California at Los Angeles; Ellen Alderman, Lizzie Borden, Gary Crowdus, Charles Musser, Maurice Schell, Leo Seltzer, Elena Simon, Martin Sklar, George Stoney, and Norman Wang.

It has been a pleasure to work with the staff of Harry N. Abrams, Inc., on this book. Senior Editor Beverly Fazio and Senior Picture Editor John K. Crowley brought to the project their enthusiasm and their exacting standards, and I am grateful for their commitment. I thank also Paul Gottlieb, Sheila Franklin Lieber, Julia Moore, and Bob McKee.

My daughter, Susan Sklar Friedman, a film editor, improved the book in many ways through her expertise and assistance, and I was supported as well by my other children, Leonard Sklar, Kate Tentler, and Justin Tentler. Adrienne Harris helped me in ways beyond measure. I am grateful to George and Norah Harris for their encouragement.

This book is dedicated to the memory of my mother, Lilyn Fuchs Sklar (1911–1992), and her sister, Frances Fuchs Dolin (1905–1993), whose father screened movies for immigrant audiences in New Brunswick, New Jersey.

Film	Arts and Sciences	World Events
1798 Robertson's Phantasmagorie	*Essay on the Principle of Population* (Malthus)	Battle of the Nile
1839 development of photography	vulcanization of rubber	China, Britain fight Opium War
1861 first color photograph	New York–San Francisco telegraph link	U.S. Civil War begins Italy unified
1872 Muybridge begins experiments	*Middlemarch* (G. Eliot)	Grant wins 2nd term as U.S. President
1876	Bell patents telephone	Battle of the Little Bighorn
1877	Edison patents phonograph	Britain annexes South Africa
1882 Marey's photographic gun	Wagner's *Parsifal*	electric light begins in U.S.
1885 film developed by Eastman	*The Adventures of Huckleberry Finn* (Twain)	transcontinental railway links Canada
1888 Kodak box camera	Van Gogh's *The Sower*	Wilhelm II becomes German Kaiser
1889 celluloid used as roll film base	Eiffel Tower erected in Paris	Oklahoma land rush
1891 Edison's lab makes Kinetograph camera	*Tess of the D'Urbervilles* (Hardy)	Brazil adopts constitution
1892 Reynaud's Théâtre Optique	Burroughs adding machine invented	Populist Party campaigns in U.S.
1893 public showing of Edison Kinetoscope	Munch's *The Scream*	Financial panic in U.S.
1894 first Kinetoscope parlor opened	Marconi builds first radio	Dreyfus case in France
1895 Lumière Cinématograph	*The Time Machine* (Wells)	Japan controls Taiwan
1896 projected films in Britain, U.S.	Puccini's *La Bohème*	McKinley elected U.S. President
1898	Curies dicover radium	Spanish-American War
1900	*The Interpretation of Dreams* (Freud)	Boxer Rebellion in China
1902 *A Trip to the Moon*	air conditioner invented	Boer War ends in South Africa
1903 *The Great Train Robbery*	Wright brothers' first flight	auto industry begins in U.S.
1905 *Rescued by Rover*	Einstein's theory of relativity	upheaval in Russia, mutiny on *Potemkin*
1908 Motion Picture Patents Company	invention of cellophane	Austria annexes Bosnia
1914 *Cabiria*	Panama Canal opens	World War I begins
1915 *The Birth of a Nation*	*The Rainbow* (Lawrence)	sinking of *Lusitania*
1917 Ufa formed	Birdseye develops frozen food	U.S. enters World War I Bolshevik revolution
1919 *The Cabinet of Dr. Caligari*	commercial air service begins	Versailles peace treaty

Part
One

EMERGENCE
OF
CINEMA

CINEMA, SOCIETY,

We should be wary of talking about origins. The medium of motion pictures (which here as elsewhere will be variously and interchangeably called film, cinema, the movies) is a case in point. While we seek to pinpoint exact beginnings to celebrate anniversaries and centennials, the fact remains that large-screen projection of multiple moving images forming a narrative has existed for centuries, delivered by a variety of technologies. Claiming to specify where things started begs more questions than it answers. Let us speak instead of an *emergence*—of cinema arising in a particular moment out of a prior history, to captivate and dominate an epoch, and destined perhaps to stand as prehistory to some other medium of moving images preparing in turn to emerge.

THE PREHISTORY OF CINEMA

A shift away from an emphasis on origins casts new light on cinema's prehistory—the period of motion picture devices and entertainments before the development of filmmaking apparatus in the 1890s. It makes possible a way of thinking about the past that does not treat the narrative of time as, inevitably, a story of progress: as if we stood on the shoulders of our ancestors, growing bigger and better with each new generation. Earlier in time does not have to mean, as it sometimes has in modern histories, less sophisticated, less civilized, more crude. While our machinery undoubtedly has grown more sophisticated, the same is not necessarily the case for human mind or character, or for people's capacity to experience what they have in complex and sophisti-

cated ways. We would do well to regard earlier times not as diminished in relation to our own, but simply in some ways different.

When this principle is applied to cinema's prehistory, what becomes apparent is a rich and varied world of screen presentations in the time before movies. If the cinema was something new for spectators of the 1890s, seeing larger-than-life projections of still and moving images was not. In Asia, shadow puppets formed a part of popular entertainment and ceremonies for centuries; their most widely known manifestation appeared on the Indonesian island of Java, where intricately perforated puppets made of thin leather, in lamplight, cast filigree shadows. Different kinds of screen entertainment appeared in early modern Europe. Inventors in the Netherlands in the mid-seventeenth century used the sun as a light source (or at night, light from a candle) to project images painted on a reflecting surface through a **lens** onto a wall. Within a few years others had devised a projector which contained light source, image, and lens all in one portable apparatus. This was called the Magic Lantern.

Magic Lanterns

Over the next two centuries magic lanterns and their entertainments became more and more elaborate. One of the most impressive magic lantern presentations was the Fantasmagorie (known in English as Phantasmagoria) staged by a Belgian, Étienne Gaspar Robert (1763–1837), who went by the name Robertson. It premiered in Paris in 1798 and later toured Europe. With his audience on one side of a translucent screen, Robertson on the other side had his lantern mounted on wheels. Moving the lantern,

1.1. Long before motion pictures began in the late nineteenth century, multiple-image screen entertainment played a significant role in popular culture. A travel-ing exhibitor brings his "peep-show" to a German country fair in an 1843 lithograph by F. Schlotterbeck.

AND SCIENCE

adjusting the lens to maintain focus, and using a shutter for dis-solves, Robertson projected a macabre specter of skeletons, ghosts, and other frightening figures simulating lifelike motion.

The development in subsequent years of dual- and even triple-lens projectors made it possible for operators to surpass Robertson's spectacle without having to match his athleticism. These machines smoothed the transition from image to image, enabling lanternists to construct complex narratives out of multi-ple slides in a manner not unlike a sequence of shots in a movie. Magic lantern entrepreneurs put together a full evening's program with segments such as travel scenes, popular science, art appreci-ation, comedy, and melodrama.

Motion Toys

As screen entertainment for public consumption expanded in the years before cinema, so too did devices proliferate for enjoying moving images privately in the home. These are often thought of merely as toys: small portable units that came with disks or paper strips containing a sequence of images which, when set in motion, gave the illusion of movement. Yet their origins lay in sci-entific experimentation. Scientists in the 1820s became intrigued with a phenomenon they called persistence of vision—the eye's capacity to retain a visual image after its source has been removed. A paper by Peter Mark Roget (1779–1869, famous later for his *Thesaurus*) prompted several efforts to construct mecha-nisms that could turn separate still pictures into a single moving image. Though the concept of persistence of vision continues to appear in film histories, the term is no longer accepted in the field of perceptual psychology; the eye's capacity to retain a visual

image has become known as "positive afterimages," and its con-nection to the perception of apparent motion is not clear.[1] No one disputes, however, that motion toys produce the illusion of motion.

Their inventors gave these devices high-sounding, tongue-twisting names. The Thaumatrope (1826, attributed to John Ayrton Paris) was simply a round card attached to a string, with separate but related drawings on either side: for example, a horse on one, a rider on the other; when the card was spun, the rider appeared to be riding the horse. The Phenakistoscope (early 1830s, several inventors) was a plate-sized, slotted disk with a sequence of draw-ings around its circle; when the disk was spun in front of a mirror, a person looking through the slots would see the drawings appear to move. The Zoetrope (1860s, also several inventors) was a bowl-like device with a strip of drawings around the interior circumference; when the bowl was spun, viewers peered through slots in the sides to watch the drawings seemingly in motion. (The name Zoetrope resurfaced in the 1970s when the United States producer-director Francis Ford Coppola used it for his production company and studio.) The Praxinoscope, developed in the 1870s in France by Émile Reynaud (1844–1918), was like a Zoetrope only it also utilized mirrors.

Théâtre Optique

The instruments soon outgrew the home. They began to compete with magic lanterns in the public entertainment sphere. Reynaud, after inventing the Praxinoscope, developed a projecting version, using a reflector and a lens to enlarge the apparatus's moving images (on the same principles of projection that had been used

1.2. A magic lantern with three lenses, enabling an operator to construct narratives out of a considerable number of separate slides in a sequence of images comparable to edited shots in later movies

1.3. A magic lantern operator carries his apparatus on his back and bangs a tambourine to attract attention, as depicted in a nineteenth-century lithograph.

1.4. The magic lantern was a device for home as well as public entertainment: H. G. Hine projects images on a wall in a lithograph from 1870.

for still images as far back as the seventeenth century). Continuing his efforts, he constructed the Théâtre Optique, an even more sophisticated projection system. He drew pictures on long bands which wound through the apparatus much like a **reel** of film moves through its own projecting device; his individual narratives contained up to seven hundred separate drawings, and went on for fifteen minutes. The Théâtre Optique made its debut in Paris in 1892 and lasted until 1900, when it was undone by competition from the cinema.

As screen entertainment, the Théâtre Optique fell just short of what cinema was to provide. Only its lack of a catchy name may

have kept it from enduring fame as a symbol of technological futility, like the Stanley Steamer, the steam-driven automobile that failed the challenge of the internal-combustion engine.

RECORDED MOVEMENT

What Reynaud's device lacked was images of movement recorded at the source. Ever since the development of still photography in the 1830s, inventors had been exploring ways to take a sequence

1.5. The Phenakistoscope was one of the earliest of the nineteenth-century motion toys. A slotted disk with a sequence of drawings was placed in a device that rotated the disk; viewed

through a mirror, the rotating drawings appeared as a single moving image. The apparatus is attributed to several inventors; this one was made by the French optician Jules Duboscq.

1.6. A Phenakistoscope disk by S. W. Fores, London, 1833

1.7. A disk made by the Austrian inventor Simon Stampfer for his machine, which he called the Stroboscope

Panoramas and Dioramas

While we focus inevitably on the late nineteenth century's historic transformation of moving image technology and culture, the end of the eighteenth century also marked significant innovation in screen entertainment. The era of the 1780s–90s saw not only Robertson's Fantasmagorie and other enhanced magic lantern programs, but also the panorama, a large-scale painting designed to take up the complete interior circumference of a circular building. What is credited as the first of these opened in Edinburgh, Scotland, in 1788, and the idea spread to London and France. (On this principle, the Walt Disney company opened at its Disneyland park in 1955 a circular moving image photographed by eleven cameras, called Circarama.) Strictly speaking, the early panoramas were not moving images, but smaller-scale versions were produced for home use, some on scrolls which could be unrolled to create an illusion of movement.

In the early nineteenth century an element of "movement" was introduced into public exhibitions of static pictures through the diorama. (One of its developers was Louis Jacques Mandé Daguerre [1789–1851], who later became an inventor of photography.) The diorama involved either a single painting or a canvas painted on both sides. Audiences sat in front of the work as shifts in lighting produced changes in the image. In the case of two-sided paintings especially, diorama shows offered narratives of visual spectacle—changes in the weather, in seasons, from day to night—that effected substantial transformations and lasted up to fifteen minutes with a single work.

As with the panorama, the magic lantern, and motion toys, the diorama concept was developed into products for home entertainment. A popular diorama toy was the Polyrama Panoptique, a viewing box into which pairs of slides could be inserted. By manipulating a hinged lid, the viewer could shift the light so as to effect a visual transformation.

1.8, 1.9. A typical shift was from day to night. This pair of slides for the Polyrama Panoptique, dated 1851, depicts the Paris-to-Rouen railway line (another new technological wonder of the era). The tracks are empty for the daylight scene, while at night the train speeds through, engine smoking.

1.10, 1.11. Another type of transformation was from exterior to interior. This pair of Polyrama Panoptique slides, also from 1851, shows the Palais Royal in Paris. Unlike the railway views, this subject also involves a change in spectator perspective.

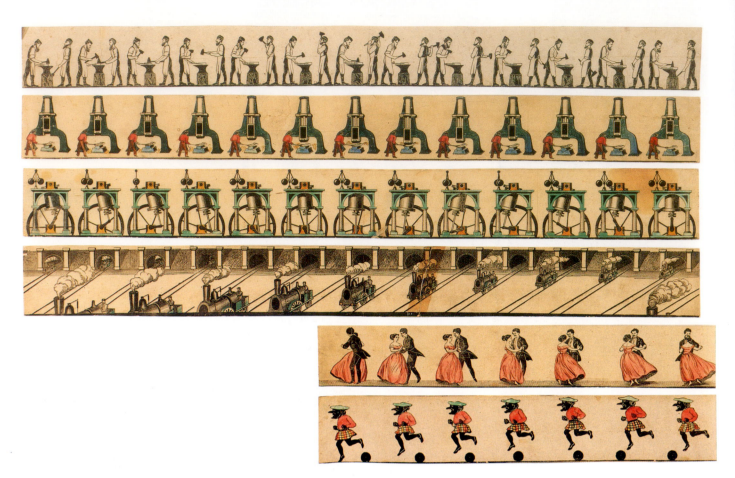

1.12. These are examples of Zoetrope strips, which would be attached to the interior of the Zoetrope, a bowl-shaped device invented in the 1860s. When the bowl was rotated, the drawings, viewed through slots in the side of the bowl, appeared to move.

of photographs rapidly enough to record a movement in all its phases, not just arrest a single image. These efforts gained the substantial support in the 1870s of the railroad tycoon and former governor of California Leland Stanford, who was determined to find out whether a trotting horse ever had all four legs off the ground at the same time. To settle the question, he hired British émigré Eadweard Muybridge (1830–1904), well-known in California as a wilderness photographer.

Muybridge's Horse

Muybridge's famous experiments, begun in 1872, culminated in 1878 with a sequence of photographs that proved, yes, a horse did have all four legs raised at once. He placed twelve cameras in a row alongside a track, spread threads across the track, and attached them to a contact with each camera's shutter. As the horse moved, its legs broke the threads, causing the cameras to operate in sequence. The result was a dozen photographs showing successive phases of a horse's gait. Within a year he expanded the system to twenty-four cameras with timed electronic controls, which made the sequence more accurate than the thread method. The international acclaim for Muybridge's

achievements prompted him to go out on the lecture circuit, and he joined the world of screen entertainment with his own version of a magic lantern device, the Zoopraxiscope. This was a projecting version of the Phenakistoscope, using rotating disks on which were painted images of horses in motion drawn from his sequence photographs (he discovered, however, that he had to elongate the drawings in order for the projected illusion of movement to look "natural"). Over the next decade he greatly publicized the possibilities for sequence photography of motion.

Étienne-Jules Marey

Among many whom Muybridge stimulated was the French scientist Étienne-Jules Marey (1830–1904), a specialist in animal motion. When he utilized the photographer's methods, however, Marey found them inadequate for recording birds in flight. He adopted a device developed by an astronomer, Pierre-Jules-César Janssen (1824–1907), for recording the transit of the planet Venus across the sun. Marey's version, developed in 1882, was a "photographic gun" equipped with a disk functioning as a shutter to record sequential images on a rotating photographic plate. This worked well to capture the flight of birds, but it was limited to

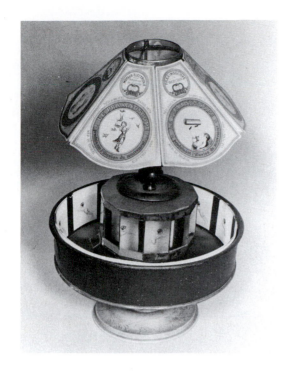

Left: 1.13. The Praxinoscope, developed by Émile Reynaud in France in the 1870s, utilized the principle of the Zoetrope, though the drawings were viewed through mirrors to produce (as promised on the lampshade) the illusion of movement.

Below: 1.14. Elaborating on the concept of the projecting Praxinoscope, Reynaud constructed a machine to project large-screen images before a theater audience, which he called the Théâtre Optique. An 1889 drawing from La Nature illustrates its operation.

twelve separate images. As a next step, Marey devised a stationary camera (called a chronophotographic camera) that could take a considerably greater number of images superimposed on one another, producing a single picture of motion for scientific study.

"Film"

The pace of development quickened. In England, France, Germany, the United States, and elsewhere during the 1880s inventors and entrepreneurs worked on machinery for motion photography. Key advances in the still photographic field came from the work of the American inventor and manufacturer George Eastman (1854–1932). In 1885, with William H. Walker, Eastman developed a new kind of recording material to replace individual coated glass or gelatin plates: sensitized paper, coated with gelatin emulsion, on a roll, called **film**. In 1888 Eastman introduced a box camera with the film roll loaded inside it, under the trade name "Kodak." A year later, the paper roll was replaced by **celluloid**, a synthetic plastic material invented in the 1870s, which utilized the chemical compound cellulose nitrate. Marey immediately took up this innovation for his chronophotographic camera, constructing a mechanism that could move roll film

through the apparatus, hold it still momentarily for an **exposure** to be taken, and systematically repeat the operation. This fulfilled his desire for an ample number of separately recorded images of movement, for research purposes. Almost alone among the many experimenters in the medium, Marey was uninterested in carrying his work forward into the world of screen entertainment.

Thomas Alva Edison

The patent offices in England and the United States began filling up with plans for motion picture inventions. All eyes naturally turned toward the famous laboratory in West Orange, New Jersey, when Thomas Alva Edison (1847–1931), creator of the phonograph and the electric light bulb, staked out his claim for primacy in the field. Decades of research and debate have considerably tempered the view, once widely held, that the development of motion pictures sprang full-blown from Thomas Edison's brow. By the time Edison expressed interest in the subject he had become in any case more a business executive than a hands-on scientist, and the actual labor of invention was assigned to employees in his lab. Edison brought to the inventors' competition, however, his own carefully crafted international celebrity and business power, and he was bound to change the way the game was played.

Edison entered the field in 1888, well behind the stage that others had attained. His lab in fact wasted a year fruitlessly attempting to develop a motion picture recording device on the model of the cylinder with which Edison had constructed a sound recording machine. It was not until Edison visited Marey in 1889 and observed the roll film mechanism that his effort began to appear practical. Though roll film was obtained from George Eastman immediately on Edison's return, the lab was occupied with other projects until 1891. In that year Edison's British employee, William Kennedy Laurie Dickson (1860–1935), constructed and demonstrated versions of both a motion picture camera, the Kinetograph, and a machine to view the pictures, the Kinetoscope.

THE KINETOGRAPH CAMERA. Dickson's crucial accomplishment was the sprocket mechanism for advancing the film. The celluloid roll was perforated at regular intervals, and a

1.15. In 1878 the British photographer Eadweard Muybridge, at the behest of California railroad tycoon Leland Stanford, set out to determine by sequence photography whether a trotting horse ever had all four feet off the ground at once. Workmen set up the experi- *ment at Stanford's farm. The shed at right contains twelve cameras whose shutters are attached to strings stretched across the track; the horse will break the strings as it trots by, thus tripping the shutter mechanisms.*

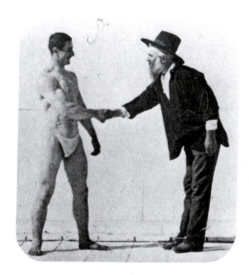

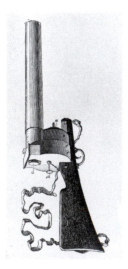

Above: 1.16. In 1879 Muybridge began to photograph sequences of humans in motion, which was to occupy much of his later career. After photographing gymnasts from the Olympic Club of San Francisco, Muybridge (at right) shakes hands with an athlete, L. Brandt.

Left: 1.17. The French scientist Étienne-Jules Marey's "photographic gun," designed to take sequential images of animals in motion

Right: 1.18. With his chronophotographic camera, Marey was able to take more photographs than with the gun; around 1890 he recorded this sequence of a pole vaulter.

1.19. The photographs resulting from Muybridge's experiments became an international sensation, demonstrating that a sequence of moving images could reveal what the eye could not see.

The dozen exposures were exhibited in Paris under the title "Les Allures du Cheval"—literally, the Horse's Gait, a French version of Muybridge's title.

toothed wheel driven by an electric motor moved the film forward with precision. (Several other early cameras also had electric motors, but such cameras were bulky and generally stationary; these gave way to hand-cranked cameras, lighter and more mobile, which required individual operators to determine film speed.) Although the first Kinetograph positioned the film horizontally in the motion picture camera (like standard still photo cameras of a later era), the improved machine moved the film vertically. With vertical placement of the roll, the Edison labs decided on a 35mm width for the film strip, which was eventually to become an industry standard. For the time being, however, early cameras utilized a variety of film widths and camera speeds.

The basis of motion picture cinematography was the exposure of individual **frames** on the film roll through a shutter mechanism. While some early cameras exposed as few as ten frames per second (f.p.s.), the Edison/Dickson camera operated at about 40 f.p.s., and that too emerged as something of a norm; later silent cameras were operated generally in the range of 18 to 22 f.p.s., and the standard for sound film became 24 f.p.s. The Edison/Dickson camera in most respects provided the basic

1.20. Thomas Alva Edison in his West Orange, New Jersey, laboratory, photographed by William Kennedy Laurie Dickson, 1893

1.21. A museum replica of Edison's Kinetoscope, showing its internal operation

1.22. The "Black Maria," Edison's motion picture studio constructed in 1893 on the laboratory grounds, with its roof open to show how sunlight entered; the photograph is from late 1894.

design for recording movement on film that has lasted with little change for one hundred years (though the electronic recording of images by video camera, is, of course, fundamentally different).

THE BLACK MARIA. Further improvements in the apparatus led to public exhibitions in 1893 and the opening of commercial viewing parlors in 1894 in the United States, France, and England. To foster the commercial development of his devices, Edison also constructed a studio on his laboratory grounds. This was a shed-like structure built on a turntable to follow the sun, with a roof that opened to let in sunlight, and walls of black tar paper. The staff called it "the Black Maria" because they thought it resembled the police patrol wagons of the era, which went by that nickname. In early 1894 vaudeville performers came over from New York to record their acts for Edison's camera. With film rolls 50 feet in length, these films lasted about twenty seconds, a single shot from

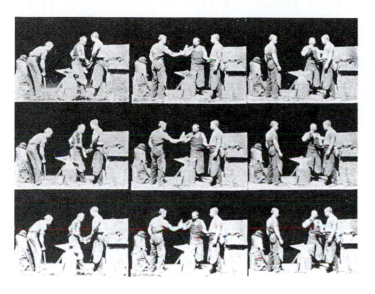

PROJECTED FILMS

By that time, however, the first projected motion pictures had already been demonstrated in France. The inventors were the brothers Auguste and Louis Lumière (1862–1954; 1864–1948), who ran in Lyons an important firm for manufacturing photographic equipment. Knowing of Edison's work, they sought to compete with an apparatus of their own. What they came up with in early 1895 was a device whose versatility surpassed any previous invention. Called the Cinématographe, it was a light-weight, hand-cranked machine that advanced the film roll through a claw mechanism. They found that it not only could operate as a camera but could be used to throw large-sized images onto a screen when it was linked with projecting equipment familiar from magic lantern shows. With their Cinématographe, they shot films and projected them for select groups repeatedly during 1895. At

Left: 1.23. Frames from Blacksmith Scene, shot in the Black Maria in early 1893. This film was featured at the first public exhibition of Edison's Kinetograph camera and Kinetoscope viewer on May 9, 1893. Using a magic lantern, individual frames were projected before an audience of several hundred; then people lined up to view the complete film in the Kinetoscope, one at a time. This event has led early-cinema historian Charles Musser to call Blacksmith Scene "the first commercial-length modern motion-picture subject to be publicly exhibited."

Below: 1.24. The Lumière Cinématographe camera depicted on a catalogue cover, 1897; when linked with a magic lantern lamp and lens, this apparatus functioned as a projector.

a stationary position, without editing or camera movement. At the same time Edison's company was manufacturing the Kinetoscope viewing machines. These were box structures containing a motor-and-shutter mechanism much like the camera's that ran a loop of positive film past an electric light source. The spectator peered through a small window to see the image. Originally the machines could only accommodate, like the cameras, 50 feet (or twenty seconds) of film, but within a few months some were modified to hold 150 feet of film, about a minute of screen time. Edison made deals with several firms to sell them both Kinetoscopes and films to show in them. A Kinetoscope parlor opened in New York in April 1894.

Edison and Dickson had apparently given little attention to the possibility of projecting their images. They continued to operate from the example of the phonograph, which had successfully been marketed in public commercial spaces with instruments for individual listening. The long tradition of magic lantern screen entertainment, however, with large-sized images projected before large-sized audiences, suggested both the technical and economic inferiority of the Kinetoscope "peep shows." Edison's achievement only spurred others to surpass him by inventing a motion picture projector. Dickson joined the effort when he left Edison's company in April 1895.

the Congrès des Sociétés Françaises de Photographie in June 1895 they filmed the delegates getting off a boat and projected the film for its subjects the following day. The premiere of projected motion pictures for the general public came on December 28, 1895, in Paris.

Inventors in Germany, England, and the United States were on their heels. In Berlin, another pair of brothers, Emil and Max Skladanowsky (1859–1945; 1863–1939), projected films with their Bioscop apparatus, which featured two film strips whose frames were alternately exposed, in November 1895. In London, the Kineopticon projector of Birt Acres (1854–1918) showed films in January 1896; it was based on a camera that Acres had earlier developed with Robert W. Paul (1869–1943), which in turn derived from Marey's chronophotographic camera (Acres went on to devise in 1899 a low-cost camera, the Birtac, for nonprofessional use—what would later be called "home movies"). The first American projector was developed by Charles Francis Jenkins (1867–1934) and Thomas Armat (1866–1948), later by Armat alone in a commercial arrangement with Edison. The projector, the Vitascope, which used sprocket wheels to advance the film, was marketed as an Edison product and made its debut on April 23, 1896, at Koster & Bial's Music Hall in New York.

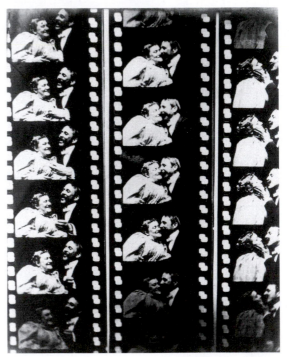

THE ADVENT OF MOTION PICTURES

Before considering more closely the films exhibited at these early screenings, we should step back for a moment to reflect once more on our subject: the emergence of motion pictures at the end of the nineteenth century. From our later position in historical time, we may say that we are observing an awesome moment launching a phenomenon that changed the world. But *why* did this happen? In the annals of technology, industry, and culture, no triumph is foreordained, no success guaranteed. Patent offices are crammed with models and drawings for inventions that never got out of the laboratory. There are innumerable stories in the world of commerce of products introduced with great fanfare that, as it turned out, nobody wanted to buy. Along with the press notices that expressed amazement at projected recordings of movement, there were other voices predicting that moving pictures, like many another novelty, would have no more than a brief moment of popularity, then pass from the scene. Let us not take cinema's triumph for granted; rather, let's look for reasons why it managed to survive and grow.

To begin at a basic, industrial level, it was important that the principal economic entrepreneurs of cinema—the Lumières in France, Edison in the United States—owned major manufacturing firms with other successful business operations. They possessed "deep pockets" to overcome the innumerable problems that could arise, and did: shortage or inferiority of films, mechanical difficulties, inadequacy of exhibition sites, and audience dissatisfaction, not to speak of legal battles or political pressures. The early history of motion pictures was far from an unbroken string of successes. Hailed at first for their startling simulations of reality, with familiarity moving pictures could easily seem inadequate to their initial premise.

Realism

What was "real" enough for the purposes of Marey's research may appear quite different in the realm of screen entertainment. Unlike the "real" world, the early moving pictures were black-and-white (two of the films shown at Edison's first projected screening were **tinted** by hand, frame by frame, but this practice was rare in the first years of cinema). Unlike the "real" world, they were silent unless accompanied by live music, voice, or sound effects. With rare exceptions the early films lasted no more than a minute or so, providing only brief glimpses or quick vignettes. A full evening's program consisting solely of movies was implausible from an entertainment point of view. Films were shown along with magic lantern projections and live presentations, and integrated as an added attraction to existing entertainment forms: variety shows, traveling lectures, carnival midways, vaudeville programs.

Reproducibility

Maybe "realism," after all, was not what spectators were looking for from the cinema. If that was the case, however, how could movies hope to compete with the magic lantern? Shows like Reynaud's Théâtre Optique offered the full possibilities of fiction and fantasy; they had color and sound, and they made for a satisfactory evening's entertainment. Again, at a basic, industrial level, the cinema possessed a capacity that the magic lantern shows could not match: reproducibility. A single negative could strike a large number of prints. They could be screened in many places simultaneously. Indeed, within weeks and months of the first public exhibition of projected movies, Lumière representatives and other operators with portable cameras had spread throughout the world, showing films and photographing new ones. By July 1896 the Cinématographe had reached Bombay, India, and St. Petersburg, Russia. Film screenings took place soon thereafter in Australia, Egypt, China, Japan.

A Global Medium

The cinema became a global phenomenon in a way the magic lantern never could. Though lantern screen exhibitions may have been familiar in all those far-flung places, lantern shows were the work of individual craftspersons, who could not match the volume and variety of the nascent cinema. In this sense the early motion picture belonged to a different world, not merely of screen entertainment but also of global communications. The 1890s also saw the development of the linotype machine for

1.27. The first film on the Lumières' inaugural program was La Sortie de l'Usine Lumière à Lyon (Workers Leaving the Lumière Factory, 1895), which showed, among other things, the large size of the Lumière company.

faster typesetting and of new rotary presses for higher volume printing of newspapers. A cheap mass press emerged which made its money not from circulation but from advertising revenue. The cinema was a part of these end-of-century transformations in information and consumption.

Visual Reporters

Much of the interest in early cinema came from its role as a visual reporter of current events. By 1898 a Lumière catalogue (the seventh issued in the space of two years) listed one thousand titles, virtually all of them **actuality films** shot by the brothers or acquired from overseas cameramen who used the Cinématographe or a portable camera from another manufacturer. Most of these films were simply scenic, but they also recorded, in the manner of a later era's television news, such scenes as the 1896 flood in Lyons and the Russian czar's visit to France. The scenics were also news of a kind; in an era of military and imperial expansion, spectators in Europe and the United States could have strategic or personal concerns for faraway places, as well as simple curiosity. Films also reconstructed important happenings and took the form, so to speak, of editorial commentary. Some early films that have survived have appeared completely inexplicable, with few internal references to guide the later spectator, but research in contemporary newspapers indicates that they were based on highly publicized events with which spectators of the time would have been familiar.

Film Propaganda

The medium's ties to newsworthy events was a significant aspect of its capacity to endure. When such happenings were scarce, cinema slumped. This was the case in New York City in early 1898, and vaudeville and variety theaters simply pulled films from their programs. Then growing hostilities between the United States and Spain gave American filmmakers a crucial boost. Photographing patriotic subjects—sometimes just a shot of the American flag waving—they joined the mass press in fomenting a war spirit over Spain's colonial possessions in the Caribbean. Using portable, hand-cranked cameras that Edison and other companies manufactured, several cameramen went to Cuba and photographed sites of military incidents there. Films of troops marching or preparing their expedition were supplemented by naval battles staged with miniature models or sham combat shot in New Jersey. Audiences cheered these films in vaudeville theaters.

Cinema and Urban Society

If information—and propaganda—were apparent aspects of the cinema's early appeal, its relation to the growth of cities at the turn of the twentieth century was also significant, though perhaps less obvious. Movies, it was true, could be shown anywhere—projectionists with their own electric generators indeed carried the medium to remote outposts. But in rural areas cinema was an occasional program or a special event, while in cities movies became part of the fabric of daily life.

The worldwide development of cities involved internal migration and external immigration, vast movement of peoples, rootlessness and cultural dislocation. It created new spaces for consumption and self-display: restaurants, department stores, covered arcades for strolling and shopping. It increased the tempo of

1.28. Arroseur et arrosé (Waterer and Watered, 1896), comedy Lumière-style, was taken from a newspaper cartoon. In the top frame, the boy steps on the hose, interrupting the flow of water, and causing the gardener to peer into the nozzle. Below, voilà!, boy removes foot, flow resumes, gardener is drenched.

life and the mingling of strangers. Emerging as a new medium on programs deriving from older entertainment forms (vaudeville, variety, magic lantern), the cinema slowly began to find a place in the experience of spectators commensurate with their habits and needs in city life. It was cheaper than many other performance events, and shorter; it could squeeze into converted spaces alongside stores, train stations, and other places that drew the mobile crowd; spectators who could not read or speak the local language could still enjoy the show.

Cinema and Women

Historians have increasingly emphasized the opportunities for social experience that cinema provided for female spectators. Theories of cinema had stressed that the medium's pleasures were almost exclusively male—that the primary place of women was on screen as objects of men's gaze. By locating cinema as an aspect of late-nineteenth-century urban consumer culture, however, it has been possible to recognize the historical importance of cinema for women. Situated among shops and cafés, the movie theater extended the world of consumption through its screen window on space, fantasy, and narrative. Female spectators, just as men, could find there the freedoms of pleasure and desire—to see, and to be seen (not just on screen). Since women have frequently made up a majority of filmgoers, the cinema's possibilities for female spectators are surely among the reasons the medium survived, took root, and thrived in modern culture.

EARLY FILMS
The Lumière Brothers

What the Lumières showed at their December 28, 1895, screening in Paris was a hit with all categories of spectators. The original program contained ten films and lasted about twenty minutes. Since the brothers had many more than ten films by the end of 1895, subsequent programs were constantly changing, and some films were retitled as well. A compilation film currently circulating that bills itself as "Films Shown at First Lumière Program" has preserved some of those early films over the decades, even though it includes some that were not shown on December 28, and excludes some that were.[2]

Because of these complications, what came first and what came a few weeks later no longer particularly matters. However the Lumières altered their programs, they began nearly all of them with *La Sortie de l'Usine Lumière à Lyon* (*Workers Leaving the Lumière Factory*), which conveyed, by the numbers pouring out of the gate, just how big an operation they ran. Work was a subject of many of the early Lumière films—including *Les Forgerons* (*The Blacksmiths*) from the first program and a slightly later, better-known film, *Démolition d'un mur* (*Demolition of a Wall*, 1896)— as were also military scenes. The film that had earlier been taken at and shown to the delegates at the photographers' congress, *Le Débarquement du Congrès de Photographie à Lyon* (*Debarkation of Photographic Congress Members at Lyon*), was also part of the first and many subsequent programs, in which were recorded, among others, the cinema pioneers Marey and Janssen. *Le Repas* on the first program, later renamed *Repas de bébé* (*Feeding the Baby*), provided a contrast to the public scenes of most of the films with its intimate glimpse of a mother and father feeding a baby, as a kind of prototype for home movies (and, for scholars, a glimpse into bourgeois family life).

1.29. The Lumières' Arrivée d'un train en gare *(Arrival of a Train at La Ciotat, 1896), a single-shot film, shows a train arriving at a station and the passengers getting off; despite its apparent simplicity, it provides evidence of how a film's visual style is shaped.*

Several of the most famous early Lumière films were not part of the first program, though often identified as being so. These include *Arroseur et arrosé* (*Waterer and Watered*, 1896), a remake of *Le Jardinier* (*A Little Trick on the Gardener*) from the first program, and *Arrivée d'un train en gare* (*Arrival of a Train at La Ciotat*, 1896). *Arroseur et arrosé* dramatizes what was a well-known cartoon sequence: Boy steps on gardener's hose, stopping flow of water. Gardener stares into nozzle, wondering what's wrong. Boy releases pressure, gardener is squirted in the face. Gardener spanks boy. This comedy was one of the earliest examples of intertextuality in the cinema—the way a text absorbs and transforms other texts, in this case the newspaper cartoon.

Arrivée d'un train en gare is a single shot of a train pulling into a station and passengers getting off. This film has attracted attention for its formal properties. From the platform, the camera observes the train in the distance approaching the station (legend has it that some spectators panicked as the engine came "closer"). The train stops; its passengers alight and move out of camera range. Rather than passing this off as simply a moment of unmediated reality, critics have pointed out its aesthetic implications, suggesting how every recorded image is an intervention, a mediation. As the train arrives, the film becomes a **sequence** of events, varying from distance to **close-up**. Though the events themselves are accidental, subject to chance (the passengers had not been coached to act in certain ways), the filmmaker's decision to set up his camera in a specific place established a certain manner of presenting the unstaged. The filmmaker was, in a way, a **director**, constructing a basic **mise-en-scène**—the French term, adopted from the vocabulary of the theater, that is widely used to denote the totality of a film's visual style: placement and movement of camera and performers, decor, lighting, all that appears before the camera.

Edison's Program

The first presentation of Edison's Vitascope four months later in New York did not have the same impact on spectators, nor has it provided grist for later critical analysis. Edison mostly put on the screen films that looked exactly like those that had been appearing in the Kinetoscope viewing machines for the previous several years—works shot inside the Black Maria against a black background, presenting moving figures in a kind of spatial void. The

one widely praised film at the Vitascope debut was a shot of crashing waves at the seaside, and it had been filmed in England by Birt Acres and supplied to Edison by Robert W. Paul.

Edison may have gotten a message when most of the acclaim went to the wave film (its original title was *A Rough Sea at Dover*, but it was changed to *Sea Waves* in the United States to make it appear a local product). Shortly after the Koster & Bial screening, Edison began to rely less on the stationary Black Maria camera and sent cameramen with portable cameras out into the world to shoot "actualities" on the model of Acres and the Lumières. During 1896 they filmed *Shooting the Chutes* at Coney Island, a waterfall, a train, a fire truck pulled by a horse, farmyard scenes, and several short outdoor comedies in the manner of *Arroseur et arrosé*.

Despite the initial successes of projected motion pictures, the early months were a time of disorder and shakeout in the new medium. Expectation exceeded technology, and technology outran manufacturing capability. Competition intensified—in addition to the primary French, British, German, and American projectors, another important machine came onto the scene: the Biograph, manufactured by the American Mutoscope Company (the firm soon changed its name to American Mutoscope and Biograph Company and eventually shortened it to Biograph Company). Soon another dozen different projecting devices were on the market.

Lumière remained dominant both in Europe and in North America, but in early 1897 United States customs officials threatened to prosecute the company's American employees because of improper customs documents—what could have led to that draconian action?—and Lumière shut down its American operations. Indeed, having put together by 1898, as we have seen, a catalogue of one thousand films, the Lumières began to curtail their motion picture activities. There has never been quite a full explanation for this, other than that the company had more than it could handle in the manufacturing of photographic and motion picture **film stock**. The Lumière catalogue of 1903 contained more than two thousand titles; then, in 1905, they abandoned film production.

Georges Méliès

Besides the Biograph company, the most significant newcomer to motion pictures after the first wave of screen projections was the magician Georges Méliès (1861–1938). He came to filmmaking from the entertainment field rather than from that of technology and invention, the background of nearly all his competitors. Since 1888 Méliès had performed magic tricks and shown lantern slides in his Paris theater (called the Théâtre Robert-Houdin, after a famous nineteenth-century French magician). When he began making films in 1896, he worked in the Lumière manner, shooting little comedies, everyday scenes, and travel views. But he also tried out a few of his own and other magicians' tricks on film. Stage illusions could be accomplished more easily just by stopping the camera and moving or substituting objects, such as in *Escamotage d'une dame chez Robert-Houdin* (*The Vanishing Lady*, 1896), where a seated woman is replaced by a skeleton. (In Edison's 1895 Kinetoscope film *Mary, Queen of Scots*, the camera was stopped so a dummy could replace a performer before a beheading was carried out; this substitution, however, was paradoxically in the service of realism, without having to sacrifice the life of a performer, while in Méliès its purpose was to go beyond

Edison's Competitors

One of the most arcane, yet significant, aspects of early movie history is the conflict over patent rights. Basically, inventors apply for patents in order to insure that they will be able to gain income from their investment of time, money, ideas, and labor—that someone else cannot simply copy the invention and sell it at a cheaper price or in a glitzier package. In the case of motion pictures, the question of patents revolved around the work of Thomas A. Edison's laboratory: could Edison or could he not claim to patent as his invention the basic mechanism of the motion picture camera?

After several rejections and extended legal struggle, Edison's claim was first upheld in 1897. Though numerous court battles were to come, Edison was quickly able to force some competitors out of business or require them to operate their equipment only if licensed by him. One that was able to resist him, however, then and for some time after, was the company operating under several different official names but generally known as the Biograph. When the Lumières gave up their activities in the United States in 1897, Biograph became the principal American film company.

Biograph began competing with Edison in the days before large-screen projection when it devised its own peep-show viewer, the Mutoscope. Its film frames were printed not on a strip or reel (as in Edison's Kinetoscope) but on separate flip cards, which were activated by a hand crank to produce the illusion of motion. Before they could market the Mutoscope, however, they needed films, and so they developed a camera, originally called the Mutograph. William Kennedy Laurie Dickson, who had devised the sprocket mechanism that became the successful basis for Edison's camera patents, assisted Biograph in constructing a mechanism that operated on different principles: rollers gripped and advanced the film. A similar apparatus was utilized in the Biograph projector.

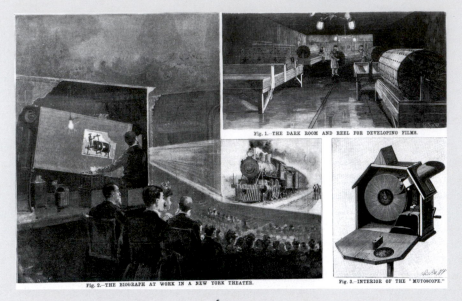

Fig. 1.—THE DARK ROOM AND REEL FOR DEVELOPING FILMS.

Fig. 2.—THE BIOGRAPH AT WORK IN A NEW YORK THEATER.

Fig. 3.—INTERIOR OF THE "MUTOSCOPE."

1.30. By 1897 the company was in full operation. An article in Scientific American magazine illustrated its varied activities. Pictured are the Biograph projector in a theater, the darkroom and drying racks for film development, and the flip-card Mutoscope, shown open on the side to reveal its mechanism.

1.31. Biograph built a studio in 1897 on the roof of its building at 841 Broadway in New York, constructed on rails so it could be rotated (like Edison's Black Maria) to make optimal use of the sun. This illustration, also from Scientific American, shows a film called Love's Young Dream (1897) in production.

realism, to create a transformation that could not be witnessed in actuality.)

Méliès brought the fantastic to the cinema—he was heir to the screen tradition of Robertson's Fantasmagorie. He has been credited as originator or precursor of such long-lasting film **genres** as horror, science fiction, and dark comedy. In the familiar dictum of film history, Méliès was the founder of cinema fantasy as the Lumières were of film realism. In Jean-Luc Godard's 1967 film *La Chinoise* (*The Chinese*), however, made in an era when many truisms were questioned, a scene presents a lecture on the early history of cinema: Méliès is the founder of realism, the Lumières of fantasy. Even such parody or excess can make the point that the past is always open to reinterpretation, redefinition of terms, and the potential transformation of accepted wisdom, just as in a Méliès film.

Notes

1. See Susan J. Lederman and Bill Nichols, "Flicker and Motion in Film," in Nichols, *Ideology and the Image: Social Representation in the Cinema and Other Media* (Bloomington: Indiana University Press, 1981), pp. 293–301.

2. Almost all the original films were later retitled, and a number of variant titles may exist. However, for the record, these are the ten films at the first screening with the titles as listed on the program: 1. *La Sortie de l'Usine Lumière à Lyon* (*Workers Leaving the Lumière Factory*); 2. *La Voltige* (*Horseback Jumping*); 3. *La Pêche aux poissons rouges* (*Fishing for Goldfish*); 4. *Le Débarquement du Congrès de Photographie à Lyon* (*Debarkation of Photographic Congress Members at Lyon*); 5. *Les Forgerons* (*The Blacksmiths*); 6. *Le Jardinier* (*A Little Trick on the Gardener*); 7. *Le Repas* (*Feeding the Baby*); 8. *Le Saut à la couverture* (*Blanket Toss*); 9. *La Place des Cordeliers à Lyon* (*The Place des Cordeliers at Lyon*); 10. *La Mer* (*The Sea*).

1.32. A poster advertising a traveling motion picture exhibitor, c. 1900. Note the orchestra conductor just below the screen image, and, on screen, a military parade, one of the patriotic subjects that proved popular in the first years of cinema.

T W O

EARLY CINEMA

Primitive cinema is a name that has often been used to describe the era of filmmaking and the culture of moviegoing in the United States and western Europe from their beginnings up to around 1910. The term's purpose is not to explain the apparent oddities in early films that sometimes provoke laughter from latter-day audiences; rather it is to make those presumed oddities understandable (and thus no longer laughable) by clarifying some fundamental differences between early cinema and what followed. It seeks to replace the notion, once quite common, that the history of film was a story of something that began as comically bad and slowly got better and better. The concept of primitive cinema suggests that early filmmakers held a different *idea* about how a film should be made, and that filmmaking did not "improve" (though there were obvious technical advances) so much as shift to an entirely new perspective on the medium. From this viewpoint, early movies become comprehensible within their own setting; also, the norms of mainstream cinema that have dominated most of the twentieth century no longer are regarded, as they sometimes have been, as the apex of an inexorable historical progress.

REDISCOVERY OF EARLY CINEMA

As a historical term, primitive cinema came into currency in the 1970s with the discovery and restoration of hundreds of pre-1910 films. This opened the way to a richer and more varied viewpoint

on the period than had been possible with the handful of surviving prints—some not in their original form—that had previously been available. The old linear perspective on the evolution of film style and technique gave way to a recognition that cinema developed through debate, controversy, and struggle. One such period of strife erupted around 1910 when the expansion of audiences, changing industrial structures, and political pressures, among other factors, exposed deficiencies in primitive cinema and led to its decline. The decade after 1910 was a time of transition—which, in the United States, also marked a shift in film production from east to west coast—that ended with the full-scale emergence of a new mode, associated with the Hollywood studio system. This new mode has sometimes been called **classical cinema**.

Early Cinema and the Avant-Garde

To a certain degree, the revised viewpoint on early cinema was formed in a framework of opposition to the standard Hollywood product of the studio era. In the 1970s, when a vigorous and influential independent film movement flourished, parallels were drawn between primitive cinema and the modern **avant-garde** as common alternatives to the mainstream mode. From the notion of film history as progressive development, many aspects of early cinema had been criticized by historians on the supposition that early filmmakers only slowly came to understand the stylistic potentials of the medium. From the new perspective, what had been seen as inadequate now came to be regarded as authentic and autonomous ways of representing time and movement on screen.

2.1. Primitive cinema became popular in amusement parks and fairgrounds as well as in urban vaudeville and peep-show entertainments. The Bioscope was an attraction at a British amusement pier around 1900; it was a projector devised for Charles Urban (1871–1942), an American who worked in Britain after 1898 as a traveling exhibitor and motion picture entrepreneur.

Film as Spectacle

Central to this reassessment was the notion of primitive cinema not primarily as a narrative story-telling medium but as a type of presentation or exhibition—similar to an act on a vaudeville program or an attraction on an amusement park midway. What drew audiences was the allure of spectacle.

In early films, the camera was likely to be stationary and at a considerable distance from the performers, mimicking the situation of a seated theatergoer. When the camera moved or a closer view of action was presented, it was in the service of spectacle rather than story, as in Biograph's *Photographing a Female Crook* (1904), where the camera (mounted on wheels or **tracks**) begins a shot with a distant view of the criminal suspect, and then advances to show in close-up her horrific grimace. A number of films, such as *Uncle Tom's Cabin* (1903), directed by Edwin S. Porter (1870–1941), drew on well-known dramatizations and were likely to follow a format of discrete scenes in the stage manner, rather than creating a close-knit moment-to-moment narrative. After the demise of primitive cinema, commentators for years derided its adherence to theatrical conventions and its inability to construct a distinctive new cinematic "language." In the revised view, however, early film provided the spectator a visual and emotional distance, a contemplative stance, whereas the later mainstream cinema sought to evoke explicit and determined audience responses.

CINEMATIC TIME

One of the most subtle areas of difference between primitive cinema and the dominant modes of later years lay in their separate approaches to temporal continuity. The modern cinema has treated time as a flow. You can leap backward in time (as in **flashbacks**, where past scenes are interwoven with a film's temporal present) or adjust its tempo (as in sequences where movement is slowed down or speeded up), but time inexorably moves forward. The primitive cinema took an attitude toward time with which we have once again become familiar through the instant replay of televised sports. You see an event, time is temporarily arrested, then you see the event again, often from camera positions different from the first, or "live," presentation. This is a form of visual simultaneity outside time's flow. Modern cinema creates an impression of visual simultaneity *within* time's flow through **editing**, showing several alternative perspectives on action while time continues its movement. Primitive cinema said, in effect, let's stop time and look at that from another angle.

Méliès

The pioneer French magician-filmmaker Georges Méliès (see Chapter 1) exemplified primitive cinema's concept of time as repeatable, rather than endlessly flowing. His 1902 fantasy film *Le Voyage dans la lune* (*A Trip to the Moon*) begins with scenes of preparation for the departure of a rocket to the moon. Then we

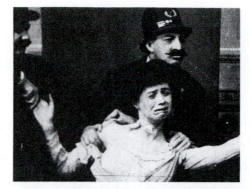

ELIZA PLEADS WITH UNCLE TOM TO RUN AWAY.

PHINEAS OUTWITS THE SLAVE TRADERS.

PHINEAS OUTWITS THE SLAVE TRADERS.

THE ESCAPE OF ELIZA.

REUNION OF ELIZA AND GEORGE HARRIS.

THE QUAKER ASSISTING THE HARRIS' TO ESCAPE.

RACE BETWEEN THE ROBERT E. LEE AND NATCHEZ.

THE ARRIVAL OF THE STEAMBOAT ROBERT E. LEE.

see the mobile human face of the moon just as it is struck in the eye by the arriving rocket. The following shot repeats the landing of the rocket, but in much closer view, as it settles down more conventionally on the moon's terrain. The same event is shown twice, and very differently.

Life of an American Fireman

Perhaps the most extended (and controversial) instance of primitive cinema's different form of temporal continuity came in Porter's *Life of an American Fireman* (1902). This mixture of actuality and fiction footage opens with a series of shots depicting the operations of a fire station as its wagons answer a call—a fire alarm is pulled, the firemen leap from bed and slide down the ladder, the wagons roll out of the station and race along the street. The film's second half, equal in length to the first, depicts a rescue scene, with interior and exterior views of the firemen carrying a woman and child from a burning house.

For years the available prints of *Life of an American Fireman* showed this rescue scene (the film's second half) as a thirteen-shot sequence. After the first shot of the woman inside the house, twelve **rapid cuts** shift the action between outdoors and indoors

Top: 2.6. Members of the Astronomic Club celebrate the announcement that a rocket will be sent to the moon, in Georges Méliès's Le Voyage dans la lune (A Trip to the Moon, 1902).

Above: 2.7. The rocket hits the man in the moon right in the eye.

The Brighton School

"The Brighton School" is a name often invoked in connection with early film history. Primarily it denotes two filmmakers who worked in the British seaside resort Brighton in the first years of cinema: George Albert Smith (1864–1959) and James Williamson (1855–1933). Along with other British pioneers, they have often been overshadowed by figures from countries that became more prominent and powerful in the early history of cinema, such as George Méliès in France and Edwin S. Porter in the United States.

The Brighton filmmakers gained renewed attention when film historians began to question traditional claims to stylistic innovation, particularly those of D. W. Griffith, who had asserted that he was the inventor of a host of filmmaking techniques. A look back at the work of Smith and Williamson, along with other early filmmakers, makes clear that certain cinematic techniques—such as **point-of-view shots**, close-ups, and moving camera shots—occurred much earlier than Griffith and others had claimed. The larger point, however, is that trying to discover who went "first," who could be called the "inventor" of a technique, is fruitless. A considerable range of stylistic elements appeared from the beginning in early cinema and were widely diffused, though their use was often haphazard; Griffith deserves credit not for inventing them but for using them in a completely different way from the earlier filmmakers, as part of a new narrative style.

Smith's and Williamson's films shared the spectacle and presentational aspects of primitive cinema that marked Porter's works. In Smith's *Grandma's Reading Glass* (1900), the gimmick, as it were, of seeing what Grandma sees is the whole point of the film. Williamson made *Attack on a Chinese Mission Station* (1900) as a re-creation of a current news event, in the manner of American films on the war in Cuba, and *Fire* (1902) as part of what amounted to a fire-rescue genre. Both Smith and Williamson made magic and trick films in the Méliès fashion. Like Porter and Méliès, their careers as filmmakers substantially ended with the transition away from primitive cinema around 1910.

However, Smith by that time had become active in developing color filmmaking. In 1906 he secured a patent on a two-color filmmaking process that utilized the Bioscope equipment of Charles Urban. It photographed black-and-white film through a rotating wheel with red and green **filters**, so that each frame was alternately exposed to one or the other filter. The black-and-white positive print was then projected with red and green lights, the red light shining on the frames exposed to the red filter, and the green light accordingly. Smith and Urban publicly introduced this system, which they called Kinemacolor, in 1908. The process was considered quite effective in giving the appearance of natural color, and Kinemacolor films were made and successfully exhibited into the 1920s, when technologies incorporating color into the film negative began to supersede it (see Chapter 8).

---

as the exciting rescue is carried out. Allowing the spectator to see multiple perspectives as the action proceeded, this was visual simultaneity of a remarkable sophistication for that early day and was regarded as the finest example of advanced editing techniques in the early cinema. The trouble is, it was not the way Porter put the film together.

This became an issue when a Library of Congress copyright submission was restored. The film's first half was exactly the same as in the extant version, but its second half, the rescue scene, was presented in just two shots: first the interior from start to finish, then, going back in time to the beginning of the rescue, the exterior from start to finish. The authenticity of this two-shot version was confirmed when an original print of *Life of an American Fireman* was discovered in the state of Maine. It showed that Porter's concepts of editing and temporality were similar to those of Méliès, and both were different from those of "advanced" editing and its notions of visual simultaneity.

When one is aware of the differing structures of perception that separate primitive from modern cinema, the way a film like *Life of an American Fireman* repeats time from varied perspectives can be more fully appreciated. After all, it is not so alien an idea. Literary texts employ a similar convention so frequently it is scarcely noticed: first an event is narrated from one character's viewpoint, then it is gone over again through the eyes of another character. But this basic literary device also points up why early films can seem confusing to later-day spectators. Temporal repetitions in literature are rooted in points of view that shape and define the action. Early cinema often failed to provide such anchors.

The sense of contemplation that early cinema fosters in spectators can easily shift over into bafflement. The screen image at times simply provides insufficient information. Who are these people? What are they doing? Where in the frame is the significant action taking place? Early audiences may have found answers to such questions by being familiar with the stories; or, in many cases, theaters employed lecturers who narrated the action, following synopses provided by the filmmaker. (There were even instances when actors were hired to stand behind the screen and read lines of dialogue.) But as the popularity of cinema grew in its first decade, and as the films became longer and their narratives more complex, spectators at that time also sometimes became puzzled. Audiences and economics were at the heart of the struggles over primitive cinema that erupted around 1910, but so too was a crisis in film style and form.

2.8. Scenes from Porter's *Life of an American Fireman (1902). The photographic reproduction of film* frames was made horizontally; the order of the images is left to right, top to bottom.

2.9. The climactic sequence from Porter's Uncle Josh at the Moving Picture Show *(1902). Seeing the screen image of an embracing couple, country bumpkin Josh* takes it literally, approaches the screen, and in his excitement tears it down, starting a fight with a behind-the-screen projectionist.

EDWIN S. PORTER

The brief history of primitive cinema is encapsulated in the career of Edwin S. Porter. Hailed in his own time and by posterity as the most important filmmaker of cinema's first decade, Porter in early 1909 was removed from his post as head of film production at the Edison company and was fired several months later. In the view of his employers, his method of filmmaking and his concept of what a film should be had become outmoded. After 1915 he was no longer active in making films, though he lived for another quarter century. Porter's strengths and limitations do not solely account for, but are central to, both the triumphs and decline of primitive cinema.

Like many other early filmmakers, Porter was drawn to cinema through an interest in its mechanical rather than its artistic development. He began his film career as a projectionist and traveling exhibitor. It was his skill with machines that led the Edison company to put him in charge of its motion picture production in early 1901. As he set about organizing the company's new studio in New York City, he helped to define the filmmaker's responsibilities in the early years. The range of his tasks is also perhaps one of the reasons later commentators have linked the primitive cinema to avant-garde practices: though he often worked with others, Porter was at various times (and sometimes all at once) the person who operated the camera, directed the actors, processed the negative, edited the film, maintained the equipment, and paid the bills.

One thing he was not able to do, at the beginning of his labors with Edison, was control the way his company's films would appear on screen. Most films were still quite brief and consisted of a single shot. To make an attractive program, a theater operator interspersed films among magic lantern slides, live entertainers, audience sing-alongs; exhibitors might construct a theme or an order for the various items on a program that relegated a film to a minor role or gave it an emphasis different from the filmmaker's purpose. One of Porter's challenges was to make longer films that could give cinema more prominence and autonomy in the exhibition setting; these necessarily involved going beyond the single-shot film, taking a series of separate shots and editing them together into a "chain" of images.

Uncle Josh at the Moving Picture Show

Among his first productions was a film that highlighted the mystery and power of cinema. *Uncle Josh at the Moving Picture Show* (1902) was an early example of a movie on one of the medium's favorite subjects: itself. (Porter's film copied an earlier production by Robert W. Paul in England.) Uncle Josh, a country bumpkin, is attending a screening of Edison films. He grows increasingly agitated as films of a dancer and an express train are shown (these were Edison releases placed within *Uncle Josh* through a **matte process**, in which portions of a negative are blanked out and then printed with another negative to make a positive containing more than one image). When the third film-within-a-film portrays a "country couple" embracing, Josh tears down the screen and wrestles with a projectionist behind it.

Cinema and Sexuality

Uncle Josh's extreme response to the country couple suggests the centrality of sexuality in early cinema. Although magic lantern slides and live vaudeville performances were not without their

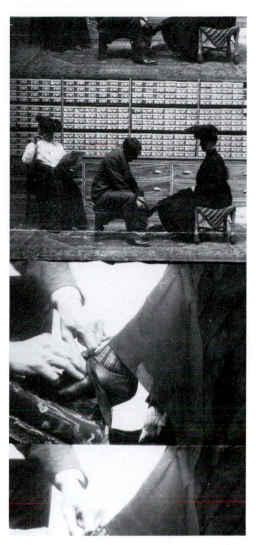

2.10. An insert shot (cutting from a wider scene to a close-up) in Porter's The Gay Shoe Clerk (1903) emphasizes the moment when the woman's skirt is raised to reveal her calf and petticoat.

suggestive elements, the cinema of spectacle could be more risqué than either, with more motion and duration than the slides, and more candor than many of the family-oriented vaudeville programs. One of Porter's contributions to the extensive genre of risqué films was *The Gay Shoe Clerk* (1903). A shoe salesman greets two women shoppers and assists one in trying on a pair of shoes. As he is tying the laces, a cut to a second shot shows his hands and her foot in close-up (this was called an **insert shot**, to designate its emphasis on a segment of a larger scene). An unseen hand raises her skirt to reveal a stocking-clad calf and petticoats. A third shot returns to the original camera position: the clerk leans over and kisses the customer; the second woman leaps up and beats him with an umbrella and then rushes her companion out the door.

Crime and Violence

The objectification of women's bodies has remained a dominant, and always controversial, aspect of cinema spectacle. It could hardly serve, however, as the foundation of a new medium's development toward greater presence in the entertainment world. More prominent in the popular theatrical and literary cultures, on which the movies also drew, was the spectacle of crime and vio-

2.11, 2.12. Contrasting how society treats rich and poor differently, Porter's The Kleptomaniac *(1905) shows a wealthy woman receiving gentle handling when caught shoplifting in a department store, while a policeman roughly captures a poor woman accused of theft.*

lence. Porter, like other filmmakers, utilized these subjects frequently, though he was unusual in sometimes treating crime as a social and moral issue rather than solely a subject for exploitation. Two examples are *The Ex-Convict* (1904), in which a man released from prison is driven by ostracism and his family's need to commit another crime (but finds redemption through a good deed he has done), and *The Kleptomaniac* (1905), which shows the justice system treating unequally a rich woman and a poor woman who are caught stealing.

The Great Train Robbery

But it was crime preeminently as spectacle that Porter emphasized in the work that was to become the most famous film of the primitive cinema, *The Great Train Robbery* (1903). This film has received so many diverse accolades—credited for establishing the Western genre, the "story" film, indeed the commercial success of the motion picture medium itself—that its character as *film* has sometimes been lost sight of. As a genre work, as a story, *The Great Train Robbery* was in no sense original: certainly not in relationship to similar works of popular literature and theater, or even to earlier films. Its power lay in its diverse demonstration of cinema's special strengths.

The Great Train Robbery encapsulated the medium's capacity to place the spectator within its space, to simulate the spectator's "presence" in movement and action. The camera's eye could situate the viewer in the midst of a scene, as when, placed atop a moving train, it observes robbers entering its field of vision from the bottom of the frame—behind the spectator's standpoint—and attacking the engine crew. With separate shots edited together, moreover, the film could give the spectator an unequaled sense of spaciousness and breadth, of having access simultaneously to multiple standpoints: the train from several angles, a station, a dance hall, several outdoor scenes. And by moving the camera, or moving the action in relation to the camera, it offered unprecedented visual immediacy: the aura of, and the terror at, witnessing senseless, violent death, as when one of the train's captured passengers bolts toward the camera, is shot by the robbers, and falls in close view before us. The spectator's vicarious vulnerability is vividly reinforced in the final shot, a close-up of a sheriff taking aim and shooting point-blank at the camera.

Challenges and Contradictions

The Great Train Robbery, while exemplary of primitive cinema, also exposed its contradictions: its capacity to involve the spectator heightened the elements of spectacle but also broke down the distanced, contemplative viewpoint that primitive cinema had inscribed. Yet the involvement it offered was more visceral than emotional, providing only fleeting opportunities for feeling, or identifying with, its fictional characters.

These contradictions were to be more fully exposed in Porter's work over the next few years. *The Great Train Robbery*'s enormous success with audiences marked a decisive turn in primitive cinema toward narrative, or story films. The Edison company's film sales (which had actually declined in 1902 from 1901) began a gradual improvement that soon turned into a spectacular leap. The first challenge was an increasing demand for "product," and that meant determining the variety of subjects an expanding production company should offer. Porter's output included further Westerns, more comedies, "chase" films (these were a type of comedy that had a brief vogue, chronicling the mishaps of people

2.13. Some early films were partially hand-tinted, to highlight a scene or object—the color of a dress, the flames of a fire. A print of Porter's The Great Train Robbery *(1903) survives with hand-tinting throughout, though only of specific elements in each scene. When the robbers shoot up the dance hall, smoke from their guns and a woman's dress are tinted yellow.*

2.14. The sheriff in The Great Train Robbery's *last shot wears a green-tinted shirt.*

running away and those trying to catch them, in alternating shots), versions of classic theater works, fantasy, and trick films.

But the more daunting challenge was to explore the logic of the contradictions that *The Great Train Robbery* laid bare. What was the relation between spectacle and narrative, between identification and emotional distancing? If they grasped the force of these issues, Porter and the Edison company may have been too preoccupied with other demands, such as maintaining volume of production, to cope with them fully. *The "Teddy" Bears* (1907) highlights the difficulty. Part of the film recounts the children's tale of Goldilocks and the Three Bears; part of it depicts the United States president, Theodore Roosevelt, in a hunting episode that led to the naming of the "Teddy Bear" doll; and another part is an elaborate sequence of "Teddy Bear" dolls animated through stop-motion photography. Spectacle is interspersed with narrative, fantasy turns into realism, and identification becomes emotional distancing in a way that causes modern audiences to gasp in astonishment, as fantasy bears with whom we have been led to identify suddenly become indifferent targets of the president's rifle. This remarkable film marked a crisis of the primitive mode.

Within less than half a decade Edwin S. Porter went from the leading filmmaker in the United States to an outmoded and fading

Dividing Up The Tasks

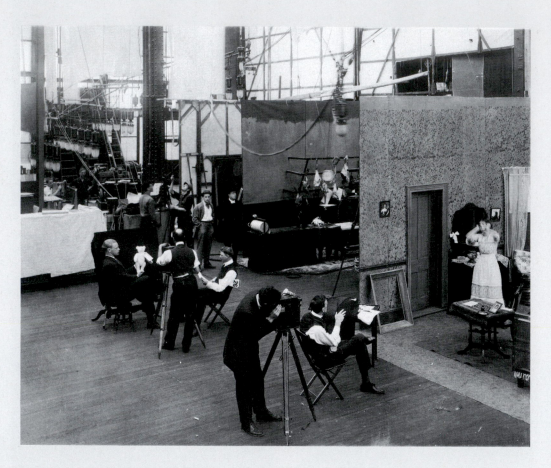

2.15. One trouble with the sun as a light source was that it cast shadows, which sometimes appeared incongruous in indoor scenes. By 1903–4 banks of mercury-vapor lamps made by the Cooper-Hewitt company had come into use; these supplied a diffuse and even light, which some cinematographers began to supplement with specific lighting (as from a light source within the images, such as a fireplace) for enhanced visual effects. Cooper-Hewitts provide lighting for filmmaking at the Edison company's studio in the Bronx, New York.

2.17. "Teddy" bears are lined up to begin their animated acrobatics, as observed through a knothole in a door, in Porter's The "Teddy" Bears (1907).

figure. (The Edison company did not survive much longer as a production entity, so the difficulties were clearly institutional as well as personal.) A way of putting this phenomenon in context would be to compare it with another rapidly expanding and transforming industry, such as computers in the late twentieth century, where enterprises founded in inventors' garages became multi-million-dollar businesses, and companies that had once led their field soon afterward went bankrupt. In the early cinema, artisans like Porter who had taken responsibility for every technical, artistic, and managerial aspect of filmmaking found themselves especially vulnerable to the industry's changing nature.

THE TRANSFORMATION OF EARLY CINEMA

The development of early cinema did not exactly take place on what one would call a level playing field. Edison, having begun to challenge his competitors in legal actions as early as the 1890s,

2.16. The Lubin Manufacturing Company's studio in Philadelphia, photographed around 1910. Three scenes are being shot simultaneously on the glass-walled stages.

A glance at the accompanying illustrations will indicate why the primitive cinema's mode of production could not last. As early as 1907, when the two studios pictured here were constructed in the United States, the demand for motion picture "product" required an increase in output that a single individual could not encompass. As late as 1907, conversely, Edwin S. Porter attempted to continue the mode of production he had developed nearly a decade earlier, as a person responsible for all facets of the filmmaking process—from preparing the story, to running the camera, to developing and cutting the celluloid strips. But under these methods he was unable to produce either the volume or quality of films that new industrial circumstances required, and in 1909 the Edison company fired him.

The mode of production that replaced the primitive was, to a degree, transitional. Production companies set up story departments to prepare **scenarios** (the word then used to describe outlines, treatments, or scripts) and write intertitles. **Cinematography** became a specialization, while postproduction tasks were given over to technicians. Directors, however, remained central to the process: in the course of working with performers and the camera operator they could improvise or alter story lines and, of course, determine the style of a film through camera placement, length of **takes**, and other on-set decisions.

These directorial prerogatives soon came into conflict with management desires that filmmaking be not only artistic but businesslike—that schedules be adhered to, budgets maintained. A new position was created, called supervisor. This figure often came from the ranks of directors, who were familiar with all phases of filmmaking, but as the industry developed what became known as the "studio system," the title shifted to **producer** and its holders came from the business and management side. Producers worked most closely with story departments, since preproduction activities such as casting, set construction, budgeting, and schedule making all depended on what was in the script. By 1913, as the trade journal *Motion Picture News* reported, companies were handing "a working script up to a director with strict orders to produce it."

continued after 1900 to file suit after suit alleging patent violations. Though the courts continued to define his role as inventor quite narrowly, his tactics harassed and financially hindered other film companies. In addition, with copyright provisions pertaining to films vague or nonexistent, companies felt free simply to make a duplicate print of someone else's film, slap on a new title, and sell it as their own. Producers combated this tactic by placing their company logos or symbols on the walls of sets, so these would show up unmistakably in shots. With duping thus hindered, pirating took the form of reshooting a competitor's film, sometimes on a straight shot-for-shot basis. Some of the large film companies opened overseas offices, the better to protect rights in their products, hastening the internationalization of the motion picture trade.

The Decline of Méliès

Not every film company, even among the most notable, was a success story. Georges Méliès in France, though he was different from Edwin S. Porter as the owner of his own company rather than an employee, also had difficulty with the changing circumstances of film production. Unlike the Edison company, the Lumières, and several other French and British producers, he did not manufacture related technical devices as an additional source of income and a capital base. His films were expensive and labor-intensive—they required multiple changes of costume, elaborate painted backdrops, and intricate trick photography (which involved stopping the camera and changing the scene to make it appear that an instantaneous magical transformation had occurred, as in a sequence where a man loses his head, headlessly hunts for it, then restores it).

Economic and structural changes in the film industry, requiring increased production and greater management organization, were probably the most severe challenges to Méliès's survival, rather than aesthetic obsolescence. Yet the unchanging conventions of his magical productions also began to fall out of favor. One of his most ambitious films, *Le Palais des Mille et une Nuits* (*The Palace of the Arabian Nights*, 1905), displays Méliès in all his grandeur and contradiction. More than twenty minutes long, it contains

Above: 2.18. An elaborate scene from Méliès's Le Palais des Mille et une Nuits *(The Palace of the Arabian Nights, 1905)*

Right: 2.19. An illustration depicts film production at the Pathé studio in Vincennes, near Paris, in 1903. The film is titled Guillaume Tell.

2.20. The comedian Max Linder in an early Pathé effort, Les Débuts d'un patineur (Max Learns to Skate, 1907). A few years later, as a director-performer, he became a world favorite. His persona as a fatuous dandy wearing a top hat and a white scarf, with a mustache and a skip step, was emulated by Charlie Chaplin.

spectacle elements of primitive cinema like women in revealing garments, dancing skeletons reminiscent of Robertson's Fantasmagorie, and a startling mise-en-scène of painted sets and magical action. Yet the narrative is hardly comprehensible, and only with the assistance of a lecturer, or previous knowledge of the legend it depicts, could audiences have followed it. After a desperate attempt to keep up with new circumstances—in 1908 he produced sixty-eight films, more than three times as many as the previous year—Méliès gradually shifted his interest back to live theater, and produced his last films in 1912.

2.21. Rover leading a father to his kidnapped daughter in Rescued by Rover (1905), a British film directed by Lewis Fitzhamon

Pathé Frères

As Méliès had succeeded the Lumières as the major figure in French film production, he was in turn surpassed by the firm of Pathé Frères, which by 1908 had become the world's largest pro-

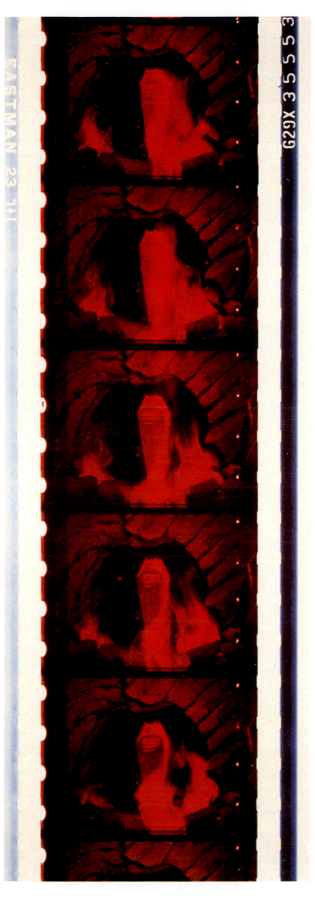

2.22. A tinted sequence from a Pathé film released in the United States as The Red Spectre (1907; original title unknown)

VITAGRAPH FILMS

12 CENTS PER FOOT

12 CENTS PER FOOT

Last Week! A TALE OF THE SEA, 750 Feet

This Week—Two positive Hits. AN ELABORATE HOLIDAY FEATURE

A NIGHT IN DREAMLAND

A FAIRY FANTASY
Copyright, 1907, by THE VITAGRAPH COMPANY OF AMERICA

Two little children are put to bed on Christmas eve by their parents, and dream of a visit to the North Pole, where many wonderful toys are seen, all imbued with life. The children have some wonderful adventures in their dream and finally are chased and captured by two big Polar bears who are just in the act of hugging them when they awaken to find that it is Christmas morning and they are in reality being hugged tight in the arms of their parents.

LENGTH, 500 FEET

A BEAUTIFUL STORY PICTURE

A CLOWN'S LOVE STORY

Copyright, 1907, by The   Vitagraph Company of America

A grotesque circus clown who is of a serious and honest disposition, loves the beautiful daughter of an old performer. She refuses him and accepts the attentions of the handsome ringmaster who later casts her off and then she finds the true worth of a clown's affection.   LENGTH, 325 Feet.

For Perfect Results use "Vitagraph" Adjustable Rheostats $20.00
"Vitagraph" Lamps $35.00

THE VITAGRAPH COMPANY OF AMERICA, { NEW YORK, 116 Nassau Street
CHICAGO, 109 Randolph Street
LONDON, 10 Cecil Court
PARIS, 15, Rue Sainte Cecile.

2.23. An advertisement for Vitagraph films from a 1907 number of Film Index (also known as Views and Film Index), an early motion picture trade paper in the United States

duction company. Originally dealing in the phonograph, the firm under Charles Pathé (1863–1957) became an important manufacturer of motion picture cameras (its professional studio camera, introduced in 1905, had its hand crank on the back instead of the side, and was favored by cinematographers), and began making films as well. The Pathé company logo, a rooster silhouette, was for a time the movie industry's most familiar symbol: besides its Paris studio, Pathé operated a studio in the United States and produced films in Russia.

Pathé led the way in 1907 in transforming the relationship between producers and exhibitors. Instead of selling film prints outright to theater operators, as had previously been the case, Pathé rented its prints, retaining ownership; this change, soon emulated by other producers, enabled the company significantly to expand its **distribution** network, and it opened offices in cities throughout the world to rent its films. Ferdinand Zecca (1864–1947) was the company's production head and principal director. Though in the forefront in quantity of production, Pathé films have been regarded by film historians generally as derivative of those of other filmmakers, with an output consisting largely of simple trick films and comedies—a judgment, like all others in cinema history, perhaps open to challenge.

Gaumont

A second French company, Gaumont, based like Pathé in equipment manufacture, also moved ahead of Méliès. Its founder, Léon Gaumont (1864–1946), looked upon filmmaking as a sideline, and so turned production over to his secretary, Alice Guy (1875–1968), with the proviso (as she later wrote) that it not interfere with her secretarial duties. From 1896 to 1905 she was the firm's only director, and produced as many as four hundred films. Later, as Alice Guy Blaché (she married Herbert Blaché, who also became a film director), she ran her own production company in the United States—at Fort Lee, New Jersey—and directed many more films from 1910 to 1920.

Britain

In Britain, a similar pattern of transformation occurred, but with a difference. While early leaders such as Robert W. Paul dropped out of the business in the manner of Porter and Méliès, their competitors were not new British entrepreneurs but French and American producers, who were said by 1910 to control together 85 percent of the British market. Perhaps the one figure with a continuous career in the early decades of British cinema, Cecil Hepworth (1873–1953), was more like Edison than Porter, a producer rather than a director. His most important production in the era of primitive cinema was *Rescued by Rover* (1905), directed by Lewis Fitzhamon. This was a particularly well constructed "chase" film with twenty-two separate shots. A gypsy steals a baby from an inattentive nanny. The dog Rover follows her to a hideaway, then fetches the baby's father and guides him to the kidnapper's lair. This was one of many films made in nearly every country about dangers posed by outsiders and criminals to the bourgeois family.

United States

Edison's legal challenges against his rivals were the shaping influence on the first decade of cinema in the United States. Biograph, Edison's most formidable competitor, had trouble raising capital and lost key personnel. The Vitagraph Company of America, another important early producer, was forced by court decisions concerning infringements of Edison copyrights and patents to pay Edison a royalty, then to cease production entirely. The firm survived by operating as exhibitors (showing European films) until another court case in 1902 limited Edison's patent rights and allowed Vitagraph to resume production. Still, given the uncertainty of the legal picture—Edison was continuing to sue others, and there was always the possibility of new judgments in Edison's favor—Vitagraph showed its films only in its own theaters until 1905, when the expanding market for films persuaded the company to build a studio in Brooklyn, New York, and offer films to other exhibitors. Vitagraph's early history is an example of the way the development of the medium was held back in the United States by legal struggles. After being curtailed for more than five years, the company—headed by J. Stuart Blackton (1875–1941) and Albert E. Smith (1875–1958)—quickly demonstrated a knack for making popular entertainment films and returned to the top rank of American producers.

2.24. A woman with two boys at a nickelodeon box office. The sign reads, ambiguously, "[blank] under 16 years of age not admitted unless accompanied by [blank] or [blank]."

THE NICKELODEON ERA

Throughout the world, around 1905, the primary site of movie exhibition began to shift from fairgrounds and vaudeville houses to permanent motion picture theaters. It is logical to assume from this movement that spectators from wealthier and more educated classes were becoming interested in films and wished to see them in new, clean, well-appointed theaters. This was certainly the case in a number of countries, though in the United States other forces were at work as well. A hot debate has been waged for some time among film historians over the relative extent to which bourgeois or working-class values and concerns shaped developments in the American cinema after 1905. However one views the American situation, it is clear that from an international perspective the primitive mode of cinema production was coming under pressure from both the higher and the lower ends of the social hierarchy.

What made the United States different in this historical moment was the rapid expansion of its industries and cities fueled by an influx of immigrants from southern and central Europe. Many of these newcomers came from agricultural regions and were new to factory work and city life. Too poorly paid to afford vaudeville prices and working such long hours that they had little time for amusements at all, this population proved a fertile opportunity for entrepreneurs, themselves often immigrants, who found a way to offer them inexpensive popular entertainment—the five-cent movie theater, or nickelodeon. It is no coincidence that these theaters first made an impact in such heavily industrialized centers of immigrant settlement as Pittsburgh and Chicago. Within a couple of years there were many hundreds of nickelodeons across the United States.

This expansion of exhibition generated enormous profits—at first for the exhibitors more than the producers. It occurred several years before Pathé led the switch from selling to renting films, so in the beginning of the nickelodeon boom producers received only their original price for a print, regardless of how many times the print was screened and how many people saw it. Once the rental system began, payment varied according to length of time, number of screenings, audience size, and box office receipts (and the exhibitor's honesty in reporting these figures). Renting films necessitated setting up a new tier of organization, the film exchange, which handled distribution of prints to exhibitors. A new level of complexity entered the industry: with higher profits came a demand for increased production, an elaborate system to control prints, and, for the first time, critical feedback from audiences, exhibitors, the expanding entertainment trade press, and concerned social and cultural organizations.

Movies and Society

This critical feedback from different groups marked the emergence of a distinct public sphere for motion pictures. The medium's qualities—and deficiencies—now became a focus for public debate. Social organizations concentrated on the moral issues, while for critics, exhibitors, and audiences the concerns were more on the aesthetic side. The nickelodeons were magnets for young people, families, and even mothers with babies, as evidenced by photos of nickel theaters with baby carriages parked outside. Those concerned for the morals of such audiences criticized the elements of violence and sexual titillation on which the cinema of spectacle often relied. Those concerned with aesthetics criticized primitive cinema for its frequent incomprehensibility. Reliance on audience familiarity with the story grew more untenable as patrons came from increasingly varied cultural backgrounds and training. Production companies expanded the plot synopses they supplied to exhibitors (to promote rentals, and also as background information for lecturers), but these sometimes contained so much more narrative information than did the screen images that they proved the critics' point.

There were complaints centering on the theaters themselves for which the producers did not bear direct responsibility. These concerned hygiene, lighting, safety, and the broader question of whether children should be exposed to alluring impressions outside the bounds of the official school and church cultures. Some wanted the movies controlled out of censoriousness, others out of a desire to uplift the medium's environment and cultural values.

Motion Picture Patents Company

Where control was an issue, Thomas Edison would eventually be sure to have his say. As the motion picture industry transformed itself, Edison had continued to pursue his legal cases. After 1907, with the shift from selling to renting films, he had a new card to play: he could put pressure on the new distribution firms, or film exchanges, to handle only films produced by companies that paid him royalties for using his patents. The overall strategy, as it had been for a decade, was to control the motion picture industry, but under the new industrial circumstances it would serve additional purposes. Only a select group of theaters that charged higher

2.25. The five-cent theater, beginning around 1905, made movies part of everyday life for immigrant and working-class Americans. When storefront operations were photographed, owners and employees often posed at the door, as at the World's Dream Theatre in St. Louis, Missouri.

2.26. Moralists' concerns about unseemly behavior in nickelodeons were countered by lantern slide advice.

prices would be given access to films, which would drive cheap working-class theaters out of business, pleasing the reformers. Producers would not suffer because fees for film rental would be raised, and the cut in demand for films would give them more time to deal with the critique of primitive cinema's film style. Beginning in late 1907 a series of producers' meetings led to a pact among Edison and a number of companies who agreed to become Edison licensees, paying royalties to Edison and participating in the plan to rationalize the industry. Among the firms joining were Pathé and Vitagraph; some production companies and film importers were excluded. A side arrangement was struck with George Eastman whereby he would supply raw film stock only to member producers. After months of fierce battles, Biograph and its allies also joined, and in 1908 the Motion Picture Patents Company, an attempted monopoly over the industry, was formed.

Censorship

One of its first acts was to cooperate with social organizations in the establishment of a National Board of Censorship. This voluntary group screened films in advance of release and recommended cutting or, on rare occasion, banning outright those it found immoral. One goal of the board was to curtail the proliferation of municipal and state censorship bodies throughout the United States. In this it was not notably successful, in large part because local groups considered the board too much in collusion with producers. The cultured, well-to-do volunteers were perhaps more effective in applying traditional aesthetic values to the movies, adding their influential voices to the chorus calling for higher standards.

The Spectator's Place

As a new power structure emerged for the industry and culture of cinema—shaped by the producers' monopoly, the censorship board, social organizations, and critics—where did the spectator, the paying customer, fit in? With primitive cinema entering a period of crisis and decline, some film historians in recent years have seen the triumph of a monolithic bourgeois ideology with the imposition of a new narrative cinema that quashed variety, experimentation, and the possibility of cultural resistance. There are certain conceptual problems, however, with this view. It is not quite accurate to regard primitive cinema as either non-narrative or antibourgeois, and the influx of working-class patrons into the nickelodeons only highlighted the need for change.

The history of cinema is not a case of either/or. The cinema of spectacle, a feature of the early era, survived primitive cinema's demise and has remained significant in mainstream genres as well as avant-garde films ever since. Though the new narrative system

2.30. Brandishing a gun, a mother (Marion Leonard) calls for help as villains attack in D. W. Griffith's The Lonely Villa (1909). Mary Pickford (face visible above mother's arm) played the eldest daughter, Gladys Egan and Adele De Garde the younger two. In the upper-left corner of the frame appears the Biograph company logo, "AB" in a circle, to deter piracy.

shaped film texts as more unitary and psychologically involving viewing experiences, moviegoers do not invariably turn into the passive, solitary, absorbed spectators postulated by some film theories. Going to the movies can be a communal event where active, oppositional viewpoints are clearly voiced, and social historians have shown how it frequently served that purpose for immigrant and working-class audiences in the years of early cinema. Nevertheless, we need to avoid romanticizing the "resisting" spectator as well.

2.31. Film lecturers generally became obsolete with the emergence of intertitles and new narrative styles around 1910, except in Japan, where the lecturer, called benshi, grew in importance through the silent period. Some became more famous than screen stars and interpreted narratives and dialogue as it suited them. Shunsui Matsuda (1924–1987), pictured at left, worked as a child-benshi (his father was also a benshi). When sound came to Japanese film in the 1930s, benshi soon were phased out. After World War II, Matsuda began collecting silent films and presenting benshi performances. A woman benshi, Midori Sawato, trained by Matsuda, is carrying on his tradition, giving performances with Japanese silent films throughout the world.

DAVID WARK GRIFFITH

No name is more closely associated with the development of narrative cinema than that of David Wark Griffith (1875–1948). Though the rediscoveries and reevaluations of early cinema have called into question many of his claims to stylistic originality, they have recast our view of his achievement rather than diminished it. The idea of originality itself is what is most suspect: all art is intertextual, and a popular hybrid form such as cinema—with its early history of pirating and duping—brazenly so. Griffith may have originated very little, but in his sustained accomplishments as a film director at the Biograph company from 1908 to 1913 he has few equals in the medium's history.

D. W. Griffith was a poet, playwright, and stage actor before entering motion picture work as a performer. His assumption of directorial responsibility at Biograph marked a shift toward

2.32. The "wheat king" has cornered the market and the price of bread doubles in Griffith's A Corner in Wheat (1909), leaving the poor to go hungry.

creative personnel from allied arts instead of inventors and mechanics like Porter. It also highlighted the increasing subdivision of creative tasks: someone else operated the camera, another department supplied the stories, and if Griffith had a hand in editing his films, he surely did not have to go into the lab and process them. This collaborative structure freed him up for his principal effort—to put on film some twenty to thirty minutes of screen time per week.

Biograph was committed to releasing two one-reel fiction films and a shorter half-reel film every week, as part of the Motion Picture Patent Company's plan to maintain a steady supply of films to participating exchanges and approved exhibitors. In the early cinema (and later to become standard terminology) a reel of film designated the film spool that was loaded onto the projector; each spool, or reel, could hold 1,000 feet or 305 meters of film. Because the amount of film on each reel varied, as did projection speeds, film duration in the silent cinema was typically given in number of reels and/or feet or meter length. With all these variables, one reel on screen might last from ten to fifteen minutes. Many films longer than one reel had been produced by 1908, and the Patent Company's decision to make the one-reel film its norm appears to reflect a business rationale—for efficiency, standard-

ization, and product flow—rather than an aesthetic or even a box office judgment. Griffith's ability to produce distinctive and innovative work under this breakneck schedule assured his and Biograph's emerging leadership.

The Lonely Villa

Griffith had directed more than one hundred films in less than ten months when he made perhaps his most important early work, *The Lonely Villa* (1909). This is—there is no other way to describe it—a direct steal from a 1908 Pathé film that has survived with its British title, *Physician of the Castle*. But it is not a shot-by-shot remake in old pirating fashion. Though the Biograph film almost exactly follows the other's narrative, the well-constructed Pathé work told its story with twenty-six shots, while Griffith more than doubled that number, to fifty-four. Both films recount a well-worn tale of bourgeois danger. Intent on robbery, or worse, criminals lure a man away from his isolated home with a false message and then proceed to terrorize his wife and children—until a last-minute rescue. *Physician of the Castle* makes effective, fast-paced use of both theatrical and exterior space. Using the same elements of mise-en-scène (inside and outside, constructed and natural space, is all there is), Griffith builds something different, what we might call narrative or **cinematic space**.

Cinematic Space

Herein lies the significance of Griffith's more than doubling the number of shots in the earlier film. Since the films are approximately the same running time, shortening the length of individual shots and increasing their number, coupled with rapid shifts from one location to another, has the effect of creating a metaspatial world, a "beyond" space or multispace that exists only on the cinema screen. Questions of temporal continuity that have been raised concerning primitive cinema—are these events occurring simultaneously or sequentially?—now become irrelevant as the **shot chain** (the shaping of a narrative through a sequence of separate shots) constructs its own screen-time and the images leap from location to location in a rapid flux. The retreating mother and children futilely barricading doors; the inexorably pursuing criminals, the madly dashing husband/father, racing against time—these form a narrative out of time and space.

Analytical Editing Style

The term for alternating among different locations is called **cross-cutting** (that is, when a series of shots cuts back and forth among two or more separate spaces). The term for shifting between positions within the same space is called **shot-countershot**, implying a relation between the camera setups in the sequence, such as two persons in the same room whose viewpoints are alternately presented. These practices are both elements of what critics have called the **analytical editing** style. This describes the way that an action or several actions that occur as continuous movements without interruption are "analyzed" or broken up into a series of discrete images, involving different camera setups and separate shots, and then reconstructed at the editing stage from individual fragments into a multi-image whole, to create a cinematic experience of time and space different from direct perception.

Narrative Intelligibility

The point was to make a film narrative intelligible without previous knowledge of its story, without the aid of lecturers, with all

2.33. Films in color became more widely available with the advent of tinting and toning, which involved bathing black-and-white positive film in a dye. This enabled the full frame image, and entire sequences, to be colored, and was less expensive and time-consuming than hand-tinting individual frames. Colors were chosen to fit mood or location: blue signifies a seaside scene in the Italian film Corradino di Svevia (Conrad of Swabia, 1909), directed by Romolo Bacchini for the Vesuvio company of Naples.

the necessary information contained within the frame, on the screen. In the analytical system of multishot scenes, increased emphasis was placed on insert shots, which had occurred less frequently in primitive cinema (such as in *The Gay Shoe Clerk*, noted above). These were close-up shots directing the spectator's attention to a specific element of a wider scene that was of narrative importance and would leave a viewer confused if it were not noticed—for example, a gun hidden in a pocket, or the location of a missing object for which characters were searching. Insert shots could heighten suspense and viewer involvement by giving the spectator privileged knowledge not possessed by characters onscreen; they guarded against a problem of the primitive cinema, where key details were sometimes so underemphasized that spectators were left puzzling in the dark.

Another element of narrative clarity was the use of **intertitles**. These frames of printed text had been utilized occasionally in earlier years but became a standard feature only as an elaboration of the new narrative system. Intertitles could announce a change of scene or location, give dialogue lines, guide the spectator by

summarizing in advance the next scene's action, or comment editorially along the lines of, "Such are the wages of sin." Along with other elements of narrative intelligibility, they placed narrative control more firmly in producers' hands; they made it less likely that exhibitors would cut or reedit films to fit their own program requirements, and, as film historian Tom Gunning has written, the new system of narration worked "as a sort of interiorized film lecturer."[1] Live voice accompaniment gradually disappeared from movie theaters, except in Japan, where the narrator—called *benshi*—grew in importance throughout the silent film period.

The shift to the new narrative mode was not an inexorable progression. It was perhaps most apparent in contemporary genres like comedy, crime, and domestic melodrama. In films drawing on literary sources there was a tendency to revert toward the presentational style of primitive cinema. Another of Griffith's significant early works, *A Corner in Wheat* (1909), was based on writings by the American novelist Frank Norris. Since *The Lonely Villa* Griffith had directed nearly seventy films, yet *A Corner in Wheat* was made with less than half the number of shots than the

2.34. Reddish tint was used for an action scene in Giovanni Pastrone's La caduta di Troia *(The Fall of Troy, 1910), produced by the Itala company of Turin.*

earlier film: twenty-four, as against fifty-four. It was among the most trenchant social critiques in early American cinema—the poor go without bread as "the wheat king" corners the market and lavishly celebrates his coup—and it adopted a slower pace with tableau-like shots of the suffering poor. (The wheat king does suffer the wages of sin, falling by accident into a bin at the granary and suffocating under the flow of the commodity that made him rich.)

Griffith's feat of personally directing more than 140 films in 1909 was a remarkable achievement, and the system of film narration he was developing would transform the medium. Yet from an industrial perspective his working methods represented the old primitive cinema as much as or more than they did the new production practices and filmmaking goals that were becoming apparent. In terms of production, Vitagraph, in contrast, utilized half a dozen directors and twice as many camera operators to make some 170 films in that same year, pointing to the large-scale operations that would characterize later studio modes of production. Outside the sway of the Motion Picture Patents Company

(which included European producers such as Pathé) filmmakers were rejecting the one-reel and half-reel lengths as industry standards. Italian director Giovanni Pastrone (1883–1959) captured attention in Europe and the United States with *La caduta di Troia* (*The Fall of Troy*, 1910), a historical **epic** two reels in length whose ambition and narrative breadth made the one-reelers look puny by comparison. As the changes of 1908–9 eliminated the contradictions of primitive cinema, they introduced new contradictions of their own: in particular, a well-regulated, upwardly mobile film industry could not curtail the desire of filmmakers and audiences alike for a medium that offered not just quarter-hour entertainments, but a place among the arts.

Notes

1. Tom Gunning, *D. W. Griffith and the Origins of American Narrative Film: The Early Years at Biograph* (Urbana: University of Illinois Press, 1991), p. 93.

THREE

FILM AS ART AND

The transformation of filmmaking in the decade after 1910 had barely begun before sweeping new claims were made for the medium in the realms of culture, philosophy, and art. Motion pictures were said to be the first new art form of the modern era. They spoke in images accessible to all nations, all ages, all stations in life. Philosophers linked the movies with their theories of perception and knowledge; psychologists compared the movies to dreams. Avant-garde writers and visual artists drew on formal properties of cinema for their own work.

Here was a new medium and art form of almost unlimited potential, in the eyes of many, yet in its everyday reality it remained predominantly an inexpensive popular entertainment, produced for profit. A debate was begun in the decade after 1910 about the relation in cinema between art and commerce. That it could be commerce was already amply proven; that it could be art—could achieve aesthetic significance for its practitioners and spectators—was becoming more certain year by year. Whether it could be both at once, and in what proportion, was a matter of contention and continues to be so to the present day.

D. W. GRIFFITH AND NARRATIVE STYLE

During the decade from 1910 to 1920 few if any films were made for other than commercial purposes, yet among commercial film-makers at least a few claimed for their work the status of art. Chief among these was D. W. Griffith. He continued as perhaps the world's most prolific filmmaker, personally directing more than

eighty one-reel films in 1910, more than seventy in 1911, more than sixty in 1912, and around forty in 1913, when he left Biograph because the company would not allow him to make longer films (several two-reel works and one of four reels, *Judith of Bethulia* [1914], which Biograph had reluctantly permitted him to direct, were released after his departure). He joined a production firm that gave him the opportunity to make films of four reels or more.

In his years at Biograph Griffith steadily advanced the narrative style he had begun to develop with such films as *The Lonely Villa*. A notable example was *The Lonedale Operator* (1911), one of the most intricately edited of the one-reel films with ninety-eight separate shots. This film definitively laid out the distinction between a **scene**, continuous action in one location, and a **shot** as a segment of a scene and of a shot chain that breaks up the scene into numerous shots. A variation on *The Lonely Villa* theme (thugs menace here not a bourgeois family but a working woman, a railroad telegrapher), *The Lonedale Operator* displays a wider range of analytical editing technique than any film before. It cuts rapidly among three or four separate locations, changes camera position within scenes, and uses close-ups and inserts for narrative information.

Griffith demonstrated his mastery of the one-reel format with two films made back-to-back in August–September 1912—*The Painted Lady*, a psychological study, and *The Musketeers of Pig Alley*, a crime melodrama. In the first film, Blanche Sweet (1894–1986, the telegraph operator of *The Lonedale Operator*) plays the prim, responsible elder daughter of a widower who misses out on the playful life of her younger sister. A man courts

INDUSTRY

3.1. *Capturing the thieves in the railway telegraph office in D. W. Griffith's* The Lonedale Operator *(1911); Blanche Sweet, as the telegrapher, is at left.*

her, only to betray her. When a burglar enters the house and she accidentally shoots him, the victim turns out to be her "sweetheart." She becomes mentally unbalanced. Moving the camera closer for more **medium shots** (less than a performer's full body, generally from head to thigh or calf) and close-ups than was typical, the film focuses on the woman's inner, emotional life; it was one of the earliest to emphasize an actor's interpretation of character, performance as well as plot.

Though a crime film, *The Musketeers of Pig Alley* was different from the hundreds of earlier films that had depicted criminals as alien invaders of bourgeois family life. It was set in the lower-class ghetto which spawned crime, but where people (as the film insists) also struggle to maintain respectable lives. Some scenes were shot on the streets of New York City's Lower East Side (**location** shooting had been common in the primitive cinema, when several long takes might comprise an entire film, but the growing emphasis on performance and on multiple camera setups made the controlled setting of the studio more suitable for the emerging narrative style); studio sets were constructed to resemble famous photographs by the reformer Jacob Riis of an underworld hideout. The film features a tense gun battle in a back alley, but it also offers touches of character and comic relief for which Griffith's dramas also became known. As a further display of his versatility, soon after this Griffith directed a romantic comedy, *The New York Hat* (1912). This film was based on a free-lance submission from a teen-age girl, Anita Loos, who later became a Hollywood scriptwriter and wrote the book *Gentlemen Prefer Blondes*.

FEATURE FILMS

The trouble was, by the end of 1912 being king of the one-reelers no longer put you on top of the motion picture trade. While the producers affiliated with the Motion Picture Patents Company, such as Biograph, pursued a conservative policy, moving only cautiously into two-reel films, others were undeterred by their attempted monopoly. New companies stepped into the vacuum with longer films. Their inspiration was the international success of a nearly one-hour (four-reel) film made in France, *Les Amours de la Reine Elisabeth* (*Queen Elizabeth*, 1912), starring the stage legend Sarah Bernhardt. That it looked back to the primitive cinema in its distant camera and tableau style did not impede this film's popularity. It carried the aura of its star attraction and the "higher" art of theater and was more readily acknowledged as aesthetically significant than, for example, the stylistics of a Griffith one-reeler. (As early as 1907 a French production company called itself Film d'Art and offered works made with performers and directors from the prestigious theater company the Comédie Française.)

By 1914, in the United States alone, more than four hundred **feature** films of four reels or more were produced by more than one hundred companies. ("Feature" remains an ill-defined term, pertaining to the principal attraction on a mixed program, rather than to any agreed-upon minimum length; over time, however, the norm for features tended to grow longer, going from less than one hour in this era to ninety minutes or more.) The best of these (on the evidence of the few that have survived) went far beyond *Queen Elizabeth* in their capacity not only to incorporate but also to advance the narrative style Griffith had pioneered.

3.2. Lillian Gish (at left) in a location shot from Griffith's The Musketeers of Pig Alley *(1912)*

The Wishing Ring

A prime example was *The Wishing Ring* (1914), written and directed in the United States by the French filmmaker Maurice Tourneur (1876–1961). Because he knew English, Tourneur had recently been sent by his French production company, Eclair, to make films at a studio they had opened in Fort Lee, New Jersey.

The Wishing Ring (made not for Eclair but for a new American company, World Film Corp.) pays homage to the theatrical origin of its story and the prestige accorded filmed plays by enclosing its narrative within a theater curtain that opens when the film begins and closes at the end. In between, however, the mise-en-scène develops a sense of cinematic space, based on the shot, rather than the theatrical space of a film like *Queen Elizabeth*. This light-hearted "Idyll of Old England," as it is subtitled, utilizes the range of analytical editing techniques articulated by Griffith — cross-cutting, changes of shot within a scene, inserts, and close-ups. What marks it further is a complex use of **deep space**: in contrast to the flat, enclosing rear walls of most studio sets, or action in only one spatial area in outdoor locations, the film's action can be observed in several planes of space receding from the camera. Contrasts between different spatial areas are enhanced by the use of light emanating from sources within the screen image (rather

3.3. The famous stage actress Sarah Bernhardt performs in Les Amours de la Reine Elisabeth *(*Queen Elizabeth, *1912), a work that popularized longer "feature" films.*

3.4. A fire provides atmospheric source lighting in Maurice Tourneur's The Wishing Ring (1914). Vivian Martin and Alec B. Francis portray the romantic couple.

than the diffuse Cooper-Hewitts or natural sunlight) to vary or focus lighting within the frame. The film ends in a flourish with a long **pan** shot (a horizontal camera movement) down a table, slowly revealing the entire cast assembled to celebrate the wedding of the romantic leads.

A Volatile Era

The period from 1910 to 1920 was among the most varied and volatile in film history. While the major transformations in film style that have captured the attention of scholars were proceeding at a rapid pace, out of the spotlight the landscape of cinema changed much more slowly. Though exhibitors began charging premium prices for special bookings of big new feature films (in 1990s terms, more like the cost of an opera ticket than a movie ticket), the five- and ten-cent theaters were still the places where most people saw films. What was shown in those theaters continued to be mainly one- and two-reelers, and comedies remained highly popular. Even as new narrative styles took root, first in the United States, then more and more internationally, a great many filmmakers still were content to work in the older presentational style, with little interest in exploring the possibilities of shot changes, camera movement, or close-ups.

The Sound of Silents

Silent films were rarely soundless. Often considerable effort went into preparing musical scores, sound effects, narrations, or even spoken dialogue to be performed at the exhibition site of films that lacked recorded sound. This is invariably a surprising discovery to later generations who are accustomed to seeing silent films played silently in classrooms or museums, or to hearing a nostalgic tinkly piano score accompanying television screenings of silent comedy classics. By comparison, as a perhaps unusual example, some early cinema audiences heard an original score by the noted symphonic and opera composer Charles Camille Saint-Saëns (1835–1921), commissioned by the French company Film d'Art to be performed with its 1908 film *L'Assassinat du Duc de Guise* (*The Assassination of the Duc de Guise*).

A historian of silent film music, Martin Marks, has analyzed scores written as early as 1895–96 for the Bioscop presentations of Emil and Max Skladanowsky in Germany. But a principal focus of activity around sound accompaniment to silent

films came in 1908–10, years that saw the beginning of a transition from the "primitive" modes of early cinema to new narrative styles. A dominant concern of the time was how much explanation and interpretation the screen images needed. Lecturers flourished in this period, and film historian Charles Musser, in a study of traveling exhibitors prepared in collaboration with Carol Nelson, discovered numerous instances of performers delivering dialogue and sound effects from behind the screen. "Humanova Talking Pictures" was the name of one company of traveling performers.

The development of new narrative styles, which included increasing use of intertitles and visual narrative explanation through analytical editing, sharply curtailed the roles of lecturers and live performers. Music, however, became even more important to motion picture presentation. In 1910 the American trade paper *Moving Picture World* began a column "Music for the Picture," and by 1912 a production company, Kalem, was offering to exhibitors (at twenty-five cents a

copy) special piano scores for its releases, composed by a pianist, Walter Cleveland Simon (1884–1958). A landmark in film music was the orchestral score composed and selected by Joseph Carl Breil for D. W. Griffith's *The Birth of a Nation* (1915), which contributed significantly to the film's success.

At the same time, inventors in the United States and Europe were working on recorded sound for motion pictures. One system was Thomas A. Edison's Kinetophone, which harked back to his ideas of a quarter century earlier for linking the phonograph and motion pictures. Edison's company made a number of films in 1913–14 with sound recorded on phonograph records that were connected to a projector and a sound amplifier in theaters. Other systems were developed and exhibited in France, Germany, and Britain before World War I. Problems with synchronization and amplification were not satisfactorily solved until the 1920s (see Chapter 8).

Despite its importance, this decade is also the era of film history about which least is known. Only a small handful of films by the best-known directors are in wide circulation, and archival collections are only beginning to be systematically viewed and evaluated. It is possible that directors and films from Brazil or India or Japan, from the Scandinavian countries or Germany or Russia, even from the dominant cinemas of France or Italy or the United States—known now, if at all, only to a few specialists—will take their place alongside the prominent figures discussed here. The materials for a full picture of the "teens" decade are still to be gathered.

EPIC FILMS

There are films that make their presence felt before they are seen. One of the earliest was *Cabiria* (1914), directed by Giovanni Pastrone for the Itala company of Turin. News of its epic form, enormous length—its original version is listed variously at 4,000 meters or eighteen reels, which would make at least three hours of running time, though later versions were cut by a third—and massive sets preceded its actual arrival in many countries, shaking the foundations of world cinema like the volcanic eruption of Mount Etna the film depicts. The Italian cinema had already made a significant impact in the international market with epic-style films on historical, biblical, and mythological subjects. The most successful thus far had been *Quo Vadis?* (1913), directed by Enrico Guazzoni (1876–1949), based on Henryk Sienkiewicz's 1896 novel about Christians and pagans in Imperial Rome during the first century A.D. Operatic in its grandeur, *Cabiria* was nearly twice the length of *Quo Vadis?* (released at 2,250 meters). It united spectacle and narrative in a manner that has made a permanent mark on film style and practices.

Cabiria

The story of *Cabiria* is perhaps of less moment to a later era than to its original audience. (An Italian literary hero of the time, soldier and poet Gabriele D'Annunzio, was hired to write the intertitles; historians dispute how much work he actually did, but

*3.7. A poster advertising the
Italian epic* Quo Vadis? *(1913),
directed by Enrico Guazzoni for
the Cines company of Rome*

the fact that he lent his name to the project was of immeasurable importance to its prestige and success.) It is set in the period of the Roman Republic, around the third century B.C., when Rome was engaged in wars with another city-state, Carthage, located in North Africa near the present city of Tunis, in Tunisia. An aristocratic Roman child, Cabiria, is kidnapped and carried off to Carthage; a Roman soldier, Fulvius Axilla, and his black slave Maciste pursue her into the dark heart of the enemy's city; after many years and innumerable harrowing adventures, they rescue her. By that time Cabiria is a beautiful grown-up woman, and she and Fulvius Axilla have fallen in love.

The awesome splendor of its mise-en-scène is what keeps *Cabiria* remarkably fresh. The city of Carthage was destroyed in the second century B.C., during the last of its wars with Rome, and no visual renderings of it survived; the film's designers were free to create a space of fantasy and horror. The Carthaginian temple to the god Moloch is its highlight. Its entrance, approached by a broad stairway dozens of feet in height, is through the fanged mouth of a three-eyed figure; inside is another huge statue of a god, a strange winged figure with an elephantine head and a roaring fire in its belly, into which young children are gruesomely sacrificed.

Maciste (played by a Caucasian actor in light blackface make-up) put his superhuman strength in service to the Romans—and to the Italian expansionist ideology of the period when the film was made. Along with similar figures in *Quo Vadis?* and a 1913 gladiator film, *Spartaco (Spartacus)*, Maciste launched a genre of strongman films that lasted into the 1920s (thirteen titles began with the character's name between 1915 and 1926) and resurfaced in the 1960s with a series again bearing the name of Maciste. English-language versions called the hero Hercules, Goliath, Colossus, Samson, Atlas, or simply The Strongest Man in the World.

The Birth of a Nation

Among those for whom *Cabiria* made the ground tremble was D. W. Griffith. His ambition was to be recognized as the world's greatest filmmaker; but the Italians were regularly raising the stakes. It was the arrival of *Quo Vadis?* in New York that prompted him in 1913 to go beyond Biograph's policy of one-reel films and make two-reel films and his own biblical epic, *Judith of Bethulia*. Merely hearing about *Cabiria*, it was reported, led him to begin planning his own big historical film, *The Birth of a Nation* (1915), and actually seeing the Italian work set him to an even more grandiose project, the omni-historical *Intolerance* (1916).

The Birth of a Nation came only fifty years—not, as in *Cabiria*'s case, two millennia—after the events it depicted. Still, some background is required to place the film in its historical context. The United States Civil War of 1861–65 between the northern and southern states had numerous causes, but many of them stemmed from the South's attempt to preserve the holding of African-Americans as chattel slaves. Slavery was abolished in the South by President Abraham Lincoln's Emancipation Proclamation during the war, and the victorious North followed a policy of Reconstruction after the war in the defeated southern states, partly in an effort to insure rights of citizenship for freed slaves. The Civil War and Reconstruction were the subjects of Griffith's film. By the early twentieth century, a new tide of racialism in the United States had swept away the gains of Reconstruction, segregation between whites and blacks had become a way of life in the South, and theorists of racial purity were advocating a reconciliation between northern and southern whites who had formerly been enemies.

As a southerner living and working in the North and seeking national approbation, Griffith chose to emphasize one particular version of the reconciliation theme: that the southern secession from the union deserved to be forgiven because southern whites had demonstrated to northern whites that their true enemies were not each other, but the threat of dilution of their common race. While proclaiming its fidelity to historical accuracy, Griffith's film subsumes the issues of chattel slavery and the southern secession within its larger subject—that racial equality places white women in danger of sexual assault.

Reviewers in the United States were quick to hail *The Birth of a Nation* as superior to *Cabiria*. If the motion picture medium had not yet proven itself a major cultural force, the film's sweeping depiction of significant events in United States history put the matter to rest. The riveting sequence of the Ku Klux Klan's ride to rescue white maidenhood had the forceful power to sweep the spectator up at least temporarily into its racist fantasy of fear and redemption. However disturbing its social implications, the

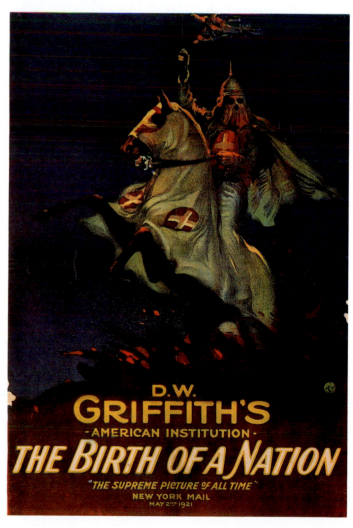

3.8. The troubled legacy of D. W. Griffith's The Birth of a Nation (1915): a poster advertising the film as an "American Institution" depicts a hooded Ku Klux Klansman.

sequence marked the most spectacular instance of analytical editing yet constructed, with its cascade of dozens of separate shots, switching rapidly back and forth between the white woman besieged by the sexual advances of a mulatto man and the gathering of the white-hooded bands who ride to save her.

The Birth of a Nation was controversial from its first screening. The National Association for the Advancement of Colored People (NAACP), a recently formed organization concerned with the rights and development of African-Americans, organized a public campaign against the film and sought unsuccessfully through legal action to have it banned. Even decades later the film often cannot be screened without protests. Its historical importance is undeniable, but as the first great American epic its legacy is more troubling than triumphant.

Intolerance

Griffith's *Intolerance* seems to have been shaped as much by his resentment against the critics of *The Birth of a Nation* as by any larger philosophical viewpoint. While he was working on a contemporary story of injustice in an urban ghetto much like the setting of *The Musketeers of Pig Alley* (a humanitarian sensitivity toward immigrants and white ethnic minorities stood in contrast to his racial views), he decided to create an epic on the subject of lack of tolerance toward others' beliefs by adding to the present-day narrative further episodes on the persecution of Jesus, the massacre of Protestant Huguenots in sixteenth-century France, and obscure but colorful struggles in ancient Babylon. These four separate narrative strands were intermingled, with the shift from one to another signaled by a repeated shot of a woman rocking a cradle.

Above: 3.9. A publicity composite shows some principal players from The Birth of a Nation.

Right: 3.10. Silas Lynch (George Siegmann) menaces Elsie Stoneman (Lillian Gish) as Opposite, above: 3.11. the Klan rides to her rescue against retreating black soldiers.

Griffith had been spending the winter months since 1910 in the Southern California community of Hollywood, where a number of filmmakers had begun to work year-round; after leaving Biograph he had relocated there for his first feature film work. For the Babylonian sequence of *Intolerance*, he built in an open Hollywood field a set that was his answer to the mammoth Carthage sets of *Cabiria*. His Babylon made Moloch's temple in the Italian film look puny by comparison; he borrowed the motif of elephantine figures, but made them twice the size of Pastrone's devouring god. The spectacle of licentiousness and carnage that he staged on this set was justified, as it were, by association with the more pious and humane themes of the other three episodes. Unlike *The Birth of a Nation* and the Italian epics, *Intolerance* was a commercial failure. One reason audiences did not find it satisfactory, ironically, was that its structure challenged the narrative conventions that Griffith more than anyone else had made the norms of filmmaking practice and spectator expectation.

Cabiria and the Griffith epics profoundly influenced cultural discourse about cinema, though their impact on the way films were made was, at least in the short run, limited. The outbreak of World War I in Europe in August 1914 cut off resources for filmmaking, curtailing production generally and precluding any grand projects. In the United States (which did not enter the war until 1917), the development of standard management and production procedures in the film industry discouraged expensive, time-consuming projects. The epics mainly affected how people talked

3.12. *D. W. Griffith directs a scene from the modern episode of* Intolerance *(1916), with Billy Bitzer operating the camera.*

Top: 3.13. Lillian Gish portrays "the woman who rocks the cradle" in the repeated scene representing "all ages" that links the four segments of Intolerance.

Middle: 3.14. Griffith planned his Babylonian sets, shown here under construction in Hollywood,

to outdo the Moloch temple of Cabiria.

Above: 3.15. A Babylonian slave market

Right: 3.16. War and conflagration bring the downfall of Babylon.

3.17. André Deed as Cretinetti, one of several popular Italian comic characters before World War I. In three years, 1909–11, Deed made nearly one hundred Cretinetti comedies for the Itala film company of Turin.

3.18. Principals of the Keystone Film Company on the studio lot: from left, President Adam Kessel, comedy stars Mabel Normand and Ford Sterling, and producer-director Mack Sennett

about film: cultural elites who had previously given scant attention to the medium could now appreciate its artistic capabilities in the framework of traditional "high" art forms such as opera, theater, and symphonic music. While there were still holdouts who deplored the movies primarily on moral grounds, with the epics of the mid-teens most educated people throughout the world accepted cinema not only as a sociological phenomenon but as the newest form of art.

COMEDY

The vast majority of the world's peoples who had access to cinema theaters did not go to the movies to debate aesthetics. They went to have a good time. All sorts of films were created to feed this appetite. As did other arts, cinema as it developed organized itself in categories or types of works, distinguished by style or subject, called **genres**. Reference works for this period have identified at least two dozen different genres within the full range of film production. Among these, a particular pride of place might be

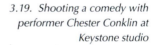

3.19. Shooting a comedy with performer Chester Conklin at Keystone studio

3.20. Keystone's The Knockout (1914), with Roscoe "Fatty" Arbuckle the boxer at left, and Charlie Chaplin the referee

3.21. Charlie Chaplin's first performance as the tramp, in the Keystone comedy Kid Auto Races at Venice (1914)

accorded to comedy. Amid all the lofty discussions of epic cinema and its status as art, one- and two-reel comedies poured out of the film companies, attracting little or no critical notice beyond the laughter of the common filmgoer.

In the trick films, risqué comedies, and chase films of the primitive cinema, performers had been anonymous figures and the comedy arose from situations. The success of Max Linder (1882–1925) at Pathé introduced the comic personality whose basic character and behavior generate comic happenings. After he began directing his own films, Max became an international star with his persona as a fop who continually finds himself in circumstances beyond his capacity to understand or control—such as how to prepare a meal for himself while his wife and servants are away. Another Pathé comic, André Deed (1884–1938), went to Italy and became a star as the character Cretinetti, sometimes translated as Foolshead, with a more **slapstick** style of performance than Linder—the term derived from the stick wielded by clowns in Punch-and-Judy puppet shows and denoted a boisterous, sometimes physically violent type of comedy.

Mack Sennett

The slapstick comedy format was developed in the United States by Mack Sennett (1884–1960), a Canadian of Irish extraction, born in Quebec. Sennett had joined Biograph as an actor around the same time as D. W. Griffith and became an active if minor member of Griffith's stable of performers. In 1909 he appeared in more than one hundred Biograph films, usually as a figure in a group or crowd; later he claimed to have written the script for *The Lonely Villa*, which, as we have seen, copied a Pathé film. By 1911 he was directing the half-reel comedies while Griffith concentrated on one-reel dramas. The next year two entrepreneurs, Adam Kessel and Charles Bauman, hired him as director at a new comedy studio, Keystone.

Sennett learned the analytical editing style from Griffith and applied it with a vengeance. Though he employed comic personalities in the Linder manner (a long list including Roscoe "Fatty"

Arbuckle, Chester Conklin, Charley Chase, Mack Swain, Mabel Normand, Edgar Kennedy, and, of course, Charlie Chaplin), they rarely got a chance to do long-take routines. Sennett preferred **rapid cutting**, so fast at times that individual shots passed in a blur. Sennett's films adapted the chase sequence from primitive cinema to this breakneck editing style, and exaggerated both to the point of parody. One constant was a failure to be solemn about the film medium. In *The Knockout* (1914), Fatty Arbuckle motions to the camera to tilt up so it won't show him changing his pants; it obliges, and he smiles sheepishly as he makes the switch below the bottom frame line.

Charlie Chaplin

Charlie Chaplin (1889–1977) entered Sennett's world dressed like a Max Linder clone, in top hat and frock coat, in his first Keystone appearance, *Making a Living* (1914). That film also revealed his fundamental difference from the French comic: where Max created humor from being befuddled, Charlie's persona was endlessly inventive. Within days after his first film the distinction was made visible by Chaplin's change of costume—his famous inspiration to dress as a tramp, unveiled in *Kid Auto Races at Venice* (1914). Though the tramp persona gave poignancy to his screen character, it did not diminish his resourcefulness or his unsurpassed ability to assume almost magically any guise at all.

Chaplin worked for a year as part of the Keystone ensemble—he appeared in thirty-five films, including the six-reel *Tillie's Punctured Romance* (1914), directed by Sennett. At Keystone Chaplin had written and directed a few of his films, but he sought complete autonomy, first with the Essanay company in 1915–16, then with the Mutual company in 1916–17, where he began to produce his films as well as write, direct, and perform in them. Many consider the dozen films he made for Mutual to be his finest concentrated achievement. They include *Easy Street* and *The Immigrant* (both 1917), films in which he demonstrated a remarkable capacity to create humorous but deeply sympathetic vignettes of immigrant and urban ghetto life. They are in a way a

Above: 3.22. Chaplin in The Immigrant *(1917), with Edna Purviance at left*

Below: 3.23. Company owner and film director Alice Guy Blaché (in white hat) with a production crew at the Solax studio in Fort Lee, New Jersey, c. 1914

tribute to the working-class audiences who were so important to the rapid development of cinema in the United States, yet they have often been described as having universal appeal across lines of nationality and social class. Chaplin's reputation has gone through ups and down over the decades. His films have been criticized for sentimentality and for lacking advanced cinematic techniques. Still, his worldwide success was a phenomenon few other artists have ever attained.

Middle-Class Comedy

Bourgeois comedy was also highly popular in the United States, reflecting perhaps the growing predominance of spectators from the middle classes. Vitagraph produced scores of domestic comedies, many with the portly comedian John Bunny (1863–1915). Alice Guy Blaché's *A House Divided* (1913), produced for her Solax company, was a typical example of the genre: a husband comes home smelling from the perfume a salesman has tried to sell to his secretary; the angry wife, after consulting a lawyer, communicates with her husband only by handwritten note; the misunderstanding is solved and they reconcile. This film is distinguished by vivacious performances by wife and secretary, the latter a gum-chewing snip.

A performer who brought a particularly youthful slant to bourgeois comedy was Douglas Fairbanks, Sr. (1883–1939), who became a highly popular figure in more than two dozen feature comedies between 1915 and 1919 before turning to costume epics in the 1920s. Fairbanks was more than a performer, writing (or signing his name to) self-help books with titles like *Laugh and Live* (1917) which stressed developing moral character and physical strength. His screen persona was a figure who found himself in comic situations that also addressed the serious question, what does it take to be a man? This was often posed in the framework of a contrast between the constraints of city life as compared to wide-open frontiers. In the comedy *Wild and Woolly* (1917), for example, Fairbanks portrays a seemingly spoiled and effete rich boy who goes to the West and through imagination and physical strength proves his worth as a man.

3.24. *Douglas Fairbanks rides the butler (Joseph Singleton) in lieu of a horse in* Wild and Woolly *(1917).*

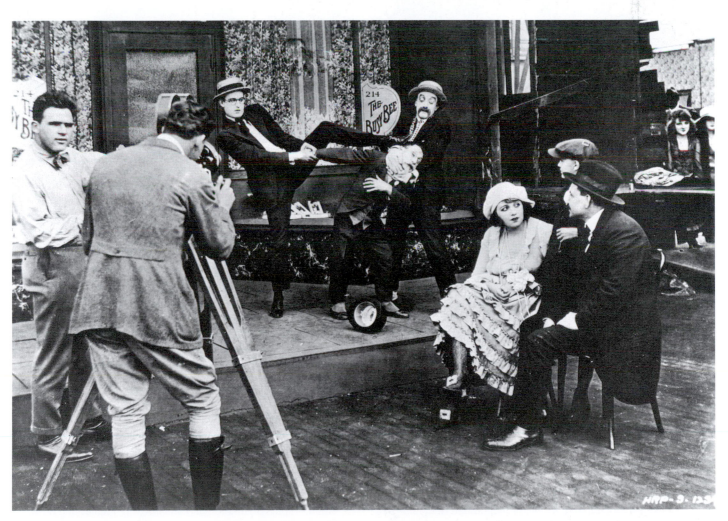

3.25. *Among the most enduring of the middle-class comedians was Harold Lloyd (1893–1971), who launched his career in the "Lonesome Luke" series of one-* *reel comedies between 1915 and 1919, produced and directed by Hal Roach. This shot of a 1918 production shows, from left, Roach with cameraman Walter* *Lundine; Lloyd, Sammy Brooks, and Snub Pollard performing; and actress Bebe Daniels talking with a visitor to the set, comedy director Henry "Pathé" Lehrman,* *whose nickname derived from the story that he got his first directing job by falsely claiming he was a French director from the Pathé company.*

Animation

Another important aspect of screen comedy after 1910 was the animated film. These films simulated motion through stop-action photography: each frame was photographed separately, with imperceptible shifts of position in the image that, when projected, appeared as movement. An early form of animation, popular beginning around 1906, went by the name of "Lightning Sketches," with cartoonists presenting for the camera exhibitions of rapid drawing that they gave as live performances. Another animation style utilized dolls or puppets: the most remarkable examples in early cinema were the work of Russian animator Wladyslaw Aleksandrowicz Starewicz (1882–1965). His most famous film was *Mest' kinematograficheskogo operatora* (*The Cameraman's Revenge*, 1912). The film concerns the infidelities of Mr. and Mrs. Beetle, one with a dragonfly, the other with a cricket, all observed and documented by a grasshopper cinematographer. When the beetles see themselves on screen at an outdoor cinema, they brawl, and the projector goes up in flames.

The emerging form of animation after 1910, however, involved frame drawings, individual drawings photographed one frame at a time. Sometimes these were combined with other animation forms, as in the films of Émile Cohl (1857–1938) in France, which sometimes mingled drawings, puppets, and live action, either through shots of the artist's hand or scenes showing performers and animation together through the matte process of printing separate negatives onto a single positive frame. Cohl's *Le Retapeur de cervelles* (*Brains Repaired*, 1911) was a film of continual figure transformations that, like primitive cinema style, found an echo in later avant-garde animations. Winsor McCay (1871–1934), an American newspaper cartoonist well-known for comic-strip series such as "Dream of the Rarebit Fiend" and "Little Nemo in Slumberland," created an animated *Little Nemo* for Vitagraph in 1911 (another example of cinema's intertextual relation with comic strips, noted as early as the Lumières' *Arroseur et arrosé*). McCay developed his work through the decade with such films as *Gertie* (1914), featuring a dinosaur, and *The Sinking of the Lusitania* (1918), a kind of animated "actuality" film concerning a German submarine's sinking of a passenger ship in 1915.

STARS

The success of the comedy genre, and in particular Charlie Chaplin's rapid rise to international fame, highlighted the basic underpinnings of cinema as the medium increasingly took on an industrial character after 1910. The organization of film companies into larger, more complex units went together with exhibition practices and audience expectation and desires to establish a production system based upon repetition and familiarity—in other

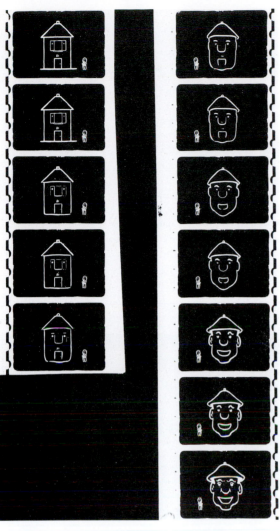

Opposite: 3.26. A scene from the Russian animated film Mest' kinematograficheskogo operatora (The Cameraman's Revenge, 1912) made by Wladyslaw Aleksandrowicz Starewicz

Left: 3.27. Frames from Le Retapeur de cervelles (Brains Repaired, 1911), by French animator Émile Cohl

Below: 3.28. Gertie the dinosaur in Winsor McCay's Gertie (1914)

Bottom: 3.29. A frame of McCay's animated "actuality" film The Sinking of the Lusitania (1918)

words, genres and stars. Genres had been part of moviemaking since the days of Edison's Black Maria; it was only with the emergence of the new narrative style—which began to emphasize emotional identification with performers/characters on screen—that stars became a factor in the medium.

Once film producers began to employ stock companies of performers who appeared frequently in one-reel releases—and played them close enough to the camera so they became recognizable personalities—spectators expressed preferences for their favorites. Exhibitors discovered that they could attract audiences by publicizing the name or face of a popular performer and began to press producers for promotional materials. Vitagraph players early in 1910 started making personal appearances at theaters near their Brooklyn studio. Trade publications began running sections on "picture personalities," and fan magazines appeared in 1911, beginning with *Motion Picture Story Magazine* and *Photoplay*. There were precedents for star status in other performance-based arts, but live performers could be in only one place, while film performers could be seen on many screens simultaneously.

Female Stars

The mystery of stardom is that no single variable—beauty, performance style, or promotional effort—can predict or determine public response. Historical accounts of the "first" stars tend actually to be concerned with the first promotions of stars. Florence Lawrence (1888–1938), who was known as the Biograph Girl at a time when that company did not publicize its players, became the subject of a promotional campaign in 1910 when the IMP (Independent Motion Picture) company hired her away. Vitagraph countered that same year by promoting Florence Turner (1885–1946) as the Vitagraph Girl, and these two campaigns have been credited as the emergence of the star system. But the careers of both women were short-lived, compared with that of Mary Pickford (1893–1979), a Canadian who got her start with Griffith at Biograph and became the most important female star in the United States with a radiant, youthful style; or of the Italian *diva* Francesca Bertini (1888–1985), a dark, fiery Neapolitan who attained international stardom in such films as the realist drama *Assunta Spina* (1915), directed by Gustavo Serena.

The most notorious instance of star promotion of the era involved a performer named Theda Bara (1890–1955). William Fox (1879–1952), an exhibitor and distributor launching the Fox Film Corp. (which would later be merged into Twentieth Century-Fox), concocted the name for Ohio-born actress Theodosia Goodman; its anagram turned out to be "Arab Death," and fanciful tales were told of her exotic origins as daughter of a sheik. Extensive promotion of Bara as a "vampire" whose seductions men could not resist preceded release of her first film, *A Fool There Was* (1915), whose narrative seemed to confirm the publicity. She popularized the word *vamp* and made nearly forty films between 1915 and 1919 before her vogue waned.

Male Stars

By mid-decade a handful of stars had become major attractions and were commanding extraordinary salaries in keeping with their importance to a film's success. The comics Linder and Chaplin were near the head of the list (it was perhaps significant that as directors they had greater control over their screen images, but audiences knew them only as performers). Besides these comic personalities and others like Fairbanks, however, few male per-

Right: 3.32. Theda Bara in Cleopatra (1917), directed by J. Gordon Edwards

Below: 3.33. Maciste at war: the former black slave of Cabiria transformed into an Italian soldier in World War I, portrayed by Bartolomeo Pagano in Maciste alpino (1916), produced by Giovanni Pastrone

SERIES AND SERIALS

Seriality occurred through both series—feature-length films that recounted the adventures of a continuing character—and **serials**, one- or two-reel films released on a weekly basis, which often ended in moments of crisis and imminent death that would be resolved only in the next installment. The most famous series concerned an arch-criminal, Fantômas, who stymies the police in five four-reel French films made in 1913 and 1914. Director Louis Feuillade (1873–1925) used a distant camera and static shots to create a contemplative viewpoint on his urban setting, rather than spectator involvement with individuals. Perhaps because of this visual style, though the series gained enormous popularity in many countries, it did not achieve international stardom for René Navarre, the actor who played Fantômas. Feuillade went on to make a ten-part series, *Les Vampires*, in 1915–16 and others later in the decade.

Many of the weekly serials featured women as protagonists. The one that gained lasting fame was *The Perils of Pauline* (1914),

formers attained star status in this early period—at least few whose reputation and aura have survived the years. One was Bartolomeo Pagano (1878–1947), Maciste of *Cabiria*, who re-created the popular role at least half a dozen times before 1920; in *Maciste alpino* (1916), produced by Pastrone, the "friendly giant" was transmigrated from a black slave to an Italian soldier fighting on the Austrian front. Another was a cowboy star spawned by the Western genre in the United States, William S. Hart (1862–1946). He was the prototype of the "good-bad man," a lean, stern loner who values his independence more than his reputation but always ends up fighting on the side of justice. Hart also directed most of his films; in *Hell's Hinges* (1916), he created a remarkable portrait of a corrupt frontier town through which he stalks, guns blazing, until the place is consumed for its sins in a spectacular fire.

For nearly all these figures, especially the men, stardom and screen character were fused. Basically their screen personas and roles were the same from picture to picture, unlike many stars of later eras who played a variety of roles in different genres. One reason for the difference may lie in the fact that seriality of screen character was at its height in the 1910–20 period.

a serial starring intrepid blonde heroine Pearl White (1889–1938). Pathé produced this and other serials starring White in the United States (she made nine different serials for the company by 1919). It combined parts of *The Perils of Pauline* with other White serials to make a new hybrid for French release, called *Les Mystères de New-York*, that created a sensation in France in 1915. Later critics have argued over whether spectators were more enthralled by White's screen triumphs or her tribulations.

FILM AND WORLD WAR I

While it changed the course of history, World War I also deeply influenced the development of cinema. Above all, it affected the film industries of Europe, several of which had been among the world leaders in the first two decades of the medium. When war broke out in August 1914, film activity in France simply stopped. Movie theaters closed, actors and technicians left the studios for the front. None of the other belligerents reacted in such a drastic way—and in Italy, which did not enter the war until April 1915, production briefly boomed. As the war dragged on longer than had been expected, filmmaking resumed in France. But overall, as combat continued until 1918, European film industries increasingly felt the effect of lost personnel, lost resources, lost markets.

United States Expansion

In the United States, which stayed out of the war until April 1917, filmmakers were in a position to take advantage of their competitors' distractions. The industry had changed radically since 1908, when the Motion Picture Patents Company had been formed to limit the number of producers, distributors, and exhibitors to Edison licensees (see Chapter 2). This effort had completely failed. Firms excluded from the Edison group continued to make films, and **independent production**, **distribution**, and **exhibition** companies managed not only to survive but to gain strength in the years when feature-length filmmaking became more common. In 1912 the United States government brought a suit against the

Patents Company as a monopoly in violation of antitrust laws, and in October 1915 a federal court decision ordered the company dissolved.

In the early part of the decade hundreds of companies had entered the motion picture business, but by 1916 new forms of concentration were beginning to take shape. A few companies from the ranks of the independents were emerging as leaders. One was formed in a merger that year among two production companies, Famous Players and the Jesse L. Lasky company, and a distributor, Paramount. Adolph Zukor (1873–1976) became president of the new firm, called Famous Players-Lasky, but the name Paramount was retained and eventually became the company name. Another, Universal, united a number of smaller companies under Carl Laemmle (1867–1939). William Fox's Fox Film Corp. was a third. Zukor, Laemmle, and Fox had all come into the motion picture field as exhibitors or distributors. Zukor and Fox in particular recognized a need to gain ownership of all three ele-

3.39. A futurist set design by Enrico Prampolini for Anton Giulio Bragaglia's Thaïs (1917); the performer is Thais Galitzsky.

ments of the motion picture business—production, exchanges, and theaters—in order to insure a steady flow of films through a vertically integrated operation.

With war disrupting European production, particularly in the powerful French film industry, American producers went after markets in Asia, Australia, and Latin America. In Europe, too, they made inroads. The war was a crisis for European civilization; it shattered ideals and empires, fostered revolutions, left cultures in shambles. American movies—the comedies of Sennett and Chaplin, the serials, the Westerns—with their sense of space, movement, and action, seemed to many a relief from the tragedies and disappointments of war. Some deplored the violence and anarchic humor of American movies as further evidence of civilization's downfall, but they were not among the mass of moviegoers. By 1918 the United States had emerged as the world leader of cinema, and it widened the gap with **production values**—elaborate sets and expensive costumes—that European cinemas could no longer afford.

Expansion produced in the United States a form of industrial filmmaking that was far removed from Edwin S. Porter's methods only a few years earlier. It came to be known as a "producer" sys-

Expressionism

Of all the early-twentieth-century art movements, the one most closely associated with cinema, at least in name, is **expressionism**—and in film as in the arts, the term is usually given a national definition, "German Expressionism." Clearly the link between expressionism and German cinema is an important one: for one thing, it helped to give status to German films after World War I as distinctive works of art. But where expressionism is concerned, neither terminology nor chronology is undisputed.

"To try to define Expressionism is a thankless task," cultural historian Walter Laqueur has written, "given the inchoate character of the movement." Many critics have found it easier to characterize expressionism not by what it was but by what it was against: naturalism, efforts to depict reality, the idea that there were artistic forms through which the "real" could be represented. The expressionists were part of pre–World War I intellectual ferment, a rebellion against the values of European bourgeois society of the late

nineteenth century. They believed that art derived from inner vision rather than from impressions of a real world or from conventions of artistic practice.

In the visual arts, expressionism began in Germany around 1905–6 and flourished in the period 1911–14 with a group of artists in Munich known as Der Blaue Reiter ("The Blue Rider"). Among its leading figures were the Russian painter Wassily Kandinsky (1866–1944), the Swiss painter Paul Klee (1879–1940), and the German painter Franz Marc (1880–1916), who was killed in action during World War I. In their 1912 book *Der Blaue Reiter*, Kandinsky and Marc asserted their movement's affinity with "primitive" art and the necessity of breaking with artistic traditions. Their own work in paintings and lithographs was generally abstract and non-representational.

Expressionism was also a literary movement, particularly in poetry and theater. In her book on expressionism in German cinema, *The Haunted Screen*, Lotte

Eisner describes an expressionist play of 1912 as one in which "Mind, Spirit, Vision, and Ghosts seem to gush forth, exterior facts are continually being transformed into interior elements and psychic events are exteriorized." These same traits she finds in German films of the World War I period and the Weimar era.

Many critics have seen expressionism in the arts as ending in 1914 with the outbreak of war. From this perspective, the expressionist mise-en-scène of *The Cabinet of Dr. Caligari* has been regarded as contrived and commercial, a calculated means to attract attention by novelty. A new viewpoint argues that in 1914–25 there emerged a second generation of expressionist artists, still seeking to express inner vision but more didactic and political. In any case, only a handful of films after *Caligari* followed its style of abstract, nonrealist set design; but the film's contemporary importance was the attention it secured to German film under the rubric of "expressionist art."

tem—so named because the person in charge was a business manager who supervised all aspects of a film's development. This person acquired story properties, approved scripts, established budgets, hired creative personnel, approved casting, maintained shooting schedules, oversaw the director's work, and had final say over editing and other postproduction work. New creative responsibilities marked a further division of labor: to the behind-the-camera jobs of scriptwriter, cinematographer, director, and editor were added important new roles for costume and set designers (also called **art directors**), who supplied those production values that enhanced American films.

Art Direction

A former New York theatrical designer, Wilfred Buckland (1866–1946), was perhaps the first to receive onscreen credit for art direction. Director Cecil B. DeMille (1881–1959) hired him to work on films such as *The Girl of the Golden West* and *The Cheat* (both 1915). Buckland worked closely with DeMille and his cinematographer in decisions about lighting, camera angles, and placement of actors in designing the overall look of a film. Stung by elite critics who delighted in attacking motion picture design for historical inaccuracies and other slips, the American designers strove for artistry within a realist style. The Italian cinema for a time was more experimental: the director Anton Giulio Bragaglia (1889–1960) incorporated styles from the contemporary futurist art movement into set designs for his *Thaïs* (1917) and *Perfido incanto* (*Wicked Enchantment*, 1918).

Danish Film

The war had an impact even on countries that stayed out of it. The Nordisk company of Denmark, with its logo of a white polar bear astride the globe, was, before 1914, next to Pathé the world's second largest film producer. Danish films were popular in Russia, Germany, western Europe, and the United States, where Nordisk's branch was called the Great Northern film company. Denmark's neutrality did not protect Nordisk from the effects of war. Perhaps because the company owned theaters in Germany, its films were banned in France and Russia, and then the Germans took over the theaters. Nordisk and Danish film never recovered.

Out of this debacle, however, emerged one of the most important film directors of the century. A scriptwriter, Carl Th. Dreyer (1889–1968), got a chance to direct for Nordisk when others left the declining company. His second film, *Blade af Satans bog* (*Leaves from Satan's Book*, 1919, released 1921), was indebted to *Intolerance*. Like Griffith's film it had four episodes, three historical and one contemporary, but Dreyer's came one after another, rather than interspersed. Its dark theme is that Satan is doomed to do evil through the ages—first, also as with Griffith, in the betrayal of Jesus; then in the Spanish Inquisition; in the French Revolution; and in the postwar struggle between Reds and Whites in Finland. Despairing and nihilistic (Satan appears in both religious and revolutionary guise), Dreyer's film displays a mastery of the screen image, using architectural space and studies of the human face in ways rarely before seen in the cinema.

Postwar German Film

Cinema was also profoundly affected, unsurprisingly, in countries where political upheaval was the greatest. In Germany, after political turmoil and attempted revolution, a republic was founded in 1919 in Weimar. During the war, the German government played

a stronger role in film than elsewhere. It launched a production company, Universum Film Aktiengesellschaft (Ufa), which went private under banking control after the war.

After the war, because of the hostility to German cultural products in the victorious allied nations, German filmmakers sought subjects or styles of such compelling interest that they would overcome resistance in the export market. One approach was the sensational costume drama concerning the histories of allied countries: if the costumes (or the removing of them) did not impress, then the behind-the-curtains representations of historical personages would capture attention. Two such works were *Madame Dubarry* (1919), concerned with France, and *Anna Boleyn* (1920), with England, both directed by Ernst Lubitsch

3.40. In the French Revolution episode of Carl Th. Dreyer's Blade af Satans bog (Leaves from Satan's Book, *1919, released 1921), Helge Nissen (left) portrays Satan, Elith Pio is Joseph.*

(1892–1947), who gained such international prominence from them that he was invited to Hollywood to direct a picture for Mary Pickford; he came, and stayed.

Expressionism

A second approach was the controversial application of avant-garde aesthetic styles in commercial films. The classic instance was the expressionist film *Das Cabinet des Dr. Caligari* (*The Cabinet of Dr. Caligari*, 1919), directed by Robert Wiene (1881–1938). Expressionism was an artistic movement in painting, theater, and literature. A revolt against naturalism, it emphasized the inner vision and personal emotional feelings of the artist. In theater and also in cinema, it took the form of abstract set design and a highly psychologized narrative. The script for *Caligari* by Carl Mayer (1894–1944) and Hans Janowitz was about a mysterious doctor, Caligari, who displays a somnambulist, Cesare, at sideshows; Cesare rises at night to murder the doctor's enemies and rivals. During production a frame structure was created so that the original narrative became a tale told by an inmate at an insane asylum—the doctor, it turns out, was the head of the asylum, the somnambulist a patient, the murders perhaps a figment of an insane person's imagination. Or perhaps not.

Top: 3.41. *Polish actress Pola Negri played the title role in Ernst Lubitsch's German film* Madame Dubarry *(1919).*

Above: 3.42. *The somnambulist Cesare (Conrad Veidt) carries the lifeless body of Jane (Lil Dagover) in the German expressionist clas-* *sic Das Cabinet des Dr. Caligari (The Cabinet of Dr. Caligari, 1919), directed by Robert Wiene.*

Above right: 3.43. *A street scene from Dr. Caligari; the doctor himself (Werner Krauss) appears left-center, with glasses.*

The designers, Hermann Warm (1889–1976), Walter Röhrig (1897–1945), and Walter Reimann, were instructed, as one later put it, to make the sets as eccentric as possible. They created grotesquely distorted spaces, tilting houses, misshapen furniture. *Caligari* remains an important and widely debated film, both for its stylistic innovations and for its provocative and ambiguous treatment of the relationships among authority, madness, and violence.

War had transformed the world of cinema. A decade that began with the first challenges to primitive cinema, and saw in its middle years a decisive shift to feature-length films, ended with new industrial structures and aesthetic ambitions in place. The United States was ready to assert its hegemony over world film distribution; European film industries were seeking artistic forms that could compete with American commercial products; and other regions and nations were struggling to establish or defend their own film cultures in the face of the formidable dominance of the major film producing countries.

FOUR

THE GLOBAL SP

What did people mean in the period after 1910 when they spoke of cinema as a universal language? The term had both idealistic and practical connotations. At its most visionary it held the promise of a global form of communication, freed from the babel of languages. Like the pictographs of ancient times, film spoke in a sign-system of images that all humankind could understand. It overcame distance and difference. There was indeed something utopian about this new medium that, unlike the railroad, operated throughout the world on a standard gauge.

Behind such lofty sentiments, however, lay utilitarian considerations. For one thing, the people who advocated cinema as a universal language were mainly from the United States. As the American film industry began to dominate the export market during World War I, it had solid commercial reasons to foster such a view. Associating itself with the idea of a universal medium was a counterargument against those who wanted to use film to represent national cultures or local interests. The notion of a universal language was a means of breaking down barriers that countries might erect against outside incursion on their own native film expression.

The universal concept also served to give special place to the new narrative style of American cinema that had been developing in the work of D. W. Griffith and others as the norm for film language. Films without such increasingly standardized American practices as rapid cutting between shots or close-ups of charac-

ters' faces might then be seen as "grammatically incorrect," or an inferior utilization of the film medium. It was difficult to argue, on the contrary, that the American style could be regarded as lock-step and one-dimensional, forcing spectators to look only at what the filmmaker wanted them to see for utilitarian narrative purposes. What if one was not interested in the narrative but wanted to look at the scenery or the decor or the fashions? Universalism implied there was only one right way to make and watch films.

The combination of the universal idea and the fact of United States domination meant that film as a global language could be understood by all humankind, but only a very few could speak it. Even as cinema moved closer to becoming a universal spectator experience, economic pressures and cultural preferences prevented film production from developing on a global scale and hindered it where it was struggling to get started. Only recently have these efforts outside the European and United States mainstream begun to receive the attention of historians. If we still do not know enough about early filmmaking in the countries that dominated cinema production, we know next to nothing about filmmaking everywhere else. While historians are hunting for more information, archivists are searching for more surviving films (it is estimated, for example, that only 4 percent of all Japanese films made *before 1945* have survived), and the fullness of our view of the past is bound to grow. For now, however, the lines of development—and underdevelopment, and arrested development—can only partly be sketched in.

FILMMAKING OUTSIDE EUROPE AND THE UNITED STATES

Brazil

Among the most exemplary instances of cinematic practice outside Europe and North America is the early history of filmmaking in Brazil. Some historians have called the years between 1908 and 1911 Brazilian cinema's *Bela Época*, or Golden Age. Around 1907, as in the Northern Hemisphere, Brazil experienced an expansion in movie theaters, followed by local production of actuality films, a few fiction films, and a unique genre called *fitas cantatas*—singing films. These were movies of operettas and stage musicals, projected with live singers behind the screen attempting to lip-synch the filmed performances. They accounted for about 25 percent of Brazilian production in 1908–10, outnumbering fiction films, while actuality films made up the majority.

Changes in distribution methods doomed this brief burst of Brazilian production. Pathé's earlier shift from selling to renting its film prints began to affect the Brazilian market around 1911. Since European or United States films would have already earned the bulk of their income in their home countries, foreign produc-

gaucha (*Gaucho Nobility*), directed by Eduardo Martínez de la Pera, Ernesto Gunch, and Humberto Cairo. This epic about the cowboys of the Argentine pampas was exported throughout the Hispanic world. Feature-length films were produced in almost all the Latin American countries during the period, while in Mexico a famous twelve-part serial, *El automóvil gris* (*The Gray Car*, 1919), directed by Enrique Rosas, Joaquin Coss, and Juan Canals de Homes, was a dramatization based on actual events—holdups by a gang driving gray automobiles—similar to contemporary television docudramas.

Japan

In Japan—which had been opened to the West only in the 1860s after nearly three centuries of isolation—a clear distinction between Japanese tradition and Western cultural importations ensured that Japanese film production would not be stifled, no matter how many films were brought in from abroad. In the 1910–20 period Japanese films remained strongly tied to theater. One genre consisted of filmed plays with live performers delivering the dialogue from behind the screen—something like the Brazilian *fitas cantatas*. Another was the "chain drama," so called because it interspersed, like links in a chain, scenes of live theatrical performance with filmed segments shot on location, or involving spectacle elements too elaborate for the stage.

READ OF FILM

ers could lower their rental prices in Brazil below what Brazilian producers needed to charge local exhibitors in order to recover their costs. Given the choice of supporting domestic production or earning higher profits, Brazilian distributors and theater operators opted for the latter, and argued in justification that overseas films were superior to those produced in Brazil. Domestic product was relegated to a minuscule position in its own home market.

By 1913, when Brazilians went to the movies, their opportunities to see a Brazilian film were infrequent. That year, French and Italian films equally dominated Brazilian screens. In 1915, when French imports disappeared because of a curtailment of production at the beginning of World War I, Italian films increased their share of the Brazilian market to two-thirds. Then when Italy entered the war, United States films took over top position in Brazil, accounting for two-thirds of imported films by 1920, and their domination grew throughout the 1920s. These developments in Brazil set a pattern for many countries.

Latin America

There were in fact several so-called golden ages in early Latin American cinema, most of them coming later than Brazil's, in that brief window from 1915 to 1920 when European film was weakened but before the big postwar export surge from United States production companies. In 1915 Argentina produced among the most popular Latin American silent films, *Nobleza*

4.1. A scene from the popular Argentine film Nobleza gaucha (Gaucho Nobility, 1915), an epic about the cowboys of Argentina's pampas

Late in the decade a debate developed over introducing a "new style" of Japanese cinema production utilizing the new narrative styles of American cinema and stories from contemporary life. One of the points of difference concerned the all-male casts from traditional Japanese theater. The figure of the *oyama* (a man playing a woman's role) was carried over into the cinema, and it was a radical departure when women first appeared in Japanese films in the early 1920s.

Colonialism

A glance at a historical atlas from 1914 would show that much of the remainder of the world's territories was the colonial possession of European nations. The effect on the development of film production under this circumstance was double-edged: on the one hand, the flow of cultural products from the metropolitan center was welcomed by colonial elites; on the other, these works were not likely to represent indigenous cultural values, the lack of which might create opportunities for local entrepreneurs.

INDIA. This was the case in India, at that time part of the British Empire, where one man apparently single-handedly launched film production in the country. The story is told that Dadasaheb Phalke (1870–1944), executive of an art printing company, saw a film about the life of Christ and determined that a film should be made about the Hindi deity Lord Krishna. He traveled to England for equipment and instruction, met there with Cecil Hepworth, producer of *Rescued by Rover*, and returned in 1912 with camera, darkroom equipment, and film stock. For his first film he chose a story from the popular legend the *Mahabharata*, and in 1913 he released a feature-length film running nearly an hour, *Raja Harishchandra* (*King Harishchandra*). No prints of this film have survived, and later historians have been unable to describe it, but segments were discovered that Phalke had apparently saved for a planned **compilation film**, and frame enlargements from these provide a sense of the film's mythic mise-en-scène. Phalke made many more films and often carried them as an exhibitor into the countryside. These works

Top: 4.2. A souvenir card for Nobleza gaucha; Humberto Cairo, a codirector of the film with Eduardo Martínez de la Pera and Ernesto Gunch, is pictured top center.

Above, left and right: 4.3, 4.4. Scenes from El automóvil gris *(The Gray Car, 1919), a Mexican crime serial directed by Enrique Rosas, Joaquin Coss, and Juan Canals de Homes*

The Father of Indian Cinema

4.5. *Dadasaheb Phalke editing footage from* Raja Harishchandra *(King Harishchandra)*

In Europe and the United States the development of cinema production was multiple and simultaneous—a number of figures were working independently at the same time. In other parts of the world, where filmmaking began a decade or more after the first film screenings, its emergence can often be pinpointed precisely to a specific group or individual. Probably in no other country has the founder's mantle been so unequivocally bestowed as in India, where film historians honor Dadasaheb Phalke as "Father of Indian Cinema."

What does it take to become the patriarch of a nation's cinema? Phalke was a forty-year-old businessman when he went to a film that changed his life. "While the *Life of Christ* was rolling fast before my physical eyes," he wrote a few years later, "I was mentally visualising the Gods, Shri Krishna, Shri Ramchandra, their Gokul and Ayodhya. I was gripped by a strange spell. I bought another ticket and saw the film again. This time I felt my imagination taking shape on the screen. Could this really happen? Could we, the sons of India, ever be able to see Indian images on the screen?"

Phalke's desire to make an Indian film became an obsession. He borrowed money to make the trip to England to buy equipment and learn how to make films; returning with a camera, a printing machine, a perforator, and raw film stock, he made a short test film with his family and used it to gain financing for the feature-length film, *Raja Harishchandra* (*King Harishchandra*), he wished to make. Placing an advertisement in a Bombay newspaper, "Handsome Faces Wanted for Films," he found a few stage players, but no suitable female performers answered his call. Though he wanted women to play female roles, he reverted to the traditional Indian stage practice of male actors performing the female parts (see fig. 4.6).

"I had to do everything," Phalke said later. "I had to teach acting. I had to write the scenario, do the photography and actual projection too. Nobody knew anything in India about the industry in 1911." Shooting in the day, doing lab work and editing in the evenings, Phalke completed the film in six months. Released in 1913, it was a major success. "I am proud to say that if I had not possessed the artistic and technical faculties required for film-making and if I had not the courage and daring," he wrote near the end of his life, "the film industry would never have been established in India in 1912."

Between 1913 and 1931 Phalke directed more than one hundred silent feature films; during the 1930s he made two sound features before retiring. A few years later, when a magazine wrote him requesting information, he replied, "The industry to which I gave birth has forgotten me." Whether he was right in this assessment, film historians in India have restored his claim as the founder of Indian film.

4.6, 4.7. Scenes from Raja Harishchandra (King Harishchandra, 1913), a feature-length film directed by Dadasaheb Phalke in India; the bathers are male actors dressed as women.

reached an audience who did not see films from western countries in the big cities. They also were exported to overseas Indian populations in Singapore and East Africa, and were the precursors of an indigenous Indian cinema that became after World War II the world leader in total film production.

AUSTRALIA. In 1900 a British commonwealth with a population predominantly of British origin, Australia as early as 1906 produced a feature-length fiction film, running more than an hour: *The Story of the Kelly Gang,* directed by Charles Tait. This narrative, based on actual events, inaugurated a genre of "bushranger" films, similar to films about western outlaws in the United States. As in Brazil, production peaked around 1911, and began to fall off for somewhat the same reasons: a group of companies came together to dominate distribution and exhibition and

had little interest in promoting or showing locally made films. Matters were made worse in 1912 when the police banned "bushranger" films as harmful to children.

CHINA. In China, film production was largely in the hands of western entrepreneurs in Hong Kong, a British possession, and the treaty port of Shanghai, where European commerce dominated. A firm owned by Americans, the Asia Company, recorded scenes of military struggle in 1912 in Shanghai, in the aftermath of the Manchu dynasty's abdication, and released a film, *Shang hai zhan zheng (War in Shanghai,* 1912). The same company produced a fiction film in 1913, *Nan fu nan qi (The Difficult Couple),* with Chinese directors, Zhang Shichuan (1889–1953) and Zheng Zhengqui (1888–1935). In 1916 Zhang set up his own Chinese company, Huanxian, the first in Shanghai, and produced *Hei ai*

DEATH OF DAN KELLY & STEVE HART

CAPTURE OF NED KELLY

4.8, 4.9. Ned Kelly was an Australian horse thief and bank robber of the 1880s who was captured after a two-year manhunt and hanged for murder. His story became a local legend and sub-

ject for popular entertainment, and was the basis for the five-reel, feature-length The Story of the Kelly Gang, *directed by Charles Tait in Australia in 1906 (few films of this length were made in*

Europe or the United States until some seven or eight years later). Australian spectators would have been familiar with the episodes depicted in these stills. A British film on the same subject, Ned

Kelly (1970), directed by Tony Richardson, featured Mick Jagger, the Rolling Stones musician, in the title role.

yuan hun (*Wrong Ghosts in an Opium Den*), filmed by an Italian cinematographer who had been in China for a decade shooting travel films. The Italian owned the camera.

This review of filmmaking in half a dozen countries outside Europe and North America—a summary of the principal industries and efforts—suggests that the notion of a universal medium reflected at least the reality of an international medium. Filmmakers traveled, from the West to elsewhere and from elsewhere to the West; films traveled, though more in a one-way flow. The question of what was "national" about films made within the borders of a country was complicated by the fact that ownership of production companies and theaters, as well as key creative personnel, frequently came from other countries and "national" cultures. What was certain was that the dominance first of European then of United States films in the world market forced a dialogue on filmmakers in other countries: Should we make films just like theirs, or be different? How do we find our own voice in the cinema?

THROUGH WESTERN EYES

An even more serious flaw in the idea of cinema as a universal language emerges from the fact of domination by Europe and the United States. All countries and peoples could see films from western countries, but when they appeared as subjects in those films they were seen, perhaps inevitably, through western eyes. If the western film industries aspired to global leadership in cinema they did not accompany that desire with an effort to construct a global perspective on human lives and cultures. While filmmakers were probably no worse than most political and opinion leaders on issues of race and ethnic difference, they were rarely capable of rising above the worst prejudices of their societies. Their representation of peoples other than themselves was far from universal in spirit; it was more often narrow, low, and mean.

Race and Ethnicity

Distinctions might be made among three types of racial and ethnic distortions found in European and United States films: those drawn, perhaps without reflection, from the common fund of stereotypes; those based on large-scale geopolitical viewpoints, which were especially stimulated by the impact of World War I on empires, colonies, and new forces in international relations; and those that may have been affected by specific circumstances, such as the debate in California, where most American movies were made, over restricting or totally banning immigration from Asia. Their sources, to be sure, were often novels, stories, and plays that had already served to legitimate and popularize opinions.

The few surviving films and the telltale titles—such as the sixteen-part United States serial *The Yellow Menace* (1916), with an "arch villain" named Ali Singh—are only the tip of the iceberg. For example, the seeming confection *Elusive Isabel* (1916) concerns a plot, according to the *Variety* review, by "all of the Latin speaking countries of the world . . . to band against the United States and finally subdue and rule the territory."[1]

Sessue Hayakawa

A point of focus for this pervasive but historically elusive subject is the remarkable film career in the United States of the Japanese actor Sessue Hayakawa (1890–1973). As a young man Hayakawa came to the United States and graduated from the University of Chicago. He joined a Japanese theater company in California and was hired for movie roles. In an era when acting styles were changing from the vigorous emoting of primitive cinema, with its distant camera, to a more compact and concentrated performance consistent with the close-up camera of the new narrative mode, Hayakawa's controlled tension and stillness on screen made him a notable figure. He appeared in more than forty films by 1920, many with his wife, the actress Tsuru Aoki. In later years he worked on stage and in European films, became a Zen

4.10. Edwin Stevens portrays the arch villain Ali Singh in a sixteen-part American serial, The Yellow Menace (1916).

4.11, 4.12. Sessue Hayakawa as Japanese art dealer Hishuru Tori, Fannie Ward as Long Island socialite Edith Hardy, in scenes from Cecil B. DeMille's The Cheat *(1915)*

priest, and returned to cinema fame with his Academy Award–nominated performance as commander of a Japanese World War II prisoner-of-war camp in *The Bridge on the River Kwai* (1957).

Hayakawa's silent film roles ran the gamut of an earlier era's stereotypes about Japanese and other Asians, particularly those living in the West. He was a valet; he was a valet who was also a spy; he was a spy who was also a diplomat. (He does not seem to have played a University of Chicago graduate.) Above all, his movies were clarion calls against sexual relations between Caucasian women and Asian men. In film after film nothing but disaster and tragedy ensue from such unions, married or illicit. Nevertheless, Hayakawa once wrote that "public acceptance of me in romantic roles was a blow of sorts against racial intolerance."[2] More likely, his romantic roles were signs of public fascination with, and dread of, what was still culturally forbidden.

THE CHEAT. The most notorious of Hayakawa's roles was as a wealthy Japanese art dealer in Cecil B. DeMille's *The Cheat* (1915). It was so inflammatory that Japanese-American groups in California protested, and in a 1918 rerelease his character was changed to a "Burmese ivory king." He is a figure in the Long Island, New York, "smart set" who is attracted to the spendthrift wife of a hardworking stock broker. She is custodian of $10,000 in the Red Cross fund to send relief supplies to Belgium, but a friend persuades her to put it in the stock market. Disaster strikes when the money is completely lost. But the Japanese man offers to give her money to cover her disgrace if she will consent to be his lover. She accepts.

Unexpectedly her husband has made a success in the market, and she manages to obtain $10,000 to pay back the art dealer, but he refuses the money. She threatens to kill herself. He hands her a gun. In a harrowing scene, they scuffle; he grabs her by the hair, and brands her shoulder with the signature iron he uses on his ivories. She fires the gun, wounding him. The husband suddenly appears, picks up the gun, and is captured as the assailant.

The husband's trial is an even more stunning sequence. The Japanese man testifies falsely that the husband shot him; the husband claims it happened while he was trying to disarm the art dealer. The verdict: guilty. Then the wife steps forward and says she fired the shot. "This is my defense," she says, and bares the brand on her shoulder. The men in the courtroom rush at the Asian man, who is barely saved from the riotous crowd. The judge sets aside the verdict and dismisses the indictment. Husband and wife walk together out of the courtroom, applauded by the spectators. As in *The Birth of a Nation*, all is forgiven in defense of racial purity. The famous dictum of Rudyard Kipling, "East is East and West is West and never the twain shall meet," is one of the film's intertitles.

Broken Blossoms

D. W. Griffith turned to this same theme in his first major post–World War I film, *Broken Blossoms* (1919). It took a markedly different approach, but came to a similar conclusion. This film was hailed in its time, as well as by later historians, as the first authentically "poetic" work of cinema art. They were referring to the camera work of cinematographer Hendrik Sartov, a former portrait photographer who used techniques of **soft focus** (diffusing the image, usually with material covering the lens) and

backlighting (lighting the subject from behind) to complement the performance of Lillian Gish (1893-1993); to the atmospheric sets of London's dockside district shrouded in smoke and fog; and to the ubiquitous use of **masking** (blocking off parts of the frame image to create different shapes within the frame). It would be difficult to imagine that they had in mind the narrative of brutality, murder, and suicide.

The framing theme is once again the unbridgeable difference between East and West. The film opens in a Chinese port city, where a "sensitive yellow man" (played by Richard Barthelmess) dreams of carrying a message of peace to barbarous Anglo-Saxons. His ineffectual attempt to stop a brawl among Caucasian sailors, where he lands unceremoniously on his backside, reveals at once the impracticality of the dream. In the next scene he is a "Chink storekeeper" in a squalid London slum, blotting out his dreams with an opium pipe.

The other protagonists are a prizefighter (Donald Crisp) and his daughter (Gish), whom he constantly abuses. After a cruel whipping at his hands, she takes refuge in the Chinese man's shop. He takes care of her, dresses her in Asian robes—and desires her "white skin." One of the most curious and contradictory intertitles in silent film reads: "His love remains a pure and holy thing—even his worst foe says this." His foes have no way of knowing, and when they find out she is in his shop they assume something quite different. The prizefighter wrecks the room where his daughter has been staying and takes her home. She locks herself in a closet and whirls about the enclosed space in terror as he smashes in the door with an ax; he drags her out and beats her to death. It is one of the most painful scenes of male violence against women in cinema history. The Chinese man fatally shoots the prizefighter and carries the daughter's body back with him before taking his own life.

Broken Blossoms is a film of many meanings. On one level it is a comment on the brutalization of European society by World War I, for which the prizefighter's behavior is a microcosm. Near the end a policeman is shown reading a newspaper and remarking, "Better than last week—only forty thousand casualties." Another scene, where one clergyman tells another, "My brother leaves for China tomorrow to convert the heathen," surely is meant to be ironic. The Chinese dream of peace is depicted as spiritually superior but also lacking power, vitality, effectiveness. It is passive, perhaps effeminate, subject to violation by the turmoil of the West. Yet the film's center lies in its subtitle: "The Yellow Man and the Girl." His fantasy of possessing the "alabaster Cockney girl" is its emotional core, in its way a greater transgression, more subject to containment and denial, than a father's murderous brutality toward his child.

German Cinema

The German cinema was also enthralled by the exotic. This may have arisen on different grounds than in the United States. Defeated in the war, Germany had lost its colonial empire. Its view of the relations between East and West was colored by its position as an outsider in postwar geopolitics.

Among filmmakers who turned their attention to foreign adventures was the Austrian artist Fritz Lang (1890–1976), who would become one of the world's most important directors, working in Germany and the United States. Lang began his film career after the war in Germany with several films on the theme of interracial romance, including *Halbblut* (*Halfbreed*) and *Harakiri*, based on

Above: 4.13. A publicity portrait of Barthelmess as "the Yellow Man"

Right: 4.14. "The Yellow Man" (Richard Barthelmess) cares for, and dotes on, the girl Lucy (Lillian Gish), after she has run away from her father's beatings, in D. W. Griffith's Broken Blossoms *(1919).*

Below: 4.15. Ressel Orla as Lio Sha, female leader of the secret society the Spiders, with a co-conspirator in Fritz Lang's Die Spinnen (The Spiders, 1919–20)

the play *Madame Butterfly* (both 1919). These were followed by his most significant work in the genre, the two-part *Die Spinnen* (*The Spiders*, 1919–20)—reconstructed by film historians in the 1970s and rereleased with English intertitles.

THE SPIDERS. Hero of *The Spiders* is Kay Hoog, San Francisco millionaire adventurer, whose nemesis is the seductive Lio Sha, female leader of the secret society the Spiders. Part One, *Der goldene See* (*The Golden Lake*), opens in a foreign setting with a native shooting a white man in the back with an arrow, just as the man is tossing a bottle with a message into the sea. California Hoog—a film ancestor of Indiana Jones—finds the message and learns that descendants of the Incas possess unbelievable treasures in Peru. The Spiders steal the message, and Hoog and his enemies race to South America. There Hoog rescues an Inca princess, Naela, from a deadly snake, and brings her back to San Francisco after all the Incas and Spiders (save Lio Sha) perish. Lio Sha offers her love to Hoog; after he spurns her,

he finds Princess Naela murdered, a spider on her chest.

Shifting attention to Asia, Part Two, *Das Brilliantenschiff* (*The Diamond Ship*), centers on a search for a diamond resembling the head of Buddha. Westerners had taken the diamond from China's Ming dynasty in the sixteenth century. If it is returned to Asia by a princess, "Asia will free itself from foreign tyranny." The Spiders want the diamond, presumably as a means to kick the foreigners out and themselves become rulers of Asia. Hoog's desire to bring the Spiders to justice for Naela's murder leads him to a secret subterranean Chinese city beneath San Francisco's Chinatown, and eventually to the Falkland Islands, where he finds the diamond. He foils both the Spiders and something called the "Asian Committee," whose East Indian operatives also want the diamond.

The film seems to posit western imperialism as a tyranny, but its hero fights to preserve it. This contradictory view might be as revisionist on the subject of East-West relations as a mainstream western cinema was capable of achieving.

ARCHITECTURAL EXOTICISM

The universal language of cinema was also spoken by the buildings in which films were shown. For the first several decades of movies their space was borrowed—from stage theaters and music halls down to sideshow tents and converted stores. Around 1910, however, architects were given the challenge to design spaces for the screening of motion pictures alone. Their choices would do nearly as much to define the meaning of cinema for twentieth-century culture as the films themselves. Almost from the beginning of their efforts, the symbols of exotic cultures would be their preference as the fantasy setting to enhance the spectator's pleasure in the moviegoing experience.

One of the first freestanding theaters constructed for motion pictures established the motif. This was the Cines-Theatre opened in 1911 on Nollendorfplatz in Berlin, Germany, a country that was among the leaders in film theater construction. It was an imposing stone structure with blank walls facing the streets on three sides. The entrance was recessed and half-domed, surmounted by a "Buddha-like statue."[3] New movie theaters in other countries also utilized western architectural styles ranging from the classical to the baroque. In the United States, Thomas W. Lamb (1871–1942), a Scottish-born architect, designed several of the famous Times Square theaters in New York (the Strand, the Rialto, and the Rivoli, opened between 1914 and 1917) in the framework of traditional European styles, as well as theaters in such other cities as Cincinnati, Kansas City, and San Francisco. By the end of the 1910–20 decade, however, "Orientalism" had come to the fore in motion picture theater design as Asian subjects had also done in the films themselves.

"Atmospheric" Theaters

The trade term for theaters in the "Oriental" style was **atmospheric.** The architect most closely associated with this approach was John Eberson (1875–1954), born in Austria, whose first "atmospheric," the Majestic Theatre in Houston, Texas, opened in 1922. While their side walls and screen prosceniums were exotic renderings derived from building styles across the globe, their interior ceilings were designed to resemble an outdoor night sky, complete with twinkling lights to represent stars and projected images of moving clouds. Eberson brought the world to the American heartland: he designed theaters in Akron, Ohio; Louisville, Kentucky; Detroit, Kalamazoo, and Flint, Michigan; Nashville, Tennessee; Wichita, Kansas; Omaha, Nebraska; and many other cities. Their designs embodied the universal language theme. Their fantasy spaces took spectators out of everyday life and placed them in a world commensurate with the spatial and temporal universalism of the movies—where styles from Asia and the Middle East met and mingled with Moorish Spain and the American Southwest. "You can step from Randolph Street—into the glory and glamor and romance of the Orient!" read the opening day advertisement crediting one of many Oriental Theaters with "bringing to Chicago the jeweled splendor of the Far East."[4] The space of fantasy lacked completely the fear and disdain western films often expressed toward Asian peoples.

Sid Grauman

The career of the theater operator Sid Grauman (1879–1950) illustrates the development of exhibition practices in first-run United States movie houses after World War I. An experienced San

Above: 4.16. Perhaps the most remarkable of the Chinese-motif theater designs in the United States, the Fifth Avenue theater in Seattle, Washington, opened in 1926. It was designed by architect R. C. Reamer in collaboration with a specialist on Chinese art, Gustav Liljestrom, reproducing designs from the Imperial Palace, the "Forbidden City," in Beijing, China.

Right: 4.17. Oriental Theater, Chicago, designed by the brothers C. W. and George Rapp of that city's architectural firm Rapp & Rapp

4.18. "Orientalism" in American movie theater design: the interior of Grauman's Egyptian theater, designed by the firm of Meyer and Holler, which opened on Hollywood Boulevard, Los Angeles, in 1922

$\mathcal{S}$howmen

It's rarely safe to declare that any aspect of the entertainment world is gone forever: styles, genres, stories, promotional campaigns that seem as old as the hills have a way of coming back (sometimes in updated technological guise) claiming to be fresher than ever. But one figure it is difficult to imagine will make a return is the old-fashioned exhibitor, the "showman" of the early decades of movies (there were surely "showwomen" as well, but their history has yet to be written).

They were personages in their communities. They staged public events to promote their theaters and individual films. They took pride in doing more than just turning on the projector, shaping varied programs of live entertainment, short films, cartoons, and newsreels along with the featured picture. They were the front-line troops of the movie business, counting the house, listening to an audience's pleasure or discontent, hearing individual voices from the crowds of moviegoers.

Running a theater was one of the best schools for learning the dogmas of "what the public wants," and from that foundation a number of exhibitors went into the production end of the business. The ranks of movie moguls were filled with former theater operators: Carl Laemmle of Universal, Adolph Zukor of Famous

4.19. Grauman (kneeling at right) chose—who else?—Mary Pickford and Douglas Fairbanks as the first stars to press their footprints into concrete at Grauman's Chinese in 1927.

Players-Lasky (Paramount), and William Fox of the Fox Film Corp., the three companies that emerged as leaders in the United States film industry around World War I, all had experience as exhibitors. Marcus Loew (1870–1927), a pioneer exhibitor, ran Loew's, Inc., a theater organization that was the parent

company of M-G-M, whose head of production, Louis B. Mayer, also began in exhibition. The Warner brothers, Harry M., Albert (1884–1967), Sam (1888–1927), and Jack L., who led the way in sound production in the 1920s at their Warner Bros. studio, started as traveling exhibitors and nickelodeon operators.

Sid Grauman, of Grauman's Chinese and other Los Angeles theaters, did not go into film production, but that did not mean he was not a producer. He produced scores of elaborate prologues between 1918 and 1934, as live entertainment introductions to feature films, and produced Hollywood previews that filled Hollywood Boulevard with crowds estimated at up to fifty thousand spectators eager to glimpse the stars arriving at Grauman's Chinese.

Grauman's legendary promotional legacy was the forecourt of Grauman's Chinese, in which movie stars implanted their hand- or footprints into concrete. The showman is reputed to have gotten the idea from a mason working on the theater construction crew, who made a special concrete mixture in which he placed his handprint as a record of his work on a job. The mason kept his formula a secret, so the story goes, and sold Grauman a batch whenever a star's prints were to be enshrined.

Francisco showman (he screened movies in a tent after the 1906 earthquake), he opened a Los Angeles theater, the Million Dollar, in 1918. The top ticket price was 25 cents.

That same year he began to offer "prologues" to feature films. These were live stage performances designed to preview and complement the movie. For example, when the Million Dollar offered *The City of Dim Faces* (1918), yet another Sessue Hayakawa interracial romance melodrama, set in San Francisco's Chinatown, Grauman's prologue was a Chinatown street facade with twenty Chinese performers. Prologues sometimes ran nearly as long as the feature and often drew more acclaim. These live performances became a key part of big-city movie programs throughout the 1920s, and companies formed to produce elaborate prologues that traveled from theater to theater. They were

phased out in the 1930s, a luxury that exhibitors could no longer afford in the economic crisis of the Great Depression. One such prologue producer, Fanchon and Marco, was the prototype for the company that provided the storyline of a 1933 musical film, *Footlight Parade*.

In 1922 Grauman opened his first fantasy theater on Hollywood Boulevard, Grauman's Egyptian. Its screen was flanked by four immense columns covered by hieroglyphics, and above the screen were four bands of pictographs stretching from one side of the auditorium to the other (a number of Egyptian-style cinemas were also constructed in Britain in the early 1920s). The most famous of Grauman's fantasy movie palaces, the Chinese Theater in Hollywood, opened in 1927. Renowned as a site for klieg-light premieres, it was also the theater where

4.20. Grauman's Chinese theater, designed by architect Raymond Kennedy of the Meyer and Holler firm, under construction on Hollywood Boulevard in 1927.

A sign in the forecourt, partially visible, indicates that Cecil B. DeMille's The King of Kings (1927) will be the premiere attraction.

movie stars pressed their hand- and footprints for posterity in the forecourt. The pagoda-style roof of Grauman's Chinese (later Mann's Chinese) is one of the most recognizable sights in cinema history.

Within months of opening the Chinese Theater, however, Grauman discovered he could no longer operate it as an independent exhibitor. The major Hollywood studios retained their important films for first-run release in theaters that they owned, denying to the independent Grauman movies of a stature that his lavish theater demanded. Grauman decided he needed to strike a deal with one of the major companies, the Fox Film Corp., in order to gain access to its hit titles. He sold his Million Dollar and Egyptian theaters, only to be replaced by Fox as manager of the Chinese (though he later returned).

4.21. Grauman's Chinese in 1929, playing Condemned, a Samuel Goldwyn production starring Ronald Colman. The shop to

the right of the theater entrance, offering "A Puff from Hollywood," is a tobacconist.

HOLLYWOOD'S GLOBAL DOMINATION

What happened to Sid Grauman in the heart of the United States motion picture industry was a microcosm of industrial domination on a global scale. The universal language of cinema had all the hallmarks of English spoken with an American accent. Several factors had led to the emergence of the United States, soon after World War I, as the strongest force in the world film marketplace: distributors and exhibitors in many countries pre-

Right: 4.22. Actress Jetta Goudal points to posters of Paramount films in foreign distribution on display at the company's studios during the 1920s; looking on, from left, are director Raoul Walsh, actor Warner Baxter, writer-producer Paul Bern, and actor Ricardo Cortez.

Below: 4.23. The first Paramount road show in Ceylon (Sri Lanka), at the Elphinstone Picture Palace in Colombo, June 18, 1931. The picture is Beau Geste *(1926), a story of colonial military adventure in Africa.*

ferred to gain higher profits by showing foreign films instead of supporting local filmmaking; European colonial control over a considerable part of the globe continued to give central place to western commerce and culture; and European (particularly French and Italian) domination of world film markets gave way because of production cutbacks during World War I, allowing United States film companies to fill the void. Another source of the new American leadership derived from developments in the United States itself.

Vertical Integration

Following the demise of the Motion Picture Patents Company, which had integrated a number of production firms under its banner, a new group of independent companies had taken over leadership of the film industry with the tactic of vertical integration (see Chapter 3). With Famous Players-Lasky in the forefront, these companies built and purchased theaters, especially first-run houses in the big cities. Though they never owned a majority of

the thousands of theaters scattered in nearly every town and village across the United States, their control over the metropolitan theaters gave them significant advantages in revenues, promotion, and publicity. They could largely determine what spectators in provincial theaters would want to see. They sold their films to independent theaters not individually but in "blocks": exhibitors had to take many mediocre films to get the one or two big hits. The system operated on volume: theaters in smaller towns played over 100 films in a year. In 1919 Paramount, the distribution arm of Famous Players-Lasky, alone distributed 139 features.

This system enabled the major United States companies to make a profit on most of their films in the domestic market; when Europe faltered, they had the product and the capital to expand rapidly into foreign markets. The statistical story of United States film domination has been recorded in different ways—sometimes as a percentage of film footage imported, taxed, or viewed by censors; sometimes as a percentage of film titles imported, screened, or viewed by censors; and only rarely by more accu-

rate methods, such as share of playdates in theaters or, most specific of all, percentage of box office admissions. Nevertheless, these different methods produce generally similar conclusions: 75 to 90 percent of the films screened in most countries during the period between the two world wars were from the United States.

The consequences for the international development of film were, to be sure, enormous. Many countries struggled to retain the foundation of a "national" film industry, while creative personnel and film financing capital moved from country to country seeking greater opportunities (these themes will be explored further in Chapter 6). Hollywood became a magnet for foreign film professionals. From Britain, Scandinavia, Central Europe, and elsewhere came not only directors and performers but creative figures such as cinematographers and art directors who brought European styles to United States films, creating an international look to American films that reinforced their claim to speak a universal language.

Government Intervention

An effort to prevent, or at least curtail, United States domination arose in the form of government protection of domestic film industries. Germany, whose government had been closely involved with developing film production, in 1921 enacted the first laws limiting film imports. The quota of foreign films was 15 percent of domestic production, measured in footage rather than film titles. Though more films came in than the quota strictly permitted, the law did keep American films from flooding the German market.

Italy, Britain, Portugal, France, Hungary, and Austria also passed film quota legislation in the 1920s. Italy's laws sought to require the country's theaters to show only Italian films one week out of every two months. Britain enacted quotas that applied both to distributors and to exhibitors; as a base figure, British films were to constitute 7.5 percent of all films handled by distributors and 5 percent of films exhibited, and these minimums were gradually to increase over a period of years. Portugal required every film program to include at least one domestically produced one-reel
(ten- to fifteen-minute) film. Legislation in France, Hungary, and Austria tried to use import quotas as an incentive to produce domestic films; for every local film a company produced (or exported), it was to receive a certain number of licenses to import foreign films.

Foreign involvement in all branches of film activity in many of these countries often eroded the laws' effects. In Britain, for example, production subsidiaries of United States companies made inexpensive films, called "quota quickies," to insure that enough "domestic" films were made to meet the quota requirements. This made a travesty of the quota's purpose to encourage development of domestic filmmaking. The advent of recorded sound films in the late 1920s put an end to the rhetoric of cinema as a universal language—but it made little difference in the distribution of power among the world's film industries.

Notes

1. *Variety*, May 5, 1916, reprinted in *Variety's Complete Science Fiction Reviews*, ed. Donald Willis (New York: Garland, 1985), p. 6.
2. Sessue Hayakawa, *Zen Showed Me the Way* (Indianapolis: Bobbs-Merrill, 1960), p. 139.
3. Dennis Sharp, *The Picture Palace, and Other Buildings for the Movies* (New York: Praeger, 1969), p. 154.
4. Advertisement for Balaban & Katz's Oriental Theatre, Chicago, in Ben M. Hall, *The Best Remaining Seats: The Story of the Golden Age of the Movie Palace* (New York: Bramhall House, 1961), p. 141.

Film	Arts and Sciences	World Events
1920 Way Down East	radio broadcasting begins in U.S.	women gain vote in U.S.
1921 The Phantom Chariot	Anna Christie (O'Neill)	famine in Russia
1922 Nosferatu	The Waste Land (T. S. Eliot)	Fascists seize power in Italy
1923 Safety Last Warner Bros. founded	two-sided recorded discs	Hitler's Beer-Hall Putsch
1924 Greed M-G-M formed	"First Manifesto of Surrealism" (Breton)	death of Lenin
1925 The Battleship Potemkin	The Great Gatsby (Fitzgerald)	general strike in Shanghai
1926 Metropolis Vitaphone demonstrated	New York–London telephone service	Pilsudski coup in Poland
1927 Napoleon The Jazz Singer	big-bang theory of universe	Lindbergh flies Atlantic
1928 The Passion of Joan of Arc	first television broadcasts penicillin discovered	Stalin takes power in U.S.S.R.
1929 The Man with the Movie Camera	A Room of One's Own (Woolf)	Wall Street crash Vatican City established
1930 The Earth	suicide of Mayakovsky	Nazis gain in German vote

Part Two

THE SILENT ERA

FIVE

HOLLYWOOD

What cultural phenomenon can compare with the global spread of United States movies after World War I? No communications medium emanating from one country had ever before extended a voice so expansively. No military power, no imperial administration, had cast its leadership so far and wide. Only the world's great religions were comparable forces with such enormous reach. To be sure, these faiths held an incomparably more important place in the lives of their adherents than did American movies. Yet films from the United States were able to connect with spectators of many beliefs.

A considerable part of this remarkable supremacy derived from a single word, which came to symbolize the American motion picture industry: Hollywood. The name was new to history. A western district of Los Angeles, at the turn of the twentieth century it had been a rural outpost, a few houses among the fruit groves. As a burgeoning motion picture community, it was able to develop its own resonance, its own mystique. New York already possessed broad cultural significance, as did Rome or Paris or Berlin. Hollywood meant only one thing: American movies.

THE RISE OF HOLLYWOOD

Hollywood was as much a generic name as a place on the map. By 1920 probably a majority of United States feature films were produced in Hollywood; still, filmmaking went on all over the Los Angeles area, in such places as Culver City, a western suburb, and an incorporated town in San Fernando Valley owned by Universal

Pictures, called Universal City. Though movies continued to be produced all over the United States, Hollywood and its environs came more and more to dominate the industry. Southern California offered inexpensive real estate, a sunny climate, and varied locales. It made possible a new lifestyle, grounded in hard work but emphasizing leisure, sports, and the outdoors. Movie people came to be called a "colony," a separate community unto themselves.

New York Production

Throughout the 1920s, New York remained a substantial center for film production. Vitagraph continued in Brooklyn, Fox and Paramount (Famous Players-Lasky) retained studios in Manhattan, and the latter firm was soon to open a new studio complex in the borough of Queens. Performers from the Broadway theater made movies in the daytime and appeared on stage at night. (With the coming of sound at the end of the decade, dozens of actors abandoned the theater and went out to Hollywood, where pay was better and work more steady.) New York partisans complain that film history has neglected the important contribution of East Coast production to American cinema. The point is well taken, though it is also the case that film production made up only a small part of New York's cultural activities, while "Hollywood" came to define a whole new moviemaking way of life.

Hollywood Studios

Hollywood (with Culver City and Universal City) was home to the vast studio lots that were central to the world's image of American filmmaking. "Here are found," wrote the Paramount company in a trade advertisement, "the huge sky-light buildings for interiors [before sound production made necessary more substantial, soundproof stages], enormous laboratories, costume and research departments, acres of out-door locations, whole cities built for sets. . . ."[1] You had to see them from an airplane to grasp their immensity. Up close, all that was visible was a nondescript gate with a guard to block entrance, and perhaps a glimpse of a standing set high above surrounding walls.

Industry Consolidation

There were several dozen such **lots**, as they were called, around the Los Angeles area in 1920, though few of course as grand as Paramount's. In the rapidly progressing vertical integration of the American movie industry (described in Chapter 4), consolidation was already setting in. More than 750 feature films were produced in the United States in 1920, slightly fewer than in each of the four previous years. Six companies and their affiliates accounted for nearly half this number. Fox Film Corp. and Paramount/Famous Players-Lasky were approximately equal at the top in terms of total releases, followed by Pathé, Universal, Goldwyn Pictures Corp., and Metro Pictures Corp. All told, about two-thirds of the films came from fewer than a dozen companies.

THE FILM DIRECTOR

To highlight the director is not to endorse an "**auteur theory**," which holds that certain "great" directors become "authors" of their films by placing a personal stylistic signature on otherwise industrial products of the Hollywood system. It is first of all a recognition of historical circumstance and archival practice: while most films from the 1920s have been lost, it is the films of famous directors (along with several world-renowned stars) that are most likely to have been preserved in archives and that continue to be circulated and screened. These films, even if by default, form the **canon** of classic works. To spotlight the director is a necessary step in reexamining the historical record. It calls attention not simply to the director's role in Hollywood but, more significantly, to how that role was debated and struggled over in the years after World War I.

Directorial Independence

If consolidation and concentration were the central developments in the United States movie industry during the 1920s, then independence marked their antithesis. **Independent production** has been a key term in American filmmaking throughout most of the twentieth century, beginning around 1910 when it was applied to

IN THE 1920S

This was but a snapshot, because the logic (and power) of concentration was overwhelming. Production companies needed their own theaters; exhibition companies needed a guaranteed source of production. Smaller companies were swiftly being absorbed by larger. By 1920 Thomas A. Edison's company had ceased feature film production, as had other important firms from the early years of cinema. By 1924 Goldwyn and Metro were absorbed into a new production company, Metro-Goldwyn-Mayer (M-G-M), a subsidiary of Loew's, Inc. The advent of sound production brought newer companies like Warner Brothers to the forefront and set off a fresh wave of acquisition and consolidation. Powerful company heads became known as "movie moguls." These included Adolph Zukor at Paramount, Louis B. Mayer (1885–1957) of M-G-M, William Fox, and brothers Harry M. Warner (1881–1958) and Jack L. Warner (1892–1978).

Mode of Production

How do we find ways of thinking about a film industry that was producing (when short films such as two-reel comedies are counted in) more than one thousand pictures a year? Genres and stars are two obvious approaches, since these were categories the motion picture companies themselves used in distribution operations. Another way is to think in general terms of the mode of production—how films are planned and produced, the contributions of craft workers such as cinematographers and film editors to the visual style and narrative movement of typical films. All these aspects will occupy our attention. But inevitably we need to raise the issue of the film director's role in the mammoth production system Hollywood was becoming.

the production companies outside the Motion Picture Patents trust. A decade later, when former independents like Fox and Universal and Famous Players-Lasky had become the industry's leaders, the independents were small production firms headed by, or named after, big-name directors and stars.

The Role of Independents

This new form of independence was out of step with vertical integration of the industry. These companies did not want to operate distribution subsidiaries and theaters: their purpose was to gain big-name directors and stars more money and more creative freedom. They needed financing to make films, distributors willing to market them, theaters willing to show them. In later eras (especially after 1948, when the U.S. Supreme Court struck down the system of vertical integration as a violation of antitrust laws), the studios were more willing to accommodate and support the independents. In the early 1920s, however, when the monopoly structure was just forming, the major studios began to gobble them up. Those that survived became part of vertically integrated units that supported independents, such as United Artists, a financing and distribution company that in the 1920s acquired theaters, or First National, an exhibitor-owned company that acquired and distributed films produced by independents.

Independence and Film Quality

Did independent production result in better films? Here the rules of the canon come into play: films from the early 1920s that have been preserved and valorized by cinema history overwhelmingly have been independent works. Among the productions of leading

The Hollywood Studios

Los Angeles, wrote architectural historian Reyner Banham, is a city of four ecologies: beaches, foothills, plains, and highways. Under the name "Hollywood," one of its western suburbs, it became the first factory town for motion pictures. Besides its varied terrain—deserts and mountains were also nearby—it offered in the 1920s a skilled work force with wage scales lower than those prevailing in other American cities. Studio complexes began to spring up on the wide open Los Angeles plains; the tallest buildings in town were the temporary sets constructed on their back lots. Decades later, with all the open spaces filled in, Hollywood remains in many ways a company town, with the company defined as the motion picture, television, and recording industries. Traces of the old Hollywood survive, though it may take a good guide and a sense of archaeology to find them.

5.1. The "Hollywoodland" sign was constructed in 1923 to advertise a real estate development in the foothills above Hollywood. Over the years it suffered from wear and vandalism, and, with the original promotional purpose gone, it was restored after World War II simply as "Hollywood." In 1978 the original letters were replaced by a completely new "Hollywood" sign. Visible over the crest of the hill in this 1920s photograph are the farms and fields of the San Fernando Valley.

5.2. Hollywood archaeology often involves knowing the corporate history of an industry that changed rapidly until its dominant forces established more stable structures in the late 1920s. This studio complex was built in 1918 on Melrose Avenue in East Hollywood by a company called Paralta Plays, Inc., which failed the same year. Its seven stages were taken over by Robert Brunton Studios, Inc., and rented to independent producers. In the year this photograph was taken, 1921, Brunton had given way to United Studios, Inc., which continued to rent it out to independents. In 1926 one of the industry's giants, Paramount Pictures, Inc., having outgrown a smaller studio on Sunset Boulevard, acquired the property and built a new studio there, with its famous Paramount Gate.

UNITED STUDIOS, INC.
M. C. LEVEE - PRES.   LOS ANGELE

LARGEST INDEPENDENT
MOTION PICTURE STUDIO
IN THE WORLD

SPENCE
Air Photos

5.3. Mary Pickford and Douglas Fairbanks were two of the four cofounders of United Artists in 1919; the next year, they married and began producing their films at the Pickford-Fairbanks Studio on Santa Monica Boulevard in Hollywood. When this photograph was taken in 1922, sets for Fairbanks's Robin Hood (1922) were under construction on the back lot. "Armies of workmen moved there, huge sets were built," Alistair Cooke described the scene in a 1940 essay on the star. "Fairbanks had made a gesture to solve Hollywood's chronic unemployment problem . . . and given orders for the largest interior ever to be built in the history of the movies." Moreover, the film was said to have the largest cast of extras of any Hollywood movie to that time, and its exterior constructions at least rivaled, if they did not exceed, D. W. Griffith's Babylonian sets for Intolerance. In 1926 the studio was expanded and renamed United Artists Studio.

studios Fox and Paramount/Famous Players-Lasky, on the other hand, few titles are remembered in film histories (a principal exception are the works of Cecil B. DeMille). As with all else in cinema history, this viewpoint is subject to revision; film historians have not yet given the period from World War I to the coming of sound the scrutiny that both earlier and later eras have received. Nevertheless, whatever changes in emphasis and evaluation may occur, the decline and fall of directorial independence is certain to remain a dominant theme of American film history in the early 1920s.

5.4, 5.5. Scenes from The Last of the Mohicans *(1920), directed by Maurice Tourneur, regarded as the outstanding visual stylist of the immediate post–World War I era. The film was completed by Clarence Brown after Tourneur was injured during production.*

D. W. Griffith, Erich von Stroheim, and the Decline of Directorial Independence

The best-known names to suffer this fate were D. W. Griffith and Erich von Stroheim. To put their cases in perspective we might first consider the situations of two important but less famous figures, Maurice Tourneur and Lois Weber.

Director of the notable early feature *The Wishing Ring* (see Chapter 3), Tourneur had grown in stature during the 1910s and was regarded as second only to Griffith among prominent directors working in the United States—and second to none as a visual stylist. In 1918 he set up his own production company, releasing through several distributors, including Paramount. *The Last of the Mohicans* (1920), based on the classic nineteenth-century American novel by James Fenimore Cooper, is considered his

Above: 5.6. The Blot (1921), a melodrama directed by Lois Weber. Claire Windsor (center) and Louis Calhern (right) portray a young couple who cross class boundaries.

Right: 5.7. Lillian Gish on a ice floe in D. W. Griffith's Way Down East (1920)

Women in Hollywood

A history of women as creative workers in Hollywood has yet to be written. Less than a handful of women directors who worked before the 1980s have been talked about, even by specialists—Alice Guy Blaché for the early years, Lois Weber after World War I, Dorothy Arzner in the 1930s, Ida Lupino after World War II—although there were considerably more. Women screenwriters are somewhat better known, but the study of women in that profession only makes more clear the fate of women directors until recently: when a job took on prestige or became high-paying, women were frequently shunted aside. The World War I era was a high point for women directors, who found more opportunities then, before the industry consolidated into a few major companies (and when women stars still headed independent production units). Women screenwriters remained prominent at the major studios until the sound era commenced, when writing, too, became almost entirely a man's profession.

5.8. Director Lois Weber with her all-male crew on the set of The Angel of Broadway *(1927), her last film of the 1920s (she was to direct a final work in 1934). Weber's career flourished in the years 1917–21, when she directed eleven films for her own production company and six more for other studios; it declined after her company shut down and producers' interest waned in the social problem films that she had emphasized.* The Angel of Broadway *was produced by Cecil B. DeMille's independent company, and featured Leatrice Joy and Victor Varconi.*

5.10. Jeanie Macpherson (1884–1946) received writing credit on nearly all of Cecil B. DeMille's films between 1914 and 1930; it is fair to say that the work of one of Hollywood's most famous directors cannot be fully assessed without taking her contribution into account (though this does not yet appear to have been done). Macpherson was an actress before she became a writer and occasionally also appeared in DeMille's films; she took a role, for example, in his Carmen (1915). Here (with goggles on her forehead) she works with a secretary on location near Santa Maria, California, for The Ten Commandments (1923), for which she was credited for both story and scenario.

5.9. Frances Marion (1886–1973) was an important screenwriter for a quarter century, and one of the few women writers who successfully made the transition from silent to sound films. She wrote scripts for Rudolph Valentino, Greta Garbo, and Lillian Gish, among other stars, and won Academy Awards for screenwriting on The Big House (1930) and The Champ (1931). Perhaps her most important professional relationship was with Mary Pickford. In 1917–18, among the years of Pickford's greatest popularity, Marion wrote scenarios for nine of the eleven films in which the actress appeared. In 1921 Pickford assigned Marion to direct the star's third United Artists picture, The Love Light (1921); they are photographed together on the set of that production. Marion directed one other film in 1921 and codirected a third in 1923, while continuing her screenwriting career until 1940.

most important film, even though Tourneur was injured during the filming and much of the direction was handled by Clarence Brown. What remains that is unmistakably Tourneur's stylistic touch are the atmospheric contrasts of light and dark in interior scenes. This visual style had a narrative counterpart in the film's sympathetic treatment of sexual desire across racial boundaries. Cora Munro is attracted to Uncas, last chief of the Mohicans. A rejected British suitor says, in an intertitle, "You! The daughter of Colonel Munro! Admiring a filthy savage!" The would-be lovers die tragically, and touch only at the moment of death.

Tourneur's opportunities for independence waned after First National, which distributed his films in the early 1920s, opened its own studio for production. He then went to work for major companies, making *Never the Twain Shall Meet* (1925) for M-G-M and *Aloma of the South Seas* (1926) for Paramount, both about romantic yearnings, eventually frustrated, between South Seas maidens and North American men. He resisted being placed under the authority of a producer, however, and in 1927 left an M-G-M film in midproduction. Returning to his native France, Tourneur directed more than twenty films in Europe in a career lasting until the late 1940s, though none gained the prominence of his early United States silents.

Lois Weber (1882–1939) followed Alice Guy Blaché as an important woman film director (Blaché's last film was made in 1920). Directing since the early 1910s, Weber established her production company in 1917 and kept it going through 1921. She wrote, directed, and produced a number of domestic dramas, including *The Blot* (1921), concerning the family life of an underpaid professor. Their genteel poverty is so galling to his wife, in contrast to the bounty enjoyed by a family of fat foreigners living next door, that she steals a chicken from their kitchen—then puts it back. Weber's gritty realism proved less popular with audiences in the 1920s than it had been in the World War I period, and she had difficulty finding directorial assignments when not her own boss.

D. W. GRIFFITH. Could the director with the greatest prestige in United States motion pictures avoid a similar fate? We do not know the specific details of any tactical errors Tourneur or Weber may have made in resisting the tide of consolidation, but those of D. W. Griffith have been thoroughly chronicled. He already had his own production company; what he wanted was his own studio, which he acquired in 1920 not in Hollywood, or even New York City, but in the suburban isolation of Mamaroneck, New York. The costs of converting an estate into a functioning motion picture facility and maintaining the property and staff created a problem of overhead expenses that other independents, who rented studio space as needed, did not have.

This affected Griffith's business relationships. Films such as *Way Down East* (1920) he chose to open as "road shows" (special bookings at premium prices before general release) because he did not want to share income with a distributor. This meant, however, that he also bore alone the costs of prints and promotion. It also had the effect of alienating small exhibitors and cutting into first-run revenues when the films were officially released.

Griffith's only big money-making film of the early 1920s, *Way Down East*, an adaptation of a late-nineteenth-century stage melodrama, did not contribute to Griffith's reputation as cinema's great innovator. But this "Simple Story of Plain People," as it was subtitled, appealed to old-fashioned tastes in a modernizing world,

and continues to exert its power a century later. A naive country girl, portrayed by Lillian Gish, is seduced and abandoned by a city slicker. She gives birth and her baby dies, in a sequence with intertitles such as "Maternity—Woman's Gethsemane." Working with a farm family when her past is discovered, she is banished into a winter storm by that melodramatic stock figure, the outraged patriarch who opens the door and points into the swirling snow. She collapses on an ice floe in a river whose current is carrying her inexorably toward a waterfall. Griffith's style of crosscutting to heighten drama and tension, familiar from *The Birth of a Nation* and *Intolerance*, here records another of its triumphs in this thrilling sequence of danger and ultimate rescue.

Griffith returned to historical epics with *Orphans of the Storm* (1921), also based on a nineteenth-century melodrama, this one with the story shifted in time and place into the turmoil of the French Revolution. Despite continued critical acclaim and box office success, Griffith could not control his expenses. He fell deeper into debt from bank loans obtained to finance pictures which, though popular, did not earn back their high costs. In 1924 he came to the end of the line as his own boss. He became a studio director for Paramount, where the former giant of American movies could not accommodate well to working as a subordinate. Griffith made his last film in 1931.

ERICH VON STROHEIM. Then there was Erich von Stroheim (1885–1957). An Austrian immigrant who claimed he was an aristocrat and a military officer, he gained success in Hollywood by playing roles as German villains in World War I movies (his enduring legend is as "The Man You Love to Hate," though the origin of this phrase remains obscure, even to his biographers). After the war he pitched a script to Universal for a project on which he would also become the director and star. The film, *Blind Husbands* (1919), a love-triangle story involving a neglected American wife and an aristocratic Austrian officer (played, of course, by von Stroheim), became one of the most auspicious debuts in United States film history. Its critical and financial success seemed to justify the director's excesses: over-budget and over-schedule, he lavished time and money on lengthy rehearsals,

5.11. Erich von Stroheim, playing another of his dissolute middle-European aristocrats, with Miss Du pont in Foolish Wives *(1922), which von Stroheim wrote and directed*

Left: 5.12. A lobby card for Foolish Wives, showing the casino set at night. Mae Busch is in circular inset, lower left.

Below: 5.13. The practice of hand-coloring individual frames was largely abandoned in the 1920s. (Foolish Wives was one of the few films of the post–World War I era in which the method continued to be used, and only some of the prints in circulation were so treated). Given Hollywood's scale of operations in the 1920s, wider audiences could gain access to films in color when the celluloid image was mechanically tinted or dyed. Film manufacturers such as Eastman Kodak prepared positive film stock with different color bases and dyes and suggested how different colors could be used to enhance dramatic moods).

details of art direction, and painstaking editing. The result was an intensity of performance and psychological realism of character unusual in American cinema.

But these were a rookie's excesses compared to his third film, *Foolish Wives* (1922). It took almost a year to produce and ran nearly a million dollars (or close to 400 percent) over the original budget. A huge set representing the casinos of Monte Carlo, a resort on the Mediterranean Sea, was built on the **back lot** of Universal City. Then a duplicate set was constructed along the California coast hundreds of miles away, showing the opposite oceanfront side of the same casinos. The director's cut was over five hours long and included segments colored by hand (common in earlier days, hand-coloring had become rare with feature films, which more frequently used mechanical tinting processes). The studio cut *Foolish Wives* by two-thirds before release. In the eyes of the film industry, von Stroheim, though a talented director, was irresponsible and insubordinate. To the press and public (aided by von Stroheim's own pronouncements) he was the first important director to emerge in Hollywood since the war, a unique artist thwarted by the narrow business values that increasingly came to dominate United States filmmaking.

His career over the remainder of the decade oscillated between these poles: fired at one company, he would receive a generous offer from another. When he was dismissed in the middle of a picture at Universal, he signed on with Goldwyn and began work on a project even more vast than *Foolish Wives*, a film based on the 1899 novel *McTeague* by the American naturalist writer Frank Norris. The result, *Greed* (1924), cost half as much as *Foolish Wives*, but the director wanted to release a nine-hour version. Goldwyn had been by this time merged into Metro-Goldwyn-Mayer, and the new company's head of production was none other than Irving Thalberg (1899–1936), the young executive who

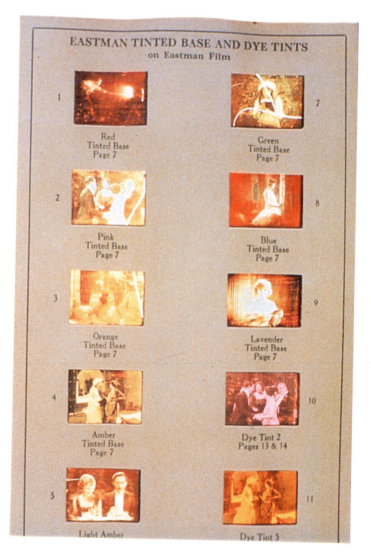

EASTMAN TINTED BASE AND DYE TINTS
on Eastman Film

1 — Red Tinted Base Page 7	Green Tinted Base Page 7 — 7
2 — Pink Tinted Base Page 7	Blue Tinted Base Page 7 — 8
3 — Orange Tinted Base Page 7	Lavender Tinted Base Page 7 — 9
4 — Amber Tinted Base Page 7	Dye Tint 2 Pages 13 & 14 — 10
5 — Light Amber	Dye Tint 5 — 11

5.14. *The* Foolish Wives *set, representing the casinos at Monte Carlo. Because Universal City's back lot, where these sets were constructed, was located well inland, another set was built by the Pacific Ocean several hundred miles away for the casino's seaside facade.*

had fired von Stroheim at Universal. M-G-M cut *Greed* by three-quarters. Even this pastiche contains some of the most remarkable sequences of cinematographic realism in American silent cinema, from extensive location shooting designed to give portions of the film the appearance of nonfiction (other segments, meanwhile, were shot in expressionist style).

These were not von Stroheim's only troubles with the studios. On *The Wedding March* (1928), Paramount executives replaced von Stroheim during editing because the director again wanted to release a film they considered too long. The von Stroheim legend was capped in 1928–29 during the shooting of *Queen Kelly*, produced by Joseph P. Kennedy (father of President John F. Kennedy) for the independent company of its star, Gloria Swanson (1899–1983). Fearful about costs and censorship problems, Kennedy and Swanson fired von Stroheim midway through production; the film was completed by others but never shown in the United States. A new restored version of von Stroheim's footage was released in

1985. By its excesses, von Stroheim's experience—and his fate—defined the terrain. The businessmen were in charge (when had they not been?). Independence for directors was rarely a production possibility within the American film industry over the next several decades.

THE POWER OF STARS

A few big-name stars were able to hold out longer against industrial consolidation. Douglas Fairbanks, Mary Pickford, and Charles Chaplin, having established (along with Griffith) their own financing and distribution company, United Artists, managed to keep control over their own work, so long as they maintained their box office appeal—and avoided Griffith's financial excesses. The enemy, perhaps, was time. Fairbanks and Pickford, in particular, had prospered on screen images of youth. How long could they remain, respectively, the juvenile and the ingenue? The question was especially pertinent when, after divorcing their previous spouses, they married in March 1920, in Hollywood's first big celebrity marriage.

Douglas Fairbanks

Fairbanks carried his middle-class boy hero over into his first several United Artists efforts, but started transforming it with *The Mark of Zorro* (1920), which marked the beginning of a shift to historical costume roles. By day he was an effete and idle young man, by night the fearless masked Zorro, fighter against an oppressive Mexican government in early-nineteenth-century Southern California. (The story was resurrected for a 1957–59 television series.) It was very much a transitional film, in terms of both Fairbanks's "double" persona and the fact that director Fred Niblo (1874–1948) frequently had difficulty capturing the star's athletic feats within the frame. But its success led Fairbanks—as he approached the age of forty—completely to adopt a new screen role, performing as the great (and ageless) adventure heroes of world literature.

First he was D'Artagnan in *The Three Musketeers* (1921), then the heroes of *Robin Hood* (1922) and *The Thief of Bagdad* (1924), based on the Arabian Nights legends. For *Robin Hood*, with Wilfred Buckland as supervising art director, his production com-

5.15. *Gibson Gowland as McTeague and Jean Hersholt as Marcus in the final sequence of Erich von Stroheim's* Greed *(1924), filmed during midsummer* *(for the sake of realism) in Death Valley, California, where temperatures reputedly reached over 140 degrees Fahrenheit.*

among the women. Their careers developed as studio employees, but both sought the independence that Fairbanks and Pickford had established for themselves through United Artists. Valentino's efforts were cut short by his untimely death; Swanson's were undercut by the debacle of *Queen Kelly*.

RUDOLPH VALENTINO. Valentino's legend as the silent era's most controversial screen lover, relegated for decades to the realm of tabloid sensationalism, has begun to attract new attention from the historical study of female spectatorship. He was a figure perhaps unique in film history, a male star whose popularity lay overwhelmingly among women fans. What were the issues of gender and sexuality that made him a signpost of contention between men and women during his brief career?[2]

His was a screen persona created by women, according to one version of his legend—particularly by screenwriter June Mathis (1892–1927), who wrote four of his most important films. Thus he was not a "manly" man, a "regular guy," so the argument went, but one whose screen appearance gave pleasure only to women. Certainly one aspect of his appeal came from his representation of the exotic—as an Italian whose characters were frequently Spanish or Hispanic American, he was the "Latin lover" whose screen romances with Caucasian women touched the same ethnic and racial boundaries as had those of Sessue Hayakawa. In *The Sheik* (1921), he plays a desert prince who abducts an aristocratic Englishwoman who had masqueraded as a slave girl; it

pany built one of the largest Hollywood sets ever; they topped it for *The Thief of Bagdad*, where the art direction and design by William Cameron Menzies (1896–1957) rivaled the immensity and imagination of *Cabiria*'s Carthage and the Babylon of *Intolerance*. In superb shape, the fortyish Fairbanks played the thief mostly bare-chested, constantly throwing his arms in the air to display his muscles. All this athleticism eventually tired the actor before it did the public, and his career petered out, it seems by choice, in the early 1930s.

Mary Pickford

Pickford was a decade younger than her new husband, but still playing child roles in her late twenties. Like him, she tried to develop her screen persona through historical costume dramas, which, though successful at the box office, displeased the fans who wished her forever young. Returning as a child, she gave the part some perverse imagination in at least one picture, *Sparrows* (1926), directed by William Beaudine (1892–1970), which combined comedy and melodrama. Pickford plays the eldest child on a swampy farm in the deep South where a cruel family keeps orphans and babies stolen from the rich. With bow lips and long braided pigtails she leads her charges through harrowing adventures to a happy ending. Personal difficulties with Fairbanks played a part in ending her career in the early 1930s; they were divorced in 1936.

New Stars of the 1920s

For publicity and marketing purposes motion picture stars became even more important during the 1920s, although top-name players appeared only in a minority of major films. Prominent in the new generation of younger stars were Rudolph Valentino (1895–1926) among the men and Gloria Swanson

Above left: 5.16. Queen Regina (Seena Owen) wields the whip on young Kitty Kelly (Gloria Swanson) in von Stroheim's Queen Kelly, *produced in 1928–29, but not publicly screened in the United States until 1985 (except for segments that appeared in the 1950 film* Sunset Boulevard, *in which Swanson portrays an aging silent star).*

Right: 5.17. Gloria Swanson as the grown-up Queen Kelly

turns out he is not an Arab but an Anglo-European.

What women want from men is also one of the questions raised in and about Valentino's films. Their heroines, as in *The Sheik*, were often ostensibly independent women who yearned to be dominated by men. In *Blood and Sand* (1922), the *femme fatale* cries out (in an intertitle), "Some day you will beat me with those strong hands! I should like to know what it feels like!" Then she bites his hand.

GLORIA SWANSON. Swanson achieved stardom in a series of contemporary social comedies directed by Cecil B. DeMille with such titles as *Don't Change Your Husband* (1919) and *Why Change Your Wife?* (1920). Temperamentally independent, though under contract to Famous Players-Lasky, she left Hollywood for New York and made her films in the company's Astoria, Queens, studio. It was perhaps her apprenticeship in Mack

Top left: 5.18. Director Fred Niblo had problems keeping the acrobatic Douglas Fairbanks (upper right) in the frame in The Mark of Zorro (1920).

Top right: 5.19. Even huge sets often started out as miniature models, with which directors and cinematographers were able to work out blocking of actors and camera placements before setting up shots on completed sets. Here actress (and producer) Mary Pickford (right) plans a shot on a miniature set for Tess of the Storm Country (1922) with, from left, cinematographer Charles Rosher, director John S. Robertson, and assistant director Robert Florey.

Above: 5.20. A lavish fantasy interior designed by William Cameron Menzies for Douglas Fairbanks's The Thief of Bagdad (1924)

Sennett's Keystone comedies that gave a double edge to her performances in society melodramas directed by Allan Dwan (1885–1981)—in *Manhandled* (1924) she does an impersonation of Charlie Chaplin's tramp, an act she repeated a quarter century later in Billy Wilder's *Sunset Boulevard* (1950). In Wilder's film she portrays a neurotic former silent star, Norma Desmond, a role that has overshadowed her own silent film career. With Erich von Stroheim playing Desmond's chauffeur, clips from *Queen Kelly* were used in the film—the first time any of that disastrous project was shown in the United States.

Charles Chaplin

Among the four founders of United Artists, Charles Chaplin remained active and autonomous the longest. His association with the company ran through the 1950s, and his filmmaking career ended in the late 1960s. Chaplin's screen persona, the tramp, was most immune to the inroads of time, seemingly age-

5.21. *Englishwoman Diana Mayo (Agnes Ayres) succumbs to the enticements of Sheik Ahmed Ben Hassan (Rudolph Valentino) in* The Sheik *(1921). In the end he is revealed to be an Anglo-European.*

5.22. Gloria Swanson portrays a
department store clerk riding a
subway to work in Manhandled
(1924). Paramount placed an
advertisement for itself above her
head on the subway car.

less if not timeless. During the 1920s he retained the persona
intact, although the volume of his output diminished. Early in the
decade he completed a First National contract with four films—
his first feature (a film longer than three reels), *The Kid* (1921), and
a second, *The Pilgrim* (1922), and the short films *The Idle Class*
(1921) and *Pay Day* (1922). Thereafter all his films were feature-
length. For United Artists he directed a drama, *A Woman of Paris*
(1923), in which he played only a token, uncredited role. His
major comedies of the 1920s were *The Gold Rush* (1925) and *The
Circus* (1928).

Many Chaplin films have remained international favorites for
decades, but the work considered among his greatest—for many,
the outstanding film of his career—was *The Gold Rush*. Here, the
poignancy and humor of the tramp character were seamlessly
blended, and sustained for more than eighty minutes, his longest
film thus far. The heart of his comedy is displayed in the "dinner"
scene: the famished prospectors, Charlie and Big Jim (Mack
Swain, a former Keystone comic), cook and eat the tramp's shoe.
"Charlie attacks the sole with a gourmet's relish," Chaplin biographer Theodore Huff describes the scene, "twists the shoe laces
around his fork like spaghetti, and sucks the nails as if they were
marrow bones."[3]

Postwar Comedians

Chaplin's competition came mainly from a new postwar generation of movie comedians. Chief among these were Buster Keaton
(1895–1966) and Harold Lloyd, who, like Chaplin, controlled
every aspect of their productions, even though others were sometimes credited as director. Both portrayed contemporary young
men coping with the modern world—Keaton as a bewildered but
ingenious figure amid the mysteries of machines, Lloyd as a bumbling but savvy bourgeois striver. In *Sherlock, Jr.* (1924), Keaton is
a movie projectionist who falls asleep and dreams himself into the
picture on screen, where he has a series of scrapes based on
rapid cuts from location to location; then he becomes a detective
in a film within the film. *The General* (1927), often considered his
finest film, places him back in history in the United States Civil
War, where he becomes a hero through a combination of imagination and dumb luck on a runaway railway engine. Lloyd's
screen persona gently mocked the middle-class ambitions of the
post–World War I era. He is indelibly remembered for precarious
scenes of danger where, out of foolishness, he finds himself hanging from flagpoles and ledges of tall buildings, as in *Safety Last*
(1923), in which he is forced to impersonate a "human fly" and
climb the outside wall of a skyscraper.

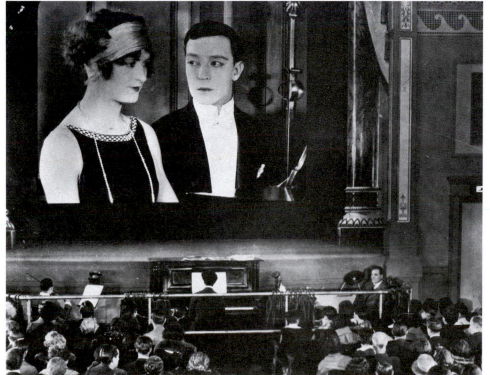

Above: 5.23. Charles Chaplin in
The Gold Rush (1925). Chaplin
modeled this scene after photographs he had seen of
prospectors climbing Chilkoot
Pass en route to the Klondike gold
fields during the Alaska gold rush
of 1898. The shot was filmed on
location at Truckee, California,
near Lake Tahoe in the Sierra
Nevada.

Left: 5.24. Buster Keaton on
screen with Kathryn McGuire in
Sherlock, Jr. (1924). Keaton plays
a motion picture projectionist
who falls asleep and dreams he is
a character in the movie he is
showing. Here he is a suave
detective.

Left, top: 5.25. Keaton in The General *(1927). As he chops firewood with total concentration to keep his steam engine running, he is oblivious to a vast army passing in the other direction behind him.*

Left, middle: 5.26. A lobby card for Safety Last *(1923) depicts comedian Harold Lloyd's travail in attempting to scale the exterior of a tall building, "and all for the love of a maid!" Mildred Davis plays the maid.*

Left, bottom: 5.27. The extensive production schedules of major studios required hundreds of craft workers with versatile skills, from carpenters to seamstresses. The staff of the makeup department at M-G-M goes about its work in 1928. Actor Jean Hersholt is in the chair at left, and department head Cecil Holland, fourth from left, works on the clown.

Max Linder, the first great silent comic, came to Hollywood in the early 1920s and performed in three films which he also produced, wrote, and directed. One, *The Three-Must-Get-Theres* (1922), was a parody of Douglas Fairbanks, with Max as Dart-in-Again. He returned to Europe, made several more films, and in 1925 committed suicide.

HOLLYWOOD GENRES

Central to the Hollywood mode of production was the concept of **genre**. A genre is a category or a type; genres are differentiated from each other by characteristics of style, technique, or narrative content. In studio productions, even before directors were

5.28. Studios promoted their films in a variety of ways, including releasing to the press a sequence of production stills, such as this one for Smouldering Fires (1924), which, with added captions, encapsulated a film's entire narrative. Pauline Frederick, who appears in all these stills, is the businesswoman in this melodrama who marries a younger employee only to give him up to her younger sister. Laura La Plante plays the sister, Malcolm McGregor the man.

assigned or performers were cast, films were planned and written in the framework of genres: What kind of film is it? A comedy; a Western; a mystery; a love story.

Genres did not originate with the movies. They were an intrinsic aspect of popular entertainment, intensified by the proliferation and diversification of cultural products in the emerging mass society. Genres came ready-made to the movies from theater, dime novels, and magazine fiction. Writers on film genre generally list from six to a dozen basic categories, depending on how fine they draw distinctions, and are capable of defining seemingly endless variations. How many kinds of comedy have been identified, for example? Comedy variants include slapstick, sophisticated, farce, parody, "comedian" or clown (featuring comic stars or personalities), and what has been called "populist" comedy—about average people, sometimes with an underlying social message. Moreover, genres can be amalgams of other genres—comedy-drama, for instance—and films could, and often did, switch genres in midreel, when cowboys, say, enter a haunted house.

This welter of generic possibility has led to containment through theories of genre. One view is that genres have a kind of life cycle, in which they grow, mature, and decline. This might help to explain why Western films, once among the most important Hollywood genres, have rarely been made in the last quarter of the twentieth century. Another approach is to link the popularity of generic categories with specific cultural and historical circumstances, which might account for genres such as horror or science fiction lying dormant in some periods and flourishing in others. Still a third places emphasis on factors within the film industry that create genre cycles leading from innovation to emulation to exhaustion.

Genre Codes

A fundamental aspect of genre filmmaking is familiarity through repetition. Genres develop codes of character type, visual style, and narrative progression. Spectators become familiar with these codes, anticipate them, and take satisfaction as they play themselves out within structures that allow, but limit, variation. The history of storytelling is not a history of incessant originality. To "make it new," however, became a supreme value of twentieth-century high art, and in this context the new mass medium of movies, as practiced by the Hollywood studios, was seen as hopelessly inartistic. We continue to grapple with this question, designating, as we have seen, the director as the potential artist in a generic and collaborative setting where writers, performers, art directors, costume designers, cinematographers, picture and sound editors, and many others contribute professional skills to the outcome.

INTERTEXTUALITY. The concept of intertextuality—how texts relate to other texts—has become central to our understanding of all the arts, even the most advanced. In the case of Hollywood, this concept describes a clear-cut practice in which films refer to other films: broadly, through shared codes, and minutely, through specific textual citations (an object, a gesture, a phrase). These small references were an intentional aspect of film production, designed to encourage filmgoing by rewarding spectators who have extensive knowledge of other films. If we could see all the Hollywood films made in a single year, or even a generous sampling, the similarities would outweigh the differences—the intertext looms as more important than the individual texts. In this sense the films that have survived and make up the canon do not have to be claimed as masterworks. They can be regarded as films that may clearly have some special distinction yet also represent a broad range of others that have been lost or, though of lesser aesthetic stature, share many common traits.

The Woman's Film

Such a work, for example, is *Smouldering Fires* (1924), belonging to that amorphous category, the woman's film. A Universal picture, directed by Clarence Brown (1890–1987) and featuring

5.29. With such varied productions as the war epic The Big Parade (1925), the realist drama The Crowd (1928), and the comedy Show People (1928), King Vidor was one of the most accomplished directors of the 1920s. Under contract to M-G-M, however, he also made films such as the swashbuckler Bardelys the Magnificent (1926), of which he later said, "I was a little ashamed of it." (He also satirized it, and the swashbuckler genre, in Show People.) Here Vidor (center, with glasses) directs a shot in a camera vehicle designed to simulate a moving carriage. John Gilbert is the actor without the hat.

5.30. *Greta Garbo during a lighting set up for* Flesh and the Devil *(1927). Director Clarence Brown stands directly behind her.*

Pauline Frederick (1883–1938) and Laura La Plante (b. 1904), it is distinguished by qualities of pace and craft that critics describe in only the most general terms and are more easily notable by their lack. Frederick plays a forty-year-old businesswoman who runs a factory inherited at an early age from her father; asexual in dress and appearance, she had no thought for romance until she falls for a young employee. He, in turn, is smitten by her younger sister. Though the executive and the young man marry, she soon discovers his true feelings and gives him up so that youth can unite with youth.

Sophisticated Comedy

Sophisticated comedy in the United States received a boost with the arrival of German director Ernst Lubitsch, hired by Mary Pickford to direct *Rosita* (1923), one of her efforts to adopt a more mature screen persona. Lubitsch credited Chaplin's *A Woman of Paris* as inspiration for a series of films that almost formed a sub-genre on their own—comedies of manners with European settings, produced by an emerging new company, Warner Brothers. These included *The Marriage Circle* (1924) and *Lady Windermere's Fan* (1925), the latter with very few intertitles, conveying playwright Oscar Wilde's epigrammatic wit through gesture and expression rather than words.

Romantic Drama

Europe was also the setting, and often supplied the performers, for romantic dramas set in the past—if far back enough in the past, they became romantic costume dramas, or historical romances, or, with sufficient swordplay, "swashbucklers." These were often the occasion for heroics by male stars such as Fairbanks and Valentino, but the genre received its greatest boost with the arrival in 1925 of Swedish actress Greta Garbo (1905–1990), with a contract from M-G-M. She brought to the screen an intensity in performing erotic passion that American cinema had rarely seen before. In her third Hollywood film, *Flesh and the Devil* (1927), she was paired with M-G-M star John Gilbert (1897–1936), and their well-publicized off-screen romance heightened interest in their on-screen love scenes.

Left: 5.31. John Gilbert and Greta Garbo in a love scene from Flesh and the Devil

Right: 5.32. After World War I ended in 1918, it took seven years for the war to be significantly represented in American cinema. Promotional efforts helped to launch the first war epic, The Big Parade, at the Astor Theatre in New York in 1925.

Above: 5.33. The Big Parade marched again when it was released with a recorded musical score and sound effects.

Opposite: 5.34. Lon Chaney in The Phantom of the Opera (1925)

War Films

Nearly a decade passed after the end of World War I before a genre began to take shape dramatizing and assessing the war experience. Valentino's first starring role in *The Four Horsemen of the Apocalypse* (1921) had dealt partly with the war, but the film industry shied away from the subject (as it did with the Vietnam War half a century later) until the success of the Broadway play *What Price Glory* by Maxwell Anderson and Lawrence Stallings in 1924. M-G-M hired Stallings to write the story for a war movie, *The Big Parade* (1925). Directed by King Vidor (1894–1982), this tale of lost innocence, with its epic battle scenes and bittersweet romance, established the recently merged studio and became the formative work of the genre.

Horror

The horror genre during the 1920s was largely the province of one performer, Lon Chaney (1883–1930), known as "The Man of a

Thousand Faces." For *The Hunchback of Notre Dame* (1923) he wore a painful harness to create the grotesque posture of his character, Quasimodo. His most famous performance was in the first film version of *The Phantom of the Opera* (1925), where again he endured hardships in creating the gruesome face of the disfigured phantom. Both works were made at Universal; though Chaney left the studio for M-G-M after *The Phantom,* Universal built on these early silent triumphs to become a leading producer of horror films in the sound era.

Melodrama

Dancing Mothers (1926), a Paramount picture directed by Herbert Brenon (1880–1958), was one of a number of "society" melodramas of the Jazz Age that capitalized on the sensational aspects of that period's changing social and sexual mores. Clara Bow (1905–1965) plays a wealthy young woman who parties at the same

5.35. Clara Bow as Kittens Westcourt, the defiant daughter of Dancing Mothers (1926). In the 1920s a woman with a cigarette was meant to be provocative.

5.36. He received his first screen credit in 1921 as assistant director Jo Sternberg, but by 1924 he was Josef von Sternberg, and in 1925, with The Salvation Hunters, he launched a career as one of the leading visual stylists among American directors. Best known for his films with Marlene Dietrich, whom he first used in the German film The Blue Angel; they went on to make six more films together in Hollywood over the next five years. This photograph is from the early 1920s.

5.37. Von Sternberg's Underworld (1927) was the first important film in the gangster genre. In France it was retitled Les Nuits de Chicago to link it with the notorious exploits of Al Capone and other Chicago gangsters. Evelyn Brent, playing "Feathers," a gangster's girl, is pictured here.

nightclub where her father pursues his affairs. The mother, attempting to thwart her daughter's relationship with an older man, awakens her own desires and perceives the empty frivolity of her spouse and child. She leaves them to start a new life abroad.

Gangster Films

Contemporary society also played a role in spawning a new type of crime film, the gangster genre. These films responded to the changes in urban crime as a result of the post–World War I amendment to the United States Constitution prohibiting the manufacture, distribution, or sale of alcoholic beverages.

Prohibition fostered powerful criminal organizations that supplied illegal liquor; their highly publicized exploits found their way into films in the later 1920s. The classic silent gangster film was *Underworld* (1927), directed by Josef von Sternberg (1894–1969) for Paramount. The director called it "an experiment in photographic violence and montage."[4] Gangster films outnumbered Westerns by the end of the decade.

Hollywood on Hollywood

If every film was in a sense reflexive of other films, there was, finally in this partial survey of Hollywood genres of the 1920s, the self-reflexive genre of films about Hollywood moviemaking. King

5.38. Paul Robeson plays an ex-convict masquerading as a clergyman, who turns out to be a figment of a woman's nightmare, in black filmmaker Oscar Micheaux's Body and Soul (1925). He's shown here with Chester A. Alexander.

the end of the 1920s (long neglected, Micheaux's work has not yet been fully catalogued). Though Micheaux and other black filmmakers made entertainment films on the model of Hollywood genres, the budgets for these works often came to less than a week's salary for a Hollywood star. The films played in black neighborhood theaters in such cities as Chicago and Detroit.

BODY AND SOUL. Few so-called race films have survived. One that did, Micheaux's Body and Soul (1925), may have been saved because it stars the famous actor and singer Paul Robeson (1898–1976). It is a complex and ambiguous work, and the extant version may have been altered from the original because of objections from censorship boards. Robeson play two roles, a young woman's respectable fiancé and a vicious ex-convict who poses as a clergyman and commits rape and murder. Then the evil preacher is revealed as a dream figure in a nightmare of the woman's mother.

Documentary Film

A different kind of alternative—with a different commercial outcome—was the "**documentary**" filmmaking of Robert Flaherty (1884–1951). A miner, prospector, and explorer in northern

Vidor's *Show People* (1928) for M-G-M was a prominent example. It presented several of the significant codes of the genre, particularly centering on the propensity of female stars to let success go to their head and lose touch with their fans, with only the benign guidance of producers to protect them from disaster.

No wonder producers invariably came out the good guys in Hollywood self-reflexive films. The United States commercial cinema had become, in the final analysis, a producers' medium. Except for the few directors and stars who retained control over their own creative endeavors, it was supervising businessmen who decided what stories would be prepared for screen treatment, who would work on them, how much would be spent to produce them.

ALTERNATIVES TO HOLLYWOOD

As a cinema culture, the United States was largely mesmerized by the Hollywood monolith. Other forms of filmmaking were carried on: educational films for classroom use, industrial films for training and promotion, films by government agencies on such subjects as health or agricultural methods. Amateur "home movie" filmmaking was getting under way by a small number of enthusiasts who used newly developed hand-held professional cameras. But these were regarded as narrow and specialized activities unrelated to cinema as art and entertainment.

Black Filmmakers

The principal exception came in efforts by African-Americans, fueled by mainstream cinema's discrimination and neglect, to create a film culture for and about black people. The most sustained achievement in black cinema in the silent period came from novelist and filmmaker Oscar Micheaux (1884–1951), whose companies produced several dozen fiction features from 1919 to

5.39. Robert Flaherty's documentary Nanook of the North (1922) was a commercial and critical success, especially in Europe, and is regarded as a foundation work of nonfiction film practice. In filming the lives of Eskimo people in northern Canada, however, Flaherty was less interested in recording what he witnessed than in discovering a "true spirit" of a people that may have been lost through modern influence. To this end he sometimes dressed his subjects in old-fashioned costumes and had them reenact for his camera traditional events that they no longer practiced.

Canada, Flaherty had begun around 1913 to make films of Eskimo life. In 1920, financed by a French fur-trading company, he returned to the north to shoot a feature-length film on the theme of the Eskimos' triumph of survival in inhospitable conditions. Flaherty sought a commercial distributor for the completed film, *Nanook of the North* (1922), and finally found one in Pathé

5.40. Flaherty went to Samoa in the South Pacific for Moana (1926) and observed the importance of dance in Samoan culture.

Exchange. No nonfiction film had received such wide theatrical distribution since the earliest days of cinema, when actuality film-making dominated the field. *Nanook* was greeted, particularly in Europe, as a masterly depiction of a vanishing "primitive" way of life. Yet Flaherty's notion of film documentary was not without controversy. Rather than merely recording what he observed, particularly among native peoples whose lives had been altered by European intrusion, he sought the "true spirit" of his subjects by restoring old-fashioned costume and staging traditional events.

After *Nanook*, Famous Players-Lasky supported Flaherty's next documentary project, in which he went to an opposite climatic extreme, the Pacific islands of Samoa, to make *Moana* (1926). However, Flaherty had a hard time persuading the distribution company, Paramount, to release the film; ultimately it was released with the promotional line, "The Love-Life of a South Sea Siren." Hollywood companies occasionally produced nonfiction films, though mostly for prestige purposes rather than from any interest in encouraging alternatives to their standard products. Flaherty tried to work within the Hollywood system for several more years, without completing any films. His career resumed in the 1930s when he went abroad and worked with funding from British government agencies and film companies (see Chapter 11).

Art Cinema

In the 1920s, primarily in Europe, film became regarded as a fresh field of experiment for artists (see Chapter 6). The concept developed of an art cinema, separate from commercial production, where a self-styled **avant-garde** sought to advance the medium by creating new aesthetic forms, such as abstract images or nonnarrative works. In United States filmmaking, however, it is almost impossible to speak of an art cinema apart from the commercial film industry in the 1920s. One of the very few such films, and perhaps the first, was the nine-minute work *Manhatta* (1921), by the photographer Paul Strand (1890–1976) and the painter-photographer Charles Sheeler (1883–1965). The film illustrated

verses from several Walt Whitman poems with images of New York City. Though not abstract, *Manhatta* attempted to convey a mood rather than tell a story; its **high-angle shots** of skyscrapers, roofs, and pedestrians viewed from above communicate a sense of the individual dwarfed by the city's cold immensity. A few years later King Vidor's M-G-M fiction feature *The Crowd* (1928) echoed *Manhatta* in its opening sequence, with similar views of the lower Manhattan skyline approached from the Staten Island ferry and shots of the blank geometric windows of an office building in which the film's protagonist toils amid vast rows of desks.

More experimental films may have been made *in* Hollywood, by otherwise commercial filmmakers trying out new techniques, than outside it. The most prominent was *The Life and Death of 9413—A Hollywood Extra* (1928), by Robert Florey (1900–1979), a director born in France, and Slavko Vorkapich (1895–1976), a Yugoslav film editor. In its eleven-minute length it displays a variety of artistic effects rarely seen in standard Hollywood products: expressionist sets (constructed as miniatures on table tops) and skewed frame images in the *Caligari* manner; unstable camera movements representing psychological states of mind; Japanese-style theatrical masks; rapid editing without regard for conventions of **continuity**. Its theme is the pathos of the Hollywood dream, as an aspirant to stardom gets a number written on his forehead, fails to find work as an extra, succumbs, and ascends to heaven, where his number is removed.

Florey and Vorkapich's ambitions were not avant-garde but mainstream like their subject's, and theirs came closer to fulfillment. Because of their professional status, *A Hollywood Extra* gained some commercial screenings. Florey was hired by Paramount; at the New York–Astoria studio he codirected the first Marx Brothers film, *The Cocoanuts* (1929), and went on to a long career as a film and television director. Vorkapich worked in Hollywood as a designer of special **montage** sequences (rapid cutting and juxtaposition of images). Their cameraman, Gregg Toland (1904–1948), became one of the movie industry's most important cinematographers, and filmed Orson Welles's 1941 classic, *Citizen Kane*.

In its own way, Hollywood was also an innovator. Its advances were in the studio mode of production, in promotion and marketing, in the development of genres and the star system. These made American movies a communications medium of unprecedented reach and power, a phenomenon to which many societies and film cultures were forced to respond, with varying feelings, from admiration to resentment.

Notes

1. *Motion Picture Studio Directory and Trade Annual 1920* (New York: Motion Picture News, 1920), n.p.
2. See Miriam Hansen, *Babel and Babylon: Spectatorship in American Silent Film* (Cambridge, Mass.: Harvard University Press, 1991), Chapter 11, "Male Star, Female Fans," and Gaylyn Studlar, "Discourses of Gender and Ethnicity: The Construction and De(con)struction of Rudolph Valentino as Other," *Film Criticism* XIII:2 (Winter 1989), pp. 18–35.
3. Theodore Huff, *Charlie Chaplin* (New York: Henry Schuman, 1951), p. 192.
4. Josef von Sternberg, *Fun in a Chinese Laundry* (New York: Macmillan, 1965), p. 216.

MGM·6072

Left: 5.41. Setting up a shot at an amusement park for King Vidor's The Crowd *(1928)*. While the scene in the film takes place at Coney Island, New York, according to the director's recollection it was shot at Ocean Park, California. James Murray and Eleanor Boardman, the leading players, are directly to the right of the camera magazine.

Above: 5.42. Scenes from Manhatta *(1921)*, a nine-minute film by photographer Paul Strand and painter-photographer Charles Sheeler. One of the first works of noncommercial "art cinema" in the United States, it used quotations from several Walt Whitman poems with shots of Manhattan, taken mostly from above to emphasize life's anonymity in the city.

SIX

THE CINEMAS OF

Nowhere did the global cinema hegemony of the United States come as a greater shock than in Europe. Since the era of European expansion began in the late fifteenth century with voyagers like Christopher Columbus, Europeans had imposed their cultures on other lands, not the other way around. Other peoples had become familiar with the experience of cultural assimilation and domination; when American movies became preponderant in their local movie theaters, it was merely another chapter in a long history. Even the insular Japanese, cut off for several centuries from outside contacts, had quickly proven themselves adept at incorporating the new flow of western phenomena into their existing culture. Only to Europeans, unaccustomed to receiving cultural products from elsewhere on terms other than their own, was the dominance of American movies seen as a crisis not only of cinema but of civilization.

The issues were aesthetic, social, and economic. From the perspective of art, Europeans wondered whether American films were intrinsically "better" than their own—whether Hollywood products possessed a pace, rhythm, and narrative drive that European cinemas could not match. From the perspective of society, Europeans asked if the popular appeal of American films was a sign of cultural deterioration, of an emerging mass commercial culture oriented toward proletarian and "feminine" values. And from the perspective of economics, Europeans questioned whether United States dominance was simply the outcome of trade tactics that Europeans themselves had previously practiced on other nations, such as cutting film rental prices below those of local producers, or gaining control of distribution and exhibition outlets.

Whatever the answers these questions evoked in the immediate circumstances after World War I, from a longer historical perspective we can say with certainty that Europeans were not deficient, compared to Americans, as filmmakers. The prominence that so many Europeans attained in United States film production, beginning with figures such as Alice Guy Blaché and Maurice Tourneur and continuing throughout the century, would suggest, if anything, their superiority. With the passage of time, it has become abundantly clear that the crisis of European cinema was not primarily of filmmaking but of finances—of postwar weaknesses in national economies that provided insufficient capital to support domestic film industries. As had occurred earlier in countries such as Australia and Brazil, motion picture executives who were more interested in making money than making films found they could profit more by importing American movies than producing their own.

GERMAN CINEMA

To this broader pattern, which adversely affected filmmaking in major prewar film-producing countries such as Denmark, Italy, and France, there was one notable exception: Germany. At the beginning of the 1920s Germany possessed a well-organized film industry which had been strengthened and strongly supported by the wartime government and then passed into private hands. Rampant inflation within Germany rendered that country unprofitable for importers (the currency was constantly losing value) but also made German exports cheaper. Much as did the United States, Germany built up its film industry by aggressively exporting films, especially to Central and Eastern Europe. When currency stabilization occurred in 1924, Germany's film exports and overall film production weakened, enabling American films and investments to make significant inroads in Germany as elsewhere. Nevertheless, Germany continued to produce around two hundred films a year throughout the 1920s, several times more than any other European nation, and maintain during most years the leading position in its home market.

The Weimar Era

Germany marks an exception also in the way historians *periodize* the past. For film history in general, the coming of sound in the late 1920s designates a division between two eras. For the German national cinema, however, the break is moved forward in time to 1933, and made on political grounds: it demarcates the end of a distinct cinematic phenomenon associated with the rise and fall of the German republic founded in the city of Weimar after World War I. Though not directly a state-controlled industry, German film from 1919 to 1933, silent *and* sound, is called **Weimar cinema**.

Nevertheless, no matter how strongly Kracauer's book has been questioned either on theoretical grounds or historical details, its thesis has proven compelling. Because the crimes of the Hitler regime were so horrific, the book leaves the impression that filmmakers were blameworthy, if for no other reason than that their works sensed and displayed the "deep psychological dispositions" that were bringing fascism to power and yet they were unable to resist it. Other historians have gone even further, suggesting that the German film industry "helped pave the way for Hitler."[2]

This is a heavy burden for films to bear. Without denying that films can have powerful ideological and emotional effects, it would be wise to think carefully through all the methodological barriers to sweeping claims for their specific historical and political impact. For example, since in the Weimar years foreign films made up around half the total screened in German theaters, do we conclude that foreign filmmakers must shoulder half the blame? Puzzles such as this have led some historians, without exactly repudiating Kracauer, to seek to change the terms of understanding. If we want to learn about how and why people make choices—or films—in a historical moment, it is fruitless to analyze them on the basis of what was going to happen years in the future.

EUROPE

FROM CALIGARI TO HITLER. A film history book published in 1947 by Siegfried Kracauer (1889–1966) encapsulated the era and the conception in its famous title: *From Caligari to Hitler*. Kracauer's book is perhaps unique in the annals of film history. Since perspectives change, and new information is constantly unearthed about the past, few history books that are nearly half a century old are widely read, let alone hotly debated. Yet this book remains at the center of any appraisal of Weimar cinema. The author had himself been a film and cultural critic in the Weimar era, but had fled Germany after the advent of Hitler's fascist dictatorship in 1933. He spent the World War II years in the United States, writing, in a new language, his history of Weimar cinema. It was subtitled *A Psychological History of the German Film*, and the issues it raised continue to be of consequence for the understanding not only of German cinema but of film as a medium of communication in society.

FILM AND NATIONAL HISTORY. Kracauer took as his thesis the viewpoint that commercial films, because they are made collaboratively to appeal to mass audiences, reveal more effectively than any other medium "deep layers of collective mentality" in a nation. Thus the study of film exposes "deep psychological dispositions" that led, in the Weimar period, to the collapse of republican government and the onset of a totalitarian regime.[1] To assess this argument fully would require almost a book in itself—it goes well beyond the role of film in society to include concepts argued over in cultural studies and psychology, such as national character or the collective unconscious.

THE KINO-DEBATTE. On these grounds, the interpretation of Weimar cinema has shifted radically. It becomes a cinema struggling to establish itself: as a commercial product differentiated from popular American films, as an artistic endeavor worthy of support from the nation's high culture establishment. This perspective emphasizes the *Kino-Debatte*—the debate over the status of cinema among the arts—that took place in Germany during the 1920s. It also stresses the way films of the Weimar cinema were shaped by the need to justify their artistic value for aesthetic elites. Directors in Germany retained the autonomy as independent artists that their Hollywood counterparts had lost. Their films were much more strongly stylized—particularly through cinematography and set design—than the standard Hollywood product, and they aimed at a far more elevated, or profound, viewpoint on history and human experience. Weimar cinema was remarkably, in this interpretation, an "art cinema," directed to minority tastes in the face of the mass popular cinema of Hollywood.

COMMERCIAL CULTURE. Between the poles of Kracauer's "collective mentality" approach and the thesis of Weimar cinema as high art has emerged a third view: recalling that the German cinema functioned fairly effectively as an industry, releasing two hundred or more domestic products a year, it seeks to place German film production not only within the context of mass psychology or high art but in the framework of twentieth-century commercial culture. From this perspective Weimar cinema emerges as a film phenomenon with its unique aesthetic and national characteristics, yet also one not unlike many others—a film industry following accustomed distribution and reception practices, seeking to build its appeal on the familiar pillars of genres and stars.

These debates over Weimar cinema suggest once again how the past exists in fluid form, constantly altering its appearance as we interpret it in new ways. In this rearrangement, one of the key concepts that has fallen out of favor is the notion that "German Expressionism" can stand as an overall term to describe Weimar films. The expressionist movement in painting, theater, and literature around World War I (see Chapter 3) had made a sensational cinematic impact in *The Cabinet of Dr. Caligari*, with its distorted sets and antinaturalistic performances. But only a handful of films in the early 1920s carried their stylizations forward, and applying the expressionist label too sweepingly to Weimar films can hamper a full sense of their relationship to the genres and intertexts of international film culture.

STIMMUNG. Like other cinema industries, Germany produced its share of comedies, romances, melodramas, social dramas, and historical epics. These films have captured critics' attention and been included in the Weimar canon much less frequently than works in genres regarded as more authentically *German*—films of the fantastic, mountain films, street films, and **Kammerspiel** (chamber films, or intimate dramas). These key genres are considered especially to convey the German preoccupation with *Stimmung*—an emphasis on mood or feeling, especially of melancholy. It was this concern with mood that led German filmmakers to give extraordinary attention to lighting and design, to communicate feelings through the play of space and light in the mise-en-scène. After the nucleus of Weimar cinema's creative talent dispersed—in the 1920s lured by Hollywood, after 1933 exiled by Hitler—what remained as its legacy to world cinema was this concern for a charged and often disquieting visual atmosphere.

German Film and Filmmakers

Categories and generalizations—particularly the perennial question, how German is it?—tend to fade into the background when confronted with the complexities of actual films. The work of Fritz

Lang is a case in point. Lang's early 1920s films are intensely associated with their time and place and have become classics of cinema history; yet, like many major works of the medium, they are also fundamentally linked to the formulas of international popular culture. Reviewers in the United States trade paper *Variety* were not entirely consumed by nationalist bias when they called Lang's films "dime-novel stuff" made for "mass appeal."[3]

LANG AND VON HARBOU. After completing the two-part adventure film *The Spiders*, Lang worked for the remainder of his Weimar career with scriptwriter Thea von Harbou (1888–1954); they were married in 1924. Their first significant collaboration was *Der müde Tod* (literally "Weary Death," released in English-language versions as *Destiny*, 1921). In its episodic structure and bleak fatalism, this film considerably resembles Dreyer's *Leaves from Satan's Book* (there is a character, Death, who, like Satan in the Danish film, is weary of the duty he must eternally perform). Visually the film is marked by exotic settings (depicting episodes in Baghdad, Renaissance Venice, and China) created by two of the *Caligari* designers, Walter Röhrig and Hermann Warm, along with Robert Herlth.

Lang and von Harbou turned to contemporary times for *Dr. Mabuse, der Spieler* (Dr. Mabuse, the Gambler, 1922). The film's scenes of speeding cars and trains, nightclubs and gambling dens, conveyed a sense of the hedonism, restlessness, and haste of post-war Germany. Yet it also utilized the conventions of prewar crime serials, like the French series *Fantômas*, with its two-part structure (each part to be shown on successive nights) and its epic battle of wits between an intrepid investigator, State Attorney von Wenk, and an arch criminal, the rogue psychoanalyst Dr. Mabuse, with many masks and a lust for power. An inside joke in the film is this exchange, in the English version's intertitles: "What is your attitude toward Expressionism, Doctor?" Mabuse answers: "Expressionism is a pastime—but why ever not? Everything today is a matter of just passing the time!"

Die Nibelungen (1924) was an ambitious effort by Lang and von Harbou to retell the ancient Nordic legend of Siegfried that composer Richard Wagner had used as the basis for his famous nineteenth-century opera cycle, *Der Ring des Nibelungen* (in the original legend, the name Nibelungen refers to Siegfried's land, his people, and his treasure). The film version differed markedly

6.1. Death (Bernhard Goetzke) demands a child, and the Young Woman (Lil Dagover) offers herself in the child's place, in Fritz Lang's Der müde Tod (Destiny, 1921).

6.2. A nightclub performance is one of the exotic scenes conveying the hedonistic atmosphere of post–World War I Berlin in Lang's Dr. Mabuse, der Spieler *(Dr. Mabuse, the Gambler, 1922).*

from the opera, particularly in the complete absence of Wagner's narrative of the decline of the gods. It was also made in two parts for successive nights' showings: the first, *Siegfried*, carries the legend to the hero's death; in the second, *Kriemhild's Rache (Kriemhild's Revenge)*, the hero's widow wages an implacable campaign to avenge his murder. The film is one of the stunning triumphs of mise-en-scène in Weimar cinema, a world of myth created in geometric design—in architecture, costume, and cinematographic spectacle.

F. W. MURNAU. Along with Lang and Ernst Lubitsch (who left for Hollywood in 1923), an important filmmaker of early Weimar cinema was F. W. (Friedrich Wilhelm) Murnau (1888–1931). Although Lang and Murnau shared cinematographers and designers, and von Harbou also wrote several Murnau films, the two directors' styles were markedly different. Lang's early films created a world of externals, of visual power; while Murnau's films did not lack for aesthetic pleasures, they were based far more than Lang's on character psychology, on interior states.

Murnau's first major work, *Nosferatu* (1922), a horror film about the legendary vampire (drawn from Bram Stoker's novel *Dracula*), plays down the supernatural visual possibilities in favor of a focus on the subtleties of human desire. The cinematography by Fritz

Arno Wagner (1894–1958), who also filmed Lang's *Destiny*, is surprisingly realist in style considering the subject, with a substantial part of the work shot outdoors and on location. Though there are moments of expressionist stylization in decor and camera angles (and in the cadaverous appearance of the vampire himself, portrayed by Max Schreck [1879–1936], with bat ears and grotesque curled fingers), the film's horror derives much of its power from its setting in daily life.

The basic Dracula narrative is familiar enough from having been retold scores of times in the movies, with every imaginable variant. Murnau's earliest version, in its ambiguous treatment of desire and evil, in its knowing simplicity, retains a startling power. After the vampire has traveled to meet her, spreading plague and death as he goes, the virtuous Mina reads in *The Book of the Vampire* that "A woman pure in heart must offer herself to Nosferatu" (in the subtitles of the English-language version), and she does so. The vampire comes to her, and at morning's light we see him crouched by her lifeless body, his fangs by her throat, sated. Too late, he realizes he has exposed himself to sunlight. Rising to leave, he clutches his heart, and disappears in a puff of smoke. His longing makes the vampire paradoxically more sympathetic than the normal, rational characters, and the tryst between Mina and Nosferatu appears a fulfillment of each one's desire and a tragic end for both.

6.3. Paul Richter as the hero
Siegfried and Georg John as
Mime Alberich in Siegfried, part
one of Lang's Die Nibelungen
(1924)

6.4. Having lingered too long
after his tryst with Mina, the vampire Nosferatu (Max Schreck),
struck by morning daylight,
clutches his heart and begins to
fade away in a double image shot
from F. W. Murnau's Nosferatu
(1922).

6.5. *Emil Jannings as the hotel doorman abjectly demoted to washroom attendant in Murnau's* Der letzte Mann (The Last Laugh, *1924)*

6.6. *The courtyard set helps to convey the mood of Leopold Jessner's* Die Hintertreppe (Back-stairs, *1921), a film without intertitles.*

Scandinavian Cinema

No countries with populations so small, British film historian Forsyth Hardy wrote in the early 1950s, had made so great a contribution to world cinema as Sweden and Denmark (and this was before Sweden's Ingmar Bergman became famous as a leading director of international art cinema). Denmark's Nordisk company was one of Europe's leading film producers before World War I (see Chapter 3). Carl Th. Dreyer of Denmark, whose directing career covered six decades, ranks among the most important figures of film history, and his work is treated throughout this book. Danish actress Asta Nielsen was a star of German silent cinema; because German films of the 1910s are so little known, her fiery, passionate performances have not received sufficient recognition.

After World War I the Swedish company Svensk Filmindustri, formed in 1919 from a merger of smaller firms, became the major production center in the Scandinavian countries. Swedish films gained international stature through the work of directors Mauritz Stiller (1883–1928) and Victor Sjöström (1879–1960). Born in Finland, Stiller began working in Swedish films in his late twenties. His principal films include *Erotikon* (1920), a comedy of manners, and *Gösta Berlings saga* (known in English as *The Story of Gösta Berling* or *The Atonement of Gösta Berling,* 1924). The latter film marked Greta Garbo's second screen appearance, and Stiller became her mentor. They went to Hollywood together in 1925 with contracts from M-G-M; whether the studio hired Stiller only to secure Garbo, or whether the actress was signed at the director's insistence, has been a matter of conjecture ever since. Stiller was able to finish only one film, *Hotel Imperial* (1927, for Paramount), before returning to Sweden, where he died in 1928.

Sjöström began directing in 1912 and also performed in both his own films and those of other directors. Two of his early Swedish films continue to circulate widely: *Berg-Ejvind och hans hustru* (literally "Berg-Ejvind and His Wife," known in English as *The Outlaw and His Wife,* 1918), filmed on location in rugged mountain terrain and admired for its realism, and *Körkarlen* (literally "The Coachman," known in English as *The Phantom Chariot,* 1921).

Sjöström went to Hollywood in the 1920s and adopted the name Victor Seastrom; he directed several notable films, including *The Wind* (1928) with Lillian Gish (see Chapter 8). Returning to Sweden in 1930, he worked thereafter mainly as an actor. His last film appearance was in Bergman's *Smultronstället* (*Wild Strawberries,* 1957; see Chapter 15).

6.7. *An intense moment in the* Kammerspiel *(chamber drama)* Scherben *(Shattered, 1921), another film without intertitles, directed by Lupu Pick. Werner Krauss portrays a railway trackman, Edith Posca his daughter.*

6.8. *Greta Garbo in* Gösta Berlings saga *(The Story of Gösta Berling), 1924*

6.9. *The Phantom Chariot's central sequence conveys supernatural events through **double images** (one shot printed over another). A dissolute man (played by Sjöström) has been knocked down in a drunken brawl; in this shot (a production still made from a frame enlargement) his soul rises from his inert body and confronts the figure of Death (Tore Svennberg), who has come as a coachman in a ghost carriage. The sequence turns out to be a dream, after which the drunken man reforms.*

In 1924 Murnau directed *Der letzte Mann* (literally "The Last Man," but given the English-language title *The Last Laugh*). Though not the first, it was the most famous Weimar silent film to appear without intertitles (in some versions circulating in the United States a single intertitle has been added, which has confused some commentators into thinking it appeared in the original). Some earlier works in the *Kammerspiel* genre also went without titles. The rationale was that in this intimate genre characters' feelings were conveyed most subtly through performance and visual effects. These included two films of 1921, *Die Hintertreppe* (*Backstairs*) directed by Leopold Jessner (1878–1945) and *Scherben* (*Shattered*), directed by Lupu Pick (1886–1931). All three titleless films were made from scripts by Carl Mayer, the most important screenwriter of the Weimar cinema, who had also coauthored the script for *The Cabinet of Dr. Caligari.*

The Last Laugh concerns an aging doorman at a posh hotel who is demoted to washroom attendant when he is unable to handle a heavy trunk. Back in his working-class apartment house his fancy uniform had been the source of his dignity and vanity, and its loss marks a crushing blow to both. "A non-German mind will have difficulty in comprehending all its tragic implications," Lotte Eisner wrote in her study of Weimar cinema, *The Haunted Screen*.[4] Tragedy or not, *The Last Laugh* was rather mitigated by a fantasy ending, in which the defrocked doorman becomes fabulously rich because an "eccentric American multimillionaire" (so described in a newspaper article that serves in place of an intertitle) dies in the hotel washroom and bequeaths his fortune to the last person who attended him.

The Last Laugh is regarded as among the greatest of Weimar silent films not for its unique "German tragedy" or its ironic/upbeat commercial ending, but as a cinematographic tour de force. If *Caligari*'s sets and performances were indeed expressions of a national aesthetic style, *The Last Laugh* was less "Germanic" in the sense that its achievements in performance and camera work could inspire filmmakers internationally. The performance of Emil Jannings (1884–1950) as the once preening, then broken, doorman was a triumph of psychological realism; and the exceptional camera work of Karl Freund (1890–1969) heightened the characterization by visualizing the doorman's viewpoint. In one central sequence, the demoted doorman attends a family wedding, after secretly reclaiming his uniform, and then gets drunk; the camera (along with editing and lab work) creates images of what he sees: distorted, elongated faces; two heads of the same person; many faces superimposed

6.10, 6.11. E. A. Dupont's Variété (Variety, 1925), a love triangle among trapeze artists, with exceptional cinematography by Karl Freund, featured (from left) Warwick Ward, Emil Jannings, and Lya de Putti. Paramount, which successfully distributed the film in the United States, soon after joined in a coproduction agreement with Ufa and M-G-M, called Parufamet.

close upon one another; blurred images; wavering side-to-side views.

Far from being incomprehensible to non-German minds, *The Last Laugh* heralded a new presence for German films in international cinema. By the mid-1920s, the novelty of American cinema had become routine. Of *Variété* (*Variety* in the United States, *Vaudeville* in Britain, 1925), a love triangle story among trapeze artists, by the German director E. A. (Ewald André) Dupont (1891–1956), the American critic Harry Alan Potamkin could write that it

"burnt its way through these United States and came near demoralizing the matter-of-fact technique of Hollywood," because of its remarkable cinematography. This was again the work of Karl Freund, shooting the narrative's high-platform acrobats, as Potamkin wrote, "from above, or from a corner, or from beneath, or from whatever point of view was demanded"—even from a camera mounted on a high swing.[5]

Hollywood was not totally demoralized; it simply intensified its importation of German film talent. Murnau and Jannings went to

California in 1926, Freund several years later. Jannings returned to Germany in 1929, after winning the first Oscar for best actor from the Academy of Motion Picture Arts and Sciences for performances in *The Way of All Flesh* (1927) and *The Last Command* (1928). Murnau died prematurely in an auto accident. After a distinguished career in film, Freund went into early commercial television, and was the cameraman on Lucille Ball's classic comedy series "I Love Lucy."

FRENCH CINEMA

The circumstances for French film culture after World War I were fundamentally different from those in Germany. Where Germany had developed its film production during the war, France had essentially sacrificed the world's leading film industry to the war effort. American films had flooded in and, despite some grumbling, generally enthralled both popular audiences and intellectuals. After the war, the French almost had to rethink their cinematic goals from the ground up. Should they make films like Hollywood's, or strive for something specifically French? Should films be long or short, popular or for an elite? All these options, and others, were tried out during the 1920s, in a period of constant change and experimentation in French film. Throughout the decade, France managed to produce roughly one-fourth the number of films made in Germany.

What was unique in postwar France was the richness of cultural life surrounding the cinema. Because of the need to reestablish cinematic institutions, as well as an early recognition of the importance of cinema to other arts, intellectuals and artists in France became much more involved with film than elsewhere. Film journals sprang up; *ciné-clubs* formed to screen movies, hear lectures, and participate in the development of the medium. Critics became filmmakers, filmmakers became theorists, theorists became critics, in a fluidity of roles and interests few other countries could match. In the United States similar activities barely existed. In Germany they centered on the *Kino-Debatte* about film's status among the arts. In France, critics and theorists committed to cinema had no doubt about its potential as art, and debated its characteristics.

Photogénie

A key concept in the emergence of French film criticism was *photogénie*—a word with broader connotations than its nearest English equivalent, photogenic. The term was coined by Louis Delluc (1890–1924), regarded as the leading critic of the period, as well as an emerging filmmaker before his untimely death. Other important filmmaker-critics who contributed to the theory and practice of *photogénie* included Jean Epstein (1897–1953), Marcel L'Herbier (1888–1979), and Germaine Dulac (1882–1942). One might think of the term as defining a dialogue between the cinematic apparatus and the actual world. Cinema stylizes actuality, in this concept, and transforms our perception of it, without altering actuality itself. It takes the real world and through cinematic techniques such as **framing** (what one chooses to include within the image frame and leave outside it), the close-up, and editing, makes it appear differently—imbued with new mystery and beauty.

As may be suspected from these definitions, French critics of the *photogénie* persuasion considered *The Cabinet of Dr. Caligari* a false step in cinema. Its expressionist-style sets and performance style they regarded as untrue to actuality; the camera had not been permitted to fulfill its function of transforming the actual, it merely recorded a staged event. These critics also faulted French commercial cinema for, in their view, emulating theatrical conventions. What mattered to them, above all, was movement. Cinema must be visual, wrote Germaine Dulac, even if that sounded redundant. The trouble was that films gave too much attention to dramatic action, when they should be focusing on "the value of the image and its rhythms."[6]

Cinégraphie

The momentum of this tendency in critical thought soon carried it away from the dialogue between cinema and actuality, and toward a concern with the properties of cinema itself—from *photogénie* to *cinégraphie*. The new theme took one of two directions: toward a "poetic" cinema, the "pure" movement of images irrespective of content or story; or toward the utilization of technique to express interior states otherwise unviewable in the actual world. Both of these interests came to be associated with avant-garde cinema, though it is worth noting that in the fluidity of French cinema practice of this period several films now regarded as avant-garde were produced and exhibited commercially.

This overall movement in French filmmaking and cinema theory has traditionally been known as French **Impressionism**, as a handy distinction from German Expressionism and also to associate its principles with the nineteenth-century Impressionist aesthetic in painting. But as Expressionism has fallen out of use as an overarching label for Weimar cinema, so too should Impressionism be used only with caution to define this aspect of French films. As early as the mid-1920s such distinctions had been erased by German films such as *The Last Laugh* and *Variety*, in which the use of the camera to create images simulating characters' altered states of perception closely resembled what has been called French Impressionism. Ironically, these German films gained more credit for this style than did the French in the international marketplace.

Most films of the French avant-garde, however, were not competing in the international film market. What gives them a special interest is the fact that they were made by the first group of men and women who thought and wrote about film, and then sought to put their ideas into practice as filmmakers. Some of the films have been dismissed by critics because they fail to fulfill the elaborate prescriptions of the filmmaker's theories, but this view sometimes does injustice to films that have intrinsic value.

FIÈVRE. Delluc's *Fièvre* ("Fever," 1921), for example, hardly matches some of his critical flights of rhetoric about *photogénie*, yet it is an intense short narrative film of considerable power. Sailors returning from a voyage tumble into a rough waterfront bar, attracting a bevy of prostitutes and setting in motion a highly charged conflict of desire among a sailor; the barmaid, his former girlfriend; his Asian wife, whom he married (flashbacks tell us) after she nursed him through an illness; and the bar owner. With its waterfront setting and exotic Asian character, the film echoes *Broken Blossoms*, and it resembles a Hollywood Western in its final sequence of a vicious fight, where the sailor is killed and the barmaid unjustly arrested. Throughout the violence the Asian woman yearns to reach a flower which, when she gets to it, turns out to be artificial.

LA SOURIANTE MADAME BEUDET. Among this group of early films, the one that has entered the film history canon most centrally is Dulac's *La Souriante Madame Beudet (The Smiling Madame Beudet,* 1923). This is in part because of feminist scholarship's interest in films by women, but Dulac and her film are sufficiently important without special categorization. Based on a stage play, the twenty-five-minute film chronicles the unhappy marriage of a provincial bourgeois wife both by observing her and by constructing her interior life. She passes the time by playing the piano and reading; as she turns magazine pages, photographs become fantasy images—a car passing over clouds, a tennis player come to life. Her husband, depicted often in tight close-up with a loutish smile, has the habit of putting an unloaded revolver to his temple when she vexes him. Unbeknownst to him, she puts bullets in the gun, but this time he aims at her when he pulls the trigger. The shot misses, and they briefly regard the horror of their estrangement. The film's final shot—the couple in overcoats on a winter day, backs to the camera, walking slowly uphill past a priest—is an apt exemplar of *photogénie,* in the pathos of its simplicity.

LA ROUE. Alongside these small, intimate films was a work that by its scope and aesthetic ambition was seen to stand as a landmark in French cinema—a landmark, unfortunately, much like the films of von Stroheim in the United States. This was *La*

Roue ("The Wheel," 1923), directed by Abel Gance (1889–1981), who had been working in the commercial film industry since the early 1910s but was consistently interested in experimenting with film form. The premiere screening of the film ran for nine hours over three days. This complete work apparently made it into general release, but soon afterward the director edited a condensed version, and over the years the original was lost and a variety of shorter prints made their way into archives. The print circulating in the United States is approximately three and one-half hours long.

Gance spent nearly a year shooting *La Roue,* almost entirely on location. Its narrative concerns the fate of a train engineer, Sisif, and his two children, an artistic boy who makes violins and a girl whom he rescued as a baby from a train wreck. From surviving prints it is perhaps impossible to recapture the excitement contemporaries felt for the film. It seems a cumbersome amalgam of Griffith-style sentimentalism (the girl's blond hair made into a halo by backlighting) and windy philosophy (the wheel as life symbol). Yet there are gritty working-class scenes of railyards, combined with what the critics admired most, "poetic" moments of montage showing the rhythm and movement of steam locomotives. In a way *La Roue* remains most fascinating as a work that evokes the importance of the steam engine and the railroad for early cinema and industrial culture.

Surrealism and Film

These eruptions of "pure" imagery in Gance's film inspired the cinematic avant-garde. A new aspect was the advent of filmmaking by Surrealist artists. Since **Surrealism**, at its most basic level, wanted to undermine the concepts of everyday reality, the Surrealists found the techniques of cinema ideal for their cause: the film image could be made to defy conventional reality in innumerable ways, as trick films had demonstrated from the earliest products of the medium.

RENÉ CLAIR. Among the first films associated with Surrealism was *Paris qui dort* (literally "The Paris That Slept," but titled in English-language versions *The Crazy Ray*, 1924), directed by René Clair (1898–1981). It tells a droll story about a scientist's "ray" that has frozen people in their tracks; what is "surreal" is not so much its style as its vision of a normal world radically altered. When a group of otherwise respectable people discover that they have escaped the ray's effects, for example, they go on a crime spree. Clair's *Entr'acte* (also 1924) was a short film originally made to be screened at a ballet performance; what we now know as a single film was first shown in two parts, one as a prologue to the ballet

6.14. Sisif (Séverin-Mars, at left) with a fellow railway worker in Abel Gance's La Roue *("The Wheel," 1923)*

6.15. The professor (Martinelli) in his laboratory with the ray machine that has stopped Paris in its tracks in René Clair's Paris qui dort *(*The Crazy Ray, 1924)

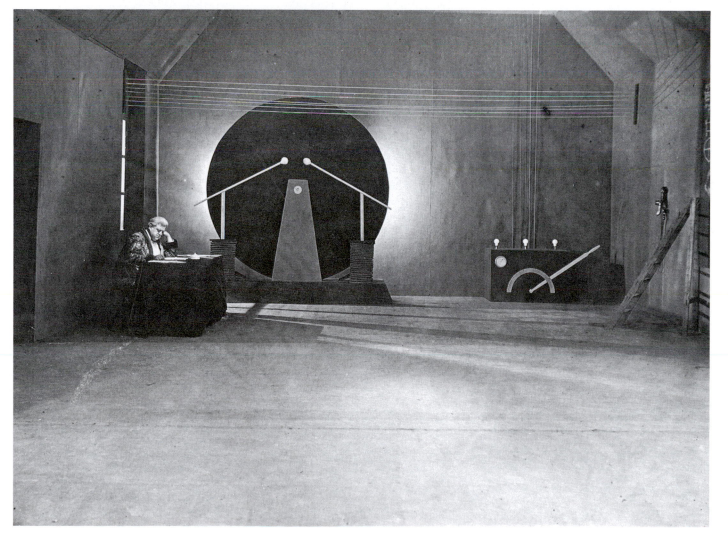

and the other between the first and second acts (the title means "intermission," or literally, "between the acts"). Its Surrealist aim was again disorientation, in a raffish comic way. Utilizing fast and slow motion, stop-action animation of inanimate objects, and other elements of trick cinematography dating back to Georges Méliès, *Entr'acte* turned primitive cinema into avant-garde art.

MÉNILMONTANT. Important contributions to the French avant-garde also came from Russian artists who emigrated to Paris after the 1917 revolution. *Ménilmontant* (1926), directed by Dimitri Kirsanov (1899–1957), was linked to Delluc's *Fièvre* through its working-class milieu, brutal violence, and symbolic use of artificial flowers. Within a realist narrative concerning the lives of two sisters in the Ménilmontant district of Paris, it displays a full range of avant-garde techniques, particularly **rapid cutting**

and moving camera shots, **superimpositions**, and **dissolves** from scene to scene that seem to defy conventional continuity; a centerpiece is a remarkable montage sequence that intersperses images of time, speed, and the human body. *Ménilmontant* achieves Louis Delluc's theoretical goals for cinema as completely as any other film of the era.

INTERNATIONAL CINEMA

The presence of Russian émigré filmmakers in Paris was one of many signs in the mid-1920s of an expanding international circulation of images and styles. Earlier in the decade, the political passions of World War I and the reaction to Hollywood's postwar domination had fueled an emphasis on cinema's importance to national cultures. While this concern continued to be debated,

Opposite: 6.16. The professor's daughter (Myla Seller) takes a rest atop the Eiffel Tower, in a tinted still from The Crazy Ray.

Right: 6.17. Artists Marcel Duchamp and Man Ray play chess on a rooftop in Clair's Entr'acte *(1924).*

Below right: 6.18. Nadia Sibirskaia in Ménilmontant *(1926), directed by Dimitri Kirsanov*

filmmakers found it increasingly necessary to cross national borders, or draw financing, personnel, or inspiration from elsewhere. Not all the talent fled to Hollywood: Germany, as well as Paris, attracted aspirants like the young British film worker Alfred Hitchcock, who went to Munich to develop his craft.

Germany

The German film industry was itself going through changes, as the stabilization of its currency in 1924 set off a crisis. With exports falling and imports rising, film companies facing financial losses found support in Hollywood, but naturally with strings attached. Ufa, the large production-distribution company set up during World War I (see Chapter 3), received a substantial loan from Paramount and Metro-Goldwyn-Mayer. In return, the three companies set up a new distribution subsidiary, Parufamet, whose main purpose was to increase American film imports to Germany. This and similar deals upset people who wanted films to portray German national characteristics, and they bought out American interests in 1927.

Above: 6.19. Though Ufa (Universum Film Aktiengesellschaft) operated one of the largest studios in Europe during the 1920s, the German company was more significant as a distributor than as a producer. This imposing complex in Neubabelsberg, outside Berlin, began in 1911 as a studio for the Deutsche Bioscop company. Ufa was founded in 1917 with financial support from the German government, became private in 1918, and began absorbing smaller firms. Ufa moved to Neubabelsberg in 1923, when it took over Decla Bioscop, which had produced The Cabinet of Dr. Caligari *and Fritz Lang's early films there, and enlarged the studio, as pictured here.*

FAUST. Several major films of the period were underrated, at least in Germany, because they were regarded as culturally more hybrid than national. Murnau's last German film before his departure to Hollywood, *Faust* (1926), was planned by Ufa with a strong international flavor. The studio cast a Swedish actor, Gösta Ekman, as Faust; a French actress, Yvette Guilbert, in a supporting role; and unsuccessfully sought Lillian Gish for the part of Gretchen. Though subtitled "A German Popular Legend," the film closely follows (without acknowledgment) the version most Europeans knew best, French composer Charles François Gounod's nineteenth-century opera. Unmistakably familiar in the

Left: 6.20. Mephisto (Emil Jannings) demonstrates his satanic powers to Faust (Gösta Ekman) in F. W. Murnau's Faust *(1926).*

Right and overleaf: 6.21–6.25. Scenes from Metropolis *(1926), Fritz Lang's futuristic vision of a modern city with fantastic skyscrapers and a sybaritic leisure class sustained by workers toiling in hellish conditions underground*

Right: 6.21. The gigantic steam engine that maintains the city's power and water supplies

framework of Weimar cinema, however, were the fantasy settings by designers Robert Herlth and Walter Röhrig, cinematographer Carl Hoffmann's moving camera and shadowy images, and Emil Jannings's performance as Mephisto, a chubby, energetic demon to stand beside Max Schreck's gaunt, languid Nosferatu.

METROPOLIS. The disquiet caused by *Faust*'s international casting, however, was minor compared to the controversy stirred by Lang and von Harbou's futuristic tour de force, *Metropolis* (1926). This stunning vision of a modern city—soaring skyscrapers with railway bridges running between upper stories, sustained by workers toiling at huge machines deep underground—was criticized for a simplistic narrative and a failure to offer other than sentimental clichés in response to the crisis of labor and management the film depicts. When Maria, an idealistic young woman who seeks to ameliorate gruesome working conditions, preaches to the workers, she tells them (in intertitles of the English-language version), "Between the brain that plans and the hands that build there must be a mediator. . . . It is the heart that must bring about an understanding between them."

Metropolis.

6.22. Curiosity has led Freder (Gustav Fröhlich), son of the Master of Metropolis, underground; volunteering to take over operation of a huge dial, he collapses from the labor.

6.23. The scientist Rotwang (Rudolf Klein-Rogge) shows the Master (Alfred Abel) a robot he has developed to replace human workers. The Master orders Rotwang to create a robot in the likeness of Maria, an idealistic woman who preaches to the workers.

6.24. Rotwang has kidnapped Maria and placed her in a device that transfers her features to a robot. Robot-Maria stands at right (Brigitte Helm portrayed both Marias).

6.25. Fomenting rebellion, the robot-Maria leads workers to crash a gate and sabotage the machinery (as part of the Master's plan to destroy the workers so robots can take over).

6.26. Lang (in white shirt) directs Gustav Fröhlich, whose character, Freder, rescues the good Maria, saves the workers, and reconciles them with his father, the Master.

These critiques are certainly pertinent, but in the sweep of cinema history they appear to miss the point. Films can indeed espouse a philosophy, an ideology, a political theory, but many of the greatest films are less likely to be paragons of narrative coherence than they are to be triumphs of spectacle and mise-en-scène. They communicate through the feelings evoked by their visual power rather than by logic. This is the case with *Metropolis*. Long after one has dismissed its narrative banalities, its powerful images remain: the fabulous city and the horrendous machinery, run by clocks and steam, for which the workers function as changeable parts.

Metropolis is the prototype of cinema's science fiction exploration of humanity's place in the modern scientific/industrial system. A scientist, Rotwang, played by Rudolf Klein-Rogge (1888–1955), who also portrayed Dr. Mabuse (and who was married to Thea von Harbou before her marriage to Lang), has constructed a robot. "Now we have no further use for living workers," he says; it is "a machine which no one will be able to tell from a human being." The Master of Metropolis, a soulless engineer rather than a greedy capitalist, orders the scientist to make over the robot in the image of Maria; rather than urge the workers toward peaceful change, as the saintly young woman had done, the robot-Maria will incite violence that will lead to their destruction.

The two Marias—the ethereal human, the demonic robot—were both portrayed by eighteen-year-old Brigitte Helm (b. 1908) in her first screen role. They are perhaps the most striking elaboration in Weimar cinema of the theme of the *Doppelgänger* or "double," the divided self, which appeared frequently in German literature and theater; another notable example was *Der Student von Prag* (*The Student of Prague*, 1926), directed by Henrik Galeen (1882–1949), which was a remake of a 1913 film of the same title. In *Metropolis*, the radical opposition of the two Marias

Below: 6.27. Greta Garbo as Grete Rumfort and Jaro Fürth as Hofrat Rumfort in G. W. Pabst's Die freudlose Gasse *(The Joyless Street, 1925)*

Bottom: 6.28. Lulu (Louise Brooks) confronts Dr. Schön (Fritz Kortner) backstage at a theater in Pabst's Die Büchse der Pandora *(Pandora's Box, 1928).*

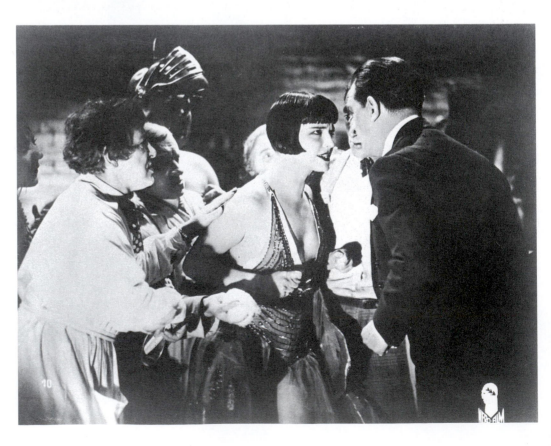

has become the focus for analyzing the film's complex interplay of sexuality and technology, gender and ideology. *Metropolis* has gained in stature as its vision continues to resonate over the decades, both in cinema and society.

Neue Sachlichkeit

The technological concerns of *Metropolis* were one sign of a cultural change in Weimar Germany and its films in the mid-1920s. This shift has often been described as a movement from Expressionism to *Neue Sachlichkeit*—rendered in English usually as New Objectivity, an emphasis not on mood and feeling, as in Expressionism, but on function and technique. New Objectivity is too sweeping a term to define a new era of Weimar cinema, just as Expressionism was too broad for the earlier period. But certainly a new stress on realism in the cinema became evident.

G. W. PABST. A leading figure in the realist trend was G. W. (Georg Wilhelm) Pabst (1885–1967). An Austrian like Lang, Pabst also began his career as a film director in Berlin. His first major work was *Die freudlose Gasse* (*The Joyless Street*, 1925), a melodramatic street film with Swedish actress Greta Garbo and Asta Nielsen (1881–1972), the Danish performer who was Weimar cinema's leading female star. Pabst became a principal director of contemporary social dramas. For his *Die Liebe der Jeanne Ney* (*The Love of Jeanne Ney*, 1927), concerning Russian revolutionaries in Paris, cinematographer Fritz Arno Wagner contributed exceptional moving camera work in exterior locations, as he had done on Murnau's *Nosferatu*.

Pabst's most famous film, *Die Büchse der Pandora* (*Pandora's Box*, 1928), was a treatment of sexual psychology based on the character, Lulu, in Frank Wedekind's turn-of-the-century

National Cinema

As a concept in film history, "national cinema" is simultaneously inevitable and questionable. Films, film technology, and filmmakers crossed national borders from the first moments of the medium. Yet many governments also regarded cinema as a key instrument of national communications, and filmmakers themselves often worked within the context of national traditions, debates, and movements in other art forms. In principle a supranational medium, in practice filmmaking was helped or hindered by state policies and by local economic and social conditions.

Italian film in the 1920s provides an intriguing case study for the idea of national cinema. Italy's films had been among the world's leaders before World War I, in both stylistic innovation and the international marketplace. Numerically production continued to rise during and after the war, reaching a peak in 1920. Then things fell apart. By 1927 only about a dozen feature-length films were produced. "The twenties were the most pathetic decade in Italian film history," film historian Elaine Mancini has written.

"The industry lacked imagination, energy, and contact with its public; it became overcrowded with speculative companies that closed one after the other, often without producing anything; and it insisted on making films in the same style and usually with the same techniques of the earlier decade."

The specific causes of this sorry state, however, are not always easy to identify. Surely the social and political turmoil surrounding the Fascist seizure of power in 1922 played a role. It disrupted financing and left the film companies uncertain about their cultural role, which contributed to their failure to innovate in style or technique. In a situation of stagnation talent fled to Berlin and Paris; the most prominent film made by an Italian abroad was *Prix de Beauté* ("Beauty Prize," 1930), directed in France by Augusto Genina (1892–1957), with a screenplay by René Clair and G. W. Pabst and starring Louise Brooks. By the late 1920s the Fascist regime had begun to develop film policies that slowly began to revive Italian production in the 1930s (see Chapter 10).

British cinema was also in a bad state during the 1920s. In 1926 only 18 British films were released by major distribution companies, out of a total of 580. A contemporary critic, C. A. Lejeune, wrote in 1931, "The British cinema has been handicapped in every way—with bad brains, shortage of money, lack of confidence, injudicious flattery, misdirected talent, unfortunate legislation." As in Italy, the particular combination of difficulties led to a stylistic and technical conservatism.

The answer to a national cinema's problems was often found in cinema's internationalism. Talent went abroad to learn, as Alfred Hitchcock did to Germany, and then returned; talent from abroad saw the opportunity and came to seize it, as was the case with Hungarian producer-director Alexander Korda, who arrived in London by way of Berlin, Hollywood, and Paris. Hitchcock and Korda were among the leaders of British cinema's recovery in the 1930s (see Chapter 10).

6.29. Jeanne Ney (Edith Jehanne) with the man she loves, Andreas (Uno Henning), outside a Paris hotel in Pabst's Die Liebe der Jeanne Ney (The Love of Jeanne Ney, 1927)

6.30. Discovering a murder victim in Alfred Hitchcock's The Lodger *(1926)*

expressionist dramas. For his Lulu, the director sought a performer who could portray not the playwright's sexual temptress, but a figure whose tragedy derives from an innocent, natural sexuality. He persuaded the young American actress Louise Brooks (1906–1985) to come to Berlin, and their collaboration was to become a legend in film history, for the riveting power of her performance as Lulu and for the transgressive sexual subject matter of the film.

With her signature cap of shiny black hair, cut in bangs low on her forehead, Brooks's Lulu was memorable in *Pandora's Box* precisely for her childlike spirit, her loose-limbed movement, her sexual ease and freedom. These qualities, however, were contradicted by the desires of others and the pressures of bourgeois society. At the end, poverty-stricken in London, her father sends her out to prostitution because he wants to eat a Christmas pudding. She meets Jack the Ripper, and it is now her desire, perhaps unconsciously, to end her travail that lures the murderer to his task.

6.31. Antonin Artaud, leading performer and theorist of French avant-garde theater, portrays Jean Massieu, a priest sympathetic to Joan of Arc, *in Carl Th. Dreyer's* La Passion de Jeanne d'Arc *(The Passion of Joan of Arc, 1928).*

6.32. Falconetti as Joan in La Passion de Jeanne d'Arc

6.33. Luis Buñuel, the film's codirector, in the opening scene of Un Chien andalou ("An Anda-lusian Dog," 1929)

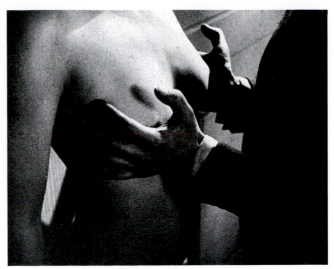

6.34. A Surrealist moment in Un Chien andalou

THE PUNISHMENT OF WOMEN

Central to the circulation of images during this period, clearly, was the issue of representing, and constructing narratives about, female sexuality. Critical scholarship in recent years has devoted intense theoretical debate to questions concerning the male gaze, to which women are subjected. But perhaps more attention ought to be paid to the physical punishments that women are made to suffer in the films.

In *Faust*, Gretchen is accused of killing her baby and is burned at the stake; in *Metropolis*, robot-Maria is set on fire as the work-ers cry, "The witch! The witch!" Lulu encounters a notorious murderer of women, and serial killings of women are also the theme of Alfred Hitchcock's first British film as director, *The Lodger* (1926), after he had directed two British-German copro-ductions made in Munich. In *The Lodger*, the male protagonist rents a room decorated with sentimental portraits of women. The last one is of a bare-breasted woman, guarded by a soldier, being readied for burning at the stake.

Whatever the psychological, social, or aesthetic groundings for such repeated aggressions, they reach a culmination with Carl Th. Dreyer's *La Passion de Jeanne d'Arc* (*The Passion of Joan of Arc*, 1928). The Danish director, who had worked in Sweden, Norway, and Germany during the 1920s, as well as his native country, was given a free hand by French producers to make a film about the fifteenth-century saint. He brought in a German cinematographer and designer and cast as Joan a stage comedy actress, Falconetti, whose memorable performance was her only appearance on film.

Joan was condemned to the stake for theological and political reasons, but Dreyer's film, particularly from an intertextual per-spective, is also powerfully about gender. The film is an onslaught of male oppression. Joan's interrogators are shot in tight close-ups, from consistently low camera positions, emphasizing their loom-ing, malign power. The spectator is placed in the female position, subjected to the male gaze—except that Joan's face in tight close-up is constantly intercut with the men, so the spectator is

simultaneously in the position of oppressor. Constant pans and dollies, off-center framings, figures rising into the frame, and the claustrophobic tight framing of faces and parts of faces make *The Passion of Joan of Arc* one of the most emotionally intense and visually rewarding works in cinema history.

The gender issues in these films make it inevitable to ask the question of cinema, who is looking? The Surrealist film *Un Chien andalou* ("An Andalusian Dog," 1929), made in Paris by the Spaniards Luis Buñuel (1900–1983) and Salvador Dalí (1904–1989), opens with a notorious sequence depicting a man (Buñuel) slicing a woman's eye with a straight razor. This violent act marks another culmination to a decade of European filmmaking—a provocation against the spectator, perhaps against a cinema turn-ing from silence to sound, but inescapably also against a woman.

Notes

1. Siegfried Kracauer, *From Caligari to Hitler: A Psychological History of the German Film* (Princeton, N.J.: Princeton Univ. Press, 1947), pp. 6, v.
2. Bruce A. Murray, "An Introduction to the Commercial Film Industry in Germany from 1895 to 1933," in *Film and Politics in the Weimar Republic*, eds. Thomas G. Plummer et al. (Minneapolis: University of Minnesota, 1982), p. 33.
3. See reviews of *Dr. Marbuse, the Gambler* (sic), June 2, 1922, and *Metropolis*, March 16, 1927, reprinted in *Variety's Complete Science Fiction Reviews*, ed. Donald Willis (New York: Garland, 1985), pp. 14, 23.
4. Lotte H. Eisner, *The Haunted Screen: Expressionism in the German Cinema and the Influence of Max Reinhardt* (Berkeley and Los Angeles: University of California Press, 1973; originally published as *L'Écran démoniaque*, 1952), p. 207.
5. Harry Alan Potamkin, "The Rise and Fall of the German Film" [1930], in *The Compound Cinema: The Film Writings of Harry Alan Potamkin* (New York: Teachers College Press, 1977), p. 305.
6. Germaine Dulac, "From 'Visual and Anti-visual Films' " [1928], in *The Avant-Garde Film: A Reader of Theory and Criticism*, ed. P. Adams Sitney (New York: New York University Press, 1978), p. 32.

SEVEN

SOVIET CINEMA

Since the collapse and disappearance of the Soviet Union as a political entity, perhaps the most intriguing question in cinema history is how the view of Soviet silent films may be transformed. For most of the twentieth century, the film practices fostered by the 1917 Bolshevik revolution in Russia (and, subsequently, other republics of the former Soviet Union) have been regarded as one of the medium's grandest experiments. Out of revolutionary ideology came an avant-garde movement whose great works challenged and inspired filmmakers throughout the world. Since that ideology has fallen into disrepute (and, even more strongly, its political institutions), its achievements in the arts will also inevitably be reexamined. What may help to preserve the reputation of Soviet silent cinema, by tragic irony, is that, like so much else, it ultimately was crushed by postrevolutionary politics, as bureaucracy inexorably triumphed over art.

As every aspect of the 1917 revolution and its aftermath undergoes new scrutiny, fresh perspectives on the history of cinema in the territories of the former Soviet Union have emerged. Filmmaking in prerevolutionary Russia, for example, was a subject long neglected, if not suppressed. It turns out to have been of substantial importance. At the time of the revolution some four thousand movie theaters were operating in Russia. The French company Pathé played a strong role in production and distribution, as in the United States, until the outbreak of World War I. Directors such as Evgeni Bauer (1865–1917) developed a distinctive style featuring a carefully lighted and decorated mise-en-scène, slow movement, and tragic endings. Following the revolution many of the old companies moved from the capital, Moscow, to southern Russia outside Bolshevik control, and con-

tinued to produce films until the early 1920s.

Although Vladimir Lenin, the Bolshevik leader, was famously quoted as saying, "Of all the arts, for us the cinema is the most important," it took several years for the new Soviet state to develop policies and plans for the medium. The question of whether control over cinema would be centralized or in local hands was decided in favor of nationalization, but that was also slow in taking effect. One of the first concrete steps was to establish a state Film School in Moscow, to replace the trained personnel who had gone south. Lacking raw film stock (with severe shortages, what was available went to make propaganda films, not student work), faculty and students spent their time theorizing about cinema rather than making films.

AGIT-TRAINS

The most important development for Soviet cinema in the first postrevolutionary years were the agit-trains. These were special trains carrying agitational (in the political sense, to present an argument or sustain a viewpoint) and propaganda materials to peasants in rural areas—there were also agit-trucks, an agit-ship, and, for severe winter conditions, agit-sleds. They contained newspapers, pamphlets, political speakers, and film equipment, both to project films (for many agit-train audiences, it was their first experience of movies) and to record images and events.

The agit-train experience was crucial to the formation of a Soviet cinema sensibility. Many of the future filmmakers went out on the trains or worked as editors on the footage that came back. Screening films outdoors under less than optimal conditions emphasized the need for brevity, speed, and movement; back in

7.1. From left, the "Countess" (Alexandra Khokhlova), the One-Eyed Man (Sergei Komarov), "Jug" (Vsevolod Pudovkin), and the Dandy (Leonid Obolensky), in Lev Kuleshov's Soviet comedy Neoby-chainiye priklucheniya Mistera Vesta v strane bol'shevikov (The Extraordinary Adventures of Mr. West in the Land of the Bolsheviks, 1924)

the cutting room, the task of taking footage from many different locations and melding it together into a coherent newsreel or documentary stressed the importance of montage, the principle that images communicate less in themselves than by their placement and juxtaposition among other images.

LEV KULESHOV

The first important figure to explore these ideas was Lev Kuleshov (1899–1970). He was eighteen years old at the time of the Bolshevik uprising—the revolution was, in effect, his university (nearly all the major Soviet filmmakers were under twenty-five during the formative period of political upheaval). The year before, when he was seventeen, the young art student had landed a job as set designer with Evgeni Bauer. He also acted, completed directing a film after Bauer's death, and directed one on his own. When the old film companies left Moscow, Kuleshov remained, casting his future with the revolution. He worked on agit-trains and on **agitkas**, the films made for agit-train screenings. One of the founders of the Film School in Moscow, he formed the Kuleshov Workshop within it to work on cinematic theories and techniques.

The Kuleshov Effect

In the workshop Kuleshov developed his views on montage. He took the position that the material of cinema was the **celluloid** film strip—pieces of film. Film art consisted of putting these pieces together to create, through montage and the spectator's perception, a cinematic composition or idea. The legendary **Kuleshov effect** was an illustration of this principle. The film

director V. I. Pudovkin (1893–1953), then a student in the workshop, tells the story about how he and Kuleshov constructed a film using a close-up of a famous Russian actor juxtaposed with three different images—a bowl of soup, a dead woman in a coffin, a girl playing with a toy bear. Spectators, according to Pudovkin, imagined that the actor was registering hunger toward the soup, sorrow toward the coffin, joy toward the girl. But the image was exactly the same all three times. The Kuleshov effect thus describes a phenomenon whereby shots acquire their meaning only in relation to other shots.

Still hampered by lack of film stock, the workshop also practiced performance exercises before an unloaded camera, with the aim of developing a direct, systematic acting style appropriate to the brief shots of a montage-based cinema. Finally, after several years, the newly formed state film organization Goskino offered Kuleshov and his group a chance to make their first film. This was the lengthily titled *Neobychainiye priklucheniya Mistera Vesta v strane bol'shevikov* (*The Extraordinary Adventures of Mr. West in the Land of the Bolsheviks*, 1924). As director, Kuleshov somewhat defensively admitted that this propaganda comedy was a commercial and industrial product rather than a fulfillment of their experiments and theories.

An American observer and his faithful cowboy bodyguard arrive in Moscow, expecting the Bolsheviks to be the "beasts" and "barbarians" pictured in American popular magazines. Their fears appear confirmed when they are set upon by counterrevolutionary rogues bent on extortion. "We have to perform some Bolshevik atrocities for the American fool," the villains proclaim in an intertitle of an English-language version. Ultimately they are rescued by genuine, nondemonized Bolsheviks and get a look at

Political Upheaval in Russia

Whatever significance the Bolshevik revolution may come to hold in world history, it will surely continue as an important context for the early history of cinema. Under the auspices of the revolution and the state it established, the Soviet Union, a major film movement attempted to forge a revolutionary aesthetic from a revolutionary ideology. Many of its key films, such as Eisenstein's *October* and Pudovkin's *The End of St. Petersburg*, celebrated the revolution itself; others, like Shub's *The Fall of the Romanov Dynasty*, proffered historical justification. Spectators of Soviet silent cinema need to know something of the background of the revolution and its consequences.

The Russian Empire was a monarchy whose emperor was known as the czar; in 1894 the heir to the Romanov dynasty, Nicholas II, became czar. Throughout the nineteenth century revolutionary movements had sprung up among students and intellectuals opposed to the autocratic rule of Nicholas's predecessors. Among the philosophies underlying these movements, the theories of the German socialist Karl Marx (1818–1883) became increasingly important.

Marx, along with Friedrich Engels, had written *The Communist Manifesto* following the failure of European revolutions in 1848. Later he wrote a three-volume analysis of the capitalist system, *Das Kapital*. In basic terms, Marx held that history is governed by laws which shape economic development; that these laws divide society into classes; and that the injustices of capitalism would drive wage laborers (the working class, or proletariat) to overthrow the political system that supported capitalism and put in its place a "dictatorship of the proletariat." This would wipe out capitalism's evils and pave the way for a classless society, called Communism.

After Russia suffered a major defeat in war with Japan in 1905, a revolutionary uprising occurred that included the formation of a *soviet*, or workers' council, in St. Petersburg. This revolution was crushed (Eisenstein's *The Battleship Potemkin* depicts one phase of it), but a radical left-wing group called Bolsheviks ("majority"), espousing Marxism, continued to advocate overthrowing the czar. Its leader, Vladimir Lenin (1870–1924), spent the years from 1897 to 1917 in exile.

When Russia entered World War I in 1914, on the side of France and Britain against Germany, it again experienced defeat and social unrest. In March 1917 a workers' revolt in St. Petersburg deposed Nicholas (who was later murdered with his family) and led to the forming of a provisional government. Returning from exile, Lenin called for a "dictatorship of the proletariat," and in October 1917 the Bolsheviks overthrew the provisional government and seized power. With Lenin at the head, the new regime in 1918 took the name All-Russian Communist Party (of Bolsheviks). It faced several years of civil war and, in the early 1920s, dire famine. In 1922 the Union of Soviet Socialist Republics (U.S.S.R.) was formed, including non-Russian territories controlled by the Communist party or its armies. This state dissolved in 1991 and its republics became autonomous.

Moscow. "Bury those New York magazines and hang a portrait of Lenin in my office," Mr. West wires home. "Long live the Bolsheviks."

Though not the first Soviet film, *Mr. West* raised clearly for the first time issues with which every state-controlled cinema has since grappled: Should films made under state auspices aspire to be art, ideology, or entertainment? To what extent are they a society's showpieces for foreign consumption, or utilitarian products for domestic audiences? *Mr. West* is a comedy that provides ample pleasures and scores some broad political points. But it is hardly a work to inspire and challenge the world.

SERGEI EISENSTEIN

Inspiration and challenge were surely among the goals of theater director Sergei Eisenstein (1898–1948) when he turned to full-time film work around the time of *Mr. West*. Within a few months of their release in 1925 his first two films, *Stachke* (*The Strike*) and especially *Bronenosets Potemkin* (*The Battleship Potemkin*), had given notice to the world of an important new presence. These were works that seemed to represent not only a personal triumph but also a revolutionary art forged in the aesthetic and ideological ferment of the new Soviet state. Though Eisenstein was soon to suffer the proverbial fate of prophets in their own countries, to those elsewhere who followed cinema and the arts the Soviet Union never had a more prestigious or persuasive ambassador.

Proletkult

Eisenstein's voluminous endeavors as the most important film theorist of his era mainly came later in his career, but even in his early theater work he was developing ideas that would have impact on his films. When his training as an engineer was interrupted by the revolution (he was nineteen), Eisenstein went into military service and eventually shifted toward the theater, working as a designer for agit-train productions. He became associated with Proletkult (the name stood for "proletarian cultural-educational organizations"), a group advocating the development of a new culture for the working classes. As designer, sometime actor, and then director, Eisenstein worked on experimental Proletkult theater productions. One strand of his efforts drew on an antinaturalistic "biomechanical" performance style, based on actors' movements rather than expressions of feeling (later, in his film work, Eisenstein preferred to cast "ordinary people" as performers rather than professional actors); another borrowed from popular entertainments like the circus and pantomime.

Theory of Montage

His first published essay, "The Montage of Attractions" (1923), though concerned with theater rather than film, related closely to the cinematic debates of the period. Like Kuleshov, Eisenstein emphasized the centrality of the spectator's response. He defined "attraction" as whatever element of a production *"that subjects the audience to emotional or psychological influence"*[1] (his italics). The stress is not on constructing a narrative or representing the actual world but on creating a shock that leads to audience perception and knowledge. In a sense Eisenstein's aesthetic harkened back to primitive cinema, with its play of spectacle rather than orderly narrative progression.

As he shifted into filmmaking Eisenstein developed and transformed his montage theories. He placed greater emphasis on what he called "**intellectual montage**," which built on the concept of "attraction" but which aimed, in the words of the French Eisenstein scholar Jacques Aumont, at "a conceptual effect . . . the production of meaning."[2] Among the techniques he favored in "intellectual montage" were synecdoche (the part standing for the whole) and metaphor (in his cinematic usage, the juxtaposition of unrelated images to generate associations in the spectator's mind). A famous example of montage as metaphor is a sequence in *Oktyabr'* (*October*, 1928), in which a shot of a soldier in a trench is **intercut** with a shot of a tank rolling off an assembly line, metaphorically shaping an intellectual perception that the soldier is being (or will be) run over by the tank.

Eisenstein moved into film with a proposal from Proletkult to the state film organization to make a series of seven films on events leading up to the Bolshevik revolution, "Towards Dictatorship of the Proletariat." *The Strike* and *The Battleship Potemkin* developed from that plan. The first film was a Proletkult project, but afterward the director and the group had an acrimonious falling-out (ostensibly from a dispute over whether Eisenstein should get a screenplay credit), and future work went forward with Eisenstein's own group of coworkers. His cinematographer Eduard Tisse (1897–1961) and scriptwriter Grigori Alexandrov (1903–1984) stayed with him.

Still, nearly all the director's films of the silent era grew out of this Proletkult concept—*October*, his third released film, was an assignment to commemorate the tenth anniversary of the 1917 revolution. We might consider the significance of these historical subjects, particularly from the viewpoint Soviet theorists placed such importance on, that of the audience. Eisenstein's historical films were addressed foremost to Soviet spectators, as works of interpretation and emotional reinforcement. "Proletarians, Remember!" exhorts the final intertitle in *The Strike*: remember how bad things used to be. They also spoke vividly to sympathizers elsewhere, who could be inspired to carry on their own struggles by visions of Soviet tribulations and triumphs. At the end of the twentieth century, however, what remains of these films' power? It's unlikely that their director would have accepted the idea that their art was separate from their ideology.

Perhaps the simple answer is that Eisenstein's films, viewed at far remove from their historical and contemporary struggles, both gain and suffer from ideology. Writing his own critique of *The Strike* some years later, the director stressed how the film was among the first to treat collective and mass action, to make the mass rather than the bourgeois individual the hero. What it failed to do, he said, was show the development of the individual within the collective. Only after the general image of the collective was established as a screen subject, Eisenstein reflected, could this deeper meaning be attained.

The Strike

This judicious perspective provides a framework for looking at Eisenstein's first film. Indeed, in *The Strike* the individual is missing. There is no humanity in the capitalists' total villainy. Yet the work well illustrates the theory of "montage of attractions." It involves the spectator not through story or logic but through a kind of dance of movement and form—movement of the mass crowds in the mise-en-scène; movement of the camera particularly as it photographs inanimate objects; and movement of the editing through rapid cutting, **dissolves** (editing two shots together so that one fades while the other emerges), **wipes** (editing so that one shot appears to push another off the screen), **double images** (printing one shot over another), **irises** (darkening part of the image to reshape the frame and highlight one part of it), and such trick devices as opening up one shot from the center of another (an unusual kind of wipe). In another essay, written shortly after completing *The Strike*, Eisenstein defended his controversial intercutting of scenes of police shooting workers with shots of a bull being killed in a slaughterhouse: it was, he said, to avoid the falseness of human death on screen while fully signaling its bloody horror (thus, one might add, an early example of metaphorical montage).

The Battleship Potemkin

The lessons of *The Strike* were applied immediately to *The Battleship Potemkin*. Drawn from events that occurred during an unsuccessful uprising against the Russian monarchy in 1905, the film depicts a mutiny aboard a naval vessel. In the first of five separate parts, or "acts," entitled "Men and Maggots," individuals were created among the sailors, and their discontent was made human and immediate through the rotten food they were given and their officers' cruelty and indifference. The mutiny itself, beginning on the ship's foredeck, is choreographed intimately rather than massively, as were the events in *The Strike*. Though filled with temporal leaps ("real time" becomes "reel time," and can be lengthened or foreshortened for psychological effects) and visual disjunctions, the editing style avoids *The Strike*'s virtuoso

7.2–7.7. Sergei Eisenstein's first film, Stachke (The Strike, 1925), aimed to make collective action rather than individual figures its focus. Though Eisenstein later saw this approach as a drawback (or at least a necessary stepping stone before individuals could be shown developing out of the col-lective), The Strike remains notable for its remarkable chore-ography of movement, performed by actors from Moscow's First Workers' Theater. These shots from the film illustrate how the director shaped visual forms both from active and static scenes.

Above: 7.8. Sailors aboard the battleship Potemkin *celebrate their successful mutiny in Eisenstein's* Bronenosets Potemkin *(The Battleship Potemkin, 1925).*

Opposite: 7.9. In The Battleship Potemkin's *Odessa Steps sequence, a mother carries her injured child up the stairs in the face of the murderous soldiers advancing down. Soon she too will be shot.*

display of effects for their own sake. Not much shorter in length than *The Strike*, *The Battleship Potemkin* has the appearance of a briefer, more direct work, moving forward tautly with an economy that seems to absorb its intricate and complex montage strategies.

ODESSA STEPS SEQUENCE. The events culminate in the Odessa Steps sequence, one of the most famous set-pieces in cinema history. As the crowds in the port city Odessa pour into the harbor area to view the liberated battleship and mourn a dead sailor, soldiers appear behind them and march down the steps, firing their rifles. From the intertitle "Suddenly . . ." (in English-language versions), which introduces a shot of empty steps and then soldiers' boots beginning their downward march, the sequence lasts about four minutes twenty seconds, and contains approximately 155 separate shots. Though it may appear a welter of crowds and individuals, close-ups and **long shots**, movement up and down, in ever accelerating tempo, the sequence also relies on specific narrative and character elements: the mother whose son is wounded and trampled, who picks up the child and confronts the soldiers, only to be shot in cold blood; the mother with the baby in a carriage, whose fall, after being shot in the stomach, sends the carriage careening down the steps; the older woman in a white scarf and pince-nez glasses, who first proposes appealing to the soldiers, then is slashed in the eye by a soldier's saber.

The baby carriage segment perhaps deserves most detailed scrutiny for a sense of Eisenstein's montage principles and editing style. Strict temporality is discarded. Separate shots of the carriage wheels, ominously moving and then precariously stopped, are intercut with the mother's fall, which is itself presented in separate, overlapping shots, elongating and repeating "real time." Over the years *The Battleship Potemkin* has received many tributes and homages from other filmmakers—for one Hollywood example, a careening baby carriage in a crucial sequence of Brian De Palma's *The Untouchables* (1987)—but few have come close to matching the intricacy and delicacy of Eisenstein's montage.

October

At twenty-six, Eisenstein perhaps knew that *The Battleship Potemkin* would be a hard act to follow. Preliminary work on a contemporary film about Soviet agricultural policy was interrupted by the assignment to make *October* (the film has sometimes been known in other countries by the title of John Reed's book on the Bolshevik revolution, *Ten Days That Shook the World*). More ambitious in scope than *Potemkin*, the film inevitably became caught up in the intense political struggles of the time. Following Lenin's death in 1924, succession to his leadership was contested by several factions. Around the time Eisenstein was completing *October*, Joseph Stalin emerged as the new Soviet leader, and his enemies and rivals, no matter how important they had been in the

7.10–7.12. Eisenstein's visual design for his film celebrating the tenth anniversary of the Bolshevik revolution, Oktyabr' (October, 1928), included scenes of individual and mass action, of bourgeois decadence characterizing the provisional government that took office following the workers' uprisings of March 1917, and of Vladimir Lenin's fiery oratory that propelled the Bolshevik seizure of power in October 1917. A man named Nikandrov (whose first name seems lost to history) was selected to portray Lenin (top) because of his resemblance to the leader. Of this controversial performance the poet Vladimir Mayakovski wrote, "Nikandrov doesn't resemble Lenin, but a statue of Lenin."

Top: 7.13. Eisenstein (with megaphone) prepares an overhead shot
of the storming of the Winter
Palace for October. His collaborator, Grigori Alexandrov (right),
was credited as coscenarist and
codirector on the film.

Above: 7.14. A tractor mecha-
nizes working methods at a
collective farm in Eisenstein's
Staroe i novoe (The Old and
the New, 1929). Other angles
indicate that the vehicle is a
"Fordson," manufactured in the
Soviet Union by the Ford Motor
Company.

revolution, had to be edited out of the finished film. Even for those historical personages who remained in the film, controversy surrounded their representation by actors. Despite its dramatic events and dynamic stylization, *October* at this distance seems static and uninvolving.

The Old and the New

The agricultural film appeared in 1929 as *Staroe i novoe* (*The Old and the New*, also known by Eisenstein's working title, *The General Line*). Political pressures also drove this film toward a heroic treatment of a peasant woman who overcomes the hostility and sabotage of ignorant neighbors to demonstrate the superiority of collective farming and mechanized agricultural methods. One of its anomalies for present-day spectators is that when the heroine succeeds in obtaining a tractor from a factory, this triumph of the Soviet system turns out to be a Ford Motor Company product, manufactured in the Soviet Union by the giant capitalist firm.

DZIGA VERTOV

Another view of cinema's role in Soviet culture came from Dziga Vertov (1896–1954), the professional name of Denis A. Kaufman. Vertov left medical school at the revolution to go into film work in Moscow. He traveled on agit-trains and as a war correspondent, and put together newsreels and documentaries from available film footage. Where Kuleshov had gone from the agit-train experience through film school teaching to fiction filmmaking, and Eisenstein through theater to historical films, Vertov learned the creative importance of film editing, and became a lifelong advocate of the documentary film.

Kino-Pravda

Vertov entered the Soviet film debates of the early 1920s with vigorous attacks on fiction film. With his brother Mikhail Kaufman (1897–1980) as cameraman and his wife, Elizaveta Svilova (1900–1976), as coeditor, Vertov formed the Cine-Eye group. They began producing a newsreel series called *Kino-Pravda*, named after the official Soviet newspaper, *Pravda* (the term meant Cine-Truth, and was revived decades later for the French documentary film movement of the 1960s, **cinema verité**). More than twenty *Kino-Pravda* episodes were released between 1922 and 1925. In his manifestos, Vertov called for an approach to montage that was at once scientific and poetic, whose core lay in the organization of movement into a "*rhythmical artistic whole.*"[3] That job belonged to the film editor, who shapes the movement of the overall work by determining the "intervals," Vertov's term for the transitions from one image to another.

Vertov's sharp polemical pen earned him opponents as well as supporters. He was criticized from many directions: for depriving images of their status as documents; for using ineffective images that needed more design and composition; for overemphasizing intertitles; for attempting to monopolize the documentary field. One who voiced this last critique was Esfir Shub (1894–1959), whose career as a film editor and documentary filmmaker has been largely eclipsed by Vertov's fame as a lone Soviet avatar of nonfiction film. In an era before archives and museums preserved film materials, Shub hunted down discarded footage and put together historical documentaries. In her first **compilation film,** *Padenie dinastii Romanovykh* (*The Fall of the Romanov Dynasty*, 1927), she crafted from what often appeared accidental or innocu-

ous images a compelling narrative of events leading up to the abdication of the Russian monarch in February 1917. This was followed by several similar works on Russian history and Soviet life.

A Sixth Part of the World

Many of the attacks on Vertov found a focus in his 1926 feature-length documentary *Shestaya chast' mira* (*A Sixth Part of the World*). This is an unabashedly propagandistic work sponsored by a Soviet trade agency. The spectator is continually addressed as "you" and is further positioned by occasional shots of a movie audience viewing the film's images on a screen. The film's uniqueness, perhaps now difficult to appreciate, lay in its sending cameramen out to the far reaches of the Soviet north, east, and south to capture images of non-Russian ethnic groups within the vast Soviet territory. Their efforts as hunters and farmers were producing export goods, the film declared, to trade for machines to build "A Model Homeland."

The Man with the Movie Camera

For the next several years Vertov played a less prominent role in the intensifying Soviet film debates. He and his Cine-Eye colleagues, it turned out, were preparing a film intended as a visual, rather than verbal, statement of their documentary theories. This was *Chelovek s kinoapparatom* (*The Man with the Movie Camera*, 1929), produced by a Ukrainian film organization. In the film's opening credits Vertov proclaimed it an experiment without intertitles, script, actors, or sets: a work aimed "to create a truly international film-language, *absolute writing in film,* and the complete separation of cinema from theater and literature."

The Man with the Movie Camera is one of the most unusual works in cinema history. It is also perhaps the most difficult of all major films, almost certainly requiring more than a single viewing to grasp some of its meanings and pleasures. A coherent summary of all it attempts to accomplish is probably next to impossible. But many with an open mind toward the varieties of filmmaking and an interest in the autonomy of the cinema image will find it one of their most memorable film experiences.

Presented on one level as a day in the life of a film team photographing places and people in Soviet cities, *The Man with the Movie Camera* is basically a film about the recording and viewing of images. Its opening sequence establishes the beginning and the end of the image-making process. A trick shot shows a camera, and on top of that a tiny cameraman with his own camera on a tripod. Then there are shots of a movie theater—first empty, then filling with spectators—and a projection booth. All these scenes emphasize the continuity of the act of looking, with metaphors such as one that links window blinds, a camera lens, and a human eye.

The cameraman's work is related to circularity. Shots of the hand-cranked camera are intercut with moving wheels of cars and bicycles. (Denis Kaufman's pseudonym, Vertov, was derived from the verb to spin or rotate; the first name, Dziga, mimicked the sound of a camera crank turning.) A regularly repeated segment of the film shows the man with the movie camera mounted in the back of an open car photographing people in a moving car beside him (perhaps they should have called the film "Two Men with Movie Cameras," to account for the cameraman in an unseen third moving car who is filming the filming).

Soon the work of Elizaveta Svilova as editor is brought into the picture. Here the materiality of the image is stressed—its existence

Top left: 7.15. Filming on location for Dziga Vertov's newsreel series Kino-Pravda ("Cine-Truth"), which ran from 1922 to 1925

Top right: 7.16. A shot from Esfir Shub's film compiled from historical footage, Padenie dinastii Romanovykh (The Fall of the Romanov Dynasty, 1927)

Above: 7.17. A split-screen image (two separate shots occupying different parts of the frame) from Vertov's Shestaya chast' mira (A Sixth Part of the World, 1926)

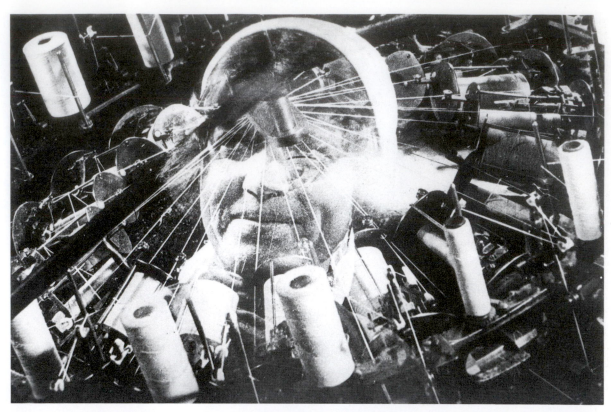

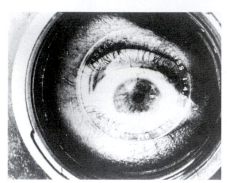

7.18–7.21. Vertov's Chelovek s kinoapparatom (The Man with the Movie Camera, 1929) concerns, among many other things, the recording, processing, and consuming of images. Vertov's concept of the "cine-eye," of the imperfect human eye giving way to the perfectible camera eye, is made manifest in a double-image shot (one shot superimposed on the other) of a human eye and a camera lens together (above). Another double image shows a woman worker superimposed on a mechanical loom, representing rolls of film that an editor weaves together into a continuous series of images (top). One such series (right) begins with an empty theater space that by superimposition fills with spectators who view the film in which they appear, and sometimes view themselves.

7.22. From left, Sergei Komarov as Hans Nelson, Alexandra Khokhlova as Edith Nelson, and Vladimir Fogel as Michael Dennin in Kuleshov's Po zakonu (By the Law, 1926), based on a story by American writer Jack London

on rolls of celluloid that are stored in long rows, studied, cut, hung from clips. The editor's work is visually compared to manicuring, sewing, and spinning. All these subjects are presented in a dizzying array of visual techniques—an incomplete list includes **split-screen** (separate images occupying different parts of the frame) shots, speeded-up action, **freeze frames** (a moving image stopped on the screen as if a still), images at a slant, stop-motion trick photography (as when the camera and tripod become animated and move by themselves), and floods of images flowing at the spectator, at times with no apparent continuity.

The third term of the image process after photographing and editing is viewing, and the audience experience is continually reintroduced—the spectators in the theater, the screen, and sometimes on the screen a shot of the audience itself. And finally there is the actual world represented amid the world of image-making and image-consuming. It shows Soviet people at work and play, marrying and divorcing, dying and being born (the film contains one of the earliest shots of a birth in cinema history). Without explanatory intertitles, the spectator unable to pick up clues from Russian-language documents or signs in the frame is often a bit lost as to what is happening. Still, for all its avant-garde techniques and theoretical ambitions, *The Man with the Movie Camera* is one of the few silent films that strongly conveys a sense of everyday life in Soviet Russia.

OTHER SOVIET FILMMAKERS

By the mid-1920s Soviet cinema was becoming firmly established. Releases rose from thirteen in 1923 to over one hundred in 1928, the first year when domestic films outpaced foreign works in box office revenues from Soviet theaters. There was a vastly proliferating body of cinema organizations whose acronyms and initials are confusing enough, without the frequent name changes that occurred. Most of the films forming the canon of Soviet silent cin-

ema were produced by the Goskino and Mezhrabpom-Russ studios in Moscow; by Sovkino, a national film body formed in 1924, with studios in Leningrad and Moscow; and the Ukrainian studio known as VUFKU, in Kharkov. The Film School was the training ground for new film personnel. Periodicals and conferences constantly debated questions of style, theme, and the cinema's social and ideological role.

The Reaction to Eisenstein

For filmmakers, however, a generally healthy competition in revolutionary zeal and cinematic innovation was almost immediately skewed by Eisenstein's achievement in *The Battleship Potemkin*. Eisenstein had virtually retired the trophy before the race had begun. Directors were faced with the equally unpromising choices of trying to emulate him or to outdo him. Kuleshov had fallen into this dilemma following Eisenstein's *The Strike* by making an elaborate science fiction thriller, *Luch smerti* (*The Death Ray*, 1925), that was heavily criticized and almost caused the Goskino studio to drop the Kuleshov group.

He sought to recover with a very different, un-Eisensteinian kind of work, *Po zakonu* (*By the Law*, 1926), an intense realist drama about gold prospectors in the Yukon, based on a story by the American socialist writer Jack London. With most of the action taking place in a small cabin, this was a Soviet equivalent to the German *Kammerspiel* genre, though in Kuleshov's style more emphasis was placed on expressive body movement by performers. Some critics saw *By the Law* as the beginning of an "actors' cinema" as a possible alternative to Eisenstein, who was less interested in performance than in casting to type.

Vsevelod Pudovkin

Another potential advocate of "actors' cinema" was Vsevelod Pudovkin, who had been a performer in the Kuleshov group, a coworker in the Kuleshov effect experiments, and author of early

7.23. Vera Baranovskaia portrays the mother and Nikolai Batalov her son in Vsevelod Pudovkin's Mat' (The Mother, 1926).

(*The End of St. Petersburg*, 1927), a few months ahead of *October*. Again Pudovkin built an individualized story line—a peasant family forced by poverty to move to the city, whence members participate in events leading from the World War to the storming of the Winter Palace. Though much of the film's treatment of the prerevolutionary era seems stylistically hyperbolic, with exaggerated villains and scenes of stock market speculation derived from Lang's *Dr. Mabuse*, the moment of revolutionary triumph is surprisingly muted, as family members find each other among exhausted Soviet soldiers.

Pudovkin's third historical fiction, *Potomok Chingis-khana* (literally "The Heir of Genghis Khan," but titled in English *Storm over Asia*, 1928), was set in the postrevolutionary era, during the Civil War period of 1918–20 when British forces invaded Soviet territory from the east. The film retains its strongest interest in segments filmed on location in Mongolia, with documentary scenes of indigenous religious rituals and ceremonies that give the work power as an ethnographic record that its political fiction has long ago lost. Another film that shifted attention to the east was

pamphlets on film technique that gave considerable attention to acting. Pudovkin's debut fiction feature as director, *Mat'* (*The Mother*, 1926), was a hybrid of several styles: avant-garde techniques à la Eisenstein, such as superimpositions; an emphasis on performance, through frequent use of expressive close-ups; and a constant recourse to natural symbolism, such as shots of ice breaking up and water flowing as metaphors for human events. Based on a novel by the popular Soviet writer Maxim Gorki, *The Mother* dealt with prerevolutionary struggles similar to those of *The Strike*. But it strongly individualized the narrative through a story of a woman who innocently betrays her son to authorities, then redeems herself by raising high the flag of rebellion just as she meets her own death.

Pudovkin outpaced Eisenstein by releasing his film on the tenth anniversary of the Bolshevik revolution, *Konets Sankt-Peterburga*

Left: 7.24. The director Vsevelod Pudovkin in a photograph from 1932, described as talking with workers from a Moscow factory who appeared in his film Dezertir (The Deserter, 1933)

Above: 7.25. A scene from Pudovkin's Konets Sankt-Peterburga (The End of St. Petersburg, 1927)

Goluboi ekspress (*The China Express*, also known as *The Blue Express*, 1929), directed by Ilya Trauberg (1905–1948), which constructs a rebellion aboard an express train as a microcosm for a society and its revolutionary potential.

Abram Room

The triumph of a performance-oriented cinema was *Tret'ya Meshchanskaya* (*Bed and Sofa*, 1927), directed by Abram Room (1894–1976). Except for a few candid moments, this love-triangle story might have been little noticed had it been made in a Western country, where romantic melodramas were produced by the dozens. But in the Soviet Union, where films with contemporary everyday settings were scarce, and both heroes and villains in prestige pictures tended to be stick figures, the film came as a revelation.

The premise behind this three-character drama is Moscow's housing problem. A worker new to the city cannot find a place to live, but an old army buddy, already shown to be an insensitive husband, offers him the sofa to sleep on. The husband goes away on a job assignment, the unhappy wife and the lodger become friends and soon lovers. When the husband returns and learns of the new relationship, he moves out, but he cannot find a place either, and returns—to the sofa. The woman now finds both men insensitive, and all three sleep alone. She learns she is pregnant. She goes to an abortion clinic but abruptly decides to leave the men and have the baby on her own.

All three performers are worth noting: Nikolai Batalov, who played the son in *The Mother*, as the husband; Vladimir Fogel, who looked like James Dean and also tragically died young, as the friend; and Ludmilla Semyonova as the wife. After the very discreetly handled tryst between the friend and the wife,

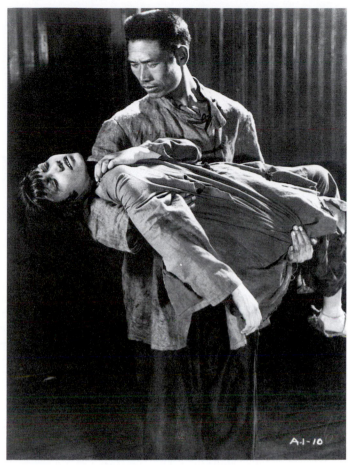

Above: 7.26. A scene from Pudovkin's Potomok Chingis-khana (Storm over Asia, *1928)*

Above right: 7.27. Goluboi ekspress (The China Express, *1929), directed by Ilya Trauberg, was subtitled in English-language versions, "An Episode from the Revolutionary Movement in the East."*

Right: 7.28. Vladimir Fogel as the friend, Ludmilla Semyonova as the wife, in Abram Room's Tret'ya Meshchanskaya (Bed and Sofa, *1927)*

Russian Art Movements

If cinema, in the phrase attributed to Lenin, was the Soviet Union's "most important art," a variety of movements and "isms" also thrived in other art forms, including painting and sculpture, poetry, and theater. Some of these movements were well established before the Bolshevik revolution, but many artists became revolutionary enthusiasts and linked their practice to revolutionary ideas, as did filmmakers such as Eisenstein and Vertov. There are conflicting viewpoints on whether the terminology of movements in other arts can be applied to cinema, although some critics and historians confidently do so.

Futurism in prerevolutionary Russia derived from Italian Futurism, a movement launched in 1909 by Italian poet Filippo Tommaso Marinetti. Disdaining what they saw as the sentimentality and nostalgia of nineteenth-century art, futur-ist poets and visual artists wanted to create works that represented the dynamism of their contemporary world, dominated by technology, movement, and speed. The leading Russian futurist was poet Vladimir Mayakovski (1893–1930), who broke with traditional rhythm and decorous language to write poetry in street vernacular. Mayakovski became an avid supporter of the revolution and was a popular poet in the 1920s, though the term "futurism" fell out of favor after 1922 when Italian futurists supported the Fascist seizure of power in Italy. As also happened to filmmakers, Mayakovski's work came under official criticism in the late 1920s for its avant-garde "formalism." He committed suicide in 1930.

Constructivism, a term that replaced futurism in the 1920s, was in a way futurism with a Soviet face. This concept viewed the artist as an "engineer": the artist united revolutionary ideology with his or her materials in order simultaneously to construct new content and new form. Even more than in futurism, the emphasis was on technology and industrial forms. Though constructivism was especially important in painting, sculpture, and architecture, it also played a significant role in Soviet theater through the work of director Vsevolod Meyerhold (1874–1940). Even before the revolution Meyerhold was developing a "biomechanical" theory of acting drawn from industrial motion analysis, emphasizing body control rather than emotion as the basis of performance (Eisenstein adapted this idea for cinema). Meyerhold became head of theater activities in the Soviet Union, but like so many other Soviet artists he was eventually attacked and purged by the regime. He was arrested in 1939 and executed in 1940.

Semyonova is sitting on the bed beside her sleeping lover. She rests her cheek on the gauze-covered metal bar of the bed frame, and then impulsively bites at the bar. It is one of those unforgettable moments of performance that remind us of cinema's capacity to reveal the complexities of human emotions.

Alexander Dovzhenko

Dominated by directors whose careers had begun on agit-trains, at the Film School, or in Moscow theater work, the Soviet film world was startled in 1928 by the emergence of the first major regional figure, Alexander Dovzhenko (1894–1956). Production had developed in Ukraine and in other non-Russian Soviet republics such as Georgia, yet these films received little attention in the main centers of the Soviet industry. Dovzhenko, who came from a peasant background and had fought with the Bolsheviks against Ukrainian nationalists in the postrevolutionary civil war, had made no impact with his first two films, shot at the VUFKU studio in Odessa. But his third feature, *Zvenigora* (1928), propelled him by its original force into the top rank of Soviet filmmakers (Zvenigora is the name of a mountain in Ukraine, and the film has always gone by its original title).

In a setting where a range of nonrealist, avant-garde techniques had by repetition almost become formulas, *Zvenigora* nevertheless managed to display an avant-garde style different from anything to which Soviet filmmakers and their sophisticated audiences had become accustomed. Its opening shot of horses galloping in **slow motion** signals the spectator to expect disorientation. The film quickly takes on the character of a fable, linking past and present in a timeless whole and shifting temporality in the manner of the magic realist style practiced in late-twentieth-century Latin American and Eastern European literature (**magic realism** was in fact a term coined in the European art debates of the 1920s). And like the later magic realist literary works, the film directs its fabulist techniques toward political allegory: in

Zvenigora, the need to discover the strengths of Ukraine's past and unite them with its Bolshevik present.

Of cinema's great works, Zvenigora is among the most neglected. Like *The Man with the Movie Camera*, its cultural references are often difficult to decipher. But there is also much to reward the spectator, who may be as surprised on first viewing as Moscow audiences were in 1928.

Dovzhenko's equivalent to *October* and *The End of St. Petersburg* as a commissioned film to commemorate the recent past was *Arsenal* (*The Arsenal*, 1929). Its subject was a 1918 event in the Ukrainian civil war—the successful defense of the Arsenal munitions plant in Kiev during a six-day attack. What makes *The*

Left and above: 7.29, 7.30. Nikolai Nademsky portrays the protean Grandfather who inhabits different eras of Ukrainian history in Alexander Dovzhenko's Zvenigora *(1928).*

Below: 7.31. A scene from Dovzhenko's Arsenal *(The Arsenal, 1929)*

7.32. Vasyl (Stepan Shkurat), the hero of collective farming, dances with joy, moments before he is murdered, in Dovzhenko's Zemlya (The Earth, 1930).

Arsenal remarkable as a film intended to be politically correct and ideologically didactic are two, perhaps connected, aspects. One is a style that frequently veers toward the absurd (as when a portrait hanging on a wall begins to move its head), giving the film at times a Surrealist atmosphere. The other is a completely unromanticized, absolutely grim treatment of violence and death, even in revolutionary struggle.

Zemlya (The Earth, 1930) is Dovzhenko's best-known but also most controversial film, and the one that earned him a reputation as a poet of the cinema. Like Eisenstein's *The Old and the New*, it deals with the contentious issue of farm collectivization, and combines a strong emphasis on the cycles of death and renewal in life and nature with touches of Surrealist humor.

Its centerpiece is a lyric-tragic sequence where Vasyl, the hero of collective farming, is walking slowly through the village at night. Then he begins to dance, and a series of shots shows him dancing alone along the village paths, radiating joy, energy, and power. Suddenly he crumples to the ground. There is a cut to a

horse lifting its head, signaling in this silent film a loud noise like a gunshot—then back to the shot of the fallen Vasyl, with a person scuttling off in the background. Vasyl's martyrdom unites the peasants on the side of collectivization and against the rich farmers who have murdered him.

ART AND IDEOLOGY

The Earth was one of the works that brought to a head a growing struggle within the Soviet film community. While some criticized the film for alleged flaws in ideological analysis or political strategy, the overriding issue for filmmakers was one of aesthetics. *The Earth* was lumped together with other works that one polemic called "Formalist obscurantism and mystical Symbolist nonsense."[4] (**Formalism** was a term almost always applied pejoratively in Soviet film debates; at the same time it could be said accurately to describe works whose emphasis was on form rather than on story, or acting.) Nevertheless, nearly every filmmaker discussed in this chapter, despite considerable variations in style and significant emphasis by some on narrative and performance, came under attack.

At stake was the issue raised when the first Soviet filmmakers dedicated themselves to creating a revolutionary art: Were films to be revolutionary as art or revolutionary because of their ideology? A few films seem to have passed both tests: principally *The Battleship Potemkin*, *The Mother*, and *The End of St. Petersburg*. But a great number of other works, perhaps especially among those admired by Western filmmakers and critics for their avant-garde style, were condemned as petty bourgeois rather than proletarian in their orientation.

Socialist Realism

The proletarian standard began increasingly to be raised in the late 1920s as the rationale for cinema in the Soviet state. In one sense this represented new policies of the Stalin era (though any comparison with Lenin's viewpoint is purely inferential, since Lenin died before there was a Soviet cinema for him to criticize); in another sense it came from new cadres of film bureaucrats who were responsible for meeting production goals and pleasing the political leadership. What mattered was not film art but a cinematic practice that could please (and also politically indoctrinate) a mass audience of workers and peasants. Like mass audiences everywhere, this one wanted genre entertainment (a desire that in the early postrevolutionary years had been satisfied by importing Western films). By raising the proletarian standard, the film industry emphasized the production of genre entertainments that were ideologically correct from a Soviet viewpoint. In the 1930s this practice was codified under the term **socialist realism**.

The Problem of Sound

Bureaucrats, both in the film industry and outside it, began to play a more active role in the filmmaking process. Projects had to be approved for political correctness before resources could be committed; completed films were subjected to further ideological tests, and held back from release if they failed. These difficulties were exacerbated by the problem of sound. The Soviet cinema was not as advanced in sound technology as were, particularly, the United States and Germany (see Chapter 8). It was difficult, however, to forge ahead with silent film production while Western countries converted fully to sound. Production fell off in 1929, and the annual number of releases continued to decline for several years after that.

Sound technology was also viewed by many critics as a fundamental challenge to the montage principle that lay at the heart of Soviet cinema's achievements. Early talking pictures, especially because of technological restraints on movement of both the camera and the actors, seemed to signal a return to the simplest form of filmed theater. In this context, several years before the first Soviet sound films appeared, directors Eisenstein and Pudovkin, along with scriptwriter Alexandrov, jointly released a "Statement on Sound." Its purpose was to lay out several theoretical arguments supporting the continuing primacy of montage in a sound cinema.

They took the view that sound was not a threat to montage but an avenue of escape from "blind alleys" into which they thought montage filmmaking had been headed. These were, first, a growing tendency by filmmakers to turn intertitles into elaborate trick shots (for example, by making words grow or shrink in size

through the duration of an intertitle, as if modulating volume); and, second, what they called "*explanatory* sequences" that slowed down montage rhythm. They advocated the use of **contrapuntal sound**.

"*The first experiments in sound must aim at a sharp discord with the visual images*," they wrote (italics in all cases theirs). They called this a "hammer and tongs" approach to create "a new *orchestral counterpoint* of visual and sound images."[5]

This statement had little effect except to please a handful of Western critics who regarded the talking picture as the downfall of cinematic art. Neither Eisenstein nor Pudovkin was involved in early Soviet sound films. In 1929 both directors were sent abroad to exploit the prestige of Soviet silent films in Europe and the United States. Pudovkin went to Germany, where he performed the lead role in a film coproduced by Soviet and German companies, *Zhivoi trup* (*A Living Corpse*, 1929, directed by Fyodor Otsep); later he lectured in Britain and Holland before returning to the Soviet Union. Eisenstein (along with Tisse and Alexandrov) stopped in a number of western European countries en route to Hollywood, where an original plan to study American movies turned into an effort to make an American movie. His major project was an adaptation for Paramount of Theodore Dreiser's novel *An American Tragedy*; when producer David O. Selznick read the script (a collaboration of Eisenstein, Alexandrov, and British writer Ivor Montagu), he called it "the most moving script I have ever read," but added, "as entertainment, I don't think it has one chance in a hundred."[6] Unable to get this or other projects approved by the studios, Eisenstein went on to Mexico to shoot a film, "Qué Viva México!," sponsored by American socialist writer Upton Sinclair. This ended in even greater disappointment when Sinclair, concerned over costs, cut off further financing and confiscated all the footage on the unfinished film. Eisenstein returned to the Soviet Union in 1932, but did not begin shooting another film until 1936.[7]

ENTHUSIASM. One of the first Soviet filmmakers given a chance to make a sound film was Vertov. His *Simfoniya Donbassa* ("The Donbass Symphony," but titled in English-language versions *Enthusiasm*, 1930), a documentary about industrial production in the Don River basin, was, characteristically, a difficult avant-garde work. There are moments of sound/image counterpoint as advocated in the "Statement on Sound," as when jazz plays on the **soundtrack** during religious scenes, but there are many other sound experiments: **synchronous sound** (sound recorded simultaneously with the image) shot on location, which was still relatively uncommon in Western cinemas, where early sound films were studio-bound; separate sounds edited to clash (or harmonize) by occurring at the same time on the soundtrack; "abstract" sound with no clear source or referent; sound juxtaposed with a blank screen.

Enthusiasm is an avant-garde triumph equal to any similar nonfiction work of the century. But it did not fare well by the proletarian standard. Though it shows many scenes of industrial and also agricultural labor, it seems to create less a feeling of joy in work than of pathos, by showing how strenuous and dangerous such labor often is. The film came under severe political criticism. It marked the end point of an effort to create an avant-garde cinema under revolutionary auspices, the lessons of which continue to be pondered within film cultures of many different political systems.

7.33. A double-image shot
from Vertov's first sound film,
Simfoniya Donbassa (Enthusiasm,
1930)

The Far-Reaching Impact of Soviet Filmmaking

Among many films and filmmakers influenced by Soviet silent cinema, one of the most interesting examples is a film that was made contemporaneously by a Japanese filmmaker who had actually not yet seen any Soviet films (when they arrived in Japan, films such as *The Battleship Potemkin* were confiscated by authorities because of their allegedly subversive political content). The film is *Kurutta ippeiji* (*Page of Madness*, 1926), directed by Teinosuke Kinugasa (1896–1982), a work thought lost for more than half a century until its rediscovery in the 1970s. Kinugasa had read accounts of Soviet montage theories, translated from German magazines, and these impelled him to make what is regarded as Japan's first avant-garde film. The work challenged almost every aspect of Japanese film conventions: it cast women in the parts previously played by *oyama* (female impersonators) and attempted to confound the *benshi* narrators by adopting a rapid, impressionistic montage style. In 1928 Kinugasa went to Moscow, where he met with Eisenstein, Pudovkin, and Alexandrov at the time of their "Statement on Sound."

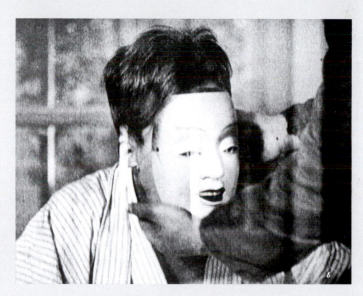

7.34. A mask from Japanese Noh theater is placed on an asylum inmate in Page of Madness.

Notes

1.   Sergei Eisenstein, "The Montage of Attractions," in *The Film Factory: Russian and Soviet Cinema in Documents*, eds. Richard Taylor and Ian Christie (Cambridge, Mass.: Harvard University Press, 1988), p. 87.

2.   Jacques Aumont, *Montage Eisenstein*, trans. Lee Hildreth, Constance Penley, and Andrew Ross (Bloomington: Indiana University Press, 1987; French edition, 1979), p. 158.

3.   "We: Variant of a Manifesto" [1922], in *Kino-Eye: The Writings of Dziga Vertov*, ed. Annette Michelson, trans. Kevin O'Brien (Berkeley and Los Angeles: University of California Press, 1984), p. 8.

4.   *Kino i zhizn* Editorial, "Film Work and the Mass Audience" [1930], in *The Film Factory*, p. 297.

5.   Sergei Eisenstein, Vsevolod Pudovkin, and Grigori Alexandrov, "Statement on Sound" [1928], in *The Film Factory*, pp. 234–35.

6.   David O. Selznick to B. P. Schulberg, October 8, 1930, in *Memo from David O. Selznick*, ed. Rudy Behlmer (New York: Viking, 1972), p. 26.

7.   The Hollywood and Mexico episodes in Eisenstein's career can be followed, respectively, in Ivor Montagu, *With Eisenstein in Hollywood: A Chapter of Autobiography* (New York: International Publishers, 1967), which contains the *An American Tragedy* script; and Sergei Eisenstein and Upton Sinclair, *The Making and Unmaking of "Que Viva Mexico!"*, eds. Harry M. Geduld and Ronald Gottesman (Bloomington: Indiana University Press, 1970).

EIGHT

THE TRANSITION

The shift from silent to sound film at the end of the 1920s marks, so far, the most important transformation in motion picture history. Despite all the highly visible technological developments in theatrical and home delivery of the moving image that have occurred over the decades since then, no single innovation has come close to being regarded as a similar kind of watershed. In nearly every language, however the words are phrased, the most basic division in cinema history lies between films that are mute and films that speak.

Yet this most fundamental standard of historical periodization conceals a host of paradoxes. Nearly every movie theater, no matter how modest, had a piano or organ to provide musical accompaniment to "silent" pictures. In many instances, spectators in the era before recorded sound experienced elaborate aural presentations alongside movies' visual images, from the Japanese *benshi* crafting multivoiced dialogue narratives to original musical compositions performed by symphony-sized orchestras in Europe and the United States. For the premiere performance outside the Soviet Union of *The Battleship Potemkin*, in Berlin, Eisenstein worked with Austrian composer Edmund Meisel (1874–1930) on a musical score matching sound to image; the Berlin screenings with live music helped to bring the film its wide international fame.

Beyond that, the triumph of recorded sound has overshadowed the rich diversity of technological and aesthetic experiments with the visual image that were going forward simultaneously in the 1920s. New color processes, larger or differently shaped screen sizes, multiple-screen projections, even television, were among the developments invented or tried out during the period, some-

times with startling success. The high costs of converting to sound and the early limitations of sound technology were among the factors that suppressed innovations or retarded advancement in these other areas. The introduction of new screen formats was put off for a quarter century, and color, though utilized over the next two decades for special productions, also did not become a norm until the 1950s.

Though it may be difficult to imagine from a later perspective, a strain of critical opinion in the 1920s predicted that sound film would be a technical novelty that would soon fade from sight, just as had many previous attempts, dating back well before World War I, to link images with recorded sound. These critics were making a common assumption—that the technological inadequacies of earlier efforts (poor synchronization, weak sound amplification, fragile sound recordings) would invariably occur again. To be sure, their evaluation of the technical flaws in 1920s sound experiments was not so far off the mark; yet they neglected to take into account important new forces in the motion picture field that, in a sense, would not take no for an answer.

TELECOMMUNICATIONS AND FILM SOUND

These forces were the rapidly expanding electronics and telecommunications companies that were developing and linking telephone and wireless technologies in the 1920s. In the United States, they included such firms as American Telephone and Telegraph (with its subsidiaries Western Electric and Bell

Laboratories), General Electric, Radio Corporation of America (RCA), Westinghouse, and others. They were interested in all forms of sound technology and all potential avenues for commercial exploitation. Their competitions and collaborations were creating the broadcasting industry in the United States, beginning with the introduction of commercial radio programming in the early 1920s. With financial assets considerably greater than those in the motion picture industry, and perhaps a wider vision of the relationships among entertainment and communications media, they revitalized research into recording sound for motion pictures. Two basic technologies were pursued: **sound-on-disc** (similar to a phonograph record) and **sound-on-film** (the optical recording of sound as an element on the celluloid film strip).

Sound-on-disc

In the 1920s sound-on-disc (which had its antecedents in Edison's nineteenth-century idea of uniting phonograph with motion picture camera) was the first to attain practical status for commercial development. Having solved the problem of adequate amplification, Western Electric was ready in 1926 with a system of disc recorder and camera powered by the same motor. The company teamed with a Hollywood studio, Warner Bros., to form the Vitaphone Corporation. At the exhibition end, the Vitaphone sys-

particularly as a spin-off of research on radio and telephone sound transmission for military purposes during World War I. In the United States the inventors Lee de Forest (1874–1961) and Theodore Case (1888–1944) presented their Phonofilm system in 1923. Case and de Forest ended their work together in 1925, and the following year Case, with his assistant Earl I. Sponable (1895–1977), devised a new sound reproducing head that could be added to existing projectors. A few weeks before Western Electric and Warner Bros. demonstrated the sound-on-disc Vitaphone, Fox Film Corporation purchased the rights to Case's sound-on-film system and called it Movietone.

Sound in Europe

In the same period as these United States developments, inventors in Denmark and Germany were making similar progress. The Danish system, developed by P. O. Pederson and Vlademar Poulsen in 1923, at first utilized separate picture and sound film reels. The Pederson-Poulsen system was utilized in Britain; in Germany, where it was known as Tonfilm; and in France, where the first French sound film was made in 1928 with the Danish apparatus. A different system that initially put the soundtrack outside the perforations on the film roll was developed in Germany by three inventors, Josef Engl, Joseph Massolle, and Hans Vogt.

TO SOUND

tem utilized a projector and turntable run by the same motor, as well as loudspeakers for sound amplification. The system was demonstrated in August 1926 with a screening of short musical films, and Warner Bros. quickly expanded into sound feature film production. Difficulties in the Vitaphone system's technology, however, soon became amply exposed—discs broke, and projectionists often had trouble correctly synchronizing disc and picture. By 1930 Warner Bros. shifted over to sound-on-film.

Sound-on-film

Sound-on-film was developed using different formats in several countries. All of these involved the optical recording of sound—turning sound waves into photographic images. Experiments with this process had been going on since the late nineteenth century. In simple terms, inventors devised a series of steps by which sounds were converted into a variable electric current that activated a modulated light beam projected onto negative film. This created the wavy streaks of white lines we see when we look at what is called a **variable-density soundtrack**. In the movie projector, the process is reversed: light projected onto the soundtrack activates a variable electrical current that is converted back into sounds.

Amplification

A working model based on these principles had been demonstrated as early as 1906. What was principally missing was a means to amplify the sound, which was not fully developed, as with sound-on-disc, until the mid-1920s. In the years between, a great many technical improvements were made in the process,

Their process, called Tri-Ergon, was put on the market by the Tonbild-Syndikat, known as Tobis, which soon merged with another firm to become Tobis-Klangfilm. This became the leading European sound company.

Patent Struggles

Patent disputes among these three systems were likely to be considerably more complicated than even the struggles over early motion picture technology. Both the Danish and German inventors had secured key patents in the United States that threatened, even against the might of the American industrial giants, to involve years of litigation and slow down the pace of sound film development, as Edison's court battles had hobbled the medium in the pioneer days of cinema. A 1930 Paris conference of patent holders attempted to reconcile patent claims and allocate rights, royalties, and territories, akin to the Motion Picture Patents Trust agreements of 1908. Though these arrangements frequently broke down over the next few years, industrial fights did not appear to hinder the advancement of sound in the major film-producing countries.

Hollywood and Sound

Despite the efforts of Warner Bros. and Fox, the largest Hollywood studios, Paramount and Metro-Goldwyn-Mayer, did not appear at first nearly so interested in converting to sound. However, the success of Warner's features produced with the Vitaphone sound-on-disc system, and Fox's determination to switch its feature film output entirely to sound, persuaded other companies to join the movement. Rapid consolidation occurred in the motion picture industry as stronger studios sought to enlarge their base of theaters, distribution exchanges, and production facilities in the wake of significant investments in wiring theaters for sound. Fox for a time took over Loew's Inc., the parent company of M-G-M, but was forced to give it up because of government pressure against motion picture monopolies and financial losses after the 1929 stock market crash. A merger was discussed, but never accomplished, between Paramount and Warner Bros. When the dust settled, these four firms—Paramount, M-G-M, Fox, and Warner Bros.—were clearly established as Hollywood's leading companies, the "majors."

RKO. The conversion to sound created a fifth "major" Hollywood studio. RCA established a movie company as a vehicle for marketing to theaters its own sound system, Photophone, in competition with Vitaphone and Movietone. RCA joined with Film Booking Office, a small studio, for its production facilities, and the Keith-Albee-Orpheum vaudeville circuit, in order to acquire its theaters and its control over the American Pathé studio. The resulting amalgam was called Radio-Keith-Orpheum, or RKO.

Conversion to Sound

In 1929 the United States motion picture industry released more than three hundred sound films—a rough figure, since a number were silent films with music tracks, or films prepared in dual versions, to take account of the many theaters not yet wired for sound. At the production level, in the United States the conversion was virtually complete by 1930. In Europe it took a little longer, mainly because there were more small producers for whom the costs of sound were prohibitive, and in other parts of the world problems with rights or access to equipment delayed the shift to sound production for a few more years (though theaters in major cities may have been wired in order to play foreign sound pictures). By 1930, meanwhile, virtually everyone making sound films had committed to sound-on-film rather than sound-on-disc, utilizing one or another of the American or European systems. The triumph of sound cinema was swift, complete, and enormously popular.

COLOR AND WIDESCREEN

We might pause for a moment and attempt one of those exercises historians occasionally resort to, the "counterfactual" question: what if? What if the sound amplification problem had not been solved and sound reproduction had come out so crude and tinny that nobody liked it? What if attention and capital had gravitated toward other potential innovations? What creative directions might the silent film have evolved in if it had not, like a prehistoric beast, been marked for extinction?

The world's film archives hold a few tantalizing possible answers. But most of us have a problem in getting to see the evidence. While important efforts are being made to preserve and restore classic silent films, it remains true that major silent film experiments with color or large-screen formats (known by the general term **widescreen**) are only rarely available for general public viewing in their original form. When they exist in the 16mm or video formats used for classroom or home screening, they are almost always presented in black-and-white versions, with standard screen dimensions.

8.1. The documentary Chang (1927) was one of several films released in Magnascope, a widescreen process in which a special lens dramatically enlarged the screen image for spectacular scenes like this elephant stampede through a village in Siam (now Thailand). Filmmakers Merian C. Cooper (1894–1973) and Ernest B. Schoedsack (1893–1979) built the structures and staged this scene, preferring not to destroy an actual village.

8.2, 8.3. One of several two-color processes used in film during the 1920s was Eastman Kodak's Kodachrome. The film was shot with two frames side-by-side, one exposed through a green **filter,** the other through red. A positive print was made of each, then these prints were again printed on opposite sides of double-coated film, one side red, the other green. These two shots are examples of the final image.

Magnascope

Some experiences were created not on film but through projection and can only be re-created using the proper equipment and setting. An example is Magnascope, a widescreen process introduced in the 1920s using a special enlarging lens. To prepare a Magnascope presentation, an extra-large screen was installed to encompass the entire area within a theater's proscenium arch. Then the wider areas of this expanse were curtained off so that only the standard screen was exposed. Two prints of a film were mounted on separate projectors, one equipped with a Magnascope lens and stronger illumination to maintain brightness over a larger area. In moments of spectacular action, such as an elephant stampede in *Chang* or the World War I aerial battles in *Wings* (both 1927), the Magnascope projector would enlarge the image to fill the vast screen space dramatically exposed to view. Magnascope was rarely seen outside a few big-city picture palaces. It was utilized for perhaps half a dozen films in the mid-1920s and several more times after World War II.

8.4. Hell's Angels *(1930) was shot partly in the two-color process Multicolor by financier Howard Hughes, in his first work as producer and director. The film about British aviators in World War I featured (from left) Jean Harlow, Ben Lyon, and James Hall.*

Animation in the 1920s

"No one mourned the passing of the silent cartoon," animation historian Leonard Maltin has written. Following the pioneer work in animated cartoons before World War I by Émile Cohl in France, Winsor McCay in the United States, and others, cartoons became somewhat routine commercial products, put on theater screens as part of short film packages that preceded feature films.

In a broader sense, animation (the filming of a series of still images so as, when projected, to create the illusion of movement) played a significant role in the development of avant-garde film. In Germany, artists Hans Richter (1888–1976) and Viking Eggeling (1880–1925) gained access to the animation tables at Ufa studio and made short films from drawings and graphic designs,

including Richter's *Rhythmus 21* (1921–24) and Eggeling's *Diagonale Sinfonie* (*Diagonal Symphony*, 1925). In the French surrealist movement, artists made films incorporating animated designs and objects, including *Le Ballet mécanique* (1924), by painter Fernand Léger (1881–1955); *Anemic Cinema* (1926), by Marcel Duchamp (1887–1968); and *Emak Bakia* (1927), by American painter and photographer Man Ray (1890–1976).

In the United States, where there was no comparable activity in avant-garde animation, critical and popular interest in animation was revived by a cartoon character named Felix the Cat, created in 1919 by Otto Messmer and produced by Pat Sullivan (1887–1933). Felix was the first animated cartoon character to be manufactured as a toy for children. Other significant producers of animated cartoons in the 1920s included the brothers Max Fleischer (1883–1972) and Dave Fleischer (1894–1979), whose main character in silent animations was Ko-Ko the

8.5. *Sound/image integration in Steamboat Willie: the goat has swallowed sheet music, so Minnie Mouse cranks its tail to produce the sound, while Mickey observes.*

Clown, and Walt Disney (1901–1966), whose silent creations included the Alice in Cartoonland series (a combination of animation and live action) and Oswald the Rabbit.

A crisis erupted for Disney in 1928 when a producer took the popular Oswald away from him. Disney and his coworker Ub Iwerks (1901–1971) created a new character, Mickey Mouse, and produced two cartoons on their own. But no distributor was willing to handle them. Disney then took a gamble: he would try to break the logjam by making another Mickey Mouse cartoon, *Steamboat Willie* (1928), as the first animated cartoon with synchronized sound.

Several cartoons made as silents had already been released with added sound tracks, but Disney developed *Steamboat Willie* with sound completely integrated into the narrative and animated movement. A bouncing ball was inked in on the film strip to guide the orchestra conductor's tempo. With neither the Fox nor Warner Bros. sound systems available to him, he found another system, Cinephone, owned by an independent producer, to record the film, and premiered it in New York without a distributor on November 18, 1928. Thereafter, as Maltin wrote, no one mourned the passing of the silent cartoon.

8.6. *Fox Film Company's Grandeur system used 70mm film (rather than the standard 35mm) to enlarge the screen image. Three Grandeur films were made, including* The Big Trail *(1930), directed by Raoul Walsh, with John Wayne and Marguerite Churchill.*

Color Experiments

More available to the typical moviegoer in the 1920s were experiments with color—which had received, over the years, nearly as much attention from inventors as sound. Color technology did not gain, as did sound, from stepped-up research impelled by military needs during World War I. On the other hand, coloring films was a simpler and less expensive process than adding sound. As early as 1905 the French Pathé company had begun to replace hand-tinting of individual film frames with tinting machines through which entire segments or scenes could be passed, to give them a "mood" coloring of a single shade—red for fires, blue for night, yellow for daytime exteriors. Pathé developed a stencil system, called Pathécolor, that colored films frame-by-frame with several colors, until a multihued image was achieved. All these processes added an artistic conception of appropriate colors to an image photographed in black-and-white.

Recorded Color

There were also efforts to record on film the original colors of the photographed subject. As with the Kinemacolor process (see Chapter 2), these began by using color filters (screens made of glass or dried gelatin, placed over the lens) both in recording and projecting the image. A scene would be photographed using two lenses, one with a red filter, the other green. A projector with two lenses would then project the black-and-white print through similar-colored filters. The blending of colors could produce on the screen, under optimal circumstances, an acceptably realistic-seeming color image. The problem, as usual, was that circumstances were frequently less than optimal. If the separate images were not perfectly matched, or projector speeds not perfectly timed, either the colors or the images would be "out of register" (examples of this uneven color matching can sometimes be seen on the Sunday newspaper comics pages).

Technicolor

Inventors worked to overcome these defects by achieving the same two-color effects with a single lens. Around World War I the Technicolor process photographed two frames through one lens, but adequate projection proved too difficult. In the early 1920s the two separate color negatives were printed on specially prepared film strips that were dyed and pasted together to form a single positive print containing all the colors the spectator would see, without the necessity of additional filters or complex projection mechanisms. Technicolor, devised principally by Herbert Kalmus (1882–1963), was the first widely successful color film process. Still, the cemented images could be out of line, and the extra thickness of the print led to problems of scratching or buckling. These drawbacks were overcome in 1928 with development of a dye transfer system that could print the separate color negatives onto a single positive film with precise registration.

The first feature-length all-Technicolor product appeared in 1922, and its biggest success was a Douglas Fairbanks film, *The Black Pirate* (1926). More commonly, the Hollywood studios utilized Technicolor for special sequences within black-and-white films. Erich von Stroheim's *The Wedding March* (1928), the M-G-M musical *The Broadway Melody* (1929), and Paramount's omnibus *Paramount on Parade* (1930) are among several dozen films originally released with Technicolor sequences that generally appear solely in black-and-white in current circulating versions.

Two-color Technicolor peaked in 1930, with nearly thirty all- or part-color productions. Its utilization was scaled back over the next several years while the company developed a three-color process, first tested in a Walt Disney cartoon, *Flowers and Trees* (1932). Three-color Technicolor began to appear in Hollywood features in the mid-1930s and remained the dominant color system for several decades even though it was used for only a small minority of films.

Multicolor

Technicolor's only competition in Hollywood came from the Multicolor process, which used a "bipack" system (two negative films placed together in the camera emulsion to emulsion, which, when exposed by a single camera lens, would record different portions of the color spectrum; these were then printed on one positive film). Multicolor had occasional use in color sequences of films such as the 1929 Fox musical *Sunny Side Up*. The financier Howard Hughes bought Multicolor in 1930 and used it in sequences of his first film, *Hell's Angels* (1930), but the system soon faded from use.

Larger Film Stock

If sound films had the backing of giant communication companies, and the big photographic firms were concerned with color film, widescreen experiments sought support directly from the motion picture studios, and they were only rarely interested. Beyond the few Magnascope presentations, widescreen productions in the late 1920s could be counted on the fingers of both hands, and after 1931 they went into hibernation for two decades.

One way to expand the screen image was by using film stock larger than the standard 35mm gauge. Several efforts with 70mm film were marketed under varied trademarks, including Grandeur, the name the Fox company gave to three widescreen presentations, *Fox Movietone Follies of 1929* and *Happy Days* (both 1929) and *The Big Trail* (1930). A variation was 65mm film, used on such films as the Warner Bros. *Kismet* and a United Artists release, *The Bat Whispers* (both 1930). M-G-M tried out a system it called Realife, which photographed film in 65mm and projected it on 35mm stock with an enlarging lens. King Vidor's *Billy the Kid* (1930) was one of only two Realife releases; the other was *The Great Meadow* (1931).

The Anamorphic Lens

Major investments in converting production and theaters to sound, coupled with the beginnings of the Great Depression following the 1929 stock market crash, persuaded movie companies they could not afford the additional costs involving new cameras, projectors, and theater screens for widescreen presentations. The process that was to revolutionize screen dimensions in the 1950s was already available, but evoked little interest. This was the **anamorphic lens**, whose principles were described in 1927 by Henri Chrétien (1877–1956), a French scientist, and developed by Chrétien and others soon after. Chrétien constructed a lens he called the Hypergonar, which, when fitted over a regular camera lens, greatly expanded the lateral range of the image that could be recorded on standard 35mm film (without affecting the vertical range). When held in one's hands, or projected with standard projection lenses, the recorded image looked compressed, or "squeezed." But when an anamorphic lens was placed over the regular projector lens, as had been done with the camera, the image would appear in its normal vertical proportions with a considerably wider horizontal field than could be recorded by regular lenses.

Aspect Ratios

The standard projected image at that time had what was known as an **aspect ratio** of 1.33:1. In other words, the screen image was one-third wider than it was high. When a Hollywood studio acquired the rights to Chrétien's anamorphic lens in the 1950s and named the process CinemaScope, the new aspect ratio reached 2.66:1, twice as wide as standard, or two and two-thirds wider than high (the soundtrack slightly reduced the picture width, and many theaters had to crop the sides further because their screens were not wide enough).

Napoléon

The greatest triumph of widescreen experimentation in the era was conceived by French director Abel Gance, who had already demonstrated visionary ambitions in *La Roue*. For *Napoléon* (1927), a biographical film on the French general and emperor, Gance devised a plan utilizing three standard screens side-by-side (an aspect ratio of 3.99:1, or half again wider than anamorphic widescreen). The completed film ran over five hours. Though much of it appeared on the single center screen, at crucial sequences the curtains would draw back to reveal the other two screens. The screens were used in variable combinations—sometimes three separate images, sometimes a central image flanked by two parts of another scene, in climactic moments action (photographed by three separate cameras) sweeping across all three screens in a single image.

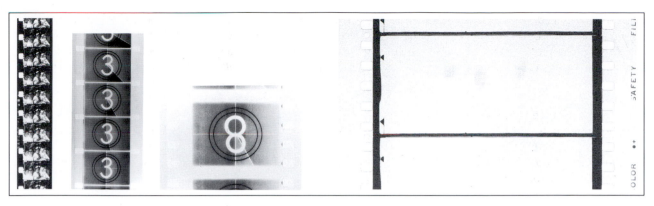

Above: 8.7. The four principal
film widths in use in the 1990s,
shown in actual size: from left,
8mm (Super 8), for home
moviemaking (though recently
supplanted by video camcorders);

16mm, often used by documentary filmmakers with hand-held
cameras; 35mm, the standard
gauge for commercial feature
films; and 70mm., utilized occasionally for features

Below: 8.8. Illustrations of standard aspect ratios, expressing the
relation of screen width to screen
height; for example, the
"Academy" ratio established in

the early 1930s by the Academy
of Motion Picture Arts and
Sciences is four units wide and
three high, expressed as 1.33:1.

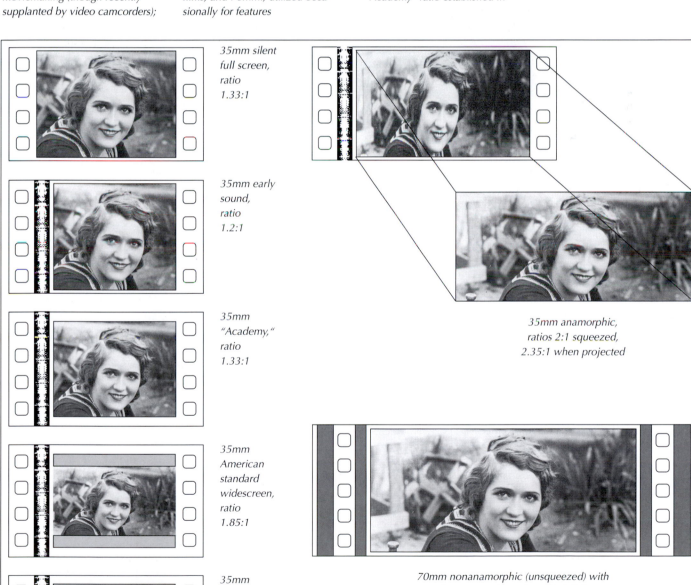

35mm silent
full screen,
ratio
1.33:1

35mm early
sound,
ratio
1.2:1

35mm
"Academy,"
ratio
1.33:1

35mm
American
standard
widescreen,
ratio
1.85:1

35mm
European
standard
widescreen,
ratio
1.66:1

35mm anamorphic,
ratios 2:1 squeezed,
2.35:1 when projected

70mm nonanamorphic (unsqueezed) with
four magnetic tracks, ratio 2.2:1

Above: 8.9. Napoléon (1927), made in France by Abel Gance, ranks as the most elaborate widescreen project in film history. It utilized three standard screens side-by-side. Sometimes three separate images appeared (top); at other times a central image was flanked by scenes that resemble each other (bottom). At key

moments (not illustrated here) a single image, photographed by three separate cameras, consumed all three screens. Lost for half a century, Napoléon was restored in the 1970s and screened in 1979 at Radio City Music Hall, New York. Albert Dieudonné (top center) played Napoleon Bonaparte.

Opposite, above: 8.10. To film the air battle scenes in Wings (1927), a camera tower was constructed in San Antonio, Texas.

Opposite, below: 8.11. William A. Wellman's Wings won the first Best Picture award of the Academy of Motion Picture Arts and Sciences; the prize statuette was later nicknamed "Oscar." Portraying World War I aviators (from left) were Charles "Buddy" Rogers, Richard Arlen, and Gary Cooper.

Gance's unique innovation was lost to history for half a century, until the American producer-director Francis Ford Coppola put his resources behind efforts by film historian Kevin Brownlow and other scholars to find as much as possible of Gance's original. With a live orchestra playing a new score composed and conducted by Carmine Coppola, a four-hour restored version of *Napoléon* with English-language intertitles premiered in 1979 at New York's mammoth surviving picture palace, Radio City Music Hall. One of the most remarkable events in cinema history was thus partially re-created and returned to circulation.

MUSIC AND EFFECTS TRACK

With neither color nor widescreen accompanying the transition to sound, what other "what ifs" remained as alternatives to talking pictures? Perhaps the most viable was the possibility of a compromise between silent and sound films, eschewing speaking voices but with a musical and effects soundtrack. Though in practical terms this was generally utilized only when silent films had been completely shot and the music and effects track added as a stop-gap, it held the promise at least of preserving the visual aesthetics of silent film.

Wings

How the silent film had evolved might be considered by taking a closer look at the first film to win an Academy Award for best picture, *Wings* (1927). In some theaters, as we have seen, it was released with Magnascope projection, and a music and effects score was added that was played variously with sound-on-disc, sound-on-film, and live accompaniment. But as a visual product of director William A. Wellman (1896–1975) and his creative personnel, except for its ambitions as a war spectacle, it can be regarded aesthetically as a typical Hollywood product.

What marks *Wings* is a breadth of stylistic variation that was soon to be lost in standard talkies. Though the film can attain stark, even brutal, realism in its battle scenes, it also employs a number of nonrealistic techniques more readily associated with Soviet avant-garde montage or the impressionistic devices of French and German cinema than with Hollywood—**double exposures** or split-screen images, subjective **point-of-view shots** (a drunk's out-of-focus vision), trick effects (oversize bubbles rising from a champagne glass), and symbolic illustrations on intertitles, such as a drawing of a whirlpool to connote danger or fate. It may be that stylistic, technological, or cultural changes would have put an end to this eclectic stylization, with its elements of what may now seem awkward sentimentality, even without the coming of

sound (recall how Eisenstein, Pudovkin, and Alexandrov in their "Statement on Sound" had complained about filmmakers turning intertitles into trick shots). But by the late 1920s such devices had become fairly commonplace in the silent cinema.

Sunrise

The most memorable work of the transition period was F. W. Murnau's *Sunrise* (1927), the German director's first American production. It is a telling anomaly of film history that this work is almost invariably described as a silent film, when in fact it was released and widely seen in its own time with a Fox Movietone sound-on-film music and effects track. *Sunrise* is regarded as one of the great triumphs of visual aesthetics in silent cinema, though, technically speaking, it was a sound film—and when critics write that the visual effects are so powerful it is as if one can also hear, they sometimes forget that they *did* hear.

With a scenario by the German scriptwriter Carl Mayer, *Sunrise* recounts a love triangle contrasting city and countryside. A vacationing city woman—a vamp in the Theda Bara mold—has ensnared a peasant farmer with beguiling tales of city life (her words are conjured on screen as impressionistic visual images). But things turn ugly when she proposes he murder his wife and make it appear an accident. The scene where the farmer takes his wife out on a lake, along with its inherent drama, is a key moment in early sound film. As they leave the shore, the soundtrack several times mixes the peal of church bells with its musical themes, and

a church spire can be seen among village buildings in the distance. He stops the boat, and looms menacingly above her. She forms her hands in a prayerful gesture. Suddenly he turns away, and at the same moment bells ring out again on the soundtrack.

This sequence poses significant issues of interpretation, particularly because the film's production history suggests that it was completely shot and edited, and Murnau had returned to Germany, before sound was added. To what extent is a religious motif apparent in the images? In the image-sound relationship, do the bells stop the husband's murderous intent, or are they a symbolic confirmation of his internally directed moral choice? As one of the earliest recorded music and effects tracks that still survives, *Sunrise* calls attention to the strong influence sound can have on shaping spectator response to the image.

The wife runs away and the husband follows, on a streetcar that seems magically to whisk them into the city center. They enter a church where a wedding is being performed and experience their own "remarriage." As they leave the church, the scene turns to a verdant natural backdrop—another of silent cinema's visual projections of feelings. They stop to kiss, and suddenly the backdrop fades and they are in the middle of a busy street. Cars slam on brakes, drivers bang their horns. The soundtrack shifts from harps and violins to horns, bells, whistles, and even voices yelling "get out of there."

On the way back a storm comes up and capsizes the boat. The husband is safe, but the wife is missing, and the night scenes of

the search for her and her eventual rescue (photographed by Charles Rosher and Karl Struss) are further instances of *Sunrise's* visual power. Scenes such as these were made more effective in the late silent period by technical developments in film stock and lighting. **Panchromatic negative film**, developed for color photography but which added considerable light sensitivity in black-and-white, was introduced in the early 1920s and became standard in 1927, with an infrared version added in 1928. Panchromatic film's light-sensitive properties let cinematographers move away from the powerful carbon arc floodlamps previously used and replace them with incandescent tungsten bulbs, which gave off a softer, more nondirectional light. It also made possible, as in *Sunrise*, day-for-night effects—shooting in sunlight scenes that appear on screen as if photographed at night.

The Late Silent Film

Panchromatic film and incandescent tungsten light shifted the late silent film toward a darker, more subtle image, particularly effective for night scenes and for the play of light and dark contrasts in the frame, or **chiaroscuro** (a technical term derived from painting, describing variations in light and shade). These cinematographic qualities were especially applied in late silent cinema to enhancing the almost iconographic status of female stars as objects to be viewed. One such figure was Lillian Gish, who appeared in an important late silent film, *The Wind* (1928), directed by Victor

Above and opposite: 8.12, 8.13. A new light-sensitive film stock, panchromatic negative, gave cinematographers Charles Rosher and Karl Struss the opportunity to create rich variations of light and dark in night scenes of Sunrise *(1927), German director F. W. Murnau's first American film. Opposite, George O'Brien, playing "the man," walks outdoors at night; above, the city square in a night scene.*

Seastrom, the Americanized name of Swedish director and actor Victor Sjöström (see Chapter 6). Another was Greta Garbo, who through 1929 continued to appear in among the last major Hollywood films without dialogue, perhaps because of apprehension about her Swedish accent. In such films as *The Kiss* (1929), directed by Jacques Feyder (1894–1948), Garbo's look was also emphasized through increasing attention to costume styling, here by the designer Adrian.

Sunrise, *The Wind*, and *The Kiss*—Hollywood films made by European directors—all displayed the range of visual stylization emblematic of late silent cinema and exemplified by *Wings*. There were split-screen images, double exposures, visualizations of inner thoughts, a blend of symbolism and realism, a stress on the performance of character psychology, and, above all, careful attention to the aesthetics of the image through visual contrasts, shadings, and the play of light. Many of these elements, and particularly the visual, gave way before the technological demands of early sound apparatus.

THE ADVENT OF SOUND
The Jazz Singer

"Wait a minute. Wait a minute. You ain't heard nothing yet." These were the prophetic first words of synchronous speech spoken by a performer in a feature fiction motion picture, by Al Jolson (1886–1950) in *The Jazz Singer*, released on October 6, 1927. The reason for precision in defining exactly the significance of Jolson's words lies in the fact that words had been spoken on screen for more than a year before *The Jazz Singer*—synchronous speech in Vitaphone short films and nonsynchronous words on soundtracks such as that of *Sunrise*. Jolson's words are important in cinema history because they were spoken in a compelling fictional narrative. *The Jazz Singer* convinced spectators that recorded sound could be more than a short film novelty or feature accompaniment, that they wanted films to talk.

Top: 8.14. A tense and atmospheric late silent film, The Wind (1928), directed by Victor Seastrom (the Swedish director and actor Victor Sjöström), featured Lillian Gish as a woman alone in a frontier cabin, beset by terrors imagined and real.

Above: 8.15. Clothes, lighting, and decor of Greta Garbo's last silent film, The Kiss (1929), were created, respectively, by costume designer Adrian, cinematographer William Daniels, and art director Cedric Gibbons. Jacques Feyder directed. Garbo appears here with Conrad Nagel.

Top and above: 8.16, 8.17. Al Jolson plays the piano and sings in The Jazz Singer, *but, more significantly, he also utters the first words of synchronous speech spoken by a performer in a feature fiction film: "Wait a minute.*

Wait a minute. You ain't heard nothing yet." A crowd of spectators waits to hear it on opening night, October 6, 1927, at Warners' Theatre in New York's Times Square.

The ground for Jolson's words had been prepared by months of activities by both Warner Bros.' sound-on-disc Vitaphone system and Fox's sound-on-film Movietone. This involved not only beginning to install speakers and amplification in theaters but also preparing production facilities to record sound. The technical conditions for sound recording were worked out in dozens of short films produced following Vitaphone's premiere in August 1926. Studio stages had to be protected from exterior sounds, and, because of the noise from its motors, the camera had to be soundproofed as well. Before adequate sound-deadening material was found, the solution was to house the camera inside a large sound-tight box with a nonreflecting window through which action could be photographed; this box was the size of a small room, because it had to be big enough to hold the technician who operated the camera, the cinematographer (who was in overall charge of lighting and camera work), and the film's director. These circumstances placed severe restrictions on **dollying** and horizontal or vertical **panning**, the kinds of camera mobility that were hallmarks of silent film style.

These drawbacks were not particularly noticeable in *The Jazz Singer* because it contained only two dialogue scenes, besides Jolson's songs, in an otherwise nontalking picture. The sentimental narrative carried spectators swiftly past any subtle technical critique. The story of a cantor's son who wants to sing jazz songs,

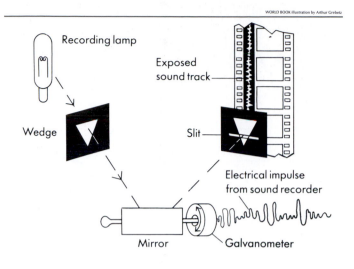

Recording lamp

Exposed
sound track

Wedge

Slit

Electrical impulse
from sound recorder

Mirror   Galvanometer

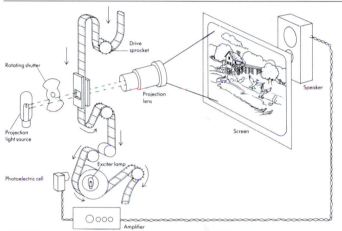

Drive
sprocket

Rotating shutter

Speaker

Projection
lens

Projection
light source

Screen

Photoelectric cell

Exciter lamp

Amplifier

Top and above: 8.19 a and b. How film sound is recorded and projected: a. Light from a recording lamp is beamed through a wedge-shaped lens onto a mirror that vibrates in response to electronic impulses from a sound recorder. The vibrating mirror reflects the beam through a slit in another lens, exposing the sound as a pattern of light and creating the soundtrack alongside the individual frames of the film image. b. In projection, an exciter lamp shines a beam through the photographed soundtrack onto a photoelectric cell, which reconverts the light pattern into electronic impulses. These are amplified and emerge from loudspeakers as the sounds that were originally recorded.

Left: 8.18. Early talkies were inhibited by stationary microphones, constraining performers' movement, and an immobile camera, enclosed in a large sound-tight box so microphones would not pick up the noise of camera motors. For the production of Gentlemen of the Press (1929) on the sound stage of Paramount's Astoria, New York, studio, an overhead microphone catches the words of performers Walter Huston and Betty Lawford; director Millard Webb sits in the folding chair (right), and cameramen George Folsey and Sam Leavitt are enclosed in the camera box behind him.

A Changing of the Guard

Few legends are more firmly fixed in motion picture history than the one immortalized in the 1952 M-G-M musical *Singin' in the Rain*: the tempestuous but squeaky-voiced silent screen star who gets her (well-deserved) comeuppance with the advent of talkies. Some legends embellish actuality; this one sugarcoats it. While there was cautionary anxiety in Hollywood about silent performers (particularly those without stage training) making the transition to sound, and reviewers of early talkies passed judg-ment on voices, very few silent stars lost their careers because of vocal inade-quacy. Some *did* lose their careers, but for other reasons, which the legend quite effectively masks.

The emblematic figure was John Gilbert (1897–1936), star of M-G-M's *The Big Parade* (1925) and Greta Garbo's love interest in *Flesh and the Devil, Love* (both 1927), and *A Woman of Affairs* (1929), as well as briefly off-screen. The principal issue was not voice, but money. Just before the advent of sound, Gilbert had signed a new contract at $250,000 per picture. This was an astronomical sum for the time, but competition for leading players was fierce and he was sought by other studios.

The problem for Gilbert and M-G-M was not sound but the economic depres-sion following the 1929 stock market crash. When the bubble burst on the excesses of the 1920s, among the real and imaginary figures on whom the pub-lic soured was the character type whom John Gilbert frequently played: the romantic lead in swashbuckling costume dramas of middle-European aristocratic intrigue. Sound complicated things not because the dashing heroes had squeaky voices but because they were asked to

rather than follow generations of ancestors into the synagogue, spoke powerfully to United States society in the 1920s, with its themes of conflict between Old World parents and native-born children, as well as the claims of contemporary popular commer-cial culture (here, jazz music and theater, but surely also the movies themselves) against traditional forms.

Jolson's Jakie Rabinowitz becomes Jack Robin in his vaudeville and stage career, and also falls in love with a woman outside his own faith—further ramifications on the theme of cultural assimi-lation. The fact that Jolson for his principal song numbers puts on minstrel-style blackface makeup, complete with nappy hair wig and oversize white lips, only exaggerates (in a way the filmmakers almost certainly were unaware of) the cultural contradictions the film portrays.

Jolson's performance of an African-American stereotype tells us much about the popular culture of that era. But contemporary spectators had eyes—and ears—more attuned to the sequence where Jakie/Jack sings to his mother and sweetly offers to take her to the amusement park at Coney Island. His father enters the frame in the background and (in a separate shot) shouts, "Stop!" Even the soundtrack music seems to falter. The father moves his

8.20. Helene Costello sings and dances in Lights of New York (1928), the first "all-talking" fea-ture film. The long takes and the restrictions on camera and per-former mobility in early talkies were less noticeable in musical numbers than in dialogue scenes.

utter insipid endearments instead of expressing emotion through silent, soulful looks.

Gilbert's early sound films flopped. Although his partisans have argued that M-G-M executives conspired against him, it seems unlikely that the studio set out deliberately to lose money on Gilbert's films. More plausible is that they were unable to find a workable formula for him and unwilling to put much money in unpromising projects already saddled with his huge salary. Rugged types with an outdoor, working-class aura, like Clark Gable, were supplanting him—and at much lower salaries. Gilbert made his last film at M-G-M in 1933; still in his thirties, he died of a heart attack in 1936.

lips again but no sound comes out. Though the remainder of the film reverts to intertitles for dialogue, it was that shouted "Stop!" that truly ended the silent era. In the long run, father could no more prevent movie performers from talking than he could keep Jakie/Jack off the Broadway stage.

Lights of New York

The powerful appeal of audible dialogue was made manifest by the success of the first "all-talking" feature, *Lights of New York* (1928). This was a mediocre gangster picture whose technical difficulties were not masked by a strong story or popular star. The film shifts awkwardly from medium long shots where actors move without speaking to medium shots where they stand still and deliver their lines. The performers stood or sat close together so as to be within range of microphones hidden in props such as telephones—the sound-on-disc system worked best when voices were recorded directly into microphones. Entire scenes were staged in lengthy takes, and camera movements were confined to slight pans permitted by the width of box windows. These limitations, of course, were not unique to *Lights of New York*; they affected virtually every talking film at this early stage of the transi-

tion: one could not even say it marked a return to filmed stage plays, because actors were able to move more freely in theaters than on sound stages. Yet few spectators complained, and more "all-talkies" quickly followed.

Sound Improvements

The difficulties involved in making early talkies were quickly overcome. While engineers worked on developing cameras with quieter motors, a temporary expedient for existing cameras was found by covering them with thick layers of sound-insulating material, called blimps or "bungalows," and the cameras came out of the oversize box. Then they were mounted on battery-operated dollies with rubber tires, which restored panning and camera mobility. Microphones were hung from long arms, called **booms**, which dangled out of camera range above the scene being filmed; these were also mounted on dollies, so freedom of movement was restored to performers. Trucks were fitted with sound-recording equipment for location work. The Mitchell Recording Camera was developed which could record both image and sound on a single film strip and was used particularly by newsreel companies as they made the transition to sound along with feature films. Within a year or two after *The Jazz Singer* and *Lights of New York*, sound film had completely recovered from the technical or aesthetic deficiencies the early talkies had demonstrated in comparison with silent cinema.

THE ART OF SOUND

Talkies, said director Rouben Mamoulian (1898–1987), were not movies. A stage director, Mamoulian was approached by Paramount's Long Island, New York, studio to assist film actors in learning to speak dialogue. He preferred to direct a film, and his first production, *Applause* (1929), was among the earliest to restore movement to the "talking" picture.

Applause

The film's story concerns an aging burlesque queen who continues to perform in order to support her daughter's education in a faraway convent. The key scene from a technological standpoint occurs when the daughter, at seventeen, returns from the convent to her mother's seedy show business milieu. The mother sits at the girl's bedside and sings her a burlesque song in lullaby style, while to herself the daughter whispers a prayer. Mamoulian, as he recalled it, wanted two things the talkies had not before done: a moving camera shot of the scene, and dual microphones to pick up both the song and the prayer. The camera box was placed on rollers, and two mikes put in place.

Though the scene lasts nearly five minutes as a single shot, it has none of the immobile, static feeling that made the **long takes** of early "all-talkies" seem interminable. The scene begins in medium long shot, the camera gradually moves in to close-ups of mother singing and daughter praying, pulls back to a medium close-up of the pair, then back again to the medium long shot

Above: 8.23. Movement returned to the image in sound films when cameras were covered with sound-insulating materials, called blimps, and placed on battery-operated dollies with rubber tires. The caption for this publicity shot for Lilies of the Field *(1930) claims that the camera followed performers Corinne Griffith and Ralph Forbes through five rooms (past twelve microphones) "in the longest shot ever attempted in talking pictures."*

Right: 8.24. Sound moved outdoors with portable recording equipment and microphones hung on poles or long arms, called **booms.** *For a location shot on* Woman Hungry *(1931; British title:* The Challenge*) near Lone Pine, California, the microphone was enclosed within a megaphone to point it in the right direction. Below the microphone, director Clarence Badger prepares a scene with performers Sidney Blackmer and Raymond Hatton.*

F.9.42.

position at which it began—all without a **cut**. The two voice recordings were overlapped by laying one negative track on top of the other and printing the positive as one sound strip.

Applause is filled with many such sound innovations. Sound was recorded outside the studio, on location. Sound is used to anticipate a scene change, with sound from the upcoming shot beginning in the final frames of the previous shot (a technical term for this form of sound editing is **pre-lap**). There were split-screen shots with **overlapping sound** coming from both images in the frame. Scenes of telephone conversations intercut both speakers, with modulations of sound tone to indicate which voice is on screen and which coming over the wires. Sound is employed without a visual source, an early example of using **off-screen sound**. **Rack focus**—change of focus within a shot—was utilized to shift sound emphasis within a scene, for example, from foreground to background sound. Finally, the soundtrack was modulated to indicate psychological perceptions of sound, similar to subjective point-of-view images.

Applause is remarkable for the range of its sound experimentation. In the American cinema, few sound films would strive for such a variety of effects. Overall the goal was sound that appeared "natural" or realistic, with impressionistic sound devices reserved for special occurrences. (Mamoulian, however, continued to experiment. In the opening sequence of his 1932 film *Love Me Tonight*, the morning sounds of Paris form into a musical accompaniment to a visual montage of the city waking up.)

8.25. Rouben Mamoulian's Applause *(1929), produced at Paramount's Astoria studio, was among the first talkies to use sound in innovative fashion. In this shot of Jack Cameron performing in a burlesque theater, what appears innovative is the chorus line.*

191

Below: 8.26. King Vidor's *Hallelujah* (1929), an early sound film with an all-black cast, combined music, religion, and melodrama. Daniel L. Haynes and Nina Mae McKinney, pictured on a lobby card, were featured players.

Bottom: 8.27. Vidor (in hat, with megaphone) directs Haynes in a sequence shot on location in an Arkansas swamp, to which post-synchronized sound was added later.

8.28. The Dixie Jubilee Singers perform a black spiritual in a religious revival scene from *Hallelujah.*

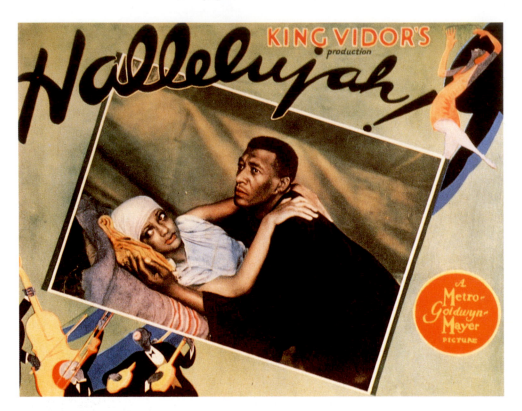

Hallelujah

Among the sound techniques demonstrated in *Applause* that were to become standard were location shooting and off-screen sound. Both were exemplified in an unusual film of 1929, *Hallelujah*, directed by King Vidor, perhaps the first major production of a Hollywood studio featuring an entirely black cast. Some of the outdoor scenes were shot silent with **postsynchronized** effects added back in the studio, but there were also exterior scenes recorded with synchronous dialogue. In these, Vidor laid down a continuous soundtrack, consisting of music or speech coming from definite on-screen locations, and then played this sound over a variety of different shot setups related to, but not showing, the sound source. The result was an expansion of the visual field, an increase in the variety of images, while maintaining a steady soundtrack that frequently comes from off-screen. (Once off-

8.29. Alfred Hitchcock's Blackmail *(1929), his first and Britain's second sound film, ranks with* Applause *for its inventive early use of sound. One instance can be described as subjective or "point-of-hearing" sound. A woman has gone to a man's flat and, resisting his advances, stabbed him to death. After returning home, in the morning at breakfast she encounters a neighborhood gossip commenting on the discovery of the victim: "A good clean, honest whack over the head with a brick is one thing. There's something British about that. But knives. . . ." The camera* pans from the speaker to the woman, then cuts to a close-up of her, and the soundtrack begins to represent the woman's auditory perception: the talk fades to unintelligibility except for repetitions of the word "knife." Her father's off-screen voice breaks into her consciousness, saying, "Alice, cut us a bit of bread, will you?" The camera pans down to show her hand, picking up the bread knife. The hand flinches on the next repetition of "knife" and another "knife" sounds like a shout, startling her and sending the knife clattering across the room. Anny Ondra plays the knifeholder.*

screen sound became familiar, it no longer required an establishing on-screen shot; the source for off-screen sound could be left to the spectator's imagination.)

SOUND AND LANGUAGE

Sound obviously had implications for the notion of cinema as a universal language. The advent of talkies threatened to render the medium no more widely comprehensible than the babel of tongues it had promised to overcome. Some producers at first attempted to deal with this problem by shooting films in several languages, replacing performers on the same set in consecutive takes. This soon proved economically impractical, and other steps were taken to overcome language barriers. In Europe, films in foreign languages were commonly **dubbed** (a term derived from "vocal doubling," to indicate the postsynchronization of a voice replacing the original), with native speakers lip-synching new dialogue. In the United States, where the audience for foreign films was largely drawn from immigrants and cinema aesthetes, films more generally were played in their original versions, with English-language translations of dialogue printed as subtitles across the screen bottom.

The Blue Angel

Perhaps the most famous dual-language production was *Der blaue Engel/The Blue Angel* (1930), which still circulates in both German and English-language versions. Directed in Berlin by the Austrian-American Josef von Sternberg, the film was a coproduction of Germany's Ufa and Hollywood's Paramount. *The Blue Angel* was more distinctive for its psychological portraits than for its use of sound. Emil Jannings, back in Germany after his brief but highly successful stint in Hollywood silents, plays Professor Immanuel Rath, a straitlaced teacher destroyed by his attraction to Lola Lola, a nightclub singer. The German actress who portrayed Lola Lola, Marlene Dietrich (1901–1992), accompanied Sternberg on his return to Hollywood, and a series of pictures Sternberg directed in the early 1930s launched her career as one of the most important stars in American cinema.

Early Sound in Germany

In Germany, the leading directors of Weimar cinema came later to sound than their United States counterparts, but their early efforts were significant. G. W. Pabst's *Kameradschaft* ("Comradeship," 1931), a didactic film advocating working-class unity between German and French coal miners on the border of

Above: 8.30. Marlene Dietrich as the cabaret singer Lola Lola in Josef von Sternberg's dual-language German-American production Der blaue Engel/The Blue Angel (1930)

Below: 8.31. The cover of a German film magazine, Illustrierter Filmkurier, depicts the theme of cross-border solidarity between French and German coal miners of G. W. Pabst's Kameradschaft ("Comradeship," 1931), in which both languages are used on the soundtrack.

the two countries, explores the boundaries of communication by freely employing both languages on the soundtrack. The film is also visually among the most fluid of early sound films. Its theme of breaking down barriers between peoples is conveyed in the cinematography of Fritz Arno Wagner, emphasizing spatial mobility through almost constant panning and tracking.

ʍ. Fritz Lang turned to sound with *M* (1931)—only his third film since *Metropolis*—and produced one of the most important works in cinema history. *M* has been freighted by the judgment of some critics that it portends the imminent triumph of fascism in Germany, but any single interpretation is likely to be inadequate for this enigmatic, elusive film. If there is any clear frame for analysis it may lie in an intertextual, authorial perspective, in Lang's long-standing preoccupation—predating his collaboration with scriptwriter Thea von Harbou—with conflicts between social authority and a secret criminal underworld. In this sense, *M* continues some of the central concerns of *The Spiders* and *Dr. Mabuse the Gambler* (see Chapters 4 and 6).

M's narrative focus is a series of murders of children. As public hysteria mounts, the police systematically, but fruitlessly, interrogate the criminal subculture. Leaders of criminal organizations call a summit meeting—famously intercut with a meeting of

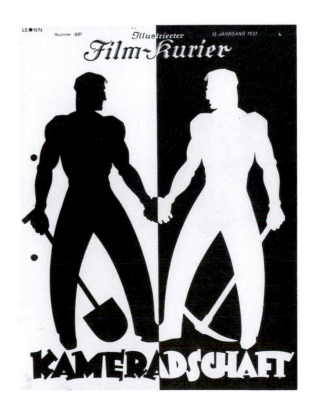

police chiefs, so that the two smoke-filled rooms soon appear interchangeable—where they determine, for the sake of their operations, to find the killer themselves. Efficiently they locate and capture him, then stage a trial in the cellar of an abandoned building. There, the killer, portrayed by Peter Lorre (1904–1964), gives harrowing testimony of his own inner torments, almost swaying the criminal spectators to sympathy. As the killer tries to escape the police arrive, and the film ends with a most ambiguous restoration of social authority.

8.32–8.34. Along with its masterly use of sound, Fritz Lang's M (1931) was a visual tour de force. Peter Lorre, playing a child murderer, is reflected in a toy-shop window with a prospective victim (above right). Later, with the criminal underground on his trail (they want to alleviate harassment from the police), he is marked with the incriminating "M" when a blind beggar recognizes his tell-tale whistle (above). Captured and tried by the underground in an abandoned factory (right), the murderer gives a harrowing account of his compulsion. An intertextual footnote: Gustav Gründgens, who played the criminal leader Schraenker (in bowler hat), became head of an important state theater during the Nazi era; a fictional version of his career was dramatized in a 1981 Hungarian film, Mephisto, directed by István Szabó.

Already a major director, Lang's work with sound demonstrated significant development as a filmmaker. Where performance and character delineation had been among the weaker elements of Lang's silent films, *M* features complex performances by, among others, Lorre, Gustav Gründgens (1899–1963) as Shraenker the criminal chief, and Otto Wernicke (1893–1965) as police inspector Lohmann, that go far beyond their stereotypical roles.

In visual style, sound enabled Lang to expand his concern with the relation between the screen frame and off-screen space. *M* is

among the first films to modulate sound as a marker of distance and as a unit in the montage construction of a sequence. As a mother calls the name of a child, the sound of her voice grows fainter as each shot change reveals a place farther away where she cannot be found (since each space is empty, the subjective effect of the lengthening distance from the mother is experienced only by the spectator, who becomes a stand-in for the absent child, and for whom the apprehension of danger grows with every new location). The final shot that symbolically confirms the child as the killer's latest victim is soundless. (One should note here not only Lang's use of sound but the cinematography of, once again, Fritz Arno Wagner, who in the same year shot *Kameradschaft* for Pabst and *M* for Lang in almost diametrically opposite styles). Later, sound is used to identify the murderer when a blind beggar hears, off-screen, the killer's characteristic whistle. With *M*, Fritz Lang created the sound cinema's first masterpiece.

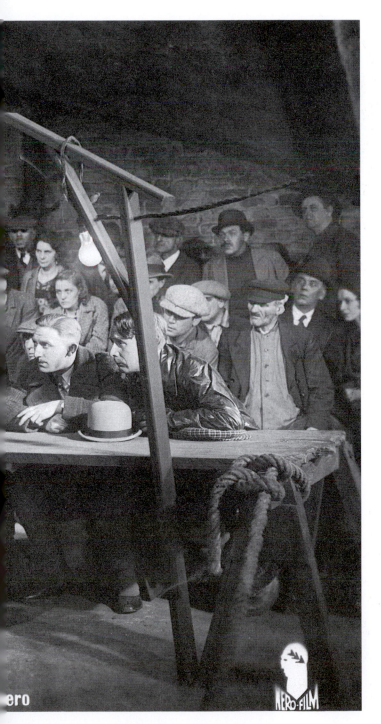

Film	Arts and Sciences	World Events
1931 M	nylon invented	Japan invades Manchuria
1932 *Scarface* first Venice film festival	first nuclear reaction	F. D. Roosevelt elected U.S. President
1933 *Duck Soup*	emigration of German artists	Hitler becomes German dictator
1934 *L'Atalante*	socialist realism doctrine in U.S.S.R.	Mao's Long March in China
1935 *The 39 Steps*	Gershwin's *Porgy and Bess*	Italy invades Abyssinia
1936 *Osaka Elegy*	*Absalom, Absalom!* (Faulkner)	Civil War in Spain Rome-Berlin Axis formed
1937 *Grand Illusion*	Picasso's *Guernica*	Japan attacks China
1938 *Alexander Nevsky*	*Homage to Catalonia* (Orwell)	Germany annexes Austria
1939 *Rules of the Game*	nuclear fission	World War II begins in Europe
1940 *The Great Dictator*	*Native Son* (Wright)	Germany occupies France
1941 *Citizen Kane*	first jet aircraft flies	U.S. enters World War II
1942 *Ossessione*	German V-2 rocket-bomb	Japan conquers Philippines
1943 *Casablanca*	Penicillin produced	Germans retreat from Russia
1944 *Ivan the Terrible*	*No Exit* (Sartre)	Allied invasion at Normandy
1945 *Rome, Open City*	U.S. drops two atomic bombs on Japan	Germany, Japan surrender

Part Three

CLASSIC CINEMA

NINE

HOLLYWOOD

When talk about the movies turns ethereal—when words like magic and myth, glamour and legend crop up—it immediately evokes, for most people, images from 1930s Hollywood. Astaire and Rogers airborne in a dance step. Garbo in a lover's embrace. Judy Garland, as Dorothy, and her little dog Toto on the yellow brick road. Grant and Hepburn chasing a leopard through Connecticut. These and scores of similar scenes from American films of the 1930s are almost invariably the associations that come to mind when we think of movies not only as enormously successful mass entertainment but as creators of a style of living— of dressing, of speaking, of romancing—that affected people throughout the world, and continues to exert its power.

Yet the world of images that Hollywood constructed—the magical and glamorous part of it, at any rate—was far removed from the surrounding world of actuality. The 1930s began with the most severe economic depression of the century and ended with the outbreak of a devastating world war. American motion picture companies were affected by these disruptions as were all institutions and peoples. Nearly all the Hollywood studios suffered financial losses during the Great Depression, which struck soon after the companies had borrowed substantial sums to finance the conversion to sound. Paramount, Fox, and RKO were among the firms whose management was temporarily controlled by courts, banks, or other debt-holders, while filmmaking policies generally continued in the hands of experienced studio executives. The studios were further challenged during the period by accusations against the morality of their films and the legality of their business practices.

THE DREAM MACHINE

Still, the Hollywood "dream machine" functioned smoothly in the public's eyes; its attraction during an era of social and political crisis can surely be explained by spectators' desires to "escape" for a few hours their own and the world's troubles into a make-believe place where happy endings were the rule. But that wish is not limited just to the 1930s. More specific to the era were the growth of mass society and the increasing cultural importance of popular commercial entertainment. Though movies had demonstrated wide appeal in earlier decades, particularly among young people, the arrival of sound films, coupled with a crisis in traditional values caused by the depression's impact on the economy and social life, catapulted the film industry to a position of acknowledged cultural power it had not possessed before.

New Talent

Talking pictures—and later, political repression overseas—also brought to Hollywood new waves of creative and technical talent. The need for dialogue lured across the continent playwrights, journalists, novelists, stage performers, and directors to motion picture work; prominent examples include director George Cukor (1899–1983), writer-director Preston Sturges (1898–1959), and performers Paul Muni (1895–1967) and Katharine Hepburn (b. 1907). In Germany, meanwhile, the rise of the fascist Nazi movement to political power sent many of that country's leading film personnel into exile, some elsewhere in Europe, many to the United States. The presence in Southern California of refugee artists in such other fields as literature and music helped to turn the once-isolated movie "colony" into a center where some of the outstanding American and European figures in the literary and visual arts turned their hands to the popular art of American movies.

Continuity and Stability

Given the range of transformations experienced by the American motion picture industry in this period, what is also remarkable is its capacity for continuity and stability. This was most evident at the top. At several leading film companies, including M-G-M, Warner Bros., and Columbia Pictures, management remained in the same hands for decades; a generation of showmen, fabled as the "movie moguls," ran the studios from the 1920s, and in some cases even earlier, right through to the 1950s. Much the same was true of behind-the-camera personnel: directors, cinematographers, designers, editors, and other craft workers moved almost *en masse* from silent to sound filmmaking with few disruptions. The consolidations and mergers that occurred in the late 1920s with the transition to sound left an industry that, despite the difficult depression period, appeared in its general structure almost exactly the same at the end of the 1930s as at the beginning.

be dropped) to gossip columnists. This form of "grooming" often had little to do with actual development of screen performance; in practice, contract players outnumbered good roles, and the production system depended on the repetition of character types rather than individuated performances. Any contract player who broke through to become a star, though well recompensed by any standard, was nevertheless grossly underpaid in terms of box office value to the studio, and not even the highest-paid stars of the 1930s earned salaries comparable to what leading stars had been paid in silent days.

THE CLASSICAL ERA

The developing star system of the 1930s marks one of the key elements of what has frequently been called the **classical** era of Hollywood cinema. As applied to the American film industry, "classic" and "classical" are loose terms with several meanings and periodizations. Most fundamentally they refer to the mode of production and aesthetic styles fostered by the vertically integrated studios—those controlling not only production but also distribution and exhibition—that took shape in the 1910s and

GENRES

The Star System

The profession most affected by the advent of talkies, quite obviously, was acting (see Chapter 8). Nearly every studio added several dozen stage-trained players to its roster during 1929–30; many flopped, but a few quickly became stars, including Spencer Tracy (1900–1967) at Fox, Irene Dunne (1898–1990) at RKO, and James Cagney (1899–1986) at Warner Bros. The arrival of so many new performers brought changes in the **star system**. With beginning players, starting from scratch, the studios sought to gain firmer control over careers and salaries than in the 1920s, when stars' salaries had soared and a few had gained considerable power to approve scripts and casting decisions. As the sound era began, virtually every aspirant for leading roles was obliged to become a "contract player" with a specific studio; only later in the 1930s did a few outstanding stars, such as Barbara Stanwyck (1907–1990) and Cary Grant (1904–1986), strike out on their own as successful "free-lancers."

The host of stage players who came to Hollywood signed contracts that by theater standards were generous, and to the average person a fortune, but by previous Hollywood norms the salaries were a mere pittance. As contract players they were generally bound for up to seven years, but the studios had frequent "options" to drop them before the contract expired. They could be loaned out to other studios (at a profit to their employer) and suspended without pay if they refused a role. The studios shaped their public images through publicity staffs who orchestrated coverage in the press and fan magazines and leaked items (not always favorable, if performers were making trouble or about to

operated until the 1950s. The "classical Hollywood system" ultimately broke up under the impact of the U.S. Supreme Court's 1948 decision in the "Paramount Case," which declared **vertical integration** illegal (see Chapter 14), as well as the challenge of television.

The concept of "classical" stresses determinative norms and uniform practices. Therefore many who use it refer only to the studio era of sound cinema (dated 1928 to 1955), thus ignoring important transformations such as the shift, with the coming of sound, away from symbolic and impressionistic stylization. "Classical" is more useful as a general term than as a descriptive and interpretive category. It helps to call attention to the prevalence of institutional procedures and styles; but if applied too sweepingly, it hinders recognition of variety, change, and the multiple struggles that go into the making of individual works.

To determine which is more important, continuity or change, is a recurrent issue in studies of the past. Perhaps the key word for American movies in this era is adaptability. The major companies and most of their important personnel weathered the changeover to talkies. They survived the Great Depression. As the 1930s went on, they rode the wave of an expanding popular commercial culture to greater profits, popularity, and social influence. Since the 1930s, subsequent waves have carried American motion pictures to both new depths and new heights. But at no other time in their history have movies played so pervasive and significant a role in cultural definition and consciousness. That is a major reason why the myths and legends of the 1930s remain so vivid.

GENRE DEVELOPMENTS

The impact of sound on Hollywood's genre system, as with everything else, was contradictory. Things stayed the same and things became different. Few if any of the dominant silent film genres were adversely affected by the advent of talkies. Conversely, few if any new genres were inaugurated as a result of sound (the one major exception was the musical with recorded sound; it drove out the staged musical prologues that had been an important exhibition feature in the silent period). There were developments within genres, to be sure, but in general these derived as much from cultural and industrial factors as from new technologies; the principal exception was comedy, where sound technology mingled with cultural changes to shape a new, highly verbal comedy style.

Gangster Films

The gangster genre, for example, responded significantly in the early 1930s to an increased public concern about crime and to an emerging literary treatment of legendary gang leaders of the Prohibition era. At least two dozen gangster pictures appeared in 1930, capped by the First National production *Little Caesar*, directed by Mervyn LeRoy (1900–1987). It was followed the next year by *The Public Enemy*, a Warner Bros. picture directed by William A. Wellman, and in 1932 by *Scarface*, a Howard Hughes film directed by Howard Hawks (1896–1977). Together these comprise the trio of works that has defined over the decades the early depression era gangster film.

All three films aroused strong public controversy. Reviewers and moralists were concerned about the graphic depiction of violence, as well as the possibility that powerful performances could turn fictional criminals into romantic heroes, whatever their violent fates. Each work indeed offered powerful performances in their gangster roles, launching three stage actors toward major

movie careers. Edward G. Robinson (1893–1973) played Rico Bandello in *Little Caesar*, James Cagney was Tom Powers in *The Public Enemy*, and Paul Muni portrayed Tony Camonte in *Scarface*. This last film was delayed, added to, and in some states reedited before it was allowed to be released, in part because of Muni's disturbing characterization of the gangster as grotesque and abnormal.

From that era forward—through decades of the genre's undiminished popularity—commentators have pondered the question of gangster films' social meaning. Do they encourage criminal behavior or do they suppress it? Are the gangsters the equivalent in modern popular culture of figures in Greek drama or Shakespearen plays, doomed overreachers who play out their fated

Left: 9.1. Paul Muni (second from left) as Tony Camonte pushed gangster characterization toward the grotesque in Scarface *(1932), directed by Howard Hawks. Karen Morley played his girlfriend, Polly; George Raft, his right-hand man, Guino Rinaldo; and Maurice Black (at left, with pistol), one of the gang.*

Above: 9.2. James Cagney, as Tom Powers, persuades a saloon-keeper to carry his brand of beer in The Public Enemy *(1931), a Prohibition-era gangster film directed by William A. Wellman.*

109-1120.

destinies, representing excesses of desire and ambition for power-less spectators to experience vicariously their rise and fall? In an essay on "The Gangster as Tragic Hero," critic Robert Warshow wrote, "He is what we want to be and who we are afraid we may become."[1]

9.3. Count Dracula (Bela Lugosi), bringing the somnambulistic Mina (Helen Chandler) into the cellar of his abbey, is discomfited to encounter a disciple, Renfield (Dwight Frye), in Dracula (1931), directed by Tod Browning.

Horror Films

The horror genre also surged in popular appeal in the early 1930s. Should we attempt to characterize spectator identification with movie monsters? The actor Lon Chaney had dominated Holly-wood horror films in the 1920s with his remarkable array of makeup and disguises. With Chaney's untimely death in August 1930, at forty-seven, after making only one sound film, the genre was open to new directions in the talkie era. What was perhaps most unusual about the first of the classic sound horror films—Dracula (1931), a Universal production directed by Tod Browning (1880–1962)—was that the vampire, far from being a grotesque as in Murnau's Nosferatu, looked quite normal. As played by the Hungarian actor Bela Lugosi (1882–1956), the fiend's other-worldly character was emphasized by lighting his eyes while leaving the rest of his face in shadow and by his heavy middle-European accent, which became the stock-in-trade of a thousand imitators delivering such legendary lines as "I never drink . . . wine."

Universal followed this success later the same year with Frankenstein, directed by James Whale (1889–1957). Its title cred-its were preceded by a filmed segment showing a man stepping out from stage curtains to deliver a "friendly warning": "I think it will thrill you. It may shock you. It might even horrify you." The performer of the monster role was identified in the opening cred-its with a question mark, and only at the end was the fabled figure with the flat-top head, plugs in the neck, and sewn-together body revealed to be Boris Karloff (1887–1969), a journeyman British actor who henceforth would be a fixture of the horror genre.

These famed works (based on nineteenth-century novels that had already been made into silent films) have generated over the decades something like subgenres in themselves. Their countless remakes, variations, and parodies include Blacula (1972), about an African prince who passes through Transylvania and becomes a vampire, and Mel Brooks's comedy Young Frankenstein (1974),

Promotion and Publicity

Hollywood motion picture companies had a word for their promotional and publicity efforts: exploitation. Much of this activity was delegated to local movie theater operators, who were sent "press books" for individual films that contained ideas for tie-in events, such as contests for patrons with film-related themes, and feature stories complete with headlines that could be offered to local newspapers. In the studio era of the 1930s, however, publicity endeavors became more closely controlled by the production companies, who increasingly promoted not only individual titles but a glamorous image of the movie world.

9.4. The work of portrait photographers and gossip columnists alike often found outlet in Hollywood fan magazines. Their contents were generally carefully controlled by studio publicists, who knew well enough, however, that movie fans needed not just good news but conflict, pathos, and mystery in the stars' life stories just as in the fictional roles they played. Photoplay was the first of the fan magazines, founded in 1911; by the 1930s readers could choose among such other titles as Motion Picture, Silver Screen, Screenland, and Modern Screen, which featured four star names on the cover reproduced here.

9.5. With searchlights piercing the night sky, and bleachers set up to accommodate throngs of fans, the Hollywood premiere was another exciting event, combining professional and personal publicity, as gossip columnists noted who accompanied whom as the stars arrived in limousines. Premieres such as this one for All This and Heaven Too (1940) at the Carthay Circle Theatre lured tourists to Hollywood, but other cities also got the opportunity to host premieres which the stars attended, and local exhibitors were encouraged to stage their own, with local celebrities.

Right: 9.6. A major role in shaping a view of Hollywood as a land of magic and enchantment was played by the studio portrait photographers. Other photographers recorded films in production and shot scene stills on the set; these men (and one woman) had their own galleries where—with access to props, costumes, and makeup specialists—they created portraits of the stars. The woman was Ruth Harriet Louise (1906–1944), sister of director Mark Sandrich (she dropped her surname from her professional name), who had a portrait gallery at M-G-M from 1925 to 1930 and an unusual contract that allowed her to photograph stars outside the studio, gave her approval over prints, and required that all reproductions be attributed to her. Among other important figures were Clarence Sinclair Bull (1895–1979), who also worked at M-G-M and became Greta Garbo's exclusive photographer, and George Hurrell (1904–1992), whose studio appointments included M-G-M, Columbia, and Warner Bros. At the latter studio, Hurrell (with right arm upraised) prepares a portrait photograph of Bette Davis in connection with the production of Juarez (1939).

Below: 9.7. Meanwhile, thousands of photographs went out free of charge to newspapers and magazines, since their reproduction was a form of free publicity. Sometimes a picture is worth a thousand words, as in this shot of Marlene Dietrich on the set of Flame of New Orleans (1941).

9.8. Dr. Frankenstein (Colin Clive, with torch at right) observes his monster (Boris Karloff) in chains, in Frankenstein (1932), directed by James Whale.

perhaps the definitive send-up. Given the historical importance of these early 1930s horror films, it is surprising how quaint they now appear—in contrast not only to the genre's truly shocking evolution, but to the enduring power and freshness of early 1930s gangster films. Their setting is Hollywood's version of English upper-class life (or in *Frankenstein*, Hollywood's version of the English upper class masquerading as German aristocrats). Despite their potential for disturbing visions and the occasional horror they depict, both films end happily, with none of the principal "normal" characters very much affected. Mina, the ambiguous and tragic heroine of *Nosferatu*, survives the vampire's bite in *Dracula* and weds her fiancé as if only a small inconvenience had occurred.

The Musical

By the early 1930s the new genre of recorded sound musicals had already gone through one cycle, and its staying power seemed uncertain. With the exception of *Applause* and a few others, early sound musicals had been hampered by restricted camera movement and the variety format taken over from stage musicals. The genre made a decisive recovery when Warner Bros. inaugurated in 1933 a series of musicals with show-business stories featuring dances and ensemble staging created by choreographer Busby Berkeley (1895–1976).

The first, *42nd Street*, directed by Lloyd Bacon (1890–1955), told the classic tale of the "raw kid out of the chorus" who gets her big chance when the leading lady breaks her ankle. "You're going out a youngster," says the director to young Peggy Sawyer (played by Ruby Keeler), "but you've got to come back a star." Besides such familiar, but compelling, stories, the Warner musicals gave free reign to Berkeley's dance spectacles. He completely freed the musical from adherence to stage conventions; having tried out overhead shots of dancers in several earlier musicals, he advanced this style in *42nd Street*, and it reached full flower in

such films as *Gold Diggers of 1933* and *Footlight Parade* (both 1933) and *Dames* (1934). *42nd Street* also offers a **tracking shot** with a male vocalist while the camera passes between the legs of female dancers. These and similar images from other films have made Berkeley's dances prime subjects for studies concerned with the mechanization, objectification, and segmentation of women's bodies in cinema.

Almost simultaneously with Berkeley's triumphs, a different musical style, which placed a more contemplative emphasis on individual performances, was emerging in the Fred Astaire (1899–1987) and Ginger Rogers (b. 1911) musicals made at RKO. (Rogers personified the transition, having appeared in *42nd Street* and *Gold Diggers of 1933*). Fred and Ginger—we seem to know no other Hollywood couple so familiarly on a first-name basis— danced together in nine films between 1933 and 1939, to music by Cole Porter, Irving Berlin, Jerome Kern, George Gershwin, and other leading popular composers, with dance direction by Hermes Pan (1905–1990). Their most prominent successes (and enduring favorites) included *Top Hat* (1935), directed by Mark Sandrich (1900–1945), and *Swing Time* (1937), directed by George Stevens (1904–1975).

Comedy

Last in this brief survey of genres, comedy received a strong boost from new writers and performers who came in with sound. Representative among the former was playwright Samson Raphaelson (1896–1983), whose stage play served as source for *The Jazz Singer*; Raphaelson brought his sardonic dialogue to director Ernst Lubitsch's sophisticated comedies twitting European upper-class society, notably *Trouble in Paradise* (1932), a Paramount film featuring Miriam Hopkins, Kay Francis, and Herbert Marshall. Inimitable among the latter was the vaudeville and Broadway comedy team the Marx Brothers (Groucho, Harpo, Chico, and Zeppo). The five anarchic comedies they made for

9.9. *Women on display in Busby Berkeley's choreography, from the "By the Waterfall" sequence of* Footlight Parade *(1933)*

9.10. *The incomparable dancing team of Fred Astaire and Ginger Rogers in* Swing Time *(1937), directed by George Stevens*

Paramount—*The Cocoanuts* (1929) and *Animal Crackers* (1930), produced at the New York Astoria studio; then, in Hollywood, *Monkey Business* (1931), *Horse Feathers* (1932), and *Duck Soup* (1933)—remain popular favorites, though deeply rooted in the ethnic humor style of their times.

THE PRODUCTION CODE AND ITS EFFECTS

Between 1933 and 1935 most of the Hollywood film studios that had suffered financial difficulties in the Great Depression's early years began to regain their stability. Their struggles shifted from the economic realm to the social and moral. The movies, as carriers of modernity into traditional communities, had always encountered hostility from some social groups. In the early 1920s the Motion Picture Producers and Distributors Association (MPPDA, later renamed Motion Picture Association of America) appointed as its president Postmaster-General Will H. Hays

9.11. Ernst Lubitsch, director of sophisticated comedies, brought his droll humor even to publicity shots, as in this photo of him directing Una Merkel for a bedroom scene in The Merry Widow (1934).

9.12. The Marx Brothers declare war in Duck Soup (1933), directed by Leo McCarey; from left, Zeppo, Chico, Harpo, and Groucho.

(1879–1954), whose task was to fend off state censorship and build good will toward movies. The coming of sound, however, again exacerbated public concern about movie morality and social impact.

In 1930, as a counterweight to outside pressure and efforts to impose federal government censorship (on top of already existing state censorship boards), the movie industry strengthened its self-regulatory mechanisms, setting up a Production Code and an office to monitor scripts and completed films. The Code offered general principles, such as "No picture shall be produced which will lower the moral standards of those who see it," and twelve sections dealing with specific prohibitions concerning topics such as crime, sex, profanity, and costuming (as examples, no nudity, and no offensive references to a character's national origin). Economic pressures, however, led producers to more license rather than less: gangster violence, risqué dialogue, and sexual candor were exploited as lures to retain a diminishing audience. The Hays Office had established a Studio Relations Committee in Hollywood to monitor Code compliance, but by 1933 critics regarded its efforts as ineffective and religious groups threatened to boycott movies.

Production Code Administration

In response to this crisis, Hays in 1934 set up a new watchdog body, the Production Code Administration (PCA), headed by Joseph I. Breen (1890–1965), with power to issue an MPPDA seal to films deemed in compliance with the Code; member companies of the MPPDA agreed not to release any film without a seal. Nevertheless, conflicts between the PCA and producers quickly became heated, as in the exchanges over the RKO production Of Human Bondage (1934), adapted from W. Somerset Maugham's novel of a sexual obsession. "It deals definitely with tangled sex relations which are highly offensive to the rank and file of our patrons," the PCA noted in an internal memo. Let them "stop cheap filth on the screen," a producer fumed in an RKO internal

9.13. *Dorothy Arzner, the only woman director in Hollywood during the early sound years,* *directs Ruth Chatterton and Clive Brook in* Anybody's Woman *(1930).*

memo, "and let distinguished, fine novels be produced in picture form."[2] After all this, the finished film was approved as conforming to the Code and presented a stirring performance by a young actress, Bette Davis (1908–1989), that launched her toward star status.

The Woman's Film

With stringent Code enforcement (the PCA carefully scrutinized scripts and costume drawings at the preproduction stage and previewed every finished film), broader cultural changes, and different ambitions among producers and filmmakers, American movies after 1934 moved closer to the social mainstream, enhancing their role as leaders in representing and defining issues of ideology and values. A case in point is the woman's film. This traditional genre was dominated in the early 1930s by a cycle dealing with the "fallen woman." After 1933 it shifted back toward more conventional society.

One of the last among the genre's controversial early 1930s works was *Christopher Strong*, a 1933 RKO production directed by Dorothy Arzner (1900–1979), Hollywood's only woman direc-

tor in the first sound years. Arzner began her career at Paramount as a film editor and scriptwriter and directed her first picture while still in her twenties. She made eleven films for Paramount from 1927 to 1932 and six more at other studios over the following decade; many of her works feature a strong, independent-minded woman who frequently meets a tragic end. In *Christopher Strong* this figure is portrayed by Katharine Hepburn in her second screen role; a famous woman aviator, she falls in love with a married man, becomes pregnant, and takes her own life by removing her oxygen mask during a flight that sets an altitude record. (Strict Code enforcement would have prohibited the pregnancy and the suicide, and the PCA later banned the film from reissue.)

Even as it began to steer away from some subjects, however, the woman's genre—now more commonly called melodrama—inevitably touched on others quite as contentious. *Imitation of Life* (1934), directed by John M. Stahl (1886–1950) at Universal, treated race relations. A widowed white woman (Claudette Colbert) and her African-American housekeeper (Louise Beavers) establish a successful business selling a pancake mix based on the black woman's secret recipe. Each has problems with a daughter. The housekeeper's daughter is so light-skinned ("Her pappy was a very, very light colored man," the mother explains) that she wants to pass for white. She renounces her mother, who dies of a broken heart. The widow's daughter falls in love with the same man her mother plans to marry, so the mother sends him away. The genre focused on the broader concerns society had demarcated as women's issues, including marriage, family, and children. Though sometimes dismissed as "weepies," melodramas dealt with fundamental human themes, even if considerably masked, as in *Imitation of Life*'s covert allusion to sexual relations between whites and blacks.

Screwball Comedy

Also at least partly attributable to the Production Code was a shift in the comedy genre after 1934 away from the ethnic, often vulgar style of early sound comedies drawing on vaudeville stage conventions (though the Marx Brothers continued to thrive, their connoisseurs lamented that they had been tamed) toward a new type of romantic comedy. Called **screwball comedies**, these films often featured quirky members of the affluent classes, held out the possibility of cross-class romance, or gave wealthy characters lessons in human values. A prototype was *It Happened One Night* (1934), the first film to sweep the top five Academy Awards— Frank Capra (1897–1991) as director, Clark Gable (1901–1960) and Claudette Colbert (b. 1905) as actor and actress, Robert Riskin (1897–1955) for screenplay, and best picture to Columbia, lifting that studio from the ranks of minor companies (derisively nicknamed "Poverty Row" because of low salaries and

9.15. Claudette Colbert as Bea Pullman (right) and Louise Beavers as Delilah, her maid, share their worries over their daughters in the woman's melodrama Imitation of Life *(1934)*, directed by John M. Stahl.

9.14. Colin Clive as Christopher Strong and Katharine Hepburn as Lady Cynthia Darrington in Christopher Strong *(1933)*, directed by Dorothy Arzner. Hepburn's "moth" costume was the creation of a free-lance designer, Howard

Greer. The studio's caption described it as "made of metal material, somewhat like that used in mesh bags, consisting of tiny, solid aluminum squares, all linked together."

picture budgets) to become one of Hollywood's "majors." Columbia's most important contract director, Capra was developing a special style of comedy based on everyday life, and loan-outs from major studios (Gable from M-G-M, Colbert from Paramount) gave him leading players for whom he could craft innovative roles. Gable plays a newspaper reporter who encounters Colbert, an heiress fleeing from an undesired wedding, on a long-distance bus ride. What begins as a scoop turns into romance on the American road.

MY MAN GODFREY. One of the most unusual screwball comedies was *My Man Godfrey* (1936), a Universal production directed by Gregory La Cava (1892–1952). It begins at a garbage dump along New York's East River. People in evening clothes, taking part in a scavenger hunt for a charity event, step out of a roadster to look for a "forgotten man"—a 1930s term for the unemployed and homeless. A derelict, after pushing one woman into an ash heap, agrees to go along with her sister. His dignity and sardonic humor impress her, and she hires him as butler for the family's Fifth Avenue mansion. The wealthy family turn out to be spoiled, selfish, and inane— "empty-headed nitwits," as the derelict-turned-butler calls them.

He, it turns out, is also from a rich family; he landed in the dump through despondency over a broken love affair. Through his butler work he pulls his life together and in the end opens a posh nightclub, the Dump, on the dump site to provide employment, food, and shelter to "forgotten men." The film's predominant point, however, is not that the poor are redeemable, but that the wealthy are.

HOWARD HAWKS. In the later 1930s director Howard Hawks emerged as a leading creative figure in the screwball subgenre. His films were notable for the questioning approach they took toward gender issues. Relations between women and men, if they sometimes appeared to be warlike, actually depended in his films on recognition of life's playfulness. This gave performers an

opportunity to be comically inventive and outrageous. In *Bringing Up Baby* (1938), made at RKO, Katharine Hepburn recast her screen persona in her role as a ditzy rich girl seeking romance with a cerebral scientist (played by Cary Grant). For *His Girl Friday* (1940), a Columbia production that remade a hit play and movie, *The Front Page*, Hawks changed one of the characters from male to female. Editor Walter Burns (Grant) and reporter Hildy Johnson (Rosalind Russell) became ex-husband and wife, making their battles more focused than in previous versions on the vexed, yet creative, relationship between love and work.

HOLLYWOOD PRODUCTION VALUES

When movie-struck Esther Blodgett (played by Janet Gaynor) arrives in Hollywood from the sticks in the first, 1937 version of *A Star Is Born* (there were two remakes: 1954 with Judy Garland, 1976 with Barbra Streisand), a printed intertitle proclaims her destination "the beckoning El Dorado, Metropolis of Make-Believe in the California Hills." Esther's rise to stardom is predicated on her sincerity and honesty, her "natural talent," yet she learns new ways to walk, speak, and wear makeup—and is renamed Vicky Lester. In its own ascent to extraordinary cultural prominence during the 1930s, the movie industry strived to maintain a careful balance with its spectators between identification and otherness:

Top left: 9.18. The movie aspirant's destination in the first version of A Star Is Born (1937), directed by William A. Wellman

Above: 9.19. The first feature film made in the three-color Technicolor process was Becky Sharp (1935), based on Vanity Fair, the nineteenth-century British novel by William Makepeace Thackeray. Director Rouben Mamoulian and production designer Robert Edmond Jones used color symbolically, particularly in the dramatic sequence of the Duchess of Richmond's ball on the eve of the Battle of Waterloo, which opens in a spectrum of colors but gradually gives way to military red.

Top right: 9.20. Becky (Miriam Hopkins) with the Marquis of Steyne (Cedric Hardwicke) and Rawdon Crawley (Alan Mowbray)

you could imagine yourself the same type as a star, but must always remember that only one in 100,000 succeeded in Hollywood.

"Tie-ups"

For the motion picture companies, movies on screen accounted for only one part—granted, the first and most important—of the relationship they sought to build with audiences. Movies served as the foundation of a cultural concept: screen stories were make-believe, and their stars were distant and different, yet those stories and stars could be vicariously emulated. One could acquire the sheet music (from a subsidiary of the movie studio) and play the songs the stars sang. One could purchase modestly priced "knockoff" dresses based on outfits worn by the stars and complexion and makeup products they endorsed. One could buy furniture, rugs, drapes, lamps—furnish a whole household—modeled on the rooms the stars lived in on-screen. The motion picture experience extended beyond the theater into everyday living through the world of "tie-ups," products drawn from the screen or promoted by film personalities. (However, movies in that era rarely displayed brand items, because exhibitors protested that they did not share in fees paid by manufacturers.)

Mise-en-scène

This cultural and economic emphasis had an unmistakable effect on American motion picture style in the 1930s. It was a significant reason why the sound cinema moved away from the stylizations and symbolization common in 1920s silent film. Technique less and less called attention to itself. In the 1930s films discussed here—works that have stood the test of time and remain lively and entertaining—there are nevertheless few occasions to exclaim over virtuoso cutting sequences or extraordinary cinematography. Superior editing and camera work are indeed amply present, but at the service of illusion and presentation, of the reality of make-believe. Hollywood's distinctive film style of the 1930s lay not in *how* one viewed but in *what* was viewed. It marked a triumph of mise-en-scène.

Costume Design

The industry spoke of **production values**, a term that referred principally to costumes and sets. In a historical epic like *The Charge of the Light Brigade*, a 1936 Warner Bros. film directed by Michael Curtiz (1888–1962), this meant period gowns, uniforms, and massed extras in ballroom and battle scenes. But for the economic purposes of "tie-ups" it connoted up-to-date fashions in clothes and decor. Edith Head (1907–1981) at Paramount, Adrian at M-G-M (see Chapter 8), and Orry-Kelly (1897–1964) at Warner Bros. were among the leading costume designers of the period. Costume design played a significant role in narrative, representation, and character development in 1930s movies, and it carried over to the commercial marketing of clothing based on movie models; publicity stills of actress Joan Crawford (1908–1977), for example, carried detailed captions explaining the stylistic features of the dresses she wore in her films.

Art Direction

Among the principal **art directors** were Cedric Gibbons at M-G-M, Hans Dreier (1885–1966) at Paramount, William Darling (1882–1963) at Fox, Anton Grot (1884–1974) at Warner Bros., Van Nest Polglase (1898–1968) at RKO, and Richard Day

Hollywood Mise-en-Scène

When French critics of the 1950s debated issues of film "authorship" (see Chapters 16 and 17) they emphasized the director's role in shaping a film's visual style, its mise-en-scène. In Hollywood's 1930s mode of production, however, though a director's influence was paramount over such elements as camera movement and the blocking of actors, a considerable part of a film's visual style might be established even before a director was assigned. After a script was approved, responsibility for translating it into a visual design would be placed in the hands of the art department. Now that notions of authorship have begun to encompass not just directors, but the collaborative nature of crafting a film, the art director's contribution deserves further attention, as these three examples attest.

Left: 9.22. Expenses were also not spared on Cain and Mabel (1936), directed by Lloyd Bacon, the third Marion Davies vehicle made at Warner Bros. by William Randolph Hearst's production company. Davies portrayed a waitress who becomes a musical comedy star. Art director Robert Haas (1887–1962) designed this set for a musical number called "I'll Sing You a Thousand Love Songs." Neither the sets, nor the songs by Harry Warren and Al Dubin, could carry this picture, which became a substantial box office failure. After one more film, Davies retired.

Below: 9.23. Stephen Goosson (1889–1973) designed this vision of a futuristic city for Just Imagine (1930), a Fox production directed by David Butler. This "city of tomorrow" represented a conception of how things might look half a century ahead, or 1980. (The narrative concerns, among other things, space travel to Mars, and humans have names like license plates, such as RT-42.) Ralph Hammeras, director of effects, supervised several hundred workmen in constructing this set at a cost of $250,000, according to studio publicity, a substantial sum at that time. Goosson and Hammeras were nominated for an Academy Award in the category Art Direction–Set Decoration; Goosson later won an Oscar for his work on Frank Capra's Lost Horizon (1937).

Left: 9.21. For The Garden of Allah (1936), producer David O. Selznick caused "a wasteland of sand" in the desert near Yuma, Arizona, to be transformed into an oasis where Charles Boyer and Marlene Dietrich (seated at left) performed a love scene under the direction of Richard Boleslawski (seated at right). To build this setting, according to studio publicity, water was "piped from five miles away and trees and shrubs brought from even greater distances. The temperature there often reached 120 in the shade during the period of the location trip." Lansing Holden and Sturges Carne were credited for art direction.

9.24. A scene from the burning of Atlanta sequence in Gone with the Wind (1939)

stages they built nightclubs, ocean liners, apartment interiors (even the occasional office) of a size, scale, and lavishness that actuality rarely, if ever, matched. In their early decades American motion picture producers had been criticized for failing accurately to depict the settings where fashionable people lived. By the 1930s such criticism was moot: the movies were in the vanguard, themselves helping to shape the fashion standards of the time.

Color

Beginning in mid-decade the studios worked color back into their visual repertory, though slowly and selectively. RKO in 1935 produced the first full-length feature film using three-strip Technicolor, *Becky Sharp*, loosely based on William Makepeace Thackeray's nineteenth-century British novel *Vanity Fair*. Following the death of the original director, Rouben Mamoulian took over the project and brought his flair for stylistic experimen-

(1895–1972), who worked for Samuel Goldwyn, a producer distributing films through United Artists. For their contemporary settings the Hollywood studios fostered the styles that have come to be known by the collective term Art Deco. This modern, streamlined look linked the movies to advanced concepts in the visual arts, architecture, and industrial design. Artists, planners, and designers were seeking aesthetic styles expressive of twentieth-century forms—the city, the machine, abstraction as a mode of representing reality. Motion picture art directors tended to shift these concepts into realms of pleasure and fantasy. On vast sound

9.26. Judy Garland as Dorothy on the yellow brick road in another popular Technicolor clas-   sic of 1939, The Wizard of Oz, directed by Victor Fleming

9.25. Producer David O. Selznick believed more strongly in Technicolor than any other Hollywood executive of the 1930s. His (and Hollywood's) great triumph of the era was Gone with the Wind, the epic of the United States Civil War based on Margaret Mitchell's novel. Selznick went through three directors (Victor Fleming, the middle one, got the credit) and "authorship" of the film could justly be ascribed to Selznick, production designer William Cameron Menzies, and art director Lyle Wheeler (all three won Academy Awards, as did Fleming; the film gained ten in all). The famous burning of Atlanta sequence was shot first, to clear the lot for other sets, with doubles filling in for the leads (even before Vivien Leigh had been cast as Scarlett O'Hara). A storyboard established the setups for seven Technicolor cameras.

tation evident from *Applause* and other films. In *Becky Sharp* this took the form of subtle changes in color patterns based on shifts in mood and narrative development. Lacking a compelling screenplay, however, *Becky Sharp* failed to excite either audiences or the industry, and it became a technological footnote rather than a landmark.

For the next several years color was utilized primarily in Westerns and other outdoor films where it was regarded as enhancing picturesque landscapes. Producer David O. Selznick (1902–1965), who had worked at Paramount, M-G-M, and RKO before setting up his own company, Selznick International, was most committed to the new technology: he used it on *A Star Is Born* and other films he distributed through United Artists, and then on the grandest production of the era, the nearly four-hour Civil War epic *Gone With the Wind* (1939), released by M-G-M, with Victor Fleming (1883–1949) credited as director. Also in 1939, and also directed by Fleming, M-G-M's *The Wizard of Oz* shifts from black-and-white to Technicolor after a tornado carries Dorothy (Judy Garland) and her dog Toto from Kansas to the Land of Oz. Though it was not yet clear that color was other than an occasional novelty, it had helped to create two popular classics.

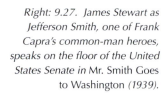

Right: 9.27. James Stewart as Jefferson Smith, one of Frank Capra's common-man heroes, speaks on the floor of the United States Senate in Mr. Smith Goes to Washington *(1939).*

Below: 9.28. Shooting Stagecoach *(1939), directed by John Ford. John Wayne as the Ringo Kid stands at the coach door.*

Above: 9.29. Henry Fonda as Tom Joad, John Carradine as Casey, in John Ford's The Grapes of Wrath *(1940), based on John Steinbeck's novel about migrant farmers in the Great Depression*

Below: 9.30. Charlie Chaplin (right) encounters the industrial machine in Modern Times *(1936), which the comic performer also produced, directed, and wrote.*

AN ESTABLISHMENT CINEMA

In the space of half a decade, Hollywood had gone from something of an outlaw cinema, in the eyes of some, to something of an establishment cinema. As the United States struggled to recover from the Great Depression, as the rise of European Fascism and the onset of war caused the nation to reconsider its history and values, the movies became increasingly important as framers of cultural and ideological discourses. Two filmmakers emerged, to industry and public alike, as key figures in Hollywood's task of cultural definition: Frank Capra and John Ford. Both directors were concerned in separate ways—Capra through social comedy, Ford with historical films and literary adaptations—with leadership: how leaders emerge in the American democratic mythology from humble roots, how they forge complex and reciprocal relations with those they lead. Between 1934 and 1941 this pair won six of eight Academy Awards as best director—three apiece.

Both were from immigrant Catholic backgrounds. Capra was born in Sicily and immigrated with his family to Los Angeles when he was six. Ford (1895–1973) was named Sean Aloysius O'Feeney when he was born in the state of Maine as the thirteenth child of Irish immigrant parents. Outsiders who became insiders, they both possessed ambition and the vision, after careers as journeymen directors, to seize the opportunity the times and the movie industry's new role afforded.

5-P-148

9.31. *Greta Garbo as Marguerite, with Rex O'Malley as Gaston, and Laura Hope Crews as Prudence in* Camille *(1937), directed by George Cukor*

Frank Capra

With roots in comedy and contemporary melodrama, Capra moved following his award-winning *It Happened One Night* toward films focusing on social values. Beginning with *Mr. Deeds Goes to Town* (1936), with Gary Cooper as the small-town man who triumphs over city slickers, Capra's work emphasized the common-sense skills and leadership qualities of "little people." After winning additional Oscars as best director for *Mr. Deeds* and *You Can't Take It with You* (1937), an adaptation of a Broadway comedy, Capra applied his themes to politics in *Mr. Smith Goes to Washington* (1939). James Stewart (b. 1908) portrayed the common-man hero, a naive young United States senator—named, with historical resonance, Jefferson Smith—who fights against corruption and for democratic values on the Senate floor.

John Ford

Ford had emerged in the silent era as a director of Westerns, and he brought to his mature work a developed view of American history. His first major recognition came with a best director award for *The Informer* (1935), based on a novel of Irish independence struggles, and another of his awards was for an adaptation of a Welsh novel, *How Green Was My Valley* (1941). But his most enduring works from the period were on American themes: *Stagecoach* (1939), his first of many Westerns filmed in the magnificent setting of Utah's Monument Valley; *Drums Along the Mohawk* (1939), on the American Revolution on the New York frontier, shot in color; *Young Mr. Lincoln* (1939), a biographical film on Abraham Lincoln's young manhood and the future president's growing sense of destiny; and *The Grapes of Wrath* (1940), a panoramic adaptation of John Steinbeck's controversial best-selling novel about Oklahoma farmers migrating to California in the Great Depression. Ford has often been regarded, and not

without validity, as an outdoor director, with special affinities for the American landscape; yet of even greater importance are group events in interior space, where the moral relationships of communities are contested and formed: a dinner table in *Stagecoach*, a courtroom in *Young Mr. Lincoln*, a migrant camp tent in *The Grapes of Wrath*. Ford's historical perspective emerged in these communal settings, emphasizing, much like Capra, the necessity of justice and respect for common people.

Ford and Capra were veterans of the silent era who achieved prominence with Hollywood's 1930s transformation. The situation was different for some of the major stars of the silent period, who had to cope, as directors did not, with maintaining or altering their screen images as they grew older and as culture changed. Charlie Chaplin and Greta Garbo are significant examples.

Charles Chaplin

At first Chaplin avoided the challenge of sound. Operating his own studio, he released only two comedies during the 1930s, *City Lights* (1931) and *Modern Times* (1936), both eagerly awaited by contemporary audiences and destined to become film classics. He retained his tramp character as a silent performer, adding only a music and effects track. Chaplin finally spoke on screen in *The Great Dictator* (1940), a satirical attack on Europe's fascist leaders, in which he plays both a dictator modeled on Adolf Hitler and one of his victims.

Greta Garbo

Garbo made the transition to sound late, but successfully, in *Anna Christie* (see Chapter 8). If anything, her throaty European accent increased her mystery and allure. A greater problem was the staying power of her continental *femme fatale* stereotype. As the 1930s went on she made fewer films, though she was acclaimed for performances in *Anna Karenina* (1935), directed by Clarence

9.32. Sylvia Sidney and Henry Fonda portray the doomed outlaw couple in Fritz Lang's You Only Live Once (1937).

Brown; *Camille* (1937), directed by George Cukor; and Ernst Lubitsch's *Ninotchka* (1939), a satire on Soviet communism where Garbo showed a flair for comedy. She retired from films in 1941, still in her mid-thirties.

European Émigrés

Hollywood in the 1930s became a place of refuge as well as opportunity for European filmmakers fleeing from political or religious persecution. With another influx of Germans added to those (like Lubitsch and Murnau) who had migrated during the silent era, the Weimar cinema's legacy was carried forward as much or more in Hollywood as in Berlin. The leading figure among post-1933 refugees was Fritz Lang, who left Germany reputedly after being asked to head the film industry under Nazi control (see Chapter 10). Lang directed his first American film, *Fury*, in 1936 and the following year rejuvenated the crime genre with the subtle, ambiguous *You Only Live Once*.

1939

The year 1939 was an *annus mirabilis* for Hollywood: a year of wonders. Along with the films already mentioned here—*Gone With the Wind, The Wizard of Oz, Mr. Smith Goes to Washington, Stagecoach, Young Mr. Lincoln, Drums Along the Mohawk, Ninotchka*—another dozen all-time favorites could easily be named, ranging from genre works like Howard Hawks's *Only Angels Have Wings* to prestige literary adaptations such as *Wuthering Heights*, directed by William Wyler (1902–1981). The year marked a high point in Hollywood's history for cultural power and self-confidence. Amid the hundreds of genre films churned out by the studios, the bedrock of the American motion picture industry's mode of production, an elite of filmmakers had coalesced with the talent and desire to create serious, ambitious films.

Still, not all agreed that this was the best of all possible cinema worlds. Along with self-confidence, some thought, came self-importance; along with cultural power, a certain grandiosity. A more pessimistic assessment of the year of wonders saw a decline in the energy and excitement of genre production (only the Western was showing some renewed signs of life) and a static, unadventurous style in the so-called "quality" films.

Right: 9.33. Walt Disney pioneered the animated feature film with Snow White and the Seven Dwarfs *(1937)*, in Technicolor, and followed it with Pinocchio *(1940)*, both based on traditional fairy tales and popular fables. His third feature, Fantasia *(1940)*, was conceived as something quite different: animated images accompanying classical and contemporary orchestral music, with Leopold Stokowski conducting the Philadelphia Orchestra and Deems Taylor, a radio commentator on music, narrating introductions to the film's seven segments. The first sequence, with Johann Sebastian Bach's "Toccata and Fugue in D Minor," began by introducing the musicians in silhouette, then shifted to abstract images.

Far right: 9.34. The third sequence, to the music of "The Sorcerer's Apprentice," by Paul Dukas, features Mickey Mouse as the apprentice. Mickey puts on the sorcerer's hat and commands a broom to do his work for him. These five frames from the segment show how things quickly get out of hand.

ORSON WELLES

If there was complacency in Hollywood, it was challenged by the arrival (significantly, in 1939) of theater and radio's boy genius, twenty-four-year-old Orson Welles (1915–1985). Welles had gained prominence at an extraordinarily youthful age as a gifted theater director and actor with the Federal Theatre Project and then his own company, Mercury Theatre Group, formed with John Houseman (1902–1988). Moving Mercury Theatre to network radio, he created front-page headlines when his 1938 Halloween eve radio broadcast adapting H. G. Wells's novel *The War of the Worlds* convinced many listeners that Martians had invaded New Jersey. RKO offered him nearly unprecedented creative freedom—the opportunity to be simultaneously producer, director, writer, and actor—and, in addition to a salary, an astonishing 25 percent share of his films' gross earnings. Hollywood veterans did not take kindly to this brash newcomer with a highly developed public egoism and a norm-breaking deal.

9.35. The most significant film produced in the American commercial cinema, by general critical consensus, is Orson Welles's Citizen Kane (1941). Few of its stylistic effects were new; what was dazzling was the way it brought to bear a variety of innovations in nearly every scene. The narrative was based on a mystery: what was the meaning of media baron Charles Foster Kane's dying word, "Rosebud"? The film investigates the question through a series of flashbacks as Kane's associates tell their stories to a journalist. In the memoir of financier Walter P. Thatcher (George Coulouris, in top hat), we learn how Kane's mother (Agnes Moorehead), after gold is discovered on her Colorado property, makes the financier the boy's guardian; Buddy Swan played Kane, age eight, and Harry Shannon his father (left).

Citizen Kane

Behind the scenes, however, Welles was gifted at gathering around him talented collaborators. Besides the Mercury Theatre performers he brought with him—including Joseph Cotten (b. 1905), Agnes Moorehead (1906–1974), and Everett Sloane (1909–1965)—he enlisted established professionals for his first production, *Citizen Kane* (1941). These included writer Herman Mankiewicz (1898–1953); cinematographer Gregg Toland, who had worked with John Ford on *The Grapes of Wrath*, among other films; and art director Van Nest Polglase. He also gave opportunities to newcomers Robert Wise (b. 1914) as editor and Bernard Herrmann (1911–1975) as composer. With a working title of "American," *Citizen Kane* was no less serious and ambitious than the works of Ford and Capra, a biographical mystery story seeking to unravel the character and cultural significance of a media baron whose dying word was "Rosebud." It incurred the wrath of a living media baron, newspaper publisher William Randolph Hearst, who felt, not without reason, that Welles's Charles Foster Kane was modeled after him.

Recognized as a major work at its release, despite the controversy generated by Hearst, *Citizen Kane* has continued to grow in stature as the American commercial cinema's most important film. It enabled the spectator not only to look through the frame at a make-believe world, but to see once again, so to speak, the frame as a constructed image: to take delight not only from stories but from the virtuosity and splendor of cinematic art.

As with D. W. Griffith's early films, no single aspect of *Citizen Kane* was entirely original or previously unknown to filmmakers, but the work's startling impact came from its total effect, the concentration, comprehensiveness, and unity of its stylistic effort. Where innovation in Hollywood tended to occur only in isolated sequences and shots, Welles strove with his collaborators to utilize multiple innovations in nearly every shot and scene throughout the entire film.

These began with the basic narrative, fragmenting the story to different voices and viewpoints, refusing linearity or unity of perspective. This was carried forward through mise-en-scène, the construction of exceptionally deep sets so that action as well as narrative could fragment into different planes of space and depth. It was augmented by long camera takes that enabled greater movement in performance and ensemble acting by the Mercury players. It was all made possible by Gregg Toland's cinematography and lighting, using camera lenses that maintained focus through the **deep space** of the sets (Toland gave credit to Welles's unusually detailed preproduction planning, which was required for building camera locations into sets for extraordinary **low-** and **high-angle shots** to convey symbolic meaning). And finally, it was embedded in the shot continuity, which used sound and lighting changes as editing devices to avoid direct cuts in favor of scene changes through camera panning or dollying, or **overlapping dissolves**.

The Magnificent Ambersons

Welles went on to write and direct (and to narrate, though not to appear in) *The Magnificent Ambersons* (1942), set in the early-twentieth-century American Middle West and based on a novel by Booth Tarkington. Before editing was completed, the United States entered World War II, and Welles went to Mexico and Brazil to begin work on a documentary entitled "It's All True," jointly sponsored by RKO and the U.S. government to strengthen ties with Latin America. While he was away from Hollywood, studio executives ordered *The Magnificent Ambersons* cut by one-third; at the same time they lost interest in the documentary and destroyed some of the footage Welles had delivered. Even the truncated version of *The Magnificent Ambersons* that survives marks a considerable achievement, and researchers have begun to uncover the remarkable and tragic tale of "It's All True," as well as some of its lost footage.

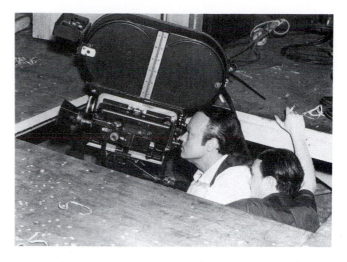

Notes

1.   Robert Warshow, "The Gangster as Tragic Hero," in *The Immediate Experience: Movies, Comics, Theatre, and Other Aspects of Popular Culture* (Garden City, N.Y.: Doubleday, 1962), Anchor edition, p. 86.

2.   Joseph I. Breen to James Wingate, memorandum, May 22, 1933, *Of Human Bondage* file, Motion Picture Association of America, Production Code Administration files, Academy of Motion Picture Arts and Sciences, Beverly Hills, California; Merian C. Cooper to B. B. Kahane, memorandum, May 25, 1933, *Of Human Bondage* file, RKO Radio Pictures archive, Los Angeles.

Above left: 9.36. The marriage of Kane (portrayed by Welles) to Emily Norton (Ruth Warrick) is recounted in a witty montage sequence of breakfast table scenes.

Top: 9.37. Low-angle, deep-focus shots were made possible by careful preproduction planning that placed the camera sometimes below floor level; here Welles checks out a setup with cinematographer Gregg Toland.

Above: 9.38. Kane's campaign for governor was photographed in another low-angle shot.

TEN

MEETING

With the advent of sound, no less than in the silent era, the prime challenge to the world's film industries was how to respond to Hollywood's competition. But as the 1930s progressed, the task took on a stronger patriotic character. As struggles among nations once again erupted into armed conflict, and regional wars expanded to engulf the globe, the motion picture medium came to be valued more than ever as an important tool of national purpose and a shaper of public consciousness. Governments as well as individuals turned their attention to nonfiction filmmaking to serve the ends of propaganda and persuasion (as will be discussed in Chapter 11), but the documentary mode rarely reached as wide an audience as narrative fiction films. This popular art thus became the focus of political intervention to a far greater extent than in any previous era. There had been numerous instances of film being used for propaganda purposes; the World War I period and the Soviet cinema were recent examples. In the 1930s, however, utilization of entertainment to communicate national ideology became widespread.

Left, above: 10.1. Alessandro Blasetti's Terra madre *("Mother Earth," 1930), emphasizing the importance of the countryside in Italian Fascist ideology, concerns an aristocratic playboy who learns to be a responsible manager of his lands. A duke, Marco (Sandro Salvini, at left), and his polished* consort Daisy (Isa Pola, second from left) enjoy hedonistic pastimes while his estates deteriorate.

Left, below: 10.2. The love of a country woman, Emilia (Leda Gloria, at left), who represents human warmth and fecundity, returns Marco to the land.

STATE CONTROL OVER CINEMA

The decade's principal innovation was the spread of state control over cinema. Except for the Soviet Union, where the state sought to control all enterprise, and the short time in Germany during World War I when government temporarily took over film production for propaganda purposes, the medium had belonged over its first three decades almost entirely to private enterprise. Governments, of course, had intervened in cinematic affairs in myriad ways, such as quotas, tariffs, and censorship, but decision making in artistic and financial matters had remained in private hands.

New models of state power over cinema emerged in the 1930s in two of the historically most important filmmaking countries, Italy and Germany. Both nations had been taken over by dictatorial regimes that exercised different forms of totalitarian, sometimes brutal, control over institutions and people—in Italy, the Fascists under Benito Mussolini, from 1922; in Germany, the National Socialists (Nazis) under Adolf Hitler, from 1933. In the Soviet Union, meanwhile, Communism was becoming more blatantly a

direct subsidies, though it left artistic control in private hands. Production gradually rose, reaching eighty or more films per year by decade's end.

For years after the Fascist regime collapsed in World War II, critics and historians ignored the films made during its rule. The works were dismissed either as crude propaganda or as frivolous, escapist pseudo-Hollywood works featuring lives of the rich in lavish settings (these latter were called *telefoni bianchi* films because their sets were furnished with white telephones, signifiers of conspicuous wealth). But a reevaluation of that era's films has begun, and it finds a more complex cinematic achievement. Of all the totalitarian governments, Fascist Italy proved most tolerant of diversity, at least in the arts. A case in point was the Centro Sperimentale, where, as Italian film historian Gian Piero Brunetta has written, antifascists were able to study and work. The regime's interest in Soviet aesthetics enabled Marxist critic Umberto Barbaro to teach Russian film theories at the school and espouse a realist aesthetic; among those who studied at the school during the Fascist period were filmmakers who emerged as leading figures after World War II, including Michelangelo Antonioni, Giuseppe De Santis, Pietro Germi, and Luigi Zampa (see Chapter 13).

HOLLYWOOD'S CHALLENGE

totalitarian dictatorship under Joseph Stalin. For all three regimes, a central purpose was to build film industries that would produce fiction films to serve state policies.

Italy

The Italian Fascist government took nearly a decade to develop its plans for cinema. Throughout the 1920s it concentrated its film activities on newsreel production, while commercial feature filmmaking fell into disarray (see Chapter 6). When the state turned its attention to the problem in the early 1930s, it found two strong models to draw upon—Hollywood and the Soviet Union. Hollywood's capitalist free enterprise mode of production showed the ability to make successful popular entertainment efficiently and in quantity; the Soviet socialist mode demonstrated the possibility of gaining wide prestige by making films combining art, ideology, and spectacle. Italy sought to adopt elements of both systems. It wanted to encourage films that merged Hollywood and Soviet styles, communicating ideology and political viewpoints in the form of popular entertainment.

The Soviet model fell into place first with the establishment in 1935 of the Centro Sperimentale di Cinematografia in Rome, a school to train filmmakers as well as develop film criticism and theory. The Hollywood model followed in 1938 with the opening of Cinecittà, a studio complex on the outskirts of Rome designed to concentrate and organize the film production process. The government also supported filmmaking through quota laws and

ALESSANDRO BLASETTI. An effective synthesis of ideology and popular style was achieved during the Fascist era in the films of Alessandro Blasetti (1900–1987), a neglected figure in film history. Beginning with *Sole* ("Sun," 1929), Blasetti directed a number of the period's important films; his career continued through the 1960s. In *Terra madre* ("Mother Earth," 1930) and *1860* (1934), two of his major works, evocative images of the rural countryside, photographed with lengthy panning camera movements, supported the ideological theme that the land and the peasantry were foundations for national values. *Terra madre* concerns an aristocrat who neglects his country estates to live as a city playboy; an unscrupulous manager plots to steal the land while the peasants who farm it are demoralized and indifferent. Awakened to his responsibility through the love of a country woman, the aristocrat returns, defeats the villain, and vows to fulfill his traditional role, rooted in the land. *1860* is a historical film about the era when Italy was united as a single nation; its story of Giuseppe Garibaldi's campaign to liberate Sicily from foreign rule focuses less on the hero than on efforts of rural people to achieve their place in the new nation.

Germany

The situation in Germany when the Nazis gained power in January 1933 was different from that of Italy. Though hard hit by world depression and domestic political turmoil, the German film industry remained a major force in international cinema, pro-

Right: 10.3. Blasetti's 1860 (1934), a historical film on the unification of Italy, treated Giuseppe Garibaldi's campaign to liberate Sicily less as a moment of heroism than as a struggle of rural people to make a place in the new nation.

Below: 10.4. Fritz Lang returned to the archcriminal of his 1922 film, Dr. Mabuse der Spieler, for a sequel he later described as a parable on Nazi "terror methods," Das Testament des Dr. Mabuse (The Last Will of Dr. Mabuse, 1933); the Nazis banned the film on the grounds that it might encourage terrorism against the state. Here Dr. Baum (Oscar Beregi, left), head of a mental institution, has fallen under the spell of Mabuse (Rudolf Klein-Rogge), and commits crimes that Mabuse orders.

ducing over one hundred films yearly and earning a third of its income from other countries. Hitler's regime was determined to take over this industry, as well as every other aspect of culture and society, and utilize cinema in spreading its ideology and strengthening its grip on the country. Within its first weeks the Nazi government set up a Ministry of Popular Enlightenment and Propaganda under Joseph Goebbels. Speaking to film industry leaders, Goebbels proposed to "radically reform German films" and praised Eisenstein's Soviet work *The Battleship Potemkin* for propagating "even the worst kind of ideas . . . through the medium of an outstanding work of art."[1]

A day after his speech, Goebbels banned Fritz Lang's *Das Testament des Dr. Mabuse* (*The Last Will of Dr. Mabuse*, 1933). The official reason given was that it endangered "public order and security"; press accounts suggested that the criminal activities of the demonic Mabuse could encourage terrorist acts against the state. In later years Lang gave an equally cogent explanation, that the film "meant to show Hitler's terror methods as a parable."[2] In

one scene (to which either Goebbels or Lang could have referred) a demented scientist, possessed by Mabuse's spirit, looks directly toward the camera and hails the criminal as an "*Übermensch*" (superman) seeking to destroy and rule by terror. Lang claimed that, after banning the film, Goebbels offered him leadership of the German film industry; though often cited in film histories, this seems wholly mythical. The Nazis took over the film industry by their practice of *Gleichschaltung* (coordination), the term used to describe the placing of cultural and industrial sectors under state domination.

Lang chose exile, as did many other film workers who opposed Hitler's authoritarianism or feared his anti-Semitic threats. Émigrés included Robert Wiene, director of *The Cabinet of Dr. Caligari*; screenwriter (later director) Billy Wilder; and actors Conrad Veidt from *Dr. Caligari* and Peter Lorre from *M*. Wiene settled in France, but Wilder, Veidt, and Lorre were among scores of German film personnel who went on to forge important careers in Hollywood. (Not all succeeded. G. W. Pabst, director of *Pandora's Box* and other major Weimar films, made only one film in Hollywood, returned to France, and eventually wound up working in the Nazi cinema.)

With filmmaking under their control, the Nazis at first produced films glorifying their party's heroes and loyal followers, beginning with *SA–Mann Brand* (*S.A. Man Brand*), *Hitlerjunge Quex* (*Hitler Youth Quex*), and *Hans Westmar, Einer von Vielen* (*Hans Westmar, One of Many*), all 1933. These followed Hitler's views that propaganda should be direct; they dealt with recent and contemporary political events, *SA–Mann Brand* completely as fiction, the other two as fictionalized biographies of martyred Nazi youth. But Goebbels was critical of these works, and even temporarily banned *Hans Westmar* as being unworthy of the memory of the hero it commemorated. Goebbels believed ideology was better absorbed by spectators in entertainment form; while the regime produced several important documentaries (see Chapter 11) as well as political fiction films, the majority of its output was comedies and dramas. When studied at all, however, these films are treated primarily as propaganda; abhorrence of Nazism has perhaps prevented the sort of revaluation that cinema of the Italian Fascist era has undergone.

DETLEF SIERCK/DOUGLAS SIRK. The works of one Nazi filmmaker have attracted interest because this figure left Germany in 1937 and later became an important director of Hollywood melodramas under the name Douglas Sirk (1900–1987). His original name was Detlef Sierck, and his most widely known Nazi film is his last one, *La Habanera* (1937; the title refers to a dance of Cuban origin), which featured Zarah Leander (1900–1981), a dark-haired Swedish actress and singer who became a leading star of wartime Nazi musicals and melodramas. Filmed in Spain, the film purports to be set in Puerto Rico, and the narrative explicitly criticizes United States' rule over the island. Leander plays a Swedish woman on a holiday who impulsively marries a swarthy charmer, Don Pedro, who is revealed as a criminal figure in league with Washington officials to suppress knowledge of an epidemic that could harm tourism and the economy. A Swedish doctor leads her back to Aryan safety while the evil don dies of the disease. This was a model of the skilled entertainment picture Goebbels advocated, with an attractive star, songs, and melodrama as framework for ideology.

10.5. *Several early films made after the Nazis gained control of the German film industry gave heroic treatment to Nazi heroes. SA–Mann Brand (S.A. Man Brand, 1933), directed by Franz Seitz, was completely fictional, while others were based on actual figures. On its poster (designed by Julius U. Engelhardt), the film is described as "a life story of our age."*

Soviet Union

The situation in the Soviet Union differed considerably from that of Italy or Germany. As those countries tried to expand their role in international film culture and display their ideologies to the world, Soviet cinema turned inward; where Italy and Germany found models in the classic 1920s Soviet silent films, the U.S.S.R. repudiated those films and criticized their makers. The history of 1930s Soviet filmmaking—long hidden through suppression or distorted by state-approved versions—is emerging like a forgotten nightmare.

Soviet cinema went through a fundamental transformation between 1928 and 1935. Factors such as the political evolution of the Soviet state, bureaucratic and personal rivalries, and Stalin's increasingly cruel and capricious dictatorship all contributed to rejection of the previous decade's achievements as formalism and a demand for "socialist realism" in cinema (see Chapter 7). In practice, "realism" often meant a simplified visual style where both heroes and villains were bigger than life. Socialist realism's

10.6. *The Nazi minister of propaganda, Joseph Goebbels, preferred to communicate ideology indirectly through entertainment films rather than blatantly as in S.A. Man Brand. Detlef Sierck's La Habanera (1937), a film concerning a Swedish woman who marries a swarthy Puerto Rican and learns to rue her choice, was a good example. Swedish actress and singer Zarah Leander, a popular star of Nazi cinema, played the woman, and Karl Martell the Swedish doctor who rescues her; they are pictured here on a ship returning to the Aryan north. Sierck left Germany after this film; he later became a noted Hollywood director with the name Douglas Sirk.*

triumph was signaled in 1936 when Eisenstein's *Bezhin lug* (*Bezhin Meadow*) was banned and attacked by Boris Shumyatsky, head of the Soviet film industry, as "anti-artistic and politically quite unsound."[3] During 1935–36 some thirty-seven films, fully one-third of total production, were banned after completion and held back from release.

The goal of this repression was not only ideological correctness but also the creation of a popular entertainment cinema, especially after the importing of foreign films was halted. As in Hollywood, genre films dominated Soviet production; though many of these were fictional dramas set in the 1917–20 era of revolution and civil war (with actors portraying Lenin and Stalin as humble leaders of the people), there were also musical comedies. Grigori Alexandrov, who had worked with Eisenstein in the 1920s, was able to accommodate to the new policy and directed the popular musical *Volga-Volga* (1938). But Shumyatsky was increasingly criticized for insufficient production and money wasted on banned films. History books report that he was "dismissed," "deposed," or "removed," but these are euphemisms: he was denounced as a saboteur and executed in July 1938.

EISENSTEIN. Shumyatsky's downfall led to Eisenstein's rehabilitation. The director was assigned a project that became the most widely known of 1930s Soviet films, *Alexandr Nevskii* (*Alexander Nevsky*, 1938). Its source lay in the Soviet regime's growing perception of the threat of Nazi Germany. Eisenstein was called upon to make a historical epic based on events in the thirteenth century, when Russians led by Prince Alexander Nevsky repelled an invasion by German knights. This was Eisenstein's first sound film, and he enlisted Soviet composer Sergei Prokofiev to write a **score**. In commercial cinema, in Hollywood and elsewhere, composers of film scores went to work only after the image continuity was completely edited. Eisenstein's close collaboration with

Right: 10.7. Sergei Eisenstein, who came under attack as "politically unsound" in the Soviet Union's era of socialist realism, was rehabilitated to make Alexandr Nevskii (Alexander Nevsky, 1938), a historical film concerning events in the thirteenth century, when Russians led by Prince Alexander Nevsky turned back an invasion by German knights. Nevsky is shown in single combat with an enemy in the decisive Battle on the Ice.

Below: 10.8. After the victory, Nevsky (Nikolai Cherkasov) addresses his warriors, prisoners, clergy, and townspeople.

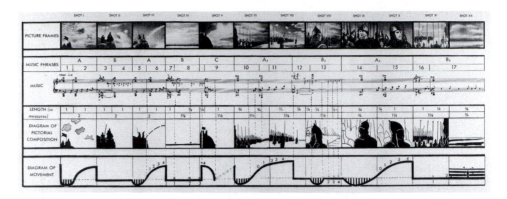

10.9. Eisenstein closely collaborated with composer Sergei Prokofiev for an unprecedented fusion of image and sound. He discussed the "audio-visual correspondence" in an essay, accompanied by this chart illustrating the relationship between music and pictorial composition in shots of the preparation for the Battle on the Ice.

Prokofiev was unprecedented: Prokofiev composed the music based on the director's sketches and shot plans, and Eisenstein cut the final footage to match movement and sound (he discusses the procedure in detail in "Form and Content: Practice," a chapter of his book *The Film Sense*). As a call to defend the Russian homeland, *Alexander Nevsky* was a political and popular success and restored Eisenstein's reputation. When the Nazis and Soviets signed a nonaggression pact in August 1939 the film was withdrawn, but it was released again after Germany invaded the Soviet Union in June 1941.

FILMMAKING OUTSIDE EUROPE

Outside Europe, United States domination in film was maintained or even grew with the coming of sound (Japan, as noted below, was a singular exception). Small and struggling film industries were burdened not only with the costs of acquiring sound equipment and wiring theaters but also in some cases (as in India and China) with the problem of multiple languages within national borders. Delays in converting to sound marked further setbacks for filmmakers seeking to compete with United States and European films in their own markets. Even more than the silent period, the first decade after sound outside Europe and Hollywood is a forgotten era of cinema history. Surviving films are little known even in their countries of origin, where they could serve as a significant cultural legacy. Circulation of such works in video format in the coming years may make more films part of a worldwide cinema history.

What is important is that, despite such odds, filmmaking persisted. In some cases it was lone individuals who struggled, in others it was businessmen with purely commercial motives. Many countries were able to produce only a handful of films annually; others got up to about a dozen. Mexico, with government support for its film industry and a quota system for its theaters, was making more than fifty films a year by the late 1930s. By 1940 India had attained third position behind Japan and the United States, with 171 films released that year, many of them song-and-dance melodramas that drew on Indian popular culture and could appeal to many different language groups in Indian society.

Japan

No film industry was more capable of responding to Hollywood's challenge than the Japanese. Japan rivaled Hollywood in volume of film production—each country averaged around five hundred features a year during the 1930s—and in industrial organization, with a powerful privately owned, vertically integrated studio system. In its home market the Japanese cinema was as dominant as Hollywood was in the United States, partially for the same reasons: studios that owned theaters showed their own films in preference to foreign competition. Domestic films claimed three-fourths of the box office at the beginning of the 1930s, and their share kept rising in an era of nationalistic fervor. Where Japanese films could not match Hollywood was in world influence, since few were screened outside the country's island borders.

Sweeping claims have been made for Japanese cinema of the 1930s, in which this cultural isolation plays a part. In a study of Japanese film published in 1979, theorist Noël Burch argued that Japan "has produced a cinema which is *in essence* unlike that of any other nation."[4] Few film scholars accept this viewpoint. It ignores Japan's broad interest in United States and European films, technologies, and cinematic practices, as well as positing an overly rigid and monolithic notion of a "Western" mode of representation. What remains of greatest value from this endeavor is its focus on the outstanding achievements of 1930s Japanese filmmaking, which deserves to be much more widely known.

One certain way that Japanese filmmaking of the 1930s differed from Hollywood's lay in the status of directors. In contrast to the Hollywood studio practice of placing control in producers' hands, Japanese directors maintained their artistic autonomy and creative independence. Like their counterparts in the United States, such as John Ford and Howard Hawks, Japan's leading directors of this era got their start in silent films, created some of the classics of the 1930s, and went on to make important films for nearly half a century. Most prominent among these figures were Kenji Mizoguchi (1898–1956) and Yasujiro Ozu (1903–1963).

KENJI MIZOGUCHI. Mizoguchi directed more than forty films before 1930; of these, only one survives, and this in an incomplete version. His films of the 1930s frequently centered on social injustices suffered by women. The first to place this theme in a contemporary setting was *Naniwa ereji* (*Naniwa Elegy*, but more generally known in English as *Osaka Elegy*, 1936). His mise-en-scène of modern offices and fashionably furnished apartments is as dark and starkly shadowed as the **film noir** interiors of post–World War II Hollywood, and the American pop songs on the soundtrack are ironic counterpoints to the oppression suffered by Ayoko, a telephone operator betrayed and cast out by all the men in her life—father, brother, boyfriend, boss. A shot displays her

entrapment: enclosed in her booth with the telephone apparatus, her face is visible only at the edge of the frame or faintly reflected from a windowpane as she observes her boyfriend accept an invitation from the boss's wife.

YASUJIRO OZU. Ozu worked often in a genre known as *shomin-geki*, films about the daily life of middle-class people. His approach mixed comedy and pathos. *Umarate wa mita keredo* (*I Was Born, But . . .*, 1932) was his first major work, winning a Japanese magazine's poll as best film in a year when two other of his films also ranked in the top ten. It concerns everyday events in the lives of two young brothers whose parents have moved into the suburbs. The camera, placed at the height of a child's eyes, moves and pans as the newcomers get picked on by local youths, skip school out of fear of a bully, and gradually make their way into the group. The poignant comedy suddenly turns dark when the neighborhood children and their fathers are invited to a boss's

10.12. Ruan Lingyo, described by film historian Jay Leyda as "one of the great actresses of film history, as perfectly and peculiarly adapted to the film as we recognize Greta Garbo to be," is finally becoming known outside China as her films from the 1930s begin to circulate internationally. In Shen nu (The Goddess, 1934), directed by Wu Yonggang, Ruan Lingyo (at left) portrays a woman working as a prostitute to support her child's education.

house to watch home movies shot at the office. The brothers see their father clowning and making faces, but when other boys say "Your father's funny," they're offended. "You're a nobody! You're a nothing!" they accuse their father (in English intertitles to this silent film). They rejoin the camaraderie of their school chums, where power and status mimic but do not reflect the adult world of class difference.

China

Among the many neglected histories of film production before World War II, one that has begun to attract international scholarly attention is China's. This interest stems in part from efforts to understand the background to the emergence of an important film movement in China in the 1980s (see Chapter 24). But it has been sustained by discoveries of a significant effort in the 1930s to make films with strong social purpose. Responding to the Japanese invasion of northeast China in 1931 and a Japanese bombing raid on the city of Shanghai in 1932, progressive Chinese filmmakers, some associated with the Communist party, began to make films exposing social problems and promoting national unity and defense.

Two exemplary works, both made in 1934, were *Shen nu* (*The Goddess*) and *Da Lu* (*The Big Road*). The first was a silent film, the other had sound effects and music, along with dialogue intertitles. Starring China's leading film actress, Ruan Lingyo (1910–1935), *The Goddess* was the first directorial effort of Wu

Mexican Cinema

In its early development Mexican cinema was strongly influenced by films made in Italy, and the histories of the two film industries follow somewhat similar patterns: a period of strength around World War I, a nadir during the 1920s, and a revival during the 1930s with state support.

Bordering the United States, Mexico was as vulnerable as any country to domination by American films, but it also made its contribution to American cinema when performers with few opportunities at home pursued careers north of the border. These included Antonio Moreno (1886–1967), a Hollywood leading man of the 1920s who was cast as Greta Garbo's lover in her second American film, *The Temptress* (1926); Dolores del Rio (1905–1983), who played important roles in Hollywood and Mexican films for more than forty years; and Lupe Veléz (1909–1944), who was typed as the "Mexican Spitfire" in a B-picture series of the early 1940s.

With the coming of sound, Hollywood studios experimented with Spanish-language production, but these films foundered, in part because Latin American audiences would not accept the medley of regional accents the performers offered. The possibility of reaching an international Spanish-language market gave new energy to Mexican filmmaking. Antonio Moreno returned from Hollywood to direct the first Mexican sound film, *Santa* (1932). The next year more than twenty sound features were produced at two studios, with budgets, according to Carl J. Mora, a historian of Mexican cinema, averaging from $5,700 to $8,500 (the cheapest Hollywood studio films of this period cost about $150,000 to produce).

In 1934 a new political administration in Mexico gave financial support to a production company, CLASA (Cinematográfica Latino Americana, S.A.), to build a modern studio, but it did not fully put in place a state cinema on the model of Italy, Germany, or the Soviet Union. Observers at the time noted that the Mexican cinema's greatest problem was that private investment looked to filmmaking for quick profits rather than to build an industry. Spain soon surpassed Mexico as the dominant producer of Spanish-language films.

10.13. El compadre Mendoza (1933), directed by Fernando de Fuentes (1894–1958), is regarded as a classic of early Mexican sound cinema. Much of the film's significance derived from its setting during the 1913–15 struggles of the Mexican revolution. Through a narrative of a landowner's unsuccessful attempts to balance his relations with competing forces, it portrays the betrayal of revolutionary ideals.

10.14. Another important film of the period, Janitzio (1934), directed by Carlos Navarro, was a narrative of Indian life in a fishing village on the island of Janitzio. It drew on Robert Flaherty's documentaries and Sergei Eisenstein's aborted filmmaking project in Mexico for a visual style conveying the character of native life through its imagery, as in this shot of fishing nets hung out to dry.

Indian Cinema

By the end of the 1930s India, though a colony of Britain until after World War II, became the third-largest film-producing country, behind the United States and Japan, and laid the groundwork for later decades when it moved to the forefront as the perennial leader in total film releases. How did this come about, especially since up until the late 1920s, as in many other lands, Indian theaters played mostly Hollywood films?

A primary reason is that the coming of sound, rather than causing a crisis or entrenching United States domination, created new opportunities. India was a country of at least fifteen major languages and many more dialects, and each language group was eager to see films with its own spoken dialogue. "Hear your Gods and Goddesses talk in your own language" was a slogan adopted by regional film producers. Filmmakers also found, however, that traditional music—which occurred in two principal forms widely shared among disparate language groups—could reach audiences across narrow linguistic barriers.

Indian sound cinema quickly became dominated by musical films. *Indra Sabha* (1932), for example, contained some seventy songs. Performers had to sing as well as act, and newcomers with appealing voices became not only stars but instant celebrities. Film music in recordings and played on radio attained an importance in Indian popular culture beyond that of the films themselves. Indian film music, however, was different from the musical scores composed for films in the United States or Europe: it put emphasis on lyrics as a continuation of spoken dialogue, with words in song carrying the narrative.

Below: 10.15. Indian film studios sought to adopt the Hollywood mode of production, employing hundreds of creative and craft workers on a permanent basis. One of the first firms utilizing this model was the Prabhat Film Company, organized in 1929 in Kolhapur and located in Poona after 1933. Among its founders was the director Rajaram Vanakudre Shantaram, who went by the professional name V. Shantaram (b. 1901). He began making sound films in 1932, and his seventh sound feature, Amar Jyoti (Eternal Light, 1936), was selected for screening at the fourth Venice film festival in Italy. A spectacle film set in a mythological past, it concerns a woman who is mistreated by her husband, but whose protests result in her son being taken from her. She forms a group of similarly illtreated women who enlist a band of pirates to fight for their side. Ultimately she is united with her son and gives up her power to him and his bride.

10.16. Another important production unit, New Theatres Ltd., was organized in Calcutta in 1930. One of the filmmakers who joined it was an independent producer, Pramathesh Chandra Barua (1903–1951), son of a rajah, who wrote, directed, and occasionally performed in his own films. Barua's films dealt with contemporary social themes and often featured a doomed hero (or heroine). One such figure was portrayed by Pahari Sanyal in Barua's Maya (Illusion, 1936).

10.17. Da Lu (The Big Road, 1934), directed by Sun Yu, concerns Chinese workers building a road to help defend against an "enemy," unnamed but clearly the Japanese. Lacking spoken dialogue, the film has an experimental soundtrack with percussion sounds when the workers playfully touch.

Yonggang (1907–1983). Though linked to the "fallen woman" genre of Hollywood and European cinema, *The Goddess* was less a genre picture than a work committed to a presentation of social conditions. A prostitute, working to support her child's education, murders a gambler who stole her money. Imprisoned, she is consoled that others have recognized her motives and will aid her child's future.

The Big Road was written and directed by Sun Yu (1900–1990), who had attended the University of Wisconsin and studied film at Columbia University in New York. It concerns a gang of road workers who struggle against a collaborationist landlord and "the enemy," clearly the Japanese. Without spoken dialogue, the film's experimental soundtrack is marked by songs and percussion sounds when the workers touch each other in playful gestures. At the end, an "enemy" airplane strafes the road and kills several workers, but their spirits rise from the dead (in **superimposition**) to help the survivors continue building the road.

BRITAIN

One national cinema that seemed in a position to gain from the coming of sound was Britain's. The British possessed a literary tradition and an imperial history that have served as sources for films made in many countries over nearly a century. They had superbly trained stage performers who spoke the English language with an elegance and clarity few Americans could match. But well-entrenched industrial patterns made it difficult for significant changes to occur. Hollywood motion picture companies dominated British film distribution and about three-quarters of the films that played in Britain were made in the United States. British actors were much in demand across the Atlantic, and many practiced their precise diction on Hollywood sound stages.

The strongest catalyst for change in British cinema was a 1927 law setting up a quota—a minimum percentage of British films theaters were required to show. The quota started at 7.5 percent

and rose annually to around 20 percent after a decade. The Cinematograph Films Act, as it was called, had an immediate impact on British production. The percentage of British films shown in theaters jumped immediately from under 5 percent to over 12 percent, and climbed to nearly 30 percent by 1936, a year when total British production surpassed two hundred films.

But what kind of films? The quota law defined a qualifying film as anything over three thousand feet in length—just over thirty minutes. The Hollywood-owned distributors found they could fulfill the requirements by financing cheap films of minimal length and quality, known as "quota quickies," that theaters rented but played only at off hours, or not at all. In quantitative terms Britain had the third-largest volume of films produced during the 1930s, but a considerable share were films hardly meant to be screened. Their principal virtue was the experience they provided aspiring filmmakers. An example is Michael Powell (1905–1990), a major British director of the World War II and postwar periods, who got his start directing forty-minute quickies in the early 1930s. Powell, who later formed a partnership with screenwriter Emeric Pressburger (1902–1988), is known for works such as *The Red Shoes* (1948) and *Peeping Tom* (1960).

In the 1930s British films were thus, like the products of most other national cinemas, primarily for domestic consumption. Particularly successful in regional and small-town theaters were popular comedies featuring music hall stars. Still, British filmmaking in its smaller way was quite as cosmopolitan as Hollywood,

10.18. Charles Laughton's portrayal of the English monarch Henry VIII as a likable lout won him Hollywood's Academy Award as best actor, and Alexander Korda's The Private Life of Henry VIII (1933) became British cinema's first big international success.

with strong ties especially to Central Europe. International coproductions with German companies were not uncommon in the late silent and early sound period. The filmmaker who successfully developed the cinematic potential of Britain's heritage and imperial history, Alexander Korda (1893–1956), came from this international milieu.

Alexander Korda

Korda, a Hungarian-born producer-director, had worked in Budapest, Vienna, Berlin, Hollywood for four years, and Paris before arriving in London in 1931 with a contract from British Paramount. He laid his foundation with quota quickies, but his desire was to crack the Hollywood market, not as the studio employee he had been, but on his own terms. Starting his own company, London Films, and backed by a distribution deal with United Artists, he scored the first big international success for a British picture with *The Private Life of Henry VIII* (1933). It was the first British film nominated for an American Academy Award, and its star, Charles Laughton, won the Oscar as best actor.

The Private Life of Henry VIII was perhaps British history as only a non-Britisher could imagine it: half historical pageant, half comic farce. Though listed as director, Korda by this time was most heavily involved as a producer, and the picture's "authorship" belongs as much to Laughton, who plays the "bluebeard" monarch with six wives as a likable lout, and its designer, Alexander's brother Vincent Korda. Korda's success enabled him to become a partner in United Artists in 1935, and he produced more than twenty films for the company over the next five years, many in the historical and imperial genres he helped to launch.

Alfred Hitchcock

The most important British filmmaker of the 1930s was Alfred Hitchcock (1899–1980). His early experience as a director of British-German coproductions (see Chapter 6) led him toward an expressionist mise-en-scène in his first sound films, but he gradually abandoned visual—and aural—symbolism for an emphasis on editing as a means of involving the spectator.

"The screen ought to speak its own language, freshly coined," Hitchcock wrote in 1938, "and it can't do that unless it treats an acted scene as a piece of raw material which must be broken up, taken to bits, before it can be woven into an expressive visual pattern. . . . You gradually build up the psychological situation, piece by piece, using the camera to emphasize first one detail, then another. The point is to draw the audience right inside the situation instead of leaving them to watch it outside, from a distance."[5]

Hitchcock's style began distinctively to emerge in *The Man Who Knew Too Much* (1934) and *The 39 Steps* (1935), made for Gaumont British, one of Britain's "major" studios. Both works dealt with espionage and international intrigue, subjects not yet part of Hollywood's genre repertory, which gave them a quality of freshness they still retain. Hitchcock utilized classically edited scene breakdowns to place spectators in a multiple field of commitments to the narrative—as moviegoers, as vicarious members of audiences within the film, and as potential participants. The palpable tension this strategy can create is exemplified in the Albert Hall concert sequence of *The Man Who Knew Too Much* as each shot builds the level of suspense and anxiety until a character screams, disrupting the concert and foiling an assassination.

The 39 Steps remains one of the most memorable films of Hitchcock's half-century career as a director, and a triumph of

Above: 10.19. *Alfred Hitchcock's* The Man Who Knew Too Much *(1934) revived the espionage genre and was another British success. From left, villains Frank Vosper and Peter Lorre, embattled hero Leslie Banks.*

Opposite: 10.20. *Escaping from spies, Richard Hannay (Robert Donat) finds himself at a political rally in Hitchcock's* The 39 Steps *(1935).*

popular cinema in the 1930s. Much of its appeal lies in Hitchcock's capacity to unite his style and themes of spectatorship and performance. The opening sequence is exemplary: four quick shots convey the spectator into a seat in an English music hall; an atmosphere of popular entertainment and audience back-talk is evoked as a performer named Mr. Memory comes on stage, and the line between performer and audience is blurred; finally, out of this welter, emerges a man who makes himself visible by asking Mr. Memory a question. This man, Richard Hannay (played by Robert Donat), will become the film's hero. Many suspenseful and exciting scenes follow, but all are founded on the premise of this first sequence. Falsely accused of murder, Hannay must continually change identities and improvise performances to solve a crime, prevent spies from stealing secrets, and forge a romance. The film returns to the music hall stage for its poignant and satisfying resolution.

Hitchcock left for Hollywood in 1938, as the ten-year boom in British cinema was ending. The scheme to compete internationally had led to increased production costs and greater borrowing, while American companies preferred to import British filmmakers rather than play British films in their theaters. In a year British production dropped 60 percent, to less than one hundred films annually, on the eve of the nation's entry into World War II in September 1939.

FRANCE

As it turned out, the strongest response to Hollywood's challenge during the 1930s came from France. In one sense, France's leading role was obvious; in another, paradoxically, surprising. The obvious reasons begin with French film culture—broader, more vigorous, more eclectic than anywhere else. The French came to terms more readily than other national film cultures with the medium's dual possibilities as popular entertainment and high art. They linked their commercial industry more closely with experimental and avant-garde filmmaking. They managed to admire Hollywood's achievement without undue resentment, while also supporting domestic productions. Their capacity for innovation in both film theory and practice was spurred by the coming of sound.

The surprising part is that France's film industry was weak at the beginning of the decade and ripe for domination. Unable to finance the transition to sound, the industry was invaded from Germany by Tobis-Klangfilm and from Hollywood by Paramount. Each set up studios near Paris to produce films in French and other languages. For Tobis, René Clair, director of the Surrealist classics *Paris qui dort* and *Entr'acte*, made a series of early sound features, including *Sous les toits de Paris* (*Under the Roofs of Paris*, 1930), *Le Million* (*The Million*, 1931), and *À Nous la liberté*

(*Give Us Liberty*, 1931). At its Joinville studio in France Paramount made an astonishing one hundred features in a year (many were multiple productions of the same narrative in different languages). But economic setbacks caused by the depression forced Paramount to abandon its French effort, and Tobis soon after retreated to Germany with the Nazi takeover of the German film industry. French filmmaking went back into the hands of the French.

Film production in France was structured differently than in any of the other major film-producing countries. After the departure of Paramount and Tobis, no major studios dominated the scene. Quota regulations were abandoned in the early 1930s, under considerable American pressure, and the government intervened little in film production (except for censorship of completed films). What emerged was an industry of small producers, able to raise financing for over one hundred new releases annually through the 1930s. If state control over cinema was a dominant trend of the decade, as in Italy and Germany, France went strongly against the grain, to a system of individual filmmakers operating independently.

Poetic Realism

If French cinema lacked a dominant trend provided by government direction or studio methods, however, shared social and

aesthetic concerns produced a distinctive style of French filmmaking in the 1930s. This was called *poetic realism*—a broad term with many meanings, yet with an overall clarity of purpose. It implied first of all fidelity to milieu: to the settings of everyday life, usually of working people and lower classes, rather than the lavish fantasy worlds that Hollywood created and the fascist cinemas of Germany and Italy emulated. Within these authentic atmospheres, characters were driven by destinies larger than themselves, by implacable fate. This could be understood through political ideology, or as a form of social determinism. Yet the "poetic" aspect of this realism was attained not only through the aesthetic evocation of social ambiance, but also by the characters' struggles to transcend fate and achieve important life goals.

JEAN VIGO. One of the most compelling visions of poetic realism was created by Jean Vigo (1905–1934) in a brief, tragic career that included only a single feature-length fiction film. The son of an anarchist who was murdered in prison during World War I, Vigo embodied in his work the anarchist ideal of forging unity through the collaboration of free individuals. On his four films—two short documentaries, the short fiction film *Zéro de conduite* (*Zero for Conduct*, 1933), and *L'Atalante* (1934)—he worked with cinematographer Boris Kaufman (1906–1980), a younger brother of Soviet documentarian Dziga Vertov. Kaufman later went to Hollywood and won an Academy Award for cinematography on *On the Waterfront* (1954). For his two fiction films Vigo utilized composer Maurice Jaubert (1900–1940), who went on to write some three dozen additional scores for French films in the 1930s. Shaping his film music to the narrative and stylistic needs of specific films, Jaubert contributed significantly to the movement of poetic realism. He was killed in action just before France surrendered to Germany in World War II.

10.21. The pillow fight in Jean Vigo's Zéro de conduite (Zero for Conduct, 1933), an anthem for students

10.22. Jean Dasté (right) as Jean, the barge captain, and Dita Parlo as Juliette, his bride, enjoy a moment of marital bliss in Vigo's L'Atalante (1934).

song about barge life. The film's sentimentality is leavened by Simon's raucous performance and sometimes leering humor (as in the scene where the woman explores his cabin and he shows her his tattoos), as well as by the ambient songs and accordion music contributed by Jaubert. Circulated for years in cut versions, a restored *L'Atalante* was released in 1990 to new acclaim as a remarkable achievement in cinema history.

MARCEL PAGNOL. A different form of realism shaped the films of Marcel Pagnol (1895–1974); heavy on dialogue, they seemed stage-bound, but they also languidly explored the everyday social world. Pagnol was a successful playwright who shifted to cinema with the coming of sound. Paramount acquired several of his stage works concerning life in the southern port city Marseilles; he wrote the screenplay for one, *Marius* (1931), directed by Alexander Korda, and produced another, *Fanny* (1932), directed by Marc Allégret (1900–1973). But Pagnol wanted greater artistic control, and in 1933 he set up his own studio in Marseilles, where he began also to direct. This venture marked Pagnol's commitment to regional cinema at a time when production was being centralized in film's "capitals": Hollywood, Tokyo, London, Berlin, Rome. His leisurely, low-key family melodramas may owe as much to this regional flavor as to his theatrical aesthetics. He directed *César* (1936), which carried forward the characters of *Marius* and *Fanny*; the three works by three different directors, but united by Pagnol's common narrative, are

Above: 10.23. Playwright Marcel Pagnol set up his own studio in Marseilles and directed César *(1936), the final film of his trilogy about everyday life in Marseilles; previously he wrote the script for* Marius *(1931) and produced* Fanny *(1932).*

Right: 10.24. Jean Gabin as the doomed François, Arletty as Clara, in Le Jour se lève *(Daybreak, 1939), Marcel Carné's classic of poetic realism*

known as the "Marseilles trilogy." Though often neglected in film history, Pagnol's legacy was refreshed in the 1980s when his writings and films served as sources for director Claude Berri's *Jean de Florette* and *Manon des sources* (*Manon of the Spring*; both 1986).

MARCEL CARNÉ. The most characteristic embodiment of poetic realism, for many critics, came in the films of Marcel Carné (b. 1909), though the filmmaker's directing career began late in the 1930s. Three important films in little more than a year—*Le Quai des brumes* (*Port of Shadows*, 1938), *Hôtel du nord* (1938), and *Le Jour se lève* (*Daybreak*, 1939)—seemed to move beyond the realm of art or entertainment into national symbolism. The working-class hero of *Le Jour se lève*, portrayed by popular star Jean Gabin (1904–1976), is significantly named François—as a woman he loves is named Françoise. Tormented by a diabolical

Zéro de conduite is less a work of poetic realism than an anthem for students. With strong ties to 1920s Surrealist films, it depicts a boys' boarding school as a world mingling the comic and grotesque. It climaxes in a spontaneous dormitory uprising, where the boys stage a pillow fight shouting, "It's war! Down with school! Down with teachers!" The scene ends with a procession filmed in slow motion with floating pillow feathers filling the screen like snowflakes. The next morning the rebels take to the roof, raise a skull-and-crossbones flag, and bombard the school's alumni day activities with a shower of tin cans. The censors saw the film's spirit of revolt as a threat to public order, and it was banned in France until 1945.

Made during the director's final illness, *L'Atalante* is a work of overwhelming lyricism and poignancy. The skipper of a river barge (the barge's name gives the film its title) marries a provincial bourgeois woman. Their life aboard ship is alternatively idyllic and troubled, complicated by an irascible, curmudgeonly first mate, portrayed by one of the stars of 1930s French cinema, actor Michel Simon (1895–1975). When they dock on the Seine near Paris, the woman, yearning for the city's lively pleasures, leaves the boat; miffed, her husband pulls up anchor and leaves without her. Apart, each is lonely and miserable. Seeking to reunite the couple, the first mate hunts for her, and finds her listening to a

sadist, François, strong and honest but also innocent and passive, impulsively shoots his antagonist. The film starts with the shooting and tells its story in **flashback**, leading up to police besieging his room and François's suicide. Though inevitably analyzed as a metaphor for France's condition on war's eve, the film holds even greater interest in its articulation of poetic realism through characters' feelings and the dynamics of human relations. Carné collaborated closely on this and all but one other of his prewar films with screenwriter Jacques Prévert (1900–1977). Maurice Jaubert also composed the scores of all but one; for *Le Jour se lève* his music was more quiet and atmospheric than what he had written for Vigo.

Jean Renoir

All labels, poetic realism included, explode before the breadth and variety of Jean Renoir's cinematic achievement of the 1930s. It was Renoir (1894–1979) who, in the face of Paramount and Tobis incursions, maintained French independent production in the early sound period with such films as *La Chienne* (*The Bitch*, 1931) and *Boudu sauvé des eaux* (*Boudu Saved from Drowning*, 1932); who led the way toward socially committed cinema in the mid-1930s with *Le Crime de M. Lange* (*The Crime of M. Lange*, 1935), the political campaign film *La Vie est à nous* (*Life Is Ours*, also known as *People of France*, 1936), and *Les Bas-fonds* (*The Lower Depths*, 1936); who raised the issues of war and history in *La Grande Illusion* (*Grand Illusion*, 1937) and *La Marseillaise*

Left: 10.25. A characteristic shot from Jean Renoir's Le Crime de M. Lange (The Crime of M. Lange, 1935): varied movement throughout the frame, movement in depth, and a sense of collective endeavor

Above: 10.26. Erich von Stroheim as German officer von Rauffenstein in Renoir's film concerning French prisoners in World War I, La Grande Illusion (Grand Illusion, 1937)

Below: 10.27. In La Règle du jeu (Rules of the Game, 1939) Renoir shaped a style—using a moving camera, long takes, depth of field, and contrapuntal sound and image tracks—that marked a strong antithesis to Hollywood's norms. Though it is difficult to convey the fullness of that style through film stills, they do represent the film's social themes, which led to its being banned in France shortly after its release. The Marquis de la Chesnaye (Marcel Dalio, at right) greets weekend guests at his country estate; they include the two men at left, aviator André Jurieu (Roland Toutain) and Octave (played by Renoir), while the marquise (Nora Grégor) stands at center.

(1938). He made so many superior films during the decade that it is almost impossible to give each its due, and topped all the rest with one of the great works of cinema history, *La Règle du jeu* (*Rules of the Game*, 1939). Yet this last prewar work was booed by French audiences, cut first by the production company and then by Renoir in an effort to create a less offending version, and banned as demoralizing by the French government after the outbreak of war.

The two Renoir works that have attained the firmest status as film classics are *Grand Illusion* and *Rules of the Game*. Both mark the most striking departure in film technique since the Soviet experiments with montage in the 1920s. Renoir's stylistic repertory included deep space in the frame, also known as **deep focus** or **depth of field**; a constantly moving camera, utilizing rack focus, or change of focus in a shot; long takes; and dissonant or contrapuntal use of the sound- and visual tracks. Into the complex mise-en-scène that this camera style made possible Renoir poured as rich and varied an array of characters as can be found in cinema.

The French critic André Bazin (1918–1958), writing in the 1950s, distinguished Renoir's style by naming it "realism" as opposed to montage, but this simply underlines how slippery and vague—how variable—notions of film realism usually are. What Bazin stressed was a style that emphasized "unity of image in space and time," as opposed to one (such as Alfred Hitchcock expounded) that breaks down an image into bits and then recon-

structs it.[6] Bazin found elements of this "realist" style in several filmmakers, including Hollywood directors William Wyler and Orson Welles, and indeed isolated aspects appear in many films. But no other director created, as Renoir did, a style so distinctive and thorough as to become, in the sum of its parts, virtually the antithesis of Hollywood's norms.

The narrative of *Grand Illusion* takes place during World War I among French prisoners of war held by the Germans; it suggests the core of common humanity shared by ordinary people in the midst of national antagonisms. Yet along with the universality of this antiwar theme, *Grand Illusion* also explores boundaries of nationality and social class. Its power rests in considerable part on its performances, an intertextual feast beginning with American director Erich von Stroheim in the role of the German officer von Rauffenstein, and including Jean Gabin, Pierre Fresnay (from *César*), and even Jean Dasté and Dita Parlo, the barge skipper and his wife from *L'Atalante*.

In *Rules of the Game* Renoir maintained the theme of social boundaries but avoided using stars and cast himself as Octave, the mediator between the film's worlds of aristocrats and servants. Its principal setting is the country estate of the Marquis de la Chesnaye, where multiple desires play out amid multiple misunderstandings on several social levels. If many films repay several viewings, the visual complexity of *Rules of the Game* demands them, to unveil the film's plural planes of action and feelings in its mobile mise-en-scène. "It is a war film, and yet there is no refer-

ence to the war," Renoir wrote in his autobiography. "Beneath its seemingly innocuous appearance the story attacks the very structure of our society."[7]

Few spectators saw the film as innocuous, and many recognized its attack on the structure of society. For some, it was enough that he had cast a Jewish actor, Marcel Dalio, and an Austrian émigré, Nora Grégor, in the roles of a French marquis and marquise. For others, it was the blend of farce and tragedy, reminiscent of *Le Mariage de Figaro,* the eighteenth-century drama by Pierre Beaumarchais in which the play of desire and misunderstanding across social classes had signaled the exhaustion of an earlier French social structure. *Rules of the Game* demonstrated the capacity of individual filmmakers, operating independently, to shape social meaning with even greater power than the propaganda works of state cinemas, and the furious reaction to the film and its subsequent banning indicated the limits of tolerance for such independence in the crisis of impending war. Not until 1959 was there a restored version of the film that closely approximated Renoir's original intentions, before cuts were made even prior to its original release. It was, significantly, on the eve of the emergence of the French New Wave (see Chapter 17) that the film's challenge to Hollywood's dominant stylistics began fully to be recognized.

Notes

1. David Welch, *Propaganda and the German Cinema 1933–1945* (Oxford, England: Oxford University Press, 1983), pp. 16–17.
2. Quotes from Lotte Eisner, *Fritz Lang* (London: Secker & Warburg, 1976), pp. 129–30.
3. Boris Shumyatsky, "The Film *Bezhin Meadow,*" in *The Film Factory: Russian and Soviet Cinema in Documents*, eds. Richard Taylor and Ian Christie (Cambridge, Mass.: Harvard University Press, 1988), p. 380.
4. Noël Burch, *To the Distant Observer: Form and Meaning in the Japanese Cinema* (Berkeley and Los Angeles: University of California Press, 1979), p. 11.
5. Alfred Hitchcock, "Direction," in *Footnotes to the Film*, ed. Charles Davy (London: Lovat Dickson and Readers' Union, 1938), pp. 7–8.
6. André Bazin, "The Evolution of the Language of Cinema," in *What Is Cinema?*, ed. and trans. Hugh Gray (Berkeley and Los Angeles: University of California Press, 1967), p. 35.
7. Jean Renoir, *My Life and My Films*, trans. Norman Denny (New York: Atheneum, 1974), p. 171.

ELEVEN

DOCUMENTARY, AND

The 1930s marked a revival of **documentary**, or nonfiction, film-making. For many filmmakers, it was an era of social and political upheaval that cried out for recording as moving images. For governments (as noted in Chapter 10), it was a moment to utilize the possibilities of film for propaganda and persuasion. Some part of this renewed interest derived from the advent of sound: actuality footage could be enhanced and dramatized with booming orchestrations and portentous narrations, which critics in later years would call "the voice of God."

Since the earliest years, when fiction supplanted actualities as cinema grew toward mass entertainment, documentaries had played only a minor role in public consciousness of the medium. Before the coming of sound, no more than a handful of nonfiction films had gained commercial distribution in Europe and the United States. The number of important filmmakers whose work was identified with documentary was equally small: Robert Flaherty, the director of *Nanook of the North* and *Moana*, the most prominent among a few explorers and adventurers who took their cameras to "exotic" corners of the world; and in the Soviet Union, Esfir Shub and Dziga Vertov, the intractable advocate of the primacy of documentary over fiction. But at the end of the 1920s Flaherty was fighting a losing battle to maintain a foothold

in the American film industry, and Vertov was facing increasing hostility from a Soviet film bureaucracy decisively committed to fiction.

Prior to 1930, nonfiction filmmaking was increasingly regarded as a branch of the emerging avant-garde film movement, rather than as a genre on its own or as an important contributor to the documentation of social actuality. A strong interest of the avant-garde was to capture the rhythms and contrasts of the modern city, and the documentary impulse went into a small group of films that have come to be labeled **city symphonies** after what was perhaps the most ambitious of them, *Berlin: Die Sinfonie der Grossstadt* (*Berlin: Symphony of a Great City*, 1927).

THE CITY SYMPHONY

Berlin: Symphony of a Great City involved Carl Mayer, scriptwriter of *Dr. Caligari*, and Karl Freund, cinematographer on *The Last Laugh* and *Metropolis*, but ultimately it was the work of Walther Ruttmann (1887–1941), who edited the film and was credited as director. Ruttmann's background was as an abstract painter and maker of abstract short films, and his interest in visualizing the modern city was to shape abstract patterns from its

11.1. *Walther Ruttmann's* Berlin: Die Sinfonie der Grosstadt (Berlin: Symphony of a Great City, *1927) sought to capture the* kaleidoscopic movement of urban life and gave its name to a group of films called "city symphonies."

daily activities. The film traces a day in the city's life, from early morning, when trains carrying commuters speed toward its center, to nightlife after dark. It refuses a viewpoint on the experience it observes, except for its delight in the movement and juxtaposition, through editing, of images as abstract forms.

A very different version of the city symphony was the first Jean Vigo–Boris Kaufman collaboration, *A Propos de Nice* (*On the Subject of Nice*, 1930). The film is strongly in the Surrealist mode, filled with visual jokes and shock cuts—a shoe being shined turns into a bare foot; a series of shots of a woman, seated in the same position but each time in a different dress, ends with her nude. Exuberant and disorderly, the film contrasts the staid, attenuated life of Nice's posh hotels with the erotic carnivalesque energy of its working-class back streets.

Historians have pointed out how this, Vigo's first film, presaged the humanistic triumph of his *L'Atalante*, while Ruttmann after 1933 pursued his empty abstractionism as a Nazi propagandist.

PROPAGANDA, POLITICS

Documentaries cannot escape analysis of their ethical or didactic purpose. From Vertov's *Kino-Pravda* newsreels (see Chapter 7) to a later generation's notion of cinema verité (see Chapter 19), non-fiction filmmakers have sometimes claimed that pointing a camera at a subject (or assembling such shots at an editing table) produced "filmed truth." Instead, most documentaries produce a lively debate about what truth is and whether the filmmaker has come close to capturing it. Unlike fiction films, which often distract us with their narratives and star performances, documentaries usually expose the fact that a film's "reality" is constructed. They enable us to ask fundamental questions: Why was the camera placed where it was? Why did this shot follow that one? What is the film trying to tell us, and what means did the filmmaker employ to present a viewpoint? These are necessary questions for the 1930s revival of the documentary, which was preeminently about presenting viewpoints.

BRITISH DOCUMENTARY

The first signs of documentary's resurgence came not in the totalitarian countries, where film industries were instruments of state policy, but in Britain, where in a somewhat different manner state policy decided to make use of film. The Empire Marketing Board (EMB), a government body responsible for promoting products of Britain, its dominions, and its colonies, began in the 1920s to explore film as a means, as the board's secretary recalled, "for bringing the Empire alive to the imagination of the public." It commissioned a feature-length film "which began gloriously with shots of society ladies impersonating the different Dominions in the Throne Room at Buckingham Palace."[1] The word "gloriously" is used in this context with irony. A new approach was called for.

John Grierson

Seizing the opportunity was John Grierson (1898–1972), after Flaherty and Vertov the most important figure in the development of nonfiction film. Born in Scotland, Grierson had gone to the United States on a fellowship in the 1920s to study public opinion and the media. There he became interested in film as a means of public communication. Grierson, in fact, is credited with coining the term *documentary* when he wrote in a 1926 review of Flaherty's *Moana* that the film possessed "documentary value." Inspired by Flaherty and Soviet filmmaking (Eisenstein rather than Vertov, whose work was little known outside the Soviet Union), Grierson proposed to the EMB his plans to communicate social

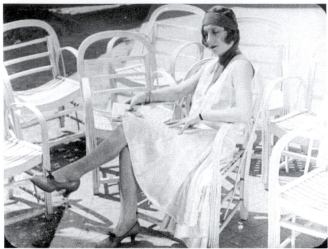

11.2–11.4. Jean Vigo, with cinematographer Boris Kaufman, created a Surrealist version of the city symphony with A Propos de Nice *(On the Subject of Nice, 1930). One of its tactics was the shock cut, as in these segments from a sequence in which a woman, seated in the same position, appears in different clothing in each shot until the final one, where she is nude.*

actuality to a wide public through cinema, and the British documentary movement was born.

The first step was a pilot project, and Grierson took on the task himself. The resulting film, *Drifters* (1929), was the only work of Grierson's career in which he took primary credit as a filmmaker. Its subject was herring fishing in the North Sea, and though, like Flaherty, it recorded humanity's encounter with the natural world, *Drifters* reversed Flaherty's concern with the survival of tradition in the face of modernity. Its focus was on change: "Once an idyll of brown sails and village harbours," said the opening intertitle, herring fishing "is now an epic of steam and steel." This, of course, was in keeping with the EMB's mandate, and the film stressed this modern industry's capacity to market its harvest "to the ends of the earth." Grierson cannily premiered *Drifters* on the same program with the first British screening of Eisenstein's *The Battleship Potemkin*. With the film's success, he was authorized to set up an EMB Film Unit.

Grierson chose to make the Film Unit a training ground for British documentary filmmakers, rather than a site for his own personal creative work. He functioned thereafter, with few exceptions, primarily as a producer. Over one hundred films came out of the Film Unit over the next four years. In 1933, when the EMB was closed, the Film Unit continued its work for the General Post Office (GPO). Fighting resistance from commercial film companies and exhibitors, Grierson fostered nontheatrical screenings, traveling exhibitions, film libraries, and journals. In 1938, after leaving the GPO, he was commissioned by a newly established body, the Film Committee of the Imperial Relations Trust, to evaluate government film endeavors in Britain's dominions. He went first to Canada, and recommended the establishment of a government film-producing unit there; the following year Canada's National Film Board was set up, and Grierson accepted an offer to become its head. His visits to New Zealand and Australia in 1940 led to similar film boards in those countries.

Flaherty in Britain

Estranged from Hollywood and unsuccessful in efforts to promote projects in Germany and the Soviet Union, Robert Flaherty approached Grierson in 1931 about making a film for the EMB. Grierson eagerly accepted him, for Flaherty brought important prestige to the new operation. But Flaherty's vision and his working methods were compatible with neither Grierson's budget nor his goals, and their collaboration was brief. Flaherty's approach was to shoot a great deal of footage of images that seemed to him compelling and gradually develop a concept of what a completed film might be about; Grierson could offer only limited funds and film stock, and he had to answer to a government bureaucracy which required a detailed script and shooting plan. Flaherty's assigned subject was industrial work, and he became interested in the methods of potters and glassblowers, but he ran out of money long before he had enough material for a film. Grierson took over the project, sent out cameramen for additional footage, wrote a script, and edited the film, which was released as *Industrial Britain* (1933). For this film and several others, The EMB struck a deal with Gaumont-British company to obtain access to sound-recording facilities and add a music track and narration.

In history's light, the deal was not such a good one. *Industrial Britain*'s soundtrack makes it the prototype of the heavy-handed documentary. Though Flaherty's images are frequently memorable, they are overpowered by the music of Beethoven and an actor's voice delivering didactic commentary directly addressed to the spectator: "And so you see, the industrial towns are not quite so drab as they seem." Its ideological message was that modern industry depended on the personal skills of individual workers, and it aimed to give assurance that the British worker took pride in tradition, craftsmanship, and quality. The film was credited somewhat disingenuously as a Grierson-Flaherty coproduction (Flaherty was nowhere to be seen after his funds were exhausted). Flaherty's name has kept it alive among documentary classics.

Industry was not really Flaherty's subject; much more vital to him was the theme of humanity's survival in nature. His EMB work was important primarily for giving him access to the British film industry, where he found producer Michael Balcon (1896–1977), a key figure of 1930s British cinema who was also Hitchcock's producer on *The Man Who Knew Too Much* and *The 39 Steps*, willing to put up a modest sum for a new documentary feature. Flaherty wanted to make a film set in the Aran Islands, in the Atlantic west of Ireland, where people lived closer to modern society than did the Eskimos of *Nanook of the North* or the Samoans of *Moana*, but still needed to wrest their living from the sea. Setting up on Aran, complete with a makeshift laboratory to process his rushes, Flaherty cast from the local populace a fictional family (father, mother, son) and shot *Man of Aran* (1934), his first sound feature documentary.

"In this desperate environment," reads an opening text, "the Man of Aran, because his independence is the most precious privilege he can win from life, fights for his existence, bare though it may be." Though it has strikingly beautiful footage of Aran's rocky cliffs battered by waves, wind, and spray, the film was controversial both in its production and in its reception. Critics charged that Flaherty ignored the actuality of the islands to substitute his own romantic vision, including the staging of a long sequence of men in a small canoe capturing a mammoth shark, an activity islanders had abandoned decades earlier.

In the 1970s American documentary filmmaker George C. Stoney (b. 1916), whose father was born on Aran, visited the islands and made with James B. Brown (b. 1950) a film about Flaherty and *Man of Aran*, called *How the Myth Was Made* (1978). As a visual text, it is one of the most interesting critical analyses of documentary ever made. It shows how action sequences were built from shots filmed sometimes days apart;

Right: 11.5. John Grierson, who is credited with coining the term documentary, *became a filmmaker with* Drifters *(1929), a film about herring fishing in the North Sea, made as a pilot project for Britain's Empire Marketing Board. The film's success enabled him to become head of the board's Film Unit and a major figure in government-sponsored filmmaking in Britain and subsequently in Canada.*

Left: 11.6. Robert Flaherty, director of pioneer silent feature documentaries Nanook of the North *and* Moana, *found work with Grierson's Film Unit in the early 1930s, but his contemplative shooting methods outran his budget. Grierson used footage from* other filmmakers to finish Industrial Britain *(1933), credited as a Flaherty-Grierson coproduction. Flaherty's images of workers at their tasks were accompanied by the music of Beethoven and a "Voice of God" narration.*

Making Man of Aran

Pat Mullen, the Aran Islander whom Flaherty chose as his go-between in relations with other residents, described how they went about finding people to appear in the film: "This is a method which Flaherty followed in all his films. He selected a group of the most attractive and appealing characters he could find to represent a family and through them he aimed to tell a story. It was always a long and difficult process, this type finding, for, as Flaherty said himself, 'It is surprising how few faces stand the test of the camera.'" Maggie Dirrane was chosen to be the mother, Tiger King the father, and Mikeleen Dillane the son, in the made-up family of the film.

Since Flaherty's aim was to show how difficult was the islanders' struggle for survival, he sometimes put his players into situations where survival indeed became a struggle. The filmmaker recounted a scene in which "we had Maggie coming up from the sea with a heavy load of seaweed dripping on her back," when she was unexpectedly hit from behind by a breaking wave and barely made it to safety, with bleeding cuts from having been thrown onto rocks. "I should have been shot for what I asked these superb people to do for the film," Flaherty wrote, "for the enormous risks I exposed them to, and all for the sake of a keg of porter and five pounds apiece. But they were so intensely proud of the fact that they had been chosen to act in a film which might be shown all over the world that there was nothing they wouldn't do to make it a success."

A school of basking sharks, averaging twenty-seven feet in length, appeared off the coast. "He was determined to include a spectacular sequence showing the islanders hunting these creatures with harpoons," wrote Paul Rotha, a Flaherty biographer, "even though no living Aran man had ever handled a harpoon, let alone pursued a basking shark with it. They would have to be taught." Flaherty prolonged production for nearly a year in order to get the shots he wanted.

11.7. *Flaherty with his nineteen-year-old assistant, John Taylor, who went on to a distinguished career in Britain as a documentary cameraman, and the spring-wound Newman Sinclair camera with which most of* Man of Aran *was shot. It had a magazine capacity of one hundred feet of 35mm film, with a running time of a little over one minute. Dozens of magazines had to be stored near shooting locations, and Taylor had to reload after almost every take.*

"Sometimes you have to lie," Robert Flaherty once said of documentary filmmaking. "One often has to distort a thing to catch its true spirit." For *Man of Aran* (1934), Flaherty wanted to capture the spirit of indomitable people wresting a living from nature on a barren island west of Ireland. It became the most controversial embodiment of his filmmaking principles—and one of the most documented of all documentary films, in his own writings, in the memoirs of others, and in the 1978 film by George C. Stoney and James B. Brown, *How the Myth Was Made.*

11.8. United States filmmakers George C. Stoney and James Brown went to Aran Island (where Stoney's father was born) to make a documentary on Flaherty's Man of Aran. Their How the Myth Was Made (1978) is an important critical analysis of film documentary. In this shot, the filmmakers record islanders driving cattle into the sea, from which the animals will be towed to a freighter. Flaherty filmed similar activity in the 1930s but did not include it in his finished film, according to Stoney, "because it did not fit into his romantic vision."

Left: 11.9. Under the auspices of Britain's General Post Office, Grierson's Film Unit produced two classics of British documentary. Song of Ceylon (1934), a poetic film concerned with religious practice and traditional crafts, was made by Basil Wright on the Indian Ocean island now known as Sri Lanka.

Right: 11.10. Night Mail (1936), made by Wright with Harry Watt, concerning a postal train's night journey, featured a score by composer Benjamin Britten and verse by poet W. H. Auden.

raises a question of documentary ethics, whether when placing a subject in a dangerous situation the filmmaker's imperative is to help the subject or get the shot; and makes clear that Flaherty deliberately excluded from his film evidence of a comfortable, prosperous life on the islands. Man of Aran "doesn't represent the life of the people here at all," says one resident, but others vigorously debate its authenticity and the islands' history. Meanwhile, film crews from all over the world came to photograph a surviving performer, Maggie Dirrane.

GPO Film Unit

The two films widely regarded as classics of the British documentary movement were produced through the GPO Film Unit: *Song of Ceylon* (1934), by Basil Wright (1907–1987), and *Night Mail* (1936), jointly credited to Wright and Harry Watt (1906–1987). Begun as an EMB film, *Song of Ceylon* (an island off the southern tip of India, now known as Sri Lanka) was supported by the Ceylon Tea Propaganda Board—no euphemisms there. On his first encounter with a non-Western society, filmmaker Wright

became more entranced with its culture than its commerce. In the Flaherty manner, he made a "poetic" film that was also ethnographic, focusing on Buddhist religious practices and traditional crafts and husbandry. It's interesting to speculate whether the board got what it was looking for. While the work implicitly criticizes the market economy's impact, its presentation of the native culture's exotic beauty could have been effective in attracting spectators to tea from Ceylon.

Night Mail recounted the journey of the Postal Special train from London to Glasgow. Like Flaherty's *Man of Aran*, but in an informational rather than "poetic" documentary context, it involved nonprofessional subjects performing scripted scenes. This gave a human dimension to the mechanics of mail delivery, also dramatized by suspenseful editing. Along with a dry, factual **voice-over**, the soundtrack offered music by composer Benjamin Britten and verse by poet W. H. Auden. Grierson read the final passage, ending with, "None will hear the postman's knock without a quickened heart / For who can bear to feel himself forgot."

11.11. Grierson and his colleagues also made films for sponsors other than government, among which two works supported by the British Commercial Gas Association were notable.

Housing Problems (1935), by Arthur Elton and E. H. Anstey, was one of the first documentaries to interview subjects on location; here a woman talks about slum conditions.

Sponsored Films

While continuing their work at the General Post Office, Grierson and his colleagues sought to branch out and find commercial sponsors for documentary filmmaking. The British Commercial Gas Association agreed to finance several films, among which were *Housing Problems* (1935), by Arthur Elton and E. H. Anstey, and *Children at School* (1937), produced by Grierson, directed by Wright. The films dealt with deteriorating housing and schools, respectively, and called for new construction, a socially progressive proposal also primarily beneficial to the gas industry. *Housing Problems* was among the first social documentaries to use direct address by interview subjects and record ambient sound on location. A mother talks about slum conditions, while the baby she holds points at the camera, and a barking dog and children's voices can be heard in the background.

FILMS OF THE LEFT

Grierson's model of government or commercially sponsored documentaries never lacked for critics. Particularly from the political left, he was attacked for drawing filmmakers into a system that would inevitably defend the status quo. *Industrial Britain* was a hymn to the quality of British workers and products; it had nothing to say about the severe problems of an economic depression that had put millions out of work. To address such social issues, and to criticize government or industrial policies they held responsible, other filmmakers organized in the early 1930s to produce documentary films.

United States

Leftist political filmmaking was not exactly without sponsorship either. In the United States, the Film and Photo League (FPL) was formed in 1930 under the auspices of Workers' International Relief, an international Communist organization that ran its own

film studio in Moscow and supported filmmaking activities in half a dozen countries. Histories of leftist filmmaking in the United States have not yet fully explored its political party connections, preferring to stress its importance in documenting events ignored or suppressed by Hollywood's newsreels.

The Film and Photo League launched the careers of several important documentary filmmakers, including Leo Seltzer (b. 1910), Leo T. Hurwitz (1909–1991), and Ralph Steiner (b. 1899). Its cameramen covered political rallies and marches, capturing historic footage of clashes between police and demonstrators, and the U.S. Army's destruction of the Bonus March encamped in

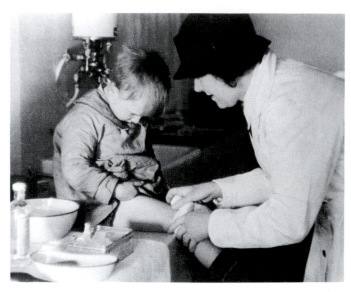

11.12. Children at School (1937), produced by Grierson and directed by Wright, emphasized

the importance of schools in children's lives, as can be seen in this shot of a nurse tending a child.

Washington, D.C., in 1932. Carrying hand-held equipment (and working without sound), the cameramen got close to the action and sometimes in the middle of confrontations. Footage was edited and screened in union halls, churches, and at FPL branches in New York and other cities. Short films with titles such as *Unemployment Special* (1931) and *Bonus March* (1932) were restored in 1982.

By 1934 the Film and Photo League was split by factional disputes about its purposes: to concentrate solely on "newsreels and documents of the class struggle," or to branch out into other forms of filmmaking, involving, for example, scripts and acted scenes. A group broke away and formed Nykino (combining New York and the Russian word for camera) to pursue a more varied cinematic practice, and, with other defections, the FPL soon dissolved. One of the earliest experiments by filmmakers associated with Nykino was *Pie in the Sky* (1935), a silent political comedy photographed by Steiner, with Elia Kazan, the future Hollywood director, as one of the performers.

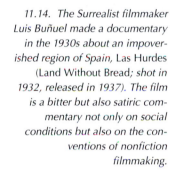

11.13. The Film and Photo League was founded in the United States in 1930 with support from Workers' International Relief, a Communist organization, to document political activities not covered by mainstream newsreels. This shot records unemployed women demonstrating in 1932 at New York's City Hall about conditions during the Great Depression.

11.14. The Surrealist filmmaker Luis Buñuel made a documentary in the 1930s about an impoverished region of Spain, Las Hurdes (Land Without Bread; shot in 1932, released in 1937). The film is a bitter but also satiric commentary not only on social conditions but also on the conventions of nonfiction filmmaking.

Europe

European political filmmaking offered several models beyond the newsreel, though the most prominent works had few imitators. One was Luis Buñuel's *Las Hurdes* (the title refers to a region of Spain; the film's English title is *Land Without Bread*), shot in 1932, but not released until 1937. This was Buñuel's only nonfiction film, but it takes the form less of a straight documentary than of a critique of the basic documentary concept from the perspective of a Surrealist aesthetics. By photographing a poverty-stricken rural region of Spain, and adding a sarcastic, outrageously humorous voice-over narration, Buñuel aimed to indict filmmakers and spectators alike for the documentary genre's complicity in the suf-

11.15. La Vie est à nous *(Life Is Ours, also known as* People of France, *1936) was an innovative political film sponsored by the French Communist party for an election campaign. A collective work, it combined documentary footage, fictional segments (Jean Renoir was one of the directors), and Surrealist political satire. In this shot, party leader Maurice Thorez speaks before portraits of Lenin and Marx.*

fering it depicts. In a notorious sequence, a goat grazes on a mountainside, as the voice-over warns of the steep terrain; then a long shot shows a goat falling, with a visible puff of smoke suggesting it was no accident.

Another prominent political effort was *La Vie est à nous* (1936), a feature-length film sponsored by the French Communist party for an election campaign. Often credited to Jean Renoir, it was a collective work, with Renoir and three others directing different segments. The film's strategy was both to expose and to transcend received notions of documentary actuality. It opens with a travelogue-like sequence extolling the strengths of French agriculture and industry, then shifts to a classroom where a teacher (played by Jean Dasté, who portrayed the sympathetic teacher in Vigo's *Zéro de conduite* and the barge captain in *L'Atalante*) repeats the points, as if the opening shots were from a film shown in school. Later it employs Surrealist techniques, showing Hitler and Mussolini speaking, the former barking like a dog, the latter sounding like a cannon.

In the film's second part a newspaper editor reads letters from readers, and these shift into fictional sequences with professional performers familiar from commercial fiction films. After three such sequences, all promoting Communist values and tactics, the film shifts to speeches by party leaders, interspersed with shots of the performers from the different acted sequences shown together as part of an audience. No other film of the era, nor for years to come, so thoroughly integrated actuality and fiction footage as part of an overall design.

Joris Ivens

The most important political filmmaker of the decade—perhaps of the century—was Joris Ivens (1898–1989). While others may have matched or exceeded Ivens's more than sixty-year career as a filmmaker, no one is likely to have traveled so far and wide: In the 1930s alone he made films in his native Netherlands, Belgium, the Soviet Union, Spain, China, and the United States; after World War II he added Australia, Eastern Europe, France, Italy, Mali, Chile, Cuba, Vietnam, and China several times again. These were not travel films but films of advocacy, yet always shot with a visual sensitivity drawn from both his political aesthetic and his early work as an avant-garde filmmaker.

Joris Ivens *Political Filmmaker*

Joris Ivens began as a filmmaker in the Netherlands making short abstract films of city scenes in the manner of Walther Ruttmann's *Berlin: Symphony of a Great City*. In 1927 he joined in forming a film club in Amsterdam, the Filmliga, whose aim was to screen new avant-garde works made in France, Germany, and the Soviet Union. Soon filmmakers also began appearing at the screenings, among whom was Vsevolod Pudovkin (see Chapter 7), who invited Ivens to show his films in the Soviet Union.

Ivens went, and he recounted in his autobiography a screening before an audience of workers. "One challenging remark was—'Why are you afraid of faces? If you could look at a face with the same frankness with which you look at a raindrop you would be wonderful.' " The comment made a deep impression on him, Ivens wrote, and so did his other experiences in the Soviet Union: he made a film there, *Komsomol* (*Song of Heroes*, 1932), and returned as a committed political filmmaker who devoted the next half century largely to making propaganda films for left-wing causes, many of which were also outstanding works of documentary art.

If anyone could claim title to world filmmaker, it was Ivens. He made films on six of the globe's seven continents, excepting only Antarctica. Many of his works were produced for government agencies, including several in the United States. His *Power and the Land* (1940), sponsored by the Rural Electrification Administration of the U.S. Department of Agriculture, was perhaps the most effective film made to promote President Franklin D. Roosevelt's New Deal policies. It focuses on a single farm family and the ways that electricity brings improvement to their productivity and their lives. He also worked on a film for the War Department documentary unit, headed by Frank Capra, that produced the "Why We Fight" series; called *Know Your Enemy: Japan*, it was completed but not released because of changes in United States policy that made the film's perspective obsolete.

One of Ivens's longest and most significant filmmaking relationships was with China. After making *The 400 Million* with John Ferno in the 1930s, he returned to China in the late 1950s to make several short documentary films and again in the early 1970s when, with Marceline Loridan, he spent three years shooting everyday Chinese life during the final years of the Cultural Revolution. The result was a series of twelve films, under the overall title *How Yukong Moved the Mountains* (1972–74), on such subjects as a Shanghai drugstore, worker discussions at a generator factory, and a disciplinary incident at a junior high school.

11.16. Ivens (left) in Moscow in 1932, working on his film Komsomol *with an assistant, Herbert Marshall (b. 1906). Marshall, who later became director of the Center for Soviet and East European Studies at Southern Illinois University, translated works of Eisenstein and wrote, among other books,* Masters of the Soviet Cinema: Crippled Creative Biographies, *on Pudovkin, Vertov, Dovzhenko, and Eisenstein.*

Misère au Borinage (*Misery in Borinage*, more generally known simply as *Borinage*, 1933), made with Henri Storck, shows Ivens's style in contrast to the newsreel approach of the American Film and Photo League. Reporting on a labor struggle in a Belgian mining district, the filmmakers spent a long period in the community, filming daily life and following events as they affected individuals. This gave the film an intimacy and sense of detail the newsreels lacked. (Decades later Storck added a voice-over soundtrack to this silent film, recording the live lecture that once accompanied its screenings.)

Ivens's major works of the 1930s were *The Spanish Earth* (1937) and *The 400 Million* (1939), a film about China codirected with John Ferno. Both films were produced in the United States and involved the participation of leaders in the arts and film industry. Novelist Ernest Hemingway wrote and spoke the commentary on *The Spanish Earth*, with music arranged by composers Marc Blitzstein and Virgil Thomson, while screenwriter Dudley Nichols wrote and actor Fredric March spoke the commentary on *The 400 Million*.

Aided by Hemingway's somber script and low-key delivery, *The Spanish Earth* superbly demonstrates Ivens's approach. The film opens simply, in a village where people bake bread, farm, and build an irrigation system. Thus rooted, the work widens out to the Civil War between Fascist rebels and the Republican government, never losing the immediacy of the personal. It is a film about death, in combat, in city streets, in villages from bombard-

Above: 11.17. Dutch filmmaker Joris Ivens, with the Belgian Henri Storck, lived among Belgian miners to make an intimate documentary of their labor struggles, Misère au Borinage *(Misery in Borinage, generally known as* Borinage, *1933).*

Below: 11.18. A scene of combat amid destroyed buildings in Ivens's documentary on the Spanish Civil War, The Spanish Earth *(1937), with commentary written and spoken by the American novelist Ernest Hemingway*

ment by German planes. "Men cannot act before the camera in the presence of death," says Hemingway. Yet behind the Spanish tragedy the irrigation work continues, and the film ends with water flowing into the fields.

Completed two years later, *The 400 Million* is a more conventional documentary. Its aim was to inform spectators about an Asian war much less familiar than the Spanish struggle and the increasing tensions in Europe. As early as 1931 Japanese troops had taken control in the Chinese territory of Manchuria. Full-scale war between Japan and China broke out in 1937, and Japan's military advance that year captured the major cities of Beijing (known at the time as Peiping) and Shanghai. *The 400 Million* covers these events through didactic historical and geographical explana-

11.19. *Chinese citizens running from an air attack in* The 400 Million *(1939), a film by Joris Ivens and John Ferno concerning China's struggle against a* Japanese invasion. Hollywood figures aided the filmmakers; screenwriter Dudley Nichols wrote and actor Fredric March spoke the film's commentary.

tions, including maps with moving lines and actors' voices impersonating Japanese generals. But the filmmakers also had another purpose, which adds to the film's historical significance: as leftists, they wanted to publicize the role of the Chinese Communists in fighting against the Japanese. They managed to include footage of Communist leaders such as Zhou Enlai, who became China's premier after the Communists gained power in 1949.

NAZI DOCUMENTARY

There were also documentaries made on the right wing of the political spectrum in the 1930s, notably in Nazi Germany. The most famous of these are *Triumph des Willens* (*Triumph of the Will*, 1935) and *Olympia* (1938), both made by Leni Riefenstahl (b. 1902). These have aroused more controversy than perhaps any

other nonfiction films yet made. Can we admire a film's artistry and abhor the ideals it propagates? "*Triumph of the Will* and *Olympia* are undoubtedly superb films (they may be the two greatest documentaries ever made)," Susan Sontag wrote in her essay "Fascinating Fascism," "but they are not really important in the history of cinema as an art form."[2] The statement seems contradictory and requires further exploration.

Riefenstahl was a dancer who began acting in an important popular genre during the Weimar period, films about mountain climbing and the mystique of the high Alps. In 1932 she directed and starred in her own "mountain" film, *Das blaue Licht* (*The Blue Light*). Adolf Hitler is said to have admired the spectacular visual effects she achieved for night scenes with smoke bombs and special filters, and he invited her to make a film of the 1933 Nazi rally in Nuremberg for his private use. This led to the major effort that went into filming the 1934 Nuremberg rally as *Triumph of the Will* and the documentary on the 1936 Olympic Games staged in Berlin. After World War II Riefenstahl was detained and investigated for Nazi activities but ultimately cleared. In later years she wrote that she had tried to get out of making the films, and that in the case of *Olympia*, the Nazi party did not finance it and attempted to prevent its release. Researchers have produced documents refuting these claims.

Triumph of the Will

The 1934 Nazi party rally was not simply an event that was filmed; rather it was planned and constructed in considerable part for the film that was to be made of it. Later spectators, recalling Hitler as an invincible dictator until his regime was defeated by the Allies in World War II, rarely have knowledge of the historical context (nor is the film much help for non-German speakers, since the original full-length version has never been subtitled in English). On June 30, 1934, Hitler purged Ernst Röhm, leader of the SA (Sturmabteilung, or Storm Troopers, a paramilitary unit of the National Socialist party), and ordered his execution; Röhm had pushed for sweeping social changes after the Nazis seized power, challenging Hitler's efforts to forge alliances with traditional military and conservative elites. Hitler planned the September rally—and the film—as a carefully choreographed pageant to show a nation united behind him, with support from the army and loyal party officials.

Riefenstahl's film was central to this purpose, since it would create a vision of the event—beginning with the famous opening sequence of Hitler's plane descending through the clouds over Nuremberg—that no participant could have experienced. She was provided with a staff of more than one hundred, along with thirty cameras. Special elevators, platforms, ramps, and tracks were constructed for her camera operators at the parade grounds and throughout the city. In the resources at its disposal, *Triumph of the Will* dwarfed all previous nonfiction films. The results are often awesomely apparent, as in its most frequently reproduced image, the high-angle shot of Hitler, flanked by two associates, walking down a wide path between the enormous massed columns of his followers.

For non-German spectators of the 1930s, what was remarkable about *Triumph of the Will* was its vivid revelation of a new politics mobilizing masses of people for public spectacle. The film's style is dedicated to driving that point home. Much of its last half consists of parade footage, with images of close-drilled units, flags, salutes, and cheering crowds endlessly repeated, and

marching music incessantly blaring on the soundtrack. The numbing quality of these sequences seems purposeful, as if to deprive the spectator of mental ability, to force acquiescence in the literally stunning power of the Nazi appeal. Riefenstahl's adherents defend the film's artistry, arguing, as has critic Richard Meran Barsam, that "At times, the spectacle . . . soars beyond the insidious propaganda."[3]

Olympia

The Olympic Games documentary was planned differently, for a different purpose. Germany had been awarded the 1936 Games before Hitler seized power; his racist ideology made the Games controversial. Riefenstahl's film aimed primarily to demonstrate that the Berlin Olympics had been a fair and friendly event in which athletes and spectators from many countries happily took part. Hitler and other Nazi leaders were shown only as faces in the crowd, cheering on the competitors.

Assessing *Olympia* is complicated by the fact that the film now exists in multiple versions. Circulating in the United States is a two-part film running three and one-half hours, with a voice-over narration in English. In recounting the men's high jump the English voice says, "America's great Negroes have the field to themselves," one sign, among several, that in this version at least the purpose was to highlight sportsmanship, rather than Nazi Germany's notorious racist ideology.

In shooting and editing, *Olympia* was a more complex project even than *Triumph of the Will*, and the film above all was a great technical achievement. (German commentators pointed out that the 1932 Olympics had been held in Los Angeles, home of the Hollywood industry, but that no comparable effort had been made to film the Games there.) The self-consciously "art" sequences that have been extracted from the film—such as the famous scene of men's diving—make up only a very small part, and some were shot in empty stadia after the competition had

Far left: 11.21. Triumph of the Will*'s most impressive moments were panoramic views such as this, presenting the awesome power of mass spectacle.*

Left: 11.22. Filmmaker Leni Riefenstahl examining footage for Triumph of the Will.

Above: 11.23. Among the highlights of Riefenstahl's Olympia *(1938), a documentary on the 1936 Olympic Games in Berlin, were spectacular sequences of men's diving, some of which were shot in empty stadia after the Games.*

Left: 11.24. Olympia *was also in part a hymn to mass spectacle, although the English-language version contains primarily reportage on competitive events.*

Above: 11.25. The United States government entered the field of documentary filmmaking with The Plow that Broke the Plains *(1936), sponsored by the Resettlement Administration of the Department of Agriculture and written and directed by Pare Lorentz. Documenting agricultural conditions, the film showed dust storms of the 1930s that turned areas of the Great Plains into a "dust bowl."*

Right: 11.26. Lorentz's second government film, The River *(1937), documented conditions caused by river flooding.*

ended. Otherwise the film consists primarily of reporting on events, with use of slow-motion cinematography the principal innovation.

Triumph of the Will and *Olympia* are important films in the history of cinema—they have had enormous impact both on films of political persuasion and on sports films. If Sontag is correct in "Fascinating Fascism" that they are not important in the history of cinema "as an art form," it may be because their artistry is compromised by their propaganda goals. To say they are "undoubtedly superb films" is to be fascinated more by Fascism than by film.

UNITED STATES

Among governments, the United States was slow to venture into documentary filmmaking—except for educational films on subjects such as how to milk a cow. Opposition from a powerful commercial film industry was one roadblock. But the administration of Franklin D. Roosevelt, establishing its New Deal program after 1933, shared the documentary impulse of governments else-

where. In 1935 the Resettlement Administration (later called the Farm Security Administration) of the Department of Agriculture set up a corps of still photographers to document social problems and programs for change, and also hired Pare Lorentz (1905–1992), a journalist and critic with no prior filmmaking experience, to produce a film about agricultural conditions.

Lorentz turned to filmmakers whose work he knew, Ralph Steiner, Leo T. Hurwitz, and Paul Strand (1890–1976), all associated with the leftist group Nykino. Conflicts soon emerged between Lorentz and the others on both political and professional grounds. Lorentz took their location footage, purchased stock footage, and worked with composer Virgil Thomson in coordinating the assemblage of sequences with a musical score. On the finished film, *The Plow that Broke the Plains* (1936), Lorentz took credit as writer and director. Like Grierson with *Drifters*, he premiered his film in Washington, D.C., on a program with European government documentaries, including an excerpt from *Triumph of the Will*.

On his next project, *The River* (1937), Lorentz used new cinematographers, including Floyd Crosby (1889–1985), who had

The March of Time

Government filmmaking was not the only documentary innovation of the 1930s. Another was *The March of Time*, a monthly documentary series produced by *Time* magazine that began in 1935 and ran until 1951. Louis de Rochemont (1899–1978), a former newsreel cameraman and editor, developed the series from an earlier *March of Time* radio broadcast. In contrast with the brief news, sports, and feature clips that made up studio newsreels, the *March of Time* releases ran around twenty-five minutes and in the first years covered three subjects in depth; around 1938 they began focusing on a single topic. The series controversially interspersed acted scenes and reconstruction of events along with actuality footage. Its hyperbolic narration and inverted syntax were parodied by Orson Welles in the "News on the March" sequence in *Citizen Kane*.

By the end of the 1930s documentary practice in the United States had grown more varied, with personnel often moving between government and independent projects. Joris Ivens made

Above: 11.27. A commercial venture in documentary filmmaking was The March of Time, *produced by* Time *magazine as a monthly series from 1935 to 1951; Orson Welles memorably parodied the series' style in the opening "News on the March" sequence of* Citizen Kane. *In the first several years the twenty-five-minute films covered several topics; later, they switched to a single theme for each number. The series was noted for its treatment of contemporary politics, as in this shot of a German-American newspaper dealing with issues of United States intervention in the European war in early 1941.*

Right: 11.28. The March of Time also covered "lifestyles," fashion, and leisure, as in this shot of contestants at a beauty pageant.

worked in Hollywood, and Willard Van Dyke (1906–1986). Both films are significant historically as the first major U.S. government efforts, but they are largely conventional exercises in documentary technique, and are no less propagandistic than Leni Riefenstahl's films. They advocate specific government programs or more generally present agricultural problems—drought, the 1930s Dust Bowl, river flooding—in a framework supporting administration policies. The temper of the times permitted them to be shown commercially in theaters (Paramount distributed *The River*), but in a different political climate after World War II, Congress placed limits on showing U.S. government propaganda films to the American people.

a U.S. government film, *Power and the Land* (1940), for the Rural Electrification Administration. Robert Flaherty returned to the United States at the invitation of Pare Lorentz to make a government film, *The Land*, released in 1942. Nykino reorganized as Frontier Films and produced several documentaries, including *People of the Cumberland* (1938), about political education and unionization in the South, which combined actuality footage and acted scenes; its directors, credited under pseudonyms, were Sidney Meyers (1906–1969) and Jay Leyda (1910–1988).

Moving away from both government and leftist filmmaking, Willard Van Dyke gained foundation support for two films of social analysis, *The City* (1939), codirected with Ralph Steiner, and *Valley Town* (1940). With a commentary by social philoso-

pher Lewis Mumford, *The City* attacks not only urban slum conditions but the modern city itself. It contrasts hectic city life—in a fast-paced comic montage that makes the urban milieu more appealing than the filmmakers intended—with an idyllic suburban environment, where "boys and girls achieve a balanced personality." *Valley Town* depicts the problems of unemployment in an industrial city where automated machinery has displaced workers. The film suggests how complicated the representation of social actuality in documentary film had become by the end of

Above: 11.29. People of the Cumberland *(1938), a film about political education in the town of Lafollette, Tennessee, combined actuality and acted scenes. Sidney Meyers and Jay Leyda directed the film but signed it with pseudonyms.*

Right: 11.30. The City *(1939), codirected by Willard Van Dyke and Ralph Steiner, used foundation support for its treatment of urban problems, contrasting grim factory-town conditions such as these with idyllic views of suburban planned communities.*

Far right: 11.31. Van Dyke's Valley Town *(1940) dealt with the plight of workers rendered unemployed by new developments in industrial technology. This shot presents a symbiosis of disused men and machines.*

the 1930s by opening with a disclaimer: "The people in this film are not actors." By the outbreak of World War II, the lines between "filmed truth" and fiction had blurred: some works called "documentaries" reconstructed events with professional performers, while other works called "fiction" interspersed actuality footage with scenes shot on stage sets. Cinema in war would serve the state more than ever, and the goals of ideology, propaganda, and national morale let no formal distinctions stand in the way.

Notes

1.   Sir Stephen Tallents, "The Documentary Film," in *Nonfiction Film Theory and Criticism*, ed. Richard Meran Barsam (New York: E. P. Dutton, 1976), pp. 56–57.

2.   Susan Sontag, "Fascinating Fascism," in *Movies and Methods: An Anthology*, ed. Bill Nichols (Berkeley and Los Angeles: University of California Press, 1976), p. 42.   The essay originally appeared in *The New York Review of Books*, February 6, 1975.

3.   Richard Meran Barsam, "Leni Riefenstahl: Artifice and Truth in a World Apart," in *Nonfiction Film Theory and Criticism*, p. 253.

TWELVE

FILM AND WORLD

In contrast to other twentieth-century wars, World War II remains most vivid in popular memory through its images on film. While novels and poetry shaped the legacy of World War I, and television news coverage captured the immediacy of later conflicts, the motion picture camera mediated the 1939–45 war. The styles of genre entertainment movies and actuality documentaries (which, as we have seen, showed tendencies to mingle in both fiction and nonfiction political and propaganda films of the 1930s) came even closer together in the war years, to shape a vision of World War II that continues in wide cultural circulation as generations pass.

When World War II began—as early as the mid-1930s in Asia, September 1939 in Europe, and December 1941 for the United States—no nation made the mistake France had done in World War I of halting film production. Cinema had risen to the status of preeminent popular medium (television had begun broadcasting on a limited experimental basis but was not to be commercially developed until after the war). Joseph Goebbels's view that propaganda is best communicated through entertainment was put into practice by every nation's film industry, while combat operations were filmed for newsreels, documentaries, and military analysis. In countries where theaters were still able to operate normally, motion picture attendance climbed throughout the war, and reached an all-time peak in the first postwar year.

UNITED STATES FICTION FILMS

From the 1930s high to the wartime low in 1945, feature film production fell by more than 40 percent in Hollywood, but studios operated as usual, even with a number of key personnel in military service, and profits soared. Much of the reduction was in inexpensive "B pictures," developed in the 1930s as the second half of double feature screenings, which were no longer necessary to attract audiences during the war. Genre production continued largely as before—comedies, musicals, mysteries, and horror films often seemed to have nothing to do with the war except to proclaim that life could go on as usual despite it.

Government supervision of Hollywood production was instituted through a new agency, the Office of War Information (OWI). Though it lacked powers of direct censorship, OWI communicated war aims and policies to the studios and could block films it disliked from overseas distribution. Broadly speaking, Hollywood welcomed guidance on war-related themes, and a general consensus prevailed between the government and the film industry. Among many propagandistic elements in Hollywood war movies, such as repeated stress on the bravery of the common soldier in combat, four major questions emerge from the war films as a whole: What was the United States fighting against, who was the enemy? How was it possible for citizens to understand that fighting the war was a choice for individuals, not something forced upon them against their will? How was the home front affected by war, and what changes could soldiers expect on their return? And finally, what were the deeper ideological implications of a struggle the United States defined as between totalitarianism and democracy? We will examine these principally through significant examples.

The Enemy

American cinema had a full stock of enemy images left over from World War I—dictatorial, aggressive, cruel to captive populations. These characteristics were carried over even into films made by émigrés from Nazi Germany, in *Hitler's Madman* (1942), directed by the former Detlef Sierck, now using the name Douglas Sirk, and in Fritz Lang's *Hangmen Also Die* (1943), with a script cowritten by the German playwright Bertolt Brecht. Both works were based on the assassination of Nazi leader Reinhard Heydrich in occupied Czechoslovakia and the reprisals against civilians that followed. Representations of the Japanese also followed the treatment of treacherous Asians in World War I–era films like Cecil B. DeMille's *The Cheat*.

The most significant film about the enemy was made before the United States entered the war. Charles Chaplin began shooting *The Great Dictator* (1940) just as war broke out in Europe in 1939. He planned it as his first speaking performance (not having spoken in his previous sound films, *City Lights* and *Modern Times*).

WAR II

Its premise was the resemblance, often noted in the 1930s, between Chaplin and Adolf Hitler, who were coincidentally born four days apart. Chaplin plays two roles, Adenoid Hynkel, dictator of Tomainia, and a Jewish barber. The film's treatment of Nazism through comedy and its focus on the persecution of Jews were both more daring than later wartime depictions of the enemy. Even half a century later the shifts in tone can strike a viewer as painful.

For cinema history one of *The Great Dictator*'s small delights is its parody of *Triumph of the Will*. Hynkel spouts gibberish German while crowds cheer on cue and marching music blares, and children and mothers in peasant garb greet the dictator, with an off-color embarrassing result. The film also more generally mocks documentary voice-over narration (not a part of *Triumph of the Will*), suggesting even as parody how central documentary forms would be to fictional representation in the war years.

The Choice

Before the Japanese attack on Pearl Harbor, United States public opinion had been sharply divided about participation in the war. One of the wartime motifs was to show involvement in the war as a moral transformation of individuals, from indifference to commitment. The decisive event was the Japanese attack itself, depicted as a betrayal of trust that wiped away petty confusions and demanded retaliation. "Sam, if it's December 1941 in Casablanca, what time is it in New York?" Rick (Humphrey Bogart) says to the piano player portrayed by Dooley Wilson. "I

bet they're asleep in New York. I'll bet they're asleep all over America," he adds, not referring to different time zones.[1] *Casablanca* (1943) went into production six months after the United States entered the war, but its narrative events were placed chronologically just before the Pearl Harbor attack. Rick's remarks point to the nation's unreadiness for war; his later actions exemplify a capacity to be roused to fight.

An unlikely adaptation of an unproduced play, with frequent script changes and an unknown finish until it was time to shoot the last scenes, *Casablanca* became nearly everyone's favorite World War II movie. It drew on familiar patterns in American popular narrative, stretching across the genres from the detective to the Western. A mysterious lone man, embittered by the past, refuses communal solidarity. Then his lost love returns to confront and console him, and he commits himself anew to his ideals. With his sardonic style and the ambiguity of his screen image, Bogart made a persuasive hero, and Swedish actress Ingrid Bergman gave their love scenes powerful romantic poignancy. The film was also unobtrusively an all-star production of European émigré performers, including Conrad Veidt, the somnambulist of *The Cabinet of Dr. Caligari*, as the Nazi Major Strasser, and Marcel Dalio, from Renoir's *Grand Illusion* and *Rules of the Game*, as a croupier.

The Home Front

Though unlike most belligerent countries the continental United States was not a site of combat, one theme of wartime policy was to assert a unity between battlefront and "home front." Like so much else in American ideology and arts, this found its strongest expression on the level of the personal. It was out of individual relations that any social implications could be drawn.

The epic home front movie was *Since You Went Away* (1944), directed by John Cromwell (1887–1979), with a screenplay by its producer, David O. Selznick. "This is a story of the Unconquerable Fortress: the American Home," the film begins, and over its three-hour duration it shows what happens in a middle-class family, living on Suburban Drive, when a husband/father goes to war, leaving behind a wife and two teenage daughters. The wife (Claudette Colbert) moves from loneliness and money worries, to news that her husband is missing in action, to training as a "lady welder" at a shipyard. Immensely sentimental, with violins tugging at your heartstrings (Max Steiner won the Academy Award for musical score), the film weaves among its private tragedies and triumphs the questions of society at large: Was the United States fighting to make a better world, or to restore a life that war had temporarily disrupted?

Ideology

These questions of why the nation was fighting led to even larger ones: What sort of people were Americans, and what were their values? It was of course enormously difficult to address such issues in film dramas. Often an attempt took the form of the

12.1. Charles Chaplin (standing, arms folded, on platform), as Adenoid Hynkel, dictator of Tomainia, in a scene from The Great Dictator (1940) parodying Triumph of the Will, *Leni Riefen-* stahl's documentary about a Nazi party rally in Germany. Chaplin's tragicomic treatment of European fascism marked the first speaking roles for the director-performer, who also played a Jewish barber.

Above: 12.2. *Casablanca (1943),*
directed by Michael Curtiz,
placed in a Nazi-occupied
Moroccan city a classic American
story of an embittered man who
regains his lost love and his
ideals. Humphrey Bogart portrays
the mysterious Rick, Dooley
Wilson his piano-playing sidekick,
in the popular nightspot called
Rick's Café Americain.

Right: 12.3. *The opening title*
card of Hollywood's epic home
front movie of World War II, Since
You Went Away *(1944). Producer*
David O. Selznick wrote the
screenplay, and John Cromwell
directed.

12.4. *In Alfred Hitchcock's*
Lifeboat *(1944), the survivors of a*
torpedoed freighter struggle for
unity and purpose, unaware, as
yet, that a German their lifeboat
has rescued (not pictured here) is
hiding his identity as a submarine
commander and exploiting their
"democratic" weaknesses; from
left, performers John Hodiak,
Henry Hull, Mary Anderson,
Tallulah Bankhead, Hume
Cronyn, and William Bendix.

Hollywood Canteen

With millions of military personnel on the move during World War II, film industries in the belligerent countries made various efforts to provide motion picture propaganda and entertainment to their armed forces. The best-documented endeavors were those of the Hollywood movie companies and their employees. Many creative and craft workers went into regular service, others made military documentaries and combat films. Star performers went overseas for personal appearances behind the battlefronts or promoted government sales of war bonds. Less than six weeks after the United States entered the war, actress Carole Lombard (1908–1942) was killed in an airplane crash while returning to Hollywood from an appearance at a war-bond rally in Indianapolis.

In the motion picture community, performers Bette Davis and John Garfield took the lead in founding the Hollywood Canteen, emulating the Stage Door Canteen in New York's theater district. This was a club open to military personnel where movie personalities entertained, mingled, or performed chores.

A 1944 Warner Bros. film, *Hollywood Canteen*, celebrates the endeavor and more generally Hollywood's contribution to the war effort, with several dozen performers appearing in the film as "themselves." It opens on a Pacific island with a motion picture unit arriving with mail and films. Then servicemen return on a Red Cross ship and arrive at the Hollywood Canteen. When a wounded soldier (a fictional figure in the film, portrayed by an actor) meets Bette Davis there, he refers to her in her fictional role in *Mr. Skeffington* (1944) and says, "I saw you on the hospital ship before you were ever released on the mainland. We see the newest pictures before you do." Another fictional soldier meets Garfield and says, "Hi, Johnny. I saw you last in Italy" (where Garfield had gone in 1943 to entertain troops). "Sure," Garfield replies, "south of Cassino. I remember."

"I used to figure that Hollywood was a place with all false fronts," says an actor performing as an enlisted man. "Nothing false about them we've seen tonight. All those famous people being friendly and democratic."

Above: 12.5. Bette Davis, the first president of the Hollywood Canteen, signs autographs for servicemen there.

Right: 12.6. One picture that did not make it overseas before it was released on the mainland (its October 1945 premiere was after the war ended) was Mildred Pierce. *This unusual poster seems to suggest (and surely represents a hope for) returning servicemen's unabated movie loyalty and desire. The small print at the bottom reads, "Have You Sent in Your Victory Loan Pledge? Let's Finish the Job!"*

12.7. The noted Hollywood director Frank Capra was called upon by the United States War Department to produce a series of films explaining to military personnel the background of World War II and United States war aims. The seven titles in the "Why We Fight" series were compiled from existing documentary and newsreel footage, with acted scenes, trick effects, and animation added. Capra directed only the first film, Prelude to War (1942), which chronicled the rise of dictatorships in Germany, Italy, and Japan with scenes such as this, depicting an Italian child being taught to give a Fascist salute.

"melting pot" platoon or crew, as in *Destination Tokyo* (1943), about a submarine reconnaissance mission to Japan; though ethnicities and regions varied from film to film, there were typically an Eastern or Southern European—from Poland, say, or Greece, both countries invaded by Germany—as well as a Jew, a middle westerner, an Ivy Leaguer, and a southerner, subsuming their differences in common purpose to win the war. This presupposed an enemy, so the question came full circle, Americans defining themselves in opposition to their foe.

Alfred Hitchcock's *Lifeboat* (1944), based on a story by novelist John Steinbeck, was one of the few films that took on the question head-on. A Nazi U-boat (submarine) torpedoes a freighter, and survivors gather in a lifeboat: wealthy and working class, men and women, black and white. They are joined by a German survivor, the U-boat captain, who conceals his rank, his English, and his compass. Torn by jealousy, rivalry, indecision, lack of leadership, the "democrats" are easy prey for the "totalitarian," who takes command and steers the boat toward his supply ship. Finally, in a frenzy of anger when the German pushes a wounded man overboard, the others gang up and beat the German to death. The film ends ambiguously, suggesting no more than that an individualist society is capable of frantic retaliation when sufficiently provoked by unmitigated evil.

UNITED STATES DOCUMENTARIES

Hollywood entertainment films, no matter how patriotically motivated, could not by themselves adequately represent the war on film. The documentary impulse of the 1930s carried over into a desire to record as much as possible of the war itself, and training thousands of military recruits also called for visual communication. Among the filmmakers who went to work in military documentary were many from Hollywood's creative talent and craft workers, including such major directors as Frank Capra, John Ford, William Wyler, George Stevens, and John Huston.

Why We Fight

The politically most important assignment went to Capra. He was asked to supervise a series of films explaining the background and goals of United States involvement in the war to service personnel, many of whom had scarcely paid attention to world events. This became the "Why We Fight" series, seven films that all U.S. Army soldiers were required to see and were also released for theatrical distribution both in the United States and overseas. These are remarkable cinematic documents, in part because they were produced with little bureaucratic supervision. Capra claims in his autobiography that when he asked the chief of staff, General George C. Marshall, what to do if he could not find out what U.S. policy was, the general replied, "In those cases make your own best estimate, and see if they don't agree with you later."[2]

The films, each approximately an hour long, began with *Prelude to War* (1942); this was followed by *The Nazis Strike, Divide and Conquer, The Battle of Britain,* and *The Battle of Russia* in 1943, *The Battle of China* in 1944, and *War Comes to America* in 1945. Capra took full directorial responsibility only for the inaugural film; Anatol Litvak (1902–1974) and Anthony Veiller (1903–1965) directed the others. Although he expressed awe at *Triumph of the Will* (which he screened after taking his assignment, and from which he took footage), Capra emulated more *The March of Time. Prelude to War* was a film of compilation and montage: It linked together actuality footage, acted scenes, trick effects (Japanese troops marching in Washington, D.C.), and animation.

12.9. Several Hollywood directors took hand-held 16mm cameras (loaded with color film) to film military action for combat documentaries. John Ford shot much of the ground footage for a film about a major engagement in the Pacific war, The Battle of Midway (1942); another cameraman, Kenneth M. Pier, recorded scenes of air combat such as the one pictured here.

12.8. Another documentary produced by Capra's unit, The Negro Soldier (1944), directed by Stuart Heisler, extolled the commitment of blacks to the war effort, without reference to the fact that the United States armed forces were racially segregated during World War II.

"What made us change our way of living overnight?" asks actor Walter Huston in the voice-over narration, and the seven films set out to answer that question, mostly by depicting the enemy's evil ambitions. The principles for which the United States was fighting were stated largely by symbol and inference: religious freedom; freedom from ideological indoctrination; freedom to be left alone.

The Negro Soldier

After completing the "Why We Fight" series, the production team Capra had assembled went on to produce another half-dozen documentaries, most significantly *The Negro Soldier* (1944), directed by Stuart Heisler. This film was fraught with implications: though the "Why We Fight" series did not explicitly proclaim the United States a land of justice and equality, it did condemn the enemy nations for injustice and inequality, particularly on racial grounds. Yet one of the U.S. institutions that remained racially segregated was the Army. Thus the film became in effect, "Why African-Americans Should Fight."

Religious freedom was again a touchstone. The film is framed as a church service, and its narrative thread is a clergyman's sermon. It gives a capsule history of black involvement in American military struggles—neglecting to mention the fact of slavery—and shows black heroes like the high-jump champions of the 1936 Olympic Games (using footage from *Olympia*). Though it followed conventional compilation documentary style, *The Negro Soldier* could not help but be radical in content. It could not justify racial segregation; it went out of its way to find scenes of blacks and whites together in military settings. This was a case of General Marshall's words coming true: President Harry S Truman integrated the armed forces by executive order after World War II.

12.10. William Wyler, with other cameramen, went on a daylight bombing raid over Germany to shoot The Memphis Belle (1944), about a B-17 "Flying Fortress" on its final mission. In a ground shot from the film, a crewman paints a bomb on the plane's fuselage to indicate a completed mission.

The Memphis Belle

William Wyler (1902–1981) had been originally assigned as director on *The Negro Soldier* but left the project when he got a chance to make a combat documentary about a B-17 "Flying Fortress" daylight air raid over Germany. The circumstances forced a drastic change in technique, especially for Wyler, notorious in Hollywood as a meticulous director who sometimes shot the same scene dozens of times before he was satisfied. His equipment for the documentary was hand-held 16mm cameras, loaded with color stock (John Ford earlier had shot color combat footage in 1942 for his seventeen-minute film of a decisive naval engagement in the Pacific, *The Battle of Midway*). Wyler and two other cameramen shot the footage, flying on combat missions at 29,000 feet in the unpressurized B-17s, where temperatures fell to 40° below zero Fahrenheit; one of the cameramen was killed in action.

The Memphis Belle (1944) focused on a specific plane whose crew was flying its twenty-fifth and final mission before rotating back to the United States. At forty-two minutes it was long enough to give not only a sense of the broader strategy of the "air front," which sent up one thousand planes with eight thousand men in a daylight bombing mission, but also the intense experience of aerial combat between the bombers and enemy fighter planes. Even after half a century of ever more spectacular visual effects in cinema, *The Memphis Belle* retains a powerful immediacy in its low-key directness. It served as the source for a 1990 British fiction film, *Memphis Belle*, directed by Michael Caton-Jones.

John Huston

Director John Huston (1906–1987) made two of the most important U.S. war documentaries, though one was altered and the other suppressed by military authorities. *The Battle of San Pietro* (1945) was the record of an infantry operation in southern Italy that cost heavy casualties. It has none of the glory or triumph of war, as even *The Memphis Belle* does; instead it shows that war is hellish and men die. The film was at first withheld, then released in a half-hour version, a third shorter than its original length (some of the cut scenes show children's fear as U.S. forces enter their village, and American soldiers giving them candy to make them smile for the camera). Both versions currently circulate.

After the war Huston went to a hospital on Long Island, New York, to make an Army documentary on "the psychoneurotic soldier"—men who suffered mental disturbance in the war. The tone

Above: 12.11. Two of John Huston's films were among the most controversial military documentaries to come out of the war. The Battle of San Pietro (1945) covered a grim campaign in southern Italy in which United States and other Allied forces suffered significant casualties; pictured are soldiers loading body bags onto a truck. The forty-five-minute film was originally withheld by military authorities and then released after being cut to thirty minutes (both versions are now available).

Right: 12.12. Huston's Let There Be Light (1946) concerned a hospital for rehabilitation of soldiers who suffered mental difficulties during the war. Frame enlargements show scenes of treatment; though the film's tone was optimistic about soldiers' recovery, it was withheld from release for more than thirty years.

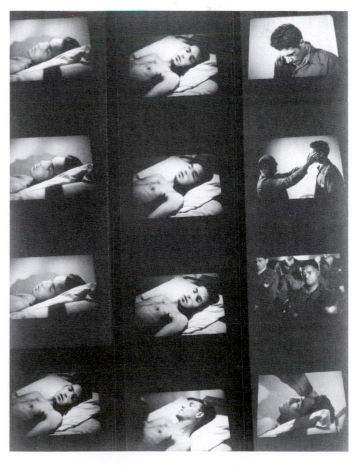

Bugs Bunny Goes to War

12.13. *Bugs Bunny masquerades as Adolf Hitler in* Herr Meets Hare, *temporarily convincing Hermann Göring.*

Like other forms of filmmaking, animation lent its services to the military struggle during World War II. One of the first examples of animation in wartime propaganda was a three-minute film, *Musical Poster #1* (1940), made for the British Ministry of Information by New Zealand artist and filmmaker Len Lye (1901–1980). Lye had been making films for the GPO Film Unit in a style he called "direct film," drawing or painting directly onto the celluloid film strip. In *Musical Poster #1*, to a soundtrack of jazz music, he animated words to spell out the message, "Careful! The enemy is listening to you." The film ends with animated letters spelling out "Shh!" with an image of a swastika, a symbol of Nazi Germany.

The Scottish-born Norman McLaren (1914–1987), who had been a colleague of Lye's at the GPO, was invited by John Grierson to set up an animation unit at Canada's National Film Board, where he launched a career as an acclaimed experimental animator with war-related animations, beginning with *Mail Early* and *V for Victory* (both 1941). His *Keep*

Your Mouth Shut (1944) was a more blunt and disturbing treatment of Lye's theme of *Musical Poster #1*: the necessity for wartime security.

But the most extensive role for animation during the war was played by Hollywood's cartoon characters. The U.S. Treasury Department commissioned a film from Walt Disney about the importance of paying taxes, and it turned into one of the studio's most memorable films of the war era, *Der Fuehrer's Face* (1943), featuring Donald Duck as a recalcitrant worker in a country ruled by the Nazis. It won an Academy Award for animated cartoons. Warner Bros. produced more than two dozen comedy shorts for a biweekly military film program, the *Army-Navy Screen Magazine,* that played along with feature films at U.S. military bases; it featured a character, Private Snafu, whose name was the slang acronym for the phrase "situation normal—all (fouled) up."

Perhaps the most militant of the cartoon figures was the Warner Bros. character Bugs Bunny, the sassy rabbit

with the greeting, "What's up, doc?" Bugs was shared among several leading cartoon directors at the studio, including Chuck Jones (b. 1912) and Fred "Tex" Avery (1908–1980), but most of Bugs's war cartoons were directed by Isadore (Friz) Freleng (b. 1906). These included *Hare Force* and *Bugs Bunny Nips the Nips* (both 1944), the latter a work that displayed the racism of wartime propaganda.

Freleng's *Herr Meets Hare* (1945) has Bugs burrowing up from underground in Germany's Black Forest and encountering the Nazi field marshal Hermann Göring. Bugs cows the Nazi by impersonating first Adolf Hitler and then Brünnhilde, the goddess of Richard Wagner's Ring cycle operas. Finally captured, Bugs is taken in a sack to Hitler's office, where he gives the Nazis a climactic fright by popping out of the bag in the guise of Joseph Stalin, the Soviet leader.

12.14. *British wartime documentaries by filmmaker Humphrey Jennings emphasized the courageous spirit of the British people under German blitzkrieg air raids. London Can Take It (1940), with scenes of bomb damage such as the overturned bus and the rubble of destroyed homes pictured here, was codirected by Jennings with Harry Watt, although the only credit it carried was the name of the narrator, American journalist Quentin Reynolds; it was produced by the British Ministry of Information primarily for United States audiences.*

of the film, *Let There Be Light* (1946), is basically upbeat, indicating that the men could be helped by psychotherapeutic techniques to resume functioning civilian lives. But its emphasis on the men's reactions to "death and the fear of death" apparently clashed with an official military view that soldiers invariably come home stronger for their war experience; this, at least, was Huston's view as to why the War Department refused to release the film. After being withheld for more than three decades, *Let There Be Light* was made available in the late 1970s.

BRITAIN

Britain entered World War II more than two years before the United States, declaring war on Germany on September 3, 1939, after the German invasion of Poland. In July 1940 Germany began bombing British cities, and in September inaugurated two months of nightly air attacks on London—what the British called the Blitz, after the German word *Blitzkrieg*, or lightning warfare. On the cinema front the response was a ten-minute film, *London Can Take It* (1940), narrated by American journalist Quentin Reynolds, and intended primarily for United States audiences.

As the film shows actuality footage of London under the bombs —the blackout, underground shelters, houses destroyed, buses upturned, buildings in rubble—Reynolds speaks of "a surging spirit of courage the likes of which the world has never known." The film sounded a theme that would shape Britain's wartime ideology, that "the people" formed an army whose unconquerable spirit would prevail.

London Can Take It carries no credits other than Reynolds's name. Its status as a work of reportage might have been undercut had it been made clear that the producer was the British Ministry of Information. The GPO Film Unit (see Chapter 11) had been placed under that ministry earlier in 1940 and renamed the Crown Film Unit. Harry Watt, of *Night Mail*, and Humphrey Jennings codirected the film.

Humphrey Jennings

After *London Can Take It*, Jennings (1907–1950) emerged as the leading figure in British wartime documentary filmmaking. Though he had joined the GPO Film Unit as early as 1934, other interests occupied him during the 1930s: He was a Surrealist painter and poet, and took part in a project called Mass Observation that combined anthropological and Surrealist interest in daily living. He developed a poetic but also comic-ironic approach to everyday life that worked effectively in his films to convey a vision of Britain's popular spirit in wartime.

Jennings's first important film was *Listen to Britain* (1942), co-directed with Stuart McAlister. "Blended together in one great symphony is the sound of Britain at war," says a speaker introduc-

12.15. *Listen to Britain (1942), codirected by Jennings and Stuart McAlister, linked the sounds and images of factory work with a* Mozart concert among other scenes that formed a picture of a varied but united nation.

ing the film through direct address to the spectator. These words link *Listen to Britain* to earlier "city symphonies" such as Ruttmann's *Berlin* and Vigo's *A Propos de Nice*, though those symphonies had been silent. Jennings and McAlister showed the value of mixing sound and image. They mingled the music of a Mozart piano concerto with the noise of a factory, and through visual editing created a montage of popular and high culture, industry and the natural landscape, forming harmonious national unity.

Fires Were Started (1943), at sixty-four minutes Jennings's longest film, combined actuality footage and acted scenes with nonprofessionals in a narrative of firefighting (German planes dropped incendiary bombs so the fires they started could overcome the blackout and help locate targets). The "players" are the men and women of the fire brigade, and the film's observations of their off-duty activities counterpoint the slowly building drama of the fire, in which one of the men dies. *Fires Were Started* was the most elaborate instance of the documentary form of which *Night Mail* and *The March of Time* were prototypes, using performance to give human depth to the recording of actual events.

Fiction Films

If films like *Fires Were Started* pushed the documentary in the direction of fiction, then the necessity of representing war equally impelled fiction films toward documentary. *In Which We Serve* (1942), a fiction film about a Royal Navy ship, opens with a sequence combining actuality footage, acted scenes, and **special effects** cinematography to construct a complex image of battle. On the ship's bridge one man remarks that the vista of sea and clouds resembles a calendar illustration; "art parts company with

reality," contradicts the captain, noting dryly that calendar pictures do not include enemy air squadrons. These are surely also self-reflexive words, highlighting the ways cinema—in a continuum from documentary through fiction—mixed artistry and actuality in its efforts to portray the experience of war.

War had a positive effect on British cinema. On its smaller scale, the British industry went through the same changes as Hollywood. The drop in production averaged around 40 percent, but theater attendance reached all-time highs. Audience and critical responses suggested that fewer pictures resulted in higher-quality films, and the themes of war and patriotism boosted exports to commonwealth countries and the United States. Resources, personnel, and script approval were controlled more tightly by the Ministry of Information than was the case with OWI in the United States, and at least one fiction film was partly financed by the ministry, *The 49th Parallel* (1941), directed by Michael Powell.

IN WHICH WE SERVE. A representative work of wartime British cinema, so far as one film can stand in for several hundred, was *In Which We Serve*. It was the most popular British film of the early war years and also a major success in the United States, where a special Academy Award was given to Noël Coward (1899–1973), the actor and playwright who wrote, produced, and starred in the film, as well as codirecting with David Lean (1908–1991). *In Which We Serve* was an idealized and ideological portrait of Britain at war as were *Casablanca* and *Since You Went Away* for the United States, and the differences are illuminating.

The film centers on a Royal Navy destroyer sunk during the

12.16. Fires Were Started *(1943),* Jennings's tribute to the men and women who fought fires started by incendiary bombs, was a documentary with nonprofessionals in performing roles.

TC·7·29.

Battle of Crete in 1941. As the captain, played by Coward, and a few other men make it to a lifeboat, several of the survivors recall their lives and past events through flashback. The captain, a seaman, and a chief petty officer are the focus of attention—a range of rank and class wider than in most Hollywood war films, where enlisted men were more commonly featured. But *In Which We Serve* is a great deal more about the style and example of leadership than the typical Hollywood war film. Coward is a model of a humane but firm leader, stoic, impassive, and understated. "We were getting a bit worried about you, Sir," says one of his rescuers. "Nothing like a good swim before breakfast," the captain replies.

In similar manner the film constructs a continuity rather than a division between battlefront and home front. Families and loved ones carry on their lives with equal stoicism, and they too experience mortal danger, as when a bombing raid kills the petty officer's wife ("Oh, I see," he says when told the news). *In Which We Serve* communicates that the British will keep a stiff upper lip and weather any crisis.

12.17. The most popular British fiction film of the early war years, In Which We Serve *(1942), was produced, written, and co-directed by playwright Noël Coward, who also portrayed the captain of a Royal Navy destroyer sunk during the Battle of Crete in 1941, shown here (at right) after being rescued with some of his men from a lifeboat.*

SOVIET UNION

It is misleading to suggest that the Soviet Union entered World War II in 1941, since the Soviets attacked Poland and Finland in 1939 and annexed the Baltic republics of Latvia, Lithuania, and Estonia in 1940. But Germany's invasion of Russia in June 1941 altered war strategy and brought the Soviets into alliance with Britain, the United States, and other countries fighting against Germany and Japan. The Soviet defense of Moscow in late 1941 was the subject of a feature documentary completed in early 1942, *Razgrom nemetzkikh voisk pod Moskvoi* (*Defeat of the German Armies near Moscow*), which as *Moscow Strikes Back* won one of several Academy Awards given in 1942 for documentary (along with *Prelude to War* and *The Battle of Midway*).

Ivan the Terrible

By the time of the battle of Moscow, the Moscow and Leningrad film industries had been moved over a thousand miles to Alma-Ata, an Asian city near the Chinese border. It was there that Sergei Eisenstein made *Ivan grozny* (*Ivan the Terrible*), the only Soviet fiction feature of the war years to have circulated widely. Conceiving the film first in two and then in three parts, Eisenstein completed Part I in 1944. It was released in 1945 and won a major Soviet award, the Stalin Prize, in 1946. The director finished Part II in early 1946, shortly before he suffered a heart attack. During his convalescence, Part II was condemned and suppressed, and completed sections of Part III destroyed. *Ivan the Terrible, Part II* was finally released in 1958, a decade after Eisenstein's death.

Left: 12.19. Sergei Eisenstein's Ivan grozny (Ivan the Terrible) concerned a sixteenth-century czar, Ivan IV, who united Russia and fought internal and external enemies. Soviet dictator Joseph Stalin admired Part I (1945) and awarded it a prize, but Part II, completed in 1946, was suppressed (to be released in 1958) and Part III abandoned. For Part I, a production shot shows a camera mounted on a crane shooting the opening sequence of Ivan's coronation.

Far left: 12.18. At the end of Part I, observing a procession of his supporters, Ivan (Nikolai Cherkasov) vows to continue his struggle.

Below: 12.20. Nazi documentaries on the outbreak of World War II pictured Germany's adversaries as the aggressors. A scene from Feldzug in Polen (Campaign in Poland, 1939), directed by Fritz Hippler, shows German fighter planes in action.

Few films make for simple readings, but *Ivan the Terrible* is more complicated than most. Are Parts I and II separate films, a two-part unit, or segments of an uncompleted trilogy? Answer: all of the above. Which takes precedence, the films' politics or their artistry? Like *Alexander Nevsky*, *Ivan the Terrible* was a historical film with contemporary meaning. The sixteenth-century czar Ivan IV unified the country, fought wars, and battled against traitors to his rule—accomplishments the Soviet leader Joseph Stalin might also have wished to claim. It is impossible not to regard *Ivan the Terrible* as historical allegory, especially because Stalin personally disapproved of Part II on the grounds that the film's czar was indecisive and insufficiently ruthless against his enemies.

Yet amidst the politics, and perhaps inseparable from them, stand the films' artistic achievements. *Ivan the Terrible* is a triumph not of montage but of mise-en-scène—of set design, decor,

Feldzug in Polen

and costumes; of carefully choreographed framing (as in the famous conclusion to Part I, where the czar observes the snaked columns of supporters bidding him to return to Moscow); and above all of the strongly theatrical linkage between the images and Sergei Prokofiev's musical score. In Part II, Eisenstein shot his first sequences in color, using it in expressionist ways to convey states of mind, rather than with the naturalistic norms of Hollywood.

GERMANY, ITALY, JAPAN

The wartime cinemas of the countries that were defeated—Germany, Italy, and Japan—have been to considerable extent consigned to historical oblivion. This is understandable. Citizens of those countries may not wish to remember the artistic products of regimes that brought defeat, disgrace, and hardship, and people from other countries abhor works of propaganda—such as Germany's anti-Semitic films or Japan's films about military triumphs in Asia—that justify criminal policies. With few exceptions surviving films are confined to archives and are screened only by specialists. Yet they are part of the historical record of world cinema and need to be understood no less fully than the films of countries that were on the winning side.

Nazi Cinema

Germany's wartime films have in particular disappeared from wider purview. Two notorious anti-Semitic films were made soon after the war started, *Der ewige Jude* (*The Eternal Jew*, 1940), described as a documentary, directed by Fritz Hippler, and *Jud Süss* (*Jew Süss*, 1940), a fiction film directed by Viet Harlan (1899–1964) and featuring, among other performers, Werner Krauss, who had played Dr. Caligari. After the war Harlan was twice put on trial by Allied authorities in occupied Germany for "crimes against humanity" for his role in making *Jud Süss*. This was considered a test case, but after both trials ended inconclusively for lack of evidence, further prosecutions were not attempted.

Early in the war several major combat documentaries also were produced, including *Feldzug in Polen* (*Campaign in Poland*, 1939), also directed by Hippler, and *Feuertaufe* (*Baptism of Fire*, 1940), directed by Hans Bertram (b. 1906), which presented Germany's enemies as the aggressors and showed German military success as occurring without harm to others. But as war progressed both overt propaganda and combat documentaries were supplanted by a policy of making primarily genre fiction films, especially historical films and contemporary melodramas of

12.21. Luchino Visconti's first film, Ossessione ("Obsession," 1942), was suppressed by Italian Fascist authorities, though they allowed it to be made. Based on James M. Cain's novel The Postman Always Rings Twice, *the film featured Massimo Girotti as Gino (center) and Clara Calamai as Giovanna, the illicit and murderous lovers.*

12.22. Japan's early propaganda films, such as the military documentary Gonin no sekkohei (Five Scouts, 1938) focused on the Japanese soldier's obligations.

private life. The historical films were allegories addressed to ideological concerns of the Nazi regime, but Propaganda Minister Joseph Goebbels, who gained even greater power after 1942, held more strongly than ever that a society that was living the tenets of National Socialism needed entertainment from its films. "On the whole, the film industry abandoned political and military subjects in favour of love stories and operettas," film historian David Welch has written; "it gave the people what they wanted, but . . . failed to capture the contemporary experiences of the masses undergoing total war."[3]

Fascist Italy

The Fascist government's efforts to develop Italian cinema reached a peak in the war year 1942, when 119 films were released. But Italy's war fortunes turned earlier than in Germany or Japan. Mussolini was ousted in 1943; his successors surrendered to the Allies, but German troops occupied most of the country (a puppet Fascist regime was set up in northern Italy), and war continued until 1945. Under the circumstances, film production fell sharply after 1943. Nevertheless, there was a sense of continuity in Italian cinema, principally because Italian Fascism, unlike German Nazism, gave certain leeway to diverse viewpoints among the filmmakers it trained and allowed to work (see Chapter 10).

The strongest case in point was *Ossessione* ("Obsession," 1942), the first film directed by Luchino Visconti (1906–1976). Visconti began his film career in the 1930s in France as an assistant to Jean Renoir, who suggested *Ossessione*'s source, James M. Cain's hard-boiled American novel *The Postman Always Rings*

Twice; French director Pierre Chenal had already adapted this for a film, *Le Dernier tournant* (*The Last Turning*, 1939). It is no surprise that Fascist authorities were upset by this tale of adultery and murder, considering that Hollywood's Production Code Administration prevented the book from being filmed for over a decade. For copyright reasons *Ossessione* was not released in the United States or Britain until the mid-1970s (M-G-M owned rights to the book, and was able to make its own film in 1946); it was never given an English-language title and continues to be known by its original name.

Though it was suppressed in Fascist Italy, *Ossessione* was allowed to be made, and became one of the most important films of the war years. It broke decisively with the "white telephone" genre of Italian Fascist cinema, as well as the allegorical and historical modes of Blasetti's films. It was set in a provincial roadside *trattoria*, where an unhappy wife and a wandering mechanic strike up the passion of the film's title. Adapting Renoir's moving camera and long-take shooting style and utilizing the gritty bluntness of Cain's prose, Visconti constructed a vision of desperation and rootlessness in contemporary Italy that stood in stark contrast to Fascist rhetoric and art.

Japan

With its military fighting in China, Japan began making war-related films as early as 1938. The Japanese military government took control of the film industry with laws modeled after Nazi Germany's film policies. Historians have debated to what extent those laws were actually put into practice—in other words, whether filmmakers were able to pursue their own artistic goals

or were forced to follow military directives. Filmmakers and scholars alike favor the view that it was possible to circumvent or undercut the orders, but it seems clear that few if any films were made that did not satisfy military needs. If directors were unwilling to make so-called national policy films they did not work; one example was Yasujiro Ozu, who made only two films between 1937 and 1947.

When Hollywood directors like Frank Capra screened Japan's first propaganda films from 1938, like *Chokoreto to heitai* (*Chocolate and Soldiers*), and *Gonin no sekkohei* (*Five Scouts*), they were surprised at how low-key and indirect they were, compared, for example, to the style developed for the "Why We Fight" series. Rather than focusing on enemy evils, as the U.S. films did, they centered on the Japanese soldier and the obligations of duty and self-sacrifice. In this they more greatly resembled British than American wartime films, and no doubt indicated fundamental differences in national ideology and concepts of the individual's relation to the state.

Fiction films also pursued the same themes, often through the genre of historical or period dramas. Kenji Mizoguchi directed the nearly four-hour, two-part *Genroku Chushingura* (*The Loyal 47 Ronin,* 1941–42), based on a famous eighteenth-century legend about feudal loyalty that was a fixture of Japanese theater and had been previously filmed more than a dozen times. Japanese film

historian Tadao Sato expressed a common critical ambivalence about this and similar works when he wrote, "These historical movies did not directly endorse militarism and can be considered progressive because the directors adhered strictly to historical accuracy. However, [they stressed] the idea of compliance with the times and the theme of the Japanese people as a fated, common body."[4]

The most important debut by a filmmaker in wartime Japan was by Akira Kurosawa (b. 1910), who directed his first film, *Sugata Sanshiro* (*Sanshiro Sugata*), in 1943. This was also a historical film but set in the Meiji era of the late nineteenth century. It recounts the training and exploits of a judo champion. A remarkable first film, with a style based on supple pans and tracking shots, Kurosawa treats it casually in his autobiography as a work of entertainment that military censors did not like. Yet one can see how its emphasis on dedication, purity, and fate places it well within the thematics of the "national policy" films.

OCCUPATION CINEMA

In its military expansion throughout Asia during World War II, Japan controlled cinema production in Korea, Manchuria, Taiwan, and those areas of China and Southeast Asia that it occupied. This filmmaking activity has only begun to be studied. In a number of

Opposite: 12.23. *Kenji Mizoguchi's* Genroku Chushingura *(The Loyal 47 Ronin, 1941–42) was a Japanese wartime "national policy" film based on an eighteenth-century drama about samurai warriors who remain faithful to their deceased nobleman. Lord Asano (Yoshisaburo Arashi, at right, with sword) attacks Kozukenosuke Kira (Manho Mimasu), an official of the shogun's court, to settle a personal grudge.*

Right: 12.24. Asano (in white) has been ordered to commit ritual suicide for his breach of court decorum; entering the courtyard where the act will occur, he acknowledges the tribute of a retainer.

12.25. The young judo student Sanshiro Sugata (Susume Fujita, right) confronts his enemy (Ryunosuke Tsukigata) in a climactic outdoor fight sequence of Akira Kurosawa's first film, Sugata Sanshiro *(Sanshiro Sugata, 1943). Though military censors did not like the work, it exemplifies several of the themes of Japan's wartime "national policy" films.*

European countries occupied by Germany during World War II, a curtain has figuratively been drawn over wartime filmmaking. The principal exception is the careful scrutiny that has been given to one of the world's major film industries, in France, during German occupation between 1940 and 1944.

France

The situation in France was enormously complex. After the French surrender in June 1940, only the northern part of the country was directly occupied by German forces, while both parts were run by a collaborationist government based in Vichy. Meanwhile, French forces outside the country under General Charles de Gaulle fought on the side of the Allies, and a Resistance movement organized within. Making films under the Vichy government was seen by many as an act of collaboration with the enemy, while others thought that filmmaking could be oppositional. Meanwhile, Jean Renoir, René Clair, Boris Kaufman, and other directors and film personnel went into exile in Hollywood.

On Germany's part, as film historian Evelyn Ehrlich has analyzed it, there were positive reasons to encourage French filmmaking: to provide entertainment for the French population; to gain profit from investment in French films; to assert the point that German domination could prove benevolent in fostering indigenous cultural production; and to bolster the one film industry that seemed capable of contesting Hollywood's domination. More than two hundred films were made in France from 1941 to 1944, with production dropping off sharply after the Allied invasion at Normandy in June 1944.

The most important filmmaker from the prewar era of poetic realism to remain in France was Marcel Carné. Like filmmakers in many other countries, he turned from contemporary to historical themes in his wartime work. The most famous film of his career, *Les Enfants du paradis* (*Children of Paradise*), was produced over several years during the German occupation but withheld from release until March 1945. This three-hour epic of theatrical and boulevard life in nineteenth-century Paris was a tribute to popular traditions, and postoccupation France hailed it as an expression of the continuity and survival of French spirit.

A far more controversial wartime film was *Le Corbeau* (*The Raven,* 1943), directed by Henri-Georges Clouzot (1907–1977). The film begins with a sour tone and grows progressively meaner, nastier, and uglier. A small-town doctor begins to receive anony-

12.26. Marcel Carné's epic Les Enfants du paradis (Children of Paradise), *made during World War II, was hailed on its release in March 1945 as testimony to the endurance of the French spirit. The film's narrative was set* amid the popular culture of mid-nineteenth-century Paris. An actress, Garance (portrayed by Arletty), mingles with admirers on the Boulevard du Temple, street of outdoor performances.

12.27. Indoors at the Théâtre des Funambules, the mime Baptiste (Jean-Louis Barrault, in white at left) performs as Pierrot.

mous letters signed by "The Raven" which accuse townspeople of various transgressions. Then a spirit of betrayal overtakes the town, as many people get similar letters, and more than one, it turns out, writes them. The doctor, played by Pierre Fresnay (who portrayed Marius in Pagnol's Marseilles trilogy and Boeldieu in Renoir's *Grand Illusion*), seems to grow in moral strength through his ordeal, but he is powerless to prevent his betrayal of another.

Le Corbeau was attacked by the right and the left, by collaborationists and the Resistance; both ends of the political spectrum saw the film as a condemnation of the French people, unpatriotic from one perspective, giving ammunition to the enemy from the other. In the postwar period it was the main target for retribution against filmmakers who worked during the war. Clouzot and scriptwriter Louis Chavance were banned from further film work; Fresnay and another performer were put in jail (after a short period the bans were quietly lifted, and Clouzot and Fresnay were back at work).

With the passage of time, *Le Corbeau* emerges more clearly as an antifascist film. It uses the same metaphorical discourse as Albert Camus did in his acclaimed 1947 novel *La Peste* (*The Plague*). The town is described (in English subtitles) as infected, polluted, suffering an epidemic. But "it can be treated and cured like any illness," says the doctor. *Le Corbeau* had the misfortune of being made in the war years, rather than after. Like *Ossessione*, it refused the allegory of history, and dared to depict the world around it.

Notes

1. Howard Koch, *Casablanca: Script and Legend* (Woodstock, N.Y.: The Overlook Press, 1973, script © 1943), p. 94.
2. Frank Capra, *The Name Above the Title: An Autobiography* (New York: Macmillan, 1971), p. 336.
3. David Welch, *Propaganda and the German Cinema 1933–1945* (Oxford, England: Oxford University Press, 1983), p. 224.
4. Tadao Sato, *Currents in Japanese Cinema*, trans. Gregory Barrett (Tokyo and New York: Kodansha, 1982), p. 43.

12.28. *In Henri-Georges Clouzot's controversial film made in occupied France,* Le Corbeau *(The Raven, 1943), Denise (Ginette Leclerc) faints during a community confrontation as townspeople display their handwriting to determine who may have written anonymous accusations signed "The Raven." The film's ambiguous hero, Dr. Germain (Pierre Fresnay), is at right.*

Film	Arts and Sciences	World Events
1946	*It's a Wonderful Life;* first Cannes film festival	U.S. TV networks begin broadcasting	United Nations meets
1947	HUAC hearings on Hollywood	aircraft breaks sound barrier	independence of India, Pakistan
1948	*Bicycle Thieves*	transistor invented	state of Israel formed
1949	*Late Spring*	*Death of a Salesman* (Miller)	Communists gain power in China
1950	*Los Olvidados*	*The Martian Chronicles* (Bradbury)	War in Korea begins, U.N. intervenes
1951	*An American in Paris*	*The Catcher in the Rye* (Salinger)	peace treaty with Japan
1952	*Ikiru*	*Invisible Man* (Ellison)	Eisenhower elected U.S. President
1953	*Ugetsu;* CinemaScope introduced	structure of DNA analyzed	death of Stalin
1954	*Senso*	color television begins in U.S.	French defeated in Vietnam
1955	*Pather Panchali*	computers begin commercial use	West Germany recognized
1956	*The Searchers*	*Howl* (Ginsberg)	Soviets crush Hungarian revolt
1957	*Wild Strawberries*	Soviets launch Sputnik satellite	Common Market in Europe
1958	*Vertigo*	stereophonic records	de Gaulle new French premier
1959	*The 400 Blows*	F. L. Wright's Guggenheim Museum	Castro takes power in Cuba
1960	*L'Avventura*	laser invented	Kennedy elected U.S. President

Part Four

POSTWAR TRANSFOR- MATION

THIRTEEN

ITALIAN NEO

Among filmmakers and critics in many countries, the experience of World War II sharpened a desire for a cinema of seriousness and social purpose. Articulations of goals for a better postwar world, combined with revelations of war's horrors, seemed to preclude a simple return to the old standard methods of skillfully producing forgettable entertainment. Wartime mingling of documentary and fiction—and the use of hand-held cameras in the midst of action—held the promise of breaking with studio-bound artificiality and forging a more direct encounter with social actuality. It is perhaps remarkable, given the constraints of commercial filmmaking, that a cinematic practice did emerge as if in response to these demands, with far-reaching consequences for world cinema. It was even more surprising that it came from a country defeated in the war, which had made little discernible impact on the international film scene for decades—from Italy, in the form of a movement known as **neorealism.**

Italian neorealism has probably been the most debated subject in the history of film. When did it begin, when did it end, what were its sources, what were its characteristics, was it new, was it realism? The questions have been unending. About the only point not in dispute concerns its impact. Hollywood's Academy of Motion Picture Arts and Sciences gave special awards to Vittorio De Sica's *Sciuscià* (*Shoeshine*, 1946) and *Ladri di biciclette* (*Bicycle Thieves*, 1948), and a nomination in the screen story category for *Riso amaro* (*Bitter Rice*, 1949), directed by Giuseppe De Santis. On winning a festival prize for *Rashomon* (1949), a film set in the distant past, Japanese director Akira Kurosawa was quoted as saying, "Of course there's nothing like happiness, so I'm happy, but if I made something more of present-day Japan, such a film as *Bicycle Thieves*, and then received a prize, there would be more meaning to it and I'd probably be happier."[1]

Like everything else concerning neorealism, this remark had to do with politics as well as art. By the time Kurosawa spoke, in 1951, neorealism had ended as a movement. Among the causes of its demise was fierce opposition from postwar Italian governments, which held that neorealist films were besmirching Italy's international reputation. A law passed in 1949 strengthening domestic exhibition of Italian films also imposed government censorship of scripts, restricted production loans to potentially controversial films, and provided for the withholding of export licenses for films that were deemed to have "slandered Italy."

Neorealism was in fact a movement very closely tied to specific historical circumstances of postwar Italy—the years between the Liberation and the consolidation of power by the conservative Christian Democrats, 1945 to 1949. These historical ties were often obscure to contemporaries in other countries who knew the films but not the Italian context, and they have been further obscured by critical propensities to discover universal meanings for humanity in the films, rather than tie them to distant parochial concerns. English titles given by United States distributors contributed to this universalization. Roberto Rossellini's *Roma città aperta* (1945) became *Open City*, losing its historical reference to Rome, and *Ladri di biciclette* became *The Bicycle Thief*, shifting meaning from the original title's plural thieves to a single one. Here we will use literal translations: *Rome, Open City* and *Bicycle Thieves.*

Neorealism's roots are many. They trace to French poetic realism, as exemplified by Marcel Carné's late 1930s films, and to the long-take, moving-camera style of Jean Renoir (critic Umberto Barbaro was in fact describing French realism when he coined the term *neo-realismo* in 1943). In Italian terms, they hark back to traditions of realism in Italian arts such as nineteenth-century literary *verismo* and to the location shooting in Italian silent regional filmmaking, as in the Naples street scenes in *Assunta Spina* (1915). From this strand of literary realism, Italian writers and filmmakers were drawn to American hard-boiled novelists of the depression era like James M. Cain, whose *The Postman Always Rings Twice* was the source of Luchino Visconti's *Ossessione*, often regarded as the first neorealist film (see Chapter 12). They also link to Italian fascism's interest in the social propaganda of Soviet silent films.

The fascist roots of neorealism are among its most controversial aspects. Of the leading neorealist directors, De Sica was a popular actor and began his filmmaking career in the fascist period, as did Rossellini, Visconti, Alberto Lattuada, Giuseppe De Santis, and others. Were elements of what came to be known as neorealist style apparent in the work of these or other filmmakers under fascism? If neorealism was already an aspect of fascist film aesthetics, what is its status as a response to revelations of war's horrors or aspirations for a better world?

BEGINNINGS OF NEOREALISM

War is always confusing, but the end of World War II in Italy was more confusing than most. In 1943 the Allies invaded from the south, Mussolini was ousted, his successors negotiated a surrender, and Germany invaded from the north. While Italy became a battleground for the Allies against the Germans, some Italians fought the Allies, some the Germans, and some each other. Rome had been considered an "open city"—that is, a place of sanctuary because of its status as a holy city—but in July 1943 the Allies bombed Rome, the government fled south into Allied-held territory, and the Germans occupied the city. The Allies entered Rome in June 1944 and Florence in August, but the Germans held the north until April 1945, when Allied and Resistance forces liberated the remainder of the country.

Roberto Rossellini

These were the events that Roberto Rossellini (1906–1977) sought to depict in the films that became the first exemplars of neorealism —*Rome, Open City* and *Paisà* (*Paisan*, 1946). "*Open City* and *Paisan* were films intended to represent a sort of balance sheet of

REALISM

It must be said that neorealist style, like most styles, does not inherently carry a particular political meaning. The most common stylistic attribute of neorealist films was **location shooting**. This was abetted by a practice of **postsynchronized** sound—dubbing of dialogue in the studio—which enabled camera movement and a more open mise-en-scène. A feature of some films was the use of nonprofessional actors. But there was more to neorealism than technique. André Bazin, the French critic who was one of neorealism's strongest advocates, wrote that "neorealism is more an ontological position than an aesthetic one. That is why the employment of its technical attributes like a recipe do not necessarily produce it."[2] In other words, more than an artistic stance, neorealism embodied an attitude toward life.

However much one finds traces of neorealist technique in earlier Italian films, it was this attitude toward life that emerged from the historical circumstances of 1945–49 that is the hallmark of neorealist cinema. Neorealism is a film movement of Liberation hope and post-Liberation disappointment. It has thus always offered an ambiguous legacy for Italian cinema. In other countries, however, and particularly in Africa, Asia, and Latin America, neorealism has made a greater impact than any other film movement of the sound era. It provided a model for a cinematic practice attempting to represent human experience outside the conventions of entertainment genres, a commitment to the possibility of rendering social actuality as art. In retrospect, what is astonishing is that a movement of so few films made over so short a time should have had such an impact on world cinema over half a century.

that period of history," Rossellini later wrote, "of those twenty years of Fascism that ended with the great drama of the war, fruit of something that had been much stronger than us and had overwhelmed, crushed, and implicated us. Once the balance sheet had been drawn up, perhaps we could start with a fresh page."[3] Rossellini's balance sheet also included a trip to Berlin to make *Germania, anno zero* (*Germany, Year Zero*, 1947). These three works make up Rossellini's "war trilogy."

Rossellini may have felt he had more reason to turn the page than others. During the fascist era, Rossellini had become prominent as a director of military propaganda films combining documentary and fiction—*La nave bianca* (*The White Ship*, 1941), *Una pilota ritorna* (*A Pilot Returns*, 1942), and *L'uomo della croce* (*The Man on the Cross*, 1943). There have been as many opinions on the moral and aesthetic implications of these works as there have been critics writing about them, but it seems clear that the director attempted a humanistic and realistic approach, within a fascist framework, not fundamentally different from his humanistic and realistic efforts in his postwar neorealist films. One looks to Rossellini's war trilogy not for the righteous fervor of retribution but for the tragic complexity of the war years. Going to his execution, the priest Don Pietro in *Rome, Open City* says, "Oh, it's not hard to die well. It's hard to live well!"[4]

ROME, OPEN CITY. Rossellini began planning *Rome, Open City* during the German occupation. The idea of an "open city" was by that time bitterly ironic, since Rome had become a site of brutal German repression—335 men were murdered in March 1944 as reprisal for the killing of 32 German military police by

Bazin and Neorealism

Not infrequently, film movements that are controversial or undervalued in their home countries find advocates and sympathetic interpreters elsewhere. Emerging in a fractious period of Italian history, when ideologues of all political hues demanded that art adhere to doctrine, neorealism was a movement that particularly needed such foreign friends. It found many, in the United States, Britain, and France; among critics, none was more important than the young French writer André Bazin (1919–1958).

Bazin had begun writing film commentary for student publications around 1943, during the war and the German occupation of France. He was already working on his theories of cinematic realism; these were imbued with a strong element of what was known as Christian personalism, which held that humans were free and could perceive but not fully apprehend the "real," which retained its mystery. His professional career began after the war simultaneously with the advent of Italian neorealism, and he became its ardent champion.

"Neorealism served Bazin's theories perfectly," his American biographer, Dudley Andrew, has written. "He found that, in nearly duplicating our everyday perception, neorealism provides the conditions under which experience can speak of its own accord, unmediated by the rhetoric of a filmmaker with a point to make or a story to tell. By choosing an aspect of reality and continuing to choose it, the neorealist concentrates on the screen what is diffused in life, allowing us to engage a subject in all its mystery."

Bazin's writings on neorealism have survived as almost the only contemporary critiques of the movement that are still read, decades later. They include "An Aesthetic of Reality: Cinematic Realism and the Italian School of the Liberation" and other essays on Rossellini, De Sica, *La terra trema*, *Bicycle Thieves*, and *Umberto D.*, originally published mainly in the French Catholic periodical *Espirit* (in English, they are collected in *What Is Cinema? Vol. II*, selected and translated by Hugh Gray). Bazin sought to add Rossellini, De Sica, and Visconti to the group of filmmakers whom he called cinematic realists, which included, among directors working at that time, Orson Welles, William Wyler, and Jean Renoir. "As in the films of Welles and in spite of conflicts of style, neorealism tends to give back to the cinema a sense of the ambiguity of reality," he wrote. "The means used by Rossellini and De Sica are less spectacular but they are no less determined to do away with montage and to transfer to the screen the *continuum* of reality."

In 1951 Bazin was one of the founders of the French film magazine *Cahiers du Cinéma*, and he became a mentor to such figures as François Truffaut and Jean-Luc Godard, critics who became French New Wave filmmakers (see Chapter 17). His theories of cinematic realism have been extensively analyzed, but one should not neglect a remark he made in a 1949 essay on *Bicycle Thieves*: "'Realism' can only occupy in art a dialectical position—it is more a reaction than a truth."

13.1. Anna Magnani, as Pina, was one of the few professional performers in Roberto Rossellini's Roma città aperta (Rome, Open City, 1945).

partisans. It was this atmosphere Rossellini wanted to convey, and many of the elements of the film's narrative are based on actual events (a legend later developed that some of the film's scenes were actually shot during the German occupation, but this is testimony to the skill of Rossellini's neorealist mise-en-scène).

Rome, Open City is as complex—and contradictory—as the events it draws upon. Parts of the film are conventional and stereotyped—its heroes are purely heroic, its villains either weak or, in the case of its Nazis, sadistic, dissipated, and androgynous in a manner that has become a staple of popular melodrama. There are moments of surprising earthy humor in the midst of critical scenes. Its centerpieces, however, are the most documentary-like sequences. Scenes of a German raid on an apartment building and a subsequent partisan attack on trucks carrying prisoners are shot from middle and long distance, but

13.2. Pina is restrained by German soldiers after her lover has been captured during a raid on an apartment building in Rome, Open City; moments later, running after the truck carrying the arrested men, she is brutally shot down.

Left: 13.3. A scene from the Naples episode of Rossellini's Paisà (Paisan, 1946): a drunken black American soldier (Dots M. Johnson) sits on a pile of rubble with a Neapolitan boy (Alfonsino Pasca) who both befriends and plans to rob him.

Right: 13.4. From the Po delta episode of Paisan: partisans recover the body of a comrade killed by the Germans, which had been floating down the river with a sign, "Partigiano" (partisan), attached.

with an intricate variety of camera locations that make them appear authentic "documents" even though there are many more setups than actuality filmmaking would have allowed. Montage was perhaps the major element of Rossellini's neorealist style rather than long takes or a moving camera, but, as Bazin argued in a wider neorealist context, "the assemblage of the film must never add anything to the existing reality."[5] Where a classical (or Soviet) montage might fill in details or point up meanings, Rossellini's montage multiplied viewpoints while leaving gaps unfilled. A striking example is the shocking scene where the Germans murder Pina, an unwed (and pregnant) mother. It comes

Above: 13.5. Barbara Hintze as Eva, Franz Krüger as Karl Heinz, members of a struggling family in postwar Berlin in Rossellini's Germania, anno zero *(Germany, Year Zero, 1947)*

Below right: 13.6. Director Roberto Rossellini (seated) during the filming of Germany, Year Zero

at the end of the nearly ten-minute sequence of the apartment-building raid, with German soldiers (and Italian fascists) looking for members of the Resistance. The style of the sequence is almost observational, its tone set by long and medium-long shots; a lesser number of medium shots portray character interaction and leaven the tension with comic touches. Suddenly, Pina sees that her lover has been captured, runs to him, and is shot down. With no break in the visual style, spectators are unprepared for the brutal turn, and in the rapid action no special shots address our feelings of mourning or rage.

Anna Magnani (1908–1973), who portrayed Pina, was a professional, as was Aldo Fabrizi (1905–1990) in the role of Don Pietro. The other performers were nonprofessionals, and their scenes of everyday domestic life are highlights of the unpretentious ensemble acting neorealism could evoke. Rossellini wrote the script with Sergio Amidei and Federico Fellini.

Considering the status it has attained as the first great work of world cinema after World War II, *Rome, Open City* was not greeted warmly in Italy when it was released in September 1945. This is not so surprising. Rossellini's "balance sheet" already

seemed like ancient history. "All must unite against a common enemy," the boy Marcello proclaims, and the film depicts such unity between the Catholic priest and Manfredi, a Communist leader of the Committee for National Liberation, both martyrs in the struggle to free Italy. But with the defeat of the common enemy, unity between right and left seemed to many on both sides a betrayal of their principles. It was with distance from the film's historical specificity, particularly in the United States, that critics and audiences could find in it a universalized humanism, an abstracted vision of solidarity and muted hope.

PAISAN. Rossellini's next film, also written with Amidei and Fellini, opened up his historical canvas to the entire Italian peninsula. *Paisan* consists of six episodes in the war, beginning with the Allied invasion of Sicily in 1943 and moving up chronologically and geographically through Naples, Rome, Florence, a monastery in the mountains, and lastly the Po delta. Each episode depicts an encounter between Italians and Americans. Several of the episodes, particularly the first three in Sicily, Naples, and Rome, focus on linguistic and cultural barriers to communication that can lead to misunderstanding, perhaps also to tragedy. The Florence and Po delta segments emphasize the partisan phase of the struggle, and here the tragic elements are more implacable, more fated. The monastery sequence suggests the possibility of the serenity of eternal values in a time of struggle and change.

The original title for *Paisan* is a colloquial form of the Italian word *paesano*, literally meaning peasant but signifying country-man and used as a term of greeting. In its broader sweep, its variety of human types (and its absence of *Rome, Open City's* stock heroes and villains), and its stark physicality of death, whether in city or countryside, *Paisan* is regarded by some critics as a more important film than *Rome, Open City*, though it has not earned the earlier film's wide acclaim or its firm place in film history.

GERMANY, YEAR ZERO. For the final film in his war trilogy, Rossellini traveled to Berlin. He wanted to examine the values he regarded as the source of the war's suffering, and to depict its

consequences for Germans. *Germany, Year Zero* was very much a message picture. The published version of the script opens with both a printed text and a voice-over stating the film's themes, though both are missing from some prints circulating in the United States. The text begins: "When an ideology strays from the eternal laws of morality and of Christian charity, which form the basis of men's lives, it must end as criminal madness."[6]

The film demonstrates how this ideology infects the life of a boy struggling to survive in the rubble and ruin of postwar Berlin. Billeted in an overcrowded apartment with his sick father, a brother in hiding because of his war record, and a sister who gets cigarettes from Allied personnel in bars to exchange for food, the boy is a bewildered figure, a waif in the hard, unforgiving street life of the defeated city. When his father repeats too often what a burden he is on the children and how they would be better off if he were dead, the boy puts poison into his father's tea and kills him. Later, after further evidence of the city's corruption and his own alienation, the boy jumps to his death from a building. *Germany, Year Zero* is remarkable for its location footage of Berlin, but its narrative seems driven more by its thesis than by the concern for humanism Rossellini showed in the two previous films of the war trilogy.

13.7. *Pasquale (Franco Interlenghi, at right), one of a pair of shoeshine boys sent to a reformatory in postwar Rome, fights a prison bully in Vittorio De Sica's* Sciuscià (Shoeshine, 1946).

Vittorio De Sica and Cesare Zavattini

If Rossellini brought neorealism to the forefront of world cinema in the immediate postwar years, the figure who sustained the movement and became its center of controversy was Vittorio De Sica (1902–1974). A popular actor during the revival of Italian cinema under the fascists in the 1930s, De Sica began directing in the early 1940s. He collaborated with scriptwriter Cesare Zavattini (1902–1989) on a notable wartime film, *I bambini ci guardano* (*The Children Are Watching Us*, 1942), that began a long-term working relationship extended through all of De Sica's neorealist films—*Shoeshine, Bicycle Thieves, Miracolo a Milano*

(*Miracle in Milan*, 1950), and *Umberto D.* (1952). De Sica's efforts to maintain neorealism in the face of governmental opposition after 1949 made him the target of political attacks for the last two of these films.

SHOESHINE. Along with Rossellini, who featured children prominently in *Rome, Open City* and in the Naples episode of *Paisan*, De Sica and Zavattini were concerned about the consequences of fascism and war for young people. *Shoeshine* focuses on two boys who earn money shining the shoes of American soldiers, get caught delivering stolen goods for an adult gang, and are sent to a reformatory. With nonprofessional performers and location shooting, the film has a grimmer and more diffuse quality than Rossellini's work, and there is little room for humanistic hope or uplift. When the boys drop off stolen blankets to a fortune teller, they ask her to read the cards for them, saying, "We have futures, too." But hope quickly closes down for them, in an authoritarian reformatory where the director covertly gives fascist salutes.

Zavattini's scripts frequently had strong elements of symbolism, and the symbolic role in *Shoeshine* is given to a horse, which the boys purchase with the money they received from delivering the stolen goods. The horse represents freedom and mobility, and at the end as one boy kills the other in a rage over accumulated betrayals and estrangements, it breaks away and vanishes in night mists. The role of cinema itself is also ambiguously symbolized by a scene where a projector is brought into the reformatory to show movies. In darkness an escape is made, the projector catches fire, and while officials cry, "light, light," a boy is trampled to death in the panic.

BICYCLE THIEVES. Cinema also figures in *Bicycle Thieves*. When Antonio, the father in the story, gets a job putting up wall posters, they turn out to be advertising sheets for American movies, notably *Gilda* (1946), showing Rita Hayworth in her dark gown and long gloves. Hollywood movies flooded into Italy after the war, not only new films but a backlog of wartime production, and audiences flocked to these rather than to De Sica's bleak neorealist work. *Shoeshine* had been a critical success in foreign countries but an economic failure in Italy; De Sica financed his next film through acting and scriptwriting, reportedly turning down Hollywood financing because it would require casting a Hollywood star.

Bicycle Thieves was the most important film of De Sica's career, standing in critical estimation alongside *Rome, Open City* as a neorealist achievement. It draws a far wider social portrait than *Shoeshine*, and its mise-en-scène is considerably more intricate through camera movement and multiple setups in a scene. It touches broadly on Italy's institutions and cultures—the government bureaucracy, political parties, the Church, popular beliefs, neighborhoods, the family, soccer. At its center is the grinding poverty of the family it portrays, exemplified in the relation between a father and a son.

While Antonio is putting up his Rita Hayworth poster, his bicycle is stolen—a brilliantly structured sequence—and with his son Bruno he searches for the thief and the bicycle. Both father and son were played by nonprofessionals (as were nearly all the other roles in the film). At wit's end, needing a bike so he can keep his job, Antonio too steals a bicycle, but so clumsily that he is immediately chased down and caught. Reprimanded rather than

Right: 13.10. Carlo Battisti as the title character with his dog Flike in De Sica's Umberto D. *(1952)*

Below: 13.11. Vittorio De Sica (center) at the premiere of Umberto D. *at the Cinema Metropolitan in Rome*

arrested—"a nice thing to teach your son"—he fades away with his son into a crowd like the horse into the mists of *Shoeshine*. A poignant and despairing work, *Bicycle Thieves* attracted audiences in Italy but, like so many other neorealist films, fell between the firing lines of the country's ideological debates—to conservatives it was impermissible to show society's flaws so brazenly, to the left it lacked analysis and a clear agenda for social change.

MIRACLE IN MILAN. The symbolic and fable-like quality of Zavattini's writing came further to the fore in *Miracle in Milan*, based on one of the scriptwriter's novels. This strange, delightful film—often described as Chaplinesque for its comic poignancy—was at once a respite from grim neorealism and a riposte against De Sica's critics, through satire rather than pathos. The film opens with a title, "Once Upon a Time," and a view of a cottage out of

a fairy tale, but another shot shows behind the cottage a vista of smokestacks and modern factories of a very contemporary Milan. An old woman discovers a foundling in her cabbage patch. She raises the boy. When she dies he goes into an orphanage, which eventually sends him out to join the city's unemployed and homeless. The boy, Totò, helps to build a shantytown and forge a community of the downtrodden, but when oil is discovered there they are threatened by the capitalist who owns the land. Using the magic powers of a white dove brought to him by the old lady's ghost, Totò helps the shanty dwellers fly away on street cleaners' broomsticks.

Though any summary makes the film sound like a neorealist social treatise (until the ending), the entire work is full of humor and wonderment. Alessandro Cicognini (b. 1906), who wrote the music for all De Sica's neorealist films, contributed a score very different from the first two, with jazz and comic motifs. By exposing power and authority to comic ridicule, *Miracle in Milan* constructs in some ways a more devastating critique than the realist films. Full of magic and fantasy achieved through a most nonrealistic special effects cinematography, the film nevertheless forcefully makes its message clear: postwar Italy offers no place and no hope for the poor.

UMBERTO D. De Sica was not in a strict sense a "political" filmmaker, in that his films did not represent party doctrines or deal with issues within the recognizable terms of partisan debate. In a way they were apolitical moral indictments, and that made them appear even more dangerous to politicians who were able to tolerate far more overtly ideological works. As he became, into the early 1950s, the last practitioner of neorealism, and the one most honored internationally, De Sica came under increasing criticism (again, both from right and left). His and Zavattini's last neorealist collaboration, *Umberto D.*, was a chamber drama, but its social critique is as strong as ever.

Right: 13.12. In Alberto Lattuada's Il bandito *(The Bandit, 1946), an Italian war veteran, Ernesto (Amedeo Nazzari), returns from a German prison camp to a disordered city and becomes a criminal. He learns that his sister has become a prostitute, but she is killed as he tries to take her away. Later, in the scene pictured, he murders the boss of the prostitution ring in the back seat of a car.*

Below: 13.13. A scene from Lattuada's Senza pietà *(Without Pity, 1948)*

The film begins with a moment of political failure: a demonstration by elderly men demanding increases in their pensions, quickly and coldly dispersed by police in jeeps. Thereafter it is the story of Umberto D. (portrayed by Carlo Battisti), an old man who cannot afford to live on his pension, and his relations with his disdainful landlady, a friendly maid, and his faithful dog Flike. His trip to the dog pound, where unclaimed animals are destroyed, is a not-so-subtle metaphor for his own plight. Similar symbolism, perhaps, can be found in his landlady's dispossessing him because of her impending marriage to a movie theater owner. Himself dispossessed from Italian cinema—at least from financing for neorealist projects—De Sica accepted Hollywood backing from producer David O. Selznick for a co-production starring American performers Jennifer Jones and Montgomery Clift, *Stazione Termini* (*Indiscretion of an American Wife*, 1953; British title, *Indiscretion*).

VARIETIES OF NEOREALISM

The question of film movements has sometimes vexed film historians, because they are never as tidy as scholarship may make them seem. Italian neorealism is perhaps as coherent as any group of films that have been designated a movement: it stemmed from specific historical circumstances, shared personnel and aesthetic styles, even had a lasting name in its own heyday (unlike Soviet silent cinema of the 1920s, which has yet to be given a satisfactory label, or Hollywood's post–World War II **film noir**, which got its name years later, in another country). Yet to all but specialists, neorealism is almost always known primarily through the works of Rossellini and De Sica. Many other styles and approaches within the movement can be suggested through a sampling of films from other directors.

The Bandit

The first postwar film of director Alberto Lattuada (b. 1914), *Il bandito* (*The Bandit*, 1946) was associated with neorealism through its focus on Italian soldiers returning from German prison camps and its location footage in Turin and the Italian Alps. But stylistically the film fits more into classical than neorealist norms, dominated by its tight close-ups of its star performers, Anna Magnani (from *Rome, Open City*) and Amedeo Nazzari (1907–1979), an Errol Flynn lookalike who was a veteran male lead from fascist cinema. Indeed it very strongly foreshadows the emerging Hollywood film noir of the same period, with its embittered but fundamentally moral war veteran who falls for a *femme fatale* and becomes a criminal. His death in the mountains after a police hunt also calls to mind the end of Humphrey Bogart's character in the Warner Bros. gangster film *High Sierra* (1941, directed by Raoul Walsh). Other Lattuada contributions to neorealism include *Senza pietà* (*Without Pity*, 1948) and *Il mulino del Po* (*The Mill on the Po*, 1949).

La terra trema

After *Ossessione* in 1942, Luchino Visconti worked as a theater director until 1947, when with initial funding from the Italian Communist party he went to Sicily to make a documentary on social conditions in one of Italy's poorest areas. Once there, he developed an ambitious plan to make a three-part film—one on fishermen, one on farm workers, one on miners. After spending seven months in the fishing village of Aci Trezza, the filmmaker

13.14. *Shooting* Il mulino del Po (The Mill on the Po, 1949); director Alberto Lattuada is under the umbrella, with sunglasses.

was able to complete only the first of these—a two-hour, forty-minute film, *La terra trema* (*The Earth Trembles*, 1948), which, however, bears a subtitle, *Episodio del mare* ("Episode of the Sea"), suggesting a larger whole.

La terra trema is neorealist aesthetics without compromise: it is filmed entirely on location and performed exclusively by nonprofessionals, Sicilian fishermen and their families. It even uses the local dialect on the soundtrack ("The Italian language is not in Sicily the language of the poor," a title reads). A voice-over narrator provides translations and commentary for Italian spectators, which may at times seem redundant to viewers of the text subtitled in English, for whom both dialect and voice-over are translated.

The film resembles Robert Flaherty's 1934 *Man of Aran*—an acted documentary, or documentary fiction, about people wresting a living from the sea. The difference lies, of course, in politics. Flaherty's people struggle only with nature, Visconti's with the ideology and practices of capitalism. His fishermen work for wholesalers who exploit them. One family, the Valastros, mortgage their house to buy a boat and break the chain of economic subservience, but bad weather destroys the boat and the family is ruined. Crudely speaking, the film's message is that you cannot fight oppression by individualistic means. Near the end the

Neorealism's Black GI

It may come as something of a surprise to see black American soldiers prominently pictured on occasion in publicity stills

and posters for Italian neorealist films. Very little has been written on this subject, but one may suggest reasons for their presence. Black troops in the United States armed forces may have been of particular interest to Italians, whose country had sought to build a colonial empire in black East Africa and had waged war against Ethiopia in the 1930s. Criticism or ridicule of American forces may have been easier to focus on black than on white soldiers, especially since Italians were familiar with the way many black characters had been made to look ridiculous in 1930s Hollywood films. Conversely, blacks as victims of injustice may have sparked sympathy from Italians who also had reason to feel victimized by the cruelties of war.

After Dots M. Johnson played the black soldier in the Naples episode of Roberto Rossellini's *Paisan* (see fig. 13.3), the prin-

cipal black performer in Italian neorealist films was the African-American actor John Kitzmiller (1913–1965), who made his debut in *Vivere in pace* (*To Live in Peace*, 1947), directed by Luigi Zampa (1905–1990). He portrays an American prisoner of war who escapes (with a white buddy) and is hidden in an Italian village guarded by a single German soldier. One night the black man gets drunk and breaks out of his hiding place, encountering the German soldier, also drunk. The two inebriates embrace and carouse through the village, declaring prematurely that the war is over.

Kitzmiller appeared in at least four other neorealist films, most notably in Alberto Lattuada's *Senza pietà* (*Without Pity*, 1948), in which he plays a black American soldier, Jerry, in the postwar setting of the port city Livorno. After falling in love with an Italian prostitute, Jerry becomes enmeshed in the city's criminal underworld, as the interracial couple struggles against injustices from both Americans and Italians. The woman is killed and Jerry drives a truck into the sea.

Kitzmiller had a small role as a jazz musician in Federico Fellini's directorial debut, *Luci del varietà* (*Variety Lights*, 1951), co-directed with Lattuada. His last film performance was as a black American pilot in a Yugoslav production, *Dolina miru* (*The Valley of Peace*, 1956), by the Solvenian director France Stiglic (b. 1919).

Above: 13.15. John Kitzmiller featured on a poster for Alberto Lattuada's Senza pietà *(Without Pity, 1948), which was undergoing a rather visible change of title; the former title, "Naufraghi," literally means "shipwreck," more generally "ruin" or "failure." The poster also suggestively shows a partially unclothed woman and alludes in smaller type to "a futile and hopeless love affair between a black man and a white girl."*

Right: 13.16. Kitzmiller as Joe, a black American soldier, on a drunken spree with the German enemy in Luigi Zampa's Vivere in pace *(To Live in Peace, 1947).*

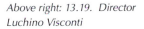

Above right: 13.19. Director Luchino Visconti

Below: 13.20. Needing money to complete Riso amaro *(Bitter Rice, 1949), Giuseppe De Santis accepted support from producer Dino De Laurentiis and, as his lead performer, the producer's young wife, Sylvana Mangano; De Santis's exposé of the exploitation of women workers turned into a torrid sex drama, as promised by this poster for the film.*

defeated fisherman looks directly at the camera and says (as the subtitle renders it), "We must learn to be good to each other and unite for our common good."

Bitter Rice

Another filmmaker with a strong commitment to Marxism was Giuseppe De Santis (b. 1917), who had worked with Visconti on the screenplay for *Ossessione*. But he applied his principles with a considerably different style as a director, particularly in his most famous film, *Riso amaro* (*Bitter Rice*, 1949). On one level an exposé of the exploitation of women hired to plant and harvest rice in a forty-day growing season, more notoriously it featured the first postwar Italian sex symbol, Sylvana Mangano (1930–1989), in tight shorts and loose blouses—and in bare-breasted scenes that seem to have disappeared from surviving prints.

Bitter Rice might have followed an approach closer to *La terra trema*, according to film scholar Michael Silverman, but the Italian Communist party, already underwriting Visconti's films, did not want to put further funds into film production.[7] De Santis was

Left: 13.21. Women at work in the rice fields in Bitter Rice, *directed by Giuseppe De Santis*

Below: 13.22. De Santis's neorealist films (like Visconti's La terra trema*) depicted the struggles of Italy's country people. In* Caccia tragica (Tragic Hunt, *1948), bandits are pitted against a farm collective.*

13.23. A scene from De Santis's *Non c'è pace tra gli ulivi (No Peace under the Olives, 1950)*

approached by producer Dino De Laurentiis, who found bank financing for the project and placed his wife, the teenage starlet Mangano, in the lead role. Mangano made the film an international sensation and paved the way for the success of such other Italian actresses as Gina Lollobrigida (b. 1928) and Sophia Loren (b. 1934). In later years Mangano became an important character actress in films of Visconti and Pier Paolo Pasolini. But for *Bitter Rice*, her presence not only made possible the financing of the film, it shifted the focus from the social issue of women workers to the torrid but distracting themes of sex, crime, murder, and suicide. Among De Santis's other neorealist works were *Caccia tragica (Tragic Hunt,* 1948) and *Non c'è pace tra gli ulivi (No Peace under the Olives,* 1950).

Story of a Love Affair

It may seem incongruous to conclude this survey on the varieties of neorealism with the first fiction feature by Michelangelo Antonioni (b. 1912), a director known for later films in a minimalist style about bourgeois alienation. But *Cronaca di un amore (Story of a Love Affair,* 1950) is of interest as a work closing a circle begun with Visconti's *Ossessione* in 1942. Though set in a Milan fully recovered from war and supporting a hedonistic bourgeoisie, the film's narrative closely resembles the plot that Visconti took from James M. Cain's novel, *The Postman Always Rings Twice:* lovers from different classes scheme to murder the woman's husband.

Events are set in motion by the husband hiring a detective to find out about his wife's past. The investigator learns of a suspicious death in 1943 involving a love triangle, and the inquiry ironically brings the wife and her former lover together again. What seems significant is the notion of interrogating the past and the precision with which crucial moments are located in the fascist era. A film about the wealthy rather than the poor, *Story of a*

13.24. *Lucia Bosè as Paola in Michelangelo Antonioni's* Cronaca di un amore (Story of a Love Affair, *1950)*

Love Affair nevertheless creates a portrait of postwar decadence and amorality firmly linked in a continuity with fascism—an updated form of the desperation and rootlessness Visconti depicted in 1942.

NEOREALISM'S LEGACY

As neorealism came to an end as a film movement in Italy, its role as a force in world cinema was just beginning. When films such as *Bicycle Thieves* and *Rome, Open City* reached countries in Asia, Africa, and Latin America, they struck aspiring filmmakers as revelations. In many countries Hollywood movies dominated the theaters, while struggling domestic film industries sought to copy Hollywood genre styles. Neorealism provided an alternative model to Hollywood—you did not need lavish sets or expensive stars; you could make a film inexpensively with your own country's landscape and people.

Centro Sperimentale

Shortly after World War II the film school founded in Rome during the fascist era, Centro Sperimentale di Cinematografia, reopened (as did the studio complex Cinecittà) under new auspices. Neorealism's influence brought to the school numerous young filmmakers from other countries. One was Fernando Birri (b. 1925) from Argentina, who enrolled in 1950. "For me," Birri later recalled, "the great revelation of the neorealist movement was that, contrary to Hollywood's tenets and example, it was possible to make movies on the same artistic level as a play, a novel, or a poem."[8] After working as an assistant to De Sica on a 1956 film, *Il tetto* (*The Roof*), Birri returned to Argentina, where he

13.25. *After studying at the Italian film school Centro Sperimentale, Argentine director Fernando Birri, among others, brought neorealism's tenets to Latin American cinema in films such as* Los inundados *(Flooded Out, 1961).*

founded a film school and made an important feature in a neo realist style, *Los inundados* (*Flooded Out*, 1961); both school and film helped to stimulate Latin America's filmmaking revival.

Another who came to Centro Sperimentale was Tomás Gutiérrez Alea (b. 1928) from Cuba, who enrolled in 1951. Gutiérrez Alea went on to become a leading feature filmmaker after the 1959 Cuban revolution. His best-known work is *Memorias del subdesarrollo* (*Memories of Underdevelopment*, 1968; see Chapter 18 for a discussion of this film in the context of the 1960s "Cinema of Liberation"). "From the beginning of the revolution," Gutiérrez Alea has said, "our artistic foundation was in fact essentially Italian neorealism."[9]

Other Influences
Many filmmakers who came of age after World War II made testimonials to neorealism. In India, Satyajit Ray (1921–1992) found inspiration in *Bicycle Thieves* for the films he began making in the 1950s that brought international recognition to his country's cinema. In China after the 1949 revolution, *Bitter Rice* provided a model for a cinema combining melodrama and social realism. "My generation," said Nelson Pereira dos Santos (b. 1928), a key figure in Brazil's **Cinema Novo** movement of the 1960s, "was profoundly concerned with the problems of the country . . . and was searching for a form of political participation in the sense of transforming reality. The synthesis (between making films and discussing national reality) was found in the model of Italian neorealism."[10]

Italian Cinema
Neorealism's legacy for Italian cinema is surely more complicated. As postwar Italy entered a period of growing prosperity amid politics as usual, both the terrors and the ideals of the mid-1940s seemed increasingly remote. Federico Fellini, who had worked on the scripts of Rossellini's *Rome, Open City* and *Paisan*, emerged as Italy's most internationally acclaimed director of the 1950s with a more private, subjective style and themes (see Chapter 15). Filmmakers of the neorealist era survived sometimes by making sex comedies featuring Italy's new generation of stars.

The film that seemed most strongly to carry forward neorealist tenets was *Accattone* (1961; the title means "beggar," and is the lead character's nickname), directed by Pier Paolo Pasolini (1922–1975), though Pasolini had not participated in the neorealist movement and spoke little about it. A protean figure, well-known as a poet, novelist, and essayist, Pasolini wrote screenplays in the 1950s before directing *Accattone* as his first film. A story of street youth who hang out and make money as pimps, *Accattone* uses nonprofessionals and location shooting, but it conveys a claustrophobia and emptiness different from neorealism's militancy or pathos. Pasolini's camera roves the faces of his subjects in medium and tight close-ups, less searching for meaning than simply recording their existence. The film breaks with realism in a lengthy dream sequence and in its use of religious motifs, such as Bach's *St. Matthew's Passion* as its music.

Past as Flashback
Films dealing with the fascist era went through a popular cycle in the 1970s, beginning with Bernardo Bertolucci's *Il conformista* (*The Conformist*, 1970), but works that touched on the crucial events of the mid-1940s appeared less frequently. Those that did often opened in a present moment and approached the past through flashback, as a protagonist's personal memory. This device was used in *Cristo si è fermato a Eboli* (*Christ Stopped at Eboli*, 1979), directed by Francesco Rosi (b. 1922), who had worked as an assistant director on Visconti's *La terra trema*. It was also the strategy of *La notte di San Lorenzo* (*The Night of the Shooting Stars*, 1982), codirected by the Taviani brothers, Paolo (b. 1931) and Vittorio (b. 1929).

Though set in the 1930s, like most films depicting the fascist era, *Christ Stopped at Eboli* derives its significance from the book on which it was based, a memoir by the writer, painter, and physician Carlo Levi of his experience in a remote village in southern Italy, to which he was banished by the fascist government in 1935; it was published in 1945, with the same title, and with *Rome, Open City* served as one of the first artistic manifestos of Liberation. *The Night of the Shooting Stars* touches on the partisan struggle, the subject of the Florence and Po delta episodes of *Paisan*. Set in August 1944, the film has as its centerpiece a remarkable sequence of fratricidal warfare, a fight between partisans and fascists in a field of tall wheat. The Tavianis favored nonprofessionals and location work in the film as a kind of homage to neorealism, but they also utilized fantasy sequences, flashbacks as reverie (within the overall flashback structure of the work), and other non-realist stylistics.

A film that attempted to encapsulate neorealism's legacy both for Italy and Italian cinema was *C'eravamo tanto amati* (*We All Loved Each Other So Much*, 1974), directed by Ettore Scola (b. 1931). It too uses flashback structure (while parodying the convention). Opening in the present, it goes back to a brief scene of partisan fighting, then traces the lives of three young partisans over the decades. One becomes a hospital orderly and remains true to his radical principles. Another becomes a wealthy businessman; this character is portrayed by Vittorio Gassman (b. 1922), the villain of *Bitter Rice*, and he gets his start through an obese, corrupt developer played by Aldo Fabrizi, the martyred priest Don Pietro of *Rome, Open City*.

The last one becomes a junior professor who loses his job defending *Bicycle Thieves* against a conservative colleague who shouts, "Films like this offend taste, poetry, and beauty. . . . Dirty laundry should be washed at home." The fired professor becomes an expert on neorealism and scores a success on a 1950s quiz show, but loses everything when he falters on a question about the boy Bruno in *Bicycle Thieves*. When asked, "Why is the boy's crying so realistic?" he answers: because the director, De Sica, put cigarette butts in his pockets. The quiz show host rejects this behind-the-camera anecdote, explaining that the correct answer is: because his father is being beaten for stealing a bicycle. Later we see actuality footage of De Sica explaining to an audience that, indeed, they got the boy to cry by putting lighted cigarette butts in his pockets (the film is dedicated to De Sica, who died in the year it was released).

In its somewhat ironic approach to neorealism, the film displays a nonrealistic style. Characters break the realist frame by making self-reflexive comments as direct address to the camera/spectator in the middle of acted scenes. Full-frame shots are partially blacked out to present a single character's internal thoughts, and shots shift from black-and-white to color and back again. "Our generation is a total failure," one of the characters says near the end, and while it does not seem likely that director Scola fully endorses this verdict, it is clear that his tribute to neorealism is also a farewell.

13.26. *Young men at a café in Pier Paolo Pasolini's* Accattone *(1961)*

Notes

1. Quoted in Joseph L. Anderson and Donald Richie, *The Japanese Film: Art and Industry* (New York: Grove Press, 1959), pp. 224–25.

2. André Bazin, *What Is Cinema? Vol. II*, ed. and trans. Hugh Gray (Berkeley: University of California Press, 1971), p. 66 (from an essay, "De Sica: Metteur en Scène," originally published in Italian in 1951).

3. Roberto Rossellini, "The Intelligence of the Present," in *The War Trilogy: Open City, Paisan, Germany—Year Zero*, ed. Stefano Roncoroni, trans. Judith Green (New York: Grossman, 1973), p. xvi.

4. *The War Trilogy*, p. 154.

5. Bazin, *What Is Cinema? Vol. II*, p. 66.

6. *The War Trilogy*, p. 353.

7. Michael Silverman, "Italian Film and American Capital, 1947–1951," in *Cinema Histories, Cinema Practices*, eds. Patricia Mellencamp and Philip Rosen (Frederick, Md.: University Publications of America, 1984), pp. 41–43.

8. Fernando Birri, "The Roots of Documentary Realism," in *Cinema and Social Change in Latin America: Conversations with Filmmakers*, ed. Julianne Burton (Austin: University of Texas Press, 1986), p. 4.

9. Tomás Gutiérrez Alea, "Beyond the Reflection of Reality," in *Cinema and Social Change in Latin America*, p. 123.

10. Quoted in Randal Johnson, *Cinema Novo X 5: Masters of Contemporary Brazilian Film* (Austin: University of Texas Press, 1984), pp. 165–66.

13.27. Anna Quadri (Dominique Sanda, at right) dances with Giulia (Stefania Sandrelli) in Bernardo Bertolucci's Il conformista (The Conformist, 1970), set in the fascist era.

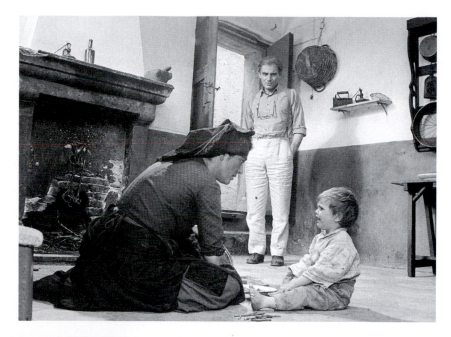

Above: 13.28. Gian Maria Volonte portrays Carlo Levi, Irene Papas his housekeeper, in Francisco Rosi's Cristo si è fermato a Eboli (Christ Stopped at Eboli, 1979), based on Levi's memoir of his banishment to a remote southern Italian village in the 1930s.

Left: 13.29. Villagers go into the fields to look for friends or foes during the wartime struggles between partisans and fascists in La notte di San Lorenzo (The Night of the Shooting Stars, 1982), a film by the brothers Paolo and Vittorio Taviani.

Below: 13.30. A reunion of former partisans Nicola (Satta Flores), Gianni (Vittorio Gassman), and Antonio (Nino Manfredi) in Ettore Scola's C'eravamo tanto amati (We All Loved Each Other So Much, 1974)

FOURTEEN

HOLLYWOOD'S

Historians of Hollywood often regard the United States film industry, with considerable justice, as a separate case in cinema history—different from other national cinemas by its size, its structure, and its success in global film domination. Yet by looking at Hollywood in comparative perspective, it is possible to view what happened there after World War II as part of a worldwide system of transformations in both cinema and society at large. Just as with Italian cinema, for example, Hollywood was subjected to decisive governmental interventions, which responded to, and served to deepen, internal divisions within the industry itself. Though it began the postwar era at the height of its success, the U.S. film industry was within half a decade beleaguered and defensive, only beginning to grasp the new challenges with which it was coping.

The events of the 1946–52 period occurred in a chronological order, but their origins and causes stretch back in some cases for decades, and they are perhaps best seen as a whole. Much of what happened involved completing unfinished business from the 1930s, postponed but also altered by the war. A good deal also was linked to emerging trends reshaping entertainment and leisure activities—ultimately, television replacing movies as primary deliverer of moving image communication. But it is important to bear in mind that television was not the principal cause of the movie industry's changes: it became an important commercial medium only after Hollywood's struggles were well under way.

POLITICAL CHALLENGES TO HOLLYWOOD

Governmental pressures experienced by Hollywood culminated actions initiated before World War II. One strand was an antitrust suit begun by the Justice Department in the 1930s that in 1948 reached the U.S. Supreme Court, where a decision was rendered against the movie industry. Another was a concern with alleged communist infiltration of the motion picture industry, which had aroused the interest of a congressional unit, the House Committee on Un-American Activities (known as HUAC), before the war, and led to traumatic public hearings beginning in 1947.

The Paramount Case

The government's antitrust suit was known as "the Paramount case" as shorthand for its full name, *United States v. Paramount Pictures, Inc., et al.* Filed in 1938, the suit charged not only Paramount but also all the other major companies (M-G-M/Loew's, Warner Bros., RKO, Twentieth Century-Fox) with violating United States laws against monopoly in restraint of trade. The government argued that the structure of the motion picture industry that had developed during the studio era—the system of vertical integration, with large companies controlling production, distribution, and exhibition (through ownership of large city theaters)—was such a monopoly.

As was usual in cases such as these, a lower court handed down a so-called consent decree, in which companies agreed to scale down offending practices. In this instance, however, the

14.1. The allure of television: a crowd gathers on a New York City street, outside the headquarters of the National Broadcasting Company, to watch a live transmission of the coronation of Britain's Queen Elizabeth II in 1953.

their contempt citations were upheld by higher courts and all ten served up to a year in prison. The motion picture industry, seeking to head off further congressional inquiry into movie content, agreed that it would no longer employ communists or alleged subversives. HUAC hearings resumed in 1951, when witnesses were required to "name names" of others they knew to be members of the Communist party, or face banishment from the industry. It is estimated that several hundred writers, performers, and directors lost their employment through the "blacklist" that lasted more than a decade. Many others came under suspicion (for example, for having joined antifascist organizations in the 1930s to which communists belonged) and to keep their jobs had to write letters repudiating their past political beliefs. The consequences for motion picture production are difficult to assess, but certainly Hollywood could ill afford to reject so many talented individuals during a period when its role in entertainment was under challenge. Some writers were able to continue working under pseudonyms or by having others take the credit, but this was not possible for blacklisted performers or directors. A breakthrough against the blacklist came in 1960 when one of the Hollywood Ten, Dalton Trumbo, received screen credit as scriptwriter for *Spartacus*, directed by Stanley Kubrick. In the

STRUGGLES

government regarded the decree as too lenient and appealed to the Supreme Court. In its *Paramount* decision, the high court supported the government and ordered decrees that would require movie studios to divest themselves of all theater ownership. That process lasted into the mid-1950s and was a major factor in the demise of the studio system that had been in place since the 1920s.

The HUAC Hearings

Simultaneously with the Paramount case came the congressional probe into alleged communist activities in the motion picture industry. That members of the Communist party worked in Hollywood was well-known; it was a legal political party, and the U.S. alliance with the Soviet Union during World War II had fostered openness and cooperation. But in a rapidly changing political climate, with a Cold War escalating between the former Allies and a domestic backlash under way against New Deal liberalism, conservatives sought to drive leftists from the communications industry. The House Un-American Activities Committee hearings of 1947 called both "friendly" witnesses (these included studio heads and performers such as Robert Taylor, Gary Cooper, and Ronald Reagan) and witnesses who did not appear voluntarily, deemed "unfriendly." Among the latter, ten were charged with contempt of Congress after they refused to answer questions such as, "Are you now or have you ever been a member of the Communist party?"

The so-called Hollywood Ten, mainly screenwriters, argued that the First Amendment of the Constitution's Bill of Rights protected the privacy of their political beliefs and affiliations, but

changing atmosphere of the 1960s the blacklist broke down and was regarded retrospectively as a nightmare of American political repression, which left behind blighted careers and ruined lives.

Audience Decline

These events came on the heels of Hollywood's most successful year in its history, 1946, in terms of motion picture attendance. Audience numbers began to decline after that, affected by population shifts to the suburbs, returning veterans concentrating on jobs and establishing families, and growing interest in outdoor and participatory leisure activities. Sales of television receivers and the development of television programming became factors in the further drop in movie attendance beginning around 1948–49. Hollywood's attempts to counter these trends began with a gradual increase in color motion pictures (color television was not substantially available until the 1960s). It reached a crescendo around 1953 with the introduction of widescreen (actually, reintroduction; see Chapter 8 for earlier widescreen innovations) and three-dimensional processes. This chapter will focus on the postwar period through 1952; the new technologies and later developments will be discussed in Chapter 16.

FILM NOIR

This period of difficulty in the American motion picture industry nevertheless saw the flourishing of perhaps Hollywood's most famous film movement—**film noir.** Distinctive in a dark and oppressive visual style, and in narratives of desperation and entrapment that defied Hollywood's conventions of happy end-

Communities and Culture

What was at stake in *United States v. Paramount Pictures Inc., et al*, the case that led to the breakup of the vertically integrated Hollywood studio system? Clearly it must have been something more than the typical suit in which the U.S. Justice Department charges a company or an industry with violating laws against monopoly in restraint of trade. In most instances the consent decrees by which these cases are settled are allowed to lapse after about twenty years; with the motion picture industry, the consent decrees that settled the Paramount case lasted nearly forty years, finally lapsing in the 1980s when motion picture production or distribution companies were again allowed to hold a financial interest in theater ownership.

Challenges to the vertical integration of the motion picture industry arose almost as soon as companies began to pursue the strategy, around World War I, of owning production studios, distribution exchanges, and theaters. This was often instigated by associations of independent exhibitors. Though the major studios owned less than 20 percent of the total number of theaters, they dominated the first-run houses in the big cities. The pictures they played in these theaters were highly publicized and eagerly sought after by thousands of smaller theaters. As distributors, however, the major companies required exhibitors to take "blocks" of films in order to get the ones they wanted, and to sign up for them sight-unseen (these practices were called "block-booking" and "blind-booking").

During the New Deal era of the 1930s, debate on motion picture industry practices shifted to the ground of communities and culture. A strong strand of thought in the United States holds that culture should be community-based; even if a community does not produce all of its own culture, as few have ever done, this viewpoint contends that "community values" should determine what cultural products are exhibited or sold. In the era of live entertainment, even when a show was produced elsewhere, communities could decide whether or not to book the road company. But motion picture industry practices, especially block- and blind-booking, were seen from this perspective as eroding community choice. The was one of the perspectives underlying the Justice Department's persistence in opening the Paramount case in 1938, sustaining it through various compromise efforts until the 1948 decision was achieved that ordered movie companies to divest their theater ownership, and continuing the resulting consent decrees for nearly four decades.

Ironically, however, motion picture divestment came at just the time commercial television was starting in the United States, with even greater potential for undermining community choice in media. As so-called "networks" emerged in television as production-distribution companies, the Federal Communications Commission limited their ownership of individual television stations; later the networks also were restricted from producing some entertainment programs. In an era of electronic delivery of cultural products, the issues of community control over culture, still very much alive, are difficult to define or implement.

ings and good triumphing over evil, film noir has influenced younger filmmakers for decades, and grown in critical importance ever since the movement was named, retrospectively, by two French critics in their 1955 book entitled *Panorama du film noir américain*.[1] (The name derived from a French series of translations of American hard-boiled detective and crime novels, called *"Série Noire,"* which gave rise to the term *roman noir*, or dark novel, hence *film noir*.)

With its themes of paranoia and betrayal, of suspicious innocence and attractive guilt, of greed and desire in a world whose moral signposts have disappeared, film noir might appear a natural outgrowth of Hollywood's postwar troubles. The film movement got its start, however, during World War II (a period to which, of course, many of its themes also apply), and its sources date back to the 1930s. These varied circumstances have generated a critical debate about the fundamentals of film noir. Was it a genre, was it a movement, was it a style? How many films belong to the film noir canon? A reference book on film noir lists nearly two hundred titles from 1944 to 1952, with 1950 as the peak year, and a rapid falloff into the mid-1950s.[2] If this seems perhaps too inclusive, there are viewpoints at the other end of the spectrum whose definitions are so precise that only a half dozen or so titles qualify as "true" film noir. Somewhere between these numerical extremes lies a film movement whose distinctive style and perspective cropped up in a wide variety of existing genres—gangster, crime, private eye, police procedural, and espionage films, even women's melodramas, historical costume pictures, and literary adaptations.

Sources of Film Noir

One of the anomalies of film noir in its historical context was that so many of its important films were drawn from hard-boiled crime and detective novels of the 1930s. These holdovers from the depression era were available in part because Hollywood's self-regulating body, the Production Code Administration, had at first refused approval for their film adaptation, then grew more lenient

(1905–1986), *Phantom Lady* by Robert Siodmak (1900–1973), *Ministry of Fear* by Fritz Lang; in 1945, *Detour* by Edgar G. Ulmer (1904–1972) and Lang's *The Woman in the Window* and *Scarlet Street*. These directors brought not only expressionist cinematography's odd angles and dark shadows but also a pessimism drawn from witnessing the rise of fascism in modern mass societies. Coincidentally, Wilder, as writer, and Siodmak and Ulmer, as codirectors, had made their film debut on a 1929 work, *Menschen am Sonntag* (*People on Sunday*), on which Fred Zinnemann (b. 1907), later the director of *High Noon* (1952), also worked.

POSTWAR ANXIETY. Along with these prewar and foreign influences, film noir was shaped by the experience of war's horrors, by the deep-rooted anxieties touched off by the dawn of the nuclear age, and by the difficult postwar adjustment faced by veterans. Moreover, after the HUAC hearings progressive filmmakers learned to couch their social critiques within familiar genre frameworks, which may help to account for the surge of noir films around 1950, just before many of the progressives were driven from the industry. Not all film noir works were concerned with criticizing society, to be sure, but in most of them something was amiss; the individual was out of step with social order and doomed to pay the consequences.

Above: 14.2. Dick Powell as private eye Philip Marlowe, with a gun at his back and facing his own grim visage, in Murder, My Sweet *(1944), directed by Edward Dmytryk*

Right: 14.3. The film noir protagonist, ensnared in the web of lawlessness: private investigator Jeff Bailey (Robert Mitchum) takes an assignment from racketeer Whit Sterling (Kirk Douglas), with assistant Joe Stefanos (Paul Valentine), in Out of the Past *(1947), directed by Jacques Tourneur.*

Film Noir Style

Film noir has been defined in terms both of narrative and of visual style. Its most common narrative element involves a male protagonist's fascination with an alluring, dangerous woman, which leads him away from certainty and order into a world of lawlessness and guilt. Formally, these stories were often told as flashbacks, with action in the present alternating with or framing past events, as the protagonist searches for his lost identity, for the place where things went wrong. These narratives of psychological distress and social disruption were also shaped by the films' visual style. Film noir emphasized dark and claustrophobic framing, with key lighting from sources within the mise-en-scène casting strong shadows that both conceal and project characters' feelings. This visual style marked a sharp break with the brightly lighted and carefully balanced look of Hollywood films of the 1930s.[3]

during the war and postwar period. The French authors of *Panorama du film noir américain* cite as the beginning of film noir *The Maltese Falcon* (1941), directed by John Huston and based on the 1930 novel of the same name by Dashiell Hammett. Others regard the emergence of film noir as dating from two 1944 films, *Double Indemnity*, directed by Billy Wilder, and *Murder, My Sweet*, directed by Edward Dmytryk; the former was adapted from the 1936 novel of the same name by James M. Cain, the latter from the 1940 novel *Farewell, My Lovely* by Raymond Chandler. Chandler cowrote the script for *Double Indemnity* with director Wilder.

GERMAN ÉMIGRÉS. Another source for film noir was German cinema of the Weimar era, with its dark psychological moods and eerie visual effects associated with expressionism. Many of the key early works of the film noir movement were directed by German (or Austrian) émigrés: in 1944, *Double Indemnity* by Wilder (b. 1906), *Laura* by Otto Preminger

Hollywood on Trial

The anticommunist crusade in the United States after World War II is widely known by the name McCarthyism, after Senator Joseph R. McCarthy (1908–1957), Republican of Wisconsin, who emerged in 1950 as a leader of the hunt for alleged subversives. A standard dictionary defines McCarthyism as follows: "public accusation of disloyalty to one's country, esp. through pro-Communist activity, in many instances unsupported by proof or based on slight, doubtful, or irrelevant evidence."

McCarthy's Senate committee was not involved in the investigation of Hollywood, which was centered in the House Un-American Activities Committee (HUAC). Besides its concern with movies, HUAC also focused on labor unions and other organizations that members of the Communist party had joined in the 1930s and the war years. But the motion picture industry and the communications field more generally were special targets of the investigators, who were supported by conservative interests opposed to what they regarded as left-wing bias in the media.

Concerned that HUAC was going to make a direct assault on motion picture content, directors John Huston and William Wyler and writer Philip Dunne took the lead in forming the Committee for the First Amendment, composed of Hollywood figures committed to defending filmmakers' artistic freedom. (HUAC did begin to probe movie content, but quickly dropped this subject in favor of concentrating on the political beliefs of individuals). Many of its members flew to Washington to be present when Eric Johnston, head of the producers association, was scheduled to testify, but HUAC crossed them up, calling instead the first of the "unfriendly" witnesses. The First Amendment group lost its zeal as members did not want to be branded as, in the language of the era, "fellow-travelers" of the left. Ten "unfriendly" witnesses refused to answer questions about their political affiliations and were cited for contempt of Congress.

Opposite: 14.4. Chairman of the House Un-American Activities Committee J. Parnell Thomas, Republican of New Jersey (right center, right hand raised), swears in the first witness, a committee investigator, as hearings begin on alleged "communist infiltration of the motion picture industry" in October 1947. Sitting at Thomas's left is first-term Congressman Richard M. Nixon, Republican of California, later president of the United States.

Right: 14.5. Members of Hollywood's Committee for the First Amendment, with Lauren Bacall and Humphrey Bogart in the lead, en route to attend the HUAC hearings

Right: 14.6. The Hollywood Ten in 1948 with their attorneys, after contesting their contempt citations (from left, front row: Herbert Biberman, attorneys Martin Popper and Robert W. Kenny, Albert Maltz, Lester Cole; second row: Dalton Trumbo, John Howard Lawson, Alvah Bessie, Samuel Ornitz; back row: Ring Lardner, Jr., Edward Dmytryk, Adrian Scott). The ten men were convicted of contempt; after their appeals were denied, all served prison terms of up to one year.

Left: 14.7. Orson Welles as Michael O'Hara and Rita Hayworth as Elsa Bannister, multiplied in a hall of mirrors in Welles's The Lady from Shanghai (1948)

Below: 14.8. Rita Hayworth, as Gilda, sings her famous "Put the Blame on Mame" number from Gilda (1946), directed by Charles Vidor.

Women in Film Noir

A significant trend in recent criticism has been to explore the representation of women in film noir. The roster of beautiful women who lure or impel men to transgression is a long one: it includes performances by Barbara Stanwyck in *Double Indemnity*, Joan Bennett in *The Woman in the Window* and *Scarlet Street*, Jane Greer in *Out of the Past* (1947, directed by Jacques Tourneur), and Rita Hayworth in *The Lady from Shanghai* (1948, directed by Orson Welles). Hayworth's famous performance in *Gilda* (1946, directed by Charles Vidor), in which she sings the sultry song "Put the Blame on Mame" while peeling off her long black gloves, has come to epitomize the *femme fatale* of film noir, though, curiously, Hayworth's character does not play that role in the film's narrative. Crudely put, while exciting the spectator this figure also warned against—and suffered—the dire consequences of sexual freedom and desire.

One distinctive mark of film noir is how well many of its works have stood the test of time. Their mordant approach is sometimes despairing, but more often it leads to a sharpened energy and surprise in visual technique and performance. For performers especially, film noir was a tonic. Barbara Stanwyck (1907–1990), Fred MacMurray (1908–1990), and Edward G. Robinson all used *Double Indemnity* to forge new screen personas. Dick Powell (1904–1963) shifted from a singing juvenile to a tough guy private eye in *Murder, My Sweet.* Dropped by M-G-M, Joan Crawford signed with Warner Bros. and won the Best Actress Oscar for her performance in *Mildred Pierce* (1945, directed by Michael Curtiz).

14.9. *A lobby card for* Murder, My Sweet *promoted Dick Powell's career change from juvenile lead in musicals to film noir tough guy.*

Narrative Innovations in Film Noir

Film noir also innovated in narrative techniques. *Double Indemnity* is marked by two temporal movements: of "real" time and remembered time. The film opens with Walter Neff (MacMurray) arriving at his office in the middle of the night and delivering into a dictating machine his confession for killing a man—"for money" (pause) "and for a woman." These words trigger a flashback that is occasionally narrated by his voice-over confession. Gradually the narrative brings "real" time and memory together, while the unusual juxtaposition of temporalities gives the spectator a premonition of what will occur/has occurred in the flashback story. Finally, they meet as Neff is about to die from the gunshot wound he suffered at the end of his flashback.

In *Scarlet Street*, another tale of allurement and murder—and a remake of Jean Renoir's 1931 French film *La Chienne*—the novelty (under Production Code rules) is that the murderer gets away with it, while another man dies in the electric chair for the crime. Because of this apparent breach of the Code, the city of Atlanta, Georgia, tried to stop the film from screening there. In an affidavit supporting the film, Joseph I. Breen of the Production Code Administration wrote, "It was our contention and belief that in this particular motion picture, the murderer was adequately punished by a higher power, working through his own conscience, which drove him to become a social outcast and a hopeless derelict."[4]

In *Detour*, the male protagonist's voice-over persistently addresses an impersonal "you"—giving the spectator the impression that he or she is the person spoken to—and assumes that the listener is smug, unsympathetic, and unbelieving. A B picture,

produced by one of Hollywood's small companies, that has become a film noir classic, *Detour* is significant in part because its genre traits shine through so strongly, unmediated by the presence of familiar stars. The man feels passive, controlled by fate and women's ambitions. His crimes are committed "accidentally" but out of deep anger and resentment.

Voice-over and flashback were persistent stylistic and narrative elements of film noir. While *Double Indemnity* carefully clues the spectator to who is speaking, when, and from where, other films use voice-over and flashback temporality more ambiguously. Often we need to inquire about the motives of narrative voices, how much they know and whether they are telling the truth, when and to whom they are speaking. If the dominant Hollywood style provided all the information spectators would need to follow the narrative, film noir seems to emphasize narrative gaps, and even the possibility of narratives that can deceive. *Invisible Storytellers*, a study of voice-over narration by Sarah Kozloff, shows that its occurrence in Hollywood films is closely linked to the rise and decline of the film noir movement.[5] Besides *Double Indemnity* and *Detour*, voice-over is a key narrative aspect of *Mildred Pierce*, *Gilda*, *The Lady from Shanghai*, and *Out of the Past*, among film noir works already noted, as well as many others.

The enduring critical question is how useful it is to apply the film noir label broadly to films of the postwar era. *Mildred Pierce*, for example, clearly demonstrates elements of film noir in its narrative structure (such as its use of the flashback) and parts of its

INDEPENDENT PRODUCTION

Though it broke with stylistic norms, the film noir movement was still very much a product of the system. With few exceptions, film noir works came out of the studio production process. A significant aspect of the postwar era, however, was a desire on the part of filmmakers to break not only with old norms but with the system itself: to set up as independent producers of their own work.

Director Frank Capra delivered the most prominent public statement of this wish in an article, "Breaking Hollywood's 'Pattern of Sameness,'" published in the *New York Times* in May 1946. "A change is in the making in Hollywood," it began, and Capra forecast that independent production would bring quality and individuality to American movies.[7] There had of course always been independent producers in Hollywood, distributing their films

Above: 14.10. Phyllis Dietrichson (Barbara Stanwyck) and Walter Neff (Fred MacMurray), lovers and murderers, meet clandestinely in a grocery aisle in Billy Wilder's Double Indemnity *(1944).*

Right: 14.11. Christopher Cross (Edward G. Robinson) talks with reporters covering the execution of a man who is innocent of the murder that Cross committed, in Fritz Lang's Scarlet Street *(1945). Joseph I. Breen defended this breach of Production Code Administration rules, in letting a guilty man go unpunished, by arguing that "the murderer was adequately punished by a higher power."*

Below right: 14.12. The claustrophobic intimacy of Vera (Ann Savage) and Al (Tom Neal) in Edgar G. Ulmer's Detour *(1945)*

visual style, but these aspects should not obscure the work's important status as a women's melodrama, where the issues of female representation are considerably different from film noir's typical concerns with male protagonists lured by *femmes fatale*. It is even more dubious to count such films as Howard Hawks's *The Big Sleep* (1946) or John Huston's *The Asphalt Jungle* (1950) as film noir if such designation deflects attention from these works as part of their primary genres, respectively private eye and crime. The same holds true for another postwar classic from a small company, *Gun Crazy* (1950), directed by Joseph H. Lewis (b. 1900). This film about an adventure-seeking couple who launch a crime spree contains few film noir aspects, but it is revealing to see from Production Code records how the code enforcement agency pushed the work in a film noir direction by proposing changes that would make the man more of an "unwilling victim" of the woman's "desire for wealth, no matter how this is obtained."[6] The original release title of *Gun Crazy* was *Deadly is the Female*.

Right: 14.13. The law confronts Mildred Pierce (Joan Crawford) after a murder in her beach house in Mildred Pierce *(1945), directed by Michael Curtiz. Her former husband Bert (Bruce Bennett) stands hatless at right.*

Below: 14.14. Director Howard Hawks (right, with glasses) working on a scene for The Big Sleep *(1946) with performers Lauren Bacall, Humphrey Bogart, and John Ridgely*

Below right: 14.15. Bart Tare (John Dall) and Annie Laurie Starr (Peggy Cummins) pulling a heist in Gun Crazy *(1950), directed by Joseph H. Lewis*

Frank Capra

The exemplary case was Capra's own endeavor. With directors William Wyler and George Stevens, Capra set up a production company, Liberty Films, with a distribution deal with RKO. All three, it should be noted, had done wartime documentary or propaganda work for the government, and their experience undoubtedly contributed to their ambitions. But Wyler had commitments to other producers he had to fulfill, and Stevens continued in military service. So it was up to Capra alone to make the first step toward independence.

through United Artists or occasionally through a major studio (as Capra had done with *Meet John Doe* in 1941), but after the war the desire to become independent was widespread. John Ford, Howard Hawks, and Fritz Lang were among many directors involved in independent companies; performers such as Humphrey Bogart set up their own independent ventures.

Independence did not produce the results Capra was looking for. There were economic reasons for bigness (and possibly also for sameness). The studios spread their overhead costs over many films; successes balanced out failures. Independents had too many eggs in one basket. Production delays or budget overruns could be financially disastrous; if audiences did not respond to their work, there was no cushion to fall back on. Though it was itself to become the norm within a few years, replacing the old studio system mode of production, independent production got off to a rocky start in the immediate postwar years, with more defeats than triumphs.

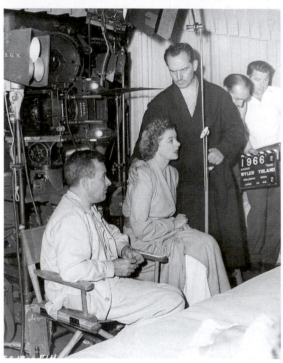

Above: 14.16. *George Bailey (James Stewart) happily reunites with wife Mary (Donna Reed) and children at the end of Frank Capra's* It's a Wonderful Life *(1946). The children are portrayed by Larry Simms, Karolyn Grimes, Carol Coomes, and Jimmy Hawkins.*

Left: 14.17. *Director William Wyler on the set of* The Best Years of Our Lives *(1946) with performers Myrna Loy and Fredric March*

Right: 14.18. *Wyler sits atop the camera boom with his crew for a shot during production of* The Heiress *(1949), based on Henry James's novel* Washington Square.

IT'S A WONDERFUL LIFE. The film he made was *It's a Wonderful Life* (1946), which drew on his award-winning prewar films such as *Mr. Deeds Goes to Town* (1936) and *Mr. Smith Goes to Washington* (1939) as well as his war work. It told a story of one of his typical figures, an uncommon common man, George Bailey, portrayed by James Stewart. Forced to give up his ambitions to travel by the necessity of taking over the family business (a savings and loan association), he remains at home while his younger brother becomes a war hero; then the business itself is threatened by a cruel and unscrupulous competitor. George attempts suicide but is saved by a guardian angel, who responds

to George's cry, "I wish I had never been born," by showing him how his community and loved ones would have fared if he had not existed. George realizes that it is better to have lived, and the angel tells him, "You've had a wonderful life." He returns home on Christmas Eve and finds that his neighbors have chipped in to save his business.

It's a Wonderful Life was an honored film of 1946 and has grown in stature over the years to become a perennial favorite of the Christmas season. But its mood of defeat and desperation was perhaps stronger than the director realized, and audiences did not respond in sufficient numbers to ensure the future of Liberty

100'52 – 2/43

Films. In 1948 Capra persuaded his associates to sell the company's assets to a studio. The failure of Liberty Films was a blow to Capra's career from which he did not fully recover.

The Best Years of Our Lives
Wyler did not get to make a film for the Liberty venture, but his first postwar film, *The Best Years of Our Lives*, made for Samuel Goldwyn, beat out *It's a Wonderful Life* for 1946 honors. It won Academy Awards for best picture, director, actor (Fredric March), supporting actor (Harold Russell), screenplay (Robert E. Sherwood), editing (Daniel Mandell), and music (Hugo Friedhofer).

The Best Years was the film Capra's was not (though Capra had deliberately declined to attempt such a work): an epic statement, nearly three hours long, on the transition from war to peacetime.

The Best Years is the story of three men returning from war to the same hometown. They represent three different branches of service and three social classes. One of the three was portrayed by a nonprofessional, Harold Russell, who had lost both hands in the war and was fitted with prosthetic devices. In addition to his supporting actor Oscar, he was given a special award for "bringing hope and courage to his fellow veterans" through his appearance in the film. The narrative centers primarily on the

than three decades as the world's most popular comic actor, Chaplin had begun to come under attack in the United States for his offscreen activities. He had been convicted in a paternity suit and tried on other morals charges (his biographers consider accusations against him in both cases to have been false). Meanwhile, his progressive political views had fallen out of step with the Cold War turn toward anticommunism.

Chaplin played into his critics' hands with *Monsieur Verdoux* (1947), his first film since *The Great Dictator*. No longer the Little Tramp and only ambiguously a comic figure, Chaplin's character seemed to confirm (in a confusion of art and life) both the moral and political charges against the actor. He played a man who murders women for profit and defends himself by saying that his business was no different from war, which was also murder for profit. The majority of reviewers and most of the public rejected the film. He went to work on *Limelight* (1952), an homage to the

Above: 14.19. Henri Verdoux (Charles Chaplin) meets a woman (Marilyn Nash) in Chaplin's Monsieur Verdoux *(1947).*

Right: 14.20. Robert Walker as John and Helen Hayes as his mother prepare to shoot a scene for My Son John *(1952); director Leo McCarey is seated at left.*

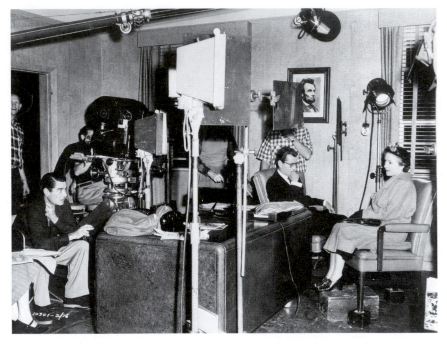

reconstruction of family life and the men's relations with women, who are represented through their roles in men's lives rather than in terms of their own wartime work or future activities.

The film was perhaps the most complete expression in Hollywood filmmaking of cinematic "realism" as expounded by André Bazin. Photographed by Gregg Toland, the cinematographer on *Citizen Kane*, it strongly favors the style identified with Jean Renoir's work in France, using long takes, a moving camera, and deep focus, with objects and people photographed in relation to each other in different planes of depth within the frame. As the film noir movement and *It's a Wonderful Life* have grown in critical estimation, however, *The Best Years* has not fared as well. It is perhaps an overly composed film, too carefully planned so as to look "natural," as compared to Renoir's fluid and supple mise-en-scène or the discomposed and artificial worlds of the films from this period that have endured.

Charles Chaplin

The independent producer with the greatest longevity entering the postwar era was Charles Chaplin, whose independent company dated to the founding of United Artists in 1919. But after more

music-hall-comedy tradition, which also featured the silent comedy star Buster Keaton. In 1952, before *Limelight* was released, Chaplin sailed for England, and the United States government rescinded his reentry permit (he remained a British subject) on the grounds that he was suspected of being an undesirable alien. Chaplin did not return to the United States for twenty years, until long after the anticommunist hysteria of the postwar era had ended. In 1972 he was given a special Academy Award "for the incalculable effect he has had in making motion pictures the art form of the century."

My Son John

In the political atmosphere in which Chaplin was barred from the United States, politicians sometimes chided the Hollywood studios for their failure to produce anticommunist films. In response, the studios turned out a few such works, but many were B pictures and most failed at the box office. Typical was an RKO film originally released as *I Married a Communist* (1950) but renamed *The Woman on Pier 13* when the original title elicited little interest. Perhaps the most ambitious anticommunist film was an independent production distributed by Paramount, *My Son John*

The Western

The most influential Western of the early postwar years was *Red River* (1948), directed by Howard Hawks as an independent production. Although Hawks's name is often associated with the Western genre, this was the veteran director's first Western after more than twenty years in Hollywood. On one level an epic tale of a historical cattle drive, the film's deeper resonance derived from the performances of John Wayne (1907–1979) as an autocratic Texas rancher and Montgomery Clift (1920–1966) as an orphan who becomes virtually the older man's son. Their characters' struggle over leadership involves issues of masculinity and male love. The film set the tone for the "psychological Western" that was to become an important phase of the genre in the 1950s.

Red River also was significant, according to Hollywood legend, because it persuaded director John Ford that John Wayne could

Aabove: 14.21. Tom Dunson (John Wayne) and Matthew Garth (Montgomery Clift) duke it out in Howard Hawks's Red River *(1948).*

Right: 14.22. Capt. Nathan Brittles (John Wayne) of the U.S. Cavalry meeting with Indian chiefs in John Ford's She Wore a Yellow Ribbon *(1949); Sgt. Tyree (Ben Johnson) is at his side.*

(1952), directed by Leo McCarey (1898–1969), a director of screwball comedies in the 1930s. Product of a harsh, religious father and a weak mother, John becomes a communist spy, but his mother discovers his secret and finds the will to turn him in.

GENRE REVIVALS

In troubled times, the Hollywood studios turned to traditional genres. The postwar years saw a revival especially of Westerns and musicals, which had been partly eclipsed during the war. These genres put on display what the movie industry saw as its trump cards over small-screen television: spectacular visual effects and sumptuous production values in costumes, décor, and color cinematography. And for filmmakers who feared to address social concerns directly in an era of political repression, genres such as the Western offered the opportunity to raise significant themes within the safer framework of conventional narratives.

act. This anecdote, like so many others, may not have been true but held a kernel of meaning: Wayne surely could act, but prior to Hawks's film, characterizations had not been developed for him that could draw out and expand his talent. Ford, whose career as a director of Westerns dated back to 1917, and who had worked with the actor in the prewar classic *Stagecoach* (1939), now crafted new roles for Wayne that helped to forge his status as an American icon.

These were in Ford's United States cavalry trilogy—*Fort Apache* (1948), *She Wore a Yellow Ribbon* (1949), and *Rio Grande* (1950). The chronology is a little tricky here, in terms of the legend, because *Fort Apache* was released before *Red River*, but Hawks's film had been delayed, and Ford had seen Wayne's performance in the editing room before embarking on *Fort Apache*. Of the three, *She Wore a Yellow Ribbon*, a color film, is the most important for Wayne's screen persona, with his elegiac portrait of an aging army officer. Thematically, *Fort Apache* is more ambitious, with Wayne playing a subordinate to an arrogant, insensitive senior officer (portrayed by Henry Fonda) who leads his troops into a massacre by Indians modeled on Custer's defeat at the Battle of the Little Bighorn. Wayne's character survives and allows the press to paint the dead officer as a legendary hero. This introduced a new element of complexity into the Western genre: simultaneously debunking the myths of United States westward expansion while suggesting that their preservation was necessary for national morale.

The development of Westerns as allegory—figurative treatment of one subject under the guise of another—was well advanced by the time of *High Noon* (1952), directed by Fred Zinnemann. Starring Gary Cooper (1901–1961) as a lawman who goes in ninety

Below: 14.23. Apache Indians in battle with U.S. troops in Ford's Fort Apache *(1948)*

Bottom: 14.24. Sheriff Will Kane (Gary Cooper) awaits his showdown with the villains in High Noon *(1952), directed by Fred Zinnemann.*

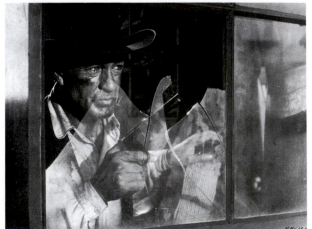

minutes from his wedding to a lonely showdown with vengeful criminals, the film was conceived by scriptwriter Carl Foreman (1914–1984) as a lesson in civics. The unwillingness of townspeople to help the lawman marked a community's failure to support authority and stand up to outside threats. This theme could be seen as applying to the Cold War, or, because Foreman was called to testify before HUAC, as an indictment of Hollywood's capitulation before the congressional investigators. The film's success, however, was due not to these figurative meanings but to its taut drama; it is one of the rare films in which narrative time and the film's duration are almost simultaneous.

The Musical

The postwar musical can almost be encapsulated in one name: Arthur Freed (1894–1973). Freed was a lyricist who became head of the musical production unit at M-G-M, and it was from that studio's Freed Unit that most of the postwar era's classic musicals emerged. Between 1946 and 1952 the Freed Unit produced eighteen musicals, highlighted by *The Pirate* (1948) and *An American in Paris* (1951), both directed by Vincente Minnelli (1903–1986), and *Singin' in the Rain* (1952), codirected by Gene Kelly (b. 1912) and Stanley Donen (b. 1924). Key performers in the Freed musicals included Judy Garland (1922–1969), Fred Astaire, and Kelly. All the Freed musicals were shot in Technicolor, with bright, rich, saturated hues.

Above right: 14.25. Manuela (Judy Garland) and Serafin (Gene Kelly) sing "Be a Clown" in The Pirate, *directed by Vincente Minnelli.*

Right: 14.26. Jerry Mulligan (Gene Kelly) dances with Lise Bouvier (Leslie Caron) in a Parisian flower market to the music of George Gershwin's "An American in Paris" in Minnelli's An American in Paris *(1951).*

Below: 14.27. Probably the most famous sequence in the most famous Hollywood musical—Gene Kelly as Don Lockwood splashes through the "Singin' in the Rain" number of Singin' in the Rain *(1952), directed by Kelly and Stanley Donen.*

Minnelli was one of the most significant directors in the genre's history, in part because he was not solely a musical specialist. Amid his postwar musicals he also directed several dramatic films, and in the 1950s he became an important director of melodramas. This experience added a depth of characterization to his musicals that was not always apparent in other works in the genre, along with an undercurrent of interest in the meaning and value of performance itself. In *The Pirate*, for example, when Judy Garland's character discovers that she can be a performer, she also learns that it is through performance that she can express her deepest feelings.

Kelly and Donen's *Singin' in the Rain*, however, is probably the most famous of all Hollywood musicals ever made—for Kelly's performance of the title song, if for nothing else. A satire on the film industry during the transition to sound, the film expressed a nostalgia and an attitude of self-reassurance—we came through that crisis, so we can get through the crisis now.

Above: 14.28. "We had faces then": Norma Desmond (Gloria Swanson) recalls her triumphs as a silent screen star, while Joe Gillis (William Holden) looks on, in Billy Wilder's Sunset Boulevard *(1950).*

Right: 14.29. Max von Mayerling (Erich von Stroheim, center right), formerly Norma Desmond's husband and director, now her butler, waits with camera crews for her to descend the stairs in Sunset Boulevard.

Hollywood on Hollywood

Singin' in the Rain belongs not only to the musical genre but also to the genre of Hollywood films about itself. These works were often self-promotional and self-congratulatory, but among those that came out in the wake of Hollywood's postwar difficulties were films dark and despairing enough to be listed as part of the film noir movement.

Leader in the mordant revisionism of Hollywood was director Billy Wilder. In *Sunset Boulevard* (1950) he carried the film noir style of narrative voice-over to audacious extremes: his narrator is a dead man, who begins his flashback story as we see his body floating in a swimming pool. The film tells of a former silent screen star, Norma Desmond (portrayed by former silent screen star Gloria Swanson), who attempts a comeback by enlisting—and ensnaring—the soon-to-be-deceased narrator, a screenwriter played by William Holden. Performing as Desmond's chauffeur (and, in the narrative, her former director and husband) was Erich von Stroheim, who *had* directed Swanson in the ill-fated *Queen Kelly*. "We had faces then," Norma Desmond says, and "I *am* big. It's the pictures that got small."

Some in the film community viewed *Sunset Boulevard* as an attack on the industry at a moment when it was most vulnerable. As legend has it, M-G-M head Louis B. Mayer shouted at the director at a preview, "You have disgraced the industry that made you and fed you."[8] But it was also immediately recognized as a classic, for its probing insights on ambition, aging, stardom and its loss, and, not least, the slippage of Hollywood's legendary aura at midcentury. *Sunset Boulevard* was as much an elegy for a lost Hollywood as *She Wore a Yellow Ribbon* was for the old West. When tempers cooled, it was nominated for eleven Academy Awards, including Best Picture and director, and won three, for story/screenplay, art direction/set decoration, and music score.

In his next film, *Ace in the Hole* (also known as *The Big Carnival*, 1951), Wilder widened the scope of his media critique to include newspapers, radio, and television. A washed-up Eastern reporter, played by Kirk Douglas (b. 1916), working in Albuquerque, New Mexico, happens upon a man trapped in a cave. He seizes on the chance to restore his career by dramatizing the incident—and prolonging the rescue effort for maximum publicity exposure. Along with the press, hordes of spectators come to the cave site, where games and rides spring up in a carnival atmosphere. There are several shots of trucks marked "The Great American S & M Corp.," a clear sign of Wilder's views (he was also producer and coscriptwriter) on the sadism and masochism involved in media-generated spectacle. The trapped man loses hope and dies, and the crowd vanishes; belatedly appalled by what he has wrought, the reporter is stabbed in a struggle and also dies. Cynical is a term often used to describe Wilder's films, though it seems a little imprecise; pessimistic and without illusions are closer to the mark.

14.30. *Newspaper reporter Charles Tatum, played by Kirk Douglas, speaks to the crowd that has gathered in the New Mexico desert to witness the attempted rescue of a man trapped in a cavern, in Billy Wilder's* Ace in the Hole *(1951).*

14.31. *Humphrey Bogart as the violence-prone Hollywood screenwriter Dixon Steele in Nicholas Ray's* In a Lonely Place *(1950), with Gloria Grahame as Laurel Gray beside him*

In the Hollywood-on-Hollywood genre, sadism, masochism, and pessimism seemed distressingly to rule. Another dark work touching on the movie industry (and one that is also often listed as a film noir) was *In a Lonely Place* (1950), directed by Nicholas Ray (1911–1979). Humphrey Bogart (1899–1957), whose independent company produced the film, plays an out-of-work screenwriter suspected of a murder. It turns out he is innocent of crimes (a last-minute script change during production), but his violent tendencies and delight in describing murder—from an artistic perspective—are unsettling to both screen characters and spectators. Hollywood is more the milieu than the subject of this work, but by implication it calls into question movie violence and the glorification of screen figures (such as Bogart had become) who use violence acceptably as tough guy heroes.

Minnelli took time out from musicals to direct an important film about Hollywood, *The Bad and the Beautiful* (1952). Kirk Douglas again plays a sadist, a movie producer who abuses creative talent—in the film, a director, a star, and a writer—in order to get them to produce their best work. Hating him, but owing their success to him, the three creative figures are ready to be beguiled into another project by the producer's imagination and energy. This was a barely hopeful ending. Hollywood's confidence appeared to be so battered by the onslaught of political, judicial, and economic challenges that the Hollywood-on-Hollywood genre seemed more capable of providing ammunition for the industry's critics than of shoring up its myths.

Notes

1. Raymond Borde and Étienne Chaumeton, *Panorama du film noir américain (1941–1953)* (Paris: Les Éditions de Minuet, 1955).

2. Alain Silver and Elizabeth Ward, eds., *Film Noir: An Encyclopedic Reference to the American Style* (Woodstock, N.Y.: The Overlook Press, 1979).

3. An article by J. A. Place and L. S. Peterson, "Some Visual Motifs in *Film Noir*," *Film Comment* 10:1 (1974), pp. 30–35, launched the detailed consideration of film noir visual style.

4. Joseph I. Breen, Affidavit, March 25, 1946, *Scarlet Street* file, Motion Picture Association of America, Production Code Administration files, Academy of Motion Picture Arts and Sciences, Beverly Hills, California. Breen's document was submitted to a court in Atlanta, which granted the plaintiffs Universal Film Exchanges and Diana Productions an injunction prohibiting the city from stopping the film from screening.

5. Sarah Kozloff, *Invisible Storytellers: Voice-Over Narration in American Fiction Film* (Berkeley and Los Angeles: University of California Press, 1988).

6. Charles R. Metzger, Memorandum for File, May 29, 1947, *Gun Crazy* file, Motion Picture Association of America, Production Code Administration files, Academy of Motion Picture Arts and Sciences, Beverly Hills, California.

7. Frank Capra, "Breaking Hollywood's 'Pattern of Sameness,'" *The New York Times*, May 5, 1946, reprinted in *Hollywood Directors 1941–1976*, ed. Richard Koszarski (New York: Oxford University Press, 1977), pp. 83–89.

8. Quoted in Maurice Zolotow, *Billy Wilder in Hollywood* (New York: Putnam's, 1977), p. 168.

14.32. Movie producer Jonathan Shields (Kirk Douglas) gives Georgia Lorrison (Lana Turner) an acting lesson in Minnelli's The Bad and the Beautiful (1952).

FIFTEEN

ART CINEMA AND

If Hollywood was having troubles after World War II, the rest of the world was hardly aware of it. American films from as far back as the late 1930s poured into European and Asian countries which had cut off imports from the United States before the war. Moreover, two of the strongest prewar film industries—those of Germany and Japan—were in the control of military occupation forces: of the United States in Japan, and of four Allied nations in Germany. Germany's film industry was further weakened as the Cold War developed and filmmaking in the Soviet zone (where the Ufa studio complex was located) split off from production in the French, British, and American zones. Under these circumstances, the powerful currents of nationalism that had shaped cinema culture before the war began to abate. They were challenged by a growing conception of a cinema without borders: that film was an international medium thriving not in response to the demands of national governments but through the artistic skills and aspirations of individuals.

The post–World War II era saw a revival of the idea of film as art, in opposition to widespread utilization of film for propaganda purposes during the 1930s and the war years. A common term was **art cinema.** Its definition was broad and general; mostly it marked a differentiation from the cinema of crass commercialism. The concept was distinct from "artist's cinema," which implied a relation to the avant-garde, and from the later notion of the film-maker as "*auteur*" (author), which found such figures working in the Hollywood studio system. Art cinema consisted of narrative fiction films whose directors brought seriousness of purpose and a taste for stylistic innovation to their work.

Art cinema was fostered at film festivals, which began to play a significant role in the postwar years as gathering places for the international film community and showcases for new work from many countries. Their prizes helped little-known filmmakers gain the attention of critics and access to a small but growing world market for aesthetically challenging films. The Venice Film Festival in Italy was the oldest such event, having been founded in 1932 as part of Fascism's revival of Italian cinema; it was canceled from 1943 to 1945 and resumed in 1946. The Cannes Film Festival in France began in 1946 and became important not only for the competitive prizes it awarded but as a marketplace for film financing and distribution deals.

INTERNATIONAL CINEMA

The international character of art cinema was shaped by the mingling of filmmakers, performers, producers, and distributors at film festivals. While a considerable share of film production continued

15.1. A public screening in the courtyard of the Palazzo Ducale (Doges' Palace) during a Venice Film Festival

OF EUROPE
ASIA

the pattern of national cinema, to be sure, there were also a number of circumstances that encouraged international cooperation or co-production. Distributors frequently held foreign currencies that could not be exchanged and could only be used in the country of origin; by assembling an international cast and crew a producer could often gain financial backing from a number of countries.

The Third Man

An example of this emerging trend was the film that won the grand prize at Cannes in 1949, *The Third Man* (1949). This thriller was nominally a British film, with direction by Carol Reed (1906– 1976), an original screenplay by novelist Graham Greene, and primary production responsibility from Alexander Korda at his London Films–British Lion company. But it was photographed in Vienna, Austria; Hollywood's David O. Selznick purchased United States distribution rights and participated in the production; and the international cast included Americans Orson Welles and Joseph Cotten (b. 1905) and the Italian actress Alida Valli (b. 1921), who had been under contract to Selznick. The film's visual style was variously compared to Italian neorealism, German expressionism, and American film noir. Perhaps its biggest selling point was its music score, written and played on a zither by Anton Karas, which became a European hit song. "The Third Man

theme" remains recognizable decades after the film's release, and, as Selznick said, "put *The Third Man* into the language" as a term relating to Cold War espionage.[1]

The film's themes were also international. Its male protagonists are both Americans, Cotten as Holly Martins, a naive writer of Western stories, and Welles as Harry Lime, a shadowy dealer in black-market drugs. They carry forward traditional types of the Innocent American and the Ugly American into the web of Cold War intrigue. The ever intrusive Selznick was deeply concerned about another American type, the Ignorant Spectator. He got the filmmakers to add a prologue explaining the four-power occupation of Vienna, and to make "the Russians the heavies, in pursuit of the girl."[2]

The Return of Buñuel

A filmmaker who benefited from a festival prize was Luis Buñuel. The Surrealist director of the avant-garde *Un Chien andalou* and the caustic documentary *Las Hurdes* (*Land without Bread*) had fallen out of the world's sight for some time. He had aided the losing Republican side in the Spanish Civil War and worked at The Museum of Modern Art in New York editing Nazi documentaries for United States distribution, but he was fired from that job when accused of communist sympathies. Basically, he had not directed

323

a film in fifteen years when he went to Mexico in 1947 and resumed his directing career. He made more than twenty films in Mexico over the next two decades before returning permanently to Europe. His third Mexican film, *Los Olvidados* (literally "The Forgotten," originally released in the United States as *The Young and the Damned*, 1950), won him a director's prize at Cannes, restored him to international prominence, and brought Mexican cinema onto the world stage.

As a film about impoverished street kids, with a strong social message, *Los Olvidados* inevitably invites comparison with De Sica's *Shoeshine*. But Buñuel was a critic of neorealism. "Neorealist reality is incomplete, conventional, and above all rational," he said. "The poetry, the mystery, all that completes and enlarges tangible reality, is utterly lacking."[3] (He did praise *Bicycle Thieves* and screenwriter Zavattini.) *Los Olvidados* presents the "real" in the form of Surrealism rather than neorealism. "The cinema," Buñuel said, "seems to have been invented to express the life of the subconscious....Yet it is almost never used to do this."[4] Mixed with scenes of abject poverty and cruelty are dreams, surreal visions, states of consciousness, and a rare (for the era) breaking of the illusion of cinematic "reality"—a boy throws an egg at the camera lens, where it shatters and drips. A film of midcentury, *Los Olvidados* unites in a single text the end of the postwar desire for a social cinema and the emergence in the 1950s of an art cinema.

Top right: 15.2. Italian actress Gina Lollobrigida in the midst of a crowd at the 1956 Venice Film Festival

Above: 15.3. Orson Welles as Harry Lime in The Third Man *(1949), directed by Carol Reed*

15.4. Pedro (Alfonso Mejía) in a dispute with his mother (Estela Inda) in Luis Buñuel's Los Olvidados (1950)

15.5. Takehiro the samurai (Masayuki Mori) and Masago, his wife (Machiko Kyo), in Akira Kurosawa's Rashomon (1950)

JAPAN

Japan's entry into the mainstream of world cinema after World War II seems, in retrospect, even more remarkable than it may have appeared at the time. As we have seen, Japan before the war maintained a film industry second in size and strength only to the United States, and in such filmmakers as Kenji Mizoguchi and Yasujiro Ozu had produced masters of the medium. But their films were rarely seen outside Japan or Japanese-controlled territories, and in Europe and North America it was a cinema barely known even to specialists. Japan had been defeated in the war, Tokyo and other cities had been nearly destroyed, and the United States occupation administration was determined to root out what it considered Japan's authoritarian value system and replace it with American-style democracy.

Perhaps fortunately, Americans had a healthy respect for the power of movies. The occupation fostered restoration of the Japanese film industry. Its censorship policies forbade "period" films on the grounds that they reinforced "feudal" values, but as the Cold War took shape the United States sought to utilize Japan's strengths rather than totally transform them, and the Japanese film industry was functioning more or less without constraint before the occupation ended in 1952. Japanese social theorists continue to debate whether the occupation had a positive or negative impact on Japanese culture (in the realm of cinema, for example, Japanese filmmakers found American restrictions less onerous than earlier Japanese censors). As a further point of comparison in film culture, postwar German cinema did not begin to make a mark internationally until the late 1960s.

Film festivals propelled Japanese cinema toward world recognition. Akira Kurosawa's *Rashomon* (1950) won the grand prize at Venice in 1951 (as well as Hollywood's Academy Award for best foreign-language film), and the director won another award for

325

Postwar British Cinema

British filmmakers seemed poised to play a significant role in the post–World War II emergence of an international art cinema. Wartime production of morale-building patriotic fiction films had boosted audiences for domestic features and established a group of talented directors, including Carol Reed, Michael Powell, David Lean, and the writing-directing team of Frank Launder (b. 1907) and Sidney Gilliat (b. 1908). Emulating the Hollywood majors, the Rank Organisation, a vertically integrated company headed by J. Arthur Rank (1888–1972), was a powerful force in production, distribution, and exhibition. And an outstanding group of British performers was doing screen work, most notable among whom was Laurence Olivier (1907–1989), who directed and starred in two Shakespeare adaptations, *Henry V* (1945) and *Hamlet* (1948), the latter of which won Hollywood's Academy Award for best picture (and won for Olivier the Oscar for best actor).

However, this foundation was not as solid as it may have appeared. As usual, the problem was Britain's relations with Hollywood. Concerned about renewed American inroads on the domestic market, the British government in 1947 placed a punishing 75 percent tax on the value of imported films. The U.S. film industry responded by refusing to send films to Britain. British producers stepped up their production commitments to make up for the absence of American films. When, after seven months, a compromise was reached and the boycott ended, Hollywood films flooded into British theaters and domestic producers suffered severe losses. What was apparently intended as a government policy to protect domestic filmmakers had actually harmed them.

In retrospect, the years 1945–48 seem a small "golden age" of British cinema. David Lean contributed *Brief Encounter* (1945), a poignant, low-key work concerning an unconsummated romance between a man and a married woman, with an exceptional performance by Celia Johnson (1908–1982), as well as two adaptations of novels by Charles Dickens, *Great Expectations* (1946) and *Oliver Twist* (1948). Reed directed *Odd Man Out* (1947), concerning a hunted Irish revolutionary portrayed by James Mason (1909–1984), and *The Fallen Idol* (1948), a thriller with the distinguished stage actor Ralph Richardson (1902–1983). Powell, with his collaborator Emeric Pressburger, made among other works an enormously popular Technicolor film concerning a young ballet dancer, *The Red Shoes* (1948).

In subsequent years, comedy became the most successful British genre in the international marketplace. The veteran producer Michael Balcon assembled a skilled comedy team at Ealing Studios. Its key figure was actor Alec Guinness (b. 1914), who had launched his film career with performances in Lean's two Dickens films and made the leap to comedy by playing eight different roles in Ealing's *Kind Hearts and Coronets* (1949), directed by Robert Hamer (1911–1963). Guinness's other important comedies included *The Lavender Hill Mob* (1951), directed by Charles Crichton (b. 1910), and *The Man in the White Suit* (1951), directed by Alexander Mackendrick (b. 1912).

15.6. *Takashi Shimura as Kanji Watanabe, a dying bureaucrat, in Kurosawa's* Ikiru *(1952)*

Shichinin no Samurai (*Seven Samurai*, 1954). Mizoguchi won various prizes at Venice for *Saikaku Ichidai Onna* (*The Life of Oharu*, 1952), *Ugetsu Monogatari* (*Ugetsu*, 1953), and *Sansho Dayu* (*Sansho the Bailiff*, 1954). It was as if Italy was passing the torch of cinematic innovation from the neorealists to the Japanese; but the Cannes festival also rang in with a best film award in 1954 to Teinosuke Kinugasa's *Jigokumon* (*Gate of Hell*, 1953), another Academy Award winner. Two general points can be made about these prize recipients: Japanese cinema's emphasis on the autonomy of directors accorded well with the 1950s' stress on art cinema; and they are all period films.

Akira Kurosawa

Kurosawa was working on a period picture, *Tora no O o Fumo Otokatachi* (*The Man Who Tread on the Tiger's Tail*), when Japan surrendered; because the film dealt with a banned subject, occupation censors held up its release until 1952. The director turned to contemporary themes in a series of postwar films, several of them highly acclaimed, before returning to a period setting with *Rashomon*. In this context one can better appreciate Kurosawa's remark (quoted in Chapter 13) that there would have been more meaning for him had he received a prize for a film about present-day Japan—he mentioned as an example *Bicycle Thieves*, but he might have spoken of his own *Yoidore Tenshi* (*Drunken Angel*, 1948), which Japanese critics consider the *Bicycle Thieves* of postwar Japan.

If *Los Olvidados*, made in the same year, stood on the cusp between social and art cinema, then *Rashomon* may be regarded as the premiere work of an art cinema to start off the second half of the century. Though its setting in a ruined temple in an indeterminate past time (twelfth century in the source story) and other

aspects of the film gave ample evidence to read it as an allegory, far more significant was its narrative method—the telling of an incident of a rape by five different people, with no effort by the filmmaker to reconcile the conflicting versions, to arrive at a single "truth." The method was not entirely novel—*Citizen Kane*, for one example, had different characters narrating their views on Charles Foster Kane's life, with an ambiguous ending—but it spoke with particular force in postwar Europe and North America (as well as Japan), where many were declaring their retreat from ideology in favor of an existential avoidance of big "truths." The film's sentimental ending, in which its common man hero, the simple woodcutter, takes home an abandoned baby, also responded to a desire for humanistic action in the face of indeterminacy.

After *Rashomon*'s prizes, Kurosawa did choose to make a kind of neorealist film: *Ikiru* (translated as "To Live," but known by its original title, 1952), concerning a dying bureaucrat who wakes up to existence and struggles through the bureaucratic maze to get a playground constructed. It continued the sentimental, humanistic tone of *Rashomon*'s ending but also presented a devastating view of bureaucratic complacency and inertia, which the film's slow pace accentuated. Kurosawa became known for his mastery of mise-en-scène in natural settings, as in *Rashomon* or the remarkable windswept final confrontation in *Sanshiro Sugata*, yet *Ikiru* also created a powerful vision of the world of petty officialdom, in dim, run-down warrens dominated by hugh stacks of bundled documents, testimony to inaction.

The director returned to the outdoors with *Seven Samurai*, an epic period film and a rousing adventure tale about a beleaguered village that gathers a small band of warriors to defend against marauding brigands. (The original film was more than three hours

Top: 15.7. Kambei, leader of the samurai (Takashi Shimura, center), directs a battle in Kurosawa's Shichinin no Samurai (Seven Samurai, 1954).

Above: 15.8. Director Akira Kurosawa on the set of Seven Samurai

long; a less impressive version with more than an hour cut out also circulates.) Kurosawa's rise to prominence employed a regular company of performers; two who became internationally known were Toshiro Mifune (b. 1920), who portrayed wild characters in the bandit of *Rashomon* and the imposter samurai in *Seven Samurai*, and Takashi Shimura (1905–1982), who played the contemplative figures of the dying bureaucrat in *Ikiru* and the samurai leader of *Seven Samurai*.

Kenji Mizoguchi

While Kurosawa gained world fame within the first decade of his career, Mizoguchi had been a filmmaker for nearly thirty years before his prize for *The Life of Oharu*, his seventy-sixth film. With support from a new production company aiming at the export market, he was able to make a series of important films before his death in 1956 at the age of fifty-eight. Several of these were on his most persistent themes, the lives of suffering women, often prostitutes and the Japanese entertainers and companions called geisha. His most renowned film was *Ugetsu*, a period work concerning a potter's encounter with the supernatural.

Ugetsu is a unique film that bears comparison with European traditions both of realism and Surrealism. Like Jean Renoir's films, *Ugetsu* utilizes a moving camera and depth of field to create an ample, complex sense of space, and, like Renoir, Mizoguchi shows the capacity to mingle farce and tragedy in the same moment. But the visual style continually bursts the bounds of realism by veering into dreams and the supernatural, as with Buñuel. Unlike either European tradition, however, or even Mizoguchi's earlier work, its tone is ultimately serene and contemplative. Real horrors have occurred—particularly to women—but in the end the potter returns to his wheel, sustained by the ghost of his murdered wife.

Gate of Hell

This multiple prize-winning film was honored primarily for its use of color. It was one of the first Japanese color films and it utilized a new color process, Eastmancolor, introduced by Eastman Kodak Company in 1950. Eastmancolor did not directly replace three-

Above: 15.9. Director Kenji Mizoguchi (with glasses) preparing a scene for Ugetsu Monogatari *(Ugetsu, 1953); Machiko Kyo (second from left) portrays the ghostly Lady Wakasa.*

Left: 15.10. Oharu (Kinuyo Tanaka) and her lover Katsunosuke (Toshiro Mifune) are discovered in Mizoguchi's Saikaku Ichidai Onna *(The Life of Oharu, 1952).*

Below: 15.11. Genjuro the potter (Masayuki Mori) and his family crossing a misty lake in a boat in Mizoguchi's Ugetsu

strip Technicolor (see Chapter 8), since the Technicolor Company had itself introduced a single lens color film pack in the 1940s, but it was considered more effective in low light circumstances and gave a less brilliant, more muted range of color tones. *Gate of Hell* was hailed for demonstrating the possibilities of the new color process; a period film set in the twelfth century, it featured elaborate, flowing, intricately tinted and patterned clothing of the ancient imperial court. In an unusual gesture, its color consultant, Sanzo Wada, won a Hollywood Academy Award for color costume design. Its director, Teinosuke Kinugasa, whose career began in 1921, even earlier than Mizoguchi's, earned a more firm place in film history with the rediscovery in the 1970s of his 1926 silent classic, *Page of Madness* (see Chapter 7).

Above and Below: 15.12, 15.13. Scenes from Jigokumon *(Gate of Hell, 1953), directed by Teinosuke Kinugasa. One of the first Japanese color films (using a new process, Eastmancolor),* Gate of Hell *won a Hollywood Academy Award for color costume design for its color consultant, Sanzo Wada.*

Yasujiro Ozu

Left out in the international recognition of Japanese filmmakers, at least initially, was Yasujiro Ozu. He did not lack for appreciation at home, however. When he resumed filmmaking after the war he quickly regained the high status he had held among Japanese critics in the 1930s. *Banshun* (*Late Spring*, 1949) and *Bakushu* (*Early Summer*, 1951) were voted top films of their year in a Japanese critics' poll, adding to three similar awards he had won before the war.

Ozu's films from *Late Spring* on look like almost no others in cinema history. Austere and simple are two words that have described these films, but they do not do justice to the audacious artistic choices the director made. Basically, the camera does not move. There may be two or three camera movements in a film depicting exterior action—the camera following bicycle riders, say, as in *Late Spring*—but interior shots completely eschew pans or dollies. In Hollywood, when an actor rises, so does the camera, so smoothly that we hardly notice; not in Ozu. In Renoir's films, the camera is constantly, imperceptibly panning or moving to reframe action; not in Ozu. Characters rise and move, the camera remains motionless.

This camera style is deployed in service of narratives in which, in the conventional sense, very little happens. In *Late Spring*, an adult daughter who doesn't want to leave her widowed father is persuaded to marry. In *Tokyo Monogatari* (*Tokyo Story*, 1953), generally regarded as Ozu's greatest film from this period, an elderly couple visit their children in Tokyo. They get in the way, go home, the mother sickens and dies, and everyone regrets that busy, cramped, and narrow lives impinge on family feelings. The combination of Ozu's style and subject is both distancing and intimate; in a world cinematic practice where family usually means melodrama, Ozu's work constructs the poignancy of the everyday as few films do. Chishu Ryo (b. 1906) and Setsuko Hara (b. 1920) became key figures in Ozu's company of actors, Ryo playing the elderly father, Hara the dutiful daughter, in *Late Spring*, *Tokyo Story*, and other films.

Right: 15.14. Shukichi Somiya (Chishu Ryu), a professor, greets his daughter Noriko (Setsuko Hara) and her friend Aya (Yumeji Tsukioka) in Yasujiro Ozu's Banshun *(Late Spring, 1949).*

Below: 15.15. Yasujiro Ozu directing Chishu Ryu (left) and Setsuko Hara in Tokyo Monogatari *(Tokyo Story, 1953)*

ITALY

Though recognition came to Japanese cinema of the postwar period in terms of individual directors, Japan could still lay claim in the 1950s to a national cinema with an industrial mode of production as in Hollywood. In Europe, however, that was less and less the case. Filmmaking had become a series of one-man (and, on rare occasions, one-woman) turns. Nowhere was this more obvious than in Italy. Neorealism, as we have seen, became moribund by the early 1950s. After *Umberto D.*, Vittorio De Sica made only three films in the 1950s; Roberto Rossellini had become enmeshed in scandal over his affair with actress Ingrid Bergman, whom he subsequently married, and the 1950s were also unproductive years for him.

15.16. Countess Livia Serpieri (Alida Valli) meets her lover Lieutenant Franz Mahler (Farley Granger) in a granary in Luchino Visconti's Senso *(1954).*

331

Luchino Visconti

The one neorealist director able to advance his work effectively in the 1950s was Luchino Visconti. He made few films, but his working method had always been slow and his output meager. *Senso* (1954), admired in its time as a beautiful Technicolor film but a retreat from neorealism into historical melodrama (and not screened in the United States until the late 1960s), has grown in stature to become regarded as one of the major Italian films of the postwar era. Its treatment of the Italian Risorgimento—the national revival of the mid-nineteenth century that led to the formation of the Italian state—is embedded in a melodrama of adultery but nevertheless raises fundamental questions of class, power, and historical meaning that make it in many ways a more effective political film than the didactic *La terra trema*. Visconti's *Rocco e i suoi fratelli* (*Rocco and His Brothers*, 1960), a remarkable working-class melodrama three hours in length, had been heavily cut for international distribution and only began circulating in its complete version in the 1990s.

Federico Fellini

The most remarkable phenomenon of 1950s art cinema—in Italy or any other place—was the rise to international prominence of Federico Fellini (b. 1920). Fellini had played a significant role in neorealism as a coscriptwriter on Rossellini's *Rome, Open City* and *Paisan*, and on important films by other directors. But when he began his career as director (after a codirecting effort with Alberto Lattuada), he made a droll absurdist comedy, *Lo sceicco bianco* (*The White Sheik*, 1952). This small work has several priceless moments, especially a parody on scenes of film production: cast and crew go to the beach to shoot a scene, but it is for a magazine that publishes serialized photo-novellas, and when the director calls out the equivalent of "action!" the actors freeze in their poses. The film launched the career of Alberto Sordi

(b. 1919), who played the Sheik, as Italy's most popular film personality of his era (though little-known outside Italy). But it was not a film that heralded Fellini's nomination, to use language that would soon be invoked, as the greatest director of the epoch.

LA STRADA. That rare acclaim came with his third film, *La strada* (translated as "The Road," but known in the United States and Britain as *La Strada*, 1954). It may be useful to approach *La Strada* first as a phenomenon, then as a film. Greeted as a masterpiece on its release, decades later it is still placed at the pinnacle of cinematic achievement by some critics and historians, while ignored or downgraded by others. *La Strada* still has fared better than its director, whose reputation has not sustained the high level it reached for a period with this and several subsequent films.

With the passing of time it is possible to see Fellini's triumph with *La Strada* as a symptom of something other than the film itself (or the director). *La Strada* spoke to and for the changing culture of an era. Whereas neorealist films, including all that Fellini wrote, were indelibly located in time and place, *La Strada*, though nominally set in postwar Italy, was bound by neither time nor place. It was not local, it was universal—not marked by society or history, but addressing the "human condition." The Road was any road and every road. To its fervent admirers, it was not a narrative like a prose work, it was cinema as poetry.

In *La Strada*, an itinerant circus strongman, Zampanò (played by American actor Anthony Quinn) buys a child-woman, Gelsomina, from her mother to be his assistant. Gelsomina was portrayed by the director's wife, Giulietta Masina (b. 1921), with a mischievous pantomime style and comic innocence that led to comparisons with Chaplin and the American silent comic Harry Langdon. Abused by the strongman, she finds support from a high-wire performer, Il Matto (The Fool, played by another American, Richard Basehart). He tells her that in God's eyes everything, even a stone, has a purpose, and she intuits that

15.17. Shooting a scene for a photo-novella about the adventures of the "White Sheik" in Federico Fellini's Lo sceicco bianco *(The White Sheik, 1952)*

15.18. *Giuletta Masina as Gelso-mina, Anthony Quinn as the strongman Zampanò, in Fellini's* La Strada *(1954)*

serving the strongman is her purpose in life. Zampanò kills Il Matto and abandons Gelsomina, but years later, when he learns of her death, he goes to a beach, alone, and cries. There are many clues in the film to suggest its intended meaning is as a Christian parable or allegory; critics have suggested that Il Matto represents Christ while Gelsomina is associated with the Virgin.

FILM AUTHORS OF THE 1950S

If Fellini became the first star of 1950s art cinema, he was soon joined at the top by Sweden's Ingmar Bergman (b. 1918). Together the pair came to represent this era of cinema, and the debates over their reputations often reflect critical disagreements about how to define film art. Though vastly different in background and temperament—Fellini from a Southern Catholic tradition, Bergman from Northern Protestantism—the two shared a taste for universalizing and a desire to place religion at the center of their filmmaking.

Ingmar Bergman

Bergman began directing films in 1946. Some of the fifteen films he made in his first decade received wider distribution after he became famous, but it was not until *Sommarnattens Leende* (*Smiles of a Summer Night*, 1955) that he achieved substantial recognition beyond Scandinavia. Perhaps it was ironic that a director later known for brooding, heavy, dark, religious, and psychological dramas should emerge internationally with a sophisticated sex comedy, but it points to a side of Bergman's sensibility that should not be ignored. This tale of sexual rivalry, jealousy, and enlightenment was indebted to Mozart's *The Marriage of Figaro*, among other works, and inspired composer Stephen Sondheim's Broadway musical *A Little Night Music* as well as the Woody Allen film *A Midsummer Night's Sex Comedy* (1982).

Bergman followed *Smiles of a Summer Night* with two films released in 1957, *Det Sjunde Inseglet* (*The Seventh Seal*) and *Smultronstället* (*Wild Strawberries*), that played the same role in his career as *La Strada* in Fellini's—they shifted his focus from comedy to cosmic themes, and elevated his status to preeminent cinematic artist. They are like *La Strada* as well in dealing with questions about God's presence in the world, life's absurdities,

15.19. Henrik (Björn Bjelvenstam) clutches a guitar in confusion as he is observed by Petra the maid (Harriet Andersson, center) and Anna, his father's young wife (Ulla Jacobsson), in Ingmar Bergman's Sommarnattens Leende (Smiles of a Summer Night, 1955).

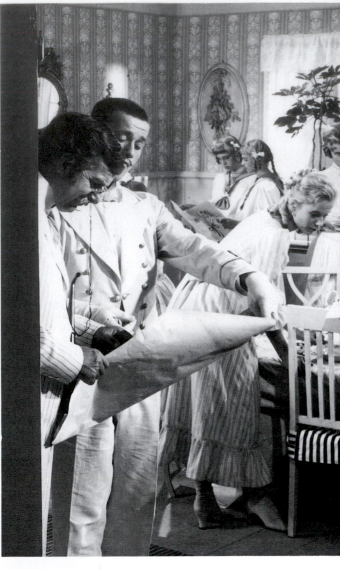

15.21. Professor Isak Borg (Victor Sjöström) recalls a scene from his youth in this split-screen shot from Bergman's Smultronstället (Wild Strawberries, 1957).

15.20. Death (Bengt Ekerot) and the Knight (Max von Sydow) play a game of chess in Bergman's Det Sjunde Inseglet (The Seventh Seal, 1957).

and the loneliness and coldness of death. *The Seventh Seal* dramatizes these issues in medieval times (as in a Japanese period film). *Wild Strawberries* was more characteristically for the director a contemporary film with links to the past: an elderly professor of medicine narrates in voice-over his thoughts while en route to receive an honorary degree. Along with the occurrences on his drive, he has disturbing symbolic dreams and also dreams in which he witnesses events of his youth at which he was not present. The profundity of its themes is leavened by a light touch of comedy, and the film offers the special poignancy of casting as the professor Victor Sjöström, the pioneer Swedish film director who had a brief Hollywood stint in the 1920s (under the name Seastrom). The professor's age in the film is exactly Sjöström's; his dream reminiscences are also by implication a look back at the youth of Swedish cinema, at the moment when it was finally attaining international recognition.

Carl Th. Dreyer

As it had with Buñuel, art cinema gave new recognition to a great but largely inactive filmmaker, Carl Th. Dreyer of Denmark. Acknowledged as one of the world's most important film artists at the end of the silent era with *The Passion of Joan of Arc* (1928), Dreyer in his first sound film, *Vampyr* (*Vampire*, 1932), made an avant-garde work in the guise of a commercial production. Eleven years passed before his next completed film, *Vredens Dag* (*Day of Wrath*, 1943), and a decade between *Tva Manniskor* (*Two People*, 1945) and *Ordet* ("The Word," but known by its original title, 1955). This latter film, however, won a prize at Venice and went on to become the director's biggest commercial success. Its narrative about a woman who dies in childbirth and is brought back to life by an act of faith continued Dreyer's focus on religious themes, dating back to *Leaves from Satan's Book* (1921), and spoke to the spiritual concerns of 1950s audiences as did many of the significant films of art cinema.

15.22. *Director Ingmar Bergman setting up a shot for* The Seventh Seal; *Bengt Ekerot sits in front of the camera.*

15.23. Johannes (Preben Lerdorff Rye) sets out candles in Carl Th. Dreyer's Ordet (1955).

Satyajit Ray

The strong cinema culture of India, like Japan's, was barely known in Europe and North America (though it exported films to other Asian countries, Africa, and the Middle East). The term "national cinema" seems inappropriate for India, since until 1947 it remained a British colony, and after independence (when the former colony was split into two nations, India and Pakistan) films were made in several languages and cultural styles. It took the era of art cinema to bring Indian film to world recognition, not as a whole, but largely in the person of a single, and hardly typical, filmmaker, Satyajit Ray (1921–1992).

Born to an intellectual family in Calcutta, Ray started his career in advertising, and was a founder of the Calcutta Film Society in 1947. His interest in making films began to develop when he met Jean Renoir in India during the making of Renoir's *The River* (1951). Further impetus came during a trip to England (just as pioneer Indian filmmaker Dadasaheb Phalke made a similar journey before making his first film) and from a viewing of De Sica's *Bicycle Thieves*, which showed Ray that a film could be made with location shooting and nonprofessional actors. He began shooting *Pather Panchali* (1955), adapted from a popular Bengali novel. The project took four years and was finally completed with financial support from the state government of West Bengal. At Cannes in 1956 it won a prize as "best human document," and Ray's career was launched.

Pather Panchali eventually became part of "the Apu trilogy"— with *Aparajito* (1956), which won a major prize at Venice, and

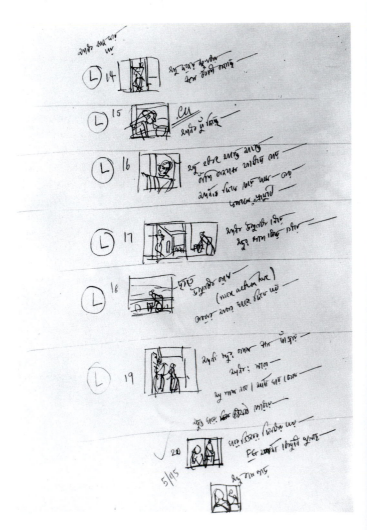

Above: 15.24. Indian director Satyajit Ray drew a series of sketches laying out his visual conception, of which this illustration is a sample page, before shooting his first film, Pather Panchali (1955).

Right: 15.25. Ray's script for Pather Panchali featured rough sketches of individual shots, to which lines of dialogue were appended. This form of screenwriting is extremely unusual, though it may relate to the fact that he was adapting a popular Bengali novel, and what he needed to add was the visual element to the book's narrative and dialogue.

Home and World

Satyajit Ray's breakthrough into the international art cinema with his first films inaugurated a debate within Indian film culture. With an immensely popular commercial film industry already in place, among the issues were: was there a need or a desire for an art cinema practice?; who would be the audience for such films?; how important was international recognition and prestige?; and what would be the cultural significance of films that might be more popular overseas than at home? These same questions have animated many national film cultures when films that may be controversial or underappreciated among domestic audiences find success in other countries.

Ray's triumphs in Europe and North America did not open doors for other Indian filmmakers; there was no general breakthrough for Indian cinema, as was the case in the 1950s with Japanese film. This should not obscure the fact that Indian films were popular in other parts of Asia, in Africa, and in the Middle East, or that other filmmakers were gaining recognition in the Soviet Union and Soviet bloc countries. Raj Kapoor (b. 1924), who began his career as a young actor with the Bombay Talkies company, became an international figure wherever popular Indian films were shown with his third work as a director, *Awara* (*The Vagabond*, 1951), a nearly three-hour melodrama with songs in which he also performed. The films of Kapoor and other Bombay filmmakers, film historian Roy Armes has written, combined "an awareness of the requirements of box office success with a clear sympathy for the poor and the oppressed."

The situation was more difficult, according to historians of Indian film, for filmmakers who attempted to be innovators or artists within the framework of the commercial film industry, without achieving the international celebrity of Ray or Kapoor. Guru Dutt (1925–1964), like Kapoor a director-performer in the Bombay cinema, was said to have taken his own life because of problems in his career following the failure of his last film as director, *Kaaghaz ke Phool* (*Paper Flowers*, 1959), which ironically was concerned with the death of a once-famous film director who had fallen on hard times. Ritwak Ghatak (1925–1976), a Bengali who following his death was characterized by Ray as a filmmaker entirely without foreign influences (unlike Ray himself, who credited the impact of Italian neorealism on his work), sought to make political films within the conventions of Indian popular melodrama. His principal works include *Ajantrik* (*Pathetic Fallacy*, 1958) and *Meghe Dhaka Tara* (*The Cloud Capped Star*, 1960).

Mrinal Sen (b. 1923) is probably the best-known Indian filmmaker in Europe and the United States after Satyajit Ray. Also from Bengal, Sen began his career in the 1950s but only began to make a mark with *Bhuvan Shome* (1969; the title is the name of the film's protagonist), a breakthrough work that utilized the Hindi rather than Bengali language and thus was accessible to wider audiences in India. A political filmmaker like Ghatak, but more internationally oriented in style, Sen has gained prizes at festivals such as Cannes and Berlin.

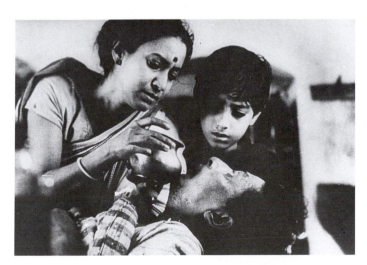

15.26. *The death of Harihar, from* Aparajito *(1956), the second film of Ray's Apu Trilogy; Karuna Banerjee as Sarbajaya (left), Pinaki Sen Gupta as the boy Apu, and Hanu Banerjee as Harihar*

15.27. *Satyajit Ray (right) directing a scene from* Kanchenjungha *(1962)*

Apur Sansar (*The World of Apu*, 1958). (The first two films also have English-language titles—*Song of the Road* and *The Unvanquished* respectively—but are generally known by their original titles, unlike the third.) The films tell the story of a young man, Apu, from birth and childhood in *Pather Panchali* to youth in *Aparajito* and manhood in *The World of Apu*. All three show the influence of neorealism in their unblinking treatment of poverty and its psychological effects on individuals, but they also link emotional states to visual representation of the natural environment, as in the symbolic shots of water in *Pather Panchali*. Indian composer and sitar player Ravi Shankar wrote and performed the musical scores for all three films.

Jacques Tati

India's experience with Ray repeated a pattern developing elsewhere in the 1950s, of an art cinema existing alongside, and obviously intersecting, a commercial cinema. In France a significant example came in the films of Jacques Tati (1908–1982), which were both highly popular with audiences and proclaimed by discerning critics as a special kind of cinematic art. Tati was director, scriptwriter, and performer in his films. He launched his enduring screen character, Hulot, in *Les Vacances de Monsieur Hulot* (*Mr. Hulot's Holiday*, 1953). This tall, pipe-smoking figure, who walked as if listing forward, was not a star comic persona in the traditional sense, but more a catalyst and observer of human

Above: 15.28. In the tradition of Max Linder, Charles Chaplin, and other comedy figures, Jacques Tati (with hat) starred as Monsieur Hulot and directed Les Vacances de Monsieur Hulot *(Mr. Hulot's Holiday, 1953).*

Above right: 15.29. A poster for Tati's Les Vacances de Monsieur Hulot *(Mr. Hulot's Holiday)*

foibles. Tati created his comedy through sight gags, but kept his camera at a distance and let the scene unfold and the spectator discover its humor without an insistent style of close-ups and inserts to pinpoint the joke. He played Hulot in three other films, *Mon Oncle* ("My Uncle," but known by its original title, 1958), *Playtime* (1967), and *Trafic* (*Traffic*, 1971).

Robert Bresson

Another French filmmaker working in the mode of art cinema, Robert Bresson (b. 1907), won less commercial success but more critical recognition than Tati, with prizes at Venice for *Journal d'un curé de campagne* (*Diary of a Country Priest*, 1950) and at Cannes for *Un Condamné à mort s'est échappé* (literally "A Condemned Man Escapes," but more generally known in English as *A Man Escaped*, 1956). Beginning with the former film, his style emphasized nonprofessional performers, use of a diary-like voice-over with very little dialogue, and a concern with religious themes. *A Man Escaped*, set during World War II, recounts the escape from prison of a Frenchman about to be executed by the Germans. It is not an adventure film so much as an account, through close observation of small details, of a man's preparation for an act for which the state of readiness is spiritual as well as

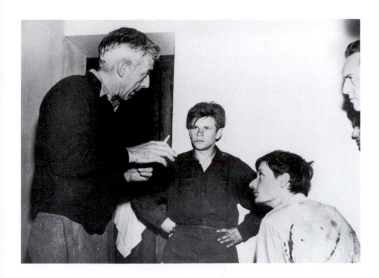

15.30. Robert Bresson (left) directing Un Condamné à mort s'est échappé (A Man Escaped, 1956); François Leterrier (lower right) portrays Fontaine, the protagonist.

tactical. Bresson added his thoughts to the 1950s debate on realism: "The supernatural in film," he said, "is only the real rendered more precise."[5]

Andrzej Wajda

One must proceed with caution in treating the emergence of postwar cinema in Eastern Europe. Countries with cinematic traditions such as Hungary, Poland, and Czechoslovakia after 1945 became socialist states and members of the east bloc under Soviet leadership—an epoch that ended around 1990 and will be subject to considerable historical revision in years to come. During the first decade after the war, a period of physical reconstruction and ideological consolidation, few films were made, and those under strict government controls. It remains a mystery not yet fully explained how a Polish filmmaker, Andrzej Wajda (b. 1926), burst on the international scene with remarkable films in the late 1950s.

Wajda's first film and two subsequent works—*Pokolenie* (*Generation*, 1954), *Kanal* (1957), and *Popiol i diament* (*Ashes and Diamonds*, 1958)—all deal with events at the end of the war. As it seems at this point inevitable to say, *Kanal* won an award at Cannes, *Ashes and Diamonds* a critics' prize at Venice. Such international recognition overwhelmed the Polish government's unease about the films. Critics generally focus on the works' dissent from official ideology, with considerably detailed analysis of their subtle opposition to party line viewpoints. Important as this independence may have been to critics outside Eastern Europe, it could not by itself have brought the films such acclaim. *Ashes and Diamonds* in particular was a visual triumph, a virtuoso example by Wajda and director of photography Jerzy Wojcik of deep-focus and long-take cinematography hardly matched in world cinema for nearly two decades, since *Citizen Kane*.

15.31. The death of Maciek Chelmicki (Zbigniew Cybulski) in Andrzej Wajda's Popiol i diament (Ashes and Diamonds, 1958)

YEARS OF FRUITION

For spectators who followed new developments in cinema, the second half of the 1950s became years of increasing excitement and anticipation. Not since the late 1920s, when films by Eisenstein, Pudovkin, Dovzhenko, and others began to arrive from the Soviet Union, had there been such a sense of renewal in the medium. Filmgoers in the United States also began to participate in the international art cinema movement; though American audiences had previously been given few opportunities to see foreign films in the country's Hollywood-dominated theaters, the breakup of the studio system and declines in Hollywood production during the 1950s led a number of theaters in cities and university towns to become "art houses" playing new and classic works from overseas. Viewing the films of Bergman, Fellini, and others, a growing number of Americans learned to regard cinema as a serious form of art (a recognition that as yet almost no one had granted to the products of the commercial film industry).

Then, at the turn of the decade, in the years 1959–60, a series of films appeared that seemed to confirm every expectation and

Below: 15.32. Nadia's party in Federico Fellini's La Dolce Vita *(1960), with the hostess (Nadia Gray) in the center*

Right: 15.33. Marcello (Marcello Mastroianni) takes friends for a nighttime drive in La Dolce Vita.

herald the arrival of a new era of cinematic art. Several were first features by French directors and will be discussed in Chapter 17 in the context of that country's emerging film movement. We will focus here on two films by directors already mentioned in this book, Federico Fellini and Michelangelo Antonioni. Fellini's *La dolce vita* ("The Sweet Life," but known in the United States and Britain as *La Dolce Vita*, 1960), and Antonioni's *L'avventura* ("The Adventure," but known as *L'Avventura*, 1960) were indexes to how both the cinema and society had changed since 1945.

La Dolce Vita

Fellini's film was a three-hour epic on Roman decadence—not ancient Rome, but Rome of 1960. To the coscriptwriter of Rossellini's 1945 film on wartime Rome, it had become "Rome, Wide-Open City." It was a place of indulgence, emptiness, and publicity, working together synergistically in a downward spiral. Witness to, and victim of, this combination was Marcello, portrayed by Italian actor Marcello Mastroianni (b. 1924) in a role that made him a star. *La Dolce Vita* locates the roots of Rome's moral decay in Italy's recent history (there are veiled references to Fascism), but the city, like the film itself, draws on an international cast: English, French, German, and Spanish as well as Italian are spoken on the soundtrack.

The film's sexual candor helped make it a sensation in 1960 (Hollywood was still operating on the 1930s Code). Since subsequent filmmaking has gone far beyond it in sexual matters, what does *La Dolce Vita* offer to later generations? Critics have noted in the opening and closing scenes—a helicopter carrying a statue of Jesus at the beginning, Marcello's inability to hear a young woman calling to him at the end—echoes of the *Divine Comedy*, the great Christian poem by the thirteenth-century Florentine, Dante Alighieri. Thus the film might be regarded as a journey through a modern hell. In cinema terms, one might recall Billy Wilder's *Ace in the Hole* (1951), and see in *La Dolce Vita* a depiction of contemporary life as a "big carnival" of spectacle, hype, and death (as when a man is trampled to death amid the

Left: 15.34. *After a screening of* La Dolce Vita *at the 1960 Cannes Film Festival, guests at a reception go fishing for bottles of whiskey in a villa's swimming pool.*

Opposite, above: 15.35. *Anna (Lea Massari) and Claudia (Monica Vitti) in Michelangelo Antonioni's* L'Avventura *(1960)*

Opposite below: 15.36. *Director Federico Fellini on location for* La Dolce Vita, *with Marcello Mastroianni and Anita Ekberg, who portrayed Sylvia, a film star*

crowds and cameras surrounding a site where children claim to have seen the Madonna).

What of the religious themes that animated *La Strada*? At the site of the recorded vision, a woman says, "If you look for God, you find Him everywhere." The characters of *La Dolce Vita* are not looking for God, and if He is looking for them, they turn away. The film is not as insistent on its religious motifs as is *La Strada*. Nevertheless, at the end the young woman whom Marcello cannot hear—signifying his lost opportunity to regain contact with innocence and a fresh start—turns her gaze toward the camera, implicating us spectators in the question of our own relationship to innocence, lost opportunities, and perhaps to God.

L'Avventura

At its premiere screening at the 1960 Cannes Film Festival, Antonioni's film was greeted by shouts and whistles from the audience (its equivalent of boos). This was perhaps a litmus test of toleration for art cinema—if art and commercialism were at opposite ends of the cinema spectrum, of how far toward art the medium could go (and still remain commercial). But thirty-five critics and filmmakers, including Roberto Rossellini, issued a statement supporting the film, and the Cannes jury voted it a special prize. The film became a cause célèbre and, after all, a commercial success.

The complaint against *L'Avventura* was that "nothing happens." Indeed, the title must be ironic, for the adventure in the film is almost purely visual and psychological: it probably rejects narrative more thoroughly than any commercial fiction feature film made to that time. Within the first twenty-five minutes, a woman disappears while on a boating trip; for nearly two hours more, her fiancé and her best friend—the latter portrayed by Monica Vitti (b. 1931) in her first important screen role—search for her and form an ambiguous attachment.

The film touches briefly on some of the themes that were central to *La Dolce Vita*: the hedonism of the wealthy, a sense of life's absurdity, celebrity and publicity, women as spectacle. But it is a work that communicates primarily through its visual structure and mise-en-scène: through tight close-ups framed in disorienting ways, contrasted with extraordinary use of deep space and objects in the distance. Italy's architectural heritage and natural scenery become, as a line of dialogue in the film suggests, a "stage setting" for empty, futile lives.

Arriving within a few months of each other in 1960, these two films—by Italian directors who had begun as filmmakers under Fascism, contributed to neorealism, and become leading avatars of art cinema—seemed to cast a critical eye back across the profound changes that had occurred in very few years. If *La Dolce Vita* and *L'Avventura* were triumphs of a successful art cinema movement that had grown up in the postwar period, they also assessed the moral costs incurred in Europe's revival since 1945, "Year Zero" of the new era.

Notes

1. David O. Selznick to King Vidor, Memorandum, May 22, 1952, in *Memo from David O. Selznick*, ed. Rudy Behlmer (New York: Viking, 1972), p. 397.

2. Selznick to Betty Goldsmith, telegram, October 16, 1948, in *Memo from David O. Selznick*, p. 386.

3. Luis Buñuel, "Poetry and Cinema" [1953], in *The World of Luis Buñuel: Essays in Criticism*, ed. Joan Mellen (New York: Oxford University Press, 1978), p. 109.

4. Ibid., p. 107.

5. Robert Bresson, in James Blue, *Excerpts from an Interview with Robert Bresson, June, 1965* (Los Angeles: self-published, 1969), p.2.

SIXTEEN

HOLLYWOOD

One might think that the most volatile and problematic aspects of film history at the present time center on those areas—such as the histories of Soviet or Eastern European cinema—where old orthodoxies have broken down, archives have been opened up, and new freedoms to see and speak have refashioned knowledge and viewpoints. Yet even well-known filmmaking practices, about which information is plentiful and full candor unimpeded, can raise complex historical questions. Hollywood in the 1950s is a case in point: there is no comparable film industry or historical era in which such a wide gap has opened up between the films that the industry itself thought important and other, different works that have become significant for later generations. This gap already existed in the 1950s, when two distinct viewpoints on Hollywood came to the fore.

DECLINE OR ARTISTIC TRIUMPH?

The first view, held within the United States film industry, was shaped by a continuation of Hollywood's experience of crisis and decline that began with the postwar drop in movie attendance, the HUAC hearings, and the Paramount case (see Chapter 14). By the early 1950s television was clearly in the ascendancy as the new mass medium of popular choice. Movies appeared to be in the same situation as the passenger trains that were just at that time losing out to air travel: a once-colossal force, now obsoles-

cent. By 1960 the weekly average of people going to the movies had fallen 63 percent since 1946. This decline led in turn to reductions in production, profits, and employment in the motion picture industry. The total number of films produced in the United States by major studios and independent companies fell below two hundred for the first time in 1959 (until World War II that figure had averaged close to five hundred). With movie attendance no longer a matter of habit but of choice, the industry placed greater emphasis on technological innovations and on "prestige" pictures drawn from "pre-sold" properties such as best-selling novels or Broadway musical hits. Films with these features were the ones the industry praised and to which it gave awards.

A different viewpoint was put forward at the same time, however, that focused not on decline but on the triumph of individual filmmakers. Advocated at first only by a few critics writing for a small film journal in France, *Cahiers du Cinéma*, over time, and with substantial modification, it has achieved a remarkable consensus as the dominant conception not only about Hollywood in the 1950s but about American commercial filmmaking as a whole. The critics of *Cahiers du Cinéma* looked at Hollywood as others saw the international art cinema: as a cinema of *auteurs*, of directors as "authors" of their works.

Although the filmmakers whom the critics found significant were in every case successful Hollywood directors, they were definitely not those most highly honored within the industry itself. And they worked within a commercial film industry, not in the framework of "art cinema" as that term applied to European and Asian directors of the 1950s. Nevertheless, the French critics regarded their Hollywood films more highly than they did the works of Europe's contemporary film artists. In one of the journal's annual polls ranking the best films of the year, Alfred Hitchcock's *Rear Window* (1954) was rated above Fellini's *La Strada*; in others, Nicholas Ray's *Rebel Without a Cause* (1955) ranked over Visconti's *Senso* and Bergman's *Smiles of a Summer Night*, Orson Welles's *Touch of Evil* (1958) over Bergman's *The Seventh Seal*, and Howard Hawks's *Rio Bravo* (1959) over Bergman's *Wild Strawberries*. Their 1957 poll, as something of a polemical statement, listed ten Hollywood films made in 1956–57 among twenty titles.

Fully to understand this iconoclastic critical stance requires a sense of its context in French filmmaking and critical discourses (to be treated in Chapter 17). For now, what is important is to know what the critics admired in the Hollywood films and filmmakers that they favored. The answer, as Jim Hillier has stressed in his English-language editions of selected *Cahiers du Cinéma* criticism from the 1950s and 1960s, is mise-en-scène. "What matters in a film," said critic Fereydoun Hoveyda, "is the desire for order, composition, harmony, the placing of actors and objects, the movements within the frame, the capturing of a movement or a look; in short, the intellectual operation which has put an initial emotion and a general idea to work. *Mise en scène* is nothing other than the technique invented by each director to express the idea and establish the specific quality of his work."[1]

IN THE

In a sense this concept of mise-en-scène, as with much else written by the *Cahiers du Cinéma* critics, was notoriously vague. But in another sense it was completely precise: it referred to a director's visual style as the whole of a film, containing of course the contributions of scriptwriter, art director, cinematographer, and others, but greater than the sum of its parts. Where the camera was placed; how the performers were blocked; what happened when the camera and the actors began to move—these were the director's responsibility, they marked his or her technique, they were the fundamental decisions that, as Hoveyda wrote, expressed the ideas and established the quality of the work.

This was not an viewpoint that sprang solely from watching Hollywood films. It derived from André Bazin's ideas about cinematic realism (see "Bazin and Neorealism," Chapter 13) and it never went so far as to put Hollywood directors at the pinnacle of cinematic achievement; the *Cahiers du Cinéma* critical consensus valued filmmakers such as Jean Renoir, Roberto Rossellini, Carl Th. Dreyer, and Kenji Mizoguchi more highly than any Hollywood figure as masters of mise-en-scène. But what is important in this context is its respectful and closely observant attitude toward films made in a commercial film industry practice. After the ideas of the *Cahiers du Cinéma* critics took hold, it became much less common for critics to dismiss Hollywood filmmakers as faceless factory functionaries, or for films to be valued solely for their scripts or their sets. Although the notion of the *auteur* has been considerably modified since it was put forward in the 1950s, to take more clearly into account collaborative contributions to film art and more nuanced ideas about individual creativity, the

concept of technique remains central. This is in contrast to the Hollywood film industry perspective of the 1950s, where what mattered most was not technique but technology.

THREE-DIMENSION AND WIDESCREEN FILMS

By 1950, nearly two decades had passed without major changes in the visual or sound technologies of motion pictures: a filmgoer in that year saw pretty much the same screen image as a spectator in 1930. A number of small advances had been made in sound recording, camera lenses, film stocks, and other technical aspects, to be sure, that had improved the viewing experience or made possible stylistic shifts in areas such as lighting or depth of field. Perhaps the most obvious change had been the replacement of two-strip Technicolor by the three-strip process in the mid-1930s, but in 1950 the number of color films screened in United States theaters still represented less than 20 percent of all releases. The Great Depression of the 1930s and then World War II perhaps created circumstances that limited technological innovation in the movies, but with attendance falling and television threatening in the postwar years, the time had come to try improving the screen image as a way to lure patrons back to movie theaters.

1950S

3-D

The first new development in the screen image to arrive in theaters was 3-D, or third-dimensionality. Like many other motion picture innovations, this one had a long history. As early as 1897 three-dimensional effects had been created with projected moving images using the principles of stereoscopy (these may be most familiar through the nineteenth century viewing devices which, when held up to the eyes, merged two pictures into a single three-dimensional image). Applied in the 1890s to magic lanterns and then to cinema, the process was called the "anaglyph" method. It utilized red and blue filters both in projection and in spectacles worn by viewers. A camera recorded images with two lenses positioned as far apart as human eyes. The two images were then projected onto a single screen, superimposed one on the other. The filters on the spectacles separated the single image back into two, and the images were then merged in the spectator's brain (as in the normal process of human seeing) back into one three-dimensional picture. Similar methods of creating three-dimensional moving images were revived briefly in the 1920s.

In the 1930s 3-D image-making was advanced through the principles of polarization, the basis of the Polaroid still camera. This also required filters on projectors and the use of spectacles by viewers; these filters separated the images through so-called polarizers that passed light only in certain planes. It enabled three-dimensional viewing of color images, as the red and blue filters did not. Polarized stereoscopic movies were screened in Germany in the 1930s and at the New York World's Fair of 1939–40. In the Soviet Union an inventor developed a process on the principle of the parallax stereogram that did not require view-

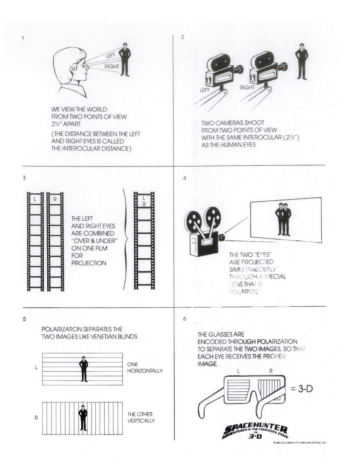

1. WE VIEW THE WORLD FROM TWO POINTS OF VIEW 2½" APART

(THE DISTANCE BETWEEN THE LEFT AND RIGHT EYES IS CALLED THE INTEROCULAR DISTANCE)

2. TWO CAMERAS SHOOT FROM TWO POINTS OF VIEW WITH THE SAME INTEROCULAR (2½") AS THE HUMAN EYES

3. THE LEFT AND RIGHT EYES ARE COMBINED "OVER & UNDER" ON ONE FILM FOR PROJECTION

4. THE TWO "EYES" ARE PROJECTED SIMULTANEOUSLY THROUGH A SPECIAL LENS THAT IS POLARIZED

5. POLARIZATION SEPARATES THE TWO IMAGES LIKE VENETIAN BLINDS

ONE HORIZONTALLY

THE OTHER VERTICALLY

6. THE GLASSES ARE ENCODED THROUGH POLARIZATION TO SEPARATE THE TWO IMAGES, SO THAT EACH EYE RECEIVES THE PROPER IMAGE.

= 3-D

SPACEHUNTER ADVENTURES IN THE FORBIDDEN ZONE IN 3-D

Above: 16.1. An explanation of the polarized stereoscopic method of creating three-dimensional images, prepared by Columbia Pictures for a brief 3-D revival in the 1980s with Spacehunter: Adventures in the Forbidden Zone *(1983)*

Above right: 16.2. Watching a 3-D film with polarizing spectacles

Right: 16.3. Advertisements like this one helped make the Warner Bros. film House of Wax *(1953) the biggest 3-D commercial success.*

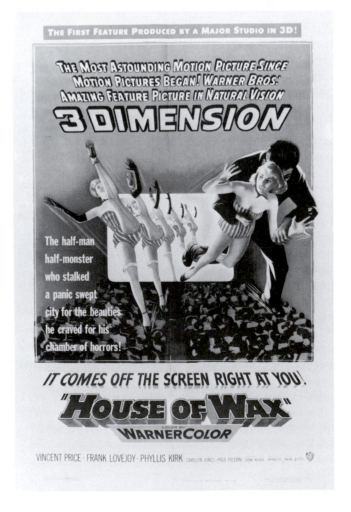

16.4. Performers Kathryn Grayson and Ann Miller come out of the screen in this publicity photo for M-G-M's 3-D musical Kiss Me Kate (1953).

ers to wear spectacles. About a dozen special theaters were constructed in the U.S.S.R. during the 1940s for screenings using this method, using back projection and special grids on both sides of the screen to perform the separations that filters accomplished in other methods. If viewers moved their heads, however, they might lose the three-dimensional effects, and this system did not catch on.

The Festival of Britain, held in London in 1951, marked the breakthrough for 3-D processes. The Festival commissioned a number of short films that were screened with the polarized stereoscopic method. Their popularity caught the attention of the United States film industry. By late 1952 the first 3-D feature film, *Bwana Devil*, produced and directed by Arch Oboler, was ready for release; a crude "African adventure" film combining travelogue footage with backlot acted scenes, it was nevertheless a novelty sensation, as spectators screamed when spears appeared to be heading in their direction. All the major studios put 3-D films into production. Warner Bros. made a huge success in 1953 with *House of Wax*, a horror thriller that went even further than *Bwana Devil* in directing threatening action toward the audience. (Interestingly, the producer of *House of Wax*, Bryan Foy, had directed the first all-talking picture, *Lights of New York*, in 1928.)

In all, twenty-three features were released by Hollywood studios in 1953 in 3-D. These included works in nearly every major genre, but featured particularly science fiction films and Westerns, in which spectacular visual effects could be utilized to draw audiences. In 1954, the number of releases was thirteen, including Alfred Hitchcock's *Dial M for Murder*. In 1955 the total was exactly one, and in 1956—zero. The 3-D craze lasted less than

three years. Viewers complained of the spectacles, poor projection, and, by and large, lousy movies. Over the interim decades, only a handful of films using stereoscopic processes have been made. Twentieth-century audiences have not applauded every technological innovation, at least not always for long. The best of the 3-D movies survive in "flat" prints, while occasional nostalgia screenings of 3-D prints are held to give new generations a chance to view a film in the 1950s way, through polarized spectacles.

Widescreen

Unlike 3-D, the widescreen processes introduced in the early 1950s did bring about a fundamental transformation in the motion picture image, even if most of them did not last a great deal longer than three-dimensionality. They included Cinerama, CinemaScope, and VistaVision, all of which eventually gave way to a different widescreen system, Panavision, developed in the early 1950s but not generally put into use until the 1960s.

Widescreen achieved at least one of the goals of the motion picture industry: marking a fundamental difference between movies and the commercial television image. After the advent of widescreen processes, few films were made in the traditional **aspect ratio**—the relation of width to height—that prevailed before the 1950s and was close to the ratio of the television screen. When widescreen films were released to broadcast television (or, later, as video cassettes) they were reduced to television's ratio either by cutting off the sides or by "panning and scanning" to highlight different areas of the frame, a form of editing for television that changes the screen image from the original. When movies began to be released for home viewing on laser disks in the 1980, original widescreen ratios were restored through "letterboxing," reducing the image in size with black borders on top and bottom. Letter-boxed movies appeared occasionally on cable television stations in the early 1990s, and one could hope that new generations would have a greater chance to see widescreen films from the 1950s in their original form.

CINERAMA. The search for a workable widescreen technology led the Hollywood studios back to the processes that had briefly appeared, then disappeared, around 1930 (see Chapter 8). However, the first widescreen process to arrive in theaters in the 1950s was new to the feature film industry. It had been tried out at the prewar New York World's Fair in a film presentation called the Perisphere, utilizing a spherical screen and eleven projectors. During World War II its inventor, Fred Waller (1886–1954), adapted the process for training in aerial gunnery. In the late 1940s Waller simplified the system down to three cameras and gave it a new name, Cinerama.

In Cinerama, the cameras widened the field of vision by photographing the same image from three different angles. When projected on a semicircular screen, the images filled the specta-

16.5. Author and radio commentator Lowell Thomas being filmed for the prologue to This Is Cinerama (1952) in which, according to the original caption, he delivered "a brief history of early attempts to bring realism and a sense of 'being in the picture' to the movie screen"

tor's peripheral vision and created a perceptual response that produced physical sensations of movement. A curved screen and the multiple projection system were installed in a New York theater and the system was previewed with a film, This Is Cinerama, in September 1952. With the opening shots of a roller coaster ride, spectators experienced a visceral reaction that recalled the legendary stories of 1890s audiences screaming at scenes of onrushing locomotives. The realistic effects were enhanced by stereophonic sound recording utilizing speakers placed around the theater auditorium. Cinerama became a headline sensation.

Despite its considerable early success, however, Cinerama was limited by several factors. Its special screen and projection system were installed in fewer than a dozen theaters in the United States, along with about thirty in other countries. Problems were reported in meshing the three projected images, and the only films made for the process in the first few years were documentary travelogues. Some fiction features were shot in Cinerama in the early 1960s, but by that time the Walt Disney Company had installed a full 360-degree circular movie screen, using eleven cameras, at Disneyland in California, and other widescreen processes had become standard. In the mid-1960s Cinerama gave up its three-camera/projector process and went to a single image system.

CINEMASCOPE. Twentieth Century-Fox acquired the rights to the anamorphic system developed by French inventor Henri Chrétien as far back as the 1920s—with a camera lens that "squeezed" a wider image onto standard 35mm film and a projector lens that "unsqueezed" it, projecting it up to twice the width of traditional screen size. Technologically updated, and renamed CinemaScope, the process was unveiled in September 1953 with The Robe, directed by Henry Koster. This form of widescreen required exhibitors only to purchase an anamorphic projection lens and widen their screens—though often they were not widened enough to accommodate the full CinemaScope image—and within two years a majority of the world's screens was equipped for widescreen.

Fox made the biggest commitment to its own process, producing more than 150 CinemaScope films from 1953 to 1960. Most of the other Hollywood studios also utilized CinemaScope for their widescreen efforts, though RKO had its own anamorphic lenses and released a few films in what it called SuperScope (before the company ceased production in 1958). Paramount, meanwhile, developed its own non-anamorphic widescreen process, called VistaVision. This involved exposing the film horizontally rather than in the normal vertical fashion, so that the wide image existed fully on the negative, instead of the anamorphic system's squeezed negative image. For positive prints, frames were reduced in size so they could fit vertically on standard 35mm film. VistaVision produced an aspect ratio of 1.85:1 (about midway between standard 1.33:1 and CinemaScope's widest 2.66:1), which seemed to many exhibitors a more practical screen size. In all its formats, widescreen fostered greater use of color and stereophonic sound, as well as experimentation with larger film stocks such as 70mm—sometimes in projection prints blown up from 35mm.

PANAVISION. Developed by Robert E. Gottschalk (1918–1982), Panavision utilized an anamorphic lens with variable aspect ratios. It was prized for its clarity and definition whether

 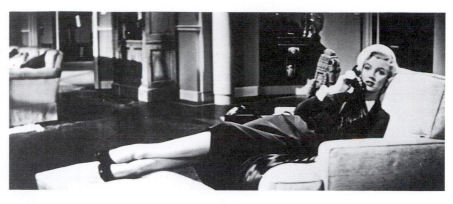

Above: 16.6. A "squeezed" shot of Marilyn Monroe in How to Marry a Millionaire (1953), photographed with an anamorphic lens on 35mm film, and an "unsqueezed" projected CinemaScope image

Below: 16.7. The climactic scene in The Robe (1953), the first film released in CinemaScope, directed by Henry Koster: Richard Burton as Marcellus Gallio and Jean Simmons as Diana (right center), choose their faith, and death, over dishonor under Rome's Emperor Caligula (Paul Robinson), at his throne in the far background.

projected anamorphically or as a wider standard image (as in VistaVision). By 1963 Panavision production outnumbered CinemaScope, and the latter process was virtually phased out by 1967.

Widescreen served as only a temporary palliative for Hollywood's audience decline. Average weekly attendance rose in the years 1954–56 as spectators returned to theaters to take a look at highly-publicized new technologies, but when their novelty wore off the deeper causes for audience loss—lifestyle changes and television—reasserted themselves. Attendance fell off sharply in 1957 and continued an inexorable drop until it leveled off in the early 1970s at a figure approximately one-fourth the total of moviegoers in Hollywood's best years (these trends and their significance will be discussed in later chapters).

Surprisingly little critical or historical attention has been paid to the impact of widescreen on filmmaking aesthetics. For those who emphasized mise-en-scène, like the *Cahiers du Cinéma* critics, widescreen was welcomed as a development that seemed to enhance the long-take and moving-camera style. Others worried that the wider image would only be further justification for banal spectacle. As with any technology, what is significant is not its inherent nature but the artistic and intellectual uses to which it is put. The aesthetics of the widescreen image deserve much closer study.

16.8. Marilyn Monroe and Jane Russell, stars of Howard Hawks's Gentlemen Prefer Blondes, immortalize their hand-prints in the courtyard of Grauman's Chinese Theater in Hollywood.

HOLLYWOOD AUTEURS

The gap between the French critics' view of Hollywood and Hollywood's view of itself was not attributable to widescreen or other technological factors. Directors whom the critics labeled *auteurs* made widescreen films, color films, even spectacle films. The difference lay perhaps in aesthetic criteria of judgment,

having to do with subjective opinions about visual artistry and thematic significance. But these distinctions also drew on assumptions about an industry and its creative workers. "There are no doubt two Hollywoods," Jacques Rivette wrote in a 1955 essay, "the Hollywood of sums and the Hollywood of individuals."[2]

Cahiers du Cinéma critics rated Howard Hawks, Alfred Hitchcock, and Nicholas Ray as the most important Hollywood directors. Hawks had received only one Academy Award nomina-

16.9. Marilyn Monroe as Lorelei Lee sings "Diamonds Are a Girl's Best Friend" in Hawks's Gentlemen Prefer Blondes (1953).

16.10. James Stewart as "Jeff"
Jeffries, a photographer who
espies suspicious doings across
his courtyard, in Alfred
Hitchcock's Rear Window (1954)

tion in a career spanning five decades, for his direction of *Sergeant York* (1941); in 1974 he was given a special Oscar as "a master American filmmaker whose creative efforts hold a distinguished place in world cinema," wording that suggests his overseas recognition. Hitchcock never won an Academy Award for directing, although he was nominated five times—for *Rebecca* (1940), *Lifeboat* (1944), *Spellbound* (1945), *Rear Window* (1954), and *Psycho* (1960). In 1967 he received the Irving G. Thalberg Memorial Award, usually given to producers. Ray was nominated only once, as the author of the original story for *Rebel Without a Cause* (1955).

Auteur Criticism

"The evidence on the screen is the proof of Hawks's genius," begins Rivette's 1953 essay, "The Genius of Howard Hawks."[3] Such hyperbole has become outmoded in critical writing, but at the time it served a salutary purpose—it stirred passions, fostered debate, got people to look at Hollywood films and the creative personnel behind them with a discriminating scrutiny as rarely before. Previous criticism had not ignored directors, but was more oriented toward studios and genres. Eric Rohmer and Claude Chabrol published a book on Hitchcock in France in 1957, at a time well before filmmakers became subjects for book-length studies in the United States (books had appeared about Chaplin, but more as a screen persona than as a director).

Auteur critics searched for the individuality of the director's style and techniques. "In the kingdom of mechanization," François Truffaut wrote of Nicholas Ray in 1955, "he is the craftsman." Prefer Hawks to Ray, Ray to Hawks, or admire them both, said Truffaut; but if you reject them both, "*Stop going to the cinema, don't watch any more films, for you will never know the meaning of inspiration, of a view-finder, of poetic intention, a frame, a shot, an idea, a good film, the cinema. An insufferable pretension? No: a wonderful certainty*"[4] (italics in original).

Not every Hollywood hero of the *Cahiers du Cinéma* critics has achieved cinematic immortality, nor have the critics' thematic concerns necessarily persisted. But to a remarkable degree, the figures in whom they were interested—rather than, for example, 1950s winners of Academy Awards for directing—are those who have continued to hold critical attention over the years. Their nearly exclusive focus on directors has been considerably revised,

however; though not discarded as a concept, the idea of the director as *auteur* has been modified by greater awareness of industrial modes of production, studio practices, and the prevalence of genres. Yet, as Rivette wrote in 1955, "we see the majority of young film-makers passing with equal facility from one genre to another, without paying much attention to their particular rules and conventions, and dealing with strongly analogous themes of their own choosing. . . . It is still better simply to trust the credits to know where you are."[5]

Howard Hawks

Hawks's key films of the 1950s, for example, were a musical, *Gentlemen Prefer Blondes* (1953), and a Western, *Rio Bravo* (1959). In the musical, starring Marilyn Monroe and Jane Russell, Hawks shifted his long-term interest in male friendships to a friendship between women. Though Monroe and Russell gave exceptional performances, they were treated as icons of female beauty, and their goals were represented as wealth and marriage (the film derived from a stage musical and a 1920s novel by Anita Loos, who created Monroe's character, Lorelei Lee, and her maxim, "Diamonds are a girl's best friend"). In the Western, starring John Wayne as a sheriff, Hawks presented a counter-version of *High Noon*'s treatment of the lone law enforcer and his community. The director's concern with the way men form relationships with women and with other men repeats themes—and dialogue—from his *Only Angels Have Wings* (1939) and *To Have and Have Not* (1944). Out of a sardonic approach to genre formulas and a capacity to elicit exceptional performances from his players, Hawks managed to shape a genre work that is simultaneously conventional and original.

Alfred Hitchcock

Hitchcock's major works of the 1950s era were *Rear Window*, *Vertigo* (1958), *North by Northwest* (1959), and *Psycho*. Each fits into a genre framework: respectively, crime, detective, espionage, and horror. Yet they all raise issues that are more common to each other than to their different genres, particularly self-reflexive questions about looking: what it means to use a camera or to be a spectator, a voyeur who sees while unobserved. None of the films is successfully reducible to brief summary (*Rear Window*: an injured photographer looking out his back window thinks he sees

Above: 16.11. James Stewart as "Scottie" Ferguson, Kim Novak as Judy Barton, in Hitchcock's Vertigo *(1958)*

Above right: 16.12. Cary Grant as Roger Thornhill, chased by a malevolent crop-duster airplane in Hitchcock's North by Northwest *(1959)*

Opposite, above: 16.13. Anthony Perkins as motel clerk Norman Bates and Janet Leigh as Marion Crane in Hitchcock's Psycho *(1960)*

Opposite below: 16.14. Alfred Hitchcock directing John Gavin and Janet Leigh in a scene from Psycho

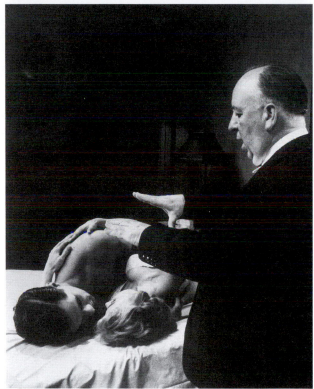

a murder; *Psycho*: a mild motel clerk turns out to be a demented killer) because external action, though amply fulfilling a spectator's desire for entertainment, is driven by psychological currents that make characters' motives and behavior far more complex.

Nicholas Ray

Ray's films of the 1950s included *Rebel Without a Cause* and *Bigger Than Life* (1956). A director who emerged after World War II, in contrast to silent cinema veterans Hawks and Hitchcock, Ray helped to develop new perspectives on the family melodrama

genre. *Rebel Without a Cause* showcases the most important performance of James Dean (1931–1955), who was killed in an automobile crash before the film was released; with only three film roles, he became an enduring cinema legend. Dean's portrayal of Jim Stark, a troubled adolescent searching for the way to become a man, influenced later views not only of the actor but of the era. In *Bigger Than Life* Ray dramatized the pressures that led a school teacher to abuse a medical drug and develop aggressive delusions of grandeur. Ray, said studio publicity for the picture, was "a man keenly interested in the neurosises of our time."[6]

GENRES AND MOVEMENTS OF THE 1950S

Hollywood was, inevitably, a cinema of genres. *Auteur* criticism, focused at first solely on directors, eventually gave way to a more comprehensive view of the varied creative contributions to film-making: individual artistry in the context of industrial codes and generic conventions. Though the films and filmmakers Hollywood honored were not the ones French critics praised, as we have seen, Hollywood's prize ceremonies of the 1950s did strongly emphasize the principle of collaborative endeavor. In the 1930s—except when a historic blockbuster like *Gone with the Wind* (1939) swept the boards—major awards normally were shared among a number of films. In the 1950s, with fewer productions, and even fewer successes, top films tended more to dominate, bringing a full range of creative effort into the limelight.

On the Waterfront

A film that briefly revived the postwar social film, with an exposé of racketeer control of New York waterfront unions, *On the Waterfront* (1954) was an important example of how collaboration was honored. In the first full year of widescreen, this standard size black-and-white film won eight Academy Awards, including those for best picture and best director, and received twelve nomi-

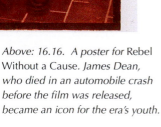

Top: 16.15. James Dean portrays Jim Stark, Jim Backus his father, in Rebel Without a Cause *(1955), directed by Nicholas Ray.*

Above: 16.16. A poster for Rebel Without a Cause. James Dean, who died in an automobile crash before the film was released, became an icon for the era's youth.

16.17. Johnny Friendly (Lee J. Cobb) trips up Terry Malloy (Marlon Brando) in On the Waterfront *(1954), directed by Elia Kazan.*

Method Acting

Although most filmgoers readily form opinions about acting, the subject of performance is one of the least analyzed aspects of film aesthetics. What exactly do actors contribute to film artistry, and how do they do it? Lee Strasberg (1899–1982), a teacher and theorist of acting and a leader of the Actors Studio, suggested that the most effective film performers were those who did not *act*. "They try not to act but to be themselves, to respond or react," he said.

This may be a debatable proposition in the sense that performers' images and roles are invariably constructed by such factors as studio publicity and genre codes, but it does relate to a central tenet of the Stanislavski method: actors were not to emote in the traditional manner of stage conventions, but to speak and gesture in a manner one would use in private life. Konstantin Stanislavski, who was a director at the Moscow Art Theatre, wrote a number of books on acting, the first of which, *An Actor Prepares*, was published in English translation in 1936. Before then, however, one of his students, Richard Boleslawsky (1889–1937), opened an acting school in New York and began teaching Stanislavskian principles (Boleslavsky went on to Hollywood and directed a number of films in the 1930s).

The first significant performance work drawing on Stanislavski's ideas was carried out by the Group Theatre, formed in New York in 1931. The Group's most famous production was a play expressing the militant radical spirit of the 1930s, *Waiting for Lefty* (1935), by Clifford Odets (1903–1963), who became a Hollywood scriptwriter and occasional director. The Group did not last beyond the 1930s, but its influence continued in Hollywood and through the formation of the Actors Studio.

After World War II, in the context of the Actors Studio, the Stanislavski method was shorn of its radical political connotations (the Group Theatre became a particular target of anticommunist investigators) and emphasized an individualized, psychological approach to acting. The "Method" required a performer to draw on his or her own self, on experiences, memories, and emotions that could inform a characterization and shape how a character might speak or move. Characters were thus shown to have an interior life; rather than being stereotyped figures representing a single concept (the villain, the heroine), they could become complex human beings with multiple and contradictory feelings and desires. It was the ability to convey the complexity—indeed the confusion—of inner feelings that made the Actors Studio–trained Marlon Brando, Montgomery Clift, and James Dean such emblematic figures for the postwar era.

16.18. "The most celebrated two-character exchange in the history of American movies," a historian of method acting, Steve Vineberg, has called the taxicab scene in On the Waterfront, *with two Actors Studio alumni, Marlon Brando as Terry Malloy and Rod Steiger as Charley (left), his older brother. Terry discovers his brother's past betrayal—"I coulda been a contender"—and Charley faces his own imminent death.*

Right: 16.19. Ben Vandergroat (Robert Ryan) and Howard Kemp (James Stewart) in life-or-death struggle in Anthony Mann's The Naked Spur (1953)

Below: 16.20. Preparing a shot for The Searchers (1956) on location in Monument Valley Utah, director John Ford demonstrates to performer Vera Miles how he wants her to welcome Jeffrey Hunter (right) with an embrace. Miles portrays Laurie Jorgensen and Hunter plays Martin Pawley, who is returning after an unsuccessful search for a girl taken captive by Comanche Indians. Olive Carey, as Mrs. Jorgensen, looks on at left.

1924) were the most famous Method actors, and their film performances revealed a male figure who was rebellious but insecure, lacking conviction, searching for the wellspring of honor and courage. Brando won the acting Oscar as the star of *On the Waterfront*. Another Actors Studio performer, Eva Marie Saint (b. 1924), won as supporting actress, and, as a remarkable tribute to the richness of performance in the film, three players were nominated in the supporting actor category, Lee J. Cobb (1911–1976), Karl Malden (b. 1914), and Rod Steiger (b. 1925).

Oscars were also won by Budd Schulberg (b. 1914) for story and screenplay, Boris Kaufman (Dziga Vertov's younger brother and cameraman and collaborator of Jean Vigo) for cinematography, Richard Day (1894–1972) for art direction, and Gene Milford for film editing. Composer Leonard Bernstein was nominated for music score.

A showcase for individual talents, *On the Waterfront* received even more attention, however, as a parable of Hollywood's political travails. Brando's character, Terry Malloy, is persuaded, after his brother is murdered by the mob, to testify against the racketeers before a crime commission. Three principals of *On the Waterfront* had testified before the House Un-American Activities Committee—Schulberg in 1951, Kazan in 1952, Cobb in 1953—and named names of others they identified as communists. Conservative commentators cited the film as an example of how "friendly" witnesses thrived in their careers, while those who refused to testify were blacklisted. Beaten up by the mobsters, Brando's Malloy becomes a Christ-like figure in a film in which what appears social devolves into the personal.

The Western

The Western continued to thrive during the 1950s. Though largely ignored within the film industry's categories of prestige, it began drawing increasing attention from critics interested in mise-en-scène. Emerging as a key figure of the genre was Anthony Mann (1907–1967), who directed an important series of Westerns between *Winchester 73* (1950) and *Man of the West* (1958),

nations overall. Director Elia Kazan (b. 1909) had been a founder in 1947 of the Actors Studio in New York, where performers were trained in a "Method" based on the precepts of Russian stage director Konstantin Stanislavski (1863–1938). The Method was an introspective, psychological style, in which actors were asked to build on their own past experience in portraying characters' emotions. Montgomery Clift, James Dean, and Marlon Brando (b.

including such others as *Bend of the River* (1952), *The Naked Spur* (1953), and *The Far Country* (1955). All except *Man of the West* starred James Stewart, an actor transforming his screen persona from the gentle domestic figure of the 1930s and 1940s into the violent, driven protagonist of Mann's Westerns, who after considerable travail found reconciliation with the social community. In films such as *The Naked Spur* Mann constructed what seemed almost chamber dramas of psychological intensity, but set in outdoor Western landscapes with the characters rendered small in deep-space cinematography.

After his cavalry trilogy of 1948–50 (*Fort Apache, She Wore a Yellow Ribbon, Rio Grande*), John Ford, the ranking master of the Western genre, made few Westerns over the next decade, though he was to return memorably to the genre in the 1960s. However, *The Searchers* (1956), little noticed on its release, has become in later critical appraisal one of his most important films and a major influence on younger directors. It was Ford's most psychological Western. John Wayne plays Ethan Edwards, like Stewart's characters an obsessed, bitter figure, searching over years for a niece kidnapped by Comanches. Having articulated in *Fort Apache* (and as he would again do in the 1962 film *The Man Who Shot Liberty Valance*) the necessity of preserving the legends of the West, even when the narrative demonstrates that they are false, Ford in *The Searchers* allowed the narrative to make its own unimpeded critique of Western myths. Its deepest poignancy derives from Wayne's portrayal of Edwards as a man whose heroism is both product and cause of a social estrangement that cannot be undone. At the end, a closing door separates Edwards from the family he has helped to reunite, as he stands awkwardly, left hand gripping right elbow (a gesture he borrowed from an actor in silent Westerns, linking his lonely figure to genre tradition).

16.21. Leslie Caron as Gigi, with Louis Jourdan as Gaston Lachaille, in Vincente Minnelli's musical Gigi (1958)

The Musical

After its successes of the 1946–52 period, the musical began to fade in importance during the later 1950s. The MGM Freed unit made fewer films—Vincente Minnelli became interested in melodrama, Gene Kelly diversified into dramatic roles, and Fred Astaire, still a remarkable dancer, was nevertheless past fifty. The genre shifted away from dance-oriented productions toward films exploiting popular singing stars like Elvis Presley (1935–1977). Minnelli nevertheless made several important traditional musicals, including *The Band Wagon* (1953), with Astaire and Cyd Charisse (b. 1921), and the enormously popular *Gigi* (1958), based on a novel by Colette, and starring French performers Leslie Caron (b. 1931), Louis Jourdan (b. 1919), and Maurice Chevalier (1888–1972). *Gigi* won the Academy Award as best picture, Minnelli won his only Oscar as director, and the film earned more than any other Freed unit production. Like *On the Waterfront* it was also a collaborative triumph, with ten awards (matched by 1961's best picture, *West Side Story*, the dance musical's last hurrah).

Film Noir

In an era of more spacious screens and more frequent color, the film noir movement held true to its dark, constrained mise-en-scène, its representation of the night world. But such films appeared less often in the 1950s and with a change of focus. Stories of restless men beguiled by *femme fatales* gave way to more institutional contexts, with narratives of key 1950s films cen-

tering on police, Cold War, and nuclear themes—and bad women trying harder to be good. Fritz Lang, who was an instigator of the movement at the end of World War II and marked its strong link to pre-1933 German cinema, directed one of its memorable works in *The Big Heat* (1953). The protagonist is a policeman fighting corruption in the force and police complicity with the mob. After his wife is murdered in a bomb attack meant for him, he is aided by the ex-girlfriend of a mobster, disfigured when the thug threw scalding coffee in her face. They form a tenuous connection that explores the moral ambiguities of character and behavior, as each discovers unexplored capacities, his for violence, hers for justice.

Samuel Fuller (b. 1911), a skilled director of action films in several genres, contributed a typically idiosyncratic work to the film noir movement with *Pickup on South Street* (1953). A pickpocket on a subway train steals the wallet of a woman who (unwittingly) is carrying communist espionage microfilm, while the FBI trails her. Agents for both sides need to find the criminal and recover the stolen goods. The film both exploits and undercuts cold war mentality in its juxtaposition of official and criminal codes of behavior. "Don't you know what treason means?" an agent asks the pickpocket, when he is found. "Who cares?" is his answer. Director Fuller and actor Richard Widmark (b. 1914) make a case for the character's defiant selfhood that the individual, rather than the state, seems better able to protect.

Robert Aldrich (1918–1983) turned the perspective on its head in *Kiss Me Deadly* (1955), featuring the sensationally violent fic-

tional detective hero of the 1950s, Mike Hammer, created by novelist Mickey Spillane. Aldrich kept Hammer's violence and his rough appeal to women (Ralph Meeker played the role) but made him a figure lacking knowledge of himself or the world in his encounter with criminals making off with "the Great Whatsit," a metaphorical box of nuclear material. The film is an exemplar of what the individual artist can bring to a modest work whose purpose was to transfer popular literature into popular film—it explores the ambiguous status of high culture in the shadow of

Above: 16.22. Dave Bannion (Glenn Ford), a former police detective avenging the murder of his wife, turns hoodlum Vince Stone (Lee Marvin) over to detectives in Fritz Lang's The Big Heat *(1953).*

Left: 16.23. Skip McCoy (Richard Widmark) comforts the battered Candy (Jean Peters) in Samuel Fuller's Pickup on South Street *(1953).*

Below: 16.24. Lily Carver (Gaby Rodgers) recoils after opening the box containing "The Great Whatsit" in Robert Aldrich's Kiss Me Deadly *(1955).*

Right: 16.25. Orson Welles as Sheriff Hank Quinlan in Touch of Evil *(1958), which Welles also directed*

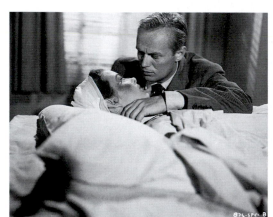

nuclear apocalypse, signaled by the conflagration with which the film ends, and in which the hero either does or does not succumb (there are two versions of the ending).

The last significant work of the film noir movement (leaving aside later revivals or homages) was Orson Welles's *Touch of Evil* (1958). Welles had not directed a film in the United States in a decade, and the opportunity he was given by Universal Studios to direct what was regarded as a genre feature again sheds light on the relation of individual artistry to industrial practice.

Recognized as a gifted collaborator as well as a one-man show, Welles worked with the studio's regular talent in cinematography, art direction, set decoration, and costumes, and created a dark, foreboding mise-en-scène quite unlike the studio's brightly lighted, spacious, widescreen color pictures on which his collaborators usually worked. Set at the Mexican–United States border, the film brings racial themes into film noir, along with a self-reflective concern with vision, spectatorship, and voyeurism in the Hitchcock manner.

1951-21

Science Fiction Visual Effects

The revival of the science fiction genre in the 1950s gave plenty of opportunities to special effects cinematographers and their coworkers. Science fiction films began dominating the Academy of Motion Picture Arts and Sciences Oscars for special effects, which previously had been awarded mainly to war films. The winner in 1949 was *Mighty Joe Young*, a giant-gorilla film from Ernest B. Schoedsack and Merian C. Cooper, who had also made *King Kong,* and in 1950 the award went to *Destination Moon* (1950), one of the first of the space travel films, shot in Technicolor.

Other science fiction winners in the 1950s were *When Worlds Collide* (1951), *The War of the Worlds* (1953), *20,000 Leagues under the Sea* (1954), and *The Time Machine* (1960). Nominated films included *Them!* (1954), *Forbidden Planet* (1956), and *Journey to the Center of the Earth* (1959). Beginning in 1963 the special effects award was divided into visual effects and sound effects.

Science fiction films of the 1950s used the standard techniques of special effects cinematographers and artists, such as miniature sets, matte paintings, model figures, and stop-action shooting. One innovation of the 1950s was the blue screen process, a kind of colored background that made possible more effective composite shots (for example, combining live action, miniatures, and matte backgrounds in the same shot) in the color films that were beginning to be made with more frequency.

L. B. "Bill" Abbott (b. 1908), a veteran special effects cameraman and director of photography who headed the special effects department at Twentieth Century-Fox from 1957 to 1972, published a detailed account of how effects are achieved in the book *Special Effects—Wire, Tape and Rubber Band Style* (1984). For *Journey to the Center of the Earth,* for example, he recounts how live rhinoceros iguanas, about twenty-four inches long, with specially made sails glued to their backs, were used to portray prehistoric monsters. Scenes in which explorers are menaced by the monsters were made by shooting live performers and iguanas separately against blue screens, then putting the shots together to make a composite of the action.

Abbott also describes creating the scenes in another important science fiction film of the era, *The Day the Earth Stood Still* (1951), in which ships from outer space land in Washington, D.C. Putting in the ships was no problem; the challenge was to show them casting a shadow when they landed. The miniature ship would have to be photographed twice, and it would have to descend at the same speed each time. The solution was found by what Abbott called "the wire, tape and rubber band method": the ship was lowered on fine wires and its descent regulated by a metronome. Thus a prop man was able to repeat the movement exactly. A white ship was shot against a black background, then painted black and shot against white. These were optically printed with location footage to show the saucer-shaped ships landing on baseball fields behind the White House.

16.26. Miles Bennell (Kevin McCarthy) seeks help in Don Siegel's Invasion of the Body Snatchers *(1956).*

Science Fiction

A rising genre of the era was science fiction. Prior to the 1950s, the occasional works in this genre tended to deal with new gadgetry or discoveries of fantastic creatures, like *King Kong* (1933). The ever-present Fritz Lang had made the major works of the genre in the silent era with *Metropolis* (1927) and a film about a rocket trip to the moon, *Die Frau im Mond (Woman in the Moon,* 1929). After World War II the development of rocketry, interest in space travel, and concern over the scientific and human consequences of nuclear power led to an upsurge in production of science fiction films. Many, to be sure, were low-budget cross-genre horror films for the expanding drive-in theater market, such as *I Married a Monster from Outer Space* (1958), that survive as late-night TV cult classics.

Some of the major works of the genre were made with new technologies: *It Came from Outer Space* (1953) in 3-D, wide-screen, and stereophonic sound; *Forbidden Planet* (1956) in CinemaScope and color; *Invasion of the Body Snatchers* (1956) in SuperScope. This last film was directed by Don Siegel (1912–

1991), an action director like Fuller, who crafted a widescreen film that looked like a dark, claustrophobic film noir. Regarded as the most enduring 1950s work in the genre (it was also remade in 1978 by director Philip Kaufman), *Body Snatchers* depicts aliens who arrive as pods and take over the bodies of unsuspecting humans, turning them into zombie-like conformists. The most eerie aspect of the film is its atmosphere of bland normality, as humanity succumbs without terror or violence; like a number of other films in the genre, in which creatures from outer space or gigantic insects menace innocent suburbanites, *Invasion of the Body Snatchers* metaphorically explored social anxieties about Cold War threats to the stabilty of domestic life.

Family Melodrama

Quite as significant a genre of the 1950s was family melodrama. Strongly linked to the traditional woman's picture, the 1950s melodrama differed in being almost solely focused on family issues—as opposed to, say, single working women or childless couples. Relations between parents and children, the transmission of values or authority between generations, came to the forefront as in Nicholas Ray's *Rebel Without a Cause* and *Bigger Than Life.*

16.28. Mitch Wayne (Rock Hudson) goes for a ride with Marylee Hadlee (Dorothy Malone) in Sirk's Written on the Wind *(1956).*

16.27. Cary Scott (Jane Wyman, right), a widow, gets quizzical looks from her children Ned (William Reynolds) and Kay (Gloria Talbott) for wearing an attractive dress in Douglas Sirk's All That Heaven Allows *(1955).*

1920); Dorothy Malone (b. 1925) won an Academy Award as supporting actress for her role in *Written on the Wind* as the wild daughter of an oil tycoon.

Minnelli's melodramas included *The Cobweb* (1956), *Some Came Running* (1959), and *Home from the Hill* (1960). Minnelli also used mise-en-scène to convey psychological moods, as in the garish colors and moving camera of the carnival scene in *Some Came Running*. The film, whose main roles were played by Frank Sinatra (b. 1915), Dean Martin (b. 1917), and Shirley MacLaine (b. 1934), explores contrasts of class more than do Sirk's films, presenting in stark terms a gap between cultural refinement and authentic feelings.

Along with Ray, the directors most closely associated with the genre were Vincente Minnelli and Douglas Sirk. Sirk, whom we saw earlier working in Nazi cinema as Detlef Sierck, left Germany in 1937 and began directing in Hollywood in 1943. In the 1950s, as a contract director at Universal, he made a series of melodramas including *Magnificent Obsession* (1954), *All That Heaven Allows* (1955), *Written on the Wind* (1956), and *Imitation of Life* (1959)—the first and last of these titles, significantly, remakes of 1930s Universal genre pictures. Working with the same creative personnel as Welles in *Touch of Evil*, Sirk devised a mise-en-scène using nonnaturalist color, distinctive decor, and reflecting surfaces to create an undertone of disorientation and disturbance in his portraits of family life. Key performers included Rock Hudson (1925–1985), Jane Wyman (b. 1916), and Lana Turner (b.

16.29. Annie Johnson (Juanita Moore) comforts Lora Meredith (Lana Turner) in Sirk's Imitation of Life *(1959).*

16.30. A back alley brawl ensues between Dave Hirsh (Frank Sinatra, center) and Raymond Lanchak (Steven Peck), while Ginny Moorehead (Shirley MacLaine) looks on, in Vincente Minnelli's Some Came Running (1958).

16.31. An "all girls" band rehearsing in Billy Wilder's Some Like It Hot (1959): on saxophone is Tony Curtis as Joe/Josephine, on bass Jack Lemmon as Jerry/Daphne, and on mandolin Marilyn Monroe as Sugar Kane.

Comedy

No survey of the period's genres is complete without a look at comedy, although it is true that 1950s comedy has been generally neglected in critical writing on the era, at least in the United States. (The split between French and Hollywood perspectives from the 1950s has subsequently been closed in every respect but one, the French esteem for comedian Jerry Lewis.) The most significant comedy directors were Billy Wilder—in addition to his work in film noir, just as Minnelli moved between musicals and melodrama—and Frank Tashlin (1913–1972). Wilder's most important comedy of the decade was *Some Like It Hot* (1959), with Marilyn Monroe, Tony Curtis (b. 1925), and Jack Lemmon (b. 1925); one of the most daring works on gender identity in Hollywood history, it featured Curtis and Lemmon posing as women in a generic, comic, and fantasized framework.

A one-time cartoon director, Tashlin became a scriptwriter in the 1940s and began directing in the 1950s. He directed the Jerry Lewis and Dean Martin comedy team in several of their most effective works, among them *Hollywood or Bust* (1956). Tashlin parodied contemporary culture, including the film industry itself. In *Will Success Spoil Rock Hunter?* (1957) his targets included

16.32. Driving west in Frank Tashlin's Hollywood or Bust (1956) are Jerry Lewis as Malcolm Smith, Pat Crowley as Terry Roberts, Dean Martin as Steve Wiley, and (in the back seat) Baron as Mr. Bascombe.

16.33. *Rita Marlowe (Jayne Mansfield) in a berth aboard a transcontinental flight with her secretary, Violet (Joan Blondell), and accessory pet (uncredited), in Tashlin's* Will Success Spoil Rock Hunter? *(1957).*

Hollywood's obsession with well-proportioned blondes, personified in the film by Jayne Mansfield (1933–1967), and the film industry's anxiety about television. Actor Tony Randall interrupts the narrative partway through to address the audience: "Ladies and gentlemen, this break in our motion picture is made out of respect for the TV fans in our audience, who are accustomed to constant interruptions in their programs for messages from sponsors. We want all you TV fans to feel at home and not forget the thrill you get from watching television on your big 21-inch screen." As he speaks the widescreen CinemaScope color image shrinks drastically to the size of a television screen, whose black-and-white image then begins a vertical roll. "Picture trouble," says Randall.

Poking fun at television was good for laughs, and for morale, but it did nothing to alter the movement of audiences away from movies to the small screen, first in the United States and then elsewhere as television broadcasting expanded. The revival of cinema in the 1960s and beyond would be initiated not in the major film industries but from their challengers, even though mainstream filmmaking would eventually be a beneficiary.

Notes

1. Hoveyda quoted in "Introduction," *Cahiers du Cinéma, the 1950s: Neo-Realism, Hollywood, New Wave,* ed. Jim Hillier (Cambridge, Mass.: Harvard University Press, 1985), p. 9.
2. Jacques Rivette, "Notes on a Revolution," in *Cahiers du Cinéma, the 1950s,* p. 94. Originally published as "Notes sur un révolution," *Cahiers du Cinéma* 54, Christmas 1955.
3. Jacques Rivette, "The Genius of Howard Hawks," in *Cahiers du Cinéma, the 1950s,* p. 126. Originally published as "Génie du Howard Hawks," *Cahiers du Cinéma* 23, May 1953.
4. François Truffaut, "A Wonderful Certainty," in *Cahiers du Cinéma, the 1950s,* p. 108. Originally published (under the pseudonym Robert Lachènay) as "L'Admirable Certitude," *Cahiers du Cinéma* 46, April 1955.
5. Rivette, "Notes on a Revolution," p. 94.
6. Twentieth Century-Fox publicity release, *Bigger Than Life* file, Academy of Motion Picture Arts and Sciences, Beverly Hills, California.

16.34. *Movie attendance may have been slipping in the 1950s but not the aura of movie stardom, which continued to be utilized in advertisements for consumer products. Actress Ruth Roman was currently appearing in* Great Day in the Morning *(1956).*

	Film	Arts and Sciences	World Events
1961	Last Year at Marienbad	U.S.S.R. begins manned space flight	Berlin Wall erected
1962	Barravento	communications satellite launched	Cuban missile crisis
1963	The Birds	The Beatles, British rock stars	Kennedy assassinated
1964	Shadows of Forgotten Ancestors	Warhol's Jackie silkscreens	China tests nuclear bomb
1965	Alphaville	first photographs of planet Mars	U.S. expands war in Vietnam
1966	The Battle of Algiers	first heart transplant	cultural revolution in China
1967	Bonnie and Clyde	One Hundred Years of Solitude (García Marquez)	Arab-Israeli Six-Day War
1968	2001: A Space Odyssey	student revolt in France	Rev. M. L. King assassinated
1969	The Sorrow and the Pity	Woodstock, N.Y., music festival	U.S. astronauts walk on moon
1970		floppy disk for computers	U.S. resumes bombing of North Vietnam
1971	Solaris	microprocessor (chip) introduced	4 Kent State University students killed at war protest
1972	The Godfather	M*A*S*H television series begins	U.S. President Nixon visits China
1973	The Spirit of the Beehive	Sondheim musical A Little Night Music	death of Mao Zedong
1974	Xala	disco music begins	U.S. President Nixon resigns
1975	Jeanne Dielman	video recorders introduced for home use	Communists control Vietnam

Part Five

THE REVIVAL OF CINEMA

SEVENTEEN

THE FRENCH

What constitutes a film movement? How do they begin, and what are their characteristics? Film historians rarely raise such questions, because the issues and criteria are not very clear. Yet a number of film movements are recognized: Soviet cinema of the 1920s; the cinema of Weimar Germany in the same era; Italian neorealism after World War II. They are marked by a burst of creativity by filmmakers working generally in close proximity and broadly sharing distinctive styles, techniques, and aesthetic values. They seem to emerge in the context of dramatic social and political transformations: respectively, in the movements cited, the Russian revolution, Germany's defeat in World War I, Italy's liberation after World War II. Film noir in Hollywood might be considered a film movement, and others outside Europe and North America not yet sufficiently known—such as the upsurge in Chinese filmmaking during the 1930s—may someday be added to the list.

In the late 1950s a new film movement suddenly broke onto the scene in world cinema: the French *nouvelle vague*, or New Wave. There is little question that the New Wave fits the criteria of a film movement, yet its contradictory aspects were also apparent. It was a national movement of French filmmakers, but its development as part of international art cinema helped to give it recognition and support. It exalted notions of cinematic artistry, yet it also aimed for popular commercial success. It was a movement that simultaneously asserted and shared its distinctiveness. The name is significant: neorealism will always carry the label *Italian* neorealism no matter where it is practiced, while the

French New Wave fostered "new waves" in other countries, and the name remains open for future appropriation.

What was most unusual about the French New Wave was that it was a movement made by figures known as critics before they were widely recognized as filmmakers. Some of their names are already familiar (see Chapter 16) as writers who shaped a new perspective on 1950s Hollywood film in the pages of *Cahiers du Cinéma*: François Truffaut; Jacques Rivette; Eric Rohmer; Claude Chabrol. They wrote criticism because it furthered their goals, while at the same time they directed short films and photographed, edited, performed in, and publicized each other's film work. With a few others—most notably Jean-Luc Godard, another *Cahiers* critic—they became the directors of the New Wave.

CRITIQUE OF FRENCH CINEMA

Though the critic-filmmakers of *Cahiers* wrote frequently about Hollywood directors, their primary concern was the situation of filmmaking in France. Their position was put most forcefully by Truffaut in a 1954 article, "A Certain Tendency of the French Cinema."[1] Truffaut attacked what he regarded as the dominant French film practice of the time: literary adaptations in which the screenplay took artistic precedence over the director's work. This "Tradition of Quality" was, in his view, a writers' cinema twice over, because it favored both the writer of the source text and the

366

writer of the screenplay. Yet he challenged the idea that this practice treated the original literary text with "faithfulness." If a literary scene was considered "unfilmable," he wrote, it was rewritten for the screen, rather than trying to find a way to express its meaning visually. In general, Truffaut's view was that French film was long on dialogue, short on attention to visual effects and to mise-en-scène. His solution was to take cinema out of the hands of *littérateurs*—literary people—and give it to film directors who were *auteurs*, whose creative efforts focused on film technique. This argument came to be called the *politique des auteurs*, literally "*auteur* policy," more often rendered in English as "*auteur* theory." Among the *auteurs* Truffaut cited were not only Hollywood directors but the French filmmakers Jean Renoir, Robert Bresson, and Jacques Tati, among others.

Truffaut and his colleagues were remarkably successful, from a critical standpoint, in their attack on the dominant French cinema: in subsequent decades, few films associated with the "Tradition of Quality" have circulated widely and few filmmakers other than those approved by *Cahiers du Cinéma* have received much critical attention. Many other writers at the time, it is true, substantially shared the critique of contemporary French films. Even a film that was hailed as a masterpiece when it first appeared, *Les Jeux interdits* (*Forbidden Games*, 1952), directed

THE NEW WAVE BEGINS

The New Wave phenomenon was not greeted with praise in every quarter. The filmmakers were subjected to the same kind of polemical attacks they had launched as writers. "The French New Wave was less a movement than a situation," British critic Ian Cameron gave a retrospective dismissal; "for a year or two, conditions favored the emergence of new directors willing to work on frequently illusory budgets at a time when the established heavyweights were producing poor results."[3] Within France their detractors called them unpolitical and self-promotional, accommodating to producers by working cheap. Moreover, it was said—accurately—that the New Wave label had come to encompass a wide variety of filmmakers who had little to do with the core of ex-critics.

No new movement arrives without criticism, as the histories of neorealism and of Soviet filmmaking of the 1920s make amply clear. But the era was disposed toward a fresh vision such as the New Wave offered. Truffaut (1932–1984), Godard (b. 1930), and Chabrol (b. 1930) were under thirty years of age when their first films made them internationally prominent. They brought to the screen the perspectives of the generation that came of age after the war.

N E W   W A V E

by René Clément (b. 1913), has fallen sharply in esteem, on the grounds that it is compromised by an overly literary screenplay. This neglect of French films of the 1950s almost certainly requires some correction, not necessarily to revive the reputation of the "Tradition of Quality," but to rediscover some important works by filmmakers such as Jean Renoir and Max Ophuls (1902–1957), the German émigré director who worked in France after 1933, Hollywood in the 1940s, and France again in the 1950s.

One director who merits renewed attention is Jean-Pierre Melville (1917–1973), whose *Bob le flambeur* (*Bob the Gambler*, 1956) was an inspiration to New Wave directors. Translating a Hollywood film noir ambience into a Parisian milieu, the film was a low-budget triumph, with deft cinematography and the gradually accelerating pace of a thriller. Its narrative of an old-time bank robber, out of prison, who gets involved in one last big heist has similarities to the Raoul Walsh film *High Sierra* (1941), starring Humphrey Bogart; but Melville shaped a comedy of manners, as he called it, rather than a gangster elegy. However, the director faulted the film on the grounds that he was forced to use a scriptwriter from the "Tradition of Quality" school in order to obtain financing. "I can't look at *Bob le flambeur* any more," he later said, "and it is because of this dialogue, which has aged terribly."[2] Truffaut used Melville's cinematographer (Henri Decaë) and one of his main performers (Guy Decomble) in his first film, *Les Quatre cents coups* (*The 400 Blows*, 1959); and in Godard's debut, *A Bout de souffle* (*Breathless*, 1960), besides sly textual references to *Bob le flambeur*, Melville himself was cast as a novelist in an airport interview scene.

17.1. Roger Duchesne (center) as Bob Montagné, gambler and underworld figure, in Jean-Pierre Melville's *Bob le flambeur* (Bob the Gambler, 1956)

The years 1959–60 (as noted in Chapter 15) had been an intense period of fulfillment for international art cinema, out of which came Fellini's *La Dolce Vita* and Antonioni's *L'Avventura*. Accompanying these films—indeed in several cases preceding them by some months—were films that marked a new beginning, the debut features *The 400 Blows* by Truffaut and *Breathless* by Godard, as well as *Hiroshima, mon amour* (1959) by Alain Resnais (b. 1922).

17.2. Eiji Okada and Emmanuelle Riva as the nameless "He" and "She" of Alain Resnais's Hiroshima, mon amour (1959)

Hiroshima, mon amour

The film that restored international attention to French cinema, preparing the way for the others, was *Hiroshima, mon amour.* Given the differences in age and experience between Resnais and the *Cahiers* critics-turned-directors, his position as a New Wave figure has often been questioned. Nevertheless, Resnais welcomed association with the New Wave, however distinctive his filmmaking style was from others in the movement. A filmmaker since his teen-age years, he worked in the 1950s as a film editor and made short documentaries, among them a famous meditation on the Auschwitz concentration camp, *Nuit et brouillard (Night and Fog,* 1955), that is closely related to *Hiroshima, mon amour.* Resnais was a director for whom the war still shaped postwar consciousness.

Hiroshima, mon amour was regarded by contemporary critics and audiences as a landmark in film history, a work of narrative complexity and philosophical depth such as the cinema had rarely seen before. With a script by Marguerite Duras, a novelist and later herself a film director, the film was partly grounded in the literary approach of the "Tradition of Quality," but Resnais transformed this emphasis by using a visual style that often played against the words, utilizing long tracking shots and tight close-ups familiar from his documentary work. The narrative concerns a French actress who has an affair with a Japanese man while she is in Japan to appear in a film about the dropping of the first atomic bomb on Hiroshima. Rooted in this personal relationship, its emotions and conversations, are subjects considerably more vast: history and memory, document and fiction, perception and visualization, the status of film as a depiction of actuality. An allusive film, austere and cryptic, it raises questions about individuality and identity in a way that film theory would pursue in the coming decades: what is human subjectivity, how is it formed? "The art of seeing has to be learned," the actress says, acknowledging that perception is a socially based activity. This profound film suggests how images and utterances both lie and tell the truth (to paraphrase a line of dialogue), and leaves the spectator to ponder the consequences of that ambiguity.

The 400 Blows

As a critic François Truffaut had attacked the "Tradition of Quality"; his first feature film, *The 400 Blows,* showed an allegiance to the visual style of filmmakers such as Jean Renoir and Orson Welles, emphasizing moving camera shots and long takes to create an open, fluid (what André Bazin had called "realist") mise-en-scène. Perhaps its strongest affinity was to the films of Jean Vigo: to the oppressive yet absurd worlds of school and adults in *Zéro de conduite,* to the joys of popular culture in *A Propos de Nice* and *L'Atalante.* Its narrative roots were autobiographical: the travails of his young protagonist Antoine Doinel were close to Truffaut's own. Precocious founder of a ciné-club as a teen-ager, Truffaut had been jailed because of his failure to pay debts and was released only through the intervention of Bazin (to whom the film is dedicated). In the film, Antoine is

Left: 17.3. Antoine Doinel (Jean-Pierre Léaud) and his friend René Bigey (Patrick Auffay) steal a typewriter in François Truffaut's Les Quatre cents coups (The 400 Blows, 1959).

Above: 17.4. François Truffaut (right) directing The 400 Blows

The Forgotten Fifties

French filmmaking of the 1950s has not recovered its reputation from the assault upon it by the critics of *Cahiers du Cinéma*. Waiting to make their breakthrough as directors of the New Wave, they attacked the films of many of their predecessors as stuffy, wordy, out of touch—elegant perhaps, but empty. The critique was so effective that it has largely eclipsed the era from historical view, including the works of filmmakers whom the New Wave directors admired.

Even the 1950s films of Jean Renoir—the one French "father" whom the New Wave was willing to acknowledge—have suffered from this general devaluation. After leaving France in 1940 and working in Hollywood during and after the war, Renoir did not make a film in France until *French CanCan* (1955; the original title was in English). This was followed by *Eléna et les hommes* (literally "Eléna and the Men," released in English as *Paris Does Strange Things*, 1956). Instead of focusing on contemporary society, as in Renoir's celebrated 1930s works, these were period films, both set in the 1880s; though lavishly praised by New Wave figures, to others they seemed artificial and nostalgic, and over the years critics have generally regarded them with perplexity or indifference. They deserve reconsideration; just as with the revaluation of 1950s Hollywood family melodrama, their visual extravagance and artifice may be seen as a strategy for social critique.

Costume films were in vogue in French 1950s cinema. Max Ophuls, the German-born director who became a French citizen in 1938, then worked in Hollywood during the 1940s, returned to France and made several elegant period works: *La Ronde* (*Rondelay*, 1950); *Le Plaisir* (*House of Pleasure*, 1952); *Madame de . . .* (*The Earrings of Madame De*, 1953); and *Lola Montès* (1955). Viewed initially by critics as beautifully stylized romantic confections, their underlying seriousness has more recently been asserted: "Ophuls' cinema," British critic Paul Willemen has written, "can be seen as the dramatisation of repression."

Other figures from the era have been more thoroughly neglected. An example is Jacques Becker (1906–1960), who had been Renoir's assistant in the 1930s and became a director during World War II. Though most of his postwar films dealt with contemporary France, his most widely known work, *Casque d'Or* (*Golden Headpiece*, 1952), was also a period film set at the turn of the century.

The filmmakers on whom the *Cahiers* critics centered their opprobrium were René Clément and Claude Autant-Lara (b. 1903), considered the leading figures of the era's "Tradition of Quality." More recently, critic Richard Roud proposed giving them a fresh evaluation by looking at what he regarded as their outstanding works of the decade: for Clément, *Monsieur Ripois* (known in English as *Knave of Hearts* or *Lovers, Happy Lovers*, 1954), made in Britain; for Autant-Lara, *La Traversée de Paris* (literally "Crossing Paris," known in English as *Four Bags Full*, 1956), a film set in the occupation period, which even François Truffaut admitted he admired "without any real reservations."

---

jailed for stealing a typewriter and held in a center for delinquent minors, from which he escapes in order to gain his first glimpse of the sea.

The performance of adolescent Jean-Pierre Léaud (b. 1944) is a key to the film's success. Grave yet comical, wise yet innocent, his portrayal of Antoine's initiation into a world of callousness and betrayal gives the film's banal events an exceptional pathos. A freeze frame on Antoine's face by the sea closes the film and leaves the future open; over the next two decades spectators got the opportunity to observe the growth of this character and performer in four other appearances of Antoine Doinel.[4]

Breathless

Even with the critical acclaim for Resnais's and Truffaut's films, it was Jean-Luc Godard's *Breathless* that became the New Wave's emblematic film, assuring the movement's place in cinema history and legend. In retrospect the differences seem self-evident, and perhaps they did at the time: *Hiroshima, mon amour* and *The 400 Blows* are concerned with the past, as history, memory, or autobiography. *Breathless* caught the moment. Besides its intellectual and aesthetic resonances, it gave spectators opportunities for identification and fantasy. It blatantly espoused its allegiance to Hollywood commercial cinema, while at the same time radically challenging conventional narrative codes through **jump cuts** (cuts that break temporal continuity in a scene by leaving gaps in time) and extended long takes shot with a hand-held camera. *Breathless* was "trendy" not in the sense of following fashion but in taking strands of contemporary culture—popular cinema, existentialism—and shaping them into an artistic creation that was simultaneously derivative and new. Looking back with a later era's vocabulary, some critics have called it postmodern.

Performance and characterization play key roles in the film's effects. Jean-Paul Belmondo (b. 1933) as the small-time hood Michel Poiccard and Jean Seberg (1938–1979) as Patricia Franchini, an American girl in Paris, are both young people searching for authenticity and a role in life. He copies the gestural mannerisms of Humphrey Bogart, commits petty crimes, and in a spontaneous existentialist moment murders a policeman. She is the quintessential American ingenue abroad, at once naive and rock hard, teetering between respectable ambition and wild adventure, which may otherwise be a way to improve her French.

17.5. Jean-Paul Belmondo as Michel Poiccard and Jean Seberg as Patricia Franchini in Jean-Luc Godard's A Bout de souffle (Breathless, 1960)

The narrative enfolds as if arbitrary, yet has the fateful inevitability of a film noir thriller.

The formulaic aspects of characterization and narrative were, in a way, the underpinning and counterpoint of the film's challenge to conventional film style. *Breathless* put the term *jump cut* into the everyday language of film technique. Jump cuts disoriented the spectator, leaving gaps in movement and camera placement. This break with standard shot continuity practice was aimed at keeping viewers attuned to the movement of performers and the vantage point from which the camera observed them. Jump cuts, like virtually every technique, go back a long way in cinema history (Orson Welles used a version of jump cutting, for example, in *Citizen Kane*), but Godard gave them more prominence than ever before, with continual surprises for spectators. *Breathless* made the New Wave synonymous with stylistic rule-breaking, a cinema of the unexpected.

Claude Chabrol

Chabrol launched his directing career earlier than Truffaut or Godard, in 1958, and he quickly moved into a commercial film-making mode. His specialty was the thriller, with a particular twist. Almost invariably it involved a surprise murder in which intimacy played a part, with the spectator invited to sympathize more with the plight of the murderer than of the victim. His visual style, shaped in his first four films with cinematographer Henri Decaë (of *Bob le flambeur* and *The 400 Blows*), emphasized a kind of heightened realism, a view of urban space that seems almost documentary yet grows increasingly dark and disorienting through the events that occur within it.[5] Chabrol developed a following among filmgoers who responded to his

17.6. Stéphane Audran as Ginette, Bernadette Lafont as Jane, kill time as shop clerks in Claude Chabrol's Les Bonnes Femmes (1960).

stark pessimism, while others deplored what they saw as a condescending amoralism.

His fourth film, *Les Bonnes Femmes* (1960), was typically controversial. The title literally means "The Good Women," but can also suggest "The Credulous Women." Four young women work in a shop and yearn for something to happen in their lives. The men they meet are boring or obnoxious, except for a mysterious motorcyclist who follows the most shy woman. He rescues her in a swimming pool incident and takes her to the country, and they appear to fall in love. Then he strangles her. The last shot of the film is of another woman, dancing with a man whose face we cannot see, and staring into the camera. In *Les Bonnes femmes*, women lead hapless or endangered lives, while men are jerks or killers—perhaps both at once.

Jacques Demy

Jacques Demy (1931–1990) had no direct connection to the *Cahiers* critics, but his first feature, *Lola* (1961), was immediately tagged with the New Wave label. To be sure, this was not entirely without premeditation on the director's part. The film opens under the titles with shots of a man driving a white Cadillac convertible with the top down: this car had already become a New Wave signature with appearances in *Breathless* and *Les Bonnes Femmes*. A suggestion is made to a character that he make friends. He replies (in the English subtitles), "I had one. Poiccard. Got himself shot," a reference to Belmondo's character in *Breathless*. Godard's cinematographer Raoul Coutard shot the film. In its fairy-tale fantasy of fate and coincidence, with a happy ending for the title character, *Lola* had little in common with the films of Truffaut, Godard, or Chabrol. Nevertheless, Anouk Aimée (b. 1932) in the role of Lola, dressed like her namesake Lola-Lola of *The Blue Angel* in a lacy costume with a dark feather boa, became an icon of New Wave imagery, along with Léaud and Belmondo.

Jacques Rivette

While Godard shot *Breathless* in less than a month, Jacques Rivette (b. 1928) spent parts of three years, 1958–60, making his

17.7. *Anouk Aimée as the title character in Jacques Demy's* Lola *(1961)*

first feature, *Paris nous appartient* (*Paris Belongs to Us*, 1961). Truffaut gave the project a boost in *The 400 Blows* when he had Antoine and his parents—in their one happy time together—go to the movies to see *Paris Belongs to Us*, though Rivette's film was two years away from release. The narrative centers on a woman pursuing information about a mysterious death that others think may be related to a worldwide fascist conspiracy. At the end the conspiracy turns out to be another character's paranoiac delusion. "Modern art is in a phase in which each work is a searching which ends by destroying itself," a *Cahiers* critic wrote, "and that is why Rivette's *Paris nous appartient* is the most significant and most resolutely modern work of the new cinema."[6] This was a generous assessment. Rivette himself retrospectively made a telling appraisal. "The style of the dialogue and the resulting style of acting bother me prodigiously," he told interviewers some years later. Though he thought at the time he was overturning the "Tradition of Quality," he realized he had done "the same thing—dialogue for effects, in the worst sense of the term."[7] By this he meant dialogue taking precedence over visual style, rather than a dynamic relationship between language and images.

FRENCH FILM IN THE 1960S

After its triumphs of 1959–60 the French New Wave was firmly established as an international phenomenon, regarded by many filmgoers as setting a new direction for cinema art. But in what sense did it hold together as a movement, after the "situation" that had launched it was over? As we have noted, earlier film movements had been closely linked to social transformations, which were prominent as subjects in their films. However, New Wave films seemed more about cinema than society. With their variety and ambiguous relationship to commercial film conventions, they carried forward the term New Wave more as a brand name than as a banner. By the early 1960s it was possible to regard the New Wave as the next wave of international art cinema.

17.8. *Françoise Prévost as Terry Yordan, Betty Schneider as Anne Goupil, in Jacques Rivette's* Paris nous appartient (Paris Belongs to Us, 1961)

François Truffaut

Truffaut's development illustrates the shift from New Wave challenge against cinematic orthodoxies to a secure place within an established filmmaking practice. After *The 400 Blows* he turned to a thriller novel by American writer David Goodis as source for *Tirez sur le pianiste* (*Shoot the Piano Player*, 1960). Early in 1962 he released another film based on a novel, *Jules et Jim* (*Jules and Jim*). These two films are perhaps the most highly acclaimed of Truffaut's career, surpassing in critical reputation any of the works he was to make over the next two decades.

For both films Truffaut utilized Godard's cinematographer Raoul Coutard, who helped to shape a visual style based on free-flowing camera movement. At the same time, contrasting to but also working in conjunction with Coutard's camera work, both films gave prominence to verbal language, in extensive voice-over commentaries—the characters' inner thoughts in *Shoot the Piano Player*, an omniscient third-person narrator in *Jules and Jim*—and in story-telling monologues within the film action. These uses of language gave the films a contemplative atmosphere, lulling and distancing the spectator into a false sense of ease just as the narratives turn toward violent action.

This capacity for incongruous juxtaposition was a hallmark of Truffaut's style. *Shoot the Piano Player* has bumbling criminals and corny jokes. A crook is telling a tall tale about his scarf being made of metal and says, "I swear on my old lady's head. May she die if I lied." Immediately there is a shot of a woman keeling over (unusually shaped as an oval iris to give it the look of a silent comedy gag). Yet our laughter at this comic death is undercut by knowledge of senseless deaths that have occurred in the narrative, and the possibility of the crook's murderous intent.

Both films, but especially *Jules and Jim* in the performance of Jeanne Moreau (b. 1928), also demonstrate Truffaut's ability to create portraits of emotionally complex women with whom spectators could empathize. (New Wave films in general are open to criticism for disdainful treatment of women characters: for example, the self-centered American girl played by Jean Seberg in *Breathless*; the aimless and gullible shopgirls of *Les Bonnes Femmes*; the complaisant dancers/prostitutes of *Lola*.) Yet

Truffaut's more appealing figures, Lena (played by Marie Dubois) in *Shoot the Piano Player* and Moreau's Catherine, die at the end of their respective films.

A spectator who saw *Jules and Jim* without knowing the history of the previous decade's critical polemics might be surprised to learn that its director had excoriated the "Tradition of Quality" in French cinema. Its emphasis on poetic dialogue and literary allusion, its psychological realism, its treatment of bourgeois lives, all seem to locate the film well within the framework of the tradition Truffaut condemned. Critics who regard *Jules and Jim* as the fulfillment of a New Wave aesthetic speak of its "vitality" and "feeling" in contrast to 1950s films and even other New Wave works. Yet from a stylistic viewpoint, this seems to be a case of a revolution incorporating what it has overturned.

Alain Resnais

One filmmaker who set off resolutely in a new direction was Alain Resnais, who followed *Hiroshima, mon amour* with *L'Année dernière à Marienbad* (*Last Year at Marienbad*, 1961).

17.11. Delphine Seyrig and Giorgio Albertazzi as "A" and "X" in Alain Resnais's L'Année dernière à Marienbad (Last Year at Marienbad, 1961)

The film carried forward the movement of Antonioni's L'Avventura toward avant-garde exploration within the framework of commercial feature filmmaking. Utilizing a script by Alain Robbe-Grillet (b. 1922), like Marguerite Duras a novelist who would become a filmmaker, Resnais further examined the issues of memory and perception within a more abstract, anti-realist visual and narrative style. In a palace-like hotel sumptuously photographed in widescreen black-and-white by Sacha Vierny, and with all the performers in formal dress, a man tries to persuade a woman that they had had an affair the year before and she had promised to leave her husband and go away with him. Characters move and talk while others stand frozen. Jump cuts show the woman standing in the same position but in different clothes. These visual devices raise questions about what spectators are seeing—is it past or present, dream or projection, his perception or hers? Language is repeated over and over, and organ music on the soundtrack lends a melodramatic urgency. Last Year at Marienbad engrosses the viewer in its philosophical puzzles.

Agnès Varda

Among directors whose careers were boosted by the New Wave's success was Agnès Varda (b. 1928). Varda was the first woman feature film director in France since Germaine Dulac and joined the Hollywood actress Ida Lupino (b. 1916) as the only women to direct commercial features from World War II through the early 1960s. Because she actually completed her first feature, La Pointe Courte (named for the fishing village in which it was shot), as early as 1955, Varda was sometimes called "mother of the New Wave," even "grandmother of the New Wave," though she was the same age as Rivette and only two years older than Godard and Chabrol.

It took Varda seven years to gain financing for a second feature (in the interim she made several fiction and documentary shorts), but she became widely known when Cléo de 5 à 7 (Cléo from 5 to 7, 1962) appeared. Divided into brief "chapters" marking short, precise periods of time, the film covers two hours in the life of a pop singer who is waiting to hear the results of medical tests for cancer. Its visual style expresses the restlessness created by her fear and anxiety, as a constantly moving camera tracks her

Right: 17.12. Corinne Marchand as Cléo in Agnès Varda's Cléo de 5 à 7 *(Cléo from 5 to 7, 1962)*

Below: 17.13. A family's moment of happiness in natural surroundings in Varda's Le Bonheur *(Happiness, 1965); the director cast an actual family, Jean-Claude and Claire Drouot with their children, for the roles.*

through the Paris streets. In a park she meets a soldier about to return to Algeria to fight in the French colonial war there; his proximity to death in war helps to forge a bond between them that will launch her toward treatment and recovery. With references to the Algerian war, it was one of the few New Wave films from the period to take notice of contemporary events (historians are beginning to unearth the censorship policies that prevented New Wave filmmakers from treating political subjects more directly).

Varda's *Le Bonheur* (*Happiness*, 1965) became a significant work for the feminist movement emerging in the late 1960s. Its focus is articulated early in the film when a man speaking from a television screen says, "Happiness may be submitting to the order of nature." In the context of the film's narrative, "the order of nature" is a concept defined by men. A young carpenter has a happy life with a wife and two small children, but he takes a lover and becomes even happier—so much so that he wants to

share his joy by telling his wife, who drowns herself in a pond. Soon the lover replaces the wife. Varda shows her in a montage taking on the wifely duties: picking up the kids from school, feeding them and putting them to bed, ironing, maintaining the house. Shot in color, beginning and ending in beautiful natural scenery, *Le Bonheur* suggests that "the order of nature" has been interpreted to foster men's happiness through women's labors.

Robert Bresson

The New Wave ascendancy also brought added attention to older filmmakers whom *Cahiers* critics championed in the 1950s. This was particularly the case for Robert Bresson. As interest grew in distinguishing French filmmaking style from that of Hollywood, Bresson was acknowledged as a pioneer who, as one critic wrote, "defined his practice as a break with Hollywood cinema."[8] Bresson's practice might be categorized as spare but unsparing. In *Procès de Jeanne d'Arc* (*Trial of Joan of Arc*, 1962),

17.14. Florence Carrez as Joan of Arc in Robert Bresson's Procès de Jeanne d'Arc (Trial of Joan of Arc, 1962)

he drew the dialogue solely from the texts of Joan's trial and interrogation, and portrayed the English as cruel instigators of her martyrdom. In *Au hasard Balthazar* (1966) the title character is a donkey whose life is traced from birth to death. The title might be translated "The Perils of Balthazar," as the donkey suffers from many forms of human evil, as do some of the humans in the film, too. Since many films adopt the visual perspective of their main protagonist, *Au hasard Balthazar* follows this logic for the donkey's point of view: much of the work is photographed at donkey-eye level, with the first shots of many scenes showing feet, legs, and torsos before we see people's faces.

JEAN-LUC GODARD

The films of Jean-Luc Godard in the 1960s raise issues that go considerably beyond the context of the French New Wave: they are a phenomenon unlike any other in cinema history. Between 1960 and 1967, after *Breathless*, Godard directed thirteen features plus seven segments in collective projects. The earliest of these works were slow to make their way into the mainstream of international cinema, but by the mid-1960s Godard's films had seized the imaginations of contemporary filmgoers in a manner different from any before or since. Other filmmakers had been equally or more prolific, others had put their films forward as cinematic innovation or social commentary, but none had combined such productivity with such immediacy. His films were like bulletins from the battlefront, as audiences eagerly anticipated their capacity to render in novel cinematic forms the exploding transformations of the era.

Yet, with the smoke long cleared from the struggles of the 1960s, a question remains about the lasting status of Godard's work, other than as symbol and symptom of an age. Perhaps a price was to be paid for productivity and immediacy: the willingness to report on the contemporary whirl had its costs in depth or coherence or aesthetic form. Perhaps also what Godard pio-

neered and accomplished has become so widely diffused, so much a part of common visual experience, that it is no longer easy to recognize in his films the power of novelty that excited spectators at the time. Since his films are overloaded with self-reflexive commentary on cinema and the arts, one might look to the texts for an aphorism appropriate to the case: in *Bande à part* (*Band of Outsiders*, 1964), a teacher writes on a blackboard, "*classique = moderne*" (classical = modern). A student interprets, "All that is new is by that fact automatically traditional."

Godard's filmmaking was the new that became automatically traditional. The same kind of claim could be made for him that had been made for D. W. Griffith half a century earlier: his techniques were not inventions, but he took the innovations of his time and forged them into a unique style that also became a touchstone of future film practice. The jump cuts of *Breathless* were not as common in subsequent films, but fresh combinations of techniques marked each new work: the use of the original

17.15. Pierre Klossowski as a farmer, with Balthazar the donkey, in Bresson's Au hasard Balthazar (1966)

camera negative (rather than printed positive) footage; tinted images; tilted shots; chapter breaks and titles; direct address to the spectator; emphasis on ambient background sound; many different types of voice-over; use of artwork, cartoons, signs, and writing as significant elements of the text. The growing importance of structural linguistics and semiotics in French intellectual life of the 1960s found expression in Godard's emphasis on language, from literary quotations to everyday speech on the soundtrack.

Cinematic References

Above all perhaps was the fascination with cinema itself: making movies, going to the movies, talking about movies. *Le Mépris* (*Contempt*, 1963) was a widescreen color film about the making of a film in Italy. Director Fritz Lang plays the role of the director; American actor Jack Palance (b. 1920) portrays the producer; French actor Michel Piccoli (b. 1925) a writer; and Brigitte

Above: 17.16. Making a film about making a film at Rome's Cinecittà studio: Jean-Luc Godard (seated on ground) directs a tracking shot for Le Mépris (Contempt, 1963); in the scene, American producer Jeremiah Prokosh (Jack Palance) gives a ride to Camille Javal (Brigitte Bardot), his scriptwriter's wife.

Right: 17.17. Godard preparing a shot inside a studio theater for Le Mépris (Contempt); seated from left in the second row are Fritz Lang (playing himself) and Georgia Moll as Francesca Vanini, a secretary and interpreter; across the aisle are Michel Piccoli as scriptwriter Paul Javal and Jack Palance as producer Jeremiah Prokosh.

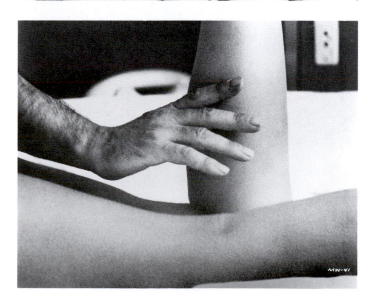

Left: 17.18. A book on Fritz Lang is bathtub reading for Camille Javal (Brigitte Bardot), with her husband Paul (Michel Piccoli) in Godard's Contempt.

Below: 17.19, 17.20. The fragmentation of love in Godard's Une Femme mariée (A Married Woman, 1964): Macha Méril as Charlotte, the hands of Bernard Noel as Robert, her lover.

Bardot (b. 1934), the reigning French sex symbol, the writer's wife. Their film is based on the epic Greek poem *The Odyssey*, perhaps a parody of the many widescreen epics on classical themes that the Italian (and Hollywood) film industries were then producing. There are aphorisms a minute on film history and technology and visual or verbal references to favored *auteurs*: Hawks, Hitchcock, Minnelli, Nicholas Ray, Rossellini. "Whenever I hear the word culture I take out my checkbook," says the American producer. Lang reminds him that the Nazi official who coined the phrase said, ". . . I reach for my gun," subtly suggesting that the effect on culture of gun and checkbook is similar. When he is introduced as the director of a Western with Marlene Dietrich (*Rancho Notorious*, 1952), Lang responds, "Personally, I prefer *M*." It was Lang's only appearance on-screen since 1917.

In *Pierrot le feu* (*Crazy Pierrot*, 1965), Hollywood *auteur* Samuel Fuller is present at a party. Asked to explain what a film is, Fuller replies, "A film is like a battleground. Love. Hate. Action. Violence. Death. In one word: emotions." Roger Leenhardt (b. 1903), whose career as a French critic and film-maker since the 1930s was a model for the New Wave, appears in *Une Femme mariée* (*A Married Woman*, 1964). In *Band of Outsiders* the camera pans past a store named *Nouvelle Vague* and in *Masculin féminin* (1966) the lead male character, played by Jèan-Pierre Léaud, pulls a prank by using the name "General Doinel" (a reference to his character Antoine Doinel in Truffaut's *The 400 Blows*) to call for a military car. Many more examples could be cited.

Top: 17.21. *A crisis moment for Ferdinand Griffon (Jean-Paul Belmondo) and Marianne (Anna Karina) in Godard's* Pierrot le feu *(Crazy Pierrot, 1965)*

Above: 17.22. *Director Jean-Luc Godard (right) discusses a scene for* Crazy Pierrot *with actor Jean-Paul Belmondo.*

Godard and 1960s Culture

These cinematic references have the effect of distancing the spectator, providing a regular reminder that one is watching a film, but they are not entirely hermetic or self-referential. Godard's project as it evolved in the 1960s linked cinema to a broad range of social developments. He was among the first film-makers to explore the consequences of the Baby Boom—the surge in birthrates after 1945—as those born in the postwar years became students and workers in the 1960s. Integral to his stylistic strategies was the effort to represent new trends in advertising and consumption, sexual relations, ideologies. His films marked a response to France's Algerian war and the United States involvement in Vietnam, the latter well before American film-makers paid attention. A "chapter" title from *Masculin féminin* became famous: "This Film Might Be Called: The Children of Marx and Coca-Cola."

If Godard's modernism was to become "automatically traditional," however, it also broke with the traditional forms of classical narrative. His films were less narratives than sequences of fragments, episodes, events, which the chapter divisions, the self-reflexivity, and the voice-over commentaries were often designed to emphasize. A paradox of Godard's films is that their break with the conventions of cinematic realism is an effort to make them more lifelike. The temporal aspect of cinema is relaxed and free-flowing in his work. Some of the most memorable scenes are "throw-away" moments, parentheses without obvious narrative purpose: in *Band of Outsiders* when a woman and her two male friends practice dance steps in a bar, or especially the sequence of the trio racing through the Louvre to set a new speed record for art appreciation.

Alphaville

One Godard film from this period that has maintained strong critical interest is, also perhaps paradoxically, the most closely linked to traditional genres. This was *Alphaville* (1965), subtitled *Une Étrange aventure de Lemmy Caution (A Strange Adventure of Lemmy Caution)*. Lemmy Caution was a private detective or government agent in a series of low-budget French thrillers beginning in 1953, portrayed by Eddie Constantine (1917–1993), an American expatriate singer turned actor. Constantine's role in *Alphaville* fuses the crime thriller and science fiction genres in a dystopian film in which the futuristic totalitarian society ruled by the computer "Alpha 60" is created out of the architecture and technology of contemporary Paris—and, Godard suggests, the political tendencies of contemporary France. But the film has, for

Godard, an uncharacteristically happy ending as Lemmy rescues the beautiful heroine portrayed by Anna Karina (b. 1940) and drives off to his home galaxy, while upbeat genre music plays parodically on the soundtrack.

FRENCH CINEMA AND SOCIETY

New Wave filmmakers besides Godard began to be persuaded that France was becoming more like "Alphaville." In February 1968 the French government of Charles de Gaulle ousted Henri Langlois (1914–1977) as director of the Cinémathèque Française, the famous Paris film library. Langlois had founded the Cinémathèque in 1935; he was one of the inspired film collectors who have been so important to cinema history, preserving films long before governments or film companies took an interest, and teaching the heritage of cinema through screenings of rare works. New Wave filmmakers called themselves "Children of the Cinémathèque." The government's action was widely criticized as a dangerous step toward seizing control over culture.

The Cinémathèque Controversy

While filmmakers around the world sent hundreds of telegrams, demonstrations were held in Paris. On February 14, 1968, several thousand people on a protest march led by New Wave filmmakers were blocked by police, and a number suffered injuries, including Truffaut and Godard. By April the government had backed down, and Langlois was restored to his position. A few weeks later the events of "May '68" began—the student

17.25. Lemmy Caution (Eddie Constantine, right) passes a nude woman in a vitrine in the totalitarian future setting of Godard's Alphaville (1965).

17.26. Eddie Constantine as Lemmy Caution draws a bead on a policeman in Alphaville; the man behind the wheel is director Jean-Luc Godard.

protests and worker strikes against what was regarded as an autocratic government—that were to reshape French intellectual life and profoundly influence film culture and theory. Truffaut later wrote, "It seems obvious that the demonstrations for Langlois were to the events of May '68 what the trailer is to the feature film coming soon."[9]

Weekend

Another preview of coming attractions was Godard's *Weekend* (1968), shot in 1967 before the events of February and May 1968. With such films as *Made in USA* (1966) and *La Chinoise* (*The Chinese*, 1967) Godard had begun to suggest that he had chosen sides between Marx and Coca-Cola; more precisely, that he was a child not only of the Cinémathèque but also of the "Little Red Book," the thoughts of Chinese communist chairman Mao Zedong. It is often a mistake to confuse what a filmmaker puts on screen with what he or she believes. *Weekend*, however, does little to alleviate the confusion.

Weekend represents two main subjects: the self-destruction of middle-class society and a revolutionary struggle against its political and economic institutions. The first half is a surrealistic treatment of social, moral, and technological breakdown, absurdist and often mordantly funny. A long tracking shot shows a traffic jam on a country road, with wrecked cars and bodies strewn on the ground. Strange characters appear from literature

and history, including one who calls himself "God" and announces "the end of the Grammatical Era and the beginning of flamboyance in every field—especially the movies." The second half shifts to tedious voice-overs on political economy and scenes of a "Liberation Front" operating in the woods outside Paris. "To overcome the horror of the bourgeoisie you need still more horror," says a voice in the film; actual scenes of killing animals and (presumably) mock scenes of cannibalism either criticize this view, parody it, contemplate it, or endorse it. *Fin de Cinéma* (End of the Movies) are the last words on-screen, and the film did mark for Godard the end of commercial filmmaking for some time.

Jacques Tati

Another modernist critique of contemporary society appeared around the same time as *Weekend*, and from an unexpected source—Jacques Tati, director/performer of the 1950s comedy *Mr. Hulot's Holiday*. Tati worked nearly ten years on an expensive production, *Playtime* (1967), which ran for two-and-one-half hours in its original release version that was a box office disaster. Shorter versions later circulated. In *Playtime* the horrors are of the spirit. Paris is portrayed as a city of glass and steel and plastic, of long blank corridors and bureaucrats in boxy offices. As it depicts a group of American tourists on their rounds of the city, the film suggests that all they get to see of historical Paris is brief

Langlois and the Cinémathèque Française

For all the important work that they do, film archivists rarely become public celebrities. Henri Langlois was an exception. He was a legendary figure even before the French government's effort to remove him as head of the Cinémathèque Française led to street demonstrations that, some observers claim, sparked the student and worker revolts of May 1968 in France.

Born in Turkey to French parents, Langlois moved to Paris in the early 1920s and began in his teens to attend screenings at ciné-clubs, where film fans pooled their funds to rent films unavailable in commercial theaters. Fascinated with the classics of silent film, he was one of many *cinéphiles* who became concerned, when sound films supplanted silents, not only that these works would no longer be screened but that they might not physically survive; some old films were already being destroyed and recycled for their chemicals. The first steps to conserve the heritage of cinema were taken in the early 1930s by museums and archives in Sweden, Britain, and the United States. In France, Langlois joined with several others in 1935 to establish the Cinémathèque Française, or French film library. He was twenty-one years old.

The goals of the Cinémathèque went beyond earlier efforts elsewhere: to preserve old films but also to screen them for the public. Moreover, while some other archives limited their collecting to "great" films, Langlois and his associates had a more eclectic policy—not yet to save everything (which in retrospect film historians wish had been possible) but to bring in a broad range of works, from art films to popular genres. In 1938 representatives of four film archives—the Cinémathèque, the Museum of Modern Art in New York, the British Film Institute, and the German Reichs-filmarchiv—founded the Fédération Internationale des Archives du Film (FIAF), which has grown to have scores of member archives from around the world.

A cofounder of the Cinémathèque was Georges Franju (1912–1987), a friend of Langlois's from ciné-club days who after World War II became a documentary and fiction filmmaker. Another important coworker was Lotte Eisner (1896–1983), a film critic who fled Germany in 1933 after the Nazis gained power and became associated with the Cinémathèque for nearly half a century, writing important studies on German silent cinema and on directors such as F. W. Murnau and Fritz Lang. Around 1940 Langlois met Mary Meerson, who became his lifelong companion and collaborator at the Cinémathèque.

Irascible and contentious, Langlois made enemies as well as friends. Some questioned his tactics during World War II, suggesting that he collaborated with German occupation forces in order to safeguard his collection. Nevertheless, after the war the Cinémathèque continued to grow as a great repository of films and documents relating to film history, and as a screening place where several generations of "Children of the Cinémathèque" have learned to love film.

17.27. *Henri Langlois (right) photographed in an airport terminal in the 1960s with Mary Meerson (center)*

flashes of the Eiffel Tower and other "sights" reflected in glass doors. Monsieur Hulot makes an occasional appearance in a film which, like Tati's earlier comedies, lets the spectator search out moments of humor in a distanced mise-en-scène.

Eric Rohmer

It is perhaps ironic that the last of the *Cahiers* critics to emerge as a prominent filmmaker, Eric Rohmer (b. 1920), found success at the end of the 1960s with films completely removed from the contemporary turmoil. Rohmer was in fact the oldest of the *Cahiers* group and had been making films for twenty years, but found wide recognition only with *Ma Nuit chez Maud* (*My Night at Maud's*, 1969) and *Le Genou de Claire* (*Claire's Knee*, 1970). These were part of what he labeled Six Moral Tales, films made between 1963 and 1972. They were chamber dramas set among the middle class, in which a man tests his desire for one woman in the moral framework of attraction to others. Serious but lighthearted, the films featured conversation about religion, philosophy, fiction, and feelings. They were antidotes to Godard's apocalyptic trajectory, further evidence that, whatever else it accomplished, the New Wave also transformed and carried forward what it had once vehemently opposed, the French "Tradition of Quality" in cinema.

How should we assess the French New Wave? It was more diffuse than earlier film movements and—with the exception of Godard—less embattled. Soviet cinema, Weimar cinema, and Italian neorealism had all been, broadly speaking, ideologically suppressed; the New Wave played itself out in diversity and individual gesture. But its importance should not be underestimated. It demonstrated that cinema remained capable of stylistic innovation. It reinvigorated French filmmaking and marked the significance of the national context even (or especially) as it took part in international art cinema; filmmakers from other countries could use the French New Wave as a model for a filmmaking endeavor simultaneously national and international. It was the first film movement of the twentieth century's second half, and it gave early attention to the economic and social configurations—the turning of culture into commodity, the blending of popular and high arts—that have marked the "postmodern condition" of the century's late decades.

Above: 17.28. A field of wrecked automobiles from Godard's apocalyptic Weekend (1968)

Left: 17.29. Jacques Tati (center) performing in Playtime (1967), which he also directed

Notes

1. François Truffaut, "A Certain Tendency of the French Cinema," in *Movies and Methods: An Anthology*, ed. Bill Nichols (Berkeley and Los Angeles: University of California Press, 1976), pp. 224–37. Originally published as "Un Certain Tendance du cinéma français," in *Cahiers du Cinéma* 31, January 1954.

2. Quoted in Rui Nogueira, *Melville on Melville* (New York: Viking, 1971), p. 55.

3. Ian Cameron, ed., *Second Wave* (New York: Praeger, 1970), p. 5.

4. In later Truffaut films, Jean-Pierre Léaud also portrayed Antoine Doinel in the "Antoine et Colette" episode of *L'Amour à vingt ans* (*Love at Twenty*, 1962), *Baisers volés* (*Stolen Kisses*, 1968), *Domicile conjugal* (*Bed and Board*, 1970), and *L'Amour en fuite* (*Love on the Run*, 1979).

5. Before *Les Bonnes Femmes*, Chabrol's films with Decaë were *Le Beau Serge* (*Bitter Reunion*, 1958), *Les Cousins* (*The Cousins*, 1959), and *A Double tour* (*Web of Passion*, 1959); thereafter he worked with cinematographer Jean Rabier.

6. Jacques Doniol-Valcroze, quoted in "Introduction," *Cahiers du Cinéma, 1960–1968: New Wave, New Cinema, Reevaluating Hollywood*, ed. Jim Hillier (Cambridge, Mass.: Harvard University Press, 1986), p. 6. The quotation is translated from "Istanbul nous appartient," *Cahiers du Cinéma* 143, May 1963.

7. Jacques Rivette, "'Time Overflowing': Rivette in interview with Jacques Aumont, Jean-Louis Comolli, Jean Narboni, Sylvie Pierre (extracts)," in *Cahiers du Cinéma, 1960–1968*, p. 317. Originally published as "Le temps déborde: entretien avec Jacques Rivette," in *Cahiers du Cinéma* 204, September 1968.

8. Jean-Pierre Oudart, "A Lacking Discourse," in *Cahiers du Cinéma, 1969–1972: The Politics of Representation*, ed. Nick Browne (Cambridge, Mass.: Harvard University Press, 1990), p. 280. Originally published as "Un Discours en défaut," *Cahiers du Cinéma* 232, October 1971.

9. François Truffaut, "Foreword," in Richard Roud, *A Passion for Films: Henri Langlois and the Cinémathèque Française* (New York: Viking, 1983), p. viii.

Below left: 17.30. Jean-Louis (Jean-Louis Trintignant) and Maud (Françoise Fabian) talk over coffee in Eric Rohmer's Ma Nuit chez Maud *(My Night at Maud's, 1969).*

Below: 17.31. Claire's knee is the focus of attention in the film named after it, Rohmer's Le Genou de Claire *(Claire's Knee, 1970); Laurence de Monaghan portrays Claire, Jean-Claude Brialy is the observer, Jérome.*

EIGHTEEN

CINEMA OF

The years 1959–60 were a watershed period in international politics, with consequences quite as profound for world cinema as events in the realm of filmmaking. In Africa, the old European colonial empires decisively crumbled, and new independent nations rapidly emerged. In Latin America, cultural renewal and political debate were fostered after guerrilla forces in Cuba overthrew the dictatorship of Fulgencio Batista y Zaldívar, who had ruled as president or from behind the scenes for a quarter century; rebel leader Fidel Castro took power on January 1, 1959. Though the pace of change was uneven, and in some places social and economic conditions deteriorated rather than got better, a sense of liberation was in the air: it was based on a desire to escape not only traditional imperial domination but the postwar polarization of the world between the two antagonistic superpowers, the United States and the Soviet Union. What began in the 1950s as a movement of the "unaligned" was regarded as a third way, and soon those nations came to be called Third World.

Though widely used, Third World is a tricky term for cinema history. Does it designate countries that stood outside the two great blocs of the Cold War era? Does it denote "underdeveloped" or "developing" countries as opposed to advanced industrialized nations? East instead of West, South rather than North? All these definitions have been applied to the term Third World, yet such countries as Cuba, China, Brazil, and Japan meet some but not others of these criteria.

During the 1960s filmmakers in these and other countries devised new names and concepts for the filmmaking practices that had developed in the wake of political and cultural change. Cuban director Julio García Espinosa proposed a concept of "Imperfect Cinema" in a 1969 essay, "For an Imperfect Cinema." He was seeking to caution against "the dangers of technique for technique's sake," as he later explained in an interview, and arguing that "attempts to challenge established conventions and seek out new approaches" were less likely to attain technical "perfection."[1] In the same year Argentine directors Fernando Solanas (b. 1936) and Octavio Getino (b. 1935) coined the term Third Cinema in an essay, "Towards a Third Cinema." They argued against both the first cinema, the Hollywood commercial model, and what they called second cinema—films by *auteurs* fostering personal expression, among which they included the works of the French New Wave. What was needed was a Third Cinema, "outside and against the System, in a cinema of liberation."[2]

For the subjects of this chapter I have chosen the title Cinema of Liberation; though not without ambiguities, it is a term that can broadly encompass the expansion and transformation of filmmaking in countries outside the European and North American mainstreams. By 1960, however, the world context for emerging cinemas had become more complicated than it had been, say, for the postrevolutionary Soviet cinema of the 1920s. Instead of one mainstream, there were two, as Solanas and Getino suggested, and each presented both models and dilemmas. Commercial filmmaking had been joined by international art cinema. The commercial mainstream provided narrative structures and genre forms that had proven accessible and popular yet often conveyed dominant values. International art cinema sought out and honored innovators, but works that met its aesthetic criteria often ran

18.1. *Ali la Pointe (Brahim Haggiag, left center) is arrested by police in an early scene of Gillo Pontecorvo's* La battaglia di Algeri *(The Battle of Algiers, 1966).*

LIBERATION

counter to political agendas and popular tastes. At an extreme, filmmakers faced the choice of reaching wide audiences using traditional commercial norms, or striving for artistry whose main impact would come through international recognition.

THE BATTLE OF ALGIERS

If any one work can be regarded as exemplifying the achievements—and ambiguities—of a cinema of liberation, it is *La battaglia di Algeri* (*The Battle of Algiers*, 1966), made by Italian director Gillo Pontecorvo (b. 1919). It was hailed on its release as one of the most remarkable political films in cinema history, and few if any political works made since can stand beside it.

In Algeria, which achieved its independence from France in 1962, an unusual (and not uncontroversial) step was taken to find a foreign filmmaker to interpret the nation's revolutionary struggle. Yacef Saadi, head of a production company, Casbah Films, approached three politically oriented Italian directors—Luchino Visconti and Francesco Rosi, in addition to Pontecorvo—before the latter went on to make the film. As a leader of the National Liberation Front during the fight for independence, Saadi perhaps had the prestige and power to go outside rather than to one of his own country's filmmakers, and to gain the public involvement that the film demonstrates. Saadi also performs in the film as a character who represents his own role in the fight. In the version released in the United States, however, Casbah Films is not acknowledged in the production credits.

Pontecorvo and his cinematographer Marcello Gatti made an extraordinary effort to give the film the appearance of a non-

fiction document, with dark, grainy black-and-white footage, even though no actuality material was used. More important is the work's insistence on the complexity, indeed the tragedy, of revolutionary struggle. No one is completely hero or villain: the French use torture and the Algerians employ terrorist bombs against civilians, and some on each side feel the anguish of these perceived necessities. The colonial power appears to achieve its goals in the events the film depicts; the liberation forces appear defeated. Yet in the final scenes of a spontaneous demonstration, as surprising to the NLF as to the French, the film asserts that the struggle has shaped a popular desire for independence stronger than revolutionary leadership or military force. In the script by Franco Solinas (1927–1982), a revolutionist, though captured and destined for torture and death, can nevertheless affirm, "the NLF has more chances of beating the French army than the French have to stop history."[3]

CHINA

On the level not of individual works but of national film practice within the framework of a cinema of liberation, China was among the first countries to deal with the issues of cinema development, following the Communist victory in the country's civil war in 1949. Its model, to be sure, was neither commercial nor art cinema, but filmmaking in the Soviet Union. During the 1950s China organized its film industry under total state control, building new studios and expanding exhibition. In 1958 production surpassed one hundred films (the only year this figure was reached until 1981), and in 1959, for the tenth anniversary of the People's

Above: 18.2. Xie Tan as the merchant Lin, Lin Bin as his wife, in Linjia puzi (The Lin Family Shop, 1959), directed by Shui Hua

Left: 18.3. Women warriors in struggle on the island of Hainan during the 1930s in Xie Jin's Hongse niangzijun (The Red Detachment of Women, 1961)

Below: 18.4. A scene from Xie Jin's Wutai jiemei (Two Stage Sisters, 1965)

Republic, special efforts went into making films that might merit attention outside China as contributions to film art.

The Lin Family Shop

The most significant of these 1959 works was *Linjia puzi* (*The Lin Family Shop*), directed by Shui Hua (b. 1916). It was based on a story by China's minister of culture, Mao Dun, that had been published in the 1930s. Setting a film in a previous era could make ideological issues more clear-cut and avoid dealing with contemporary controversies. *The Lin Family Shop* centered on a merchant family beset by debts, official corruption and coercion, and the consequences of Japanese aggression. The merchant is less a capitalist villain than a victim, yet the film makes clear—partly through a voice-over—that his failures led to even greater suffer-

ing among workers and the poor. Though its ambiguity of characterization was an aspect of its artistry, the film soon came under criticism for perpetuating an old-fashioned literary model and inadequately treating the situation of workers and peasants.

Xie Jin

In contrast to the literary emphasis of *The Lin Family Shop*, director Xie Jin (b. 1923) was a successful popular filmmaker using genre forms to convey political messages. His *Hongse niangzijun* (*The Red Detachment of Women*, 1961) was also set in the past, but took the form of a revolutionary action-adventure. American film historian Jay Leyda, who was working as an adviser in Beijing at the time, wrote a critical report on the film's "abstract time, abstract place, stereotyped characters, and illogical action."[4] It

China's Film Generations

Perhaps uniquely among the histories of national cinemas, Chinese film is organized around the concept of generations. It was only with the "fifth generation" of the 1980s that the work of Chinese filmmakers became widely known internationally, as impressive films by young directors began appearing at festivals (see Chapter 24). Their success stimulated interest in China's first generation of the 1930s (see Chapter 10), whose works had long been unavailable, even in China. The middle three generations, however, remain little known.

One reason for this lack of recognition is the damage to careers (and in some cases, lives) suffered in all three generations through political turmoil or persecution in the years of the "Cultural Revolution" from the mid-1960s to mid-1970s. Members of the second generation, which began work during the 1940s before the Communists gained power in 1949, were particularly affected. Zheng Junli (1911–1969), who directed two important post–World War II films, *Yijiang Chunshui Xiang Dong Liu* (*A

Spring River Flows East*, 1947, as co-director) and *Wuya yu maque* (*Crows and Sparrows*, 1949), died in prison; Cai Chusheng (1906–1968), Zheng Junli's co-director on *A Spring River Flows East*, also died, according to film historian Paul Clark, "under the pressure of military harassment." Nor did the third generation, made up of directors who started under the new regime in the 1950s, go unscathed; Shui Hua, director of *The Lin Family Shop*, was persecuted in the Cultural Revolution and did not make a film between 1965 and 1981.

The fourth generation, Beijing Film School graduates of the early 1960s, were harmed in that their careers were postponed for more than a decade when filmmaking was halted during the Cultural Revolution. This group also suffered artistically, as Xie Fie, vice-president of Beijing Film Academy and codirector (with U Lan) of *Xiangnü Xiaoxiao* (*Girl from Hunan*, 1985), described in a 1984 essay, "My View of the Concept of Film": "For years we were accustomed to being saturated with ideas. Our knowledge and

point of view were not gained through personal experience and independent thinking; these were swept away by the mainstream. It is natural that the only thing gained from this was our lack of a unique and a fresh point of view, and the lack of personality in our artistic ideas and styles."

Amid this persecution and disruption a career of remarkable longevity was forged by Xie Jin, who began as an assistant director in 1948, the era of the second generation; directed his first film in 1954, and thus is designated a member of the third generation; and continued as an active filmmaker into the 1990s, as the only Chinese director prior to the fifth generation to gain wide international recognition. After *Two Stage Sisters*, Xie Jin was unable to make a fiction feature over the next twelve years. In 1980 he directed one of the first Chinese films to express criticism of abuses of power by public officials in the People's Republic, *Tianyunshan chuanqi* (*The Legend of Tianyun Mountain*).

18.5.   Chinese film director Xie Jin

18.6. A funeral scene in Barravento (1962), Glauber Rocha's film concerning a fishing community in Bahia, Brazil

was not a film that would rate a place in international art cinema, but it won the top prizes at China's first Hundred Flowers film awards. In 1965 Xie Jin directed *Wutai jiemei* (*Two Stage Sisters*), a melodrama that was widely admired when it began to circulate internationally in the 1980s.

Two Stage Sisters was among the last significant Chinese films for some years. The Chinese Cultural Revolution plunged the country into chaos from the mid-1960s for more than a decade, and was particularly hostile toward artists and intellectuals. Film-making stopped completely in China during 1967–69, and over the next few years the only films made were of revolutionary ballets (including a 1971 dance version of *The Red Detachment of Women*, not to be confused with Xie Jin's 1960 film). Filmmakers

and critics were imprisoned. According to later accounts, critic Ju Baiyin died from persecutions he suffered because of a 1962 article, "Monologue on Cinematic Innovation."[5]

CINEMA NOVO IN BRAZIL
The most prominent film movement to arise as part of a cinema of liberation was **Cinema Novo** (New Cinema) in Brazil, emerging in the early 1960s (though Solanas and Getino in their essay "Towards a Third Cinema" included Cinema Novo in their second category, films of personal expression by individual *auteurs*). Cinema Novo was not the outgrowth of a revolutionary change in government, as in China or Algeria, but it was strongly affected by

state policies, both liberal and reactionary. More than almost any other filmmaking practice, Cinema Novo embodied the multiple struggles and contradictions involved in the idea that cinema could be a liberating force.

Cinema Novo developed in the aftermath of a failed effort to establish a commercial film industry in Brazil. A production company, Vera Cruz, had been set up in 1949 with a plan to import foreign directors and make expensive prestige productions—a kind of instant Tradition of Quality—that could compete in both the domestic and international markets. The effort collapsed on both counts, and closed down in 1954. In its wake, younger filmmakers turned to the Italian neorealist model of low-cost films concerned with social issues and were buoyed by the French New Wave's emphasis on *auteurs*. In a period of political liberalism, when the country's economic development was widely debated, filmmakers found bank financing for works dramatizing the nation's social ills.

The movement had barely been launched when a military coup took over in 1964—and tightened its grip with repressive measures in 1968. Filmmakers were able to continue their work, however, and their rhetoric became even more militant. They began to identify their efforts with Latin America as a whole and with a Third World struggle against European neocolonialism; they also proclaimed as a unique cultural expression an indigenous "tropicalism"—a conjunction of the cultural forms of native Brazilian peoples with the popular arts—that set their practice apart from the European aesthetics of neorealism and the French New Wave.

Glauber Rocha

The most widely known Cinema Novo filmmaker was Glauber Rocha (1938–1981), who also formulated one of the movement's manifestos in a brief 1965 essay, "An Esthetic of Hunger." There

he speaks of Cinema Novo as "these sad, ugly films, these screaming, desperate films where reason does not always prevail," yet that "will ultimately make the public aware of its own misery."[6] Rocha's reputation rests on four films he made in the 1960s before going into exile from Brazil in 1970: *Barravento* ("The Turning Wind," but known by its original title, 1962), *Deus e o diabo na terra do sol* (*Black God, White Devil*, 1964), *Terra em transe* (originally released in English as *Land of Anguish*, but more recently known by a more literal translation, *Earth Entranced*, 1967), and *Antônio das Mortes* (1969; known in English by its original title, the name of its lead character).

Barravento is often regarded as Rocha's best film, an understandable though problematic judgment, since the director claimed that he was working on the film only as a producer until the original writer-director left the project at midpoint and he stepped in to finish it. Formally the most traditional of Rocha's films, *Barravento* concerns the lives of black men and women in a fishing community in Bahia, in Brazil's impoverished northwest. It depicts the economic exploitation of the fishermen in terms similar to Visconti's *La terra trema*, but gives greater attention to the music, myths, and folk religious practices of Afro-Brazilian culture. The film seems clearly Rocha's in inaugurating what was to become a pervasive rhetoric of his work—the possibility of unexpected transformation, of a world turned upside down. The notion of "the turning wind" is defined in an opening epigraph: "Barravento is the moment of violence when sea and earth become changed, when life, love and social standing may be subjected to sudden change."

Black God, White Devil and *Antônio das Mortes* pursue this concept of reversal. They are linked texts—the first black-and-white, the second color, separated by five years and several sudden changes in Brazilian politics. They shift the location from the seacoast of *Barravento* to the northwest backlands, a region of

18.7. Othon Bastos (center, with hat) as Corisco, last of the backland outlaws, in Rocha's Deus e o diabo na terra do sol (Black God, White Devil, 1964)

Right: 18.8. Maurício do Valle as the hired killer Antônio das Mortes in Rocha's Antônio das Mortes *(1969)*

Below: 18.9. A political rally in Rocha's Terra em transe *(Land of Anguish/ Earth Entranced, 1967)*

18.10. *Fabiano (Atila Iorio) and Vitória (Maria Ribeiro) carry their belongings and children across a dry landscape in Nelson Pereira dos Santos's* Vidas secas *(Barren Lives, 1963).*

legendary outlaws and millennial religious movements. Their styles expand the ritualism of *Barravento* toward greater theatricality and pageantry, with folk ballads on the soundtrack interpreting events and commenting directly to the spectator. Central to both works is the hired killer Antônio das Mortes, a massive, bearded figure wearing a scarf, a cape, and a leather hat. Refusing introspection ("I know nothing about myself," he says), in the first film he hunts down and slays Corisco, last of the backlands outlaws, the *cangecieros*.

In *Antônio das Mortes*, we learn (Brazilian audiences presumably would already have known this) that the events of *Black God, White Devil* were set in the 1930s. Three decades have gone by, and an older Antônio, haunted by his past, returns to the backlands. Industry and investment are beginning to make inroads, but a *cangeciero* and a religious movement have reappeared like ghosts. Antônio experiences a change of heart, seeks forgiveness for his killing, and says, "Now I understand who the real enemy is"—the landowners and other powerful figures who have hired him to kill. He also proclaims his own obsolescence, saying to an intellectual fighting alongside him in a gun battle, "Fight with your ideas—they're worth more than I am." Winner of a prize at the Cannes Film Festival, *Antônio das Mortes* evoked considerable debate over its "esthetics of violence" (which was an

alternative title sometimes given to Rocha's essay "An Esthetic of Hunger").

Land of Anguish/Earth Entranced, made between the two backlands films, is concerned with Brazilian intellectual life, which Cinema Novo filmmakers began to examine after the 1964 military coup. It focuses on a poet who aspires to be active and influential as a journalist and advisor to politicians. In the opening sequence, after a coup has ousted his allies, the poet impulsively refuses to concede defeat. He drives through a police blockade and is mortally wounded. The film's central section is a flashback retrospective of his political life, leading up to the crisis with which it began. Exploring the relationship between art and power, it chronicles the failure of an intellectual who played the political game, rather than, as Antônio das Mortes advised, fighting with ideas.

Nelson Pereira dos Santos

The filmmaker whose work strikingly represents the shift from neorealism to "tropicalism" is Nelson Pereira dos Santos (b. 1928). A decade older than Rocha, he had made documentaries and features in the 1950s and worked as an editor on *Barravento*. His *Vidas secas* (*Barren Lives*, 1963) dramatized the "esthetics of hunger" that Rocha had later proclaimed. Based on a classic

18.11. *"Tropicalism" in Pereira dos Santos's* Como era gostoso o meu Francês *(How Tasty Was My Little Frenchman, 1971)*

1930s novel of the northwest backlands, the film depicts a poor family's struggle to survive in the face of economic exploitation, police oppression, and a harsh environment. Though the novel was compared to John Steinbeck's *The Grapes of Wrath*, the film has closer affinities to Italian neorealism, which dos Santos acknowledged. Fabiano, the father of *Barren Lives*, is akin to Antonio, the father of *Bicycle Thieves*, as well-meaning men overwhelmed by circumstances, fading into oblivion in an inhospitable world.

By 1971, dos Santos was challenging European culture in *Como era gostoso o meu Francês* (*How Tasty Was My Little Frenchman*). Set in the sixteenth century, and shot in color largely with a hand-held camera, the film presents "tropicalism" in its native state, with its tribal men and women unclothed. A French man is captured by a tribe and made a slave, prior to the time when he will be killed and eaten. The film presents moments of brutality and of fellowship in the encounter between European "civilization" and tropical "primitivism," while emphasizing through periodic intertitles Europe's colonial discourse of racial superiority. Conditioned by familiar narrative conventions about the lone hero among strange peoples, the spectator awaits a "happy ending": his deliverance, perhaps accompanied by his native wife. But the wife blocks his escape, and the happy ending belongs to the tribe. Cannibalism is a social fact, rather than the grisly shock Godard made it in *Weekend*, and also a metaphor: Europe's presence in the new world has been "digested" and turned into something no longer recognizable as European.

LATIN AMERICAN CINEMA
Cuba

Besides Brazil's Cinema Novo, the other major new component in Latin American filmmaking of the 1960s was the Cuban revolution. Other countries continued to struggle with the traditional difficulties of cinemas on the margin of the mainstream—foreign domination of exhibition, inadequate production funding, limited international recognition. But Cuba, soon after the Castro government gained power in 1959, initiated a radical break with its past, including these structures of cinematic subordination.

Rapidly escalating mutual antagonism with the United States led Cuba to align with the Communist bloc. Political tensions rose to new heights with the 1961 Bay of Pigs invasion by Cuban exiles supported by the United States, followed by the 1962 Cuban missile crisis in which nuclear war was threatened after the United States discovered that the Soviet Union was building missile bases in Cuba (the crisis ended when the Soviets agreed to dismantle the bases). As Castro's government transformed itself into a communist regime, it became clear that Cuba's new model of socialist filmmaking practiced some of the familiar constraints of other socialist cinemas, including ideological control and repression of dissidents. Nevertheless, for many in Latin America and elsewhere the Cuban experience encouraged renewed idealism and the possibility of utilizing cinema for social change.

In March 1959 the Castro government established the Instituto Cubano del Arte y Industria Cinematográficos (Cuban Institute of Cinematographic Art and Industry), known by its acronym, ICAIC. Among its tasks were the training of filmmakers, documenting the country's political transformation, finding films for theaters after Hollywood distributors withdrew from the country because of the U.S. government's prohibition of commerce with Cuba, and fostering filmmaking styles commensurate with political ideology. This latter question became acute after Cuba defeated the American-backed invaders at the Bay of Pigs. In that charged atmosphere, a short film was banned because it showed scenes of Havana low life considered offensive to the "Revolution." The debate that erupted among intellectuals and artists climaxed when Fidel Castro himself delivered a speech, "Words to the Intellectuals," which closed with the phrase: "Within the Revolution, everything, against it, nothing."[7]

Nearly a decade passed before Cuba began to produce significant fiction feature films. In 1968 Cuban filmmaking made its mark with two works that received wide international attention, *Memorias del subdesarollo* (*Memories of Underdevelopment*), directed by Tomás Gutiérrez Alea (b. 1928), and *Lucía*, a film by Humberto Solás (b. 1942).

MEMORIES OF UNDERDEVELOPMENT. From his studies at Rome's Centro Sperimentale di Cinematografia (along with fellow Cuban Julio García Espinosa, later the theorist of "Imperfect Cinema"), Gutiérrez Alea brought back a neorealist approach to filmmaking. But by the later 1960s, developments like the French New Wave and Cinema Novo, as well as his own analysis of Cuban circumstances, led him to a more eclectic, self-reflexive style. Combining actuality with fiction footage, material from television and other films, and scenes foregrounding the making of the text itself, *Memories of Underdevelopment* is an exploration of the politics of representation as much as a realist depiction of a social world. Based on a novel with the same original title (but translated in English as *Inconsolable Memories*), the film is set in the crucial period between the Bay of Pigs and the following year's missile crisis. Its protagonist, Sergio, is a middle-class man who has refused to flee with his family to Miami but is also unable to commit to the new regime. Neither revolutionary nor counter-revolutionary, he is "nothing"—a figure formed by underdevelopment and living detached and alienated, without meaning. *Memories of Underdevelopment* is a subtle portrait of an old Cuba passing away and a new Cuba struggling to be born.

LUCÍA. Solás came from a different generation than Gutiérrez Alea. As a teenager he fought as an urban guerrilla against the Batista dictatorship, and he began making films at ICAIC before he was twenty. For *Lucía*, his breakthrough work, he developed a strongly melodramatic approach, while filming with an almost constantly moving hand-held camera. Committed to a postrevolutionary revision—and revisioning—of Cuba's history, Solás frames that effort in *Lucía* through three episodes concerned with different women named Lucía. The first Lucía is an unworldly aristocrat, a fool for love who is tricked into betraying her countrymen during the 1890s struggle against Spanish colonialism. The second Lucía is an idealistic middle-class woman of the early 1930s whose love for a revolutionary ends in tragedy after the violent overthrow of an earlier dictator fails to change business as usual. The third episode is set in "196-," and its Lucía is a revolutionary in her own right, but she struggles with her bridegroom against *machismo*, traditional male privilege and possessiveness which the Revolution has not (yet) reformed. For its scope, variety, and energy, *Lucía* remains a vivid achievement of political cinema.

Right: 18.12. Sergio Corrieri as Sergio, immobilized between revolution and counter-revolution, in Memorias del subdesarollo (Memories of Underdevelopment, 1968), directed by Tomás Gutiérrez Alea

Below: 18.13. Sergio and Elena (Daisy Granados) visit Ernest Hemingway's house in Cuba, turned into a museum, in Memories of Underdevelopment.

Above: 18.14. A scene after battle in the first episode of Lucía (1968), directed by Humberto Solás

Right: 18.15. Women on strike in the second episode of Lucía, set in the 1930s; Eslinda Núñez (right) portrays this Lucía.

Argentina

Drawing inspiration from Cuba among other sources, a group in Argentina called Cine Liberación (Liberation Cinema) made a remarkable political film, *La hora de los hornos* (*The Hour of the Furnaces*, 1968), codirected by Fernando Solanas and Octavio Getino (who the following year published their manifesto "Towards a Third Cinema"). Though normally classified as a documentary, the film's purpose in part was to explode such categorizations in order to make spectators perceive and think freshly, about both politics and communications forms. It is a work of political advocacy cast in avant-garde style—a collage film utilizing a wide variety of image/sound juxtapositions and contrast editing, printed text, still images, borrowed scenes from fiction films, acted sequences, advertisements, voice-over, and sound effects. The full-length film, in three parts, ran to four hours and twenty minutes; only Part One, a ninety-minute segment dealing broadly with the subject of neocolonialism, generally circulates in the United States. The second and third sections, concerned more specifically with the Argentine situation, contained suggested break points for audience discussion.

Part One presents the view that violent rebellion is an appropriate response to the social disorders caused by existing forms of domination. Among its most striking visual sequences is a montage of scenes from a slaughterhouse interspersed with shots of advertisements for foreign products, suggesting that a dependent culture and economy are linked to a life-destroying system. The film is dedicated to Ché Guevara, the Cuban revolutionary killed in 1967 while leading a guerrilla group in Bolivia, and other "patriots who have fallen in the struggle for the liberation of Latin America." In contrast to its fast-paced editing style, Part One ends with a shot of Guevara's face, filmed after his death, held on-screen for three minutes, while drums beat on the soundtrack.

Bolivia

Another significant work of political advocacy, made as narrative fiction, was the Bolivian film *Yawar Mallku* (*Blood of the Condor*, 1969), directed by Jorge Sanjinés (b. 1936). It dramatized charges that members of the United States Peace Corps (called "Progress Corps" in the film) were sterilizing Indian women without their consent in an obstetrics clinic. Both the Bolivian and United

Above: 18.16. A scene of military action in La hora de los hornos (The Hour of the Furnaces, 1968), codirected by Fernando Solanas and Octavio Getino

Left: 18.17. Members of an Indian community in the mountains of Bolivia in Yawar Mallku (Blood of the Condor, 1969), directed by Jorge Sanjinés

States governments sought unsuccessfully to suppress the film, while experts supported its accusations. Peace Corps activities ended in Bolivia two years after the film's release.

AFRICAN CINEMA

With nations throughout the continent achieving independence in the period around 1960, Africa might have appeared primed to play a central role in the emerging cinema of liberation. Substantial impediments existed, however, to the growth of filmmaking. Foremost was the lack of economic development of any sort in the former European colonies, leaving cinema as a low priority for scarce financial resources. Moreover, the colonial powers, especially France in the regions it had previously ruled, maintained control over film distribution. As had been the case since the early twentieth century in countries outside the large film-producing nations, local theaters played cheap foreign imports in preference to indigenous works. Filmmaking in the newly independent countries of Africa barely got under way in the 1960s, and did not become a significant practice for another decade or more.

Ousmane Sembene

The founder of feature filmmaking in black Africa, or Africa south of the Sahara desert, was Ousmane Sembene (b. 1923) of Senegal, a major figure both in literature and film. After fighting with Free French forces under Charles de Gaulle during World War II, Sembene spent the postwar years as a dockworker in France, where he began publishing fiction written in French. Around the time of Senegal's independence, he came to the view that in order to communicate with a substantially nonliterate population in his home country, he needed to make films. Sembene studied filmmaking in Moscow and returned to Africa in the early 1960s as a writer and film director.

Sembene made the first black African feature film with La Noire de . . . (Black Girl, 1966), followed by Mandabi ("The Money Order," but known by its original title, 1968), Emitai (1971), Xala (1974), and Ceddo (1977). Though surely his work belongs to a cinema of liberation, Sembene largely eschewed the technical innovations of the Latin Americans. His style has sometimes been called "classical," but it is more accurate to describe it as "realist" in the sense that André Bazin used the term. He utilized careful composition in the frame, medium shots, and long takes with lit-tle camera movement. His mise-en-scène seems tailored for the audience he wished to reach, providing ample time and space for spectator interrogation of the image. Through subtle handling of décor, costume, language, performance, and narrative, he fash-ioned a critique of colonialism and neocolonialism quite as powerful as could be found in more modernist filmmaking styles.

BLACK GIRL. Sembene's first feature dealt with colonialism in its production as well as its narrative. Co-produced by a French company, it was shot largely in France, with a French cinematog-rapher and editor, mostly French performers, and the French language almost exclusively on the soundtrack. These French con-tributions, as Senegalese filmmaker and critic Paulin Soumanou Vieyra has written, were thought to insure "high technical quality, as per the French brand image."[8] Unmistakably, however,

18.19. El Hadj (Thierno Leye, right) dances with his second wife, Oumi (Younouss Seye), as he prepares to marry a third wife in Sembene's Xala (1974).

18.18. Thérèse N'Bissine Diop portrays Diouana, an African woman who goes to France to work for a French family in La Noire de . . . (Black Girl, 1966), directed by Ousmane Sembene.

Sembene's viewpoint shaped the film. It was based on one of his novels, which in turn had been developed from a newspaper account of an African woman's suicide in France. A young black woman arrives in France as an employee of a French family for whom she had worked in Dakar, Senegal. The imperious wife inexplicably treats her as a prisoner and drudge, while the alco-holic husband is ineffectual. The despairing woman slits her wrists in a bathtub. The film is most intriguing as a sketch of colo-nial mentality, exemplified by a French family that exposes its racism and weakness outside the colonial setting.

XALA. By 1974, the time of *Xala*, Sembene had an international reputation as a filmmaker (he was already widely known as a novelist) and was able to finance the film entirely within Senegal. Nevertheless, his target was neocolonialism, in a masterly tragi-comedy whose seriousness gradually emerges from what seems at first lighthearted satire. The opening sequence set the tone: declaring their independence from colonial influence, Senegalese

businessmen kick out the Frenchmen who run their business asso-ciation; then the French deliver briefcases filled with cash and return as "advisers."

One of the businessmen, El Hadj, uses his new wealth to take on a third wife. "Modernity must not make us lose our Africanity," says a colleague, referring to the male practice of polygamy. But El Hadj has received a curse—the Xala, pronounced ha-la—and cannot fulfill his sexual duties with his new young wife. His fail-ures multiply, and he loses both his business and the new wife. The curse had been placed on him by one of the poor people he had previously cheated or ignored, and the film ends in a stark scene of El Hadj submitting to be spat on by beggars, as a means of lifting the Xala. As in other works, Sembene uses language as a key to power and consciousness in a neocolonial environment. El Hadj, who speaks French with his colleagues, grows angry when a daughter addresses him in the native language, Wolof; but when he is under attack he asks to defend himself in Wolof and is told that he is "racist, sectarian, reactionary."

Egypt

In North Africa as well as sub-Sahara Africa distinctions among filmmaking practices have been made on regional, geopolitical, cultural, linguistic, and other grounds. But it is still useful to think about the whole continent—of Africa, as one regards Latin America or Asia—while keeping narrower divisions in mind. In these terms, Africa's strongest commercial film industry was in Egypt, which for decades had managed to produce up to forty or fifty films a year for a small urban audience and African export. An internationally prominent filmmaker who emerged from this industry was Youssef Chahine (b. 1926; sometimes spelled in English "Shahin"), who had studied acting at the Pasadena Play-house in California and began directing films in the early 1950s. In 1953 Chahine gave a first film role to Omar Sharif (b. 1932), an Egyptian actor who became a popular figure in world cinema. Changes in internal politics made it possible for Chahine to shift from genre work to a neorealist style, and his most important film of the period, *Al-Ard* (*The Land*, 1969), resembled the Brazilian

Black African Filmmaking

18.20. Photographed at a 1978 retrospective, "Senegal: Fifteen Years of an African Cinema, 1962–1977," at the Museum of Modern Art in New York, are Senegalese filmmakers (from left) Paulin Soumanou Vieyra, Ben Diogaye Beye, and Ousmane Sembene.

"African cinema is not going to be built outside Africa," filmmaker Med Hondo has said. "African cinema has to be built in Africa, by and for Africans." Unfortunately, through much of the first quarter century of African independence, these views were difficult to put into practice. The building of an African cinema by and for Africans has been hampered not only by the legacies of colonialism, which include foreign domination of film distribution, but also by the reluctance of some African governments to foster the development of free and creative (thus potentially critical) film cultures.

With the principal exception of Ousmane Sembene and other Senegalese directors, African filmmaking in the 1960s and 1970s consisted to a significant extent of films made by exiles. Hondo (b.

1936) is an example. Born in Mauritania in northwest Africa (his full name is Mohamed Abid Hondo), he launched his career in France and continued to make his films there. Writing about the complexities of exile, Hondo has nevertheless maintained that he had "established a national cinema, even though conceived and put together outside my country. For, if exile remains as the worst thing, what is essential, in the heart of that worst, is to be conscious of what has to be struggled against." His films include *Soleil O* (*O Sun*, 1970), *Les Bicots-nègres, vos voisins* (*The Nigger-Arabs, Your Neighbors*, 1973), and *West Indies* (1979). *Sarraounia* (1986), a historical film on the colonial era, was Hondo's first work set in Africa.

Another exile, Haile Gerima (b. 1946), left Ethiopia to study in the United States and stayed to become a filmmaker and educator in the context of black American cinema. He returned to Ethiopia in 1974 to make his only African film, *Mirt sost shi amit* (*Harvest 3,000 Years*, 1975), an unusual work, shot with a 16mm camera, concerning the life of a peasant family.

Senegal was among the first African countries to develop a broad film culture, in part because filmmakers who had trained in France chose to return. A pioneer was Paulin Soumanou Vieyra (1925–1987), who has been called "the father of Senegalese cinema." As a student in France in the 1950s, he codirected a short film made with other black African filmmakers, *Afrique sur Seine* (*Africa on the Seine*, 1955). In Senegal he made short documentaries and became the leading historian of African cinema, with four books published (in French) between 1969 and 1983. In 1981 he directed his only feature film, *En Rési dence surveillée* (*Under House Arrest*).

Another Senegalese filmmaker who studied in France was Safi Faye (b. 1943), considered the first black African woman to direct feature-length films. Trained in ethnography as well as in filmmaking, she returned to make two documentary features in Senegal, *Kaddu Beykat* (*Letter from My Village*, 1975) and *Fad Jal* (*Come and Work*, 1979).

18.21. *Mohsen Mohiedine as Yehia in Youssef Chahine's* Iskindria . . . Leh? (Alexandria . . . Why?, *1978)*

Barren Lives, a realistic treatment of rural life set in the 1930s. An autobiographical work, *Iskindria . . . Leh? (Alexandria . . . Why?,* 1978), set in the Egyptian city of Alexandria during 1942, also received wide attention.

THE NIGHT OF COUNTING THE YEARS. A remarkable Egyptian work that gained international recognition was *El Mumia* (*The Night of Counting the Years,* 1969), directed by Shadi Abdelsalam (1930–1986). This spare film concerns conflicts within a mountain tribe that plunders secret tombs of ancient pharaohs. An intense work, with a close-up camera style and an eerie musical score, it has the generic form of a mystery but also deals with subtle issues of history, archaeology, and class relations. It was Abdelsalam's only fiction feature, though he later made several documentaries.

Right: 18.22. A scene from El Mumia (The Night of Counting the Years, *1969), directed by Shadi Abdelsalam*

Below: 18.23. Nagisa Oshima directing a scene from Shinjuku dorobo nikki (Diary of a Shinjuku Burglar, *1969)*

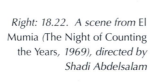

Below: 18.24. Militant students in Nagisa Oshima's Nihon no Yoru to Kiri (Night and Fog in Japan, 1960)

Right: 18.25. Japanese officials take time out for food and drink while pondering what to do about a man who has survived his execution in Oshima's Koshikei (Death by Hanging, 1968). The man, R. (Yun do-Yun), lies on the mat at left, with a symbolic figure identified as his "sister" (Akiko Koyama).

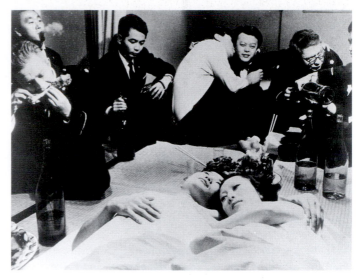

THE JAPANESE "NEW WAVE"

To include Japanese filmmaking within a chapter on cinema of liberation may seem incongruous. Japan had gone through an occupation, but had not experienced a revolution, nor colonialism or neocolonialism in the senses that those issues had been addressed by filmmakers in Latin America or Africa. Nevertheless, it is important to recognize the new generation that emerged in Japan around 1960 as political filmmakers. Newspaper accounts designated this group as the Japanese *nouvelle vague* in imitation of the French movement that had captured world attention. The term has stuck, but the Japanese "New Wave" has not gained the broad international recognition accorded earlier or more recent Japanese filmmakers. This may be because many of their key films are topical and devoted to social concerns. A more apt comparison than the French New Wave, if one were necessary, would be to Brazilian Cinema Novo.

The central figure associated with the Japanese "New Wave," Nagisa Oshima (b. 1932), has disputed that the new directors constituted a movement at all. They were young filmmakers who were going through the traditional course of career development in Japan by working as assistant directors in the major studios. Their chance to become directors arose because Japanese film attendance, as in the United States, was declining, and the studios hoped that younger directors could make films appealing to the youth audience. In the late 1950s Oshima, Shohei Imamura (b. 1926), Masahiro Shinoda (b. 1931), and others directed their first films.

Nagisa Oshima

While training as a filmmaker, Oshima had also written polemical film criticism, which may have been why other writers made the analogy to the critic/filmmakers of the French New Wave. When Oshima began directing in 1959 the Shochiku studio, his employer, got more than it bargained for. From the beginning his films raised disturbing social issues and depicted social conflicts. The studio withdrew his fourth film, *Nihon no yoru to kiri* (*Night and Fog in Japan*, 1960) from circulation within days of its release. Thereafter Oshima formed his own production company.

NIGHT AND FOG IN JAPAN. This controversial film focused on student activism in Japan during the 1950s, which was much stronger in those years in Japan than in North America or Europe. Student protests focused on Japan's security treaty with the United States (known in Japan as "Ampo") on the grounds that this alliance might lead to a resurgence of Japanese militarism. Demonstrations were held against the treaty throughout the 1950s and these erupted in violence in June 1960 when the agreement between the two countries was renewed. The film is set at a wedding where different generations of militants are gathered. In long takes (there are fewer than fifty shots in the nearly two-hour film) the camera pans and roves among the guests, who debate past events that are shown in extended flashbacks. Offering conflicting accounts of the past, the film as a widescreen color production occasionally resembles a 1950s Hollywood melodrama, with a revolutionary group replacing a family as its center. Oshima's viewpoint clearly supports the younger generation's critique of the student movement's failures, which are blamed in part on the authoritarian tactics of the Japanese communist party. *Night and Fog in Japan* condemns the older generation for refusing to face up to past mistakes. The director at this point had not yet seen Resnais's documentary *Night and Fog* (see Chapter 17) from which he borrowed the name; his point was not to make a comparison with World War II concentration camps but to suggest that darkness and obfuscation stem from an unwillingness to take historical responsibility.

DEATH BY HANGING. Oshima's most critically acclaimed film of the 1960s was *Koshikei* (*Death by Hanging*, 1968), based on an actual case in which a man born in Japan to Korean parents was hanged for murdering a Japanese woman. In the fashion of Buñuel's *Land Without Bread*, it begins as what appears to be an obsessive documentary on the death penalty and executions. Then the condemned man survives, and the film changes tone toward a different kind of surrealism, with Japanese officials debating law, ethics, and religion with increasing hysteria as they try to figure out a proper way to hang the man again. Oshima's target was Japanese racism and ill treatment of Koreans living in Japan. Perhaps understandably, critical admiration did not help the film become a success with Japanese audiences.

Shohei Imamura

Within Japan, Imamura has been a more highly regarded film-maker than Oshima, though it took several decades for his 1960s films to begin circulating internationally. Imamura's work viewed Japanese society through a stance of detached observation, as opposed to Oshima's impassioned critique. He began his career at Shochiku in the early 1950s as an assistant to Yasujiro Ozu on such films as *Tokyo Story* (see Chapter 15), and though his style and interests as a director differed from Ozu's, he was seen as a similar figure whose works represented qualities authentically "Japanese." All his films from 1959 through 1968 rated highly in the annual critics' poll, and two—*Nippon konchuki* (*The Insect Woman*, 1963) and *Kamigami no fukaki yokubo* (*The Profound Desire of the Gods*, 1968)—were ranked first.

THE PORNOGRAPHERS. Imamura's best-known work from the 1960s outside Japan has been *Jinruigaku nyumon* (*The Pornographers*, 1966), based on a novel with the same title by Akuyuki Nozaka that has also been widely translated. An academic-sounding subtitle, "Introduction to Anthropology," indicates the director's typical strategy of detachment from his subject. Narrating events in the life of a confused, unhappy man who makes cheap 8mm pornographic films, Imamura's work also uses a visual style of framing devices to distance the spectator: long shots taken through windows, doorways, and even through a fish tank, which holds a carp that also figures significantly in the film. *The Pornographers* provided a glimpse at the underside of Japanese culture—its sexual obsessions, small-time gangsters, and petty corruptions—conveyed with pathos and humor.

Masahiro Shinoda

Like Imamura, Shinoda got his start at Shochiku as an assistant to Ozu; like Oshima, the studio launched him as a director with youth-oriented subjects. When he was able to establish himself

on his own, however, Shinoda shifted his work toward a formal exploration of style in period films. His most notable work in this broad generic framework was *Shinju ten no Amijima* (*Double Suicide*, 1969), the top-ranked film for its year in the critics' poll. The film was based on the classic Japanese play by Monzaemon Chikamatsu, *The Love Suicide at Amijima*, first presented in 1720 in the Bunraku puppet theater, later adapted for the Kabuki stage, and made into several films.

DOUBLE SUICIDE. Shinoda's approach was to examine the historical and aesthetic implications of a human narrative created for puppet performance. In the opening credit sequence the director himself appears backstage at a Bunraku production, planning a scene in a telephone conversation with his scriptwriter. He is wearing the black clothing and stocking mask of a *kuroko*, the stagehands who move about the puppet stage but by convention are regarded as "invisible." After the credits, however, the narrative commences with human performers rather than puppets. Nevertheless, *kuroko* stagehands are present in many shots assisting in the action, and sometimes they are shown in close-ups as a kind of silent chorus to the narrative movement of character destinies. Shinoda also cast performer Shima Iwashita (b. 1941) in dual roles as a man's wife and as his courtesan-lover; this is a further treatment of social and performance conventions, whereby a man can ignore and betray a woman in one role, and passionately join her in a love suicide in the other. Though set in the past, *Double Suicide*'s reflexivity also addresses its contemporary present: it depicts a tradition- and rule-bound society in which rebellion leads to self-destruction rather than liberation.

The legacy of the cinema of liberation that emerged in the 1960s was profound but contradictory. What it accomplished above all, in the wake of historic movements for national independence from colonial rule and other political transformations, was to give new energy and purpose to filmmaking outside North America and Europe. It brought into world cinema culture a new

Right: 18.26. Pornographers at work in Shohei Imamaura's Jinruigaku nyumon (The Pornographers, *1966)*

Opposite: 18.27. Shima Iwashita portrays the woman, Kichiemon Nakamura the man, in Masahiro Shinoda's Shinju ten no Amijima (Double Suicide, 1969).

generation of filmmakers from Africa, Asia, and Latin America who used both familiar and innovative styles to comment on the historical traditions and political structures of their societies. They demonstrated once again the capacity of film to represent social actuality and to express new viewpoints. But to what extent could they comprise a "Third Cinema," in the words of Solanas and Getino, "outside and against the System"? With few exceptions, the cinema of liberation shaded over into the cinema of *auteurs*—a subcategory of the international art cinema, even if a fresh and exciting one—because of the need for private or government financing, and critical recognition in the international market-place, as conditions for its existence.

Notes

1. Julio García Espinosa, "Theory and Practice of Film and Popular Culture in Cuba," in *Cinema and Social Change in Latin America: Conversations with Filmmakers*, ed. Julianne Burton (Austin: University of Texas Press, 1986), pp. 247, 248. "For an Imperfect Cinema" was originally published as "Por un cine imperfecto" in *Cine cubano*, nos. 66–67 (1970), and a translation appears in *Twenty-five years of the New Latin American Cinema*, ed. Michael Chanan (London: British Film Institute/Channel Four Television, 1983).

2. Fernando Solanas and Octavio Getino, "Towards a Third Cinema," in *Movies and Methods: An Anthology*, ed. Bill Nichols (Berkeley and Los Angeles: University of California Press, 1976), p. 52. Originally published as "Hacia un tercer cine," *Tricontinental* (Havana), no. 13 (October 1969).

3. Franco Solinas, screenplay, trans. PierNico Solinas and Linda Brunetto, in *Gillo Pontecorvo's "The Battle of Algiers"*, ed. PierNico Solinas (New York: Scribner's, 1973), p. 122.

4. Leyda quotes his own report in Jay Leyda, *Dianying: An Account of Films and the Film Audience in China* (Cambridge, Mass.: The MIT Press, 1972), p. 303.

5. Reported in *Chinese Film Theory: A Guide to the New Era*, eds. George S. Semsel, Xia Hong, and Hou Jianping (New York: Praeger, 1990), pp. xx, 149.

6. Glauber Rocha, "An Esthetic of Hunger," in *Brazilian Cinema*, eds. Randal Johnson and Robert Stam (Austin: University of Texas Press, 1982), pp. 70–71. Originally published in Portuguese in *Revista civilização brasileira*, no. 3 (July 1965).

7. Quoted in Michael Chanan, *The Cuban Image: Cinema and Cultural Politics in Cuba* (London: British Film Institute, 1985), p. 106.

8. Paulin Soumanou Vieyra, "Five Major Films of Sembene Ousmane," in *Film & Politics in the Third World*, ed. John D. H. Downing (New York: Praeger, 1987), p. 32.

NINETEEN

THE NEW DOC

The transformations of world society and cinema around 1960 also propelled a significant revival of documentary filmmaking. But why, one may ask, did the nonfiction film need to revive? When last extensively observed in these pages, documentary was thriving through both government-sponsored and political advocacy filmmaking. The strong sense of social purpose fostered by the war seemed to provide ample incentive to continue the development of actuality production in the postwar period. Yet documentary, having been so important to world cinema in the 1930–45 era, suffered through a generally fallow period from 1945 to 1960. What happened?

There are two principal answers: the cold war, and broadcast television. The cold war rivalry between the United States and the Soviet Union heightened sensitivity in western nations to the propaganda and ideological aspects of nonfiction film. Government support of filmmaking on social or economic problems (such as 1930s works by the Crown Film Unit in Britain or the U.S. Farm Security Administration) became too controversial. At the same time, the advocacy films produced by left-wing groups that had been active in the depression years largely vanished in the face of political persecution. In the United States and Britain documentary filmmaking turned toward nonpolitical treatment of such subjects as the arts or distant locales. Commercial corporations played a more significant role as sponsors of nonfiction films; projects that would have been called propaganda if governments or advocacy groups had produced them now were categorized as "public relations." Standard Oil Company, for example, provided

the funds for Robert Flaherty to make his last film, *Louisiana Story* (1948), a documentary on life in the bayous that integrated drilling for oil into Flaherty's lifelong themes of traditional folkways and their relationship with nature.

Television changed cinema's role in visual reporting as well as filmmakers' techniques and styles. Live television broadcasts of sports and major public events challenged and quickly vanquished the short newsreels that had been a part of motion picture programs in many countries. In the United States, where commercial television advanced most rapidly, many theaters had abandoned newsreels by the early 1950s. Live television gave viewers a sense of direct experience and participants an opportunity to speak in their own voices; it offered the possibility that something unplanned and unexpected might happen. Eventually viewers would learn that television rarely provided an unmediated transmission of actuality, that the medium constructed its own perspectives (through commentary, camera position, and editing) that shaped its presentation of events. In the first years of television, however, these seemed inconsequential alongside the newsreels' often hyperactive montage style, booming music, and obtrusive "voice of God" narrations.

Despite the increasing availability of lightweight portable 16mm cameras, the technology for documentary filmmaking initially did not keep up with the changes brought about by television's electronic transmission. Sound recording posed the most difficult problems. Synchronized sound recorded optically onto film required a controlled environment and a sound crew—a recordist, a mixer, and a boom operator. In Italian neorealist

UMENTARY

fiction films this limitation was overcome through postsynchronization, dubbing voices and adding effects in a studio, but this solution was rarely satisfactory to documentary filmmakers trying to capture actual events.

During the 1950s, however, technology began to be developed for easier on-site sound recording. Magnetic tape replaced optical recording on film, lightweight recorders that could be operated by one person were introduced, and synchronized sound was freed from a direct cable link to the camera, removing restrictions on the mobility of image or sound recording. By the end of the 1950s a technological groundwork was laid for the emergence of new documentary film styles that offered even greater immediacy and directness than was available, at that time, through television technology.

CINEMA VERITÉ

The famous term for the new documentary style was **cinema verité**—literally, film truth. It was derived by French filmmaker Jean Rouch (b. 1917) from Soviet documentarian Dziga Vertov, who named a newsreel series *Kino Pravda*—"Film Truth"—after the Soviet Communist party newspaper *Pravda*—"Truth" (see Chapter 7). However, when Rouch used the concept for the first time in *Chronique d'un été* (*Chronicle of a Summer*, 1961, made with Edgar Morin), emphasis was placed not on film as truth, but (as an English subtitle translates the voice-over) on "an experiment in filming the truth."

Jean Rouch

Rouch's background was as an ethnographic filmmaker working in Africa after World War II. One of his most widely known films of the period was *Les Maîtres fous* (*The Mad Masters*, 1955), a half-hour color film about a religious sect in colonial British West Africa (later Ghana) that performed ceremonies of "possession" mimicking the protocols of colonial governance. The film was criticized by both colonialists and anticolonialists, as well as by animal rights advocates who objected to scenes of rituals in which a dog's throat is cut and participants drink its blood.

CHRONICLE OF A SUMMER. Rouch's critics suggested that he turn his attention to the customs of his own country. *The Mad Masters* and Rouch's other ethnographic films had been traditional documentaries whose "voice" belonged to the filmmaker, through post-synchronized voice-over narration, rather than to the filmed subjects. In the late 1950s, however, he learned of innovative work being done with new technologies by Québec filmmakers in the French-language unit of Canada's National Film Board, and he invited director and cinematographer Michel Brault (b. 1928) to work with him as camera operator on a documentary about people living in Paris. The other major collaborator was Edgar Morin (b. 1921), a sociologist and film theorist, who is credited as codirector.

As "an experiment in filming the truth," *Chronicle of a Summer* brought the filmmakers out from behind the camera—or the off-screen recorded voice-over—and placed them among its subjects. At the beginning Rouch and Morin are shown on screen discussing with a woman, Marceline, whether it was possible to

Ethnographic Film

Ethnography is defined as "a branch of anthropology dealing with the scientific description of individual cultures," and ethnographic film—the creation of a visual record concerning an individual culture—has become an expanding part of the field. What counts as an ethnographic film, however, and what are appropriate methods and procedures in making such films, remain open to intense debate.

Almost all the works designated as ethnographic films have been made by Europeans and North Americans venturing to other parts of the world to film native cultures. The earliest such films (though on North American subjects) were *In the Land of the War Canoes* (1914), made by the photographer Edward S. Curtis (1868–1952) among the Kwakiutl Indians of the Canadian province British Columbia, and Robert Flaherty's *Nanook of the North* (1922). The first films made explicitly from ethnographic research were based on thousands of feet of footage taken by the noted anthropologists Gregory Bateson and Margaret Mead in Bali and New Guinea during the 1930s; in 1952 they released six short films edited from this material, including *Trance and Dance in Bali* and *Childhood Rivalry in Bali and New Guinea*.

The next generation of ethnographic filmmakers—exemplified in France by Jean Rouch and in the United States by John Marshall (b. 1932), who made *The Hunters* (1958) among the Bushmen of the Kalahari Desert in southern Africa—faced new questions raised by changing theoretical concerns in both ethnography and documentary film. How much did the presence of cameras actually alter the behavior of filmed subjects, thus rendering the films "inauthentic"? Could filmmakers retain the stance of "observer" or should they record their own interaction with the subjects in a more "participatory" mode? Was it in fact possible to combine ethnographic standards with effective filmmaking, or did one have to take precedence over the other?

These issues were debated as ethnographic filmmaking rapidly developed in the 1960s. One model project involved a collaboration between filmmaker Timothy Asch and anthropologist Napoleon Chagnon; after Chagnon completed his fieldwork among the Yanomamö people of southern Venezuela, he returned with Asch to shoot footage illustrating his published research, resulting in *The Feast* (1970) and other films.

Another experiment was devised by communications scholar Sol Worth and anthropologist John Adair to test a theory that modes of visual expression derive from the structure of language. In 1966 they gave cameras to eight Navajo people in the southwestern United States who had never made films before. These filmmakers produced twenty short films for Worth and Adair's "Navajos Film Themselves" series. The hypothesis had been that they would communicate visually the worldview embodied in the Navajo language and provide an "authentic" ethnographic record, but the results were inconclusive; for one thing, the filmmakers were familiar with the visual styles of commercial films and had preconceptions of how a film should look.

19.3. A French man and an African student talk in a stairwell in Jean Rouch and Edgar Morin's "experiment in filming the truth," Chronique d'un été (Chronicle of a Summer, 1961), the foundation work of the cinema verité documentary style.

conduct a conversation in a "natural" manner with a camera present. Rouch tells her, "Anything you object to can always be cut." Morin states that the goal is to make a film about how people live.

Interviewers with microphones confront people on the street and ask, "Are you happy?" There are discussions around dinner tables; confessional scenes in tight close-ups; conversations on factory work, race relations, African independence, the Holocaust. At the end the participants are shown gathered in a screening room as they comment both for and against a provisional version of the film-in-progress. Morin insists that the film, "unlike normal cinema, reintroduces us to life," but its subject seems more the filmmakers themselves and their ideas about making a film about life. The final shots are of Rouch and Morin, discussing how difficult their project was and the further troubles they anticipate.

Chris Marker

Along with Rouch, Chris Marker (b. 1921) is also identified as a leading practitioner of cinema verité, but his work further complicates the concept. His four-hour documentary on Parisian life, *Le*

Right: 19.4. Police mobilize against demonstrators in Chris Marker's portrait of Paris in May 1962, Le Joli Mai (The Lovely Month of May, 1963).

Below: 19.5. Workers lay pavement in Marker's Lettre de Sibérie (Letter from Siberia, 1958), while a voice-over offers three different viewpoints on the scene.

Bottom: 19.6. A still that is really a still: Chris Marker's La Jetée (The Jetty, 1964) consisted entirely of still photographs.

Joli Mai (*The Lovely Month of May*, 1963), is more concerned with presenting his own viewpoint than in letting "life" speak for itself.

In other films Marker experimented with documentary form. In *Lettre de Sibérie* (*Letter from Siberia*, 1958), he repeats a banal sequence—a bus and a car at an intersection, a passing man, workers laying pavement—three times. The first time a voice-over interprets the scenes in glowing positive terms, the second time it is highly critical, and the third time its words are neutral and "objective." Where is "film truth" to be found? With animated footage, a mock advertisement for reindeer, and occasionally rhyming voice-over, *Letter from Siberia* sends up conventional documentary. *La Jetée* (*The Jetty*, 1964) is a haunting science fiction film consisting of still photographs and a voice-over narration. Marker's work is shaped more by avant-garde subjectivity than a search for "film truth."

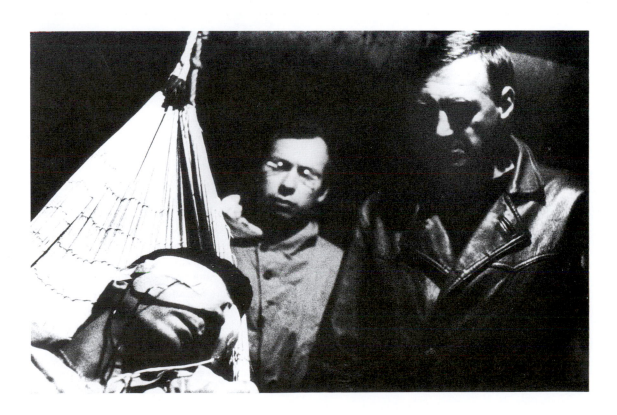

19.7. Senator and presidential candidate John F. Kennedy poses for a photograph during the Wisconsin primary campaign in Primary (1960), the first major "direct cinema" work made in the United States, by Drew Associates. Al Maysles, one of four camera operators, filmed this scene.

1924), it was a production unit of the broadcasting division of the Time-Life publishing corporation. Its aim was to produce for television films on subjects covered in *Life* magazine, with the same immediacy and intimacy for which *Life's* photographic style was noted. Drew was producer, reporter, and narrator, while cinematography was in the hands of filmmaker Richard Leacock (b. 1921), who had photographed Flaherty's *Louisiana Story*. Others joined the group who would later become known as important documentary filmmakers on their own, including Maysles and D. A. Pennebaker (b. 1930).

PRIMARY. Drew Associates's first significant film, *Primary* (1960), was also their most notable, both as film history and political history. Its subject was the Democratic party's 1960 presidential primary contest in Wisconsin between U.S. Senators Hubert H. Humphrey and John F. Kennedy, who, of course, later won the nomination and the presidential election. This was the first behind-the-scenes motion picture view of an American political campaign—as Drew's voice-over claims, accurately if not

DIRECT CINEMA

Though it became a familiar label for the new documentary techniques, cinema verité seemed a term that claimed too much while defining too little. Alternative English-language names were coined that described not the lofty goals of documenting "truth" but a way of regarding the process of filming with hand-held cameras and synchronized sound. Observational cinema was such a term, and the one most widely adopted was **direct cinema**, attributed to filmmaker Albert Maysles (b. 1926).

Drew Associates

Coinciding with developments in Québec and France, a group of United States filmmakers began to work out new documentary techniques at Drew Associates. Headed by Robert Drew (b.

19.9. A shot from the famous opening sequence of D. A. Pennebaker's documentary concerning musician Bob Dylan, Don't Look Back (1967). Dylan (right) holds the message cards; poet Allen Ginsberg stands at left.

19.8. Mr. and Mrs. Andrew Fischer, parents of quintuplets, are feted with a parade in their hometown, Aberdeen, South Dakota, in A Happy Mother's Day (1963), a film by Richard Leacock and Joyce Chopra.

elegantly, "seen close-up, as there's never before been captured by the camera." Four camera teams were utilized, with Leacock, Maysles, Pennebaker, and Terrence Macartney-Filgate (b. 1924), a British filmmaker who had become a prominent documentary director with Canada's National Film Board, filming the candidates' activities. The potential for hand-held cameras with synchronized sound was demonstrated in a famous tracking shot as a camera operator follows Kennedy making his way through a crowd of supporters, conveying a visceral sense of the campaign's excitement, movement, and human variety (the shot has been credited to Maysles).

Left: 19.10. D. A. Pennebaker (left) filming Jimi Hendrix for Monterey Pop (1968)

Below: 19.11. Jimi Hendrix performing at the 1967 Monterey, California, International Pop Festival in Pennebaker's Monterey Pop

A HAPPY MOTHER'S DAY. Drew Associates closed down in 1963, after which Leacock and Pennebaker formed their own production company, and Maysles teamed up in another company with his brother David (1932–1987). Leacock's first post-Drew film was *A Happy Mother's Day* (1963), made with Joyce Chopra (b. 1938). Like the Drew films, it was undertaken with corporate sponsorship, and deals in a similar manner with a behind-the-scenes look at a newsworthy event (in this case, the birth of quintuplets to a family in Aberdeen, South Dakota). *A Happy Mother's Day* made clear the differences between American direct cinema and the French cinema verité effort to depict "life" by filming the private activities of ordinary people. It carried forward the direct cinema tendency to make films on topics that were also involved with press coverage, publicity, or promotion (this may be linked to the fact that many direct cinema films were produced for television rather than for theatrical exhibition).

D. A. Pennebaker

Pennebaker's feature documentaries also drew on this public context, but in a way that helped to stimulate exhibitors' interest in booking nonfiction films for theatrical audiences. *Don't Look Back* (1967) and *Monterey Pop* (1968) were both concerned with popular music and appealed strongly to young audiences for whom television and video did not yet provide sufficient images of their musical favorites. *Don't Look Back* gave a behind-the-scenes view of Bob Dylan's 1965 tour of Britain. Photographed almost entirely by Pennebaker (in contrast to the multiple camera operators of films such as *Primary*), it displays a kinetic visual style rarely attempted so extensively before—almost constant camera movement, along with frequent pans, zooms, and refocusing within a shot. *Monterey Pop* was a concert film of the 1967 Monterey, California, International Pop Festival. It presented thirteen performances by rock and popular music groups, interspersed with shots of the crowd, who by this time in 1960s culture, in dress, hair, and demeanor, were definitely part of the show.

Maysles Brothers

The films of Albert and David Maysles, codirected with Charlotte Zwerin (b. 1931), brought into sharper focus the issues arising in direct cinema documentaries. After several films dealing with celebrities or musicians in the Drew style, the Maysles brothers made *Salesman* (1969), described by Stephen Mamber, a historian of direct cinema, as "the most important product of American cinema verite."[1] It was among the first works in the new documentary style to deal with ordinary life. The filmmakers followed salesmen from the Mid-American Bible Company on the road and into the homes of Roman Catholic parishioners, potential customers for illustrated Bibles. The film centers on the develop-

Above: 19.12. Bible salesman Paul Brennan makes his pitch in Salesman *(1969), a film by Albert and David Maysles, codirected with Charlotte Zwerin.*

Below: 19.13. Members of the Hells Angels motorcycle group involved in a fight during a 1969 Rolling Stones rock concert at Altamont Speedway in California, in a scene from Gimme Shelter *(1970), by the Maysles brothers and Charlotte Zwerin*

Right: 19.14. In a shot from Gimme Shelter, *filmmakers David Maysles (left) and Albert Maysles (center) show musician Mick Jagger scenes from the film on a flatbed editing machine. They are watching an edited sequence in which a member of the Hells Angels group fatally stabs a man at the Rolling Stones' Altamont concert. Spectators also see the footage as it is stopped and repeated, and hear Jagger's reaction: "It's so horrible."*

ing crisis of one salesman, whose success diminishes as his spiels grow shriller. Mamber and other critics have raised such questions as whether the filmmakers' presence caused the crisis, or whether the film was constructed through fictional techniques to create a stronger narrative and make a potentially dull subject more dramatic. *Salesman* followed the direct cinema convention (unlike the films of Rouch or Marker) of keeping the filmmakers off-screen, maintaining a kind of fiction of invisibility and neutrality.

In *Gimme Shelter* (1970), a film on the Rolling Stones rock group and their controversial 1969 concert at Altamont Speedway in California, the Maysles brothers broke this convention, and it is worth giving attention to their purpose in doing so. They appear at the opening of the film and periodically thereafter, showing footage to Mick Jagger and other Stones on a flatbed editing machine; gradually it becomes clear that they are watching the same edited scenes of the concert that we spectators also see.

This material is a far cry from the mellow *Monterey Pop*. Two years had radically changed the music world and American youth culture. There are shots of selling and taking drugs, bad trips, nudity, violence, and growing disorder, while musicians plead for people to "stop hurting each other."

The Maysles had more than twenty cameras at the concert, and one of them captured on film the fatal stabbing of a man by a member of the Hells Angels motorcycle group. The filmmakers show this scene to Jagger on the editing machine, repeating the image and stopping the frame for him and for us. "It's so horrible," Jagger comments. This unusual self-reflexivity provides a way both to use the murder footage and to construct a frame so that spectators do not experience it with the immediacy and intimacy for which direct cinema normally strove.

Frederick Wiseman

An important filmmaker in the new documentary techniques who was not associated with the Drew group was Frederick Wiseman (b. 1930). To distinguish his approach from theirs, Wiseman used the term "reality fiction," explaining that the filmmaker creates "a form which has a life of its own, and that form is a fiction because it does not exist apart from the film."[2]

Wiseman's films focused on institutions. His first documentary, *Titicut Follies* (1967), concerned a prison hospital for the mentally ill in Massachusetts. After initial public screenings, the state took legal action to suppress the film on the grounds that consent had not been obtained from the subjects who had been photographed. (The film's defenders countered that Massachusetts did not want the public to see the horrible conditions that the work revealed.) *Titicut Follies* was banned from general distribution for more than two decades, until an agreement reached in 1991 permitted its rerelease. Wiseman's *High School* (1968), filmed at Northeast High School in Philadelphia, was also controversial and withheld from screening in that city. Some saw the film as an attack on the school, or high schools in general, while others found exploitative the filmmaker's approach to his subjects.

DOCUMENTARY FILM AND THE VIETNAM WAR

The escalation of United States military involvement in Vietnam sparked a revival of propaganda and advocacy filmmaking. The models for such films, whether by governments or political

Top: 19.15. A scene from Frederick Wiseman's Titicut Follies *(1967), a film concerning a prison hospital for the mentally ill in Massachusetts; through court action, the state was able to ban the film from general distribution until 1991.*

Above: 19.16. A classroom scene from Wiseman's High School *(1968)*

groups, stemmed from the 1930s and World War II. The imperative to persuade seemed to rule out techniques of cinema verité or direct cinema, which at least rhetorically presented themselves as more purely observational or neutral. Traditional documentary techniques such as musical soundtracks and an emphasis on montage dominated the first nonfiction films about Vietnam. These works once again raise questions about the role of technique in a film's political effectiveness: do we respond to such films largely through our previous political opinions, or can effective film technique persuade us to change our views?

Why Viet-nam

The United States Department of Defense accompanied the military buildup that began in 1964–65 with a half-hour film, *Why Viet-nam* (1965). Its title echoed the World War II *Why We Fight* series, as did its primary purpose of orientation for service personnel and, as well, its style. One of its efforts is to link Communist "aggression" in Vietnam with familiar images of Hitler and to caution against the appeasement that contributed to World War II. Another is to counter the notion that the United States was opposing a "war of liberation" similar to liberation struggles elsewhere

19.17. Loin du Viet-nam (Far
from Vietnam, 1967), a collective
work by French filmmakers produced by Chris Marker, was one
of many films of the late 1960s
that fought an "image war" over
United States involvement in
Vietnam.

in the world (see Chapter 18). The film makes its points through
almost constant narrative voice-over, as well as speeches by
President Lyndon B. Johnson and other officials. One shot has
Secretary of State Dean Rusk speaking directly into the camera for
more than three minutes. A well-known historian, Henry Steele
Commager, attacked the film in a national magazine as a
distortion of history and linked it to the world of totalitarian
thought-control depicted in the famous novel by George Orwell,
Nineteen Eighty-Four. After the success of government propaganda documentaries during World War II, Commager's article
marked the failure of such efforts to bolster support for United
States policy in Vietnam.[3]

Hanoi Tuesday the 13th
Films critical of United States involvement in Vietnam used many
of the same types of images as appeared in *Why Viet-nam*: peasants working in rice fields, suffering children, dead bodies,
flag-draped coffins. What enabled these images to communicate

a certain message in one film and the opposite in another? To a
considerable extent, the answer lies in the shaping context the
filmmaker created through editing and sound accompaniment.
Hanoi Martes 13 Diciembre (*Hanoi Tuesday the 13th*, 1967), by
Cuban filmmaker Santiago Alvarez (b. 1919), consisted largely of
footage shot in North Vietnam in December 1966, presented in
significantly different ways from the United States government
film.

Hanoi Tuesday the 13th begins with color images from
historical Vietnamese paintings, with a voice-over text by the
nineteenth-century Cuban writer José Martí about struggles
against foreign domination. This is followed by a surrealist montage concerning President Johnson, suggesting in comic, brutal
images his birth as a monster. In contrast, the Vietnam footage is
accompanied by a gentle, upbeat musical score, without commentary. *Hanoi Tuesday the 13th* attempts to persuade not
through factual argument or exhortation but by an eclectic mix of
humor, elegy, and shock.

The Image War

The Vietnam war prompted filmmakers in many countries to produce advocacy works, almost all of them opposed to United States involvement. Political filmmaker Joris Ivens (see Chapter 11) made two films in Vietnam, *Le Ciel, la terre* (*The Sky, the Earth,* 1965) and *Le Dix-septième Parallèle* (*The Seventeenth Parallel,* 1968), and contributed footage to *Loin du Viet-nam* (*Far from Vietnam,* 1967), a collective work by French filmmakers produced by Chris Marker and including segments by Agnès Varda, Jean-Luc Godard, and Alain Resnais, among others. These works, and some made by the North Vietnamese government, circulated widely in Europe, although many were banned from the United States. After *Why Viet-nam,* however, United States government film activities about the war were minimal. Hollywood director John Ford participated in a project for the United States Information Agency intended for overseas showing, *Vietnam! Vietnam!* (1972), but the film was withdrawn after only a few screenings. The United States conceded the war of images several years before it withdrew from Vietnam.

DOCUMENTARY RENAISSANCE

The post-1960 period also experienced a renaissance of nonfiction filmmaking that was connected to neither the techniques nor the aesthetic claims of cinema verité. The strongest impetus for this aspect of the documentary revival, as with the development of direct cinema in the United States, came from television, which by the 1960s had almost completely supplanted the feature film industry as a medium of news and information. Networks and programming bodies in several countries established documentary units and financed the production of nonfiction films for television broadcast. Many of these harked back to earlier documentary models and used traditional techniques such as interviews and re-editing existing footage. Some made a lasting mark as films through the quality of their cinematic style or the significance of their perspectives. A few were so controversial that they never made it to television and were distributed instead as films in theatrical release.

Point of Order

Television was the source of the original material used in *Point of Order* (1964), a compilation film made by Emile de Antonio (1920–1989). In 1961 the filmmaker acquired some 188 hours of footage from the CBS television network of a famous 1954 congressional investigation, the so-called Army-McCarthy hearings, which had been broadcast live and recorded by filming a television screen (a motion picture image of a television broadcast was known as a kinescope recording; before the development of videotape, it was the only way to preserve live programs). The hearings were held by a U.S. Senate subcommittee chaired by Senator Joseph R. McCarthy, whose name often designates the 1950s era of anticommunism in the United States (see Chapter 14). The televised proceedings were believed to have undercut McCarthy's power by exposing his behavior to a large national audience, especially after Joseph N. Welch, a counsel for the U.S. Army at the hearings, responded to one of the senator's accusations by saying, "Until this moment, Senator, I think I never really gauged your cruelty or your recklessness . . . have you no sense of decency?"

De Antonio claimed not to have been aware of earlier compilation films—he said he learned of Esfir Shub's 1920s Soviet films reedited from existing footage (see Chapter 7) only after completing *Point of Order*. In reducing thirty-six days of testimony to less than one hundred minutes of film, de Antonio constructed a highly condensed version of what an opening voice-over calls "the greatest political spectacle" in the history of American democracy. The phrase calls attention not only to the hearings themselves but also to television's new role in shaping the con-

19.18. *Senator Joseph R. McCarthy (right) with an assistant, Roy M. Cohn, at 1954 hearings of McCarthy's U.S. Senate subcommittee, in a scene from Emile de Antonio's* Point of Order *(1964); de Antonio edited his film from 188 hours of CBS television footage that had been recorded by filming the live broadcast image from a television screen, in a process called kinescope recording that preceded the development of videotape.*

duct and reception of such events. *Point of Order* was a success in theatrical release and restored interest in the compilation documentary.

In the Year of the Pig

For his documentary on the war in Vietnam, *In the Year of the Pig* (1969), which also circulates as *Vietnam in the Year of the Pig,* de Antonio went not to one source but to hundreds. An advocacy film, opposed to United States policy in Vietnam, the work survives many others with similar purpose because of its rare historical footage obtained by the filmmaker from sources in several countries. One unusual sequence, showing Vietnamese Communist leader Ho Chi Minh aboard a French warship in 1945, de Antonio claimed to have secretly removed from a French military film archive. Senator Joseph R. McCarthy puts in an appearance as well, asserting, "If we lose Indochina, we will lose the Pacific, and we'll be an island in a Communist sea." Also using powerful contemporary footage shot for television network news broadcasts, the film makes its impact through a collage of moving and still images, interviews, and voice-overs. It was nominated for an Academy Award as a feature documentary.

The War Game

A work that received an Academy Award for feature documentary was one of the most controversial nonfiction films of the decade, *The War Game* (1965), directed by British filmmaker Peter Watkins (b. 1935). Watkins had become known as a producer of "documentary reconstruction" films, restaging and shooting historical events so that it appeared as if cameras had been present in cinema verité fashion. He gained backing from the British Broadcasting Corporation (BBC), the public television entity in Britain founded by royal charter and ostensibly independent of government control, to make a film for television about Britain's civil defense preparation for nuclear war. The film is shaped as a documentary reconstruction of a possible future event: a nuclear attack on Britain. Watkins's strategy was to reverse a standard practice of similar films that regarded present time as "real" and the future as a fantasy: instead, *The War Game* treats the present as a fantasy (at least concerning the adequacy of civil defense preparations) and the future it depicts as all too real.

The War Game is a polemical film arguing that nuclear war could happen and that civil defense efforts would not protect people from its terrible consequences. It uses an amalgam of techniques: hand-held shots with conspicuous panning and tracking (here cinema verité style is evoked to enhance the appearance of "filmed truth") but also music, printed text, and a dominating voice-over that speaks menacingly in a future conditional tense: "This could be the way . . ."; "It is very possible that . . ."; "The results would be . . . almost inevitable." Drawing on data from the most damaging bombing raids of World War II, the film dramatizes such potential postwar horrors as police shooting severely

Above: 19.19. A military image from de Antonio's compilation documentary on the Vietnam war, In the Year of the Pig (1969)

Below: 19.20. Police confront protesters in The War Game *(1965), Peter Watkins's "documentary reconstruction" on how Britain's civil defense preparations might cope with a future nuclear war.*

19.21. Actuality footage from Vichy France during World War II in Marcel Ophuls's four-and-one-half-hour documentary on the experience of war in the town of Clermont-Ferrand, Le Chagrin et la pitié (The Sorrow and the Pity, 1969)

wounded casualties, hunger riots, and executions of civilians by firing squads. Several hundred nonprofessional performers agreed to participate in the harrowing production, many wearing gruesome makeup to appear as victims of radiation burns and other injuries. The BBC refused to broadcast the film, but it was released for theatrical exhibition through the British Film Institute.

The Sorrow and the Pity

Another documentary made for television but banned from broadcast—at least in the country that was its subject—was *Le Chagrin et la pitié* (*The Sorrow and the Pity*, 1969), directed by Marcel Ophuls (b. 1927). Son of the German émigré director Max Ophuls, the filmmaker was born in Germany and raised in France and the United States. In the 1960s he directed feature fiction films in France and worked for German and French television networks as a journalist and documentary filmmaker. An independent production, *The Sorrow and the Pity* was financed by German and Swiss television. It focused on the experience of World War II in a French town, Clermont-Ferrand. The complete version ran four and one-half hours in two parts. French television refused to consider the work, and it was released in theaters as a single film cut to just over four hours. In the United States, where it was among the longest films to play in commercial exhibition up to that time, it also was nominated for an Academy Award as a feature documentary.

The Sorrow and the Pity examined the myths of French politics and daily life under the Vichy regime, after France's defeat by Germany. Ophuls and his crew shot some sixty hours of interviews among townspeople with different social backgrounds and political viewpoints, from collaborators with the Nazis to resistance fighters. They interspersed selections from the interviews with archival and newsreel footage from the war period. In its slow accumulation of detail, *The Sorrow and the Pity* became not a collage like *In the Year of the Pig* but a meditation, not a polemic but an elegy. The controversy it evoked arose from its insistence on looking behind the legends and discovering that evil existed and suffering could be terrible, that history is more often grievous than heroic.

Tokyo Olympiad

The major feature documentary of the 1960s decade not funded by or intended for television was *Tokyo Orimpikku* (*Tokyo Olympiad*, 1965), a widescreen color film produced by the Japanese company Toho and directed by Kon Ichikawa (b. 1915), a prominent filmmaker who previously had made more than forty fiction features in a twenty-year career. The occasion was the 1964 Olympic Games in Tokyo, the first time this event had been held in Asia, as the voice-over narration repeats several times. The production unit employed over five hundred people, used more than one hundred cameras, and shot seventy hours of film, which Ichikawa edited into a two-part film running just under three hours. It was an enormous box office success and ranked number two in the Japanese critics' poll of best films of the year.

Inevitably *Tokyo Olympiad* invites comparison with Leni Riefenstahl's *Olympia* (see Chapter 11). Ichikawa's film quietly evokes memories of the earlier work when, at the end, after a Japanese runner has finished third in the marathon run, the voice-over remarks that the Japanese flag was being raised in the main stadium for the first time in twenty-eight years—since, that is, the 1936 Games in Berlin. *Tokyo Olympiad* goes out of its way to avoid nationalistic fervor, giving emphasis instead to new African nations participating in the Games for the first time after gaining independence: the most intimate sequence concerns a runner from Chad, a country four years old that sent two athletes and a coach. Though Japanese athletes are shown competing for—and sometimes winning—gold medals in gymnastics, wrestling, box-

Canada's National Film Board

By the 1960s, Canada was perhaps the last country to remain steadfast—or at least bureaucratically committed—to the vision of government-sponsored documentary filmmaking that had animated figures such as John Grierson in Great Britain and Pare Lorentz in the United States during the 1930s (see Chapter 11). State production was a fixture, to be sure, in socialist countries, and elsewhere government agencies produced films to further policies and programs, but Canada's National Film Board (NFB), founded in 1939 by Grierson, retained and even strengthened its purpose (in the words of a 1950 National Film Act) to "promote the production and distribution of films designed to interpret Canada to Canadians and to other nations."

The political and social turbulence of the 1960s, however, posed tests for the coexistence of state sponsorship with filmmakers' free expression. One such test was the NFB series "Challenge for Change" inaugurated by filmmaker Colin Low (b. 1926) in 1967, whose aim was to give people who were the subjects of documentary films the power to shape the content and form of those films. In 1969 the government formally mandated "Challenge for Change" to make films "to prepare Canadians for social change." Nevertheless, most films made for the series were traditional advocacy documentaries in which filmmakers maintained control of film technology and their subjects expressed their viewpoints by speaking on camera. American filmmaker

George C. Stoney, a producer for the series, was criticized when he actually put cameras in the hands of Mohawk Indians, who then staged a demonstration while making a film, *You Are on Indian Land* (1969).

Another test came with the growth of political radicalism and nationalist feeling in Québec. Filmmakers at the NFB's French-language unit in Montreal had gained international recognition for documentary techniques that presaged cinema verité and direct cinema, and their nonfiction films became increasingly political in the 1960s. "It would long remain one of the most contradictory historical facts that this boisterous birth of a 'national' Québecois cinema occurred inside a Canadian government apparatus, which never intended it and always renounced it," Québecois film critic Réal La Rochelle has written. Matters came to a head in 1970 with what Canadian film historian Peter Morris has called "the most notorious example of direct NFB censorship," when the NFB banned *On est au coton*, a feature documentary on Québec textile workers by Denys Arcand (b. 1941), on the grounds that it promoted class warfare and national disunity; the film was finally released in 1976.

Meanwhile, the NFB continued to produce innovative documentaries outside its political controversies. Michael Rubbo (b. 1938) made several self-reflexive feature documentaries, including *Waiting for Fidel* (1974), in which the filmmaker visits Cuba with a Canadian politician and a media baron, who never quite get to meet their host, Cuban President Fidel Castro.

19.22. Canadian politician Joey Smallwood (in glasses) meets Cuban youth in Michael Rubbo's Waiting for Fidel *(1974).*

19.23. *Women sprinters leave the starting blocks in Kon Ichikawa's widescreen color documentary on the 1964 Olympic Games held in Tokyo, Japan,* Tokyo Orimpikku *(Tokyo Olympiad, 1965).*

ing, judo, and women's volleyball, the images convey a viewpoint quite different from the conventional: it is as if these athletes experience the agony of victory, and the glory of defeat. A sequence depicting Japan's triumph over the Soviet Union in the women's volleyball final, for example, only briefly shows the players' elation after the winning point; this is followed by lengthier shots of the Japanese team's male coach standing by himself, looking awkward and downcast, and then of the Japanese players crying, with somber music on the soundtrack.

By the end of the 1960s the innovations of cinema verité and direct cinema had redefined and been incorporated into standard documentary film practice. Nonfiction filmmaking continued to thrive into the 1970s, in the framework of the styles and techniques of the previous decade, though without its larger claims of "filmed truth." Hand-held cameras with synchronized sound gave new life to the documentary of political advocacy, of which the most notable work of the 1970s was *La Batalla de Chile* (*The Battle of Chile*, 1975–79) a three-part film directed by the Chilean filmmaker Patricio Guzmán (b. 1941) on the political struggles in his country culminating in 1973 with the military overthrow of the government of Salvador Allende; imprisoned in Chile after the 1973 coup, Guzmán went into exile the following year and completed the film in Cuba.

The rise of the feminist movement in the United States, as well as the end of the era of McCarthyism, fostered a form of advocacy filmmaking that often involved autobiography, biography, and historical reminiscence, rediscovering the forgotten or suppressed histories of feminist and radical political movements in the American past. It was not a fallow time, as the period from World War II to the 1960s can be described, so much as a time of retrospection and revision, an effort to find out what remained valid or vital from the past, as part of moving forward.

Notes

1. Stephen Mamber, *Cinema Verite in America: Studies in Uncontrolled Documentary* (Cambridge, Mass.: The MIT Press, 1974), p. 161. Mamber adapted the French term to describe American nonfiction filmmaking by dropping the accents.
2. Ira Halberstadt, "An Interview with Fred Wiseman," in *Nonfiction Film Theory and Criticism*, ed. Richard Meran Barsam (New York: Dutton, 1976), p. 303.
3. Henry Steele Commager, "On the Way to 1984," *Saturday Review*, vol. 50 (April 15, 1967), pp. 68–69, 80–82.

TWENTY

AMERICAN AND TRANS

The image of the United States in the 1960s, even more than for many other countries, is of sweeping cultural and social change. In the popular imagination the era begins in hope and ends in tragedy, marred by political assassinations, the quagmire and conflict of the Vietnam war, and growing racial confrontation; while drugs, a sexual revolution, and rock 'n' roll transform the moral landscape. All these phenomena did in fact occur, but when, and whom did they affect? The watershed years of "the sixties," broadly speaking, were concentrated late in the decade, and their most profound effect was on young people. Like many other established cultural institutions, American commercial films lagged far behind the vanguard of change. Even as the Hollywood studios began to participate fully in exploring and representing new trends, they were going through one of the worst economic periods in their history.

Indeed, while the 1960s marked an era of widespread achievement in world cinema—with new wave movements in France and Japan, Brazil's Cinema Novo, a cinema of liberation, and important documentaries, among others—for the United States film industry it was a decade largely of crisis. We have already seen how the introduction in the mid-1950s of technological innovations such as widescreen only temporarily halted the post-war decline in motion picture attendance. Average weekly attendance began to stabilize in the 1960s, at less than half the numbers even of the 1950s. By the mid-1960s operating "four-wall" (enclosed) movie theaters numbered less than half the figure of 1945. In 1963 some 121 feature fiction films were produced in the United States, an all-time low.

The American motion picture industry was becoming vulnerable to external economic forces to an extent not encountered since the early years of the Great Depression. Through decades of internal struggles and change, many Hollywood studios had remained rocks of stability: Jack L. Warner had supervised production at Warner Bros. for more than forty years (1923–67), and other motion picture executives held leadership positions for nearly as long. But in the 1960s, weakened economically, the studios became takeover targets. In 1962 MCA Inc., the talent agency, gained control of Universal. Paramount was acquired by Gulf + Western in 1966, United Artists by the Transamerica Corporation in 1967. Warner Bros. merged with Seven Arts Productions in 1967 and was taken over two years later by Kinney National Service Corporation. These changes marked the beginning of frequent corporate realignments that have continued for decades.

Despite dismal statistics and management turnover, Hollywood remained the world's most powerful and influential film production center. As filmmakers, the movie companies responded to their multiple challenges mainly by accentuating a defensive position. In the early 1960s they became committed more than ever to the 1950s "prestige" picture mentality, concentrating on big-budget genre extravaganzas based on popular Broadway musicals, novels, and classic stories. Twentieth Century-Fox scored the greatest success with this strategy and also suffered the biggest disaster. Its 1965 production *The Sound of Music*, directed by Robert Wise (b. 1914), became the outstanding box office triumph in film history up to that time, nearly doubling the receipts of the previous leader, M-G-M's *Ben-Hur* (1959). But Fox also lost more than $10 million on a single picture, *Cleopatra* (1963), which with a production cost of $37 million may rank, in real dollar terms, as the most expensive motion picture in cinema history.

THE EARLY 1960S

The early years of the 1960s are a neglected period in American film history, a time with no clear direction. Movements and genres from film noir to the family melodrama had lost their force, and beneath the top layer of expensive "prestige" pictures the codes of moviemaking that had shaped Hollywood's mode of popular filmmaking through the sound era appeared in question. Amid the uncertainty, a few bold cinematic endeavors stood out.

John Ford

The veteran director John Ford, who had made his first Western in 1917, was among a handful of pioneers entering his sixth decade of active filmmaking—others included Raoul Walsh (1887–1980) and Allan Dwan (1885–1981). In the 1960s Ford opened to question the conventions of the Western genre in which he had worked and, by implication, the historical myths of the American west. *Sergeant Rutledge* (1960), though a melodramatic film concerning a black cavalry soldier falsely accused of a crime, had the merit of bringing more prominently to the screen the role of African-Americans in western expansion; Woody Strode (b. 1914) portrayed Sgt. Braxton Rutledge. *Cheyenne Autumn* (1964) narrated the desperate effort of a small group of Cheyenne Indians to escape a reservation and return to their home territory. In their context, these were unusual attempts to revise the standard treatment of racial issues in the Western genre.

The Man Who Shot Liberty Valance (1962) more broadly considered the myths of European expansion in the West—the idea of how a "wilderness" was transformed into a society. While *Sergeant Rutledge*, *Cheyenne Autumn*, and Ford's other Westerns of the period were photographed in color, *The Man Who Shot*

FILM : TURMOIL FORMATION

20.1. The outlaw, the dude, and the quiet hero of the old West: from left, Lee Marvin as Liberty Valance, James Stewart as Ransome Stoddard, and John Wayne as Tom Doniphon in John Ford's The Man Who Shot Liberty Valance (1962)

Liberty Valance was black-and-white. Its mood was elegiac, its visual tones dark. The cast included performers who had appeared in Ford Westerns since the 1930s and were themselves icons of Western mythology, such as John Wayne, Andy Devine (1905–1977), and John Carradine (b. 1906). A United States senator (played by James Stewart) returns to the town of Shinbone for a funeral. In flashback, to newspapermen, he recounts the town's story. As a young attorney, he had championed the law against violence (personified by the symbolically named outlaw, Liberty Valance). Ironically, however, his rise to eminence was based on a mistaken belief that he had killed the outlaw. At the end of his story, when he asks that the truth be told, a newsman replies, "This is the West, sir. When the legend becomes fact, print the legend." Yet as many critics have pointed out, Ford "prints" both sides. The film suggests the inevitability of legends, but also their costs in deception and inauthenticity, for individuals as for history.

Alfred Hitchcock

Another veteran, whose career stretched back nearly as many years as Ford's, Alfred Hitchcock created in *The Birds* (1963) perhaps the most enigmatic and protean of his more than fifty films. It carried to a further level the suspense and menace found in *Vertigo* (1958) and *Psycho* (1960); its external action was more spectacular, its psychological motifs more elusive. In genre terms, *The Birds* draws on horror and science fiction: birds such as crows, sea gulls, and sparrows flock together and attack humans in the bucolic setting of Bodega Bay, north of San Francisco. Yet the film does not quite adhere to these traditional genres—it offers neither explanation nor resolution.

The Birds was a triumph of technique, deriving in part from new sound technology. The film utilized no background music; instead composer Bernard Herrmann shaped a soundtrack from natural and electronic sounds, almost as a score. Rapid montage

Right: 20.3. Artist Albert Whitlock painted this sketch for a composite shot in The Birds. *The scene in the film combined live action, a matte painting by Whitlock, and other special effects. Robert Boyle designed the production.*

Below: 20.2. Sea gulls fly off after an attack that ignites a gasoline station fire in Alfred Hitchcock's The Birds *(1963).*

Right: 20.4. Director Alfred Hitchcock, accompanied by dogs, makes his signature walk-on appearance in The Birds.

Below: 20.5 Birds invade the Brenner home in the climactic sequence of The Birds; *from left, Tippi Hedren as Melanie Daniels, Rod Taylor as Mitch Brenner, and Jessica Tandy as Mrs. Brenner. This shot was achieved by special effects cinematography: the performers went through their actions without the presence of the birds, who were added through the matte process.*

Right: 20.6. A brainwashing session for prisoners of war in the Korean conflict, in John Frankenheimer's The Manchurian Candidate *(1962): Lawrence Harvey as Raymond Shaw sits beside the table; Frank Sinatra as Bennett Marco is to the left.*

Below: 20.7. The war room in Stanley Kubrick's Dr. Strangelove, or How I Learned to Stop Worrying and Love the Bomb *(1964); Peter Sellers portrays Dr. Strangelove (left center, in dark glasses), one of his three roles in the film.*

and startling overhead shots—as if from "bird's eye" view—contribute to the film's unsettling effect on spectators. *The Birds* was not a political film but it pointed to underlying concerns about the fragility of the planet. The film marked a subtle shift from the science fiction films of the 1950s that conveyed social and political themes allegorically through fantasy elements, such as the alien pods of *Invasion of the Body Snatchers* or the giant ants mutated through atomic radiation in *Them! The Birds* locates its sense of anxiety more subtly within everyday life, implying that humans more generally may be responsible for disrupting the order of nature, and that nature will take its revenge.

Politics and Film

Like *The Birds*, the films that revived the subject matter of contemporary politics in the early 1960s did not inject fantastic elements into everyday life so much as they regarded everyday life as if it were itself fantastic. The period's groundbreaking work was *The Manchurian Candidate* (1962), directed by John Frankenheimer (b. 1930). Based on a popular novel, the film took up the theme of what historians have called "the paranoid style of American politics." It opens during the Korean conflict of the early 1950s and gradually reveals a bizarre episode of brainwashing—a term used to describe the enemy's efforts forcibly to indoctrinate prisoners of war. The incident is part of a Communist plot to gain control of the United States presidency, with the mother of a brainwashed soldier as the secret agent at the core of the plan. The film culminates in a tense sequence at a national political party convention, where the ex-soldier, after discovering how he has been duped and used, assassinates his mother and her husband, a candidate, with a long-range rifle, then takes his own life. *Variety*'s reviewer proclaimed that *The Manchurian Candidate* "restores a topical excitement to American films which has been almost totally lacking. . . ."[1] However, after the assassination of President John F. Kennedy in November 1963, the film was withdrawn and was not rereleased until the late 1980s.

With *The Manchurian Candidate* quickly out of circulation, the film that became emblematic of a new political viewpoint was *Dr. Strangelove, or How I Learned to Stop Worrying and Love the Bomb* (1964). Director Stanley Kubrick (b. 1928) took a subject of even greater worldwide portent, nuclear holocaust, and treated it as satiric black comedy. Another avatar of the "paranoid style," a demented air force general, persuaded that the "international communist conspiracy" is out to sap and impurify "all of our precious bodily fluids," sends a squadron of nuclear bombers on a preemptive strike against the Soviet Union. As political and military leaders strive to prevent catastrophe, a host of contemporary attitudes are mocked: cold war posturing, macho militarism, hand-wringing liberalism, Russians and Americans alike. Perhaps the film's most chilling aspect is not the absurd behavior it parodies but its representation of conventional behavior: the matter-of-fact professionalism and ingenuity with which the last surviving bomber crew, against all obstacles, manages to drop a bomb on a target. The film ends with a shot of a mushroom cloud from a nuclear explosion while on the soundtrack are heard the lyrics of a sentimental popular song, "We'll meet again, don't know where, don't know when. . . ." *Dr. Strangelove* deflated the standard political wisdom of the era with its grim humor as effectively as few other films in the history of world cinema.

20.8. Abbey Lincoln and Ivan Dixon portray a young black couple beginning their life together in a southern town in Nothing but a Man *(1964)*, directed by Michael Roemer.

MOVIES AND SOCIAL MOVEMENTS

In general, the American film industry was unprepared for the accelerating pace of change in the 1960s. During the Great Depression and World War II, Hollywood had demonstrated a remarkable capacity to shape social myths and mediate perceptions of public events through memorable narrative fictions; in the early 1960s, however, that skill was not available. Turnover in management and continuing box office decline left the studios with inexperienced leadership and an uncertain sense of their audience. Producers favored Broadway musicals and historical costume dramas. Young people turned to the emerging culture of rock music for their social myths and viewpoints on public events.

The Civil Rights Movement

Of all the contemporary movements for social change, Hollywood was perhaps least able to respond to the civil rights movement. The struggle of black Americans that had surged in the late 1950s and early 1960s in protest against racial segregation soon expanded into a wider effort to improve social conditions and enhance economic opportunity. A historic turning point was a 1963 march on Washington, D.C., where the Rev. Martin Luther King, Jr., delivered a famous speech with the repeated words "I have a dream" on the steps of the Lincoln Memorial. These events marked a challenge to the United States film industry. It had traditionally followed a so-called southern strategy of avoiding subjects or scenes that might disturb dominant white racial attitudes; this was justified on the grounds that otherwise exhibitors in southern states would cut prints or reject films entirely. The studios offered generalized appeals for racial understanding, such as *Lilies of the Field* (1963), concerning a black workman who helps European nuns build a chapel in the desert. African-American actor Sidney Poitier (b. 1924) won an Academy Award for best actor for his performance in the film, but there was little of "topical excitement"—of direct engagement with contemporary issues—in such works.

20.9. *In the Academy Award–winning best picture of 1967, In the Heat of the Night (1967), directed by Norman Jewison, the police chief of a southern town,*

Bill Gillespie (Rod Steiger), learns to get along with black Philadelphia police detective Virgil Tibbs (Sidney Poitier).

The first 1960s film to significantly treat contemporary black themes was a non-Hollywood independent production, *Nothing but a Man* (1965), which was also important for demonstrating that feature fiction films made outside the dominant mainstream could achieve commercial success. It was a collaboration between Michael Roemer (b. 1928), credited as director, and Robert Young (b. 1925), credited as cinematographer; experienced documentary filmmakers working on their first feature film, they raised production money from individual investors and a film laboratory. The film centers on the efforts of a black couple (played by Ivan Dixon and Abbey Lincoln) to establish life as a family in a small southern town. Through understated daily events it evokes the pain and loss in lives deprived of dignity and human rights. This small film remains a pioneering work on the African-American experience.

Hollywood and Racial Issues

Hollywood's breakthrough on racial subjects came in 1967, with the Academy Award–winning best picture, *In the Heat of the Night*, directed by Norman Jewison (b. 1926), and the year's second top box office success, *Guess Who's Coming to Dinner?*, directed by Stanley Kramer (b. 1913). These did not focus on the African-American experience in the manner of *Nothing but a Man*; rather, their narratives concern hostile whites finding racial reconciliation by encountering a superior black individual, who is the only prominent black character in the films. This figure was

portrayed in both works by Poitier, in *In the Heat of the Night* as a northern homicide detective who gets involved in a murder investigation in a southern town, in *Guess Who's Coming to Dinner?* as a scientist engaged to a white woman. Poitier wears a suit and tie in almost all his scenes in both films.

The Graduate

The surprise hit of 1967–68 was *The Graduate* (released in late 1967), directed by Mike Nichols (b. 1931). It was second only to *The Sound of Music* in box office receipts for the 1960s. The film struck a chord as no other work of the era with the "baby boom" generation of young people born after World War II who were in college during the 1960s. A twenty-year-old college graduate returns to the materialistic milieu of his parents and falls into an affair with the wife of his father's partner. Despite hard work and scholastic honors, his life seems without purpose. "It's like I've been playing some kind of game," he says, "but the rules don't make any sense to me. They've been made up by all the wrong people. I mean no one makes them up. They seem to have made themselves up." With soundtrack music by Simon and Garfunkel and an acclaimed performance by actor Dustin Hoffman (b. 1937) as the mordant youth, *The Graduate* seemed to speak for a generation that was raised in affluence but found itself facing an uncertain future.

Demise of the Code

The Graduate's affair between a young man and a married older woman was one of many signs in the mid-1960s that the moral prohibitions of the Motion Picture Production Code, monitored since 1934 by the Production Code Administration, had become a dead letter for Hollywood filmmakers. The Code had been under challenge since the 1950s, when works of the international art cinema gained prestige and critical praise with their more sophisticated treatment of sexuality. By the 1960s, the social consensus that supported the Code had collapsed. Sexual candor was more apparent in advertising, literature, and public behavior. Not only international art films but also independent low-budget "exploitation" films, featuring nudity and sexual escapades, provided increasing box office competition. In periods of economic distress, such as this one was for the motion picture industry, producers habitually turned to sensational content in an effort to attract patrons. In 1966 Jack Valenti, a former special assistant to President Lyndon B. Johnson, became head of the Motion Picture Association of America, the producers' organization that operated the Code, and began an effort to arrive at a new self-regulation device.

The Rating System

The outcome was the replacement of the Code in 1968 by a rating system, modeled after similar systems in Britain and other countries. The original ratings included "G" for general audience; "M," suggested for mature audiences—adults and mature young people; "R," restricted, persons under 16 years admitted only with an adult; and "X", no one under 16 admitted. These have been periodically revised, so that "M" became "PG," to stress the importance of "parental guidance" in young people's choice of motion pictures, and then was divided into "PG" and "PG-13," while "X" was replaced in the early 1990s by "NC-17" to avoid stigmatizing Hollywood commercial films with a label that had been eagerly claimed by pornographic works.

A Code and Rating Administration took over from the Production Code Administration and looked at finished films rather than supervising scripts, lyrics, and costumes, as the PCA had done. Its ratings were advisory for parents rather than mandatory for exhibitors; whether ticket sellers vigilantly enforced the age limitations or requirements for adult accompaniment is open to question, though many theater operators refused to book films rated "X." The rating categories reflected specific standards with regard to such subjects as profanity or illicit sex, but overall their application has seemed arbitrary to many filmgoers: gruesome violence does not disqualify a film from a "PG" rating, while filmmakers and ratings administrators haggle over a few frames of sexual explicitness that demarcate an "R" from an "NC-17."

The "Film Generation"

The Graduate's success also seemed to signal renewed excitement about cinema among college-age youth. The young audience's tastes and preferences had an immediate impact, even on reviewers' judgments. The prime example was *Bonnie and Clyde* (1967), directed by Arthur Penn (b. 1922), produced by and starring the young actor Warren Beatty (b. 1938). It was initially

20.10. The surprise box office hit of the late 1960s, The Graduate *(1967), directed by Mike Nichols, spoke to a generation raised in affluence but facing an uncertain future. Title character Ben* Braddock (Dustin Hoffman) *experiences both affluence and uncertainty as his girlfriend's mother, Mrs. Robinson (Anne Bancroft), strikes a suggestive pose.*

dismissed by many critics as little more than an excessively violent genre picture, based on the careers of notorious 1930s bank robbers Clyde Barrow and Bonnie Parker, portrayed by Beatty and Faye Dunaway (b. 1941). But when many young filmgoers embraced the film's doomed lawlessness as a metaphor for their own social alienation, several critics wrote extraordinary revisions of their earlier views. *Bonnie and Clyde* became a major box office success and was soon regarded as a harbinger of the revival of traditional genres.

Appeals to youth, combined with novelty or daring, marked several surprise hits of the late 1960s. One was *Easy Rider* (1969), directed by Dennis Hopper (b. 1936) and produced by Peter Fonda (b. 1940), who were also the lead performers. With popu-

From Exploitation to Sexploitation

In the lexicon of the film industry, the term "exploitation" originally described special forms of publicity or promotion—for example, people dressed in costumes standing outside theaters to attract attention. Since the 1930s, however, a second meaning for the term has become dominant: low-budget independent films dealing with subjects made taboo by the Production Code, such as drugs and sex hygiene.

Exploitation films flourished in the 1950s as production declined at the major studios. They became regular fare at many drive-ins and small theaters catering especially to young audiences looking for thrills and titillation. A relatively mild version (in historical hindsight) was the "teenpic" genre of the era, dealing with high school rebels, which was more transgressive in advertising posters than in the films themselves.

"Many of the films are overtly 'lower-class' or 'low-brow' in content or art direction," write V. Vale and Andrea Juno in their introduction to a book on exploitation films, *Incredibly Strange Films*. "However, a high percentage of these works disdained by the would-be dictators of public opinion are sources of *pure enjoyment and delight* [their italics], despite improbable plots, 'bad' acting, or ragged film technique. At issue is the notion of 'good taste,' which functions as a filter to block out entire areas of experience judged—and damned—as unworthy of investigation."

What has been labeled a "breakthrough" in the exploitation field came in 1959 when Russ Meyer (b. 1922), a photographer for *Playboy* magazine, directed *The Immoral Mr. Teas*, concerning a man who has the ability to view women in everyday life as if they were nude (the spectator, of course, sees what he sees). Through the 1960s exploitation films broke down the boundaries of sexual subject matter along with, but consistently ahead of, Hollywood films; the genre of taboo topics merged with the mainstream when Meyer, "King of the Nudies," directed *Beyond the Valley of the Dolls* (1970) for Twentieth Century-Fox.

By the 1970s exploitation had largely become sexploitation—and transgression had turned into pornography, defined as "soft-core" or "hard-core" depending on the degree of explicitness. As critic Jim Morton has written, "there is no true continuum from early exploitation films to modern hardcore porn." The former was always intended for a theatrical audience, while the latter grew out of pornographic films screened privately at clubs and parties. Despite efforts to prosecute filmmakers or exhibitors of pornographic films (sometimes successfully), hard-core became big business in the 1970s, playing openly in theaters in many parts of the country. With the advent of videocassette players, however, the genre shifted to video and became once again a private affair.

Above: 20.12. Arthur Penn's Bonnie and Clyde (1967) spoke to a late 1960s sense of social alienation in its dramatization (and romanticization) of 1930s bank robbers Clyde Barrow and Bonnie Parker. Here the Barrow gang makes a bittersweet visit to Bonnie's family: from left, Faye Dunaway as Bonnie, Warren Beatty as Clyde, Gene Hackman as Buck Barrow, Estelle Parsons as Blanche; the two men in left foreground are unidentified.

Right: 20.13. Bonnie Parker (Faye Dunaway) dies in a hail of bullets from law officers in one of the controversial scenes of heightened violence in Bonnie and Clyde.

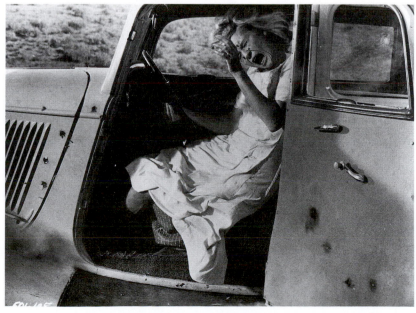

Right: 20.14. Preparing a shot for the final sequence of Midnight Cowboy (1969) with performers Dustin Hoffman and John Voight

Below: 20.15. Hollywood meets the New York counterculture in Midnight Cowboy (1969), directed by John Schlesinger. Jon Voight as Joe Buck is photographed by performers in Andy Warhol's avant-garde films, Viva and Gastone Rossilli, while Dustin Hoffman as Ratso Rizzo looks on (in the credits, Rossilli and Viva play characters named Hansel and Gretel McAlbertson).

MC-23

20.17. Cinematographer Haskell Wexler's first film as a director, Medium Cool (1969), set in Chicago at the time of the 1968 Democratic party national convention, concerned the politics of shooting film; Peter Bonerz as Gus (with sound recorder) and Robert Forster as John (with camera) are a television crew going after shots of an automobile accident.

20.16. John Wayne starred in, and codirected with Ray Kellogg, The Green Berets (1968), a film that supported United States policy in Vietnam and was one of the few mainstream features made about the Vietnam war while U.S. troops were fighting. In the uniform of a U.S. Army special forces colonel, Wayne sets up a shot for the film.

lar rock songs as the music score, this low-budget film served as a primer to the counterculture of the late 1960s, as two drug dealers, after making a big score, set off on their motorcycles "in search of America." Their journey carries them to a "hippie" commune in the southwest and to an encounter with an alcoholic civil rights lawyer, portrayed by Jack Nicholson (b. 1937), before they meet a brutal destiny on a highway in the American South.

Another was *Midnight Cowboy* (1969), the first American film of English director John Schlesinger (b. 1926), which featured Jon Voight (b. 1938) as a naive Texan who dreams of becoming a New York gigolo and Dustin Hoffman as an urban derelict who befriends the Texan—a role sharply divergent from his affluent youth in *The Graduate*. Probably because it depicted homosexuality, the film was among the first Hollywood features to receive an "X" rating, but that did not deter it from box office success and an Academy Award as best picture. The film also introduced spectators to the urban counterculture when the protagonists attend a party at the Factory, the loft-studio of artist and independent filmmaker Andy Warhol (see Chapter 23).

Political Films

In the midst of the divisive political struggles of the late 1960s, it was less likely that filmmakers could construct popular fictions on the issues that offered the originality and appeal of works like *The Manchurian Candidate* or *Dr. Strangelove*. The era's convulsive

event, the Vietnam war, was largely avoided as a subject by American feature filmmakers for over a decade. The principal exception was *The Green Berets* (1968), starring John Wayne, who also co-directed with Ray Kellogg. Wayne portrays a U.S. Army special forces colonel who persuades a skeptical newspaperman of the soundness of United States policy in Vietnam.

From a different political viewpoint, cinematographer Haskell Wexler (b. 1926) made his debut as a director with *Medium Cool* (1969). The film combines actuality footage of protests at the 1968 Democratic party national convention in Chicago with a fictional story of a television cameraman whose attitude that his work is simply technical is altered by his discovery of the moving image's ideological power and political complicity.

GENRE REVISION

The revision of genres was Hollywood's form of participation in the cultural tumult of the late 1960s. Nearly everywhere in American society the fundamental tenets of social relations and ideology were being held up to scrutiny; Hollywood's version of such basic doctrines was the traditional system of genres. Of course, genres had always lent themselves to interrogation. Though marked by codes and conventions, they had also been malleable and open, able to accommodate through allegory issues too hot to handle in direct realist form. In a sense (and contrary to views holding genres to be locked into rigid formulas or organic phases), genre revision had been going on throughout the history of genres, a constant and continuing process keeping genres vigorous through self-critique and self-parody. But genre revision in the late 1960s drew greater attention, because of its involvement in the era's cultural debates, as well as its role in the film industry's period of crisis.

20.18. Sam Peckinpah's The Wild Bunch (1969) considerably raised the level of graphic violence in mainstream Hollywood features; here Warren Oates as Lyle Gorch and Ben Johnson as Tector Gorch take part in a bloody battle.

The Western

Nowhere was this more clearly seen than with Western films. As the civil rights movement at home expanded from African-Americans to other minority groups, including American Indians, the Vietnam war overseas opened up questions about historical conflicts over territorial expansion and warfare against indigenous nonwhite peoples. If few films other than *The Green Berets* concerned Vietnam directly, nevertheless the war entered movies allegorically through the Western, while it cast new light on the historical American West. Freed from Production Code restrictions, issues of violence and racism entered the late 1960s Western film in ways that made John Ford's earlier self-critique seem tentative by comparison.

THE WILD BUNCH. Directed by Sam Peckinpah (1925–1984), *The Wild Bunch* (1969) made *Bonnie and Clyde*'s treatment of violence appear tame. At the same time, it presented a strikingly different viewpoint on violence: whereas in *Bonnie*

and Clyde violence grew out of social disorder, in *The Wild Bunch* violence appeared fundamental to human behavior. Under the title credits young boys and girls watch in awe and delight as red ants attack and kill a scorpion, and children figure in the film as both victims and perpetrators of violence. The film opens and concludes with the most graphically bloody scenes yet to appear in an American film. Vietnam is an unspoken presence as the work (set in 1914 along the border of Texas and Mexico) places its American protagonists, aging outlaws, across the border in the midst of the Mexican revolution, which is depicted as a civil war of guerrilla fighters against corrupt generals.

A technical tour de force, utilizing slow-motion shots and intricate editing to convey its brutal images of war and death, *The Wild Bunch* remains controversial even as its graphic violence has become more commonplace in cinema. Some critics hail it as the greatest Western ever made; others note its racism and misogyny, as well as an uncompelling narrative.

LITTLE BIG MAN. The director of *Bonnie and Clyde*, Arthur Penn, turned to Western revision in *Little Big Man* (1970). The film combines the picaresque tale, the Western tall story, and a more serious effort to reimagine the historical West through the reminiscences of Jack Crabb, who claims to be 121 years old and the only white survivor of the epic defeat of the U.S. cavalry commanded by Gen. George Armstrong Custer by Indians at the Battle of the Little Bighorn. Portrayed by Dustin Hoffman, Jack is a survivor of an Indian raid who is reared as a member of the Cheyenne tribe. There he learns to view other whites as strange creatures who "do not seem to know where the center of the earth is," as his adoptive grandfather, Chief Old Lodge Skins, tells him. *Little Big Man* is one of several films from the period that sought to redress Hollywood's traditional treatment of Indians as murderous savages. Instead it brings to the foreground actual instances of atrocities against Indian women and children committed by U.S. forces in the historical West.

Robert Altman

Director Robert Altman (b. 1925) emerged in the early 1970s almost as a one-man show of genre revision. He took on, among others, the war film, the Western, and the detective genre in a critically acclaimed series of films between 1970 and 1975. His feature film *M*A*S*H* (1970) retains its striking originality, even though its characters and setting attained worldwide familiarity through a weekly series of the same name that became one of the most popular shows in American television history. With an Academy Award–winning screenplay by Ring Lardner, Jr. (b. 1915), one of the formerly blacklisted Hollywood Ten (see Chapter 14), the film brought together the Vietnam era's disillusionment, Hollywood's new candor about sex and violence, and the stylistic daring of the European art film to create a surreal dark comedy of war. Displacing its themes from its own times to the early 1950s, at a mobile army surgical hospital during the Korean war, the film reflexively comments on its own genre

Hollywood's Indians

Historically speaking, Hollywood's racism has been no worse—though also no better—than the racism in other modes of communication, such as newspapers or school textbooks. But in representing Native Americans, feature films, as a story-telling form, may have had incalculably greater influence on cultural perceptions than other media. Indians have not "merely" been cast as marginal, stereotyped figures, as have other ethnic and minority groups. Rather, in the most significant popular narrative of United States history, they play a central role, as The Enemy, whose defeat and decimation are necessary conditions for fulfillment of the nation's destiny.

"We have seen the tipi and the buffalo hunt, the attack on the wagon train and the ambush of the stagecoach until they are scenes so totally ingrained in the American consciousness as to be synonymous with the very concept of the American Indian (to non-Indian minds at any rate and, unfortunately, to many Indian minds as well)," writes Ward Churchill, of Creek and Cherokee Métis

background, a critic and essayist in American Indian studies. Churchill points out that the representation of American Indians in Hollywood movies is largely confined to the place and time of the European population's westward expansion, from the 1820s to the 1880s on the Great Plains. "There is no 'before' to this story," he suggests, "and there is no 'after.' "

Historians of the Western genre have often seen a progressive trend in the representation of Indians after World War II, beginning with films such as *Broken Arrow* (1950), directed by Delmer Daves, and *Apache* (1954), directed by Robert Aldrich, and continuing through the period of broader genre revision of the late 1960s–early 1970s. "The Western's increasing emphasis on frontier discrimination against the Indian paralleled growing contemporary sensitivity about social injustice toward blacks," film historian John H. Lenihan has written.

From the Indian perspective articulated by Churchill, however, this viewpoint offers little comfort. He argues that even

films purporting "to provide an 'accurate and sympathetic treatment of the American Indian' (of yesteryear)" are shaped by a "Eurocentric" perspective, almost always with non-Indians cast in major Indian roles, and often with the narrative told through a European's viewpoint. He does not exempt from this critique revisionist Westerns such as *Soldier Blue* (1970), directed by Ralph Nelson; *A Man Called Horse* (1970), directed by Elliot Silverstein; and *Little Big Man*. "To date, all claims to the contrary notwithstanding," Churchill writes, "there has not been one attempt to put out a commercial film which deals with native reality through native eyes."

Churchill concedes that *Dances With Wolves* (1991), directed by and starring Kevin Costner, was a breakthrough production, with Indians cast in Indian roles more than ever before in a Hollywood film. Nevertheless, this too, in his eyes, is a Eurocentric film, a "Lawrence of South Dakota" to stand beside films of empire such as *Lawrence of Arabia*.

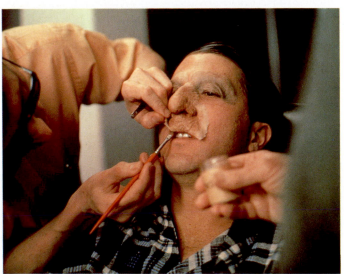

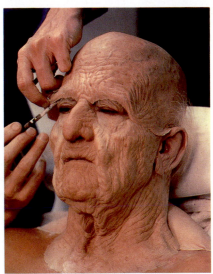

Top: 20.19. Arthur Penn's Little Big Man (1970) revised the Western genre's treatment of Native Americans as murderous savages; in the film, white Europeans more aptly fit that description. Its narrative centers on Jack Crabb (Dustin Hoffman), captured as a youth by the Cheyenne tribe, shown here with Chief Old Lodge Skins (Chief Dan George) and members of the tribe.

Above: 20.20, 20.21. Makeup artists prepare Dustin Hoffman for his scenes as the elderly Jack Crabb, who claims to be 121 years old, in Little Big Man: the beginning and the end of the process.

Above: 20.22. Staff members of a mobile army surgical hospital during the Korean conflict gather to observe Major Hot Lips Houlihan taking a shower in Robert Altman's M*A*S*H (1970). Seated on either side of the dog are Elliott Gould (left) as Trapper John McIntyre and Donald Sutherland as Hawkeye Pierce.

Right: 20.23. Altman's McCabe and Mrs. Miller (1971), an innovative work in sound editing, featured Warren Beatty as John McCabe, a small entrepreneur in a Pacific Northwest frontier town who is murdered by a mining company's hired killers.

Above: 20.24. Gary Lockwood
as Frank Poole (left) and Keir
Dullea as David Bowman try to
speak confidentially outside
the hearing of HAL 9000 in
Stanley Kubrick's 2001: A Space
Odyssey (1968). The red beam
on the console outside their space
capsule indicates their effort is
futile—HAL is reading their lips.

Right: 20.25. Director Stanley
Kubrick (holding camera) sets
up a shot of a violent assault in
A Clockwork Orange (1971).
Malcolm McDowell
portrays Alex (left).

through loudspeaker announcements promoting World War II films screening at the hospital camp. At the end the loudspeaker barks out, "Tonight's movie has been *M*A*S*H*. Follow the zany antics of our combat surgeons as they cut and stitch their way along the front lines"—a mordant commentary on war and its transformation into cinematic entertainment.

SOUND INNOVATIONS. In addition to its contrasting visual style, with sharp cuts from humor to moments of crisis, *M*A*S*H* gave emphasis to new styles in sound editing that had developed in the 1960s and gained particular prominence in Altman's work. These included bleeding sound from one image to another, especially sound that forecast a change of scene; more extended forms of sound/image juxtaposition; and an overlapping of sounds so that a medley of voices and background noise or music prevents the spectator/auditor from easily identifying a dominant communication.

Altman carried this last technique even further in *McCabe and Mrs. Miller* (1971), with Warren Beatty and British actress Julie Christie (b. 1941). This revisionist Western, set after 1900 in a Pacific Northwest frontier town, centers on an aspiring small businessman who runs a saloon and a brothel until he is destroyed, literally murdered, by a mining company's hired killers—a frog swallowed by an eagle, in one of the film's metaphors. Set mostly at night, and in snow and rain, the film is a tragicomedy of a "little guy" who fails to find a miraculous Hollywood happy ending.

Detective Genre

Genre revision was blatant in Altman's *The Long Goodbye* (1973), based on a Raymond Chandler novel featuring hard-boiled detective Philip Marlowe, a figure memorably portrayed on screen by Humphrey Bogart in *The Big Sleep* (1946). Screenwriter Leigh Brackett (1915–1978), who collaborated on the 1946 classic, wrote the screenplay for Altman's Marlowe film, in which the detective has turned into a bumbling anachronism in 1970s Los Angeles. Played by Elliott Gould (b. 1938), Marlowe is confused and abused until the last moments, when he responds to the insults of a friend who has betrayed him by pulling out a gun and calmly shooting the man. The song "Hooray for Hollywood" sounds over the closing shots.

Kubrick and Science Fiction

Following *Dr. Strangelove*, director Stanley Kubrick turned to the science fiction film. Though significant in the 1950s, this remained a relatively minor genre, associated with B pictures and movies made for the drive-in audience. Kubrick's *2001: A Space Odyssey* (1968) marked not so much a revision of the genre as a reinvention. Much of its $11 million production cost went into special effects cinematography that created spectacular vistas of spaceships and interplanetary travel and opened new possibilities for the genre. Its narrative suggested the necessity for humanity's rebirth through contact with the unknown of outer (and inner) space. Partly satirical, partly visionary—and to some critics murky, pretentious, and overlong (Kubrick cut nineteen minutes from the film after early unfavorable reviews)—*2001: A Space Odyssey* has grown in stature as a landmark work that revived a genre.

Kubrick's *A Clockwork Orange* (1971) was also set in the future, though its visionary quality comes through language and political allegory rather than special visual effects. It centers on a

youth gang that speaks an argot combining Russian and English word forms and goes out at night to commit what its narrator-protagonist calls "the ultra-violent"—gang fights, robberies, and assaults. Captured after a murder, the hooligan leader undergoes behavioral modification treatment designed to make him sick at the idea of violence (as part of the cure, he is made to watch *Triumph of the Will* and Nazi newsreel footage). Ultimately the government chooses to use his violent character rather than suppress it. Once again Kubrick creates an ambiguous world where humor coexists with horror, and the film's flamboyance holds interest beyond its deficiencies of narrative coherence.

Hollywood Left and Right

It is always risky to assign political labels like right or left, liberal or conservative, to commercial fiction films. Most works are open to multiple interpretations; and the political terms themselves are often difficult to pin down, especially in relation to fictional narratives. Nevertheless, genre revision does seem clearly linked with some form of political liberalism. Films that called attention to historical atrocities against Indians (*Little Big Man*) or the arbitrary power of large corporations in western development (*McCabe and Mrs. Miller*) addressed issues that were being raised by protest groups in American society. The period of genre revision beginning in the late 1960s was among the most politically progressive eras of Hollywood filmmaking.

Energized by the revisionists, traditional genre films began a comeback. Paradoxically, in the framework of revisionist critique, more conventional works appeared politically conservative. An example was *Dirty Harry* (1971), directed by Don Siegel, previously best known for the 1956 genre film *Invasion of the Body Snatchers*. After years of working in Italian "spaghetti Westerns"—films set in the American West made in Italy during the 1960s by Italian directors (often using American-sounding pseudonyms)—Clint Eastwood (b. 1930) emerged in the film as a major star, portraying San Francisco police inspector Harry Callahan, a fearless, independent figure who in previous eras might have pleased spectators across the political spectrum. Yet many critics regarded Harry's heroic efforts to stop a deranged killer, in defiance of his superiors' caution and legalisms, as a form of right-wing extremism. A more convincing case for the conservatism of conventional genre films might be made for *The Exorcist* (1973), directed by William Friedkin (b. 1939), a film that brought the horror genre back into first-run theaters. It posited the weakness of science and secular reason against demonic evil, which only religious faith could combat.

THE "MOVIE BRATS"

In the early 1970s Hollywood began to recover from its economic crisis. A central factor was a significant shift in marketing strategy. For decades the film industry had followed a pattern of releasing films gradually, a few cities at a time. A film's run would last a year or more as it slowly passed through the exhibition system, from larger to smaller theaters. In the early 1970s, the studios started to utilize national television advertising, and they placed films in hundreds of theaters throughout the country simultaneously, so as to capitalize on the extensive coverage of their promotional campaigns. People in smaller towns could see first-run films at the same time as moviegoers in Los Angeles or New York. Though advertising and print costs were higher, studios

20.26. The heroic individualism of San Francisco police inspector Harry Callahan (Clint Eastwood) was regarded by many critics as a form of right-wing extremism in Dirty Harry (1971), directed by Don Siegel.

20.27. Linda Blair as Regan, possessed by the devil in The Exorcist (1973), directed by William Friedkin, which brought the horror genre back to first-run theaters

sound. Among the many first-time directors of that period, the film school graduates were particularly prepared to make the big-budget, genre-oriented films the new marketing required. Though attuned to youth values, they were not primarily rebels or revisionists; their film studies had forged a link with the industry's past. Looking back a few years later, writers Michael Pye and Lynda Miles called them "movie brats, true children of Hollywood . . . heirs to the great tradition of American cinema."[2] Principal figures among them included Francis Ford Coppola (b. 1939), a graduate of the University of California at Los Angeles; George Lucas (b. 1944), a graduate of the University of Southern California; and Martin Scorsese (b. 1942), a graduate of New York University. An exception to the film school pattern among the "movie brats" was Steven Spielberg (b. 1947), a self-taught film-maker who attended California State University at Long Beach.

Francis Ford Coppola

Like a number of other young filmmakers and performers, Coppola broke into Hollywood by working for independent producer Roger Corman (b. 1926), who became a legendary figure turning out low-budget horror, science fiction, and other B-movie genre films for drive-ins. Coppola's first major studio assignments were as a writer, and he shared an Academy Award for the story and screenplay of Patton (1970), directed by Franklin J. Schaffner. In 1969 he founded a production company in San Francisco, American Zoetrope, named after the precinema moving-image device. He produced George Lucas's first science fiction film, THX-1138 (1971), and meanwhile directed several films for other companies. Versatile, independent-minded, but ambitious for success as Hollywood traditionally measured it, Coppola was a pioneer and prototype of the new generation. Still, Paramount was taking a chance when the studio picked him to cowrite and direct a "prestige" project, a film based on Mario Puzo's best-selling novel about an Italian organized crime family, The Godfather.

could demand a greater percentage of the box office in return for making their top pictures available more widely.

Individual films rarely before had held the possibility of creating such an immediate nationwide mass impact. Could filmmakers create works that would justify the promotional effort and sustain audience interest? The revival of traditional genres was clearly linked, in part, to these new marketing techniques. But such genres now carried a greater weight than they had in the past. Instead of occupying a series of niches appealing to specific audience tastes (Westerns for men, melodramas for women, and so forth), they had to appeal broadly across the fragmented American cultural scene, and especially to the young people who made up the largest part of the audience.

To answer this need, the studios turned to a surprising source—young filmmakers recently graduated from university filmmaking programs. In the crisis of the late 1960s the industry had welcomed new talent to an extent not seen since the advent of

20.28. *Francis Ford Coppola's path-breaking* The Godfather *(1972) briefly held the record as all-time box office champion. Marlon Brando (right) portrayed the leader of an organized crime family, Don Vito Corleone, and Al Pacino his son and successor, Michael.*

THE GODFATHER. Coppola faced several challenges. The "prestige" formula—top stars in big-budget adaptations—had grown stale, and a number of expensive films had flopped. In any case, he had only one star, Marlon Brando, and a cast of unknowns. Organized crime was a highly conventionalized genre subject. Moreover, *The Godfather* (1972) was among the first films marketed under the new strategy of wide simultaneous national distribution. It is difficult to imagine retrospectively that its success was not assured, but no one could have imagined the extent of its triumph. It more than vindicated the new marketing plan, surpassing *The Sound of Music* as the all-time box office leader (a position it held only briefly, as *The Exorcist* and soon other films went even higher). Its theme music, by composer Nino Rota, was heard everywhere, and the phrase "I'm going to make him an offer he can't refuse" became part of the language. *The Godfather* became an instant classic, not only for its popularity but as a powerful, path-breaking film.

Coppola depicted the violence and power of organized crime but also emphasized strong positive values of ethnic heritage and family loyalty. The film offered an epic perspective on mid-twentieth-century American social history and at the same time was a study in character and behavior, abetted by acclaimed performances by Al Pacino (b. 1940), Robert Duvall (b. 1931), and James Caan (b. 1939), as well as Brando. Neither strictly a traditional genre film nor a revisionist work, *The Godfather* fused both impulses into a new genre synthesis, traditional in style, reflective in tone, that pleased spectators of nearly every outlook.

George Lucas

Coppola served as executive producer on Lucas's *American Graffiti* (1973), which also became one of the top popular successes of the early 1970s. Lucas's film carried further than *The Godfather* a mood of nostalgia for seemingly better past times—in the case of *American Graffiti*, the early 1960s. The film's narrative takes place over one night in 1962 in a California central valley town, in a teenage car culture of drive-in restaurants, cruising the main street, and drag-racing at dawn. It portrays innocent youth on the verge of life decisions. Then it shatters that aura of innocence with printed texts at the end, indicating what the future was to hold for some of its fictional protagonists after the narrative's closure (however, only for the males).

Martin Scorsese

After directing several independent features, including one produced by Corman, Scorsese made his breakthrough with *Mean Streets* (1973). Not a box office hit like Coppola's or Lucas's films, it was highly esteemed by critics. It centers on young men in Manhattan's Little Italy, a neighborhood from which the soaring Empire State Building can be seen, but which in Scorsese's film has the claustrophobia and conservatism of an Italian provincial village. The film's visual style, emphasizing constant, chaotic movement within dark, enclosed spaces, helps to shape an ethnic milieu lacking Coppola's epic myths of organized crime and family values and a youth culture without Lucas's nostalgia and innocent hope. *Mean Streets* also brought to prominence a young actor, Robert De Niro (b. 1943), who gave an unusual performance as an irresponsible, trouble-making youth.

Steven Spielberg

Youngest of the "brats," Spielberg was hired as a television director on the strength of a short film he made as a college student. One of his made-for-television films, *Duel* (1971), was expanded for release in theaters overseas; it was a compelling, surreal horror film concerning a man driving to a business meeting who is terrorized by an eighteen-wheel tank truck whose driver's face is never seen. Spielberg's feature film debut was *The Sugarland Express* (1974), a tragicomic genre film in the tradition of road movies about doomed young couples on the run. With cine-

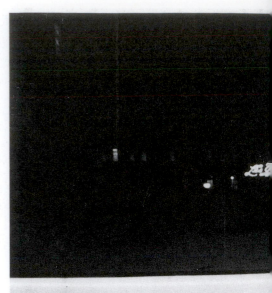

matography by Vilmos Zsigmond, the film was a visual tour-de-force, choreographing scores of law enforcement vehicles, their red lights flashing, as if they were dancers in a Busby Berkeley musical. It updated such predecessors as *You Only Live Once* (1937) and *They Live by Night* (1948) by turning the criminal chase into a 1970s-style media event with crowd participation, by-standers kissing the fugitives, giving them presents, or stealing their possessions as souvenirs.

The Sugarland Express made a strong impression and completed a transition. Hollywood's doldrums of the 1960s were over. A new generation of filmmakers was in place, confident of a future for the American motion picture industry whose contours

no one, as yet, could fully imagine. In the next few years these filmmakers, along with a few others, would seek to expand the styles and the box office potential of the genres they had inherited.

Notes

1. *Variety*, October 17, 1962, p. 6.
2. Michael Pye and Lynda Miles, *The Movie Brats: How the Film Generation Took Over Hollywood* (New York: Holt, Rinehart and Winston, 1979), p. 12.

Opposite, above: 20.29. Johnny Boy (Robert De Niro) escorts some newfound friends into a bar in New York's Little Italy in Martin Scorsese's Mean Streets (1973).

Opposite, below: 20.30. Lou Jean (Goldie Hawn) calls for her child in Steven Spielberg's tragi-comedy of a doomed couple leading a wild police chase, The Sugarland Express (1974); Michael Sacks as Officer Slide and William Atherton as Clovis Poplin, with arm out to restrain Lou Jean, are partially visible in the front seat.

Above: 20.31. Mels drive-in, where the teenagers hang out in George Lucas's American Graffiti (1973)

Film	Arts and Sciences	World Events
1976 Man of Marble	soft landing of spacecraft on Mars	Carter elected U.S. President
1977 Star Wars	Pompidou Center opens in Paris	death of Elvis Presley
1978 The Marriage of Maria Braun	test-tube baby born in England	John Paul II becomes Pope
1979 My Brilliant Career	Pink Floyd's The Wall	Khomeini takes power in Iran
1980 Raging Bull	John Lennon murdered	Reagan elected U.S. President
1981	MTV music video network begins	AIDS epidemic recognized
1982 E.T. The Extra-Terrestrial	audio compact disks introduced	death of U.S.S.R. leader Brezhnev
1983	A Chorus Line becomes longest running Broadway show	U.S. invades Grenada
1984 The Home and the World	Bruce Springsteen's Born in the USA	India leader Indira Gandhi assassinated
1985 Ran	Live Aid concerts in Britain, U.S.	hijacking of cruise ship Achille Lauro
1986 Blue Velvet	space shuttle Challenger explodes	nuclear reactor accident at Chernobyl, U.S.S.R.
1987 Wings of Desire	L.L. Cool J's Bigger and Deffer	Iran-Contra scandal in U.S.
1988 The Thin Blue Line	Libra (DeLillo)	Bush elected U.S. President
1989 A City of Sadness	The Mambo Kings Play Songs of Love (Hijuelos)	Berlin Wall comes down
1990	Sinéad O'Connor's I Do Not Want What I Haven't Got	Nelson Mandela freed in South Africa Iraq invades Kuwait
1991 Raise the Red Lantern	U2's Achtung Baby	breakup of U.S.S.R.
1992 Daughters of the Dust	All the Pretty Horses (McCarthy)	Clinton elected U.S. President

Part Six

THE EXPAN-SION OF CINEMA

TWENTY-ONE

EUROPEAN 1960S

As film and the twentieth century passed more or less simultaneously through the decades, and new mediums like television rose to challenge the cinema's status, pundits and promoters stopped speaking of motion pictures as a universal language. Yet the medium's standard gauge remained—a technological practice growing in importance, even if it was more and more taken for granted. Throughout the world most feature fiction films, works intended for theatrical distribution, were shot on 35mm stock (a few features used 70mm, and avant-garde and documentary filmmakers frequently shot in 16mm or sometimes 8mm). Basically, a film made anywhere in the world could be taken directly from its shipping can, wound onto a projector, and screened almost everyplace else.

This standardization may appear so familiar as to be not worth remarking, but its significance becomes clearer by comparison with the lack of standardization in television and video. During the development of commercial television after World War II, countries adopted different standards for the medium's screen image, and these carried over into multiple formats for receiving sets, cassette recorders, tapes, and other equipment. Manufacturers exacerbated differences in the marketing of non-compatible products. These technological barriers are among the reasons why it is not yet possible to speak of a world television culture in the same manner that we think of cinema as an international phenomenon, even as television has become a more popular and pervasive medium.

THE INTERNATIONAL MEDIUM

As television's challenge to cinema attendance expanded from the United States to other countries in the 1960s and 1970s, internationalization of the film medium also accelerated. This process dated to cinema's earliest years, when films, financing, theater ownership, filmmakers, performers, and technicians crossed international boundaries almost as soon as the first film prints had come off the drying rack. In the 1960s, however, the phenomenon became even more widespread and more public: international co-productions mingled stars (and financing) from several countries, directors and performers worked in a number of countries (and languages) without emigrating or changing their citizenship, as had been more commonly the case in the international movement of film personnel.

21.1. Carl Th. Dreyer's last film, Gertrud (1964), was a controversial work of long takes with little movement of camera or characters. Nina Pens Rode portrayed the title character, shown here with Axel Strøbye as Axel Nygren; behind them is a tapestry depicting a naked woman attacked by dogs.

FILMS OF THE
AND 1970S

Carl Th. Dreyer

A living model of the international filmmaker was Carl Th. Dreyer, a pioneer (like John Ford) whose career had begun in the World War I era and continued into the 1960s. The Danish director had begun as a scriptwriter when Denmark's film industry was one of the most powerful in Europe, but the war closed its markets, and by the time Dreyer began directing his country's prominence had passed. He was able to make only fourteen films in a career covering more than five decades (just five after the advent of sound), and fully half of those outside Denmark, in Germany, France, Sweden, and Norway. Dreyer, however, was perhaps one of a kind, a filmmaker whom few others would be tempted to emulate.

The final film of his career, *Gertrud* (1964), released when he was seventy-five years old, made that point forcefully. Based on a 1906 play, the film consists almost entirely of long-take scenes (fewer than ninety individual shots for a nearly two-hour film) in which the camera rarely pans or moves, and the performers are equally immobile. Produced in Denmark and premiered in France, the film was sharply attacked by critics in both countries as "uncinematic." For others, however, its paucity of montage or movement serves to heighten its emotional intensity (and, rather than standing outside the boundaries of acceptable filmmaking

practices, to expand those boundaries, like an avant-garde film).

Gertrud's title character is a woman who rejects men who she feels cannot love her completely, though such complete love means to her suffering and unhappiness. She finds solace in work and solitude, yet holds firm to her belief in *Amor Omnia*: Love is Everything. The film's powerful contradictions—moving images that hardly move, love that is everything but seems unattainable—are apt correlatives for a work looking simultaneously forward and backward; for spectators who can appreciate those contradictions, *Gertrud* can be among their most memorable filmgoing experiences.

THE QUESTION OF NATIONAL CINEMA

The growing internationalization of film production made even more problematic the question of national cinema. Though countries no longer blatantly protected their own film industries through quotas and other restrictive practices, many were still concerned with promoting film production as a means of addressing national history and cultural values in a popular medium. Yet

both prestige and profits could be greater if films attracted the interest of the international market. In a further twist, filmmakers who succeeded internationally would soon be invited to expand their horizons beyond the nation, toward co-productions, or to the mecca, Hollywood.

British Cinema

A perennial case study for the question of national cinema is Britain, where filmmaking for decades had been subordinated to Hollywood domination. During World War II patriotism had fostered a national spirit in British films. By the 1950s, however, several of the leading directors had shifted toward an international stance, sometimes called "Mid-Atlantic" cinema—midway, as it were, between London and Hollywood. David Lean and Carol Reed both excelled in Hollywood productions mingling British and American personnel. Two of Lean's spectacle films dealing with war and empire won Academy Awards for both best picture and director, *The Bridge on the River Kwai* (1957) and *Lawrence of Arabia* (1962).

The "Angry" Generation

A new group of young filmmakers emerged in the 1950s seeking to restore the representation of everyday social life to the British cinema. Several got their start as critics (as was the case also in France) for a short-lived but influential film journal, *Sequence*, published by the Oxford University Film Society from 1946 to 1952. Others began as nonfiction filmmakers, participants in the Free Cinema Movement of the mid-1950s that emphasized docu-

menting working-class life. Chiefly they lacked a defining promotional label, like the French *nouvelle vague*; by default they were associated with the "Angry Young Men" playwrights and novelists whose works they frequently adapted for the screen.

TONY RICHARDSON. A key figure in their transition to feature filmmaking was Tony Richardson (1928–1991), a stage director who formed a production company to direct *Look Back in Anger* (1959) and *The Entertainer* (1960) from plays by John Osborne. His greatest success with adapting British literature, however, came not with a contemporary work but an eighteenth-century classic by Henry Fielding: *Tom Jones* (1963), shot in color with financing from United Artists, followed *Lawrence of Arabia* in winning the Academy Award for best picture, and Richardson succeeded Lean with the director's award. He, too, had become "Mid-Atlantic."

An exemplary work of the short-lived British movement to depict working-class life in fiction features was *Saturday Night and Sunday Morning* (1960), produced by Richardson and directed by Karel Reisz (b. 1926). It was adapted from an Alan Sillitoe novel, and the author wrote the screenplay. *Saturday Night and Sunday Morning*'s bleak mise-en-scène, dominated by a noisy factory floor, gritty workers' flats, and raucous pubs, links it to traditions of film realism such as Grierson's social documentaries, French poetic realism, and Italian neorealism. Sillitoe also wrote the screenplay for *The Loneliness of the Long Distance Runner* (1962), which was based on one of his short stories and directed and produced by Richardson.

What was often most significant about Britain's early 1960s social realist films was not their narratives or settings but their

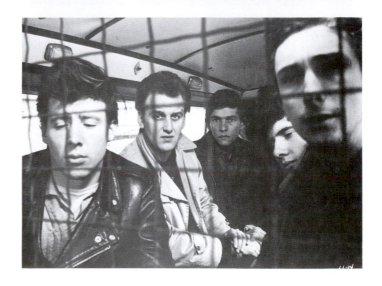

Left: 21.2. "Mid-Atlantic" in the Middle East: a scene from David Lean's epic Lawrence of Arabia *(1962) shot on location in Jordan. The film received ten Academy Award nominations and won in seven categories.*

Top right: 21.3. "Mrs. Waters" (Joyce Redman) seduces Tom Jones (Albert Finney) over a tavern meal in a famous scene from Tony Richardson's Tom Jones *(1963).*

Middle right: 21.4. Working-class life in British cinema: lathe operator Arthur Seaton (Albert Finney) in Saturday Night and Sunday Morning *(1960), directed by Karel Reisz*

Bottom right: 21.5. Tom Courtenay as Colin Smith (third from left) in a police van in Tony Richardson's The Loneliness of the Long Distance Runner *(1962)*

exceptional performances; in *Saturday Night and Sunday Morning* actor Albert Finney (b. 1936), in his first important role, portrayed the working-class figure Arthur Seaton, a rebellious, hard-drinking lathe operator. The character has no illusions about social improvement; he wants only to protect what he believes to be his autonomy and self-empowerment. Finney creates him neither as hero nor villain but as a man in conflict, who slowly gains awareness of his responsibility toward the women in his life. The film's muted ending points him toward family life, but offers no clear promise either of autonomy or of responsibility in his future. Finney gained international recognition for his title role in *Tom Jones;* director Reisz followed Richardson into co-production work. By 1963 the impulse to make socially conscious films about contemporary British life had largely waned.

EASTERN EUROPEAN AND SOVIET FILM

The emergence of Eastern European filmmaking on the international film scene during the 1960s marks a different kind of case study, one that vividly illustrates a premise of this book's approach to history: present-day change inevitably alters our understanding of the past. A generation after the 1960s film renaissance, the socialist regimes of Eastern Europe suddenly disintegrated, their ideologies repudiated by their own peoples. The startling changes of the 1990s, transforming sovereignties and boundaries, could not but cast history, and film history, in a new light.

The post–World War II nations of Eastern Europe—here we will be considering Czechoslovakia, Yugoslavia, Hungary, and

The Fate of Eastern Europe's Film Industry

Who will have a stake in the history of filmmaking in the former Communist regimes of Eastern Europe? In many of the countries themselves, national identities and political boundaries have swiftly been reshaped since the collapse of Soviet hegemony. With nations such as East Germany, Yugoslavia, and Czechoslovakia no longer existing in the form they did from the end of World War II to 1989, it remains to be seen whether the films they produced will hold value for the cultural heritage and historical memories of new societies.

Among Eastern European countries, however, one that has strong grounds for maintaining a vital link to its recent film history is Poland. With Andrzej Wajda as a world-renowned figure, Poland's film culture can draw on four decades of a frequently reflexive and critical filmmaking practice with ties to reform movements in the wider society. Polish critics and historians have begun taking a fresh look at films from the Communist period to see whether changed historical circumstances have produced new ways to interpret and appreciate those works. One film little known outside Poland that has been praised is *Rekopis znaleziony w Saragossie* (*The Saragossa Manuscript*, 1965), directed by Wojciech Has (b. 1925), a narrative of fantasy adventures set in the eighteenth century.

Figures from Poland's first postwar generation of filmmakers whose works merit renewed attention include Jerzy Kawalerowicz (b. 1922) and Andrzej Munk (1921–1961). Kawalerowicz gained international recognition second only to Wajda among Polish directors, winning prizes at Venice for *Pociąg* (*Night Train*,

1959), at Cannes for *Matka Joanna od Aniołów* (*Mother Joan of the Angels*, 1961), and at Berlin for *Śmierć Prezydenta* (*Death of a President*, 1977). *Night Train* and *Mother Joan of the Angels* are social parables set in enclosed spaces (a train car and a convent) that were deliberately vague as to place and time. *Death of a President* is a historical film based on the assassination of Poland's president in 1922; Polish audiences regarded it as a political parable for their own time. Munk was a prolific filmmaker in the 1950s who died in an automobile accident while making *Pasażerka* (*The Passenger*), a film concerning World War II death camps; it was completed by others and released in 1963.

The early works of Krzysztof Zanussi (b. 1939), a key figure of Poland's next generation, also deserve reconsideration. Zanussi's first feature, *Struktura kryształu* (*The Structure of Crystals*, 1969) was named best film of the year by Poland's critics; like much of his later work, it posed issues of science, philosophy, and morality through intellectual debates between characters. Other important films with similar themes included *Barwy ochronne* (*Camouflage*, 1976) and *Constans* (*The Constant Factor*, 1980). Like Wajda, Zanussi worked frequently outside Poland in the 1980s, making films in West Germany with funding from German state television.

Poland—fell under Soviet influence, and their film industries became part of the state apparatus. Governments decided who would make films and what kinds of films they would make; governments promoted some films and banned or censored others. What actually constitutes film history becomes a more pressing question for these regimes than in almost any other case. Is there a basic narrative of national film history, of creativity and reception? Only if it can include some account of the films made but shelved and never seen except by censors. How does this version compare to the narrative of international recognition, based on those films sent to festivals and overseas exhibition? And how will either of these versions relate to the histories that still remain to

be written, of the "national" cinemas in "nations" that proved to be makeshift and temporary, which nevertheless produced many long-known works that need to be freshly appraised and long-suppressed works that need to be discovered and circulated. An example of the latter, among many, are the films of the Czech woman director Vera Chytilová (b. 1929), for many years unavailable either at home or abroad.

More obviously than elsewhere, Eastern European films are linked to politics. Though each country had its own internal dynamics, the early 1960s (following the near-nuclear confrontation between the United States and the Soviet Union during the 1962 Cuban missile crisis) became in general a period of new cul-

21.6. Shifting from socialist realism's heroic themes to small incidents of everyday life, Miloš Forman's Lásky jedné plavovlásky (Loves of a Blonde, 1965) gained recognition for the Czechoslovak "New Wave"; Vladimir Pucholt played Milda and Hana Brejchová was Andula.

tural initiatives. Western Europe and the United States discovered Eastern European cinema; from 1966 to 1969 fully half the titles nominated for best foreign-language film at the Hollywood Academy Awards came from Eastern Europe and the U.S.S.R. The most dramatic expression of new filmmaking energies came in Czechoslovakia, where the film movement that flowered between 1963 and 1968 earned the name, as in France and Japan, "New Wave." The effort of Czech films to question and revise social values seemed to presage and herald the political movement of 1968 known as "Prague Spring," when reformers attempted to replace a dictatorial regime with a new form of "socialist democracy." This

attempt at peaceful political transformation within a Communist country was countered by Soviet bloc military intervention in August 1968, and both the Prague Spring and the Czech New Wave were crushed.

Czechoslovakia

The first signs of the Czech New Wave came in the early films of Miloš Forman (b. 1932). Forman had studied scriptwriting rather than directing at the state film school, and thereby managed to escape being inculcated, as most other postwar Czech directors had been, in the official aesthetic of Soviet-style "socialist realism." His third film, Lásky jedné plavovlásky (Loves of a Blonde, 1965) won a prize at Venice and gave the New Wave international recognition. Instead of socialist realism's heroic themes, Forman's films focused on small incidents in everyday life; Loves of a Blonde concerns the romantic yearnings of a young woman in a provincial town who works at a shoe factory.

THE FIREMEN'S BALL. Forman's most ambitious New Wave film was Hoři, má panenko! (The Firemen's Ball, 1967), another work of small incidents that in this case build into a tragicomedy of social disintegration, incompetence, and corruption, and shape a devastating allegorical critique of the socialist system. While fire officials ogle the women chosen for a beauty contest, a man's house burns and all the raffle prizes are stolen. In sorting out the practical and moral issues, someone asks (in the dubbed English-language version), "What about those people who bought tickets and didn't steal anything?" The answer comes: "They could have. There was no one stopping them. It's their own fault." The Firemen's Ball, significantly, was an international co-production between Barrandov Studios in Prague and an Italian company. Forman was in France preparing another international project when Soviet bloc troops invaded Czechoslovakia in 1968. He

21.7. A scene from the beauty contest in Forman's tragicomic Hoří, má panenko! (The Firemen's Ball, 1967)

445

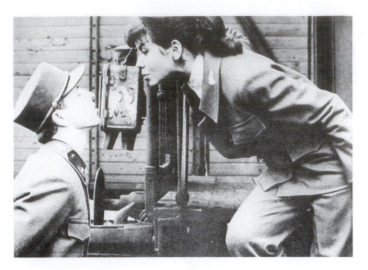

21.8. Sexual desire linked with the struggle for freedom: Václav Neckár as Milos and Jitka Bendová as Masa in Jiří Menzel's *Ostře sledované vlaky* (Closely Watched Trains, 1966), set during the German occupation of Czechoslovakia during World War II

went into exile and thereafter worked primarily in the United States, where he won the best director Academy Award for *One Flew over the Cuckoo's Nest* (1975) and made popular works such as *Hair* (1979), *Ragtime* (1981), and *Amadeus* (1984). He also became codirector of the Film Division at Columbia University in New York.

CLOSELY WATCHED TRAINS. The Czech New Wave's emblematic film was *Ostře sledované vlaky* (Closely Watched Trains, 1966), directed by Jiři Menzel (b. 1938). Like *The Firemen's Ball* it linked tragicomedy and social critique in the form of satire, but it was set during World War II, and the Nazi occupiers of Czechoslovakia were safer targets than contemporary bureaucrats. The film's break with socialist conventions, however, came in its treatment of sexuality. As with Forman's films, comic yet profound sexual longings are mingled with the struggle for freedom; here the heroic sacrifice of a young train dispatcher emerges unexpectedly yet seamlessly from his development as a man. *Closely Watched Trains* won the 1967 Hollywood Academy Award for best foreign language film. It was

banned in Czechoslovakia after the 1968 invasion; repudiating his earlier work, including *Closely Watched Trains*, Menzel continued his career in Czechoslovakia.

Yugoslavia

Sexuality was also central to the cinematic approach of Dušan Makavejev (b. 1932), a Serb who was the first filmmaker to gain international prominence from Yugoslavia, a country formed after World War I that broke up into separate republics in the early 1990s. In his debut feature film, *Čovek nije tica* (*Man Is Not a Bird*, 1966), he shot his performers in the French New Wave manner, with a hand-held camera alongside passersby in the street. The film's metaphors of hypnosis, and of man's incapacity to fly like a bird, hint at the pathos of working-class lives in a region of mines and factories. After making several more innovating features on similar themes, Makavejev shifted to a surreal style treating sexuality and society more generally, and left Yugoslavia for international production.

Meanwhile, in 1967 director Aleksandar Petrović (b. 1929) made what was hailed as the most important work in Yugoslav film history, *Skupljači perja* (*I Even Met Happy Gypsies*), a prize winner at the Cannes film festival. Also utilizing a hand-held camera style, the film focused on the lives of Yugoslavia's Gypsy people, with the soundtrack in Gypsy dialect. Its title was poignant and ironic, like the song lyric from which it was drawn.

Above: 21.10. A scene from Aleksandar Petrović's *Skupljači perja* (I Even Met Happy Gypsies, 1967), hailed as the most important work in Yugoslav film history

Left: 21.9. Dušan Makavejev's first feature, *Čovek nije tica* (Man Is Not a Bird, 1966), concerned the pathos of working-class lives in a mining and factory district of Yugoslavia; Janez Vrhovec plays Jan Rudinski, Milena Dravic was Rajka.

21.11. Ritual in Miklós Jancsó's Még kér a nép (Red Psalm, 1972); *photographed in lengthy takes by a constantly moving camera, this* eighty-four-minute film by the Hungarian director contained only twenty-seven shots.

Hungary

Among the most unusual feature film styles originating in Eastern Europe during the 1960s was that of Hungarian director Miklós Jancsó (b. 1921). His films were not narratives in the conventional sense, even though many depicted events in Hungarian history familiar, at least, to domestic audiences. There was little characterization, performance, or even spoken dialogue, as opposed to songs or declaimed words. The works were akin to folk ballets, with choreographed crowd movement, songs, dances, and patterned motion, all photographed by a constantly moving camera in lengthy takes. His eighty-four-minute film *Még kér a nép* (*Red Psalm*, 1972) consists of only twenty-seven shots. Songs, poems, and declamations, meanwhile, address basic philosophical issues of Marxism, socialism, and popular struggle. Jancsó won the award for best director at Cannes for *Red Psalm*.

Other important Hungarian filmmakers included Márta Mészáros (b. 1931) and István Szabó (b. 1938). Mészáros made her first feature, *Eltávozott nap* (*The Girl*), in 1968 and was one of the few women filmmakers whose works circulated internationally during the 1970s. Relationships between women and the social conditions of women in Hungary formed the themes of a number of her works, such as *Örökbefogadás* (*Adoption*, 1975), concerning an older and a younger woman who are both involved with the same man. Szabó's characteristic subjects were recent history and the relationship between the present and the past, as in *Tüzoltó utca 25* (*25 Fireman's Street*, 1973), in which inhabitants of an old house in Budapest recount their dreams and memories. In 1981 his *Mephisto* (1981), a Hungarian production with a German-language soundtrack, won the Hollywood Academy Award for best foreign film; it was adapted from a novel based on the life of German actor Gustav Gründgens (1899–1963), who played the criminal leader Schraenker in Fritz Lang's *M* and went on to become a prominent performer-director in the Nazi era.

Soviet Union

If an international perspective on a nation's films inevitably is shaped by works that circulate across borders, the Soviet Union marks a special case. For several decades after 1945 the Soviets sent abroad only a few films, generally adaptations from classic Russian writers like Tolstoy or Chekhov, or works stressing what were called "universal human themes" such as the injustice and futility of war; an example of the latter was *Letyat zhuravli* (*The Cranes Are Flying*, 1957), a World War II film directed by Mikhail Kalatozov (1903–1973), which won the award for best film at Cannes. These rather bland or safe films did not prepare spectators outside the Soviet Union for the stylistic daring of several Soviet filmmakers whose works began to circulate internationally in the mid-1960s and who were immediately hailed as masters of the medium, even as they experienced obstruction and punishment at home.

SERGEI PARADZHANOV. One of the most striking stylistic achievements in world cinema since World War II was *Teni zabytykh predkov* (*Shadows of Forgotten Ancestors*, also known as *Wild Horses of Fire*, 1964), directed by Sergei Paradzhanov (1924–1990), a Soviet Georgian who worked at the Dovzhenko

Above: 21.12. Ivan (Ivan Nikolaichuk) gets a bath in Teni zabytykh predkov (Shadows of Forgotten Ancestors, 1964), directed by Sergei Paradzhanov. Though derided by Soviet authorities, this work, made by a Soviet Georgian at a Ukrainian film studio, was one of the most striking stylistic achievements in world cinema since World War II.

Right: 21.13. Andrei Tarkovsky's Soviet space epic Solaris (1971) was more concerned with inner than outer space; "We don't want other worlds," says a character, "we want a mirror." Donatas Banionis portrayed Kris Kelvin (back to camera).

studio in Kiev, the Ukraine. Set in an earlier century in the Carpathian region, the film is rich in folkloric elements, costumes, rituals, and songs. As in Jancsó's works, however, narrative hardly matters, especially since the frequent chants and song lyrics go untranslated in subtitled versions. The film is a visual tour de force, using symbolic colors and nonrealistic tinting, slow motion, character viewpoint shots, soundtrack manipulation, multiple exposure, and a constantly moving hand-held camera that at times makes rapid full-circle pans, in part to emphasize themes of circularity.

A tribute both to the potentialities of cinema and to ethnic traditions within the Soviet Union, *Shadows of Forgotten Ancestors* was derided in its home country and Paradzhanov's career hampered by authorities. He was finally allowed to make another film, *Sayat nova* (*The Color of Pomegranates*, completed in 1969), with similar themes and visual style, but it was shelved and reedited by others before its release in 1972. In 1974 Paradzhanov was arrested and sentenced to prison on a variety of charges; his persecution clearly was related to his championing of ethnic and national values against the policy of the Soviet government. International as well as domestic protests gained his release in 1977.

ANDREI TARKOVSKY. The Russian filmmaker Andrei Tarkovsky (1932–1986) experienced similar though less severe difficulties over his mystical, highly symbolic style of filmmaking, and before his early death he had left the Soviet Union to work abroad. His historical epic *Andrei Rublev* (1966), based on the life of a monk and painter of holy icons who lived in the fourteenth and fifteenth centuries, was shelved by authorities, who demanded that scenes depicting nudity and what they regarded as excessive violence be cut. Requests from foreign festivals won the film an unofficial screening at Cannes in 1969, where it won the international critics' prize, and the circulation of a single print finally achieved release of the uncut version.

Tarkovsky's *Solaris* (1971), a nearly three-hour epic of space exploration, would make a good (though lengthy) double feature with Kubrick's *2001: A Space Odyssey*. Like most of Tarkovsky's work, *Solaris* is concerned with nature, childhood, and history, with dreams, memory, and imagination. "We don't want other worlds," says one character (in English-language subtitles), "we want a mirror."

Poland

Andrzej Wajda, the first postwar Eastern European director to gain international fame in the 1950s (see Chapter 15), returned to that era as a subject in *Człowiek z marmuru* (*Man of Marble*, 1976). A student of film directing in her early twenties, portrayed by Polish actress Krystyna Janda (b. 1952) in her first film role, wants to make her diploma film on a worker-hero of the early 1950s. She screens black-and-white footage from the archives (some actuality material, some artfully re-created, including a 1950s title card with "A. Wajda" as assistant director) while tracking down figures from the past. They, in turn, relate their stories in the *Citizen Kane* manner, in flashback sequences (in color in *Man of Marble*). The young filmmaker discovers that the man she investigates, while originally a "hero" through manipulation and publicity, became an authentic hero through adversity. Meanwhile, school officials shelve her uncompleted film. *Man of Marble* was not shelved, but it did elicit strong displeasure from the government. Foregoing showy stylistics, the film synthesized an era of Eastern European history and filmmaking.

Man of Marble marked what a Polish critic called Wajda's "second debut"; he went on to make several films dealing with contemporary Polish political life, including *Bez znieczulenia* (*Without Anesthesia*, 1978) and *Człowiek z żelaza* (*Man of Iron*, 1981), concerning the Gdansk shipyard strike of 1980 and the beginnings of the Solidarity movement.[1] In the 1980s Wajda moved to international co-production, notably with *Danton* (1982), a French-Polish film dealing with the French Revolution.

21.14. *Jerzy Radziwilowicz as Mateusz Birkut, being filmed as an exemplary worker for a propaganda documentary, in Andrzej Wajda's* Człowiek z marmuru *(Man of Marble, 1976)*

Above: 21.15. In Michelangelo Antonioni's first film in English, Blow-Up (1966), a photographer, Thomas (David Hemmings), maintains control of his surroundings during a fashion shoot with a model (Verushka).

Right: 21.16. Losing his control over the image, Thomas peers through a magnifying lens in Blow-Up at an enlargement of a photograph he has taken in a park, in which he believes he can discern a murder being committed.

EUROPEAN CINEMA WITHOUT BORDERS

By the late 1960s, the unification of western Europe seemed a possibility in the realm of cinema, though not yet in the institutions of government. Film had become a medium surpassing national borders, with international productions almost the rule rather than the exception.

Blow-Up

The era's famous example, highlighting the trend, was Michelangelo Antonioni's first film in English, *Blow-Up* (1966). The film involved an Italian producer, director, and screenplay; British location, cast, and crew; and a Hollywood distributor, M-G-M. But it was the film's themes, rather than its behind-the-scenes components, that made it seem a transformative work for contemporary culture as well as for cinema.

Its protagonist is a fashion photographer who, at the film's beginning, has just taken photographs inside a men's shelter for a book oriented toward social realism, in the manner of British early 1960s working-class films. When he begins to process some last shots taken in a park, he discovers through repeated enlargements what he thinks is a murder. He wanders through London, taking in a rock concert and a marijuana party, as questions of what is real, and how to act, become more and more muddled. At the end, he encounters a mime troupe, two of whom are pantomiming a tennis game without a ball. A player motions the photographer to fetch the imaginary ball. He gestures picking it up and throwing it, and then, with the camera aimed on his face, the soundtrack conveys the sound of a ball bouncing and striking a racquet. If in earlier films, such as *L'Avventura*, Antonioni was concerned with vision and perception, here he turns toward the multiplication and manipulation of images. The photographer has abandoned realism for a postmodern sensibility. *Blow-Up* won the award for best film at the Cannes film festival.

Luis Buñuel

The Spanish director Luis Buñuel, after nearly two decades in Mexico, returned to Europe in the mid-1960s to make a last group of films in combinations of French, Italian, and Spanish co-production. These works, of which *Le Charme discret de la bourgeoisie* (*The Discreet Charm of the Bourgeoisie*, 1972) is perhaps the best known, have been grist for political, psychoanalytic, and other forms of analysis yet resist being pinned down.

The Discreet Charm of the Bourgeoisie is both crashingly obvious and cunningly elusive. Three men and three women are interrupted on numerous occasions as they prepare to dine; some incidents turn out to be dreams (only the men are dreamers), and one dream is even dreamt within another; the men are drug smugglers who are protected because one is an ambassador from a Latin American dictatorship; periodically the six are shown walking confusedly on a country road. To label the film "surreal" would be to go against the grain of its elusiveness, yet one might say that Buñuel's brand of surrealism remained fresh over nearly half a century of filmmaking. Like much of his work, the film is at once absurd, cruel, pointed, and, above all, funny.

Alain Tanner

Filmmaking in Switzerland gained recognition in the 1970s through the works of director Alain Tanner (b. 1929), who utilized French as well as Swiss production financing, and collaborated frequently on screenplays with British novelist and art critic John Berger. In his best-known film, *Jonas qui aura 25 ans en l'an 2000* (*Jonah Who Will Be 25 in the Year 2000*, 1976), Tanner chronicled four men and four women from the "post-1968" generation coming together to form a loose collective, with education for the future, such as for the newly born Jonah, a chief concern. The film proclaims that "politics is finished"—at least one kind of 1960s ideological struggle—but it proposes stylistically what might be called a politics of the imagination. Through black-and-white footage inserted among the color narrative, characters' fantasies,

21.17. *The bourgeoisie take an enigmatic stroll down a country road in Luis Buñuel's* Le Charme discret de la bourgeoisie (The Discreet Charm of the Bourgeoisie, 1972); *from left, Mme. Thévenot (Delphine Seyrig), Mme. Sénéchal (Stephane Audran), the Ambassador (Fernando Rey), M. Thévenot (Paul Frankeur), Florence (Bulle Ogier), and M. Sénéchal (Jean-Pierre Cassel).*

21.18. *The "post-1968" generation gathers for a meal in Alain
Tanner's* Jonas qui aura 25 ans en
l'an 2000 *(Jonah Who Will Be 25
in the Year 2000, 1976).*

mental images, and alternative scenarios are presented, opening
up other realms than the characters' present circumstances—a
survival of possibility through the cinematic rendering of inner
lives.

Lina Wertmüller

Along with its preoccupation with the legacy of neorealism (see
Chapter 13), Italian cinema also shifted toward internationalism
during the 1970s. A prominent figure in this trend was Lina
Wertmüller (b. 1928), whose films of the 1970s gained her an
international audience behind only Fellini and De Sica among
postwar Italian directors. They also brought popularity to her frequent lead performer, actor Giancarlo Giannini (b. 1942).

Works such as *Travolti da un insolito destino nell'azzurro mare
d'agosto* ("Swept Away by a Strange Destiny on an Azure August
Sea," known as *Swept Away*, 1974) and *Pasqualino settebellezze*
("Pasqualino Seven Beauties," known as *Seven Beauties*, 1976),
took on significant political and human themes (in *Seven
Beauties*, the Nazi death camps), though in a style featuring gross
sexuality and grotesque caricatures. These successes led to a
multipicture contract with a Hollywood studio that was canceled
after her first English-language film, *The End of the World in Our
Usual Bed in a Night Full of Rain* (1978), failed with critics and at
the box office.

Bernardo Bertolucci

The young Italian Bernardo Bertolucci (b. 1940), who had
become a prominent director while still in his early twenties,
moved into the international sphere in the 1970s with *Ultimo
tango a Parigi* (*Last Tango in Paris*, 1972), an Italian-French co-
production starring American actor Marlon Brando. The film was
promoted as the most sexually explicit mainstream work yet to be
released, though for candor it could not compete with the
hard-core pornographic films just then appearing in theaters.
Nevertheless, its notoriety made it a box office success, and
Bertolucci secured the funds to make an epic on Italian history,
Novecento (*1900*, 1976).

Originally running over five hours, on its release *1900* was
exhibited in two parts or cut by more than an hour in overseas
distribution; some years later the full-length version again circulated. With Italian, French, and German production financing,
Bertolucci used an international cast that included American performers Robert De Niro, Burt Lancaster (b. 1913), and Sterling
Hayden (1916–1986); Gérard Depardieu (b. 1948) and
Dominique Sanda (b. 1948) from France; Canadian Donald
Sutherland (b. 1934); and, from Italy, the pre–World War I diva
Francesca Bertini. Coming from different generations and modes
of production, the performers had difficulty meshing their accustomed acting styles, and like many star-laden international
productions the film seemed to lose the focus of its narrative, a

sweeping effort to portray Italian society from 1900 to the end of World War II. International co-productions provided filmmakers financing and opportunities, but there were often drawbacks among the gains.

Padre Padrone

Were there alternatives? For financing, one source of support was government entities, such as Europe's state-run television networks. For subjects, a shift from internationalism led to the internal periphery, to local settings so remote that even "nation" (from the micro-perspective) might be a questionable category. Such a trajectory was taken by *Padre padrone* ("My Father, My Master," but known as *Padre Padrone*, 1977), directed by Paolo and Vittorio Taviani, with financing from the Italian state television, RAI (Radiotelevisione Italiana). The film dramatized an autobiography by a thirty-five-year-old linguistics scholar, Gavino Ledda, who had been an illiterate shepherd on the Italian island of Sardinia until he joined the army at age eighteen, where he learned to read and write, and to speak Italian instead of dialect. Besides its unusual subject, *Padre Padrone* was notable for its use of sound to render inner consciousness, not only of individuals but also of groups in a Babel of voices and even of animals. It won both the best film award and the international critics' prize at Cannes.

Below: 21.19. Giancarlo Giannini (standing, center) as the title character of Lina Wertmüller's Pasqualino settebellezze (Seven Beauties, 1976)

Above: 21.20. Director Lina Wertmüller (left) during the production of Seven Beauties; *cinematographer Tonino Delli Colli holds the camera.*

Right: 21.21. Bernardo Bertolucci's Novecento *(1900, 1976) was a five-hour epic depicting Italian society from 1900 to the end of World War II; typical of many international co-productions, the work was undercut by the difficulty of meshing acting styles of performers from many countries. Shown here is American actor Robert De Niro in the role of Alfredo Berlinghieri.*

Below: 21.22. Efisio Ledda (Omero Antonutti) disciplines his son Gavino (Saverio Marconi) in Padre padrone *(Padre Padrone, 1977), directed by Paolo and Vittorio Taviani.*

The Spirit of the Beehive

Another version of the peripheral or local were cinemas in countries outside Europe's center, for political or other reasons. An example is Spain, ruled by the dictatorship of General Francisco Franco from the late 1930s, the end of Spain's Civil War, until his death in 1975. Without international stars or financing, an outstanding Spanish film of the era, *El espíritu de la colmena* (*The Spirit of the Beehive*, 1973), directed by Victor Erice (b. 1940), focused on a locality impinged on by the wider world, in the form of cinema.

Constrained by censorship, the film dealt with historical and social issues through visual and aural metaphors, the darkness and silence of a rural house without electricity around 1940. Its thematic metaphor was the 1931 horror classic *Frankenstein*, shown in a village hall. Six-year-old Ana (portrayed by child performer Ana Torrent) believes the monster is a spirit who lives nearby; she thinks she has found him in a mysterious fugitive

21.23. Isabel (Isabel Tellería) whispers to her sister Ana (Ana Torrent) as they watch the 1931 horror classic Frankenstein in

Victor Erice's El espíritu de la colmena (The Spirit of the Beehive, 1973), a Spanish film set around 1940.

whom she aids, but he is killed in a night raid. Film historian Virginia Higginbotham has suggested that the monster is also a metaphor for Spain itself, a country without memory.[2] *The Spirit of the Beehive* takes a place along with *The Discreet Charm of the Bourgeoisie, Jonah Who Will Be 25 in the Year 2000*, and *Padre Padrone* as European works whose techniques and visions demonstrated new possibilities for cinematic portrayal of human emotion.

NEW GERMAN CINEMA

Among European countries in the 1970s, nowhere was the complex dialogue between national cinema and internationalism more problematic than in Germany—that is, in West Germany, known as the Federal Republic of Germany. This country had been formed from the occupation zones of Britain, France, and the United States after World War II, while the eastern zone occupied by the Soviet Union also became a separate country, East Germany, known as the German Democratic Republic (with the collapse of Eastern European communism Germany reunited in 1990).

Alone of the major countries defeated in World War II, West Germany had not been able to revive its strong cinematic heritage. Italy had produced neorealism, Fellini, Antonioni, and a vigorous group of successors. Japan had brought forth (or back) Mizoguchi, Ozu, Kurosawa, and the New Wave. Germany's cinematic heritage, one might say, had emigrated to Hollywood, where Lang, Wilder, and Sirk were major figures among dozens of other former German film personnel. In the 1950s West Germany fostered a genre of *Heimat* (homeland) films centering on sentimental domestic themes. Few West German films circulated abroad, and West Germany's film theaters were dominated by foreign films.

Young German Film

At a 1962 film festival a group of West German filmmakers, organized under the name Young German Film, agitated for state support of cinema. By 1965 an agency had been set up to grant production loans, and a new generation of West German filmmakers began to make feature films. Significant debuts were made by directors such as Volker Schlöndorff (b. 1939) with *Der junge Törless* (*Young Törless*, 1965), Alexander Kluge (b. 1932) with *Abschied von gestern* (literally "Farewell to Yesterday," but released in English as *Yesterday Girl*, 1966), and Werner Herzog (b. 1942) with *Lebenszeichen* (*Signs of Life*, 1967), among others. Additional funding came from other government agencies, and in the 1970s, as elsewhere in Europe, state-operated West German television added support for feature filmmaking. Young German Film was transformed into New German Cinema, and began to find fame and attract audiences everywhere—except in Germany. New German Cinema presents the paradox of a filmmaking practice financed in its home country that was principally discussed and appreciated abroad—a cinema that was national in production and international in reception. A few filmmakers and movements will serve to exemplify the issues of West German Cinema (others will be discussed in Chapter 23 as part of the avant-garde).

Rainer Werner Fassbinder

Perhaps the most remarkable phenomenon of New German Cinema was the brief but prolific career of Rainer Werner Fassbinder (1946–1982), who died, apparently from a drug overdose, at age thirty-six. Few other directors in cinema history have matched his productivity: in a thirteen-year career, from 1969 to 1981, Fassbinder directed nearly forty films for theaters and television, counting as only one a miniseries, *Berlin Alexanderplatz* (1979–80), that ran fifteen and a half hours in fourteen parts. In the early years, working with a group of performers with whom he also wrote and directed plays, Fassbinder made films quickly and cheaply, shooting a feature often in less than ten days. Yet even the roughest of these works is not without compelling interest: Fassbinder and his "anti-theater" company aimed to transgress taboos and puncture social and ideological mythologies. It is difficult to single out any one film as the most representative, the likeliest to endure. "It's the entirety of the *oeuvre* [an artist's complete works] that must say something special about the time in which it was made," Fassbinder said, "otherwise it's worthless."[3]

What was special about Fassbinder's work might be called, too grandly, his treatment of the political economy of human desire. Many of his films dealt with sexuality, and among his controversial works were *Die bitteren Tränen der Petra von Kant* (*The Bitter Tears of Petra von Kant*, 1972), concerning lesbian relations, and *Faustrecht der Freiheit* (literally "Fist-Right of Freedom," but released in English as *Fox and His Friends*, 1974), about homosexual men. But Fassbinder insisted that his central focus was less on sexual behavior than on the power relations among people sexually involved with one another, including elements such as social class, age, ethnicity, and beauty. Another of his significant films on this theme was *Angst essen Seele auf* (*Fear Eats the Soul*, also known as *Ali: Fear Eats the Soul*, 1973), which explores the dynamics of a marriage between a Moroccan working man and a German woman twenty years his senior.

Fassbinder made a substantial international box office success for the first time with *Die Ehe der Maria Braun* (*The Marriage of Maria Braun*, 1978), which also brought acclaim to actress Hanna Schygulla (b. 1943), an early coworker of Fassbinder's who had appeared in nearly half his films. Set between the war years and the mid-1950s, *The Marriage of Maria Braun* marked a turn toward history for the director: three of his last four features—*Lili Marleen* (1980), *Lola* (1981), and *Die Sehnsucht der Veronika Voss* ("The Longing of Veronika Voss," released in English as

Filmmaking in Europe's Dictatorships

Dictatorship did not end in western Europe after the Allies were victorious in World War II. Two fascist governments that had been founded in the 1930s, but that did not participate militarily in the war, managed to last fully another generation—in Spain, where Francisco Franco held power from 1936 until his death in 1975, and in Portugal, where the regime established by António de Oliveira Salazar in the early 1930s continued until 1974, four years after Salazar's death. Unlike Italy and even Nazi Germany in the 1930s, Spain and Portugal in the first postwar years pursued film policies centering primarily on censorship and propaganda.

In the early 1960s, however, new currents emerged in the film cultures of both countries. Seeking to project an image of liberalization to strengthen its links to the European community, Spain fostered a "New Spanish Cinema" to correspond with other new waves of the era. The first Spanish filmmaker of this generation to gain international recognition was Carlos Saura (b. 1932) with *La caza* (*The Hunt*, 1966), a film that utilized a hunting party as an allegory to explore the legacy of Spain's Civil War. Beginning the following year with *Peppermint frappé*, most of Saura's films over the next decade featured American actress Geraldine Chaplin (b. 1944), daughter of Charles Chaplin. His most notable work of the period was *Cría cuervos* (literally "Raise Ravens," released in English as *Cria!*, 1976), an intense family drama with political overtones.

The easing of restrictions in Portugal revived the career of the country's most important filmmaker, Manoel de Oliveira (b. 1908), who began directing in the 1930s but had not been permitted to make a film between 1942 and 1956. Among his works over the next two decades that played a leading role in the development of Portuguese cinema were *O acto da primavera* (*Spring Mystery Play*, 1963), combining documentary and fiction based on traditional passion plays; *O passado e o presente* (*The Past and the Present*, 1971), a comedy; *Amor de perdiçao* (*Doomed Love*, 1978), and *Francisca* (1981), films that link stylized decor with narratives of frustrated passion.

Greece had a shorter experience of dictatorship in the postwar period when a military junta seized power and ruled the country from 1967 to 1974. The political turmoil leading up to the coup was the subject of one of the most highly praised political films of the postwar era, *Z* (1969), an Algerian-French co-production directed by Constantin Costa-Gavras (b. 1933), a Greek-born filmmaker who became a French citizen and worked in France and the United States. Despite the dictatorship, Greece's most significant filmmaker, Théo Angelopoulos (b. 1935) began his career in the junta years with *Anaparastassi* (*Reconstruction*, 1970), a murder mystery that displayed his characteristic style, combining long takes and tracking shots. Two of Angelopoulos's films have won the top prize at the Venice Film Festival, *O Megalexandros* (*Alexander the Great*, 1980) and *Topio stin Omichli* (*Landscape in the Mist*, 1988).

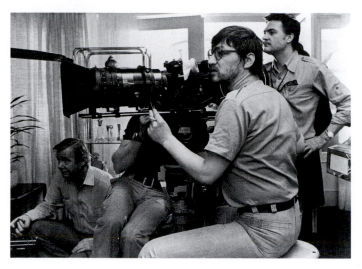

21.24. Rainer Werner Fassbinder (with glasses) sets up a shot for Die Reise ins Licht—Despair (Despair, 1977).

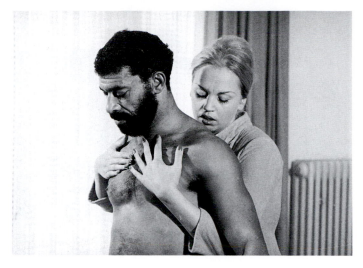

21.25. Among Rainer Werner Fassbinder's many works on the themes of sexuality and power was Angst essen Seele auf (Fear Eats the Soul, 1973); Ali (El Hedi Ben Salem) is shown here with Barbara (Barbara Valentin), a woman not his wife.

Veronika Voss, 1981)—also centered on women's lives as markers of social and psychological struggles in the postwar period. An admirer of Hollywood's family melodramas, particularly the work of the German émigré Douglas Sirk, Fassbinder revived the genre and infused it with new political and historical resonance.

Germany in Autumn

One of the unique projects of New German Cinema—perhaps also in cinema history—was the collective film *Deutschland im Herbst* (*Germany in Autumn*, 1978). There had been numerous films with multiple directors, even some addressing contemporary political issues, but few if any similar works directly responded to an immediate crisis through such an extensive collaborative endeavor. Nine directors were credited on the film, including Fassbinder, Kluge, and Schlöndorff. The background was a series

21.26. Die Ehe der Maria Braun (The Marriage of Maria Braun, 1978) was the first of several Fassbinder melodramas exploring post-1945 Germany through the lives of women; Hanna Schygulla played the title role.

of events in fall 1977 involving the kidnapping of an industrialist, later found murdered; the hijacking of a passenger jet to Somalia, where German police stormed the plane and rescued hostages; and the suicides, or murders, of three urban guerrillas in a prison. These events threw the Federal Republic into crisis, which the film sought both to depict and to contest through a complex mix of documentation, historical analogy, and fictional treatments. It would be asking too much to find such a film fully coherent, but its overall tone was to warn against the state's exercise of authoritarian power. Among its most powerful segments is Fassbinder's, an intensely autobiographical sequence in which his relations with his lover and his mother become enmeshed in political disputes and paranoia.

Women Filmmakers

Individual women directors were working in a number of countries during the 1970s, but West Germany was among the few where a women's film practice took root as part of (sometimes in conflict with) the decade's feminist movement. A key figure was Helke Sander (b. 1937), who was also editor for some years of *Frauen und Film* (Women and Film), the only regularly published feminist film journal in Europe. Sander's first feature was *Die allseitig reduzierte Persönlichkeit—Redupers* (*The All Round Reduced Personality—Redupers*, 1977), a diary film combining fiction and documentary, in which the writer-director also played the leading role as a free-lance photographer in Berlin. The film is suffused not only with the struggles of women artists and activists to gain serious attention for their perspectives but also with an acute consciousness of a city and a culture splintered by the omnipresent Berlin Wall (erected by East Germany in 1961, the wall was torn down in 1989).

GERMANY, PALE MOTHER. Perhaps the most important fiction film by a West German woman filmmaker was *Deutschland, bleiche Mutter* (*Germany, Pale Mother*, 1979), directed by Helma Sanders-Brahms (b. 1940). Its title was taken from a 1933 poem by Bertolt Brecht, written at the time of Hitler's rise to power, a

translation of which reads, in part, "O Germany, pale mother / How you sit defiled / Among the peoples." The film shares traits both with *Redupers* and Fassbinder's late historical works: the narrative takes the form of a family melodrama covering the Nazi period and the postwar years, while on the soundtrack a woman's voice comments on events as if they were scenes from her own autobiography. Among its other stylistic features is a depiction of Berlin after the war combining actuality footage along with new material made to appear as if it were newsreel shots, part of the film's approach to issues of representation and perception.

Impact of Hollywood

As United States culture had influenced West Germany during the years after World War II, so the lure of Hollywood began to

Above: 21.27. Director Helke Sander performing the role of Edda Chiemnyjewski in her film Die allseitig reduzierte Persönlichkeit —Redupers *(The All Round Reduced Personality—Redupers, 1977)*

Right: 21.28. Helma Sanders-Brahms's film concerning the life of a German woman in the 1930s and 1940s, Deutschland, bleiche Mutter *(Germany, Pale Mother, 1979), combined actuality footage with new material made to look as if it were newsreel shots, as in this scene of Helene (Eva Mattes) amid the rubble of postwar Berlin.*

attract New German filmmakers as their movement matured. Schlöndorff's *Die Blechtrommel* (*The Tin Drum*, 1979) won the Hollywood Academy Award for best foreign-language film—a landmark recognition for postwar West German cinema—as well as the prize for best film at Cannes, and the director within a few years was working mainly in the United States. Herzog had a brief fling with Hollywood studio distribution with *Nosferatu— Phantom der Nacht* (*Nosferatu the Vampire*, 1979), released through Twentieth Century-Fox.

WIM WENDERS. The exemplary case of Hollywood's impact on New German Cinema, however, was Wim Wenders (b. 1945). In the 1970s Wenders made several films exploring relations between German and American cultures, including *Alice in den Städten* (*Alice in the Cities*, 1973) and *Der amerikanische Freund* (*The American Friend*, 1977). One character says to another in his

458

Im Lauf der Zeit ("In the Course of Time," released in English as *Kings of the Road*, 1976) that the Americans "have colonized our subconscious."

Wenders went to Hollywood in the late 1970s at Francis Ford Coppola's invitation to direct *Hammett* (1982), based on a novel about the detective fiction writer Dashiell Hammett. After Coppola, as executive producer, ordered major revisions, only about one-third of the released film was Wenders's work. Wenders remained in the United States for much of the 1980s, and works such as *Paris, Texas* (1984) suggested that he had become, like Schlöndorff and the British directors of the early 1960s, a "Mid-Atlantic" filmmaker. But he returned to Germany to make *Der Himmel über Berlin* ("The Sky over Berlin," released in English as *Wings of Desire*, 1987), a strikingly imaginative film in black-and-white and color, for which he won the best director

prize at Cannes. In the sky over Berlin, angels hover unseen by human adults (but not by children or the film's spectators) and descend to mingle with people, hearing their inner thoughts. Falling in love with a trapeze artist in a circus, an angel portrayed by Swiss actor Bruno Ganz (b. 1941) gives up his angelhood to share the human condition—the director's symbolic return to Europe from the sky over the mid-Atlantic.

Above: 21.29. Bruno Ganz as the angel Damiel with Peter Falk (playing himself as an actor making a film in Berlin) at a street food stand in Der Himmel über Berlin *(Wings of Desire, 1987), directed by Wim Wenders.*

Top: 21.30. Solveig Dommartin as Marion, a trapeze artist for whom Damiel gives up his angelhood, in Wings of Desire

Notes

1. Marcel Lozinski, quoted in Boleslaw Michalek and Frank Turaj, *The Modern Cinema of Poland* (Bloomington: Indiana Univ. Press, 1988), p. 66.

2. Virginia Higginbotham, *Spanish Film under Franco* (Austin: University of Texas Press, 1988), p. 119.

3. Norbert Sparrow, "'I Let the Audience Feel and Think': An Interview with Rainer Werner Fassbinder," *Cineaste*, vol. 8, no. 2 (1977), p. 21.

TWENTY-TWO

HOLLYWOOD

However future generations assess the last quarter of the twentieth century in Hollywood, for contemporaries the era was revolutionary in many ways. A revolution occurred at the box office, as new marketing techniques led to unprecedented financial returns for the most successful films. A revolution took place simultaneously for movies as private entertainment: by 1990 more than two-thirds of United States households had acquired video cassette recorders, and many preferred to watch films on cassettes at home; in addition, cable television offered a variety of movie channels and the opportunity to order recent films on a "pay-per-view" basis. And a revolution was in the making in industrial ownership, as Japanese and other foreign companies acquired major Hollywood studios, and other movie companies merged with publishing corporations, in efforts to shape globally oriented technology/information/entertainment conglomerates. Perhaps the least revolutionary aspect of United States filmmaking in the period was what appeared on screen.

FINANCIAL REVOLUTIONS
Box Office

We have already observed (in Chapter 20) how Hollywood came out of its economic doldrums in the early 1970s through innovative marketing strategies featuring wide simultaneous distribution of important films, backed by national television advertising. Films such as *The Godfather* and *The Exorcist* broke box office records, but were soon surpassed by an even more striking phenomenon:

films that became marketing events in themselves, spinning off tie-in products such as clothing and toys, and attracting young persons to return and see them more than once. The path-breaking work was *Jaws* (1975), directed by Steven Spielberg, whose monster shark became an instant artifact of commercial folklore (greatly aided by John Williams's menacing music for the film) and later the centerpiece of a motion picture studio theme park. *Jaws* was the first film to go over $100 million in domestic rentals (the distribution company's share of the box office), and by 1993 it remained eighth on the all-time box office list.

The implications of *Jaws* and the mega-hits that followed were far-reaching. Filmmakers began to shape more films for the young spectators who consumed the toys and other tie-in products and formed the repeat audience. Special effects became increasingly important to please the same age group, as did films based on familiar comic book characters, from *Superman* (1978) to *Batman* (1989). Hit films generated sequels—not a new phenomenon, though it was novel to name them with Roman numerals (by 1993 *Star Trek* was up to VI, and other perennial favorites trailed at V or IV). As movie theaters changed from single-auditorium houses to "multiplex" layouts with up to a dozen or more screens, a handful of blockbuster films dominated exhibition more than ever before, each appearing simultaneously on anywhere from a thousand to two thousand screens.

Home Video

Yet this form of concentration was countered by the revolution in the opposite direction, toward home video consumption of movies. Video cassette recorders went through rapid technological development beginning in the 1970s, and became almost a standard appliance in the United States home. For many it was accompanied by the "camcorder" video camera, replacing 8mm or Super-8mm celluloid film as the choice for home moviemaking. But more commonly it was used for viewing feature films on cassettes rented or purchased at the video stores that sprouted up in every town. Initially producers charged a high price for individual copies because the principal buyers were video store owners, but they soon discovered a phenomenon the industry called "sell-through": if cassette prices were lowered to compare with the cost of a book, it was possible to sell millions of copies to consumers who wanted to keep a film in their "video libraries." The Walt Disney Co.'s estimated net earnings from video sales of its animated film *Beauty and the Beast* (1991) were higher than the net profits from theatrical box office returns of any film in history.

In addition, a smaller but still substantial number of film fans acquired laser disk players, which provided a sharper image than video and faster scanning to specific scenes of films recorded on disks. Special editions of films on disk often included extra materials such as footage that had been cut from release prints, trailers, screen tests, or interviews, and these features also began to be added to many video versions of films. Sales of video, laser disk, pay-per-view, and cable television rights became major sources of

RECOVERY

revenue for the major studios and of critical importance for producers of lower-budget films; often crowded out of theaters by the blockbusters, such films could sometimes come close to earning back their costs from sales of home video and cable television rights.

The New Conglomerates

The video revolution fostered the notion that "synergy" could be created between "hardware" and "software"—that technology, information, and entertainment all could be more effectively utilized through combined endeavor rather than standing alone. Hollywood studios, which in the 1960s had become subsidiaries of insurance companies and parking lot chains, now attracted the interest of publishers and video equipment manufacturers. Major developments at the end of the 1980s included acquisition of Twentieth Century-Fox by the News Corp., an international publishing and broadcasting company based in Australia; the merger of Warner Communications, parent of Warner Bros., with Time, Inc., the publishing firm, to form Time Warner; the purchase of Columbia Pictures and Tri-Star by the Japanese manufacturer Sony Corp., and of MCA-Universal by the Matsushita Electric Industrial Co., makers of video products. Although Hollywood studios in earlier eras had owned record companies or radio stations that promoted, for example, movie theme songs, these new conglomerations brought media and communications to unprecedented levels of interrelationship. Under the same corporate umbrella subsidiaries could turn one product into many—a movie, a book, a soundtrack album; and newspapers and magazines owned by the same corporation could review them all.

THE NEGLECTED "GOLDEN AGE"

The changes wrought by the revolutionary developments in marketing, distribution, technology, and finance beginning in the mid-1970s drew attention away from an unusual period of Hollywood filmmaking, one that coincides with the industry's revival in the early 1970s. Film critic Pauline Kael has suggested that this era, rather than the more commonly designated decades of the 1930s and 1940s, was Hollywood's authentic "Golden Age." It was surely a brief age, half a decade at most. Among the cultural factors that may have shaped it was a strong national mood of self-questioning following the United States defeat in Vietnam, further exacerbated by President Richard M. Nixon's resignation in the wake of the Watergate scandal. In addition, the postwar baby boom generation, which had developed a taste for serious popular filmmaking, was at the height of its youth-audience influence.

Among the most significant films from this mini–"Golden Age" were Francis Ford Coppola's *The Conversation* and *The Godfather Part II* (both 1974); *Chinatown* (1974), directed by Roman Polanski (b. 1933); and Martin Scorsese's *Taxi Driver* (1976). A common thread running through these and many of the era's other works is a concern with the interweaving of personal and institutional power; most proffer endings suffused with tragedy, pessimism, or ironic ambiguity.

Francis Ford Coppola

After *The Godfather*, the biggest box office success to that point in film history, Coppola wrote and directed *The Conversation*, a work modeled on the European art film. Antonioni's *Blow-Up* was a reference point for Coppola's film, which concerns a man who works with sound rather than images: an eavesdropping expert, he records a conversation which, as he reconstructs it from many hidden microphones, seems to him to involve plotting a murder. A film of considerable visual as well as aural subtlety, *The Conversation* was a box office flop but has grown in stature as a work of cinematic art.

In the same year as *The Conversation*, Coppola directed one of the first important sequels of the era, *The Godfather Part II*. Like many sequels it was less successful financially than the original, but its admirers found it a deeper, darker, more powerful film. It carried the Godfather saga both backward and forward in time, interspersing scenes of the youth and early manhood of Vito Corleone (Marlon Brando's Godfather figure, now portrayed by Robert De Niro) with the narrative of his son and successor, Michael (again, Al Pacino). This film, more sharply than the first, emphasizes organized crime as a business enterprise, deeply enmeshed in political manipulation. "We're both part of the same hypocrisy," Michael tells a United States senator. The work develops a tragic motif by depicting a profound contradiction in Michael's inherited ideology of the family, imposing on him a code of behavior that inexorably destroys his family life. After *The Godfather* revitalized the gangster genre, *Part II* challenged it in the spirit of genre revision.

Roman Polanski

Polanski's *Chinatown*, from a screenplay by Robert Towne (b. 1936), was another revisionist work. The Polish director had become one of the earliest exiles from Eastern European cinema (see Chapter 21) after his first feature film, *Nóz w Wodzic* (*Knife in the Water*, 1962), a prizewinner at Venice, was attacked by the Polish government. Working in Europe and the United States, Polanski made several quirky horror films, jarring but genial, and brought this macabre style to what seems at first glance a genre detective film. But *Chinatown*'s private eye, J. J. Gittes, portrayed by Jack Nicholson, is beyond his depth in a world of political and sexual power and corruption. Set in the 1930s, the film's narrative frame (based on historical events) concerns behind-the-scenes maneuvering to assure sufficient water supplies for Southern

California's development. The film made "Chinatown" a shorthand metaphor for hidden links between economic power and corrupt politics.

Martin Scorsese

Scorsese's *Taxi Driver*—with a screenplay by Paul Schrader (b. 1946)—was perhaps the most disturbing work among this group. A Marine Corps veteran, Travis Bickle (portrayed by Robert De Niro), drives a New York taxi and speaks with growing disturbance over what he sees as the city's filth and human scum. His

Top left: 22.1. After scoring the biggest box office success up to that point in film history with The Godfather, *Francis Ford Coppola made a work modeled on the European art film,* The Conversation *(1974), with Gene Hackman as eavesdropping expert Harry Caul.*

Bottom left: 22.2. Al Pacino (right) as Michael Corleone and Lee Strasberg as Hyman Roth in Coppola's The Godfather Part II *(1974); it was the first film performance for Strasberg, director of the Actors Studio and famous teacher of "Method" acting.*

Top right: 22.3. Roman Polanski's Chinatown *(1974) made its title a metaphor for hidden links between economic power and corrupt politics; Jack Nicholson portrayed J. J. Gittes, a private eye out of his depth in a world of political and sexual power and corruption.*

Bottom right: 22.4. "You talking to me?" Travis Bickle (Robert De Niro) trains for confrontation in Martin Scorsese's Taxi Driver *(1976).*

The Roughness That Only Life Has

For a brief moment in Hollywood's short "Golden Age" of the mid-1970s it appeared that director John Cassavetes (1929–1989) had made it, on his own terms, into the mainstream. His film *A Woman Under the Influence* (1974), which he had not only produced but also managed to distribute through his own independent company, had won unusual critical acclaim: in an era when American commercial cinema seemed unable to create significant roles for women, here was a work with a full, intense, emotional, anguishing portrait of a woman from a working-class family. For her performance as Mabel Longhetti, Gena Rowlands (b. 1934), the director's wife, was nominated for an Academy Award as best actress and Cassavetes won nomination as best director—remarkable recognition for a film that was not released by a major studio.

Cassavetes's first film, *Shadows* (1959), began as an exercise for an improvisational acting workshop he was teaching and helped to launch the movement of independent non-Hollywood filmmaking of the 1960s (see Chapter 23). Critic and filmmaker Jonas Mekas contrasted the first version of *Shadows* with *Citizen Kane*: Orson Welles's film was an attempt at destroying life and creating art, Mekas said, while Cassavetes's work made an attempt at catching (and retaining) life. "*Shadows* breaks with official staged cinema, with made-up faces, with written scripts, with plot continuities," Mekas wrote. "Even its inexperience in editing, sound, and camera work becomes a part of its style." Though Mekas became angry with Cassavetes for producing a longer

and more conventional version of *Shadows*, his words aptly describe all of Cassavetes's best work: improvisational, unorganized, visceral, with a roughness (as Mekas wrote) that only life has, it resembled few other films in either independent or Hollywood cinema.

Shadows gave Cassavetes opportunities to direct Hollywood films, but he was uncomfortable and generally unsuccessful when working under studio auspices. Originally an actor, he emulated the tactics of Orson Welles's later career, taking on acting assignments to earn money for his own filmmaking ventures. Among other roles, he portrayed the husband who makes a pact with the devil in Roman Polanski's *Rosemary's Baby* (1968).

Cassavetes's moment in the mainstream (on his own terms) was indeed brief. As Hollywood began to consolidate its new era of blockbuster epics (with fewer pictures taking up more screens), Cassavetes continued his unorthodox mode of independent production and self-distribution. After *A Woman Under the Influence*, his *The Killing of a Chinese Bookie* (1976, revised version 1978) barely made it into theatrical release, while *Opening Night* (1978) played only one week in one Los Angeles theater. These three films comprise a remarkable trilogy of independent production; with their release in video format, one of the most original directors in American cinema may finally find an audience.

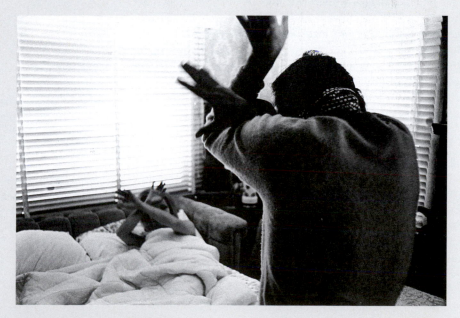

22.5. *Director John Cassavetes prepares a scene with actress Gena Rowlands for* A Woman Under the Influence *(1974).*

inchoate rage becomes focused simultaneously on a pimp and a political candidate, both of whom are linked to women about whom Travis obsesses. If the character's voice-over "diary" and preparations for violence are not enough to rattle the spectator, the soundtrack is also suffused with high-pitched New York street noise and an alternately jazzy and eerie music score by Bernard Herrmann, composer for *Citizen Kane* and many Alfred Hitchcock films. The film's violence, controversial at the time, has come to seem less distressing than its psychological atmosphere, as Travis's taxi glides through white clouds of steam escaping from manhole covers in the street, metaphors for his compressed anger and hatred of the city as an "open sewer."

Other "Golden Age" Films

Other important films from this condensed "Golden Age" included Miloš Forman's *One Flew Over the Cuckoo's Nest*, the 1975 Academy Award best picture; Robert Altman's *Nashville* (1975); *All the President's Men* (1976), directed by Alan Pakula (b. 1928), centering on newspaper reporters investigating the Watergate scandal; and *Network* (1976), directed by Sidney Lumet (b. 1924), in which an angry television anchorman exhorts his viewers to open their windows and shout, "I'm mad as hell and I'm not going to take it anymore." This phrase became a promotion tag line for the movie and began appearing as a bumper sticker on automobiles, expressing a widely felt frustration in an era of political corruption and military defeat.

Above and top: 22.6, 22.7. Producing the special visual effects for Star Wars: *artist Chris Evans paints a matte for the background of a shot; a model maker is barely visible amid the miniature set of a rocky promontory.*

THE NEW BLOCKBUSTER

"May the Force be with you." This mystical salutation, hinting of subordination to a supernatural Higher Power, replaced *Network*'s angry outcry within a year as Hollywood's most prominent promotional slogan. It came from *Star Wars* (1977), directed by George Lucas, the phenomenal success that surpassed *Jaws* by 50 percent at the box office, realizing a little less than $200 million in rentals and launching the new blockbuster era of United States cinema. Through 1993 it has been topped only by Steven Spielberg's *E. T. The Extra-Terrestrial* (1982), which attained $228 million in rentals. By the end of the 1980s decade, of the top ten all-time box office hits, Lucas and Spielberg had been involved with eight—Spielberg as director of five, Lucas as director of *Star Wars* and producer of five others, including three of Spielberg's films.

Star Wars

Lucas's science fiction epic was an almost completely unexpected triumph. Blockbuster pictures since the 1950s—including the most recent, *The Godfather*, *The Exorcist*, and *Jaws*—had been

Above: 22.8. Spaceships in battle hurtle between canyon walls, in George Lucas's Stars Wars *(1977); John Stears, John Dykstra, Richard Edlund, Grant McCune, and Robert Blalack shared an Academy Award for the film's special visual effects.*

Right: 22.9. Products licensed by George Lucas's production company, LucasArts, in connection with the release of The Return of the Jedi *(1983)*

drawn from best-selling novels, Broadway musicals, or similar well-known sources, and had usually featured star performers. In contrast, *Star Wars* had an original script (by Lucas) and no stars. Though there had been some memorable science fiction films in the previous decade, notably Kubrick's *2001: A Space Odyssey* and *A Clockwork Orange*, the genre was not normally a box office leader. Beyond the film's remarkable special effects, the secret of its success lay in its cultural stance. "Like a breath of fresh air," wrote the trade paper *Variety*'s reviewer, "*Star Wars* sweeps away the cynicism that has in recent years obscured the concepts of valor, dedication and honor. . . . An audience, first

Opposite, above: 22.10. The Saturday matinee serial returns as blockbuster epic: Harrison Ford as Indiana Jones in Raiders of the Lost Ark *(1981), directed by Steven Spielberg.*

Opposite, below: 22.11. Elliott (Henry Thomas) confronts adults in Spielberg's E.T. The Extra-Terrestrial *(1982), the most successful film at the box office in cinema history,*

Below: 22.12. The ghostbusters of Ghostbusters *(1984), directed by Ivan Reitman: from left, Dr. Peter Venkman (Bill Murray),*

Dr. Egon Spengler (Harold Ramis), Dr. Raymond Stantz (Dan Aykroyd)

Below: 22.13. This promotional logo helped make Ghostbusters *the most successful comedy at the box office in United States film history.*

entertained, can walk out feeling good all over."[1] *Star Wars* repudiated the bitter realism of the mid-1970s "Golden Age"—and offered an antidote.

Star Wars was a children's film for all ages. It was less a conventional genre movie than a feature-length version of the old Saturday matinee serials featuring fictional space adventurers like Buck Rogers and Flash Gordon. But its narrative and imagery also drew on standard figures out of World War II films—callow young men who learn bravery, uncommitted cynics (like Rick in *Casablanca*) who throw their weight behind the forces of good. At one point the *Star Wars* saga was planned to encompass nine films, of which, over the next decade, two more were made: *The*

Empire Strikes Back (1980), directed by Irvin Kershner (b. 1923), and *The Return of the Jedi* (1983), directed by British filmmaker Richard Marquand (1938–1987). These climbed, respectively, to fifth and third on the all-time box office list.

Indiana Jones

The adventure blockbusters managed well without big-name performers. Actor Harrison Ford (b. 1942) was one of the few whom they made into stars. While playing the cynic, Han Solo, in the *Star Wars* trilogy, he created an even more famous screen character, Indiana Jones, in another trio of Saturday serial-type adventure movies, *Raiders of the Lost Ark* (1981), *Indiana Jones and the Temple of Doom* (1984), and *Indiana Jones and the Last Crusade* (1989). All three were collaborations between Spielberg as director and Lucas as producer. Though earthbound rather than space adventures, they were no less dependent on fantasy and special effects. Set in the World War II era, they sometimes uncomfortably dredged up discarded racial stereotypes in their depiction of non-Caucasian characters. "Indy," however, was all hero as he fought the good fight against German Nazis. All three films earned theatrical box office rentals of over $100 million.

E.T. The Extra-Terrestrial

A year after *Raiders of the Lost Ark*, Spielberg (without Lucas's participation) made *E.T. The Extra-Terrestrial*, the most successful film in cinema history to date. Its focus is on two lost boys—the California suburbanite Elliott, adrift amid a fractured family, and the extraterrestrial left behind by his spaceship. Spielberg's camera views the world from E.T.'s height, observing its many oppressive male authority figures mostly from the waist down. Like Spielberg's earlier *Close Encounters of the Third Kind* (1977), *E.T.* combined contemporary social themes with its fantasy and special effects. A human and an alien child suffer and triumph together, only to separate at the end. *E.T. The Extra-Terrestrial* may come closer to sweeping away cynicism once and for all in the world than any other motion picture.

Blockbuster Comedies

Comedy became a part of the new blockbuster phenomenon with the unexpected box office triumph of a spoof on college fraternity life, *National Lampoon's Animal House* (1978), directed by John Landis (b. 1950). Much of its success was credited to the manic performance style of John Belushi (1949–1982), a comic actor making his film debut after gaining wide popularity on the youth-oriented late-night television program *Saturday Night Live*. A showcase for young comic performers, the same series also propelled Bill Murray (b. 1950) and Dan Aykroyd (b. 1950), both from Canada, and later Eddie Murphy (b. 1961) into film careers. Murray and Aykroyd appeared in the biggest comedy hit of the 1980s, *Ghostbusters* (1984), directed by Ivan Reitman (b. 1947), also from Canada. Murphy took the lead role in the second top comedy hit, *Beverly Hills Cop* (1984), directed by Martin Brest (b. 1951).

New Stars

Besides Harrison Ford and the *Saturday Night Live* comedians, the new blockbuster created few other stars. One was Sylvester Stallone (b. 1946), whose first major success was as an aspiring boxer from Philadelphia in the inspirational film *Rocky* (1976), directed by John G. Avildsen (b. 1936). As author also of the

22.14. Along with John Belushi, Bill Murray, and Dan Aykroyd, among others, comedian Eddie Murphy went from the late-night television program Saturday Night Live to motion picture stardom; here he portrays Axel Foley in Beverly Hills Cop (1984), directed by Martin Brest.

22.15. John Rambo (Sylvester Stallone) single-handedly wages war in Vietnam in Rambo: First Blood Part II (1985), directed by George P. Cosmatos.

22.16. The former weightlifter Arnold Schwarzenegger became one of the major stars of the 1980s in roles such as the title character in The Terminator (1984), directed by James Cameron.

Rocky screenplay, Stallone became the first performer since Charles Chaplin and Orson Welles to receive Academy Award nominations as both actor and screenwriter for the same film. *Rocky* generated numerous sequels, which Stallone also directed as well as writing and playing the title role (*III* and *IV* actually surpassed the original as box office hits). Meanwhile, he created on-screen an even more emblematic cultural figure, the character John Rambo in *First Blood* (1982), directed by Ted Kotcheff (b. 1931), and *Rambo: First Blood Part II* (1985), directed by George P. Cosmatos (b. 1941). An angry, violent Vietnam war hero, Rambo returns to Vietnam in *Part II* to wreak vengeance and rescue Americans supposedly still held as prisoners of war. Rambo became for many an image of national bellicosity and of a desire to exorcise defeat in Vietnam.

Another performer who became popular with a strong-man screen persona was the Austrian former weightlifter Arnold Schwarzenegger (b. 1947). He developed a following in military and science fiction action films such as *The Terminator* (1984), directed by James Cameron (b. 1954), and *Predator* (1987), directed by John McTiernan (b. 1951). Unlike Stallone, however, he brought a slightly ironic performance style to his super-hero roles, and he became an even bigger star when his capacity for comedy and a perhaps incongruous intellectuality were built into his screen characters. These traits became apparent in two films directed by Ivan Reitman: *Twins* (1988), in which the blond strong man plays the naive and brainy twin brother of short, dark Danny DeVito; and *Kindergarten Cop* (1990), in which he portrays an undercover policeman who takes over teaching a kindergarten class in order to protect a child and catch a killer.

U.S. FILMS AND FILMMAKERS

Future historians may give less weight to the new blockbuster phenomenon than we have here, since box office success has rarely been a predictor of which films will gain lasting significance. But in the 1980s and beyond these works shaped the context of United States filmmaking. They dominated exhibition; they set the standards by which others were judged. Stanley Kubrick, for example, an outstanding filmmaker by any measure, attempted a blockbuster with *The Shining* (1980), from a horror novel by Stephen King. Kubrick expressed the hope his film would do half as well as *The Empire Strikes Back*; in the end it earned less than one-fourth as much at the box office as the *Star Wars* sequel. *The Shining* was a profitable film but failed to satisfy grandiose aspirations. Production budgets soared in the 1980s, in part because of similar hopes, yet the trade paper *Variety* reported that only one-fourth of films that cost $14 million or more to produce earned back production costs at the domestic box office. These factors weighed on filmmakers whether they aimed at blockbusters or not. Meanwhile, there were many kinds of American films and filmmakers, and a number for whom Hollywood was more of a metaphor than a place of work. Kubrick, for example, was permanently based in Britain, George Lucas in northern California, and filmmakers such as Woody Allen and Martin Scorsese in New York.

Woody Allen

The filmmaking and marketing practices of the writer-director-performer Allen (b. 1935) offered one of the clearest alternatives to the blockbuster approach. On a small scale, on the east coast,

22.17. *Woody Allen won Academy Awards as director and coscreenwriter on* Annie Hall *(1977), as well as being nominated as best actor for his role as* Alvy Singer *in the film, an unusual feat of individual recognition; Alvy (right) shown outside New York's Beekman Theater.*

he tried to maintain operations similar to those of the former studio era: he worked steadily, making at least one film a year, and insisted that they be distributed slowly, city by city, in the old "platform" method. He reasoned sensibly that few of his films were amenable to a thousand simultaneous openings in suburban shopping mall theaters (this practice altered in 1992 after Allen's personal life became front-page news and he also changed distribution companies; his film *Husbands and Wives* opened—none too successfully—in close to a thousand suburban theaters).

Most of Allen's films featured an unprepossessing central figure, a neurotic urban Jewish man portrayed by Allen himself, who struggled in a tragicomic way with daily life and the cosmos. His most significant critical and financial success was *Annie Hall* (1977), which beat out *Star Wars*, among other films, for the Academy Award as best picture. That year Allen also won awards as director and coscreenwriter, and was nominated as best actor, surpassing Stallone (as well as Chaplin and Welles) for breadth of individual recognition.

Several other Allen films were also box office successes, including *Manhattan* (1979), concerning an older man's infatuation with a younger woman, and *Hannah and Her Sisters* (1986), which

22.18. Robert De Niro played a U.S. soldier in Michael Cimino's The Deer Hunter (1978), the first significant Hollywood feature film concerning the American experience of the Vietnam war.

22.19. Prizefighter Jake La Motta (Robert De Niro) knocks out Tony Janiro (Kevin Mahon), and the referee (Martin Denkin) orders him to his corner in Martin Scorsese's Raging Bull (1980).

dealt with the rivalries and desires among three sisters and the men in their lives. Perhaps Allen's most innovative and challenging work was *Zelig* (1983), in which the director portrays a chameleon-like man in the 1920s who takes on the character of his surroundings and can pass as, among other things, a baseball player, a Chinese man, and an intimate of the famous; the work parodies film biographies while at the same time questioning social concepts of identify and selfhood.

Michael Cimino

The blockbuster phenomenon also provided its exemplary object lesson, in the career of director Michael Cimino (b. 1940), who was controversial both in triumph and disaster. His triumph was *The Deer Hunter* (1978), Academy Award winner as best picture and widely regarded as the first significant Hollywood fiction film imaginatively portraying the American experience of the Vietnam war, at home and overseas. Moving performances by a strong cast, headed by Robert De Niro, outweighed for many spectators imbalances in the film's structure and narrative, yet others were angered by what they regarded as its racism toward Asians and flagrant departure from the historical record.

Lingering dispute over *The Deer Hunter* affected attitudes toward Cimino's next film, *Heaven's Gate* (1980), which became a financial flop of historic dimension. With production costs that rose to around $36 million, the film became symbolic of extravagance and waste in the production process. Running three hours, thirty-nine minutes, the epic of Wyoming frontier history was ravaged by critics and lasted only a week in theaters. A version seventy-two minutes shorter was later released, but the film earned back only a small fraction of its costs, and in the wake of its failure the United Artists company, which financed the film, was taken over by M-G-M. Cimino's advocates compared him to Erich von Stroheim as a visionary martyred by the Hollywood system. The original version of *Heaven's Gate*, fortunately for students and scholars of film history, can be seen on video cassette. Though it has structural and narrative difficulties similar to *The Deer Hunter*, without the performances that carried the earlier film, *Heaven's Gate* deserves attention as an attempt to extend the revision of the Western genre through an epic reimagining of the development of the American West.

Martin Scorsese

Among the early 1970s "movie brats," Martin Scorsese most consistently pursued a traditional career as a commercial director (while Lucas and Spielberg went into producing as well as directing blockbusters, Coppola tried to establish his own Hollywood studio, incurring extensive losses that affected his own filmmaking endeavors). Nevertheless, when two of Scorsese's most interesting personal projects, *The King of Comedy* (1983) and *After Hours* (1985), made negligible impact at the box office, it appeared that his artistic goals might be incompatible with the commercial system. He recovered, however, with a more conventional work, the aptly named *The Color of Money* (1986), and he managed to sur-

vive substantial public controversy over the portrayal of the life of Jesus in *The Last Temptation of Christ* (1988), based on a novel by Nikos Kazantzakis.

Earlier, Scorsese directed what many critics considered the outstanding Hollywood film of the 1980s decade, *Raging Bull* (1980), a dark, pitiless fictional portrait based on the life of prizefighter Jake La Motta. The film was shot in black-and-white, unusual for its time, with additional color sequences made to appear as if they had been shot by the characters as home movies. It featured a remarkable performance by Robert De Niro as La Motta; the actor, trim and athletic in youthful sequences, gained weight to portray the paunchy, jowly older man. From *Mean Streets*, their first film together, through *Taxi Driver*, *Raging Bull*, and *The King of Comedy*, Scorsese and De Niro formed one of the most significant director-performer working relationships in American film history. It continued in *GoodFellas* (1990), a satirical film concerning the activities of organized crime, and *Cape Fear* (1991), a remake of a 1962 crime drama.

David Lynch

An even more unconventional career within the commercial film industry was that of David Lynch (b. 1946). He made his first feature, *Eraserhead* (1976), as a student project at the American Film Institute's Center for Advanced Film Studies. This disturbing, dreamlike film became a fixture on the "midnight movie" circuit that sprang up in the mid-1970s in a few big city theaters, cultivating audiences for offbeat "cult" films.

His first commercial feature, *The Elephant Man* (1980), was like *Raging Bull* shot in black-and-white and also based on an actual

22.20. David Lynch's The Elephant Man *(1980) was based on an actual life story of a nineteenth-century British man*

who suffered from a grotesquely disfiguring disease; John Hurt, swathed in a mask, portrayed the title chararacter, John Merrick.

life story, this of a nineteenth-century British man who suffered from a grotesquely disfiguring disease. *Blue Velvet* (1986) was yet another unsettling work, using garish colors as a counterpoint to the mystery and malevolence it depicted behind the facade of a "normal" American small town. Critics ranked *Blue Velvet* alongside *Raging Bull* among important works of the decade; a British writer called Lynch "the most provocative and inspired director in the American mainstream."[2] *Twin Peaks*, a television series concerning mysterious transgressions in a small northwestern town that Lynch launched in 1989 as producer and sometime director, offered considerable provocation and occasional inspiration, but little of either was evident in the feature films *Wild at Heart* (1990), a road movie, and *Twin Peaks: Fire Walk with Me* (1992), which closed out the television series and solved its mysteries.

22.21. Ranked by critics among the most important films of the decade, David Lynch's Blue Velvet (1986) depicted mystery and malevolence in a "normal" American small town; Dean Stockwell (left) played Ben, Dennis Hopper Frank Booth.

Ridley Scott

British director Ridley Scott (b. 1939) made two significant films in Hollywood nearly a decade apart, *Blade Runner* (1982) and *Thelma and Louise* (1991). Both sparked critical and cultural debate. Based on a novel by science fiction writer Philip K. Dick, *Blade Runner* was a futuristic film noir, concerned with crime and duplicity in a nightmarish urban world early in the twenty-first century. Though not particularly successful when it opened, and faulted by critics for weak narrative and static images, the film became increasingly admired and discussed as a "postmodern" work, portraying a future where technological wizardry marks a thin veneer over social malaise and decay, while differences erode between humans and robots. *Blade Runner* was rereleased in 1992 in a longer version described as "the director's cut."

Below left: 22.22. The "postmodern" vision of Blade Runner *(1982), directed by Ridley Scott, included a nightmarish cityscape of the future in which technological wizardry marks a thin veneer over social malaise and decay.*

Below: 22.23. An artist's sketch for a scene from Blade Runner. *Lawrence G. Paull was production designer on the film.*

Bottom: 22.24. Thelma and Louise (1991), directed by Ridley Scott, created controversy by placing two women in the familiar genre role (formerly occupied by two men, or a male-female couple) of fugitives on the run from the law; Thelma Dickinson was portrayed by Geena Davis (left), Louise Sawyer by Susan Sarandon.

Thelma and Louise created immediate furor. With a screenplay by woman writer Callie Khouri (b. 1958), it resembled a genre film concerning fugitives on the run from the law, but it transmuted genre conventions by making its runaways two women. Though scores of American films had romanticized male characters in crime films involving car chases, holdups, and violent death (as well as male and female couples in works such as *Gun Crazy* and *Bonnie and Clyde*), a controversy arose over placing two women in those mythologized scenarios. Some critics hailed *Thelma and Louise* as a feminist work empowering to women, while others objected to the film's associating women with genre violence.

Oliver Stone

For controversy, however, no Hollywood figure of the era surpassed writer-director Oliver Stone (b. 1946). As a scriptwriter for works such as *Midnight Express* (1978, directed by Alan Parker) and *Scarface* (1983, directed by Brian De Palma), his films had been notable for their violence and brutality. As a director, his works took aim at contentious issues in a blunt, punchy, realist style, mixed with blatant use of caricature and symbolism. A veteran of active service in Vietnam, Stone won the Academy Award for best picture with *Platoon* (1986), hailed by many Vietnam veterans as the most authentic rendering in fiction film of their war experience. No film in decades aroused such acrimony as Stone's *JFK* (1991), which presented the 1963 assassination of President John F. Kennedy as a conspiracy among government officials. Strongly criticized in many editorials and commentaries, *JFK* nevertheless reopened a national debate over the assassination and its political and social consequences, as well as the role of feature fiction films in representing and interpreting past historical events.

22.26. *Playing hooky in a 1961 Ferrari: Ferris Bueller (Matthew Broderick, behind the wheel), Sloane Peterson (Mia Sara, left),* and Cameron Frye (Alan Ruck, rear) in Ferris Bueller's Day Off (1986), directed by John Hughes; Cameron's father owns the car.

John Hughes

Writer-director John Hughes (b. 1950) merits consideration particularly in relation to the status of genre filmmaking in late-twentieth-century Hollywood. Genres had been at the core of Hollywood studio production, as we have seen in earlier chapters, and their influence persisted through the eras of genre revision, the "movie brats," and the blockbuster. But by the 1980s few filmmakers were content to make just plain genre films (as opposed to revisionist or reflexive or hybrid works) and even less to carve out a niche, an identity, as genre filmmakers. Hughes was an exception. In the mid-1980s he directed a series of "teen" films—among them *Sixteen Candles* (1984), *The Breakfast Club* (1985), and *Pretty in Pink* (1986)—that depicted the perennial struggles of teenage life in the setting of affluent suburbia. Then, in *Ferris Bueller's Day Off* (1986), which became his biggest box office success, Hughes stepped over to the reflexive mode, treating teen fantasies and anxieties both seriously and as farce comedy. The film was couched at times in a pseudo-documentary form, with the leading character lecturing or hectoring the camera/spectator.

Women Directors

Though the rise of a feminist movement in the 1970s did not greatly alter Hollywood's status as a male-dominated industry, women did take prominent roles as producers and screenwriters, and more women directors made commercial features than ever before. Women directors helped to revitalize the teen film genre that John Hughes later commanded. Amy Heckerling (b. 1954) made her feature debut with *Fast Times at Ridgemont High* (1982), which featured young actor Sean Penn (b. 1960), while Martha Coolidge (b. 1946), a former independent feminist documentary filmmaker, contributed *Valley Girl* (1983) and *Real Genius* (1985) to the genre. Coolidge later directed *Rambling Rose* (1991), a film admired for the performances of actresses Diane Ladd and Laura Dern, who in actuality are mother and daughter.

Susan Seidelman (b. 1953), whose film *Smithereens* (1982) became the first American independent feature accepted in the prize competition at the Cannes film festival, began as a commer-

22.25. *Sergeant Elias (Willem Dafoe) is killed in Oliver Stone's film on the Vietnam war,* Platoon *(1986).*

cial director with a comedy, *Desperately Seeking Susan* (1985), that introduced a young pop singer, Madonna [Ciccone]. Films by directors such as Heckerling, Coolidge, and Seidelman raised anew (as in the cases of Lois Weber and Dorothy Arzner decades earlier) the question of whether women could bring gender-based sensibilities to the conventionalized Hollywood mode of production. "Without being a feminist film," Seidelman said of *Desperately Seeking Susan*, "*Susan* has a distinctly female point of view. . . . A man would have directed differently, a man certainly wouldn't have written that script."[3]

Independents

A feature of post-1975 United States filmmaking was increased opportunity for independents to enter the mainstream. Independent production companies had always existed within the Hollywood system, but this was different—filmmakers mostly working outside Hollywood, whose films would previously have screened on the nontheatrical, museum, or college circuits, now got a chance at theatrical distribution.

One aegis for this change was a proliferation of North American film festivals, where independent films gained publicity and demonstrated audience interest. Among the first was the New York Film Festival, founded in 1963, followed by even bigger events in such cities as Chicago, Montreal, San Francisco, and Toronto. In 1980 actor Robert Redford (b. 1937) launched the Sundance Film Festival in Park City, Utah, solely as a showcase for independent features and documentaries. From these events many independent works found theatrical distributors.

Above: 22.27. Jeff Spicoli (Sean Penn, center) with shirtless surfer pals in Fast Times at Ridgemont High *(1982), directed by Amy Heckerling*

Top right: 22.28. Director Martha Coolidge sets up a shot for Real Genius *(1985).*

Above right: 22.29. In a supporting role, pop singer Madonna made her leap to stardom as the title character in Susan Seidelman's Desperately Seeking Susan *(1985).*

While filmmakers such as Martha Coolidge and Susan Seidelman moved from independent production to Hollywood, others maintained varying degrees of distance from the dominant industry. Significant figures included John Sayles (b. 1948) and Jim Jarmusch (b. 1953), based respectively in Hoboken, New Jersey, and New York City. A novelist before and during his film career, Sayles worked within the commercial system as a screenwriter to help finance his independent features, beginning with *Return of the Secaucus Seven* (1980), a rough but energetic work concerning a reunion of 1960s radicals. In later films, such as *Matewan* (1987) and *City of Hope* (1991), Sayles continued to deal with progressive social topics. Jarmusch found backing for a feature film, *Stranger Than Paradise* (1984), from European producers

Hollywood in the 1970s recognized but was unable to respond to a paradox: in American society at large the women's movement and feminism were having a major impact, while in commercial films important roles for women were in significant decline. A simple (but hardly sufficient) explanation for this state of affairs is that a male-dominated industry found itself incapable either of perpetuating traditional conventions for female characters or of creating new ones. New opportunities that opened up for women to direct did not necessarily resolve the problem, since most women directors wanted to demonstrate they could handle any script or genre, not just specialized women's stories.

What could women performers without good roles do about it? A number of male stars of the era had gained significant power to shape their projects and even to

direct them; the question was whether any female stars possessed similar influence. One woman clearly of that rank was the singer-actress Barbra Streisand (b. 1942); after she won an Academy Award for her first film role, as Fanny Brice in *Funny Girl* (1968), directed by William

Wyler, she was in fact taken to task by critics for not choosing more adventurous roles or working with leading directors during the 1970s.

In 1983 Streisand undertook to produce, cowrite, direct, and star in *Yentl*, based on a short story by Isaac Bashevis

22.30. Director Penny Marshall (left) with Robert De Niro, who portrays a patient in a neurological hospital in Awakenings *(1990).*

22.32. Financed by European producers and television networks, director Jim Jarmusch made his mark as an American independent with Stranger Than Paradise *(1984), with John Lurie as Bela "Willie" Molnar and Eszter Balint as Eva.*

Singer in which a young Jewish woman in an Eastern European *shtetl* (village), denied education because of sex discrimination, masquerades as a boy in order to pursue her studies. Some critics regarded the film as a "megalomaniac extravagance," while others admired it and

pointed out that similar projects by male stars rarely received such dismissive comments. Streisand returned as producer, director, and star of *The Prince of Tides* (1991), to which responses were also divided. The film was nominated for an Academy Award as best picture but

Streisand was not nominated as director.

A television star (on the situation comedy *Laverne & Shirley*), Penny Marshall (b. 1942) turned to film directing in the mid-1980s, but not as a director-performer. She had a considerable success with her second film, *Big* (1988), a sentimental comedy concerning a twelve-year-old boy who is transformed overnight (in size, not in mind) into an adult; actor Tom Hanks (b. 1957) played the lead role. Her next films, *Awakenings* (1990), concerning a doctor and his patients in a hospital for neurological diseases, and *A League of Their Own* (1992), dealing with women who play professional baseball in a women's league during and after World War II (with Geena Davis and Madonna among the lead performers), were also criticized for sentimentality but became substantial box office hits.

22.31. Director Barbra Streisand (right) preparing a scene for Yentl (1983) with performers Amy Irving and Mandy Patinkin.

and television networks, which had become significant supporters of United States independents. This spare black-and-white film won praise for its minimalist irony. Jarmusch brought subtle comedy and an international cast of performers to further films, such as *Down by Law* (1986) and *Mystery Train* (1989), in which he explored contemporary anomie.

AFRICAN-AMERICAN FILMMAKERS

The openness to independents was particularly significant for African-American filmmakers. While films such as *Nothing but a Man* and performances by Sidney Poitier brought new perspectives to representations of blacks in United States cinema during the 1960s (see Chapter 20), opportunities had been slower to come for black directors.

This began to change at the end of the 1960s decade, when noted magazine photographer Gordon Parks (b. 1912) directed—as well as produced, wrote, and composed the music for—*The Learning Tree* (1969), based on his own autobiographical writings. However, his very different second film, *Shaft* (1971), an urban crime thriller featuring a black private detective portrayed by Richard Roundtree (b. 1937), was considerably more influential. A surprise box office hit, *Shaft* launched two sequels, a television series, and a short-lived film movement known as "blaxploitation" films (the term combined the words *blacks* and *exploitation*).

These violent crime and action films filled a subgenre niche for urban black audiences for several years before blockbusters began to dominate exhibition. More than three dozen blaxploitation films were made in the period from 1972 to 1975; black filmmakers, including Poitier, Ossie Davis (b. 1917), Gordon Parks, Jr. (1935–1979), and Ivan Dixon (b. 1931), the male lead performer in *Nothing but a Man*, got to direct a few.

Melvin Van Peebles

Without minimizing the experience and exposure blaxploitation films offered black directors and performers, it is clear that the movement was more concerned with traditional genre conventions than it was with expressing black viewpoints on contemporary society. A filmmaker who laid the groundwork more directly for a distinctive black perspective in fiction features was Melvin Van Peebles (b. 1932). Even earlier than Gordon Parks, Van Peebles made the first important film of the 1960s by a black director, *La Permission* (*The Story of a Three-Day Pass*, 1968), but it was produced in France, where Van Peebles had gone to get his start as a director. His Hollywood opportunity came with *Watermelon Man* (1970), a comedy about a white who turns black. Its principal (perhaps only) virtue was that it provided income Van Peebles used to fund an independent project, *Sweet Sweetback's Bad Asssss Song* (1971), in which he also played the lead role.

A violent, controversial film, expressing black anger and dedicated to "all the Brothers and Sisters who had enough of the Man," *Sweet Sweetback* developed myths of rebellion similar to those in the films of Brazilian Glauber Rocha and other filmmakers of the Cinema of Liberation (see Chapter 18). Independently distributed, it became a major success with black audiences. When "blaxploitation" films swept the market, however, Van Peebles shifted to television and theater. Nevertheless, *Sweet Sweetback* remained as a marker for a new generation when black independents found it possible to break into the mainstream more on their own terms in the 1980s.

Spike Lee

The first black filmmaker to exploit the new opportunities was Spike Lee (full name Shelton Jackson Lee, b. 1957). Lee made a distinctive debut with an independent feature, *She's Gotta Have It* (1986), a film shot in twelve days, partly in color and partly black-and-white, on a $175,000 budget funded largely by foundation grants. Lee was writer, director, editor, and one of the lead performers, and he used four members of his family in the cast and crew. A skillful promoter, he quickly branched into music video and book tie-ins for the film, and turned the slight, bespectacled character he portrayed, Mars Blackmon, into a partner of basketball star Michael Jordan in television commercials that Lee directed. *She's Gotta Have It* was not universally applauded: many critics faulted the work as a sex farce at the expense of its lead female character.

Gaining backing from a major studio, Lee showed his iconoclastic approach by making an unconventional, challenging film, *School Daze* (1988), a musical set at a black college that centers on conflicts between light-skinned and dark-skinned blacks. Later films continued his exploration of controversial issues in race relations, with an eclectic visual and narrative style combining realist and anti-realist techniques: *Do the Right Thing* (1989) deals with racial violence growing out of tensions at an Italian-American pizza parlor in a black neighborhood of Brooklyn, New York; *Jungle Fever* (1991) focuses on a love affair between a black man and an Italian-American woman.

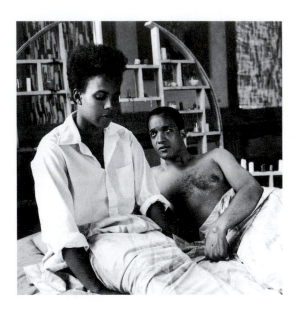

Above: 22.33. Nola Darling (Tracy Camila Jones) and Jamie Overstreet (Redmond Hicks) discuss their relationship in She's Gotta Have It *(1986), Spike Lee's debut feature as a director; he also wrote the screenplay and edited and performed in the film.*

Left: 22.34. Clifton (John Savage) meets his neighbors in a predominantly black and Puerto Rican neighborhood of Brooklyn, New York, in Spike Lee's Do the Right Thing *(1989). Clifton wears the insignia of the enemy, a Boston Celtics basketball jersey with the number of a white player, Larry Bird.*

Left: 22.35. Youths in south central Los Angeles dancing at a barbecue to welcome home Doughboy Baker (portrayed by Ice Cube) from jail in Boyz N the Hood *(1991), directed by John Singleton*

Below: 22.36. Director John Singleton (second from right, with glasses) prepares a scene for Boyz N the Hood *with performers Ice Cube (in driver's seat) and Cuba Gooding, Jr. (right); also in the car are performers Regina King and (in the back seat, from left) Redge Green and Dedrick D. Gobert.*

Based in Brooklyn, New York, Lee ran a production company and opened a retail store to sell books, music, and clothing related to his films. Baseball caps with the logo "X" appeared throughout the country months before Lee's film *Malcolm X* (1992), an epic biography of the militant black figure who gained fame in the 1960s, was released. With *JFK* of the previous year, *Malcolm X* demonstrated how ambitious historical films can significantly awaken awareness and revise debate on controversial recent events.

New Black Filmmakers

Lee's box office success made clear that a substantial audience existed for films expressing black viewpoints. In 1991, two decades after *Shaft*, another black film movement began, one far more concerned with black perspectives and giving voice to young black filmmakers. More than a dozen films by black directors were released that year, a higher total of mainstream commercial films than in the entire 1980s decade, and many were debut features.

The most prominent was *Boyz N the Hood* (1991), directed by twenty-three-year-old John Singleton (b. 1968), which Columbia Pictures distributed as a mini-blockbuster, opening the film simultaneously in nearly one thousand theaters. *Boyz N the Hood* was a strongly realist treatment of black life in south central Los Angeles, focusing on the struggles of young men to grow up amid gang violence. Black critic Armand White assessed the film's significance, writing that in *Boyz N the Hood*, "black teens see life in terms of survival," while in the 1980s teen genre, "white teens see it in terms of fun."[4]

BEYOND FORMULA

By the early 1990s, a vigorous movement of independent filmmakers appeared to be thriving within the framework of a dominant commercial filmmaking practice that continued to emphasize blockbusters, sequels, and traditional genres. Some film industry executives conceded that their formulas and conventions, while frequently popular and financially successful, lacked the combination of entertainment and artistry that had been a hallmark of American commercial cinema in the past.

"Hollywood movies aren't as good as they used to be," said Jeffrey Katzenberg, the chairman of Walt Disney Pictures.[5] A nostalgia for more adventurous filmmaking eras was evident, and some commentators hoped for a revival of the late 1960s atmosphere when new talent and new ideas reshaped American film (though not wishing, one assumes, for the extreme financial distress the film industry suffered in that period).

While no single awards season makes a trend, some critics saw a possible sign of renewal in the prevalence of independent and foreign films among nominees for Hollywood's 1993 Academy Awards (at least eight of the twenty nominations for best picture, actor, actress, and director came from such titles). Among films with the most nominations were *Howards End* (1992), from a novel by E. M. Forster, by the veteran literary adapters director James Ivory (b. 1928) and producer Ismail Merchant (b. 1936), and *The Crying Game* (1992), an unusual political thriller by Irish director Neil Jordan (b. 1950). In the event, the best picture award went as expected to *Unforgiven* (1992), in which director and lead performer Clint Eastwood not only restored vitality to the Western genre but also demonstrated a capacity for genre revision reminiscent of the 1960s; Eastwood also won the directing award.

Secrets of Sound

When film theorists speak of cinematic realism, they almost invariably refer solely to the screen image. Debates over Italian neorealism, for example, rarely find any impediment to the concept of realism in the fact that sound was not recorded simultaneously with the image but added later in a studio (indeed this has been seen as an enhancement to realism because it freed the camera for mobile location shooting).

Is film sound realistic because it resembles our conception of the sounds of the actual world, because it enhances the properties of visual realism, or because it is recorded from actuality? If the last of these three definitions is chosen, then very little film sound is "real"—in a strict sense, only the sound-tracks of cinema verité or direct cinema documentaries (and a few fiction films) that use only sound directly recorded with the image. Even in feature films that record synchronized dialogue, a substantial portion of the soundtrack is created in postproduction. Two of the places where that occurs are the Foley stage and the mixing studio.

Who is the only person to have a film credit named after him? The answer is Jack Foley, an early innovator of special sound effects in radio and movies. The men and women who make such effects have become known (and receive screen credit) as "Foley artists." Their job is to supplement the work of the sound recordist, who concentrates on dialogue when a shot is made. They pro-

duce the incidental noises that make up the sound background in a scene, such as footsteps, doors closing, the rustle of clothing; their sounds can call attention to facets of the visual image and advance the narrative just as insert shots do. They also create sounds that for obvious reasons cannot be directly recorded: Foley artists have a habit of citing as an example the sound of a head being hit, which they make by smashing a watermelon.

All the sounds for a film come together in the mixing studio to make a film's single soundtrack: the dialogue recorded during a shot, additional dialogue rerecorded in postproduction (known as ADR), the Foleys, other effects (usually from a stock sound library; for example, the sound of a jet airplane taking off), and music. As many as one hundred separate recorded tracks may be premixed to reduce the number the mixers work with to two or three dozen. Each of the premixed tracks is connected to a fader on the mixing board that controls the level of each sound to be recorded on the final track.

The film's director, working with sound editors and a mixer, makes decisions as to the level and equalization of the different elements. The completely mixed track is then recorded on an optical negative and placed alongside the image frames. Thus is "realistic" sound created through artistry and artifice.

Top: 22.39. *The Walt Disney–M-G-M studio adjacent to Walt Disney World near Orlando, Florida, functions as a working motion picture studio as well as a nostalgic re-creation of legendary Hollywood. An aerial photograph of the complex shows studio buildings in the background and, in the foreground, "Hollywood Boulevard" leading to a replica of Grauman's Chinese Theater.*

Above left: 22.40. *For the music video promoting his album "Bob on Bob," the title character of* Bob Roberts *(1992), a singer and political candidate portrayed by Tim Robbins, parodies the title*

sequence of D. A. Pennebaker's documentary film on singer Bob Dylan, Don't Look Back *(1967); Robbins also directed.*

Above right: 22.41. *Ex-gunfighter William Munny (Clint Eastwood) prepares to resume his trade in* Unforgiven *(1992), directed by Eastwood. The revisionist Western won four Academy Awards—as best picture, for Eastwood as director, Gene Hackman as supporting actor, and Joel Cox for editing. Eastwood was also nominated in the acting category, marking the first time he had received such recognition as actor or director.*

Notes

1. *Variety*, May 25, 1977, p. 20.
2. Steve Jenkins, review of *Blue Velvet*, *Monthly Film Bulletin* (London), vol. 54 (April 1987), p. 99.
3. Jane Root, "Céline and Julie, Susan and Susan: An Interview with Susan Seidelman," *Monthly Film Bulletin*, v. 52 (October 1985), p. 328. The screenplay of *Desperately Seeking Susan* was written by Leora Barish.
4. Armand White, "Flipper Purify and Furious Styles," *Sight and Sound*, vol. 1, no. 4 (NS) (August 1991), p. 10.
5. Quoted in Janet Maslin, "Is a Cinematic New Wave Cresting?" *The New York Times*, December 13, 1992, Sec. 2, p. 1.

TWENTY-THREE

THE CINEMATIC

The French term *avant-garde* signifies a vanguard—those who march in front, keep ahead of the pack. In the arts, it defines creators who break with standard conventions and push beyond accepted limits of form. In cinema, vanguard filmmakers have been designated by such terms as "experimental" or "underground." Earlier chapters gave attention to avant-garde filmmaking from the era prior to World War II. Here further manifestations of noncommercial or anti-mainstream cinema will be traced through the postwar decades. It has been a period of diverse and sometimes contradictory trends for avant-garde filmmaking, containing extreme forms of film experiment along with greater opportunities for vanguard filmmakers to move closer to the mainstream.

In the World War II era, fascism and war drove many of Europe's avant-garde filmmakers into exile. Hollywood companies played an important role in their support, as the studios also had done with other film workers. Among pioneer vanguard figures, for example, René Clair, maker of *Paris qui dort* and *Entr'acte* (see Chapter 6), spent the war years in the United States directing fiction features. Luis Buñuel, maker of *Un Chien andalou*, worked in New York and later in Hollywood, where he was hired to dub features into Spanish. While these circumstances were shaped by war's disruptions—Clair returned to France after the war and Buñuel (as we have seen) went on to Mexico and eventually to Europe—they suggest a more complex relationship between Hollywood and the avant-garde than one might assume. Mainstream cinema served not only as an aesthetic antagonist for vanguard filmmakers but also as a source for imagery, an occasion for commentary or parody, and sometimes a goal. As it

happened, not entirely by coincidence, the film that launched the postwar avant-garde movement was made privately in Hollywood during the war, not far from the studios' doors.

MAYA DEREN

The film was *Meshes of the Afternoon* (1943), a fourteen-minute work by Maya Deren (1917–1961) with Alexander Hammid (b. 1907). It has become one of the most famous avant-garde films in cinema history and perhaps the best documented, thanks to a remarkable publishing project, *The Legend of Maya Deren*, by VèVè A. Clark, Millicent Hodson, and Catrina Neiman, which has compiled in two volumes more than a thousand pages of documents, interviews, and film criticism covering the first thirty years of Deren's life (with more books to come on her later years).

Born in Russia and brought to the United States with her family as a child, Deren was preparing a book on dance and traveling with a dance company when she arrived in Los Angeles, where she met and married Hammid, a filmmaker in exile from Czechoslovakia. Deren took up photography and poetry. In late spring 1943, just before moving to New York, the couple decided to make a film. They shot it with a 16mm camera without sound (a music soundtrack was added years later) and without a scenario, planning shots as they went along and performing the roles themselves.

Meshes of the Afternoon has been described in many ways—as a film poem, a dream film, a trance film, as a work that forms a bridge between the prewar European Surrealist avant-garde and the postwar self-exploratory "New American Cinema." Deren

23.1. Maya Deren performs in Meshes of the Afternoon *(1943), the film by Deren and Alexander* Hammid that launched the post–World War II avant-garde movement.

AVANT-GARDE

portrays a woman who enters an apartment, sits down in an armchair, and falls asleep. The film's images then become her increasingly disorienting and violent dreams, shot at odd angles and in slow motion. Household objects take on ominous character in the dream sequences, and her "self" splits into three identical figures, two of whom appear together in double-exposure shots. Just as one of the dream women appears to stab the sleeping woman with a kitchen knife, a man (Hammid) intervenes and waking life seems to return. But at the end the man finds the woman dead in the armchair. Nearly every shot of *Meshes of the Afternoon* conveys a distinct beauty and mystery, and repeated viewings suggest few pat psychological or symbolic explanations.

In New York, working on her own, Deren continued to make short dreamlike films and to promote her film aesthetics through screenings and writings. After the war, communities of filmmakers, critics, and audiences formed in the United States on both east and west coasts. New York's Cinema 16 was established as a film society on the model of prewar European "ciné-clubs." In San Francisco, the Museum of Art inaugurated a historic series, Art in Cinema, that screened European avant-garde classics and the works of Deren and her contemporaries, such as *The Potted Psalm* (1946) by Sidney Peterson (b. 1905) and James Broughton (b. 1912), who collaborated on this debut film and then went on separately to careers as independent filmmakers. Another significant first appearance was *Fireworks* (1947), a symbolically homoerotic work by a seventeen-year-old filmmaker, Kenneth Anger (b. 1930), who had been making short films since he was eleven. An "underground" film culture gradually developed in the United States in the first decade after the war. But it was not until

the late 1950s–early 1960s, when the country entered a period of political and cultural transformations and a crisis in mainstream filmmaking also became apparent, that independent and avant-garde films began to make wider impact.

ALTERNATIVE FILMS OF THE 1960S

Among all the possible designations for the vanguard film movements of the 1960s, "alternative" works best because it is most broad—it encompasses the experimental and the underground, the filmmakers who called themselves New American Cinema, the emergence of gay-related films, and any other subcategories identifiable in the world of noncommercial cinema. What held them together was expressed in *The Connection* (1961), a film by Shirley Clarke (b. 1925), when a character who is making a documentary film explains his aesthetic approach: "I'm not interested," he says, "in making a Hollywood picture."

Shirley Clarke

Clarke's *The Connection* brought to the surface of its narrative a question that was central to nearly all aspects of alternative filmmaking: what it means to shoot a film, and to be filmed—to look and to be looked at. In adapting Jack Gelber's drama about heroin addiction, performed on stage and for the film by the Living Theatre, the director and the playwright (who wrote the script) added the framing device of a filmmaker and his cameraman making a film in a drug addicts' pad. In the course of

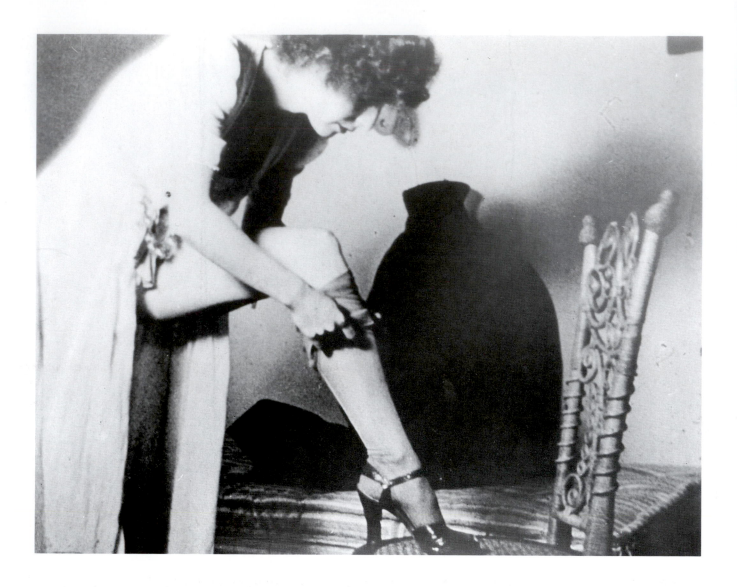

Clarke's film the fictional filmmaker becomes hooked on the drug himself, and his final words are addressed to the cameraman and, through the lens, to the spectator: "It's all yours now." Besides the implied appeal here both for artistic and for social action, *The Connection* amply conveys the potential for danger and destructiveness in filmmaking, as well as in drug taking.

Stan Brakhage

Another name for alternative filmmaking was "personal" film, to distinguish it from the films of an industry and to suggest that an alternative mode of production could be one person with a camera, or even one person splicing together or scratching on found footage. Stan Brakhage (b. 1933) once made a film by sticking flower petals and moth wings between strips of splicing tape (*Mothlight*, 1963). Brakhage was perhaps the most direct successor to Maya Deren as a "film poet," and indeed his film aesthetics were more closely aligned with contemporary poetry than the vague notion of "film poet" would suggest.

Prolific as a writer, lecturer, and filmmaker, Brakhage made more than one hundred films since beginning his career in the 1950s. A centerpiece was *Dog Star Man* (1964), a multipart film that links consciousness, nature, and myth through superimposed images and manual manipulation of the film surface with paint

and scratches. After finishing *Dog Star Man*, he took the work apart and made an even longer film, *The Art of Vision* (1965), which played the superimposed images separately and then together in different combinations. Brakhage's concern with seeing and being seen was carried forward in a radically different style in *The Act of Seeing with One's Own Eyes* (1971), a meditation on autopsies conducted in the Pittsburgh morgue.

Kenneth Anger

The precocious filmmaker of *Fireworks* took the personal film in a different direction from Brakhage, toward magic, ritual, and a critical engagement with popular culture through image and sound. His most widely known film, *Scorpio Rising* (1963), counterpointed its images with commercial rock-and-roll songs of the 1950s and early 1960s, and the music and his own photographed scenes of a motorcycle gang initiation were in turn juxtaposed with still photographs and clips from Hollywood films and television programs. Both comic and portentous, *Scorpio Rising*'s aesthetic is linked, as several critics have suggested, to Sergei Eisenstein's "Montage of Attractions" (see Chapter 7), in which the shock of perception from the clash of linked images is more important than the underlying narrative.

Opposite: 23.2. A scene from The Potted Psalm (1946), the debut film of Sidney Peterson and James Broughton, who went on to separate careers as independent filmmakers

Right: 23.3. A drug addicts' pad in Shirley Clarke's The Connection (1961); at left, William Redfield portrays documentary filmmaker Jim Dunn, who becomes hooked on heroin while shooting a film about it.

Below: 23.4. Frame enlargements from Stan Brakhage's Dog Star Man (1964), in which the filmmaker superimposes images and manually manipulates the film surface with paint and scratches.

Below right: 23.5. A member of a motorcycle gang in Scorpio Rising (1963), a film by Kenneth Anger linking the gang's initiation ceremony with scenes from commercial popular culture

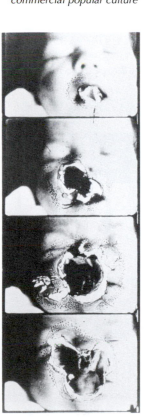

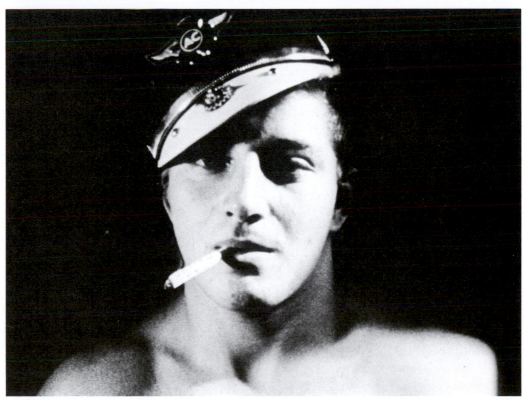

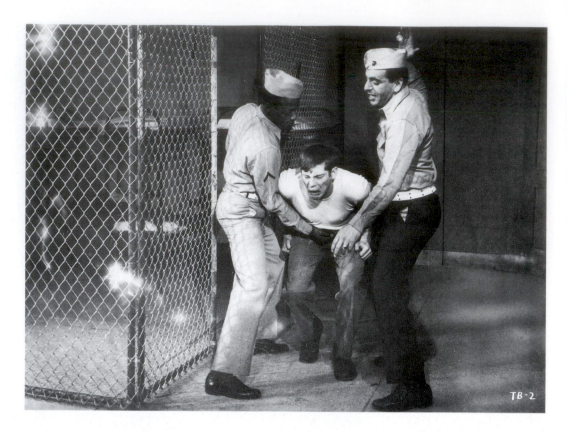

23.6. Corporal punishment for a prisoner in a U.S. Marine Corps base prison in The Brig (1964); Jonas Mekas shot the film by restaging the Kenneth Brown play in an all-night session with members of the Living Theatre stage company.

Jonas Mekas

Born in Lithuania, Jonas Mekas (b. 1922) came to the United States in 1950 after years in European displaced persons' camps and became the key organizing figure of New American Cinema, as well as a filmmaker. He was the founder in 1955 and longtime chief editor of *Film Culture* magazine, which chronicled the underground and avant-garde; an influential columnist on independent film for the New York weekly newspaper *The Village Voice* (the columns were collected in his book *Movie Journal: The Rise of a New American Cinema, 1959–1971*); an organizer of the Film-makers Cooperative in 1961, which distributed independent films, and the Film-makers Cinematheque in New York in 1963, which exhibited them; and a founder in 1970 of Anthology Film Archives in New York, which screens films and houses an archive and library of printed materials pertaining to independent films.

In 1964 Mekas made *The Brig*, one of the remarkable films of the period. Like *The Connection*, it derives from a stage production by the Living Theatre, of a play by Kenneth Brown set in a U.S. Marine Corps brig, or base prison. After the play closed, Mekas restaged it during a marathon all-night session and shot his film as he walked among the performers carrying a camera and sound recording equipment. The result is a harrowing, claustrophobic rendering of dehumanization and oppression.

Michael Snow

Canadian filmmaker Michael Snow (b. 1929), who worked in New York during the 1960s, was a leading figure in a late 1960s movement that became known as "structural film." If, as we have seen, a central project of alternative filmmaking was to foreground the act of making a film, the experiences of seeing and being seen on film, structural films gave primacy not to the filmmaker's consciousness but to the technological workings of the apparatus. In structural film, critic P. Adams Sitney has written, "the shape of

the whole film is predetermined and simplified, and it is that shape which is the primal impression of the film."[1] Snow's *Wavelength* (1967) is a forty-five-minute fixed-camera zoom (it consists of several shots spliced together, because of the length limits of film rolls) going from the widest to the smallest field of vision. His ↔ (also known as *Back and Forth*, 1969) shows a continual series of panning—movements from left to right, right to left. In both films events occur, sounds are heard, people are glimpsed; but human activities are decentered, peripheral to the inexorable movement of the machine for seeing, which takes on seemingly a life and a story of its own.

23.7. The mise-en-scène of Michael Snow's *Wavelength* (1967), a principal work in the "structural film" movement, which gave primacy to the technological workings of the filmmaking apparatus.

Above: 23.8. A promotional still from Andy Warhol's Chelsea Girls *(1966) superimposes the performers (clockwise, from upper left) Eric Emerson, Ingrid Superstar, and International Velvet.*

Right: 23.9. Paul America (born Paul Johnson) portrays the title character in Warhol's My Hustler *(1965), a film concerned with looking and being looked at.*

Andy Warhol

The most significant alternative filmmaker of the 1960s may turn out to be the famed Pop artist Andy Warhol (1928–1987). Warhol encompassed many of the categories of alternative filmmaking— he made both structural films and narrative fiction works—and at the same time exploded the most cherished category, that of the individual artist. He exemplified contemporary theories about "the death of the author."[2] Warhol operated what was in effect the alternative cinema's version of a motion picture studio at the Factory, his loft space in New York. While standard filmographies list him as producer and director of "Warhol" films from 1963

23.10. Johanna Fähmel (Martha Ständer) shoots at a former Nazi in Nicht Versöhnt (Not Reconciled, 1968), a film by Jean-Marie Straub and Danièle Huillet; the Cologne cathedral looms behind her.

until 1968 (when he was shot and wounded by a woman at the Factory), and as producer, with Paul Morrissey (b. 1939) as director, thereafter, the question of who wrote, shot, or directed which "Warhol" films is far from settled, and perhaps irrelevant. They were as much products of a worldview and a mode of production as the films of M-G-M—though quite different in nearly every respect.

Most of Warhol's films were not widely seen when they were made and for several decades were almost entirely out of circulation. When many became available again after Warhol's death, they generated considerable interest, and Warhol's work seems certain to become more familiar. His first films were of stationary objects, shot without sound and in black-and-white, with no camera movement and little movement in the screen image. *Sleep* (1963) was a six-hour film of a man sleeping, and *Empire* (1964) an eight-hour film of the Empire State Building, whose aesthetic interest derives from the changing gradations of light and darkness in the black-and-white image. Nearly everyone who came into the Factory was filmed in static close-up for the length of a film roll, three and one-half minutes; selections from these moving image photographs were assembled in *The Thirteen Most Beautiful Women* (1964) and *The Thirteen Most Beautiful Boys* (1965). "You could do more things watching my movies than with other kinds of movies," Warhol told an interviewer in 1967. "You could eat and drink and smoke and cough and look away and then look back and they'd still be there. It's not the ideal movie, it's just my kind of movie."[3]

Warhol began making sound films, with scripts and performers, in 1965. *Chelsea Girls* (1966) was his most circulated film, and indeed it marked a breakthrough of alternative cinema into commercial exhibition. The film consisted of twelve reels each thirty-five minutes in duration, but two reels were projected side-by-side, so the viewing time was about three and one-half hours. Though a narrative order was later suggested for the reels, Warhol's original idea was to let the projectionist decide which reels to show in whatever order and juxtaposition. Each reel was set in a separate room of New York's Chelsea Hotel, where figures from the 1960s "underground" acted out their personas. Among Warhol's dozens of other films, *My Hustler* (1965) has attracted attention as an important early work exploring issues of gay culture and style through the alternative cinema's inevitable concerns, looking and being looked at, in lengthy, single-take scenes.

EUROPEAN ALTERNATIVE CINEMA

Alternative cinema played a different role in Europe than in the United States after World War II. With festivals fostering an art film aesthetic within the commercial system, vanguard filmmakers such as Robert Bresson in France could find places for themselves as part of the mainstream. New Wave movements gave opportunities to young filmmakers earlier than in Hollywood, and challenging figures ranging from Alain Resnais, in France at the end of the 1950s, to Rainer Werner Fassbinder, in West Germany at the end of the 1960s, were able to pursue commercial careers. European experimental and underground filmmaking did significantly expand during the 1960s, but few from this group became well known to international audiences, most notable among them the Austrian Peter Kubelka (b. 1934) for his intense short abstract films such as *Unsere Afrikareise* (*Our Trip to Africa*, 1966). It was only in the 1970s that a distinctive alternative film practice developed, largely in the context of feminist-oriented filmmaking, even though some feminist filmmakers released their work commercially.

Jean-Marie Straub and Danièle Huillet

The most significant precursors to the 1970s movement were Jean-Marie Straub (b. 1933) and Danièle Huillet (b. 1936), a husband-wife filmmaking team. Born in France, they worked in Germany during the 1960s and in Italy thereafter. Though they shared screen credit, with Huillet's name coming first, many critics referred to their work solely as Straub's—a sign of the necessity for greater recognition of women's contribution to cinema. Their first feature-length film, *Chronik der Anna Magdalena Bach* (*Chronicle of Anna Magdalena Bach*, 1968) addressed the historical subject of a male artist, the eighteenth-century composer Johann Sebastian Bach, through the consciousness of his wife. A controversial work dealing with recent German history in a framework of formal experimentation was *Nicht Versöhnt oder Es hilft nur Gewalt, wo Gewalt herrscht* (*Not Reconciled, or Only Violence Helps Where Violence Rules*, 1968). The film condenses a well-known novel by German author Heinrich Böll, *Billiards at Half-Past Nine*, into less than an hour of screen time, mixing scenes from various historical periods without clear differentiation, and using nonprofessional actors who were coached to speak their lines in stilted ways. Its break from conventional narrative coherence and performance style marked *Not Reconciled* (the short title by which the film is known) as among the most radical avant-garde works produced in Europe since World War II.

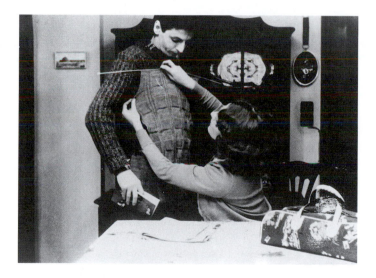

Chantal Akerman

Among the first filmmakers born after the war to gain prominence in alternative cinema was Chantal Akerman (b. 1950). Born in Belgium, Akerman began making films there while in her teens and in her early twenties spent several years in New York developing her work in the context of North American vanguard filmmaking. Her later films synthesized two strands of avant-garde aesthetics, the poetic subjectivity deriving from Deren and Brakhage and the rigorous structuralism associated with Snow. Critics have called her style "minimalist," since her films utilize a realist mise-en-scène but eschew conventional narrative plots.

Her best-known film, *Jeanne Dielman, 23 quai du Commerce, 1080 Bruxelles* (1975), concerns a Brussels woman who has male

visitors during the day while her teenage son is away at school. Portrayed by Delphine Seyrig (1932–1990), who played the woman in Resnais's *Last Year in Marienbad* and appeared in films of Truffaut and Buñuel, the character Jeanne Dielman follows a stolid routine without expression. Over the film's three-hour, forty-five-minute screen time, the persevering spectator becomes immersed in the mundane details of her daily activity and as agitated as she by slight disruptions. Jeanne's final brief eruption into murderous violence seems grounded in the atmospheric tension of Akerman's focus on minutiae, rather than psychological explanation or narrative logic.

With support from a West German television network, along with Belgian and French sources, Akerman made a significant but also ambiguous step from alternative cinema toward the traditional mainstream European art film with *Les Rendez-vous d'Anna* (literally "Anna's Meeting Places," the film circulates under its original title, 1978), concerning the travels and emotional life of a young woman filmmaker. In this and subsequent films Akerman tried to develop the commercial possibilities of women's alternative cinema by situating feminist viewpoints within more conventional narrative and genre frameworks. A number of other women filmmakers attempted this shift in the 1980s, and British critic Pam Cook assessed the mixed outcome: "A refusal to compromise aesthetic principles has resulted in the discovery that minimalist rigour and anti-narrative experiment do not necessarily travel well." Cook described a "between-cinemas limbo," neither fully alternative nor completely commercial, as a zone where some films by European and North American women filmmakers ended up during this period.[4]

Laura Mulvey–Peter Wollen

The films cowritten and directed by British filmmakers Laura Mulvey (b. 1941) and Peter Wollen (b. 1938) hold interest not only for their place in a feminist-oriented alternative cinema but because the filmmakers were also important film theorists. Wollen wrote *Signs and Meaning in the Cinema* (1969), a groundbreaking

Left: 23.11. Jeanne Dielman (Delphine Seyrig) measures the sweater she is knitting for her son Sylvain (Jan Decorte) in Chantal Akerman's Jeanne Dielman, 23 quai du Commerce, 1080 Bruxelles *(1975).*

Below: 23.12. A mother and child in Riddles of the Sphinx *(1977), a film by the film theorists Laura Mulvey and Peter Wollen*

work on authorship and film semiology, the science of signs; Mulvey in 1975 published perhaps the most influential theoretical article of the era, "Visual Pleasure and Narrative Cinema," utilizing psychoanalytic theory to postulate pleasure in narrative cinema as a consequence of representing women as objects for men to look at.[5] As filmmakers, supported by the British Film Institute (BFI) Production Board, their works, such as *Riddles of the Sphinx* (1977), explored feminist themes in a style combining structural aesthetics and minimalist narrative.

Sally Potter

A short film that gained attention for its feminist revision of an opera classic was *Thriller* (1979), made by British filmmaker Sally Potter (b. 1949). The thirty-three-minute work interrogates Giacomo Puccini's *La Bohème*, the popular opera set in the bohemian world of nineteenth-century Paris. In the opera the poet Rodolfo and the poor, sickly seamstress Mimi fall in love, separate, then reunite just before Mimi's death. In Potter's film Mimi returns after her death to conduct a kind of inquest as to its cause. The "reincarnated" Mimi asks herself, "What if I had been the subject of this scenario instead of its object?," questioning the way she has no choice in the narrative but to be vulnerable, passive, and doomed, simply because a young woman's death is a convenient source of sentimental or thrilling effects. Her inquest concludes that she was "murdered" by the conventions of popular narrative. Potter went on to make a feature film, *The Gold Diggers* (1983), with funding from the BFI Production Board and a unit of the British Broadcasting Corporation (BBC), that employed a production crew entirely of women. It was photographed by cinematographer Babette Mangolte (b. 1941), who also shot Akerman's *Jeanne Dielman* and works by United States avant-garde filmmakers.

Valie Export

Of the first wave of European alternative women's films of the 1970s, one of the most impressive, though among the least known, is *Unsichtbare Gegner (Invisible Adversaries, 1978)*,

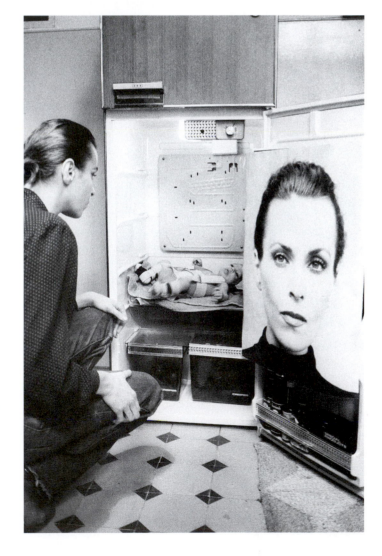

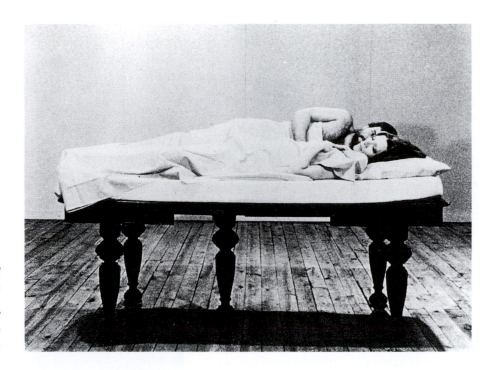

23.15. Dempster Leech and Renfreu Neff in Yvonne Rainer's *Film About a Woman Who . . .* (1974), a collage work concerned with issues of the 1970s feminist movement in the United States

made by Austrian filmmaker Valie Export (b. 1940). With a woman photographer-videomaker as its protagonist, the work is linked with Helke Sander's *Redupers* (see Chapter 21), which also features a woman photographer (Sander appears in *Invisible Adversaries* in a televised speech). The film is concerned with the notion of the human "double." The photographer fears that aliens have taken over human bodies, as in the 1950s Hollywood science fiction film *Invasion of the Body Snatchers*. In one scene the woman and her boyfriend are arguing, while their images on video monitors repeat their words a second later; then the video images speak first, and the humans repeat the lines a second later. The work expands from personal psychology to confront Austria's twentieth-century history and examine what it sees as the nation's repressive institutions.

ALTERNATIVE CINEMA IN THE 1980s

By the mid-1980s the place of alternative filmmaking in cinema culture had changed fundamentally from what it had been only a decade or so previously. The vitality and visibility of a separate avant-garde film movement, with a distinct audience and critical community, had considerably diminished. Yet alternative filmmakers who pursued unconventional styles and espoused unorthodox viewpoints were finding greater opportunities than ever before to secure commercial distribution (to be sure, not on a blockbuster scale, but in "art cinemas" in big cities and university towns) and attract mainstream critical attention. As a consequence, distinctions between vanguard cinema and independent narrative films became blurred. It seemed possible that the pace of experimentation in film form had slowed (defining film form in this context as an aspect of artistic practice, rather than of commercial innovation in such areas as computed-generated manipulation of the image).

Yvonne Rainer

The leading alternative woman filmmaker in the United States following Maya Deren and Shirley Clarke was Yvonne Rainer (b. 1934), a former dancer who began making short films to screen during live performances in the 1960s. Her first feature-length work, *Lives of Performers* (1972), drew on her performance pieces and emphasized issues of women's identity and the role of power in sexual relations that were central to the feminist film movement (Mangolte was cinematographer on this and two subsequent Rainer films). Rainer's works have been characterized as collage cinema. *Film About a Woman Who . . .* (1974), for example, utilizes image juxtapositions and image/sound contrasts, such as voice-over with a blank screen, still frames alternating with moving images, on-screen text, and voice-overs speaking sentence fragments. Her subjects ranged from intimate desires to public policies, and her treatments fulfilled the 1970s feminist tenet, "the personal is political." *The Man Who Envied Women* (1985) integrates fictional segments (in which characters extensively discuss and quote from contemporary theorists such as Michel Foucault, the French philosopher whose works explored the relation between power and knowledge) with actuality footage of a hearing on housing for artists in New York's lower east side.

Lizzie Borden

One of the most unusual films to come out of the feminist film movement was *Born in Flames* (1983), a futurist political fantasy made by Lizzie Borden (b. 1954). In style the work is a hybrid of conventional narrative and direct cinema techniques, shaping the spectator's awareness that what was ostensibly set in the future quite deliberately concerned the present. In the film's not so distant future, a social democratic revolution has taken place in the United States, but women have not benefited. Militant women organize and protest, suffer repression, and turn to violence. The work was vigorously debated among political and women's groups as to whether it offered serious political analysis or genre filmmaking with a political veneer. Borden also made *Working*

Girls (1986), concerning women in a New York brothel, with a similar amalgam of narrative and documentary styles. Another feminist filmmaker working with narrative in a vanguard framework was Bette Gordon (b. 1950), whose Variety (1983) focused on a woman ticket seller at a pornographic movie theater, ambiguously exploring sexuality and pornography.

Raúl Ruiz

Though border crossings by filmmakers had been common in cinema history, the experience of exile—of separation or expulsion from one's home country—nevertheless held a special meaning. Filmmakers had been forced into or had voluntarily chosen exile from Russia after 1917, from Germany and other European countries under Fascism, and from Czechoslovakia after 1968, among many instances; in the world of the avant-garde, prominent exiles included Dimitri Kirasanov from Russia to Paris in the 1920s (see chapter 7) and Jonas Mekas from Lithuania to New York in the 1950s. A figure who brought renewed focus on exile and alternative cinema was Raúl Ruiz (b. 1941), a Chilean filmmaker who was compelled to leave his country following a violent military coup in 1973. Ruiz eventually settled in France and launched a prolific career in theater, video, and film under the auspices of L'Institut National de l'Audiovisuel (National Audiovisual Institute).

The hallmark of Ruiz's filmmaking is an intense storytelling style whose purpose seems ironically to call into question the coherence of narrative, the capacities of stories to tell anything at all except their own indeterminacy. His narratives often take the form of seeking an answer to a puzzle that the narrative itself poses, and the answer turns out to be another philosophical riddle. In L'Hypothèse du tableau volé (The Hypothesis of the Stolen Painting, 1978) a collector tries to uncover the hidden meaning of a series of paintings by staging more and more elaborate tableaux vivant ("living pictures," in which people hold the poses of subjects in paintings), which place in question not only narrative but the moving image itself. Les Trois Couronnes du matelot (Three Crowns of the Sailor, 1983) opens with a murder; the murderer, to effect his escape, agrees to listen to a sailor tell his life story. At the end of the sailor's strange, disjointed narrative the murderer murders the storyteller (perhaps a few spectators may have felt the same urge). But the murdered sailor appears again—incoherent or not, narrative will always be with us.

Wayne Wang

Support for alternative filmmaking by governments or public institutions, common in many countries, became a factor in the United States with the establishment in 1965 of the National Endowment for the Arts (NEA) and in 1967 of the American Film Institute (AFI), which received federal funding through the NEA. Among films awarded production grants from these two bodies, a work that gained wide attention was Chan Is Missing (1983), a seventy-six-minute feature film produced on a minuscule budget of $23,000 by Wayne Wang (b. 1949). Born in Hong Kong, Wang set out to depict the complex cross-cultural life of San Francisco's

Daughters of the Dust

23.18. Three women of the Peazant family embrace during a reunion/leave-taking in Julie Dash's Daughters of the Dust (1992); from left, Eula (Alva Rodgers), Nana (Cora Lee Day), and Yellow Mary (Barbara O.).

When *Daughters of the Dust* (1992), directed by Julie Dash (b. 1952), became the first feature film by an African-American woman to attain commercial theatrical distribution in the United States, it was a case not of alternative filmmaking accommodating itself to the mainstream but of the opposite: the mainstream opening up to new filmmaking visions. Dash's work on black culture and family life on the Sea Islands off the coast of South Carolina and Georgia, set at the beginning of the twentieth century, gave voice in particular to the consciousness of African-American women as had rarely, if ever, been accomplished in a feature film before.

Even as a special case—as an African-American woman—Julie Dash in her development as a filmmaker exemplifies in many ways the transformations of her generation. Growing up in New York City, in her teenage years she attended a workshop in filmmaking at the Studio Museum of Harlem and began shooting film. It was the late 1960s-early 1970s and, "because of the political climate of the times," as she told an interviewer, the documentary form was in demand. "You could just grab a camera and shoot, shoot, shoot. There was so much stuff on the street happening and you could just shoot it and then come back and edit it into story. We had a goal, at one point, of doing newsreels for the community. Everything was community oriented."

But Dash discovered there was a difference between the demand for issue-related documentaries and what people in the community would actually go and see. Though narrative fiction was in disrepute among young black filmmak-ers in the era of conventionalized blax-ploitation action films, nevertheless audiences wanted narratives—that they could relate to. After graduating from City College of New York with a degree in film production, Dash went to the heart of narrative fiction filmmaking: Los Angeles. She won admission to the Center for Advanced Film Studies at the American Film Institute and developed her filmmak-ing style, particularly, she has said, from working with an international group of students who eschewed the formulas of commercial feature films.

Dash gained attention with *Illusions* (1983), a thirty-four-minute fiction film concerning a black woman who passes for white to become a Hollywood studio executive during World War II. She worked for nearly a decade on *Daughters of the Dust*. The film depicts a pivotal moment when descendants of black slaves decide to leave the Sea Islands for the north. The characters are poised between old and new, between memories of their African ancestors and the values of the new world. Dash conveys their division and reconciliation with dream-like, magical images, shifts in the tempo of movement, and close attention to cul-tural details such as language and cuisine. "I can't really say it's like any other film that I've ever seen," Dash has commented, "but I knew that it had to exist."

23.19. A scene from L'Hypothèse du tableau vole (The Hypothesis of the Stolen Painting, 1978), directed by Raúl Ruiz, a Chilean filmmaker working in France, whose films are narratives concerning the indeterminacy of narratives.

Chinatown, where people were divided not only between old values and new, but also by allegiances to Taiwan or the Communist mainland. The filmmaker used a cinema verité style for his fictional work, with long-take close-ups and outdoor scenes shot with a hand-held camera.

In *Chan Is Missing*, a taxi driver searches for a friend, whose disappearance has created an absence (as in Antonioni's *L'Avventura*) in which what remains becomes more mysterious than the disappearance itself. With funding from Hong Kong, Wang made another film set in San Francisco's Chinatown, *Dim*

23.20. *Independent Chinese-American filmmaker Wayne Wang made his first feature,* Chan Is Missing *(1983), on a budget of* $23,000; *Marc Hayashi played Steve and Wood Moy portrayed Joe.*

Sum—A Little Bit of Heart (1985). His later films include *Eat a Bowl of Tea* (1989), concerning a Chinese family in New York after World War II, and *Life Is Cheap . . . But Toilet Paper Is Expensive* (1990), in which an Asian-American becomes involved in underworld intrigue in Hong Kong.

Atom Egoyan

After years of assisting co-productions of Hollywood genre films, Canada's public film agencies helped to support independent and alternative cinema in the 1980s. Atom Egoyan (b. 1960, in Egypt) was among those who emerged under the aegis of funding from the Ontario Film Development Corp. and other government sources. His feature narratives—including *Next of Kin* (1984), *Family Viewing* (1987), *Speaking Parts* (1989), and *The Adjuster* (1991)—revived alternative cinema's concern with looking and being looked at, in a mise-en-scène where modern electronic communications, from home video to visual teleconferencing, have attenuated face-to-face relationships. Meanwhile, some characters struggle to retain artifacts and memories of their ethnic heritage.

23.21. *The films of Atom Egoyan, a Canadian filmmaker born in Egypt, concern characters struggling to retain memory and ethnic heritage in a world of modern electronic communications; in* Family Viewing *(1987), Stan (David Hemblen) and Sandra (Gabrielle Rose) watch TV.*

ALTERNATIVE NONFICTION

Among the convergences of cinema practices after the 1970s, one of the most interesting was a movement within nonfiction film-making toward the avant-garde. The two kinds of filmmaking had been linked in the past, in such works as Ruttmann's 1927 film *Berlin: Symphony of a Great City* (see Chapter 11). But in the 1960s, with the ascendancy of cinema verité style and the growing importance of television in financing documentary films, a rhetoric of "truth" and an ethic of journalistic "objectivity" dominated the nonfiction field. By the 1980s, however, cinema verité had largely faded as a movement, remaining as a stylistic marker denoting "documentary authenticity" in fiction films such as *Born in Flames*. Its legacy in criticism and theory was to open the debate in nonfiction film about looking and being looked at that was taking place more generally in alternative filmmaking (although, as we have seen, Shirley Clarke had raised the issue as early as 1961 in *The Connection*). A few nonfiction filmmakers explored further the implications of an aesthetic in which "truth" and "objectivity" gave way to indeterminacy and subjectivity.

23.22. *A scene from Chris Marker's "film essay,"* Sans soleil *(Sunless, 1982), an experiment in nonfiction form*

Chris Marker

For Chris Marker these developments represented not convergence but continuity. Though often discussed as a participant in the cinema verité movement, Marker had always been no less close to the avant-garde, as we have seen in discussing films such as *Letter from Siberia* and *La Jetée* (see Chapter 19). Another of his works that became a touchstone for formal experimentation in the nonfiction form was the 1982 film *Sans soleil* (*Sunless*; on screen the title appears in three languages: Russian, English, and French). This has been called a "film essay," as adequate or inadequate a name as any for a film of which one critic has written, "the only possible synopsis for *Sans soleil* would be, as though in a Borges story, the film itself (and even this would be inadequate)."[6] *Sans soleil* consists of a series of interspersed images, largely scenes from daily life in Japan, along with sequences shot in Africa and Iceland, and a segment analyzing Alfred Hitchcock's *Vertigo* through stills and shots of the film's San Francisco locations. On the soundtrack, along with music and electronic sounds, a woman's voice reads from what are said to be letters from a photographer. The work can also be described as a meditation, one that leaves room for the spectator to connect with his or her own meditations on the many topics which the film evokes.

First-Person Documentary

Another way nonfiction filmmakers found to move away from claims of truth and objectivity was to make themselves the center of their film, with all their prejudices and obsessions—in short, their subjectivity—on display. Sometimes such works were presented as salvage jobs, substitutes for conventional documentaries the filmmakers intended but failed to make. The completed film would probe the professional and personal problems that prevented the original project from getting made. (Meanwhile, the spectator would hope that the work on screen would illuminate themes of greater depth than the filmmaker's self-involvement.)

Roger & Me

One independently made nonfiction work, *Roger & Me* (1989), linked its filmmaker's self-involvement with larger issues so successfully that a major Hollywood studio purchased the rights to distribute it. The filmmaker, Michael Moore (b. 1954), who introduces himself on screen through childhood home movies, was an unemployed journalist from the city of Flint, Michigan, which had suffered economic difficulties following the closing of automobile factories there. Moore's unsuccessful efforts to interview Roger Smith, then chairman of the General Motors Corp., serve as a frame for the filmmaker's views on American politics and society. By presenting himself as a clownish figure in a baseball cap, running shoes, and battered winter coat, Moore provokes laughs that

sugarcoat the film's political polemic. Some critics complained that the film dispensed with objective journalistic standards (as in shifting the temporal order of events), raising again the question of the nonfiction filmmaker's obligations to "truth."

Errol Morris

A radical approach to this issue was taken by filmmaker Errol Morris (b. 1948), who frequently expressed the view that cinema verité had set documentary film back forty years. Morris was known among followers of nonfiction film for an idiosyncratic work concerning pet cemeteries, *Gates of Heaven* (1978), and another on a small town, *Venice, Florida* (1981), before he gained national attention in the United States for *The Thin Blue Line* (1988). The film, which aided in securing the release of a man convicted of murdering a policeman in Dallas, Texas, explores the 1976 events through interviews with the convicted man, his companion on the night of the murder, witnesses, and public officials. But its innovative and controversial segments involve reconstructing events in a highly stylized mise-en-scène with performers enacting the roles of actual persons, accompanied by a minimalist musical score by composer Philip Glass. These scenes demonstrate with minute attention to detail the portentous significance of slight variations in supposed eyewitness accounts.

The Thin Blue Line straddles a contradiction, aiming at aesthetic and practical goals that may seem at odds. It postulates the indeterminacy of "truth" on film and in human memory, while asserting within the framework of legal "truth" that a man was unjustly convicted for a crime he did not commit. Its success in both areas made it one of the most provocative nonfiction films of its era.

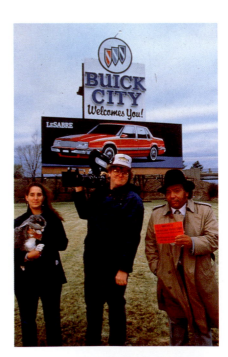

Above left: 23.23. Filmmaker Michael Moore (center) with two of the residents of Flint, Michigan, who appear in his film Roger & Me *(1989)—Rhoda Britton, a woman who breeds rabbits, and Fred Ross, a deputy sheriff who delivers eviction notices*

23.24. Reenacting the murder of a policeman in Errol Morris's The Thin Blue Line *(1988); the film aided in securing the release of a man convicted (falsely, according to the film) of the murder.*

The Duration of Shoah

In their horror and moral complexity, the events of World War II have drawn extraordinary efforts from nonfiction filmmakers to document and comprehend them. Filmmakers have shown an exceptional need for *duration* in recording their search for witnesses and traces, their interviews and sometimes confrontations with people whose memories of war are often clouded by evasion, justification, or pain. *The Sorrow and the Pity* (1969), Marcel Ophuls's film on the French town of Clermont-Ferrand during World War II, ran four and one-half hours (see Chapter 19); more recently German filmmaker Helke Sander has made a three-and-one-half-hour film on German women raped by Russian soldiers at the end of the war and the children born from those encounters, *Befreier und Befreite / Krieg-Verwaltigungen-Kinder* (*Liberators Take Liberties—War, Rapes and Children*, 1992).

One of the longest nonfiction films ever made—certainly the longest to receive commercial distribution—is *Shoah* ("Annihilation," 1985), a work by French filmmaker Claude Lanzmann (b. 1925) on the subject of Nazi extermination camps in Poland during World War II. Part I runs four hours, thirty-four minutes, Part II four hours, fifty-two minutes, for a total of nine hours, twenty-six minutes. The filmmaker has spoken of the film not as a documentary or as a historical work but as an allegory, implying that the Nazi extermination policies of World War II, rather than being a historical aberration or an event fixed firmly in the past, are part of a continuum extending into the present. Nevertheless, the film's techniques are generally similar to those of Ophuls, Sander, and other documentary filmmakers, utilizing interviews and a search for historical traces. Its uniqueness lies in its duration, its slow, repetitious compiling of detail and evidence to make the case that extermination was a deliberate policy, that many people knew of it, that the Holocaust did happen.

How is one to evaluate such a film—as film? Many critics praised *Shoah*, but few analyzed it. There was surprise and disquiet when critic Pauline Kael offered "a dissenting view." "I found *Shoah* logy and exhausting right from the start," she wrote; "sitting in a theatre seat for a film as full of dead spaces as this one seems to me a form of self-punishment." Journalist and historian Timothy Garton Ash put the issue in another light: "This deadly repetition, this exhaustion, this *having* to sit through it, is an essential part of Lanzmann's creation. He deliberately uses the dictatorial powers of the director to lock you in a cattle wagon and send you for nine and a half hours down the line to Auschwitz." According to critic J. Hoberman, "The essential question here is one of identification. . . . In its structure *Shoah* encourages the viewer to identify with the victims." The spectator's pain and exhaustion, Hoberman suggests, is a deliberate outcome of Lanzmann's "formal intelligence."

23.25. A shot appearing repeatedly in Claude Lanzmann's Shoah (1985): a moving train approaches the gate to the Auschwitz extermination camp of World War II.

la fin du voyage.

23.26. Filmmaker Rosa von Praunheim (left) and Dieter Dicken (second from left) portray gay entrepreneurs who downplay the threat of AIDS because of possible adverse effects to their business, a sauna club, in von Praunheim's Ein Virus kennt keine Moral (A Virus Knows No Morals, 1989).

GAY AND LESBIAN CINEMA

Changing mores in North America and Europe in the 1970s made more visible the lives and culture of homosexual men and women, and the AIDS epidemic beginning in the 1980s brought to society and cinema an explicitness about sexual behavior that had hitherto been unrepresented. The development of gay cinema largely followed this public trajectory, moving from the works of filmmakers such as Kenneth Anger and Andy Warhol to an extensive and varied film practice that ranged from independent narrative features to avant-garde works.

Rosa von Praunheim

A filmmaker whose works spanned the decades after 1970 with a highly individual style was the West German Rosa von Praunheim, who was born Holger Mischwitzki in Riga, Latvia (b. 1942). Making films in both Berlin and New York, von Praunheim adopted from the beginning of his career a confrontational approach, offering little comfort to spectators of any persuasion and explicitly disavowing inspirational and optimistic treatments of gay life. In the 1980s he made a series of films concerning AIDS that, like his earlier works on homosexuality, aimed to provoke outrage and spectator response.

Ein Virus kennt keine Moral (*A Virus Knows No Morals*, 1989) took the form of grim satire. Many reactions to the AIDS crisis are held up to ridicule, including those of the medical profession, the press, politicians, psychotherapists, and even those of gays themselves (von Praunheim portrays a gay entrepreneur who denigrates the AIDS threat because he runs a profitable sauna club). The film ends in bitter farce as AIDS sufferers are shipped off to the island of Helgoland (renamed Hellgayland) and a militant army of the sick kidnaps a politician.

Isaac Julien

A film that brought together many of the trends in alternative cinema during the 1980s was *Looking for Langston* (1989), by black British filmmaker Isaac Julien (b. 1960). As a member of the Sankofa workshop in Britain, Julien had worked on nonfiction films whose aim was to establish blacks as subjects in cinema— as people who looked, both from behind the camera and on screen, rather than only being looked at.

Though *Looking for Langston* may have been launched as a nonfiction project about the black American poet Langston Hughes (1902–1967), Julien ended up by shaping the work as an aesthetic amalgam—at once documentary and fiction, gay cinema, black cinema, narrative, and avant-garde. Juxtaposing historical actuality footage with a highly stylized mise-en-scène, the forty-six-minute black-and-white film is a work of contemplative and troubled exploration, suggesting that race, sexual preference, and desire are subjects that are difficult to categorize in simple, programmatic ways.

Lesbian Filmmaking

Works by women in the lesbian independent cinema have reached general audiences less often than works by von Praunheim, Julien, and other gay male filmmakers, in part because many women's films have been addressed to issues of identity and spectatorship within their own community. A film concerning a romantic relationship between two women that gained commercial distribution, *Desert Hearts* (1985), directed by Donna Deitch (b. 1945), seemed to some critics more closely linked to Hollywood narrative conventions than to lesbian film or cultural practice. New German Cinema (see Chapter 21), with its more fluid relations between narrative and avant-garde styles, and state television subsidies for subcultural works, perhaps more clearly offered a place for lesbian filmmaking within art cinema.

In that context, West German filmmaker Ulrike Ottinger (b. 1942) became a significant figure with works such as *Madame X: Eine absolute Herrscherin* (*Madame X: An Absolute Ruler*, 1977), an adventure fantasy concerning a group of women who heed a call offering "gold, love, and adventure" and join pirate queen Madame X on her voyages. Another West German filmmaker, Monika Treut (b. 1954), brought a spirit of adventure back to the community in *Die jungfrauen Maschine* (*The Virgin Machine*, 1988), a comic film in which a German woman journalist enters the lesbian culture of San Francisco.

Notes

1. P. Adams Sitney, *Visionary Film: The American Avant-Garde* (New York: Oxford Univ. Press, 1974), p. 407.

2. See Roland Barthes, "The Death of the Author," in *Image-Music-Text,* trans. Stephen Heath (New York: Hill and Wang, 1977), pp. 142–48, and Michel Foucault, "What Is an Author?" in *The Foucault Reader,* ed. Paul Rabinow (New York: Pantheon, 1984), pp. 101–20.

3. Gretchen Berg, "Nothing to Lose: Interview with Andy Warhol," *Cahiers du Cinéma in English,* no. 10 (May 1967), p. 42.

4. Pam Cook, review of *Golden Eighties* (1986), directed by Chantal Akerman, in *Monthly Film Bulletin,* Vol. 54 (March 1987), p. 67.

5. Mulvey's essay is collected along with other of her writings in Laura Mulvey, *Visual and Other Pleasures* (Bloomington: Indiana Univ. Press, 1989), pp. 14–26.

6. Steve Jenkins, review of *Sans soleil, Monthly Film Bulletin,* Vol. 51 (July 1984), p. 195. The reference is to Jorge Luis Borges, Argentine writer of metafictional short stories.

Above: 23.27. A scene from Isaac Julien's Looking for Langston *(1989); the film branches out from a nonfiction treatment of the black American poet Langston Hughes to explore issues of race, sexual preference, and desire.*

Right: 23.28. Valentine Nonyela (left) as Chris and Mo Sesay as Caz in Julien's Young Soul Rebels *(1991), a feature-length narrative fiction film that deals with black and gay cultures in 1970s Britain in the framework of a murder mystery*

TWENTY-FOUR

THE GLOBAL OF

Cinema at the end of the twentieth century and its own first century presents a choice of perspectives. If you choose to observe the medium from a certain angle you are likely to emphasize Hollywood's resurgence—the worldwide domination of blockbuster movies, the penetration by entertainment conventions into indigenous cultures in the globe's most remote corners. If you shift the viewpoint you might notice, on the contrary, a further spread of cinematic activity, a rising to respect and recognition of filmmakers whose nations of origin had rarely before appeared on the motion picture map. With a little dexterity you could keep both angles in view at once, and see that the situation remained what it had been for several generations, of interpenetration, dialogue, and struggle. On one side stand the metropolitan cinemas, those of Hollywood and Europe, not just profiting but also assisting and absorbing. On the other stand countries on the periphery, not necessarily new to cinema but to the international film marketplace, and filmmakers with new visions facing old temptations.

For the North American spectator, however, one perspective is unequivocal: world cinema is no longer confined to classrooms and museums. Films from Argentina, Brazil, Canada, and Spain became box office successes in the United States during the 1980s, expanding the experience of overseas filmmaking beyond the traditional purveyors of foreign art films, France, Italy, and the Scandinavian countries. Films from Asia, Africa, and Latin America were screened on public and cable television and became available on video cassettes. Widening the horizon of the North American filmgoer may be a very small step in the larger picture, yet it was still a critical ingredient in the development of a sophisticated and open view of world filmmaking. People of different national, ethnic, and racial backgrounds were not only being spoken for and spoken to in cinema, they were speaking in their own voices, creating their own images—and being seen and heard.

AUSTRALIAN CINEMA
To choose Australia as a case study to begin a consideration of late-twentieth-century world cinema may appear unrepresentative, since that English-speaking country exhibited national, but not ethnic or racial, characteristics different from the mainstream. Like Britain in the 1960s, however, Australia vividly exemplified the dilemmas of national cinema in the 1980s and beyond. Australia's achievement in shaping a viable national cinema from the ground up raised the same questions that British cinema had faced two decades earlier, and that other cinema movements

would confront as they emerged into the international arena: what kind of success were they aiming at, and where?

Australia, it could be argued, had been poorer in cinema than many countries. With its theaters dominated by United States and British films, the country produced only a few sound films before World War II and barely any in the quarter century after the war. Finally, in 1970, in recognition of cinema's role in national cultural expression and identity, it set up a government organization, the Australian Film Development Corp. (later renamed the Australian Film Commission) to finance domestic filmmaking. The results were impressive: over one hundred feature films produced in the 1970s, and by the end of the decade Australian filmmakers received international recognition in the form of Hollywood Academy Award nominations. *My Brilliant Career* (1979) was nominated for costume design and *Breaker Morant* (1980) for screenplay.

History and Culture

My Brilliant Career, directed by Gillian Armstrong (b. 1950), and *Breaker Morant*, directed by Bruce Beresford (b. 1940), were in certain ways exemplary models for an emergent national cinema because of their capacity to speak simultaneously to domestic and international audiences. Both were set in the past, at the turn

24.1. Sybylla Melvyn (Judy Davis) playing with her beau Harry Beecham (Sam Neill) in My Brilliant Career (1979), directed by Gillian Armstrong, one of the films that gained Australian cinema international recognition. The heroine turns down her suitor to pursue a literary career.

ADVANCE CINEMA

of the twentieth century when Australia's nationhood was being formed, and both offered historical insights with contemporary resonance. *My Brilliant Career*, directed by a woman and drawn from a 1901 novel by a young woman writer in which the heroine chooses her artistic vocation over romance and a respectable marriage, addressed feminist concerns. *Breaker Morant* was based on an actual incident in the Boer War, fought in South Africa, in which three Australian men serving in the British Army were convicted and executed, so the film asserts, more for geopolitical reasons than for the war crimes of which they were accused. Besides its specifically Australian connotations, the film dealt broadly with questions of imperialism and the sacrifice of individuals in the name of state power.

These historical dramas were also markers of historical change in international film culture. The new or resurgent national cinemas of the 1960s had offered gritty realism, as in the case of British cinema, or trenchant treatments of contemporary society, as in the French, Brazilian, or Japanese new waves. By 1980, however, nearly all the films made outside the United States that were successful in the international market were from two genres: period works like *My Brilliant Career* and *Breaker Morant*, or contemporary comedies. This flight from contemporary realism held true in Australian cinema for domestic audiences as well. Social

issues were most effectively raised in genre format—in the apocalyptic futurist dystopias *Mad Max* (1979) and *Mad Max II: The Road Warrior* (1981), directed by George Miller (b. 1945), or occult thrillers *Picnic at Hanging Rock* (1975) and *The Last Wave* (1977) by director Peter Weir (b. 1944), which dealt with relations between Euro-Australians and the country's Aboriginal people.

"Mid-Pacific" Cinema

With new visions did indeed come old temptations. By the early 1980s a substantial number of Australian filmmakers had decamped to Hollywood. Armstrong, Beresford, Miller, and Weir all began directing in the United States, along with Fred Schepisi (b. 1939), who had made an important period film on Aboriginal themes, *The Chant of Jimmie Blacksmith* (1978). Performers Mel Gibson (b. 1956) from *Mad Max and Mad Max II*, Judy Davis (b. 1956) from *My Brilliant Career*, and Bryan Brown (b. 1947) from *Breaker Morant*, among others, also made the leap to Hollywood. Though several of these figures continued to work in both countries, one heard little of "Mid-Pacific" cinema in the same manner as twenty years earlier, when the term "Mid-Atlantic" was coined to describe the films made in Hollywood by British filmmakers or in Britain by Hollywood studios. The Pacific was wider than the

24.3. Max Rockatansky (Mel Gibson), a lawman in the bleak future world of Mad Max (1979), an Australian film directed by George Miller, gets the drop on a member of a renegade motorcy- cle gang. Miller directed two pop- ular sequels, Mad Max II: The Road Warrior (1981) and Mad Max Beyond Thunderdrome (1985).

24.2. Accused of war crimes in the Boer War, three Australian officers in the British Army confer with their counsel in Bruce Beresford's Breaker Morant (1980); from left, Major J. F. Thomas (Jack Thompson) with the defendants Lt. Harry Morant (Edward Woodward), Lt. Peter Handcock (Bryan Brown), and Lt. George Witton (Lewis Fitz- Gerald). As in the actual incident on which the film was based, the three men are convicted and executed.

Atlantic and Australian culture less familiar (or marketable) than the British. After its intense moment of international recognition, Australian cinema lost through the defection of its leading film- makers its clear delineation as a national cinema: henceforward its achievements would be regarded as individual rather than national.

CINEMA OF THE "THREE CHINAS"

Following Australia's revival of the 1970s, the most significant film movement of the next decade came from Chinese cinema—not only from mainland China but also from the film industries of Hong Kong and Taiwan. These were designated the "three Chinas" to demarcate the cultural and political differences that underlay each cinematic practice: China, a socialist country after 1949; Hong Kong, a British colony on the Chinese coast, sched- uled to become part of China in 1997; Taiwan, an off-shore island ruled by Nationalist exiles from China since the 1940s. (Some even spoke of "four Chinas" to include Chinese-American cinema exemplified by filmmakers such as Wayne Wang.) By the 1990s, however, there were signs of convergence and collaboration among these disparate cinemas.

China

Around 1970, filmmaking was as negligible in China as in Australia, though for wholly different reasons. After the "Cultural Revolution" instigated by Chinese Communist Party chairman

Mao Zedong had completely shut down the film studios from 1967 to 1969 (see Chapter 18), production gradually resumed in the 1970s, but the cultural role of cinema remained uncertain. As television ownership became more widespread after the early 1980s, motion picture attendance began to drop. Chinese film- makers sought to retain their audience with an amalgam of ideology and popular genres: biopics on national heroes, films about hardship and injustice in the era before Communism, works on the World War II struggle against the Japanese (often with added *kung fu* action). Veteran director Xie Jin used the conven- tions of family melodrama for a more critical view of the recent past in *Furong Zhen* (*Hibiscus Town*, 1986), a film that became controversial because it traced how families in a rural village suf- fered over the years (particularly during the Cultural Revolution) from the excesses of Communist political dogma.

THE FIFTH GENERATION. The most significant develop- ment for Chinese cinema came with the reopening of the Beijing Film Academy in 1978, after more than a decade of inactivity. Many in the entering class, though from privileged backgrounds, had spent their teen years and early twenties as farm or factory workers, or even as militant Red Guards during the Cultural Revolution. As filmmakers they wanted to overthrow what they regarded as Chinese film's moribund narrative and stylistic formu- las. Graduating in 1982, their group became known as the "Fifth Generation" of Chinese filmmakers.

Though film authorship is generally ascribed to the director, Fifth Generation collaborations complicate that notion in the case of Chinese film. Academy graduates worked together in different

24.4. Qin Shutian (Jiang Wen, left) and Hu Yuyin (Liu Xiaoqing), condemned to be streetsweepers during China's Cultural Revolution, marry in a secret cer- emony in Xie Jin's melodrama on the effects of political ideology on a rural Chinese village, Furong Zhen (Hibiscus Town, 1986).

Below: 24.5. Lao Gar (Xie Yuan), assigned as a schoolteacher in a remote region of China during the Cultural Revolution, stands amid a symbolic landscape of burned tree stumps in Chen Kaige's Haizi Wang (King of the Children, 1987).

Above: 24.6. Director Chen Kaige (left) with cinematographer Gu Changwei shooting King of the Children

roles to create a new visual style for Chinese cinema: a mise-en-scène of open landscape and the colors of land and sky, in place of what they saw as artificial studio interiors in conventional Chinese film style. Chen Kaige (b. 1952) directed *Huang Tudi* (*Yellow Earth*, 1984), the first Fifth Generation film to gain international attention, and *Da Yuebing* (*The Big Parade*, 1986), using Beijing classmate Zhang Yimou (b. 1950) as cinematographer on both films. Zhang became a director with *Hong Gaoling* (*Red Sorghum*, 1987), using another classmate, Gu Changwei (b. 1957) as cinematographer. Gu Changwei also shot Chen Kaige's *Haizi Wang* (*King of the Children*, 1987).

Though Chen Kaige and Zhang Yimou worked together and with common collaborators, their styles differed. Chen's films are reminiscent of a filmmaker such as Hungary's Miklós Jancsó, using a moving camera, long shots, and long takes to focus on group activities in open spaces; Zhang's *Red Sorghum* and later works are more melodramatic, treating the social context of private lives with a rich visual palette of bright colors. But with others of their generation, they shared a common purpose: to leave behind the political abstractions and symbolism of earlier Chinese filmmakers and depict the workings of politics and ideology at a more human level. They wanted to put on film the daily life they had observed in the countryside during the Cultural Revolution. *Yellow Earth* and *Red Sorghum* are emblematic as titles: both are set in rural China during the 1930s. Chen Kaige's *The Big Parade* depicts the arduous efforts of a military squad training to march in the annual national day parade in Beijing's Tiananmen Square. *King of the Children* concerns a young man assigned to teach in a rural school during the Cultural Revolution.

As Fifth Generation films began to win admirers at overseas festivals beginning in 1987—a major breakthrough came when *Red Sorghum* won the top prize at the Berlin film festival in 1988—they came under strong criticism in China. These works were regarded as insufficiently respectful of official dogma, at the least. Their aesthetic concern for visual and narrative subtlety was treated as elitism, overly sophisticated for the dwindling mass audience. Chinese critics thus repeated the debates about socialist filmmaking that had begun in the Soviet Union in the 1920s: Should films be propaganda or art? Should they please the masses or impress the world? By the late 1980s the leading Fifth

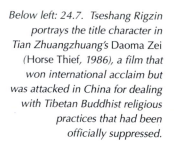

Below left: 24.7. Tseshang Rigzin portrays the title character in Tian Zhuangzhuang's Daoma Zei *(Horse Thief, 1986), a film that won international acclaim but was attacked in China for dealing with Tibetan Buddhist religious practices that had been officially suppressed.*

Right: 24.8. Songlian (Gong Li), a college student who has agreed to become the fourth wife of an older man in China during the 1920s, waits in her house while the master decides which of his wives he will sleep with each night, in Zhang Yimou's Dahong denglong gaogao gue *(Raise the Red Lantern, 1991).*

Generation directors were facing choices similar to those that confronted many filmmakers in many countries over the decades: stay at home with inadequate funding, carping criticism, and possible censorship, or go abroad, where financing and critical respect were available (but one's work might lose the cultural detail and national specificity that had made it significant in the first place). These deliberations were placed in a tragic context with the so-called Beijing massacre of June 4, 1989, when the Chinese army crushed the student and workers' movements for democracy that had broken out throughout China during the spring. The policies of cultural liberalization that had permitted students to speak out for political reform had also allowed the Fifth Generation to flourish, and after June 4 more stringent controls over expression were restored.

WU TIANMING. One of the most important figures in Chinese film, Wu Tianming (b. 1939), head of the Xi'an film studio in central China, was in the United States on June 4 and spoke out against the military crackdown. He refused to return to China and settled in Southern California, where he worked on several film projects that have not yet been produced. Originally an actor, Wu began directing films in the 1980s and made one of China's major works of the decade, *Lao Jing* (*The Old Well*, 1986), with Zhang Yimou as a cocinematographer and also a lead performer. Elected studio administrator by a vote of workers, Wu Tianming brought Fifth Generation filmmakers to Xi'an by encouraging their projects (such as *Red Sorghum* and *King of the Children*) after other studios had discouraged or tried to interfere with their previous work. In addition to Zhang Yimou and Chen Kaige, Wu Tianming

supported another of their Beijing classmates, director Tian Zhuangzhuang (b. 1952), in the production of a controversial work, *Daoma Zei* (*Horse Thief*, 1986). International critics admired its meditative beauty and ethnographic freshness, while in China the film was attacked for its lack of conventional narrative continuity and its focus on Tibetan Buddhist religious practices that had been officially suppressed.

CO-PRODUCTIONS. Despite changes in the cultural climate and the film industry after 1989, Zhang Yimou and Chen Kaige were able to continue making films in China because their international reputations enabled them to attract foreign funding. Zhang Yimou directed *Ju Dou* (1990) with Japanese financing and *Dahong denglong gaogao gue* (*Raise the Red Lantern*, 1991) with

backing ostensibly from Hong Kong; both works were nominated for a Hollywood Academy Award in the category of best foreign-language film released in the United States. Chen Kaige made *Bian Zou Bian Chang* (*Life on a String*, 1991) with production support from British and German sources. All three films were visually striking, though they lack the political resonances that energized the filmmakers' earlier work. Zhang Yimou made an effort to reconnect with Chinese audiences with *Qiu Ju Da Guansi* (*The Story of Qiu Ju*, 1992), a film set in contemporary rural China concerning a farm woman's struggles with bureaucracy, shot in a realistic style (though retaining the director's characteristic rich color) and using mainly nonprofessional performers.

Taiwan and Hou Hsiao-hsien

A name appears as an executive producer on *Raise the Red Lantern* that might have startled any spectator who recognized it: Hou Hsiao-hsien (b. 1947), better known not as a producer but as Taiwan's most important director of the 1980s. What was this film director from Taiwan doing on a Hong Kong/China co-production? The answer lies in the murky territory where cinema meets politics. The production company was not from Hong Kong but from Taiwan, though a Hong Kong entity was nominally listed so that the film did not appear to breach the official enmity between China and Taiwan. Cinema was pioneering in collaboration where politics still openly feared to tread.

Along with Edward Yang [Yang Dechang][1] (b. 1947), Hou Hsiao-hsien launched Taiwan's "new wave" in the early 1980s, developing cinema as art and social commentary in a setting dominated by commercial martial arts films and costume melodramas. Working under constraints of government censorship, Hou Hsiao-hsien forged an oblique, contemplative style built around deep-focus cinematography, focusing on intimate details of family life and subtle distinctions of class, generation, and language. Among his significant works were *Tongnian Wangshi* (*The Time to Live and the Time to Die*, 1985), *Lainlian Feng Chen* (*Dust in the Wind*, 1986), and *Niluohe Nuer* (*Daughter of the Nile*, 1987). When restrictions on dealing with Taiwan's history were eased following the death in 1988 of Chiang Ching-Kuo, son of the founder of Nationalist rule on the island, Hou made one of his most challenging works, *Beiqing Chengshi* (*A City of Sadness*, 1989), dealing with the era after 1945 when the native Taiwanese people passed from being dominated by the Japanese, who had ruled the island as a colony since 1895, to being dominated by the Nationalist Chinese from the mainland. Edward Yang, who studied filmmaking at the University

of Southern California and works in a more melodramatic style, has made films about contemporary urban life such as *Quingmei Zhuma* (*Taipei Story*, 1985) and *Kongbufenzi* (*The Terrorizer*, 1986).

Hong Kong

Hong Kong's film industry had centered on commercial martial arts and genre movies until young filmmakers inaugurated a "new wave" in the 1980s. More closely tied to commercial filmmaking than was the case with its counterparts in Taiwan and mainland China, Hong Kong's new generation gained international attention through stylish treatments of familiar themes. Works that were produced as popular entertainment for the Asian market— such as *Yanzhi Kou* (*Rouge*, 1987), a sumptuous ghost story that moves between Hong Kong in the 1930s and 1980s, directed by Stanley Kwan [Guan Jinpang] (b. 1957)—attracted art cinema audiences in other countries for their vivid production design, sensational narratives, and often incisive social commentary. John Woo [Wu Yusen] (b. 1948), who began directing action pictures in his twenties, made an international success with his eighteenth film, *Diexue Shuang Xiong* (*The Killer*, 1989), a violent but also self-reflexive underworld melodrama. Woman director Ann Hui [Xu Anhua] (b. 1947) became widely known with a film depicting brutal treatment of people attempting to escape from Vietnam, *Touben Nuhai* (*Boat People*, 1982), that was controversial because Hong Kong was frequently the destination of Vietnamese refugees. She moved the Hong Kong new wave toward a more personal cinema with an autobiographical work, *Haktou Tsauhan* (*Song of the Exile*, 1989), concerning a woman with a Chinese father and a Japanese mother.

THE END OF SOVIET CINEMA

The Soviet Union ceased to exist as a political entity following the failure of an attempted coup in August 1991; shortly thereafter Soviet leader Mikhail Gorbachev gave up his post, and with him into the proverbial dustbin of history went the policies and concepts that had animated the world during the 1980s as Gorbachev sought to overcome his country's difficulties through *glasnost*, or reform. With the former Soviet Union divided into some fifteen separate republics, most of them attempting to transform state-supported economies, the status of film production, along with many other enterprises, was in question. What is clear is that 1991 marks an end point, and film historians were only beginning to assess the impact of *glasnost* on cinema when Soviet film, as it had been known for seven decades, disappeared with the state that had supported it.

"Shelved" Films

The brief history of "*glasnost* cinema" was epitomized by an episode at the 1987 Moscow film festival, when director Alexander Askoldov (b. 1932) publicly requested that his first film, made two decades earlier but never released, be shown at the festival. It was, and Askoldov's *Komissar* (*The Commissar*, 1967) became an international success and a symbol of the Soviet Union's suppressed cinema.

"Shelved" was the film world's term for films completed but placed on a shelf in a vault, rather than screened for audiences. "There had been no reason for shelving them except bureaucratic caution," wrote a Soviet film historian in a sentence through which the entire history of a cinema, if not of a nation, might be read.[2] There were reasons aplenty, once the censors determined that a film contained material contrary to official viewpoints—on religion, for example, or on ethnicity, morality, or even editing or camera work. (In *The Commissar*, set in 1920 during Russia's civil war, the censors objected to a sequence in which a character has a prevision of the Holocaust; when the director refused to cut it, the film was shelved.)

After Askoldov's public plea, a number of films were released that had been made in the 1960s and 1970s and shelved for a decade or more. Woman director Kira Muratova (b. 1934) gained distribution for two works, *Korotkiye vstrechi* (*Brief Encounters*, 1968) and *Dolgiye provody* (*The Long Farewell*, 1971) that had been banned because their representation of relations between men and women was regarded as too gloomy. When she returned to filmmaking in the *glasnost* era and caused controversy with *Astenicheskii sindrom* (*The Weakness Syndrome*, 1989), which used profanity and displayed male frontal nudity, the film was nevertheless released. "Once the censored shelf was emptied," write film historians Andrew Horton and Michael Brashinsky, "no new shelf for glasnost films could be created."[3]

Repentance

Earlier in the *glasnost* era, important films were still subjected to delaying tactics on the part of authorities. This was the case with another controversial work, *Monanieba* (*Repentance*), made in 1984 by the Georgian director Tenghiz Abuladze (b. 1924) but not released until 1986.

24.12. Ketevan Barateli (Zeynab Botsvadze, left), a cake decorator who preserves the memory of a demolished church through her cakes, is told of the death of her town's dictatorial mayor in Mona-nieba (Repentance), directed by Georgian filmmaker Tenghiz Abuladze. Made in 1984 and released in 1986, the film was the first direct effort in Soviet film to depict totalitarian dictatorship within the Soviet Union itself.

24.13. Vera (Natalya Negoda) gives the cold shoulder to her high school classmate Andrei (Andrei Fomin) in one of the most sexually candid of Soviet glasnost films, Malenkaya Vera (Little Vera, 1988), directed by Vasily Pichul.

Repentance marked the first direct effort by a Soviet filmmaker to depict the workings of a totalitarian dictatorship within the Soviet Union itself. "Immense press coverage, a flow of letters from the moviegoers, heated debates, tears, blessings, and rejoicing on the best part of the public and the stubborn opposition and ill-feeling of a minority adhering to the principle, 'Let the sleeping dogs lie,' " greeted the film's release in the U.S.S.R., according to film historian Neya Zorkaya.[4] The film shapes its treatment of the past through surreal comedy and a narrative structure involving trial testimony, flashbacks, and dreams. The dictator, the mayor of a town in the Soviet state of Georgia, is an all-purpose figure resembling Hitler and Mussolini as well as the Soviet Union's own Joseph Stalin. He sings opera arias to his victims, and his police are spear-carrying knights in armor who greet people they are about to arrest by saying, "Peace unto this house." Yet the work's generality and narrative subjectivity do not mitigate its grim perspective on the Stalin era, particularly through the ideological double-think that clothes terror in platitudes such as (in the English-language subtitles), "That which serves the common good is moral," and, "I'm only fulfilling the will of the people."

Little Vera

Prohibitions on dealing with ideology and history were not the only taboos Soviet filmmakers sought to transgress in the 1980s. Depicting sexuality was also a goal of the new openness. The most prominent work to explore this theme was *Malenkaya Vera* (*Little Vera*, 1988), directed by Vasily Pichul (b. 1961). The film was promoted for its candor in presenting nudity and sexual relations, yet it is equally as revealing for its social realism, its portrayal of a far from utopian Soviet society of bleak industrial landscapes and disfunctional family life marked by alcoholism and violence.

With the collapse of the Soviet Union, an era of socialist aesthetics and aspirations in cinema, one of the most significant shaping forces on the medium, had come to an end in the place of its origin (though continuing in various forms in China, Cuba, and elsewhere). What was ahead for cinema in Russia, Ukraine, and other former republics of the U.S.S.R.? Hollywood films were popular in theaters, and entrepreneurs set up "videotheques" to celebrate the new freedom by showing "erotic" films on videotape. Speaking of the situation in Russia, Vasily Pichul told an interviewer that unless filmmakers can meet these different challenges, "we'll go under and we'll be reduced to making advertisements, pop promos or television programs. There's every chance that Russian cinema can become an important part of the cultural life of the country. That possibility exists, and if we don't make use of it, we'll lose it."[5]

INTERNATIONAL ART CINEMA

With the decline of the socialist model, the strongest remaining alternative to the Hollywood style of narrative fiction filmmaking was international art cinema. Supported largely through co-production by a combination of private capital, governments, and television networks, by the 1980s this film practice had become almost a broad-based genre in itself. Though there were important exceptions (to be noted), international art cinema took on a classic quality, drawing on history and literature for its sources, with a high level of visual polish and little in the way of aesthetic innovation. It occupied a third position in the global structure of mainstream cinema, with Hollywood on one side and various national film industries, producing popular narratives for domestic audiences, on the other.

Satyajit Ray and Akira Kurosawa, both of whom had been charter members, so to speak, of international art cinema when it formed in the 1950s, continued working into the 1980s (and in Kurosawa's case, the 1990s). During the 1980s new filmmakers from Japan, North America, and Europe became part of the movement, as well as from countries not previously associated

24.14. *Maia Morgenstern as Nela in* Le Chêne (The Oak, *1992*), *a Romanian film directed by Lucien Pintilie; traveling in the provinces just before the overthrow of the country's Communist dictatorship, Nela encounters a polluted land and a morally indifferent people.*

Post-Communist Cinema and Le Chêne (The Oak)

"For writers of history text-books," military historian Michael Howard has stated, "1989–1990 will mark a caesura as definitive as those of 1814–15, 1918–19, or 1945." For writers (and readers) of film history textbooks, the questions that follow the dramatic historical break caused by the collapse of Communist regimes in the former Soviet Union and Eastern Europe are: what happens next in film production, and who will pay for it?

One answer came for Romanian direc-tor Lucian Pintilie (b. 1933) when he attended a conference organized by the French Ministry of Culture in 1990 on the subject of post-Communist cinema in Eastern Europe. The French government and private French companies expressed willingness to finance co-productions, and Pintilie was offered a grant to make a film. "I was speechless," he later told an interviewer.

Well he might have been. Pintilie had not made a film for more than a decade.

As a young director he had shown exceptional ability with his first two films, *Duminica la ora 6* (*Sunday at 6*, 1965) and *Reconstituirea* (*Reconstruction*, 1969), the latter of which Mira Liehm and Antonin J. Leihm, authors of *The Most Important Art: East European Film After 1945*, describe as "the best film to emerge from Romania during the sixties, indeed one of the pinnacles of European cinema during that decade." But his work was banned or delayed from release, and in the early 1970s he was sent into exile; in the 1970s and 1980s he directed plays for theaters in France and the United States.

Following the overthrow of the regime of Romanian dictator Nicolae Ceausescu in 1989, Pintilie returned to his homeland as director of the Cinema Creation Studio of the Ministry of Romanian Culture. With his French funding, he said, "I took advantage of these exalted and confused times, which were the aftermath of the revolution, to start production immediately." The result was *Le Chêne* (*The Oak*, 1992), a film that was shot in Romania with postproduction work done in France. It played at festivals in France and the United States and was released commercially in the U.S. in 1993.

The Oak is set in 1988, in the next to last year of the Ceausescu dictatorship. After the death of her father, who had been a member of the *Securitate* (secret police), a young woman carries his ashes to a provincial town in a journey marked by brutal surprises. She passes through a country polluted morally and physically, drowning in trash and human indifference. The film's tone is angry, but its style is surreal tragicomedy. It marks an assured and impressive beginning for a possible new era in cinema.

"Co-production is the only means of survival for our cinema," Pintilie has said, "because no matter how high the costs in Romania, workers can still be found for very cheap. Let's take advantage of our misery. We can still produce important films for not a lot of money. If we do not understand this, in two years at most, our cinema will close shop."

with art films for international audiences. Several broke with the classic mold at least to the extent of treating contemporary life, and sometimes more.

Satyajit Ray

Ray's career in the context of Indian cinema marks a vivid case in point, and the title of his 1984 film, *Ghare-Baire* (*The Home and the World*), seems to symbolize the two poles of Indian filmmaking. In the 1980s India produced by far the largest number of films of any country—nearly one thousand annually. In the genre tradition established in the 1930s, many were highly codified music-dramas featuring enormously popular stars. Avidly attended by Indian audiences, these works were seen elsewhere in Asia and Africa but rarely by non-Indians in North America or Europe. Ray was the only Indian filmmaker widely known to international art cinema audiences. His most familiar work still remained his earliest, the Apu trilogy (see Chapter 15) and other films made between 1955 and 1960, when he was an exciting figure in the art cinema movement then just emerging.

The Home and the World was Ray's twenty-sixth feature in a thirty-year career to that point. Funded by the National Film Development Corporation of India, a government body, it became one of the director's most popular films. It was based on a novel by Indian writer Rabindraneth Tagore concerning a love triangle amid political struggles in early twentieth century Bengal. With subtle color cinematography enhancing its period mise-en-scène, the film depicts a clash between two kinds of nationalism, one presented as narrow and divisive, the other as cosmopolitan and humane. It is not difficult to see the work also as a parable about two kinds of filmmaking, one for home, one for the world.

Akira Kurosawa

Kurosawa in Japan was in a similar position, though by the 1980s Japan's movie audience had been heavily depleted by competition from television. More than a decade Ray's senior, Kurosawa became the medium's ranking elder in the 1980s as had been Buñuel in the previous decade and figures such as Ford and Hitchcock in the 1960s. Nevertheless, Kurosawa found it almost

Left: 24.15. Nikhilesh (Victor Banerjee, right) accompanies his wife Bimala (Swatilekha Chatterjee) along the corridor that marks the symbolic bridge between private and public spheres in Satyajit Ray's Ghare-Baire *(The Home and the World, 1984).*

Above: 24.16. Director Akira Kurosawa on location for Kagemusha *(1980) with American directors Francis Ford Coppola (center) and George Lucas (right), whose efforts to find an American distributor for the film helped secure the funds to produce it.*

Left: 24.17. Members of a family faction and their retainers in Akira Kurosawa's Ran *(1985), a version of Shakespeare's* King Lear *set in sixteenth-century Japan; from left, Taro Takatora Ichimonji (Akira Terao), Jiro Masatora Ichimonji (Jinpachi Nezu), Saburo Naotora Ichimonji (Daisuke Ryu), Kageyu Ikoma (Kazuo Kato), and Tango Hirayama (Masayuki Yui).*

24.18. Grandfather's death confronts a modern Japanese family with the fact that they don't know how to conduct themselves at a traditional funeral in Juzo Itami's popular comedy Ososhiki (The Funeral, 1984).

impossible to raise money for his projects within his own country. "It was difficult for outsiders to understand why Japan's foremost director was not working," film historian Audie Bock has written. "The basic reason was that the Japanese film industry had entered a decline in the late 1960's and the budget for a Kurosawa film was no longer affordable."[6]

This judgment seemed borne out when Kurosawa's *Dodesukaden* (1970), running more than four hours, became his first film to lose money at the box office. Discouraged and beset by illness, the director attempted suicide in 1971. His film career was ultimately rescued by overseas financing. *Dersu Uzala* (1975) was funded by the Soviet Union and made in that country. *Kagemusha* (1980) became possible only when Francis Ford Coppola and George Lucas persuaded Twentieth Century-Fox to purchase foreign distribution rights. And *Ran* (1985) was co-produced with a French company. These last two works, both set in feudal Japan, told tragic stories amid visual splendor in costume and mise-en-scène. Seeming to regain energy as he neared his eightieth birthday, Kurosawa made *Akira Kurosawa's Dreams* (1990) for a Hollywood company and, returning to Japan, directed *Hachigatsu-no-Kyoshikyoku* (*Rhapsody in August*, 1990), a film concerned with a family's memories of the dropping of an atomic bomb on Nagasaki, Japan, in 1945 at the end of World War II.

Juzo Itami

The principal new figure of Japanese mainstream filmmaking who became part of international art cinema was Juzo Itami (b. 1933). An actor and son of a film director, Itami was past fifty when he completed his first film as director, *Ososhiki* (*The Funeral*, 1984). A popular hit in Japan, the film was a bittersweet comedy about a modern family's effort to conduct a funeral when a grandfather dies. They watch an instructional video on how to behave and make the "correct expressions" at a funeral, finding their legs unaccustomed to the kneeling and squatting required by tradi-

tional ceremonies. Itami went on to make additional comedies that gained greater success overseas than in Japan, including *Tampopo* (1986), on the subject of eating, and *Marusa no Onna* (*A Taxing Woman*, 1987), featuring a woman tax inspector.

Québec Film

Filmmaking in Canada's French-speaking province of Québec was marginal twice over—to the country's dominant English-language culture, and to the cinema of France. It was further burdened by political suppression in the 1970s and thereafter by ill-considered government policies that hampered the development of Canadian filmmakers. Nevertheless, followers of the medium were aware that exceptional work was being produced by Québecois filmmakers, including films such as *Mon Oncle Antoine* (*My Uncle Antoine*, 1971), directed by Claude Jutra (1930–1986); *Les Ordres* (*Orders*, 1974), directed by Michel Brault, who had been cinematographer on the famous French cinema verité film *Chronicle of a Summer*; and *Les Bons Débarras* (*Good Riddance*, 1980), directed by Francis Mankiewicz (b. 1944).

When Canadian film policy changed in the 1980s to support domestic filmmakers, however, director Denys Arcand seized the opportunity to gain a foothold in international art cinema with a film whose title alone assured attention: *Le Déclin de l'empire américain* (*The Decline of the American Empire*, 1986). The work centered in fact on the sexual lives and frank sexual talk among a group of history professors; the title derives from a professor's theory that societies decline when personal desires take precedence over common goals. Choosing to continue working from the margin, even after this success brought offers from Hollywood and Europe, Arcand made *Jésus de Montréal* (*Jesus of Montreal*, 1989), concerning an actor who portrays Jesus in a Passion Play and himself becomes a Christ-like critic of materialism and immorality. Québec filmmaking's status in international art cinema was enhanced with the critical success at the 1992 Cannes film festival of *Léolo* (1992), a film by director Jean-Claude Lauzon (b. 1953) concerning the difficult family life of a small boy in Montreal.

24.19. A women's sauna is an occasion for frank sexual talk in Québec filmmaker Denys Arcand's Le Déclin de l'empire américain (The Decline of the American Empire, 1986); clock-wise from top left: Diane (Louise Portal), Dominique (Dominique Michel), Louise (Dorothée Berryman), and Danielle (Geneviève Rioux).

The Films of Aki Kaurismäki

One of the pleasures of cinema is the possibility of discovering the world through the medium—of continually finding films from faraway places with unfamiliar landscapes and fresh perspectives. But in an era of co-productions and international cinema culture, what is it exactly that one discovers? The question is prompted by the emergence of Aki Kaurismäki (b. 1957) of Finland as a significant new figure on the world film scene in the 1990s.

It's probably fair to say that few if any Finnish filmmakers attained international recognition before Kaurismäki and his brother Mika (b. 1955) began making films (first together, then separately) in the 1980s. Their first project was *Valehtelija* (*The Liar*, 1980), Mika's diploma film at the Hochschule für Fernsehen und Film (Higher School for Television and Film) in Munich, Germany, which Aki wrote and in which he performed. "We were greatly influenced by Godard and Truffaut," Aki has said. "We stole shamelessly from them."

Aki Kaurismäki's own films as a director—beginning in 1983, he has made nine in the period of a decade—have continued to draw on an eclectic mix of French New Wave, European art cinema, Hollywood film noir, and B-picture road movies. As with some other filmmakers of his generation, his works seem to represent a heritage of moviegoing rather than any specific cultural time or place. Yet the lack of a specific social referent (or perhaps it should be described as an excess of social referents) does not detract from the pleasures of his films. Two works released in 1989, *Leningrad Cowboys Go America* and *Tulitikkutehtaan Tytto* (*The Match Factory Girl*), demonstrate his range and style.

Leningrad Cowboys is an absurdist road movie concerning a Soviet rock band's bumbling travels through the United States to Mexico. Dressed in dark suits, with long pointed shoes and hair arranged in foot-long forelocks, they carry with them a coffin containing the body of a band member who apparently froze to death while practicing outdoors (the coffin has holes to allow the deceased's long pointed shoes and forelock, as well as the handle of his guitar, to protrude, and is packed with ice to hold beer). When they find success playing at Mexican weddings, a sip of tequila revives the apparent dead man.

The Match Factory Girl is completely different. "I decided to do a picture that would make Robert Bresson seem like a director of epic action pictures," Aki Kaurismäki has said: in other words, to make a film that would be more austere than the most austere. The oppression and betrayal of a Finnish worker, and her acts of revenge, are shot with long takes from a camera that rarely pans or moves. But the implacable logic of this bleak film is exhilarating. More recently Kaurismäki directed *I Hired a Contract Killer* (1990) in Britain and *La Vie de Bohème* (1992), based on the book that was the source for Puccini's opera, in Paris.

24.20. From left, bohemians Rodolfo (Matti Pellonpää), Marcel (Andre Wilms), and Schaunard (Kari Väänänen) in Aki Kaurismäki's La Vie de Bohème (1992)

24.21. Pepa Marcos (Carmen Maura) seems to like the idea of a bed on fire in Spanish filmmaker Pedro Almodóvar's Mujeres al borde de un ataque de nervous (Women on the Verge of a Nervous Breakdown, 1988).

Pedro Almodóvar

No filmmaker made a more sensational international debut in the 1980s than Spain's Pedro Almodóvar (b. 1951). In the cultural ferment following the end of Francisco Franco's dictatorship in Spain, Almodóvar moved from alternative filmmaking in Super-8 and 16mm formats to a transgressive position within the Spanish and international art cinemas. His concerns with homosexuality and melodrama made him appear a successor to Germany's Rainer Werner Fassbinder (see Chapter 21), but Almodóvar crafted a sunnier, more bizarre combination of comedy and disorder: he could be tragic without quite being serious. A series of features from 1982 to 1987—including works with provocative titles like Laberinto de pasiones (Labyrinth of Passions, 1982) and La ley del deseo (Law of Desire, 1987)—built a cult following in Europe and North America. He broke through to wider audiences with Mujeres al borde de un ataque de nervous (Women on the Verge of a Nervous Breakdown, 1988). A key figure in Almodóvar's work was Carmen Maura (b. 1946), a versatile comic performer who appeared in nearly all his features through Women on the Verge. Subsequent films such as ¡Átame! (Tie Me Up! Tie Me Down!, 1989) and Tascones lejanos (High Heels, 1991)—which happened to be without Maura—raised the question whether Almodóvar's style of excess could survive translation to the mainstream.

THE GLOBAL VOICE OF CINEMA

By the last decade of the twentieth century, cinema had come closer to becoming a global medium of communication—not just a form whereby messages went from the center to the periphery, but one in which messages from the periphery could reach and affect the center. In an age of television and facsimile machines, film might appear expensive, slow, and outmoded for effective communicative effort, yet as long as imagination and artistry were powerful tools to open minds and shape visions, cinema appeared to hold a fundamental place in global culture as the medium began its second century.

Yilmaz Güney

The world has its share of "unknown" cinemas—unknown not to their practitioners and audiences but to mainstream criticism and historiography. Indian film qualified as an unknown cinema in this sense despite being numerically the world's largest; a similar case was Turkey, where in the early 1970s nearly three hundred films were produced annually, mostly action films and popular melodramas (as in India). But Turkey became known to the cinema community when Yol (The Way, 1982), by filmmaker Yilmaz Güney (1937–1984), won a top prize at the Cannes film festival.

Güney had been a famous actor at the height of Turkey's film productivity, but when he turned to directing in the 1970s he clashed with the country's repressive regime. A political activist, he was accused of sheltering students wanted by police and was imprisoned more than two years without trial; after his release in 1974 he was almost immediately again arrested on a charge of murder and sentenced to twenty-four years in prison. Nevertheless while in prison he was able to prepare the script for Yol, and Serif Gören took over as director. In 1981 Güney escaped and went to Switzerland, where he edited the film (Swiss and German companies co-produced the work). After Yol he made his last film, Le Mur (The Wall, 1983), in France. Both Yol and The Wall deal with prison life in Turkey, a country the filmmaker accuses of being a prison on both sides of the wall. Though the films are not completely immune from the power relations they mean to oppose (for example, they seem to accept the dependent social status of women in Turkish society), within their limited framework they are powerful exposés of oppression.

The Official Story

Another work concerning oppression became the biggest international success in Argentina's film history—La historia oficial (The Official Story, 1985), directed by Luis Puenzo (b. 1949), which won a Hollywood Academy Award for foreign-language film. The

24.22. Seyit Ali (Tarik Akan) vainly tries to carry his wife, Ziné (Serif Sezer), on a trek through heavy snow in Yol (The Way, 1982), a film by Turkish filmmaker Yilmaz Güney, who completed the work in Switzerland after escaping from a prison in Turkey; Serif Gören took over as director during Güney's imprisonment.

24.23. Guards conduct an inspection of young prisoners in Yilmaz Güney's Le Mur (The Wall, 1983), a film the director made in France concerning prison life in Turkey.

film is set in 1983, in the waning days of the military dictatorship that ruled Argentina from 1976 and waged a "dirty war" of torture and murder against alleged subversives. It centers on a middle-class teacher of Argentine history in a high school who gradually discovers that the infant she had adopted was born in prison to a mother who had been seized and became one of the "disappeared."

The teacher's crisis of conscience is echoed in her classroom. "No people can survive without memory," she piously tells her pupils. "History is the memory of the people." But her sanctimony is undercut as she learns in her own life how memory can be elided, distorted, suppressed. "History," cries a rebellious student, "is written by assassins." Portraying the painful enlightenment of a conventional woman, Norma Aleandro (b. 1941), who had herself fled the country in 1976, won an award for her performance at the Cannes film festival.

Brazilian Cinema

A military dictatorship lasting several decades ended in Brazil in the 1980s, and Brazilian filmmakers also turned to history as a setting for their reflections on oppression. Nelson Pereira dos Santos made *Memorias do carcere* (*Memories of Prison*, 1984) based on memoirs of imprisonment during the 1930s by the writer whose novel was the source for the director's Cinema Novo

classic *Barren Lives* (see Chapter 18). Oppression in class and gender terms was the subject of *A hora de estrela* (*Hour of the Star*, 1985), directed by Suzana Amaral (b. 1933) from a novel by Brazilian writer Clarice Lispector. Amaral was an unusual figure who began filmmaking in her late thirties after raising nine children, went to film schools in Brazil and the United States, and made *Hour of the Star*, her first feature, past the age of fifty. Though some critics found the film's treatment of a young peasant woman's bleak city life to be in the Cinema Novo tradition, the

Left: 24.24. Returning from a seven-year exile, Ana (Chunchuna Villafañe, lett) reveals to her old schoolfriend Alicia (Norma Aleandro) that she was tortured by the military during Argentina's "dirty war," in Luis Puenzo's La historia oficial (The Official Story, 1985). Ana also tells Alicia that babies born to women in prison were given to supporters of the regime, news that impels Alicia on a quest to discover the true origins of her adopted child.

Above: 24.25. Macabéa (Marcélia Cartaxo, right), a lonely peasant woman working in the city, strikes up a short-lived friendship with a building worker, Olímpico (José Dumont), in A hora de estrela (Hour of the Star, 1985), directed by Brazilian film-maker Suzana Amaral.

director rejected any connection. Her work indeed lacked the militancy of the earlier movement, yet it provided ample opportunity for spectator involvement in its social and human themes through a combination of naturalism, fatalism, and fantasy. There was also a memorable script, by the director and Alfredo Oroz: when her boyfriend rejects the young woman he tells her, "You're a hair in my soup."

Middle Eastern Cinema

Among the "unknown" cinemas at the end of the twentieth century, in the sense defined above, were those of Middle Eastern countries—including Iran, the Arab world, and Israel. All films (including Hollywood's) contain cultural codes that may be indecipherable to foreigners, but the problem is exacerbated for cinemas such as those in the Middle East where the cultures themselves are not familiar to outsiders. Even in a work widely distributed internationally, such as the Israeli film *Me'Achorei Hasoragim* (*Beyond the Walls*, 1984), overseas spectators are likely to overlook the issue of ethnic differences among the Israeli characters that is an important narrative element and of which domestic audiences would be keenly aware.

Directed by Uri Barbash (b. 1946), *Beyond the Walls* gained international attention for its treatment of the conflict between Israelis and Palestinians. Set within a prison (which had become

Above: 24.26. Guards overlook a prison courtyard in the Israeli film Me'Achorei Hasoragim *(Beyond the Walls, 1984), directed by Uri Barbash.*

Below: 24.27. A contemplative moment between bride and bridegroom in Noce en Galilée *(Wedding in Galilee, 1987), by the Palestinian director Michel Khleifi*

Top: 24.28. Students in a Mali village prepare for high school examinations in Finyé (The Wind, 1982), directed by Souleymane Cissé.

Above: 24.29. A young boy, Bila (Noufou Ouedraogo, standing at center rear), observes the women of his village in Yaaba (1989), directed by Burkina Faso film-maker Idrissa Ouedraogo.

24.30. Idrissa Ouedraogo of Burkina Faso, director of Yaaba (1989) and Tilai (1990)

in the 1980s one of cinema's leading metaphors), the film follows Yilmaz Güney in suggesting that society itself has become a prison—or, in this case, has shackled itself through the perpetuation of stereotypes and divisive violence. Though cinematically conventional and somewhat contrived, *Beyond the Walls* nevertheless searches for a new basis of cooperation between Israelis and Palestinians within the symbolic space "beyond the walls."

A Palestinian treatment of similar themes was *Noce en Galilée* (*Wedding in Galilee*, 1987). This was the first feature of Palestinian director Michel Khleifi (b. 1950), who had studied film in Belgium and gained funding for the work from Belgian and French government sources. Set in a West Bank village, under Israeli military occupation since the 1967 war, the film clearly represents occupation as a kind of imprisonment (and an old man recalls that the Turks and the British had been earlier occupiers of the same territory). The narrative concerns a village leader's agreement to invite the Israeli military governor to his son's wedding in order to obtain permission to continue the ceremony past the curfew hour. Though the wedding is also a kind of metaphorical space, the film widens out to show how politics informs not only group relations between Palestinians and Israelis but also the basic ties of family and society, the relations between parents and children, women and men, even bride and groom.

African Cinema

No less unknown was the cinema of sub-Saharan or black Africa. Some observers suggested an antipathy on the part of European festivals and distributors to African films dealing with the history of European colonialism in Africa. An example cited is *Camp de Thiaroye* (*Camp Thiaroye*, 1988), codirected by the noted Senegalese filmmaker Ousmane Sembene (see Chapter 18) with Thierno Faty Sow; the film is set in Senegal in 1944 and deals with discrimination and brutality against black African soldiers who had fought with the Free French Army during World War II. The African films that gained broad international exhibition in the 1980s were set in enclosed tribal worlds, with apparently timeless themes.

After Sembene, the most widely known African filmmaker was Souleymane Cissé (b. 1940) of Mali, who studied for eight years at the Moscow film school as a photographer, projectionist, and director. His principal films, *Finyé* (*The Wind*, 1982) and *Yeelen* (*The Light*, 1987), emphasized landscape, myth, and cultural tradition. "I hope in the future to be able to make films in which the ancient depths of African culture will surge up again," Cissé has said. "A cinema imitating that of America or Europe will be in vain. We must immerse ourselves in our own sources."[7] A similar impulse animated the work of Idrissa Ouedraogo (b. 1954) of the West African country Burkina Faso (formerly Upper Volta), whose films *Yaaba* (1989) and *Tilai* (1990) were also concerned

with traditional village life. Both these works were made as co-productions with France and Switzerland, with additional funding support from sources in Britain, Italy, and Germany.

THE PRESENT AND THE PAST

"We should be wary of talking about origins," were the words with which this book began. As motion pictures celebrate their centennial, we should again be wary of making claims not only for beginnings but also for the present and the future. A hundred years of cinema comprise a remarkable epoch: they have witnessed the development of a vast commerce, a dazzling technology, sophisticated forms of popular entertainment, many enduring works of art (and documentation), and untold social consequences. Yet the past guarantees no future. Film history (as was also noted at the beginning) may become some other medium's prehistory. "Virtual reality" images and interactive narratives are already at hand as the twentieth century comes to a close.

Nor does the present guarantee the past. History is never finished, and rarely stays the same for long. As the writing of this book comes to an end, film history looks different than it did when the work was started. Countries and their film cultures have disappeared, lost or suppressed films have reappeared. The past is not a seamless whole, to be packaged and put away, but a site to be rediscovered, struggled over, and reshaped. This book has sought to lay the groundwork for readers to participate in the invigorating and unending task, the remaking of film history.

Notes

1. Taiwanese and Hong Kong filmmakers frequently adopt English-language first names; when that is the case their Chinese names are given in brackets.
2. Neya Zorkaya, *The Illustrated History of Soviet Cinema* (New York: Hippocrene Books, 1989), p. 305. The book was "published by arrangement with Novosti Press Agency Publishing House, Moscow, U.S.S.R."
3. Andrew Horton and Michael Brashinsky, *The Zero Hour: Glasnost and Soviet Cinema in Transition* (Princeton, N.J.: Princeton Univ. Press, 1992), p. 35.
4. *The Illustrated History of the Soviet Cinema*, pp. 305–6.
5. Quoted in Evgeny Tsymbal, "Into a New World," *Sight and Sound*, Vol. 2, No. 7 (NS) (November 1992), p. 33.
6. Audie Bock, "Translator's Preface," in Akira Kurosawa, *Something Like an Autobiography*, trans. Audie E. Bock (New York: Alfred A. Knopf, 1982), p. vii.
7. Quoted in James Leahy, "Stories of the Past—Souleymane Cissé," *Monthly Film Bulletin*, Vol. 55 (November 1988), p. 348.

Selected Bibliography

This bibliography offers a selection of works in English for further reading and reference. Many titles cited for early chapters, such as biographies, critical studies, and national cinema histories, also pertain to later chapters.

GENERAL REFERENCE

Finler, Joel W. *The Hollywood Story*. New York: Crown, 1988.

Gray, John. *Blacks in Film and Television: A Pan-African Bibliography of Films, Filmmakers, and Performers*. New York: Greenwood Press, 1990.

Halliwell, Leslie. *Halliwell's Film Guide*, 8th edition. Edited by John Walker. New York: HarperCollins, 1991.

Hanson, Patricia King, and Stephen L. Hanson. *Film Review Index, Vol. 1: 1882–1949, Vol. 2: 1950–1985*. Phoenix, Ariz.: Oryx Press, 1986, 1987.

Katz, Ephraim. *The Film Encyclopedia*. New York: Crowell, 1979.

Kuhn, Annette, with Susannah Radstone, eds. *Women in Film: An International Guide*. New York: Fawcett Columbine, 1990.

Leonard, Harold, ed. *The Film Index: A Bibliography, Vol. 1. The Film as Art*. New York: The Museum of Modern Art, 1941, 1966.

MacCann, Richard Dyer, and Edward S. Perry, eds. *The New Film Index: A Bibliography of Magazine Articles in English, 1930–1970*. New York: Dutton, 1975.

Magill, Frank N., ed. *Magill's Survey of Cinema: English Language Films: First Series*. Englewood Cliffs, N.J.: Salem Press, 1980.

———, ed. *Magill's Survey of Cinema: Foreign Language Films*. Englewood Cliffs, N.J.: Salem Press, 1985.

Monaco, James, and the editors of Baseline. *The Encyclopedia of Film*. New York: Perigee Books, 1991.

Roud, Richard, ed. *Cinema: A Critical Dictionary*. New York: Viking Press, 1980.

Slide, Anthony, ed. *The American Film Industry: A Historical Dictionary*. New York: Greenwood Press, 1986.

———. *The International Film Industry: A Historical Dictionary*. New York: Greenwood Press, 1989.

Thomas, Nicholas, ed. *The International Dictionary of Films and Filmmakers*, 2nd ed. Chicago: St. James Press, 1990.

FILM HISTORY AND HISTORIOGRAPHY

Allen, Robert C., and Douglas Gomery. *Film History: Theory and Practice*. New York: Alfred A. Knopf, 1985.

Bordwell, David, Janet Staiger, and Kristin Thompson. *The Classical Hollywood Cinema: Film Style & Mode of Production to 1960*. New York: Columbia Univ. Press, 1985.

Ferro, Marc. *Cinema and History*. Translated by Naomi Greene. Detroit: Wayne State Univ. Press, 1988.

Gomery, Douglas. *Shared Pleasures: A History of Movie Presentation in the United States*. Madison: Univ. of Wisconsin Press, 1992.

Jowett, Garth. *Film: The Democratic Art*. Boston: Little, Brown, 1976.

Kaes, Anton. *From Hitler to Heimat: The Return of History as Film*. Cambridge, Mass.: Harvard Univ. Press, 1989.

Mellencamp, Patricia, and Philip Rosen, eds. *Cinema Histories, Cinema Practices*. Frederick, Md.: Univ. Publications of America, 1984.

O'Connor, John, ed. *Image as Artifact: The Historical Analysis of Film and Television*. Malibar, Fla.: Krieger, 1990.

Sklar, Robert. *Movie-Made America: A Cultural History of American Movies*. New York: Random House, 1975.

Sklar, Robert, and Charles Musser, eds. *Resisting Images: Essays on Cinema and History*. Philadelphia: Temple Univ. Press, 1990.

Sorlin, Pierre. *European Cinemas, European Societies*. London: Routledge, 1991.

———. *The Film in History: Restaging the Past*. Totowa, N.J.: Barnes & Noble, 1980.

Staiger, Janet. *Interpreting Films: Studies in the Historical Reception of American Cinema*. Princeton, N.J.: Princeton Univ. Press, 1992.

Williams, Alan. *Republic of Images: A History of French Filmmaking*. Cambridge, Mass.: Harvard Univ. Press, 1992.

FILM THEORY AND CRITICISM

Arnheim, Rudolf. *Film as Art*. Berkeley: Univ. of California Press, 1957.

Bazin, André. *What Is Cinema?* Vols. I and II. Translated by H. Gray. Berkeley: Univ. of California Press, 1971.

Bordwell, David. *Narration in the Fiction Film*. Madison: Univ. of Wisconsin Press, 1985.

Burnett, Ron. *Explorations in Film Theory: Selected Essays from Ciné-Tracts*. Bloomington: Indiana Univ. Press, 1991.

Carroll, Noël. *Mystifying Movies: Fads and Fallacies in Contemporary Film Theory*. New York: Columbia Univ. Press, 1988.

Caughie, John, ed. *Theories of Authorship: A Reader*. London: Routledge & Kegan Paul, 1981.

Hoberman, J. *Vulgar Modernism: Writings on Movies and Other Media*. Philadelphia: Temple Univ. Press, 1991.

Mast, Gerald, Marshall Cohen, and Leo Braudy, eds. *Film Theory and Criticism: Introductory Readings*, 4th ed. New York: Oxford Univ. Press, 1992.

Metz, Christian. *The Imaginary Signifier: Psychoanalysis and the Cinema*. Translated by Celia Britton, Annwyl Williams, Ben Brewster, and Alfred Guzzetti. Bloomington: Indiana Univ. Press, 1982.

Mulvey, Laura. *Visual and Other Pleasures*. Bloomington: Indiana Univ. Press, 1989.

Naremore, James. *Acting in the Cinema*. Berkeley: Univ. of California Press, 1988.

Nichols, Bill, ed. *Movies and Methods: An Anthology*. Berkeley: Univ. of California Press, 1976. *Volume II*. Berkeley: Univ. of California Press, 1985.

Penley, Constance, ed. *Feminism and Film Theory*. New York: Routledge, 1988.

Rosen, Philip, ed. *Narrative, Apparatus, Ideology: A Film Theory Reader*. New York: Columbia Univ. Press, 1986.

Stam, Robert. *Subversive Pleasures: Bakhtin, Cultural Criticism, and Film*. Baltimore: Johns Hopkins Univ. Press, 1989.

Chapter 1: Cinema, Society, and Science

Barnes, John. *The Beginnings of the Cinema in England*. New York: Barnes & Noble, 1976.

Barnouw, Erik. *The Magician and the Cinema*. New York: Oxford Univ. Press, 1981.

Chanan, Michael. *The Dream That Kicks*. London: Routledge & Kegan Paul, 1980.

Coe, Brian. *The History of Movie Photography*. New York: Eastview Editions, 1981.

Cook, Olive. *Movement in Two Dimensions*. London: Hutchinson, 1963.

Fielding, Raymond, ed. *A Technological History of Motion Pictures and Television*. Berkeley: Univ. of California Press, 1967.

Frazer, John. *Artificially Arranged Scenes: The Films of Georges Méliès*. Boston: G. K. Hall, 1979.

Hammond, Paul. *Marvelous Méliès*. New York: St. Martin's, 1974.

Hendricks, Gordon. *Eadweard Muybridge: The Father of the Motion Picture*. New York: Grossman, 1975.

———. *The Edison Motion Picture Myth*. Berkeley: Univ. of California Press, 1961.

MacDonnell, Kevin. *Eadweard Muybridge, the Man Who Invented the Moving Picture*. Boston: Little, Brown, 1972.

Reiniger, Lotte. *Shadow Theatres and Shadow Films*. New York: Watson-Guptill, 1970.

Chapter 2: Early Cinema

Blaché, Alice Guy. *The Memoirs of Alice Guy Blaché*. Translated by Robert and Simone Blaché, ed. Anthony Slide. Metuchen, N.J.: Scarecrow Press, 1986.

Bruno, Giuliana. *Streetwalking on a Ruined Map: Cultural Theory and the City Films of Elvira Notari*. Princeton, N.J.: Princeton Univ. Press, 1993.

Burch, Noël. *Life to Those Shadows*. Translated and edited by Ben Brewster. Berkeley: Univ. of California Press, 1990.

Elsaesser, Thomas, with Adam Barker, eds. *Early Cinema: Space— Frame—Narrative*. London: British Film Institute, 1990.

Fell, John L. *Film and the Narrative Tradition*. Norman: Univ. of Oklahoma Press, 1974.

———, ed. *Film Before Griffith*. Berkeley: Univ. of California Press, 1983.

Gunning, Tom. *D. W. Griffith and the Origins of American Narrative Film: The Early Years at Biograph*. Urbana: Univ. of Illinois Press, 1991.

Hansen, Miriam. *Babel and Babylon: Spectatorship in American Silent Film*. Cambridge, Mass.: Harvard Univ. Press, 1991.

Iris, No. 11 (Summer 1990), Special Issue, "Early Cinema Audiences."

Musser, Charles. *Before the Nickelodeon: Edwin S. Porter and the Edison Manufacturing Company*. Berkeley: Univ. of California Press, 1991.

———. *The Emergence of Cinema: The American Screen to 1907*. New York: Scribner's, 1990.

Musser, Charles, in collaboration with Carol Nelson. *High-Class Moving Pictures: Lyman H. Howe and the Forgotten Era of Traveling Exhibition, 1880–*

1920. Princeton, N.J.: Princeton Univ. Press, 1991.

Pearson, Roberta E. *Eloquent Gestures: The Transformation of Performance Style in the Griffith Biograph Films.* Berkeley: Univ. of California Press, 1992.

Chapter 3: Film as Art and Industry

Bowser, Eileen. *The Transformation of Cinema, 1907–1915.* New York: Scribner's, 1990.

Brownlow, Kevin. *Behind the Mask of Innocence.* New York: Alfred A. Knopf, 1990.

Budd, Mike, ed. *The Cabinet of Dr. Caligari: Texts, Contexts, Histories.* New Brunswick, N.J.: Rutgers Univ. Press, 1990.

Cherchi Usai, Paolo, and Lorenzo Codelli, eds. *Before Caligari: German Cinema, 1895–1920/Prima di Caligari: Cinema tedesco, 1895–1920.* Pordenone: Biblioteca dell'Immagine, 1990.

———. *The Path to Hollywood, 1911–1920/Sulla via do Hollywood, 1911–1920.* Pordenone: Biblioteca dell'Immagine, 1988.

Crafton, Donald. *Before Mickey: The Animated Film, 1898–1928.* Cambridge, Mass.: MIT Press, 1982.

———. *Emile Cohl, Caricature, and Film.* Princeton, N.J.: Princeton Univ. Press, 1990.

deCordova, Richard. *Picture Personalities: The Emergence of the Star System in America.* Urbana: Univ. of Illinois Press, 1990.

Leprohon, Pierre. *The Italian Cinema.* Translated by Roger Greaves and Oliver Stallybrass. New York: Praeger, 1966, 1972.

Mottram, Ron. *The Danish Cinema before Dreyer.* Metuchen, N.J.: Scarecrow Press, 1988.

Robinson, David. *Chaplin: His Life and Art.* New York: McGraw-Hill, 1985.

Schickel, Richard. *D. W. Griffith: An American Life.* New York: Simon & Schuster, 1984.

Silva, Fred, ed. *Focus on The Birth of a Nation.* Englewood Cliffs, N.J.: Prentice-Hall, 1971.

Chapter 4: The Global Spread of Film

Anderson, Joseph L., and Donald Richie. *The Japanese Film: Art and Industry,* Expanded ed. Princeton, N.J.: Princeton Univ. Press, 1982.

Barnard, Tim, ed. *Argentine Cinema.* Toronto: Nightwood Editions, 1986.

Barnouw, Erik, and S. Krishnaswamy. *Indian Film,* 2nd ed. New York: Oxford Univ. Press, 1980.

Cherchi Usai, Paolo, and Lorenzo Codelli. *The DeMille Legacy/L'eredità DeMille.* Pordenone: Biblioteca dell'Immagine, 1991.

Hall, Ben M. *The Best Remaining Seats: The Story of the Golden Age of the Movie Palace.* New York: Bramhall House, 1961.

Johnson, Randal. *The Film Industry in Brazil: Culture and the State.* Pittsburgh: Univ. of Pittsburgh Press, 1987.

Johnson, Randal, and Robert Stam, eds. *Brazilian Cinema.* Austin: Univ. of Texas Press, 1982.

King, John. *Magical Reels: A History of Cinema in Latin America.* London: Verso, 1990.

Leyda, Jay. *Dianying: An Account of Films and the Film Audience in China.* Cambridge, Mass.: MIT Press, 1972.

Mora, Carl J. *Mexican Cinema: Reflections of a Society,* rev. ed. Berkeley: Univ. of California Press, 1989.

Ramachandran, T. M., ed. *70 Years of Indian Cinema*

(1913–1983). Bombay: Cinema India-International, 1985.

Sharp, Dennis. *The Picture Palace, and Other Buildings for the Movies.* New York: Praeger, 1969.

Thompson, Kristin. *Exporting Entertainment: America in the World Film Market 1907–1934.* London: British Film Institute, 1985.

Chapter 5: Hollywood in the 1920s

Brownlow, Kevin. *The Parade's Gone By. . . .* New York: Alfred A. Knopf, 1969.

———. *The War, the West, and the Wilderness.* New York: Alfred A. Knopf, 1979.

Durgnat, Raymond, and Scott Simmon. *King Vidor, American.* Berkeley: Univ. of California Press, 1988.

Everson, William K. *American Silent Film.* New York: Oxford Univ. Press, 1978.

Hake, Sabine. *Passions and Deceptions: The Early Films of Ernst Lubitsch.* Princeton, N.J.: Princeton Univ. Press, 1992.

Koszarski, Richard. *An Evening's Entertainment: The Age of the Silent Feature Picture, 1915–1928.* New York: Scribner's, 1990.

———. *The Man You Loved to Hate: Erich von Stroheim and Hollywood.* New York: Oxford Univ. Press, 1983.

Merritt, Russell, and J. B. Kaufman. *Walt in Wonderland: The Silent Films of Walt Disney/Nel paese delle meraviglie: I cartoni animati muti di Walt Disney.* Pordenone: Biblioteca dell'Immagine, 1992.

Petrie, Graham. *Hollywood Destinies: European Directors in America, 1922–1931.* London: Routledge & Kegan Paul, 1985.

Rotha, Paul. *Robert J. Flaherty: A Biography.* Edited by Jay Ruby. Philadelphia: Univ. of Pennsylvania Press, 1983.

Chapter 6: The Cinemas of Europe

Abel, Richard. *French Cinema: The First Wave, 1915–1929.* Princeton, N.J.: Princeton Univ. Press, 1984.

———. *French Film Theory and Criticism: A History/Anthology, Vol. I, 1907–1929.* Princeton, N.J.: Princeton Univ. Press, 1988.

Bordwell, David. *The Films of Carl-Theodore Dreyer.* Berkeley: Univ. of California Press, 1981.

Eisner, Lotte H. *Fritz Lang.* New York: Da Capo, 1976.

———. *The Haunted Screen: Expressionism in the German Cinema and the Influence of Max Reinhardt.* Berkeley: Univ. of California Press, 1952, 1973.

———. *Murnau.* Berkeley: Univ. of California Press, 1964, 1973.

Flitterman-Lewis, Sandy. *To Desire Differently: Feminism and the French Cinema.* Urbana: Univ. of Illinois Press, 1990.

Forslund, Bengt. *Victor Sjöström, His Life and Work.* Translated by Peter Cowie. New York: New York Zoetrope, 1988.

King, Norman. *Abel Gance: A Politics of Spectacle.* London: British Film Institute, 1984.

Kracauer, Siegfried. *From Caligari to Hitler: A Psychological History of the German Film.* Princeton, N.J.: Princeton Univ. Press, 1947.

Monaco, Paul. *Cinema and Society: France and Germany during the Twenties.* New York: Elsevier, 1976.

Petro, Patrice. *Joyless Streets: Women and Melodramatic Representation in Weimar Germany.* Princeton, N.J.: Princeton Univ. Press, 1989.

Plummer, Thomas G., with Bruce A. Murray, Linda Schulte-Sasse, Anthony K. Munson, and Laurie Loomis Perry, eds. *Film and Politics in the Weimar Republic.* Minneapolis: Univ. of Minnesota, 1982.

Rentschler, Eric, ed. *The Films of G.W. Pabst: An Extraterritorial Cinema.* New Brunswick, N.J.: Rutgers Univ. Press, 1990.

Chapter 7: Soviet Cinema

Aumont, Jacques. *Montage Eisenstein.* Translated by Lee Hildreth, Constance Penley, and Andrew Ross. Bloomington: Indiana Univ. Press, 1987.

Dovzhenko, Alexander. *Alexander Dovzhenko: The Poet as Filmmaker.* Edited and translated by Marco Carynnyk. Cambridge, Mass.: MIT Press, 1973.

Eisenstein, S. M. *Selected Works, Vol. I: Writings, 1922–34.* Edited and translated by Richard Taylor. London: British Film Institute, 1988.

Kenez, Peter. *Cinema and Soviet Society, 1917–1953.* Cambridge, Eng.: Cambridge Univ. Press, 1992.

Kepley, Vance, Jr. *In the Service of the State: The Cinema of Alexander Dovzhenko.* Madison: Univ. of Wisconsin Press, 1986.

Kuleshov, Lev. *Kuleshov on Film: Writings of Lev Kuleshov.* Translated and edited by Ronald Levaco. Berkeley: Univ. of California Press, 1974.

Leyda, Jay. *Kino: A History of the Russian and Soviet Film. With a New Postscript and a Filmography Brought up to the Present.* Princeton, N.J.: Princeton Univ. Press, 1960, 1983.

Petric, Vlada. *Constructivism in Film: The Man with the Movie Camera, a Cinematic Analysis.* Cambridge, Eng.: Cambridge Univ. Press, 1987.

Taylor, Richard, and Ian Christie, eds. *The Film Factory: Russian and Soviet Cinema in Documents.* Cambridge, Mass.: Harvard Univ. Press, 1988.

———. *Inside the Film Factory: New Approaches to Russian and Soviet Cinema.* London: Routledge, 1991.

Tsivian, Yuri, with Paolo Cherchi Usai, Lorenzo Codelli, Carlo Montanaro, and David Robinson, eds. *Silent Witnesses: Russian Films 1908–1919/Testimoni silenziosi: Film russi 1908–1919.* Pordenone: Biblioteca dell'Immagine, 1989.

Vertov, Dziga. *Kino-Eye: The Writings of Dziga Vertov.* Edited by Annette Michelson, translated by Kevin O'Brien. Berkeley: Univ. of California Press, 1984.

Youngblood, Denise J. *Soviet Cinema in the Silent Era, 1918–1935.* Austin: Univ. of Texas Press, 1980, 1991.

Chapter 8: The Transition to Sound

Altman, Rick, ed. *Sound Theory, Sound Practice.* New York: Routledge, 1992.

Brownlow, Kevin. *Napoleon: Abel Gance's Classic Film.* New York: Alfred A. Knopf, 1983.

Cameron, Evan William, ed. *Sound and the Cinema: The Coming of Sound to American Film.* Pleasantville, N.Y.: Redgrave, 1980.

Flynn, Caryl. *Strains of Utopia: Gender, Nostalgia, and Hollywood Film Music.* Princeton, N.J.: Princeton Univ. Press, 1992.

Geduld, Harry M. *The Birth of the Talkies: From Edison to Jolson.* Bloomington: Indiana Univ. Press, 1975.

Gorbman, Claudia. *Unheard Melodies: Narrative*

Film Music. Bloomington: Indiana Univ. Press, 1987.

Hilmes, Michelle. *Hollywood and Broadcasting: From Radio to Cable.* Urbana: Univ. of Illinois Press, 1990.

Milne, Tom. *Rouben Mamoulian.* Bloomington: Indiana Univ. Press, 1969.

Walker, Alexander. *The Shattered Silents: How the Talkies Came to Stay.* London: Harrap, 1978, 1986.

Walker, Joseph B., and Juanita Walker. *The Light on Her Face.* Hollywood: ASC Press, 1984.

Weis, Elisabeth, and John Belton, eds. *Film Sound: Theory and Practice.* New York: Columbia Univ. Press, 1985.

Chapter 9: Hollywood Genres

Altman, Rick. *The American Film Musical.* Bloomington: Indiana Univ. Press, 1989.

Carringer, Robert L. *The Making of Citizen Kane.* Berkeley: Univ. of California Press, 1985.

Cavell, Stanley. *Pursuits of Happiness: The Hollywood Comedy of Remarriage.* Cambridge, Mass.: Harvard Univ. Press, 1981.

Dyer, Richard. *Heavenly Bodies: Film Stars and Society.* New York: St. Martin's Press, 1986.

Gallagher, Tag. *John Ford: The Man and His Films.* Berkeley: Univ. of Calif. Press, 1986.

Heisner, Beverly. *Hollywood Art: Art Direction in the Days of the Great Studios.* Jefferson, N.C.: McFarland, 1990.

Jacobs, Lea. *The Wages of Sin: Censorship and the Fallen Woman Film, 1928–1942.* Madison: Univ. of Wisconsin Press, 1991.

McBride, Joseph. *Frank Capra: The Catastrophe of Success.* New York: Simon & Schuster, 1992.

Roddick, Nick. *A New Deal in Entertainment: Warner Brothers in the 1930s.* London: British Film Institute, 1983.

Roffman, Peter, and Jim Purdy. *The Hollywood Social Problem Film: Madness, Despair, and Politics from the Depression to the Fifties.* Bloomington: Indiana Univ. Press, 1981.

Schatz, Thomas. *The Genius of the System: Hollywood Filmmaking in the Studio Era.* New York: Pantheon, 1988.

———. *Hollywood Genres: Formulas, Filmmaking, and the Studio System.* New York: Random House, 1981.

Shadoian, Jack. *Dreams and Dead Ends: The American Gangster/Crime Film.* Cambridge, Mass.: MIT Press, 1979.

Sklar, Robert. *City Boys: Cagney, Bogart, Garfield.* Princeton, N.J.: Princeton Univ. Press, 1992.

Weales, Gerald. *Canned Goods as Caviar: American Film Comedies of the 1930s.* Chicago: Univ. of Chicago Press, 1985.

Chapter 10: Meeting Hollywood's Challenge

Abel, Richard. *French Film Theory and Criticism: A History/ Anthology, Vol. II, 1929–1939.* Princeton, N.J.: Princeton Univ. Press, 1988.

Burch, Noël. *To the Distant Observer: Form and Meaning in the Japanese Cinema.* Berkeley: Univ. of California Press, 1979.

Eisenstein, Sergei. *Film Form: Essays in Film Theory* and *The Film Sense.* Edited and translated by Jay Leyda. New York: Harcourt, Brace, 1942, 1949.

Hay, James. *Popular Film Culture in Fascist Italy: The Passing of the Rex.* Bloomington: Indiana Univ.

Press, 1987.

Kirihara, Donald. *Patterns of Time: Mizoguchi and the 1930s.* Madison: Univ. of Wisconsin Press, 1992.

Landy, Marcia. *Fascism in Film: The Italian Commercial Cinema, 1931–1943.* Princeton, N.J.: Princeton Univ. Press, 1986.

Mancini, Elaine. *Struggles of the Italian Film Industry during Fascism, 1930–1935.* Ann Arbor, Mich.: UMI Research Press, 1985.

Richards, Jeffrey. *The Age of the Dream Palace: Cinema and Society in Britain, 1930–1939.* London: Routledge, 1984.

Salles Gomes, P. E. *Jean Vigo.* Berkeley: Univ. of California Press, 1971.

Sesonske, Alexander. *Jean Renoir: The French Films, 1924–1939.* Cambridge, Mass.: Harvard Univ. Press, 1980.

Truffaut, François. *Hitchcock,* rev. ed. New York: Simon & Schuster, 1983.

Turk, Edward Baron. *Child of Paradise: Marcel Carné and the Golden Age of French Cinema.* Cambridge, Mass.: Harvard Univ. Press, 1989.

Welch, David. *Propaganda and the German Cinema, 1933–1945.* Oxford, Eng.: Oxford Univ. Press, 1983.

Chapter 11: Documentary, Propaganda, and Politics

Aitken, Ian. *Film and Reform: John Grierson and the Documentary Film Movement.* London: Routledge, 1990.

Alexander, William. *Films on the Left: American Documentary Film from 1931 to 1942.* Princeton, N.J.: Princeton Univ. Press, 1981.

Barnouw, Erik. *Documentary: A History of the Non-Fiction Film.* New York: Oxford Univ. Press, 1974.

Barsam, Richard Meran. *Nonfiction Film: A Critical History.* New York: Dutton, 1973.

Buchsbaum, Jonathan. *Cinema Engagé: Film in the Popular Front.* Urbana: Univ. of Illinois Press, 1988.

Campbell, Russell. *Cinema Strikes Back: Radical Filmmaking in the United States, 1930–1942.* Ann Arbor, Mich.: UMI Research Press, 1982.

Fielding, Raymond. *The March of Time, 1935–1951.* New York: Oxford Univ. Press, 1978.

Graham, Cooper C. *Leni Riefenstahl and Olympia.* Metuchen, N.J.: Scarecrow Press, 1986.

Lorentz, Pare. *FDR's Moviemaker: Memoirs and Scripts.* Reno: Univ. of Nevada Press, 1992.

MacCann, Richard Dyer. *The People's Films: A Political History of U.S. Government Motion Pictures.* New York: Hastings House, 1973.

Snyder, Robert L. *Pare Lorentz and the Documentary Film.* Norman: Univ. of Oklahoma Press, 1968.

Sussex, Elizabeth. *The Rise and Fall of British Documentary: The Story of the Film Movement Founded by John Grierson.* Berkeley: Univ. of California Press, 1975.

Swann, Paul. *The British Documentary Film Movement, 1926–1946.* Cambridge, Eng.: Cambridge Univ. Press, 1989.

Chapter 12: Film and World War II

Aldgate, Anthony, and Jeffrey Richards. *Britain Can Take It: The British Cinema in the Second World War.* Oxford, Eng.: Basil Blackwell, 1986.

Basinger, Jeanine. *The World War II Combat Film:*

Anatomy of a Genre. New York: Columbia Univ. Press, 1986.

Dick, Bernard F. *The Star-Spangled Screen: The American World War II Film.* Lexington: Univ. Press of Kentucky, 1985.

Ehrlich, Evelyn. *Cinema of Paradox: French Filmmaking Under the German Occupation.* New York: Columbia Univ. Press, 1985.

Hodgkinson, Anthony W., and Rodney E. Sheratsky. *Humphrey Jennings: More Than a Maker of Films.* Hanover, N.H.: Univ. Press of New England, 1982.

Jennings, Mary-Lou, ed. *Humphrey Jennings: Film-Maker, Painter, Poet.* London: British Film Institute, 1982.

Koppes, Clayton R., and Gregory D. Black. *Hollywood Goes to War: How Politics, Profits, and Propaganda Shaped World War II Movies.* New York: Free Press, 1987.

Lant, Antonia. *Blackout: Reinventing Women for Wartime British Cinema.* Princeton, N.J.: Princeton Univ. Press, 1991.

Schindler, Colin. *Hollywood Goes to War: Films and American Society, 1939–1952.* London: Routledge & Kegan Paul, 1979.

Silverman, Stephen M. *David Lean.* New York: Abrams, 1989.

Thompson, Kristin. *Eisenstein's Ivan the Terrible: A Neoformalist Analysis.* Princeton, N.J.: Princeton Univ. Press, 1981.

Chapter 13: Italian Neorealism

Armes, Roy. *Patterns of Realism: A Study of Italian Neo-Realist Cinema.* London: Tantivy, 1971.

Bondanella, Peter. *Italian Cinema: From Neorealism to the Present.* New York: Ungar, 1983.

Brunette, Peter. *Roberto Rossellini.* New York: Oxford Univ. Press, 1987.

Dalle Vacche, Angela. *The Body in the Mirror: Shapes of History in Italian Cinema.* Princeton, N.J.: Princeton Univ. Press, 1992.

Greene, Naomi. *Pier Paolo Pasolini: Cinema as Heresy.* Princeton, N.J.: Princeton Univ. Press, 1990.

Liehm, Mira. *Passion and Defiance: Film in Italy from 1942 to the Present.* Berkeley: Univ. of California Press, 1984.

Marcus, Millicent. *Filmmaking by the Book: Italian Cinema and Literary Adaptation.* Baltimore: Johns Hopkins Univ. Press, 1993.

———. *Italian Film in the Light of Neorealism.* Princeton, N.J.: Princeton Univ. Press, 1986.

Nowell-Smith, Geoffrey. *Luchino Visconti.* Garden City, N.Y.: Doubleday, 1968.

Overbey, David, ed. *Springtime in Italy: A Reader on Neo-Realism.* London: Talisman Books, 1978.

Chapter 14: Hollywood's Struggles

Ceplair, Larry, and Steven Englund. *The Inquisition in Hollywood: Politics in the Film Community, 1930–1960.* Garden City, N.Y.: Anchor Press/Doubleday, 1980.

Dick, Bernard F. *Radical Innocence: A Critical Study of the Hollywood Ten.* Lexington: Univ. Press of Kentucky, 1989.

Doane, Mary Ann. *The Desire to Desire: The Woman's Film of the 1940s.* Bloomington: Indiana Univ. Press, 1987.

Fordin, Hugh. *The Movies' Greatest Musicals: Produced in Hollywood USA by the Freed Unit.* New York: Ungar, 1984.

Hirsch, Foster. *The Dark Side of the Screen: Film Noir.* San Diego: A. S. Barnes, 1981.

Kaplan, E. Ann, ed. *Women in Film Noir.* London: British Film Institute, 1978, 1980.

Kozloff, Sarah. *Invisible Storytellers: Voice-Over Narration in American Fiction Film.* Berkeley: Univ. of California Press, 1988.

McCarthy, Todd, and Charles Flynn, eds. *Kings of the Bs: Working Within the Hollywood System, An Anthology of Film History and Criticism.* New York: Dutton, 1975.

Maltby, Richard. *Harmless Entertainment: Hollywood and the Ideology of Consensus.* Metuchen, N.J.: Scarecrow Press, 1983.

Navasky, Victor S. *Naming Names.* New York: Viking, 1980.

Polan, Dana. *Power and Paranoia: History, Narrative, and the American Cinema, 1940–1950.* New York: Columbia Univ. Press, 1986.

Ray, Robert B. *A Certain Tendency of the Hollywood Cinema, 1930–1980.* Princeton, N.J.: Princeton Univ. Press, 1985.

Silver, Alain, and Elizabeth Ward, eds. *Film Noir: An Encyclopedic Reference to the American Style.* Woodstock, N.Y.: Overlook Press, 1979.

Telotte, J. P. *Voices in the Dark: The Narrative Patterns of Film Noir.* Urbana: Univ. of Illinois Press, 1989.

Walsh, Andrea S. *Women's Film and Female Experience, 1940–1950.* New York: Praeger, 1984.

Chapter 15: Art Cinema of Europe and Asia

Bock, Audie. *Japanese Film Directors.* Tokyo: Kodansha, 1978.

Bondanella, Peter. *The Cinema of Federico Fellini.* Princeton, N.J.: Princeton Univ. Press, 1992.

Bordwell, David. *Ozu and the Poetics of Cinema.* Princeton, N.J.: Princeton Univ. Press, 1988.

Chatman, Seymour. *Antonioni: Or, the Surface of the World.* Berkeley: Univ. of California Press, 1985.

Cowie, Peter. *Ingmar Bergman: A Critical Biography.* New York: Scribner's, 1982.

Donner, Jörn. *The Films of Ingmar Bergman: From Torment to All These Women.* Translated by Holger Lundbergh. New York: Dover, 1964, 1972.

Hirano, Kyoko. *Mr. Smith Goes to Tokyo: Japanese Cinema under the American Occupation.* Washington, D.C.: Smithsonian Institution Press, 1992.

Mellen, Joan. *The World of Luis Buñuel: Essays in Criticism.* New York: Oxford Univ. Press, 1978.

Moss, Robert F. *The Films of Carol Reed.* New York: Columbia Univ. Press, 1987.

Nyce, Ben. *Satyajit Ray: A Study of His Films.* New York: Praeger, 1988.

Richie, Donald. *The Films of Akira Kurosawa,* rev. ed. Berkeley: Univ. of California Press, 1984.

Robinson, Andrew. *Satyajit Ray: The Inner Eye.* Berkeley: Univ. of California Press, 1989.

Schrader, Paul. *Transcendental Style in Film: Ozu, Bresson, Dreyer.* Berkeley: Univ. of California Press, 1972.

Chapter 16: Hollywood in the 1950s

Belton, John. *Widescreen Cinema.* Cambridge, Mass.: Harvard Univ. Press, 1992.

Biskind, Peter. *Seeing Is Believing: How Hollywood Taught Us to Stop Worrying and Love the Fifties.* New York: Pantheon, 1983.

Byars, Jackie. *All That Hollywood Allows: Re-reading Gender in 1950s Melodrama.* Chapel Hill: Univ. of North Carolina Press, 1991.

Ciment, Michel, ed. *Elia Kazan: An American Odyssey.* London: Bloomsbury, 1988.

Deutelbaum, Marshall, and Leland Poague, eds. *A Hitchcock Reader.* Ames: Iowa State Univ. Press, 1986.

Doherty, Thomas. *Teenagers and Teenpics: The Juvenilization of American Movies in the 1950s.* Boston: Unwin Hyman, 1988.

Gledhill, Christine, ed. *Home Is Where the Heart Is: Studies in Melodrama and the Woman's Film.* London: British Film Institute, 1987.

Halliday, Jon. *Sirk on Sirk.* New York: Viking Press, 1972.

Harvey, Stephen. *Directed by Vincente Minnelli.* New York: Museum of Modern Art/Harper & Row, 1989.

Lucanio, Patrick. *Them or Us: Archetypal Interpretations of Fifties Alien Invasion Films.* Bloomington: Indiana Univ. Press, 1987.

Modleski, Tania. *The Women Who Knew Too Much: Hitchcock and Feminist Theory.* New York: Methuen, 1988.

Vineberg, Steve. *Method Actors: Three Generations of American Acting Style.* New York: Schirmer, 1991.

Chapter 17: The French New Wave

Browne, Nick, ed. *Cahiers du Cinéma, 1969–1972: The Politics of Representation.* Cambridge, Mass.: Harvard Univ. Press, 1990.

Crisp, C. G. *Eric Rohmer: Realist and Moralist.* Bloomington: Indiana Univ. Press, 1988.

Hillier, Jim, ed. *Cahiers du Cinéma, the 1950s: Neo-Realism, Hollywood, New Wave.* Cambridge, Mass.: Harvard Univ. Press, 1985.

———, ed. *Cahiers du Cinéma, 1960–1968: New Wave, New Cinema, Reevaluating Hollywood.* Cambridge, Mass.: Harvard Univ. Press, 1986.

Insdorf, Annette. *François Truffaut,* rev. ed. New York: Touchstone, 1978, 1989.

Monaco, James. *Alain Resnais.* New York: Oxford Univ. Press, 1979.

———. *The New Wave: Truffaut, Godard, Chabrol, Rohmer, Rivette.* New York: Oxford Univ. Press, 1976.

Mussman, Toby, ed. *Jean-Luc Godard: A Critical Anthology.* New York: Dutton, 1968.

Narboni, Jean, and Tom Milne, eds. *Godard on Godard: Critical Writings on Jean-Luc Godard.* New York: Da Capo, 1972, 1986.

Nogueira, Rui. *Melville on Melville.* New York: Viking, 1971.

Rivette, Jacques. *Rivette: Texts and Interviews.* Edited by Jonathan Rosenbaum, translated by Amy Gateff and Tom Milne. London: British Film Institute, 1977.

Roud, Richard. *A Passion for Films: Henri Langlois and the Cinémathèque Française.* New York: Viking, 1983.

Wood, Robin, and Michael Walker. *Claude Chabrol.* New York: Praeger, 1970.

Chapter 18: Cinema of Liberation

Armes, Roy. *Third World Film Making and the West.* Berkeley: Univ. of California Press, 1987.

Burton, Julianne, ed. *Cinema and Social Change in Latin America: Conversations with Filmmakers.* Austin: Univ. of Texas Press, 1986.

Chanan, Michael. *The Cuban Image: Cinema and Cultural Politics in Cuba.* London: British Film Institute, 1985.

———, ed. *Twenty-five Years of the New Latin American Cinema.* London: British Film Institute/Channel Four Television, 1983.

Clark, Paul. *Chinese Cinema: Culture and Politics since 1949.* Cambridge, Eng.: Cambridge Univ. Press, 1987.

Desser, David. *Eros Plus Massacre: An Introduction to the Japanese New Wave Cinema.* Bloomington: Indiana Univ. Press, 1988.

Diawara, Manthia. *African Cinema: Politics & Culture.* Bloomington: Indiana Univ. Press, 1992.

Downing, John D. H., ed. *Film & Politics in the Third World.* New York: Praeger, 1987.

Georgakas, Dan, and Lenny Rubenstein, eds. *The Cineaste Interviews: On the Art and Politics of the Cinema.* Chicago: Lake View Press, 1983.

Johnson, Randal. *Cinema Novo X 5: Masters of Contemporary Brazilian Film.* Austin: Univ. of Texas Press, 1984.

Malkmus, Lizbeth, and Roy Armes. *Arab and African Film Making.* London: Zed Books, 1991.

Pfaff, Francoise. *The Cinema of Ousmane Sembene, a Pioneer of African Film.* Westport, Conn.: Greenwood Press, 1984.

———. *Twenty-five Black African Filmmakers: A Critical Study, with Filmography and Bio-Bibliography.* New York: Greenwood Press, 1988.

Solinas, PierNico, ed. *Gillo Pontecorvo's "The Battle of Algiers."* New York: Scribner's, 1973.

Ukadike, N. Frank. *Black African Cinema.* Berkeley: Univ. of California Press, 1993.

Chapter 19: The New Documentary

Benson, Thomas W., and Carolyn Anderson. *Reality Fictions: The Films of Frederick Wiseman.* Carbondale: Southern Illinois Univ. Press, 1989.

Grant, Barry Keith. *Voyages of Discovery: The Cinema of Frederick Wiseman.* Urbana: Univ. of Illinois Press, 1992.

Heider, Karl G. *Ethnographic Film.* Austin: Univ. of Texas Press, 1976.

Levin, G. Roy. *Documentary Explorations: 15 Interviews with Film-Makers.* Garden City, N.Y.: Doubleday, 1971.

Mamber, Stephen. *Cinema Verite in America: Studies in Uncontrolled Documentary.* Cambridge, Mass.: MIT Press, 1974.

Nichols, Bill. *Representing Reality: Issues and Concepts in Documentary.* Bloomington: Indiana Univ. Press, 1991.

O'Connell, P. J. *Robert Drew and the Development of Cinema Verite in America.* Carbondale: Southern Illinois Univ. Press, 1992.

Rosenthal, Alan, ed. *The Documentary Conscience: A Casebook in Film Making.* Berkeley: Univ. of California Press, 1980.

———, ed. *New Challenges for Documentary.* Berkeley: Univ. of California Press, 1988.

Stoller, Paul. *The Cinematic Griot: The Ethnography of Jean Rouch.* Chicago: Univ. of Chicago Press, 1992.

Waugh, Thomas, ed. *"Show Us Life": Toward a History and Aesthetics of the Committed Documentary.* Metuchen, N.J.: Scarecrow Press, 1984.

Worth, Sol, and John Adair. *Through Navajo Eyes: An Exploration in Film Communication and Anthropology*. Bloomington: Indiana Univ. Press, 1972.

Chapter 20: American Film: Turmoil and Transformation

Chown, Jeffrey. *Hollywood Auteur: Francis Coppola*. New York: Praeger, 1988.

Ciment, Michel. *Kubrick*. Translated by Gilbert Adair. New York: Holt, Rinehart & Winston, 1980.

Goodwin, Michael, and Naomi Wise. *On the Edge: The Life and Times of Francis Coppola*. New York: Morrow, 1989.

Kolker, Robert Phillip. *A Cinema of Loneliness: Penn, Kubrick, Scorsese, Spielberg, Altman*, 2nd ed. New York: Oxford Univ. Press, 1980, 1988.

McGilligan, Patrick. *Robert Altman, Jumping Off the Cliff: A Biography of the Great American Director*. New York: St. Martin's, 1989.

Mordden, Ethan. *Medium Cool: The Movies of the 1960s*. New York: Alfred A. Knopf, 1990.

Pye, Michael, and Lynda Miles. *The Movie Brats: How the Film Generation Took Over Hollywood*. New York: Holt, Rinehart & Winston, 1979.

Russo, Vito. *The Celluloid Closet: Homosexuality in the Movies*, rev. ed. New York: Harper & Row, 1981, 1987.

Seydor, Paul. *Peckinpah: The Western Films*. Urbana: Univ. of Illinois Press, 1980.

Talbot, David, and Barbara Zheutlin. *Creative Differences: Profiles of Hollywood Dissidents*. Boston: South End Press, 1978.

Wood, Robin. *Arthur Penn*. New York: Praeger, 1970.

Chapter 21: European Film of the 1960s and 1970s

Elsaesser, Thomas. *New German Cinema: A History*. New Brunswick, N.J.: Rutgers Univ. Press, 1989.

Goulding, Daniel J. *Liberated Cinema: The Yugoslav Experience*. Bloomington: Indiana Univ. Press, 1985.

Hames, Peter. *The Czechoslovak New Wave*. Berkeley: Univ. of California Press, 1985.

Higginbotham, Virginia. *Spanish Film under Franco*. Austin: Univ. of Texas Press, 1988.

Hill, John. *Sex, Class and Realism: British Cinema 1956–1963*. London: British Film Institute, 1986.

Hopewell, John. *Out of the Past: Spanish Cinema after Franco*. London: British Film Institute, 1986.

Knight, Julia. *Women and the New German Cinema*. London: Verso, 1992.

Kolker, Robert Phillip. *Bernardo Bertolucci*. New York: Oxford Univ. Press, 1985.

Lawton, Anna, ed. *The Red Screen: Politics, Society, Art in Soviet Cinema*. London: Routledge, 1992.

Le Fanu, Mark. *The Cinema of Andrei Tarkovsky*. London: British Film Institute, 1987.

Liehm, Mira, and Antonín J. Liehm. *The Most Important Art: East European Film after 1945*. Berkeley: Univ. of California Press, 1977.

Michalek, Boleslaw, and Frank Turaj. *The Modern Cinema of Poland*. Bloomington: Indiana Univ. Press, 1988.

Paul, David W., ed. *Politics, Art and Commitment in the East European Cinema*. New York: St. Martin's, 1983.

Portuges, Catherine. *Screen Memories: The Hungarian Cinema of Márta Mészáros*. Bloomington: Indiana Univ. Press, 1993.

Witcombe, R. T. *The New Italian Cinema: Studies in Dance and Despair*. New York: Oxford Univ. Press, 1982

Chapter 22: Hollywood Recovery

Anderegg, Michael, ed. *Inventing Vietnam: The War in Film and Television*. Philadelphia: Temple Univ. Press, 1991.

Bach, Steven. *Final Cut: Dreams and Disaster in the Making of Heaven's Gate*. New York: Morrow, 1985.

Bliss, Michael. *Martin Scorsese and Michael Cimino*. Metuchen, N.J.: Scarecrow Press, 1985.

Champlin, Charles. *George Lucas: The Creative Impulse, Lucasfilm's First Twenty Years*. New York: Abrams, 1992

Dittmar, Linda, and Gene Michaud, eds. *From Hanoi to Hollywood: The Vietnam War in American Film*. New Brunswick, N.J.: Rutgers Univ. Press, 1990.

Guerrero, Edward. *Framing Blackness: The Politics and Culture of the Black Image in American Cinema*. Philadelphia: Temple Univ. Press, 1993.

Lee, Spike. *Five for Five: The Films of Spike Lee*. New York: Stewart, Tabori & Chang, 1991.

Monaco, James. *American Film Now: The People, the Power, the Money, the Movies*. New York: Oxford Univ. Press, 1979.

Mott, Donald R., and Cheryl McAllister Saunders. *Steven Spielberg*. Boston: Twayne, 1986.

Ryan, Michael, and Douglas Kellner. *Camera Politica: The Politics and Ideology of Contemporary Hollywood Film*. Bloomington: Indiana Univ. Press, 1988.

Thompson, David, and Ian Christie, eds. *Scorsese on Scorsese*. London: Faber & Faber, 1989.

Van Peebles, Melvin and Mario. *No Identity Crisis: A Father and Son's Own Story of Working Together*. New York: Simon & Schuster, 1990.

Wood, Robin. *Hollywood from Vietnam to Reagan*. New York: Columbia Univ. Press, 1986.

Chapter 23: The Cinematic Avant-Garde

American Federation of Arts. *A History of the American Avant-Garde Cinema*. New York: American Federation of Arts, 1976.

Clark, VèVè A., Millicent Hodson, and Catrina Neiman. *The Legend of Maya Deren: A Documentary Biography and Collected Works, Vol. I, Part One, Signatures (1917–42), Vol. I, Part Two, Chambers (1942–47)*. New York: Anthology Film Archives/Film Culture, 1984, 1988.

Dyer, Richard. *Now You See It: Studies on Lesbian and Gay Film*. London: Routledge, 1990.

James, David E. *Allegories of Cinema: American Film in the Sixties*. Princeton, N.J.: Princeton Univ. Press, 1989.

———, ed. *To Free the Cinema: Jonas Mekas & the New York Underground*. Princeton, N.J.: Princeton Univ. Press, 1992.

MacDonald, Scott. *A Critical Cinema: Interviews with Independent Filmmakers*. Berkeley: Univ. of California Press, 1988.

O'Pray, Michael, ed. *Andy Warhol: Film Factory*. London: British Film Institute, 1989.

Rabinovitz, Lauren. *Points of Resistance: Women, Power & Politics in the New York Avant-Garde Cinema, 1943–1971*. Urbana: Univ. of Illinois Press, 1991.

Rainer, Yvonne. *The Films of Yvonne Rainer*. Bloomington: Indiana Univ. Press, 1989.

Rosenberg, Jan. *Women's Reflections: The Feminist Film Movement*. Ann Arbor, Mich.: UMI Research Press, 1983.

Roud, Richard. *Jean-Marie Straub*. New York: Viking, 1972.

Sitney, P. Adams, ed. *The Avant-Garde Film: A Reader of Theory and Criticism*. New York: New York Univ. Press, 1978.

Sitney, P. Adams. *Visionary Film: The American Avant-Garde*. New York: Oxford Univ. Press, 1974.

Tyler, Parker. *Underground Film: A Critical History*. New York: Grove Press, 1969.

Chapter 24: The Global Advance of Cinema

Berry, Chris, ed. *Perspectives on Chinese Cinema*. London: British Film Institute, 1991.

Chen Kaige, Wan Zhi, and Tony Rayns. *King of the Children* and *The New Chinese Cinema: An Introduction*. London: Faber & Faber, 1989.

Goulding, Daniel J., ed. *Post New Wave Cinema in the Soviet Union and Eastern Europe*. Bloomington: Indiana Univ. Press, 1989.

Horton, Andrew, and Michael Brashinsky. *The Zero Hour: Glasnost and Soviet Cinema in Transition*. Princeton, N.J.: Princeton Univ. Press, 1992.

Lent, John A. *The Asian Film Industry*. Austin: Univ. of Texas Press, 1990.

Lewis, Glen. *Australian Movies and the American Dream*. New York: Praeger, 1987.

McFarlane, Brian. *Australian Cinema*. New York: Columbia Univ. Press, 1988.

Pendakur, Manjunath. *Canadian Dreams and American Control: The Political Economy of the Canadian Film Industry*. Toronto: Garamond Press, 1990.

Pines, Jim, and Paul Willemen, eds. *Questions of Third Cinema*. London: British Film Institute, 1989.

Semsel, George Stephen, ed. *Chinese Film: The State of the Art in the People's Republic*. New York: Praeger, 1987.

Semsel, George S., Xia Hong, and Hou Jianping, eds. *Chinese Film Theory: A Guide to the New Era*. New York: Praeger, 1990.

Shohat, Ella. *Israeli Cinema: East/West and the Politics of Representation*. Austin: Univ. of Texas Press, 1989.

Véronneau, Pierre, and Piers Handling, eds. *Self Portrait: Essays on the Canadian and Quebec Cinemas*. Ottawa: Canadian Film Institute, 1980.

Glossary

Academy ratio A standard **aspect ratio** for the screen image, established by the Academy of Motion Picture Arts and Sciences in the early 1930s; the width is four units and the height is three, which is expressed as 1.33:1.

actuality films, actualities Terms used in the early years of cinema to denote nonfiction films or newsreel-type footage.

aerial shot A shot taken from the air, as from an airplane, helicopter, balloon, or camera operator with a parachute; also, can denote a **high-angle shot** from a camera mounted on a crane.

agitkas Films made to be shown on the agit-trains and other vehicles that carried propaganda materials to peasants in rural Russia following the Bolshevik revolution of 1917.

analytical editing A critical term applied to the formation of a narrative style in early cinema, in which an action or several actions that occur as continuous movements without interruption are "analyzed," or broken up into a series of discrete images, involving different camera set-ups and separate shots, and then reconstructed at the editing stage from individual fragments into a multi-image whole, to create a cinematic experience of time and space different from direct perception; **montage** became the more common term for this editing style.

anamorphic lens A lens developed by French scientist Henri Chrètien in the late 1920s which, when fitted over a regular camera lens, greatly expanded the lateral range of the image that could be recorded on standard 35mm film (without affecting the vertical range). The image recorded with an anamorphic lens looked compressed or "squeezed," but when projected using an anamorphic lens over the regular projector lens, it would appear in its normal vertical proportions with a considerably wider horizontal field than could be recorded by regular lenses. This lens was the basis for CinemaScope, introduced in the 1950s.

animation A type of filmmaking generally involving a series of drawings or the manipulation of inanimate objects, filmed one frame at a time; the drawings or objects appear animated (give the illusion of motion) when the filmed frames are projected; more recently, animated films have been created through computer graphics.

art director The person who designs and supervises the construction of sets and works with set decorators and others in planning a film's decor.

art film A term used in different eras to valorize a certain type of filmmaking as more "artistic" than regular commercial production: in early cinema it denoted films allied with traditional arts, such as theater, while since the 1950s it has signified narrative commercial features made by directors with seriousness of purpose and a goal of stylistic innovation.

aspect ratio The relation between the height and width of the screen image; see **Academy ratio** and **widescreen.**

atmospherics The trade name for motion picture theaters built in the 1920s–30s with exotic fantasy decor and interior ceilings designed to resemble an outdoor night sky, complete with twinkling lights to represent stars and projected images of moving clouds.

auteur theory A viewpoint developed in the United States in the 1960s echoing the French *politique des auteurs,* or "*auteur* policy," a critical polemic of the 1950s that stressed the director as "author" of a film through the imprint of a personal visual style.

avant-garde The French term for the vanguard, those in the forefront; in cinema, it generally signifies non-commercial cinema that experiments with new forms or subjects.

backdrop A painted scene behind live-action performers, adapted from stage productions in early cinema by filmmakers such as Georges Méliès.

backlighting Lighting a subject from behind, which creates a halo effect emphasizing hair or profile while leaving the face in shadow.

back lot Open areas on the grounds of Hollywood studios where exterior sets for films were constructed; these also held standing sets, such as "New York street" or "Western street," that were used repeatedly.

Bioscop Motion picture projector first demonstrated in November 1895 in Germany by the brothers Emil and Max Skladanowsky, in which the frames of two film strips were alternately exposed.

blocking The positioning of performers in a scene and planning of their movements.

boom The long pole from which a microphone is hung, in synchronous sound recording; the device holds the microphone out of camera range and permits performers freedom of movement beneath it.

B-pictures A term deriving from the "B units" set up by Hollywood Studios in the 1930s to produce inexpensive films to be shown as part of double-features, a common exhibition practice of that era; B units were closed down in the 1940s, but the term has been retained to describe low-budget, genre-oriented features.

camera The apparatus that records motion-picture images by exposing and advancing individual frames on a film roll.

camera angle The position of the camera in relation to the subject being photographed.

canon The body of films considered especially significant and worthy of study at a particular time.

cel A transparent sheet made of **celluloid** used in the production of animation films; developed around 1914, it enabled animators to save labor by drawing stationary backgrounds on a cel and using it continually with cels containing images of movement, photographing a single image from the layered cels.

celluloid A synthetic plastic material invented in the 1870s, originally utilizing the chemical compound cellulose nitrate, that replaced paper as the basis for the film roll in the late 1880s; later, a more general term for motion pictures.

chiaroscuro A technical term derived from painting, describing variations in light and shade.

Cinema Novo A Brazilian film movement of the 1960s, literally "New Cinema," concerned with social issues.

cinematic space The metaspatial world that is created on the cinema screen through a sequence of separate shots (**shot chain**) that constructs its own screen-time and spatial relationships; also know as filmic space.

Cinématographe Motion picture apparatus developed by Auguste and Louis Lumière in France that functioned both as a camera and as part of a projection device; recorded and screened films in 1895 leading up to the first showing of projected motion pictures to the general public on December 28, 1895, in Paris.

cinematographer The person in charge of setting up the camera and the lighting on a shot, who in some productions is also the camera operator; on Hollywood films, this figure is generally credited as **director of photography.**

cinematography The art and practice of motion-picture photography.

cinema verité A style of **documentary** filmmaking emerging in France at the end of the 1950s that emphasized the use of hand-held cameras and synchronous sound as technologies for filming "truth." The name, which literally means "film truth," derived from Soviet filmmaker Dziga Vertov's 1920s newsreel series *Kino Pravda* ("Film Truth").

city symphony A type of **documentary** film, often associated with the avant-garde, that seeks to capture the rhythms and contrasts of the modern city; it takes its name from Walther Ruttmann's *Berlin: Die Sinfonie der Grossstadt* (*Berlin: Symphony of a Great City*, 1927).

classical cinema A critical term referring to the mode of production and aesthetic styles fostered by the Hollywood studios that took shape in the 1910s and operated until the 1950s; the concept stresses determinative norms and uniform practices.

close-up A head and shoulders shot of a performer; a shot showing an object in detail.

compilation film A film compiled and edited from preexisting footage.

constructivism A movement in the arts that replaced **futurism** in the Soviet Union after Italian futurism became associated with the new fascist government in Italy. The concept viewed the artist as an "engineer": the artist united revolutionary ideology with his or her materials in order simultaneously to construct new content and new form, with emphasis on technology and industrial forms.

continuity A general term for the structuring and linkage of shots and sequences in a film; it also implies a smooth movement from image to image that maintains legibility of action and narrative for the spectator.

contrapuntal sound A counterpoint or disjunction between visual images and sounds; the concept was elaborated by Soviet filmmakers Sergei Eisenstein, Vsevolod Pudovkin, and Grigori Alexandrov in their 1928 "Statement on Sound."

crosscutting A term for alternating shots among different locations, as when a series of shots cuts back and forth among two or more separate spaces.

cut A direct change of shot in a film, rather than one that is made gradually, as with **dissolves** or **fades**; also, the word the director calls out to stop the photographing of a shot.

deep focus The photographic technique of keeping the entire image in sharp focus, no matter how far from the camera; it permits a mise-en-scène in which action can occur at different distances.

deep space The distant portion of the visual field, farthest from the camera, when it remains in focus and is utilized as part of the mise-en-scène.

depth of field The term describing the distance from the camera that remains in focus in a shot.

direct cinema The name used in the United States, as an alternative to *cinema verité*, for new documentary practices of the 1960s utilizing hand-held cameras with **synchronous sound**; the term placed emphasis on technique rather than results.

director In fiction filmmaking, the person who has the overall creative responsibility for turning a screenplay into a visual motion picture text; the basic tasks of a director are preparing and positioning performers for a shot, and supervising other personnel in establishing the technical aspects of production (such as camera positioning and lighting for a shot) and completing post-production work (such as editing the film and preparing the soundtrack). In nonfiction filmmaking, directors may also carry out such tasks as cinematography, sound recording, or editing.

director of photography The person in charge of setting up the camera and the lighting on a shot; in major studio productions, a different person operates the camera during the shot.

dissolve The transition from one shot to another, involving **fades**. A dissolve may be a **fade-out** to a blank screen (often black, sometimes white) and then a **fade-in** to a new shot, or a **lap dissolve** (short for overlapping), in which one shot fades while the next gradually becomes visible.

distribution The aspect of the film business involving the delivering of films from producers to theaters (exhibitors); distribution companies also may finance film production, and bear the initial costs of advertising and promoting a film.

documentary A term coined in the 1920s and still widely used to describe nonfiction films, that is, films that are made to record or document social actuality.

dolly A wheeled vehicle holding the camera and operator for shots involving camera movement; also the process of moving the camera on such wheels.

double exposure A type of **multiple exposure** involving two images, achieved by rewinding exposed footage and running it through the camera again.

double image An effect achieved by printing one shot over another.

dubbed, dubbing Terms derived from "vocal doubling," to indicate the postsynchronization of a voice replacing the original.

editing The process of assembling individual shots of a film into a visual continuity.

editor The person who assembles the individual shots of a film into a visual continuity.

epic A film **genre** generally dealing with historical subjects and emphasizing **production values** such as extensive location shooting, big sets, elaborate costumes, and large casts.

establishing shot The opening shot of a scene, usually in **extreme long shot**, that establishes its location; it can function as a **master shot** but

more often precedes it.

exhibition The film industry term for the operation of motion picture theaters.

exposure The process of exposing film to light and recording images through control of the size and duration of the opening through which light strikes the photographic film in a camera.

Expressionism A movement in the arts in early-twentieth-century Europe, especially Germany, that was opposed to naturalism and efforts to depict reality. Expressionists believed that art derived from inner vision rather than from impressions of a real world or from conventions of artistic practice. The term has been used to describe German filmmaking practices after World War I, exemplified by *The Cabinet of Dr. Caligari*, that emphasize non-realistic sets, supernatural themes, and the psychic states of protagonists.

extreme long shot A location shot taken from a considerable distance.

fade The gradual change of light signaling the beginning or end of a shot; a **fade-in** begins with a dark screen and brightens to become a completely visible scene, while a **fade-out** begins with a fully lighted scene and darkens to blackness.

fast motion A shot that makes people or objects appear to be moving faster than their normal speed, achieved by photographing fewer feet of film per second than standard, or by speeding up projection.

feature The principal attraction on a mixed program; in early cinema the term came into use with films of four reels (40 minutes to one hour) or more. Over the decades the length of feature films has increased to a range between 100 minutes and two hours, with many longer.

fill light A light that adds to a scene illumination to areas that the **key light** does not cover.

film Originally, a substance composed of sensitized paper, coated with gelatin emulsion, on a roll, developed in 1885 by George Eastman and William H. Walker; later, a generic name for the material on which still and motion pictures are photographed; also, a general term for motion pictures.

film noir A film movement in Hollywood cinema from World War II to the late 1950s, perhaps the only such movement to be named retrospectively (by French critics in a 1955 book). With many sources and definitions, film noir works are distinguished by their dark and oppressive visual style and narratives of desperation and entrapment that defied Hollywood's conventions of happy endings and good triumphing over evil.

film stock Sensitized celluloid made into perforated rolls that are exposed in motion picture cameras. In the first decades of cinema film stock was made from cellulose nitrate, which was highly flammable; this was replaced around 1950 by a cellulose triacetate base. Images are recorded on a light-sensitive coating on the celluloid, called emulsion. Changes in the chemical composition of the emulsion affect its sensitivity; the development of **panchromatic negative film** is an example.

filter A glass or gelatin material fitting over a camera lens that alters the light passing through onto the film.

flashback A scene from past time inserted in a

film's temporal present.

flash-forward A scene implying or forecasting future time inserted in a film's temporal present.

floodlamps Carbon-arc lamps that illuminate a scene with bright, undirected light.

focus The standard for sharp definition of the image.

formalism A doctrine in film theory and filmmaking practice that emphasizes aesthetic form rather than story.

frame The individual photographic image on which motion pictures are recorded.

framing The act of placing the camera in relation to performers and objects that determines what will be included within the image frame and what left outside it.

freeze frame An individual film frame that is reprinted on the celluloid strip, so that when projected it appears as a still image.

futurism A movement in the arts launched in 1909 by Italian poet Filippo Tommaso Marinetti. Disdaining what they saw as the sentimentality and nostalgia of nineteenth-century art, futurist poets and visual artists wanted to create works that represented the dynamism of their contemporary world, dominated by technology, movement, and speed. Futurism was also important in Russia.

gaffer The chief electrician on a film crew; moves and places lighting under direction of a cinematographer or director of photography.

genre A category or type of production, in film and other arts; genres are differentiated from each other by characteristics of style, technique, or narrative content.

grip Member of a film crew who moves the crane or dolly on which the camera is mounted.

high-angle shot A shot taken from above.

Impressionism A critical term sometimes applied to French film theory and practice of the 1920s that stressed the "pure" movement of images irrespective of content or story, or the utilization of techniques to express interior states; the term was meant to link these approaches to the nineteenth-century Impressionist aesthetic in painting.

independent production In the United States film industry, denotes films distributed by major companies but not produced by them, or non-Hollywood or noncommercial feature film production.

insert shot A shot, usually in close-up, that emphasizes a segment of a larger scene.

intellectual montage A concept developed by Soviet filmmaker Sergei Eisenstein as part of his theoretical work on the principles of **montage**, dealing with the way the placement of shots lends meaning to each shot and creates a conceptual effect that gives a larger meaning to an entire sequence of shots; intellectual montage includes techniques such as synecdoche (the part standing for the whole) and metaphor (in his cinematic usage, the juxtaposition of unrelated images to generate associations in the spectator's mind).

intercutting A term for interweaving scenes or sequences from separate times or locations in a film's continuity; though sometimes it is used as a synonym for **crosscutting**, the latter term generally implies a more direct narrative link between simultaneous events.

intertitles Frames of printed text inserted

between shots during the silent era (and less frequently later) to announce a change of scene or location, give dialogue lines, guide the spectator by summarizing in advance the next scene's action, or comment editorially.

iris The technique of darkening part of the image to reshape the frame and highlight one part of it.

jump cut A cut that breaks temporal continuity in a scene by leaving a gap in time.

Kammerspiel Chamber films, a genre in German silent cinema of the 1920s; several of these works were made without intertitles, on the grounds that, in these intimate dramas, characters' feelings were conveyed most subtly through performance and visual effects.

key light The principal light used to illuminate a scene; **high key** lighting indicates a brightly lit scene, **low key** a darker scene.

Kinemacolor A two-color filmmaking process introduced in 1908 in Britain by George Albert Smith and Charles Urban. It photographed black-and-white film through a rotating wheel with red and green filters, so that each frame was alternately exposed to one or the other filter. The black-and-white positive print was then projected with red and green lights, the red light shining on the frames exposed to the red filter, and the green light accordingly. Kinemacolor films were exhibited into the 1920s.

Kineopticon Motion picture projector introduced in Britain by Birt Acres in January 1896.

Kinetograph The motion picture camera developed in 1891 for Thomas A. Edison by his laboratory employee W. K. L. Dickson.

Kuleshov effect A concept developed by Soviet film director Lev Kuleshov at his acting workshop in the 1920s, that describes a phenomenon whereby shots acquire their meaning only in relation to other shots.

lens An optical device, usually made of glass, with one or both sides curved, that refracts light rays onto the surface of photographic film inside a camera; also used in projectors to enlarge the film image.

lighting The illumination of a camera subject.

location shooting Filming scenes away from a studio lot.

long shot A shot photographed from sufficient distance to include a character's full body and to convey a sense of the spatial dimensions of the setting.

long take An unbroken shot that involves duration longer than normal for a particular cinema practice, and generally includes camera movements to record actions and objects that would otherwise be filmed in separate shot set-ups.

low-angle shot A shot taken from below.

magic lantern The name for pre-cinema devices that projected large-screen images of slides and often created the illusion of motion.

magic realism A literary and film style in which fable-like and seemingly miraculous events are presented realistically; the term was used in European art debates of the 1920s, but is most commonly associated with works of political allegory in Latin America.

Marxism The doctrines deriving from the theories of the German socialist Karl Marx (1818–1883), founder of Communism. In basic terms, Marx held that history is governed by laws which shape economic development; that these laws divide society into classes; and that the injustices of capitalism would drive wage laborers (the working class, or proletariat) to overthrow the political system that supported capitalism and put in its place a "dictatorship of the proletariat." Marxism helped to shape filmmaking practices in the Soviet Union and other socialist countries.

masking Blocking off part of the photographed image either to alter the visible area (as with an **iris** effect) or in preparation for a **special effect**, such as a **matte process** shot.

master shot A take that establishes the complete space and action of a scene; in the editing process, it will normally become part of an edited sequence including other types of shots, such as **inserts, close-ups, shot-countershot** combinations, etc.

matte process Blocking off (**masking**) part of the photographed image so that a separately photographed image may be printed with it to give the appearance of a single shot.

medium shot A shot showing less than a performer's full body, generally from head to thigh or calf.

microphone The apparatus that picks up sound waves and converts them to electronic impulses.

mise-en-scène A French term, adapted from the vocabulary of the theater, denoting the totality of a film's visual style: placement and movement of camera and performers, decor, lighting, all that appears before the camera.

mixing (mix) These are terms that pertain both to the recording and editing of sound. The sound mixer is the person on the set who records dialogue during filming. **Mix** also denotes the final sound edit in which dialogue, music, and sound effects tracks are mixed together to make up a film's master soundtrack.

mogul A popular term for the heads of the major Hollywood film companies during the era of the studio system from the 1920s to the 1950s; it derives from the Mongol conquerors of India in the sixteenth century.

montage The French term for film editing; it denotes a theoretical concept and an aesthetic practice that puts emphasis on the placement of shots in relation to one another, on the grounds that images communicate less in themselves than by their juxtaposition among other images.

multiple exposure A special effect in which two or more images are printed over one another in a single frame.

multiple image frame A film frame that contains two or more distinctly separate images occupying different spaces in the frame.

narration Spoken words on the soundtrack, either from a **voice-over** or on-screen figures, that comment upon a film's events or characters; the term can also apply more generally to the structure, technique, or theories of narrative form.

narrative A type of visual or written text that generally tells a fictional story, as opposed to texts that are, for example, descriptions or explanatory treatises.

narrative film The term for acted fictional story films, in distinction from other filmic categories such as documentary or non-narrative film.

negative cost An industry term for the cost of producing a finished film, separate from later expenses such as making additional prints, advertising, and promotion.

neorealism An Italian film movement after 1945 with a concern for representing social actuality through a style emphasizing location shooting and the use of nonprofessional actors; though neorealism lasted only a few years in Italy, it had a strong influence on filmmakers seeking to depict issues of contemporary society in Latin America and elsewhere.

newsreel Short films of actuality footage on contemporary events, generally made up of a number of brief items; several Hollywood studios, as well as news organizations, released weekly newsreels to be screened on a theater's program before the feature film, until television news took over their function in the 1950s.

new wave A term frequently used to denote the emergence of a new generation of younger filmmakers in a country; deriving from the *nouvelle vague* in France at the end of the 1950s, it was also applied to movements in Japan and Czechoslovakia in the 1960s.

nickelodeon A term for store-front movie theaters that emerged in United States cities after 1905 and generally charged five cents (a nickel) for a ticket.

nonfiction film A film type that generally involves actuality filmmaking; the term has come into widespread use as a synonym for **documentary**.

nonsynchronous sound As opposed to **synchronous** sound, sound that is not recorded simultaneously with the visual image, or that does not necessarily appear to be emanating from a specific screen source; also known as **asynchronous sound**.

off-screen sound Sound employed without a visual source, but assumed to be related to action or events outside the frame image.

off-screen space The utilization in a film of action occurring outside the visual range of the frame image.

overlapping dissolve Same as **lap dissolve**; see **dissolve**.

overlapping sound Voices, music, or sound effects occurring at the same moment in a film, competing for the spectator's attention, or rendering each other illegible.

pan Generally describes a horizontal camera movement, though one can also speak of a vertical pan.

panchromatic negative film A type of film stock introduced in the 1920s that became standard around 1927, with an infrared version in 1928. Developed originally for color photography, it added considerable light sensitivity in black-and-white, allowing cinematographers to use softer, more nondirectional lighting. It also made possible day-for-night effects (shooting in sunlight scenes which appear on screen as if photographed at night).

Phenakistoscope A motion toy (early 1830s, several inventors), consisting of a plate-sized, slotted disk with a sequence of drawings around its circle; when the disk was spun in front of a mirror, a person looking through the slots would see the drawings appear to move.

point-of-view shot A shot that represents the viewpoint of a character, showing what the person is looking at; it can also represent a character's psychological or physical state, for example a blurred or tilted image for what a drunken person is seeing.

postsynchronization Adding synchronized sound to a shot or sequence during postproduction to make it appear as if the sound were recorded simultaneously with the image.

Praxinoscope A motion toy, developed in the 1870s in France by Èmile Reynaud, similar to the **Zoetrope,** with the addition of mirrors.

pre-lap A technical term for a stylistic feature of sound editing in which, in anticipation of a scene change, sound from the upcoming shot begins in the final frames of the previous shot.

primitive cinema A term used in film historiography to denote the era of filmmaking and the culture of moviegoing up to around 1910. Its purpose is to clarify some fundamental differences between early cinema and what followed not by suggesting that early film was deficient but that early filmmakers held a different idea about how a film should be made, and to make their works comprehensible within their own setting.

process shot A shot in which live-action performance is filmed on a studio set in front of a projected image on a translucent screen, to make it appear as if the actors are performing on location.

producer The person responsible for the financial and logistical aspects of a film production, such as budgeting, schedule-making, and set construction; he or she may also oversee the work of creative personnel and exercise authority over artistic aspects of the production.

production values An industry term for elements of mise-en-scène that are thought to enhance a film's appeal to audiences, such as expensive-looking costumes, elaborate set designs, picturesque location shots, or large casts of extras.

projector The apparatus that illuminates, enlarges, and advances film frames to cast the appearance of moving images on a screen or other surface.

propaganda film While efforts to persuade spectators to adopt a point of view take many forms, this term generally denotes films made for the purpose of advocating specific policies or viewpoints of governments or groups.

rack focus Change of focus within a shot.

rapid cutting A term denoting an editing style utilizing a series of very brief shots.

raw stock Film footage before it is exposed.

realism An aesthetic doctrine or practice that emphasizes the effort to represent actuality. In film theory, the concept is strongly associated with the French critic André Bazin, who advocated styles such as the **long take** and **deep focus** cinematography that he regarded as allowing the "real" world to speak for itself.

reel The spool on which film is wound for projection. Also, a unit for measuring film duration: in early decades, projection reels held 1000 feet (or 305 meters) of film; since projection speeds varied in the silent era, film length was often stated in number of reels (or feet, or meters) rather than minutes.

reverse angle shot A shot that reverses the angle of vision of the previous shot, often used to switch points of view, as when two people are facing each other.

reverse motion Action that appears to occur backwards, for example, a diver leaping out of the water and ending up poised on the diving platform. This effect can be achieved by running film backwards in the camera and projecting it normally, or by printing footage so it runs in reverse through the projector.

road show In U.S. film exhibition, special showings, often at higher prices, before general release.

scenario A term used in the early decades of cinema to describe written outlines, treatments, or scripts for films.

scene A unit within the narrative or continuity of a film, defined by variable elements such as time, place, or the completion of an action.

score The musical portion of a film's soundtrack, written by a composer or compiled from existing works by a musical director.

screenplay The written text of a film prepared prior to production, containing dialogue to be spoken by performers and such other elements as breakdowns of shots and scenes, descriptions of decor and locations, or specific instructions as to camera distance and movement.

screwball comedy A movement or sub-genre in American film during the 1930s of romantic comedies, often featuring quirky members of the affluent classes, holding out the possibility of cross-class romance, or giving wealthy characters lessons in human values.

scriptwriter The author of a screenplay.

sequence A unit within the narrative or continuity of a film, generally composed of a related group of shots; **sequence shot** refers to a long take that involves multiple changes of position by performers and by the camera.

serial A fictional narrative made up of one- or two-reel films released on a weekly basis, each installment often ending in moments of crisis and imminent death that would only be resolved in the next; the format was most popular when first introduced in the period between 1910 and 1920, but continued into the 1940s.

set A space constructed or utilized for shooting a film.

shot The basic unit of a film, consisting of an **exposure** from a single camera made without interruption.

shot chain The shaping of a narrative through a sequence of separate shots.

shot-countershot A term for a sequence of shots that shift back and forth between positions within the same space, such as when two persons are in conversation and the shot sequence shows each one alternately.

slapstick A boisterous, sometimes physically violent type of comedy, highly popular in the period from 1910 to 1920; the term derived from the stick wielded by clowns in Punch 'n' Judy puppet shows.

slow motion A shot that makes people or objects appear to be moving more slowly than their normal speed, achieved by photographing more feet of film per second than standard, or by slowing down projection.

socialist realism A doctrine developed in the Soviet Union from the late 1920s that opposed formal experimentation in cinema and other arts and called for narratives and styles capable of delivering political indoctrination to a mass audience of workers and peasants.

soft focus Reducing the sharpness of the image by manipulation of the lens or by interposing material such as gauze between the lens and the object being photographed.

sound effects Sounds other than dialogue or music recorded during production, or added or enhanced in postproduction.

sound-on-disc A technology for recording motion picture sound on a disc similar to a phonograph record, extensively utilized in the late 1920s, particularly by the Vitaphone Corporation, but largely abandoned by 1930 in favor of sound-on-film recording.

sound-on-film A technology for recording motion picture sound directly onto the film strip by the optical recording of sound through turning sound waves into photographic images.

sound stage A shooting stage that has been sound-proofed.

soundtrack The track on the edge of a film strip that contains the dialogue, sound effects, music, and narration for a film; it can be recorded optically (see **variable-density soundtrack**) or magnetically, on iron oxide in the manner of a tape recorder.

split-screen The printing of two or more distinctly separate images on the same film frame.

special effects The term for creating images other than by conventional photography, either by visual or mechanical means; abbreviated as FX.

star system The management and promotion of performers to determine their screen roles and enhance their box office appeal; the term is generally associated with Hollywood's studio era, but versions of the star system operated in many countries.

stop-motion photography Stopping the camera to make a change in the scene being photographed; used for **trick films** (for example, to make it appear as if a character has magically disappeared), **special effects,** and **animation**.

storyboard A series of drawings made in planning a film's visual continuity, to determine shot sequences, camera location and angles, and other elements.

studio The physical plant of a motion picture company, comprising its offices, laboratories, shops, stages, etc.; also, a general name for a motion picture company.

subtitles Words printed on the visual image, usually to translate dialogue from one language to another.

superimposition The printing of one separately photographed image over another, to achieve a **trick** or **special effect,** for example the appearance of a spirit or ghost.

Surrealism A movement in the arts emerging primarily in France in the 1920s, with the aesthetic aim of undermining concepts of everyday reality and utilizing dreams, fantasy, and the unconscious in artistic creation; associated with the cinematic **avant-garde**.

synchronous sound Sound recorded simultaneously with the visual image or synchronized with the image so that it appears to be emanating from the actions of persons or objects on the screen.

take The act of photographing a specific shot; takes are frequently repeated, and consecutively numbered, and the most effective ones are selected by the director and editor in the post-production editing process.

Technicolor A motion picture color process developed principally by Herbert Kalmus in which first two, then three separately colored negatives were photographed through a single lens and then printed together on one positive film strip. Two-color Technicolor was introduced in the 1920s and replaced with three-color in the early 1930s; the Walt Disney cartoon *Flowers and Trees* (1932) was the first three-color Technicolor release.

television A moving image technology developed in the 1920s that became linked to home viewing after the 1940s. The television camera converts the image that it photographs into electronic impulses; these are scanned by an electron beam and transmitted by electronic signals, either by broadcast antenna or coaxial cable, to a television receiver in which the signals are reconverted into impulses that reformulate the image.

Thaumatrope A motion toy (1826), attributed to John Ayrton Paris, consisting of a round card attached to a string, with separate but related drawings on either side.

tilting Turning the camera so that the photographed image appears to be observed at other than a right angle.

tinting Painting individual frames of black-and-white film by hand, or bathing film footage in colored dyes, to achieve color effects.

tracking shot A shot made with a moving camera, sometimes mounted on rails or tracks; see also **dolly.**

trick film A term used in early cinema to denote a film whose spectacle or narrative action derived from **special effects** cinematography.

variable-density soundtrack The wavy streaks of white lines on the side of a film strip that represent optically recorded motion picture sound; light projected onto the soundtrack activates a variable electrical current that is converted back into sounds.

vertical integration A term denoting industrial structures in the United States and elsewhere, in which a single company operates production, distribution, and exhibition facilities; in the U.S., this form of ownership was declared illegal by the Supreme Court in 1948, but allowed to resume in the 1980s.

videotape Magnetic tape for recording images shot with a video camera; since the 1970s, a vast market has opened for videocassette recorders (VCRs) in the home, used for recording television programs or playing feature motion pictures or other material rented or purchased at video stores.

Vitaphone A motion picture sound system utilizing **sound-on-disc** technology introduced in 1926 by the Vitaphone Corporation, formed by the Western Electric company along with the Hollywood studio Warner Bros.

Vitascope First American motion picture projector, developed by Charles Francis Jenkins and Thomas Armat, marketed as a product of Thomas A. Edison and used at the premiere motion picture screening in the United States on April 23, 1896, at Koster & Bial's Music Hall in New York.

voice-over Narration or dialogue in a film that comes from another time or space than that of the screen image.

Weimar cinema The general term for filmmaking in Germany from 1918 to 1933 during the Weimar Republic, from the end of World War I to the seizure of power by Adolf Hitler and the Nazis. The name derives from the city of Weimar, where a republic was established in 1918 following Germany's surrender.

wide-angle lens A lens with a shorter focal length than standard, that produces a wider field of vision.

widescreen A term describing screen images wider than the standard **Academy ratio** of 1.33:1. An anamorphic lens can create a screen image twice as wide as the standard, 2.66:1. Since the 1950s most films have been shot with aspect ratios ranging from 1.6:1 to 1.85:1.

wipe An editing technique that makes it appear as if one shot is pushing another off the screen.

Zoetrope A motion toy (1860s, several inventors) consisting of a bowl-like device with a strip of drawings around the interior circumference; when the bowl was spun, viewers peered through slots in the sides to watch the drawings seemingly in motion.

zoom shot A rapid magnification or telescoping effect (or its opposite), made possible by a zoom lens of variable focal length that permits the effect to occur in continuous smooth movement.

Zoopraxiscope A magic lantern projection device developed c. 1882 by Eadweard Muybridge on the model of the **Phenakistoscope,** using rotating disks to show drawings based on his motion photographs.

Filmography

This filmography contains the following information for films mentioned in this book: original language title; English title or translation, if any; country of origin; year of release; director; running time (silent films are indicated and running times given at 18 frames per second, unless otherwise noted); black-and-white or color; special formats; production company; and availability in the United States on videotape (V=VHS, NTSC format) or laser disc (LD). Films are listed in alphabetical order by original title. In a few cases complete information was not available.

↔ (Back and Forth). U.S., 1969. *Dir.* Michael Snow. 52 min., color.

A Bout de souffle (Breathless). France, 1960. *Dir.* Jean-Luc Godard. 90 min., b/w. SNC. V, LD.

Abschied von gestern (Yesterday Girl). West Germany, 1966. *Dir.* Alexander Kluge. 90 min., b/w. Kairos Film/Alexander Kluge/Independent.

Accattone. Italy, 1961. *Dir.* Pier Paolo Pasolini. 120 min., b/w. Cino del Duca/Arco. V.

Ace in the Hole (aka The Big Carnival). U.S., 1951. *Dir.* Billy Wilder. 111 min., b/w. Paramount.

acto da primavera, O (Spring Mystery Play). Portugal, 1963. *Dir.* Manoel de Oliveira. 94 min., color. Manoel de Oliveira.

Act of Seeing with One's Own Eyes, The. U.S., 1971. *Dir.* Stan Brakhage. 32 min., color.

Adjuster, The. Canada, 1991. *Dir.* Atom Egoyan. 102 min., color. Ego Film Arts.

Afrique sur Seine (Africa on the Seine). France, 1955. *Dir.* Paulin Soumanou Vieyra. 22 min., b/w.

After Hours. U.S., 1985. *Dir.* Martin Scorsese. 97 min., DuArt Color. Warner Bros./Geffen/Double Play. V, LD.

Ajantrik (Pathetic Fallacy). India, 1958. *Dir.* Ritwik Ghatak. 102 min., b/w. L&B Films International.

Akira Kurosawa's Dreams. Japan/U.S., 1990. *Dir.* Akira Kurosawa. 119 min., color. Kurosawa Productions. V, LD.

Alexandr Nevskii (Alexander Nevsky). U.S.S.R., 1938. *Dir.* Sergei Eisenstein. 112 min., b/w. Mosfilm. V, LD.

Alice in den Städten (Alice in the Cities). West Germany, 1973. *Dir.* Wim Wenders. 110 min., b/w. Filmverlag der Autoren. V.

allseitig reduzierte Persönlichkeit—Redupers, Die (The All Round Reduced Personality—Redupers). West Germany, 1977. *Dir.* Helke Sander. 98 min., b/w. Basis-Film Verleih.

All That Heaven Allows. U.S., 1955. *Dir.* Douglas Sirk. 89 min., Technicolor. Universal-International.

All the President's Men. U.S., 1976. *Dir.* Alan J. Pakula. 138 min., Technicolor. Warner Bros./Wildwood. V.

All This and Heaven Too. U.S., 1940. *Dir.* Anatole Litvak. 140 min., b/w. Warner Bros. V.

Aloma of the South Seas. U.S., 1926. *Dir.* Maurice Tourneur. 90 min., b/w, silent. Famous Players-Lasky.

Alphaville. France, 1965. *Dir.* Jean-Luc Godard. 98 min., b/w. Chaumiane/Filmstudio. V.

Amadeus. U.S., 1984. *Dir.* Miloš Forman. 160 min., Technicolor, Panavision. Saul Zaentz. V, LD.

Amar Jyoti (Eternal Light). India, 1936. *Dir.* V. Shantaram. 163 min., b/w. Prabhat Film Co.

American Graffiti. U.S., 1973. *Dir.* George Lucas. 110 min., Techniscope. Universal/Lucasfilm/Coppola Company. V, LD.

American in Paris, An. U.S., 1951. *Dir.* Vincente Minnelli. 113 min., color. Metro-Goldwyn-Mayer. V, LD.

amerikanische Freund, Der (The American Friend). U.S./France/West Germany, 1977. *Dir.* Wim Wenders. 123 min., color. Road Movies/Wim Wenders/Westdeutscher Rundfunk/Les Films du Losange. V, LD.

Amor de perdiçao (Doomed Love). Portugal, 1978. *Dir.* Manoel de Oliveira. 260 min., color. Instituto Português de Cinema/Centro Português de Cinema/Radiotelevisão Portuguesa/Cinequipa/Tóbis Portuguesa.

Amours de la Riene Elisabeth, Les (Queen Elizabeth). France, 1912. *Dir.* Louis Mercanton. 43 min., b/w, silent. Film D'Art.

Anaparastassis (Reconstruction). Greece, 1970. *Dir.* Theodoros Angelopoulos. 100 min., b/w. George Samiotis Productions.

Andrei Rublev. U.S.S.R., 1966. *Dir.* Andrei Tarkovsky. 185 min., b/w. Mosfilm. V.

Anemic Cinema. France, 1926. *Dir.* Marcel Duchamp. 7 min., b/w, silent.

Angel of Broadway, The. U.S., 1927. *Dir.* Lois Weber. 82 min., b/w, silent. DeMille/Pathé.

Angst essen Seele Auf (Ali: Fear Eats the Soul). West Germany, 1973. *Dir.* Rainer Werner Fassbinder. 94 min., color. Tango Film. V.

Animal Crackers. U.S., 1930. *Dir.* Victor Heerman. 97 min., b/w. Paramount. V, LD.

Anna Boleyn. Germany, 1920. *Dir.* Ernst Lubitsch. 100 min., b/w, silent. Union/Ufa.

Anna Christie. U.S., 1930. *Dir.* Clarence Brown. 86 min., b/w. Metro-Goldwyn-Mayer. V.

Anna Karenina. U.S., 1935. *Dir.* Clarence Brown. 95 min., b/w. Metro-Goldwyn-Mayer. V.

Année dernière à Marienbad, L' (Last Year at Marienbad). France, 1961. *Dir.* Alain Resnais. 94 min., b/w. Terra/Tamara/Cormoran/ Precite/Como/Argos/Cinete/Silver/Cineriz. V.

Annie Hall. U.S., 1977. *Dir.* Woody Allen. 93 min., De Luxe. United Artists. V, LD.

A nous la liberté (Give Us Liberty). France, 1931. *Dir.* René Clair. 93 min., b/w. Film Sonore/Tobis Film. V.

Antônio das Mortes. Brazil, 1969. *Dir.* Glauber Rocha. 95 min., color. Glauber Rocha/Mapa. V.

Anybody's Woman. U.S., 1930. *Dir.* Dorothy Arzner. 80 min., b/w. Paramount.

Apache. U.S., 1954. *Dir.* Robert Aldrich. 91 min., Technicolor. United Artists/Hecht-Lancaster. V.

Aparajito (The Unvanquished). India, 1956. *Dir.* Satyajit Ray. 127 min., b/w. Epic Films. V.

Applause. U.S., 1929. *Dir.* Rouben Mamoulian. 80 min., b/w. Paramount. V.

A propos de Nice (On the Subject of Nice). France, 1930. *Dir.* Jean Vigo. 45 min., b/w, silent. Lozinski.

Apur Sansar (The World of Apu). India, 1959. *Dir.* Satyajit Ray. 117 min., b/w. Satyajit Ray Productions.V.

ard, Al (The Land). Egypt, 1969. *Dir.* Youssef Chahine. 130 min., color. O.G.E.C.

Arriveé d'un train en gare (Arrival of a Train at La Ciotat). France, 1896. *Dir.* Louis Lumière. 1 min., b/w, silent. Société Lumière.

Arroseur et arrosé (Waterer and Watered). France, 1896. *Dir.* Louis Lumière. 1 min., b/w, silent. Société Lumière.

Arsenal (The Arsenal). U.S.S.R., 1929. *Dir.* Alexander Dovzhenko. 99 min., b/w, silent. VUFKU.

Art of Vision, The. U.S., 1961–65. *Dir.* Stan Brakhage. 270 min., b/w and color, silent.

Asphalt Jungle, The. U.S., 1950. *Dir.* John Huston. 112 min., b/w. Metro-Goldwyn-Mayer. V, LD.

Assassinat du Duc de Guise, L' (The Assassination of the Duc de Guise). France, 1908. *Dir.* Charles Le Bargy. 13 min., b/w, silent. Film D'Art.

Assunta Spina. Italy, 1915. *Dir.* Gustavo Serena. 66 min., b/w, silent. Caesar Film.

Astenicheskii sindrom (The Weakness Syndrome). U.S.S.R., 1989. *Dir.* Kira Muratova.

Atalante, L'. France, 1934. *Dir.* Jean Vigo. 89 min., b/w. Nounez-Gaumont. V.

!Atame! (Tie Me Up! Tie Me Down!). Spain, 1989. *Dir.* Pedro Almodóvar. 101 min., color. El Deseo. V, LD.

Attack on a Chinese Mission Station. Britain, 1900. *Dir.* James Williamson. 2 min., b/w, silent. Williamson.

Au hasard Balthazar. France, 1966. *Dir.* Robert Bresson. 95 min., b/w. Parc/Athos/Ardos/Svensk Filmindustri.

automóvil gris, El (The Gray Car). Mexico, 1919. *Dir.* Enrique Rosas, Joaquín Coss and Juan Canals de Homs. 12 episodes, 24 reels, b/w, silent. Enrique Rosas and Azteca Films S.A.

avventura, L'. Italy, 1960. *Dir.* Michelangelo Antonioni. 145 min., b/w. Cino del Duca/PCE/Lyre. V, LD.

Awakenings. U.S., 1990. *Dir.* Penny Marshall. 121 min., color. Columbia. V, LD.

Awara (The Vagabond). India, 1951. *Dir.* Raj Kapoor. 170 min., b/w. RK Films.

Bad and the Beautiful, The. U.S., 1952. *Dir.* Vincente Minnelli. 116 min., b/w. Metro-Goldwyn-Mayer. V, LD.

Bakushu (Early Summer). Japan, 1951. *Dir.* Yasujiro Ozu. 135 min., b/w. Shochiku. V.

Ballet mécanique, Le. France, 1924. *Dir.* Fernand Léger. 10 min., b/w, silent. Fernand Léger/Dudley Murphy.

bambini ci guardano, I (The Children Are Watching Us). Italy, 1942. *Dir.* Vittorio De Sica. 85 min., b/w. Scalera/Invicta.

Bande à part (Band of Outsiders). France, 1964. *Dir.* Jean-Luc Godard. 95 min., b/w. Anouchka/Orsay. V.

bandito, Il (The Bandit). Italy, 1946. *Dir.* Alberto Lattuada. 88 min., b/w. Lux.

Band Wagon, The. U.S., 1953. *Dir.* Vincente Minnelli. 112 min., Technicolor. Metro-Goldwyn-Mayer. V, LD.

Banshun (Late Spring). Japan, 1949. *Dir.* Yasujiro Ozu. 108 min., b/w. Ofuna. V.

Bardelys the Magnificent. U.S., 1926. *Dir.* King Vidor. 126 min., b/w, silent. Metro-Goldwyn-Mayer.

Barravento ("The Turning Wind"). Brazil, 1962. *Dir.* Glauber Rocha. 76 min., b/w.

Barwy ochronne (Camouflage). Poland, 1976. *Dir.* Krzysztof Zanussi. 100 min., color. Tor Film Unit.

Bas-fonds, Les (The Lower Depths). France, 1936. *Dir.* Jean Renoir. 92 min., b/w. Albatros. V.

batalla de Chile, La (The Battle of Chile). Cuba/Chile, 1975–79. *Dir.* Patricio Guzmán. 287 min., b/w. Equipe Tercer Ano Productions.

Batman. U.S., 1989. *Dir.* Tim Burton. 126 min., color. Warner Bros. V, LD.

battaglia di Algeri, La (The Battle of Algiers). Italy, 1966. *Dir.* Gillo Pontecorvo. 135 min., b/w. Casbah/Igor A. V, LD.

Battle of Britain, The. U.S., 1943. *Dir.* Anthony Veiller. 52 min., b/w. U.S. War Department. V.

Battle of China, The. U.S., 1944. *Dir.* Frank Capra, Anatole Litvak. 67 min., b/w. Army Pictorial Service. V.

Battle of Midway, The. U.S., 1942. *Dir.* John Ford. 17 min., Kodachrome/Technicolor. U.S. Navy/20th Century-Fox.

Battle of Russia, The. U.S., 1943. *Dir.* Anatole Litvak. 80 min., b/w. U.S. War Department. V.

Battle of San Pietro, The. U.S., 1945. *Dir.* John Huston. 45 and 30 min. versions, b/w. U.S. Army

Pictorial Service.

Bat Whispers, The. U.S., 1930. *Dir.* Roland West. 82 min., b/w, 65mm. United Artists. V, LD.

Beau Geste. U.S., 1926. *Dir.* Herbert Brenon. 120 min., b/w with color sequences, silent. Paramount.

Beauty and the Beast. U.S., 1991. *Dir.* Gary Trousdale, Kirk Wise. 84 min., color. Walt Disney Company/
Silver Screen Partners IV. V.

Becky Sharp. U.S., 1935. *Dir.* Rouben Mamoulian. 84 min., Technicolor. Pioneer/RKO. V.

Befreier und Befreite/Krieg-Verwaltigungen-Kinder (Liberators Take Liberties—War, Rapes and Children). Germany, 1992. *Dir.* Helke Sander. 210 min., color. Bremer Institut Film—Fersehen/Helke Sander Filmproduktion/Journal Film Klaus Volkenborn/WDR.

Beiqing Chengshi (A City of Sadness). Taiwan, 1989. *Dir.* Hou Hsiao-Hsien. 160 min., color. Artificial Eye/3-H/Era International.

Bend of the River. U.S., 1952. *Dir.* Anthony Mann. 91 min., Technicolor. Universal-International. V.

Ben-Hur. U.S., 1959. *Dir.* William Wyler. 217 min., Technicolor, Camera 65. Metro-Goldwyn-Mayer. V, LD.

Berg-Ejvind och hans hustru (The Outlaw and His Wife). Sweden, 1918. *Dir.* Victor Sjöström. 136 min., b/w, silent. Svenska Biografteatern. V.

Berlin Alexanderplatz. West Germany/Italy, 1979–80. *Dir.* Rainer Werner Fassbinder. 14-part series, 975 min. total, color. Bavaria Atelier/RAI-TV2.

Berlin: Die Sinfonie der Grosssstadt (Berlin: Symphony of a Great City). Germany, 1927. *Dir.* Walther Ruttmann. 70 min., b/w, silent. Fox Europa.

Best Years of Our Lives, The. U.S., 1946. *Dir.* William Wyler. 163 min., b/w. RKO/Goldwyn. V, LD.

Beverly Hills Cop. U.S., 1984. *Dir.* Martin Brest. 105 min., Technicolor. Paramount/Don Simpson/Jerry Bruckheimer. V, LD.

Beyond the Valley of the Dolls. U.S., 1970. *Dir.* Russ Meyer. 109 min., De Luxe, Panavision. 20th Century-Fox. V.

Bez znieczulenia (Without Anesthesia). Poland, 1978. *Dir.* Andrzej Wajda. 131 min., color. Group X/Film Polski.

Bhuvan Shome. India, 1969. *Dir.* Mrinal Sen. 96 min., b/w. Mrinal Sen Productions.

Bian Zou Bian Chang (Life on a String). Germany/Japan/Britain/China, 1991. *Dir.* Chen Kaige. 104 min., color. Beijing Film Studio/China Film Co-Production Corp./Serene Productions/Pandora Film.

Bicots-nègres, vos vousins, Les (The Nigger-Arabs, Your Neighbors). France, 1973. *Dir.* Med Hondo. 130 min., color.

Big. U.S., 1988. *Dir.* Penny Marshall. 102 min., DuArt Color/De Luxe. 20th Century-Fox. V, LD.

Bigger Than Life. U.S., 1956. *Dir.* Nicholas Ray. 95 min., Eastmancolor, CinemaScope. 20th Century-Fox.

Big Heat, The. U.S., 1953. *Dir.* Fritz Lang. 90 min., b/w. Columbia. V, LD.

Big House, The. U.S., 1930. *Dir.* George Hill. 88 min., b/w. Metro-Goldwyn-Mayer.

Big Parade, The. U.S., 1925. *Dir.* King Vidor. 150 min., b/w, with Technicolor sequences, silent. Metro-Goldwyn-Mayer. V, LD.

Big Sleep, The. U.S., 1946. *Dir.* Howard Hawks. 113 min., b/w. Warner Bros. V, LD.

Big Trail, The. U.S., 1930. *Dir.* Raoul Walsh. 125 min., b/w and color, Grandeur (70mm widescreen). Fox. V.

Billy the Kid. U.S., 1930. *Dir.* King Vidor. 95 min., b/w, Realife. Metro-Goldwyn-Mayer.

Birds, The. U.S., 1963. *Dir.* Alfred Hitchcock. 119 min., Technicolor. Universal. V.

Birth of a Nation, The. U.S., 1915. *Dir.* D. W. Griffith. 185 min. (16 f.p.s.), b/w, silent. Epoch. V, LD.

bitteren Tränen der Petra von Kant, Die (The Bitter Tears of Petra von Kant). West Germany, 1972. *Dir.* Rainer Werner Fassbinder. 124 min., color. Tango Film. V.

Blackmail. Britain, 1929. *Dir.* Alfred Hitchcock. 78 min., b/w. BIP. V, LD.

Black Pirate, The. U.S., 1926. *Dir.* Albert Parker. 76 min., Technicolor, silent. Douglas Fairbanks Productions. V, LD.

Blacula. U.S., 1972. *Dir.* William Crain. 92 min., color. American International. V, LD.

Blade af Satans bog (Leaves from Satan's Book). Denmark, 1919 (released 1921). *Dir.* Carl Th. Dreyer. 133 min., b/w, silent. Nordisk Film.

Blade Runner. U.S., 1982. *Dir.* Ridley Scott. 117 min., Technicolor, Panavision. Warner Bros./Ladd/Blade Runner Partnership. V, LD.

blaue Engel, Der (The Blue Angel). Germany, 1930. *Dir.* Josef von Sternberg. 98 min., b/w. UFA. V, LD.

blaue Licht, Das (The Blue Light). Germany, 1932. *Dir.* Leni Riefenstahl. 77 min., b/w. Sokal/Leni Riefenstahl Film. V.

Blechtrommel, Die (The Tin Drum). West Germany, 1979. *Dir.* Volker Schlöndorff. 142 min., color. United Artists/Franz Seitz/Bioskop/GGB 14KG/Hallelujah/Artemis/Jadran/Film Polski. V.

Blind Husbands. U.S., 1919. *Dir.* Erich von Stroheim. 90 min., b/w, silent. Universal.

Blood and Sand. U.S., 1922. *Dir.* Fred Niblo. 80 min., b/w, silent. Paramount. V, LD.

Blot, The. U.S., 1921. *Dir.* Lois Weber. 70 min., b/w, silent. Lois Weber Productions.

Blow-Up. Britain/Italy, 1966. *Dir.* Michelangelo Antonioni. 110 min., Eastmancolor. Metro-Goldwyn-Mayer/Carlo Ponti. V, LD.

Blue Velvet. U.S., 1986. *Dir.* David Lynch. 120 min., color. De Laurentiis. V, LD.

Bob le flambeur (Bob the Gambler). France, 1956. *Dir.* Jean-Pierre Melville. 100 min., b/w. Jenner/Cyme/Play Art/OGC. V, LD.

Bob Roberts. U.S., 1992. *Dir.* Tim Robbins. 102 min., color. Polygram/Working Title, in association with Barry Levinson and Mark Johnson/Live Entertainment. V, LD.

Body and Soul. U.S., 1925. *Dir.* Oscar Micheaux. 50 min., b/w, silent. Micheaux Film Corp.

Bonheur, Le (Happiness). France, 1965. *Dir.* Agnès Varda. 79 min., color. Parc Films.

Bonnes Femmes, Les ("The Good Women"). France, 1960. *Dir.* Claude Chabrol. 102 min., b/w. Paris/Panitalia/Hakim.

Bonnie and Clyde. U.S., 1967. *Dir.* Arthur Penn. 111 min., Technicolor. Warner Bros./Seven Arts/Tatira/Hiller. V, LD.

Bons Débarras, Les (Good Riddance). Canada, 1980. *Dir.* Francis Mankiewicz. 109 min., Eastmancolor. Les Productions Prisma.

Bonus March. U.S., 1932. *Dir.* Leo Seltzer. 12 min., b/w. Film and Photo League.

Born in Flames. U.S., 1983. *Dir.* Lizzie Borden. 80 min., color. Jerome Foundation.

Boudu sauvé des eaux (Boudu Saved from Drowning). France, 1932. *Dir.* Jean Renoir. 87 min., b/w. Haik/CCF. V.

Boyz N the Hood. U.S., 1991. *Dir.* John Singleton. 107 min., color. Both, Inc. V, LD.

Breaker Morant. Australia, 1980. *Dir.* Bruce Beresford. 107 min., color. New World. V, LD.

Breakfast Club, The. U.S., 1985. *Dir.* John Hughes. 97 min., Technicolor. A&M/Universal. V, LD.

Bridge on the River Kwai, The. Britain, 1957. *Dir.* David Lean. 161 min., Technicolor, CinemaScope. Columbia. V, LD.

Brief Encounter. Britain, 1945. *Dir.* David Lean. 86 min., b/w. Cineguild. V.

Brig, The. U.S., 1964. *Dir.* Jonas Mekas. 68 min., b/w.

Bringing Up Baby. U.S., 1938. *Dir.* Howard Hawks. 102 min., b/w. RKO. V, LD.

Broadway Melody, The. U.S., 1929. *Dir.* Harry Beaumont. 102 min., b/w and Technicolor segments. Metro-Goldwyn-Mayer. V, LD.

Broken Arrow. U.S., 1950. *Dir.* Delmer Daves. 92 min., Technicolor. 20th Century-Fox. V.

Broken Blossoms. U.S., 1919. *Dir.* D. W. Griffith. 105 min. (16 f.p.s), b/w, silent. United Artists/D. W. Griffith. V, LD.

Bronenosets Potemkin (The Battleship Potemkin). U.S.S.R., 1925. *Dir.* Sergei Eisenstein. 75 min., b/w, silent. Goskino. V, LD.

Büchse der Pandora, Die (Pandora's Box). Germany, 1928. *Dir.* G.W. Pabst. 97 min., b/w, silent. Nero Film. V.

Bugs Bunny Nips the Nips. U.S., 1944. *Dir.* Friz Freleng. color. Warner Bros. V.

Bwana Devil. U.S., 1952. *Dir.* Arch Oboler. 79 min., Anscolor 3-D. United Artists.

Cabinet des Dr. Caligari, Das (The Cabinet of Dr. Caligari). Germany, 1919. *Dir.* Robert Wiene. 90 min. (16 f.p.s), b/w, silent. Decla-Bioskop. V, LD.

Cabiria. Italy, 1914. *Dir.* Giovanni Pastrone. 116 min., original length 4000 m., b/w, silent. Itala Film. V.

Caccia tragica (Tragic Hunt). Italy, 1948. *Dir.* Giuseppe De Santis. 89 min., b/w. Lux/ANPI.

caduta di Troia, La (The Fall of Troy). Italy, 1910. *Dir.* Giovanni Pastrone. 27 min., b/w, silent. Itala Film.

Cain and Mabel. U.S., 1936. *Dir.* Lloyd Bacon. 90 min., b/w. Warner Bros.

Camille. U.S., 1937. *Dir.* George Cukor. 108 min., b/w. Metro-Goldwyn-Mayer. V.

Camp de Thiaroye (Camp Thiaroye). Senegal/Algeria/Tunisia, 1988. *Dir.* Ousmane Sembene. 152 min., color. Metro/SNPC/ENAPROC/SATPEC.

Cape Fear. U.S., 1991. *Dir.* Martin Scorsese. 128 min., color. Universal/Cape Fear Inc./Amblin Entertainment/Cappa Films/Tribeca Productions. V, LD.

Carmen. U.S., 1915. *Dir.* Cecil B. DeMille. 51 min., b/w, silent. Jesse L. Lasky Feature Play Co.

Casablanca. U.S., 1943. *Dir.* Michael Curtiz. 99 min., b/w. Warner Bros. V, LD.

Casque d'or (Golden Headpiece). France, 1952. *Dir.* Jacques Becker. 96 min., b/w. Speva/Paris.

caza, La (The Hunt). Spain, 1966. *Dir.* Carlos Saura. 87 min., b/w. Elias Querejeta Productions. V.

Ceddo. Senegal, 1977. *Dir.* Ousmane Sembene. 117 min., b/w. Films Domirêve.

C'eravamo tanto amati (We All Loved Each Other So Much). Italy, 1974. *Dir.* Ettore Scola. 124 min., b/w and color. Dean Cinematografica-Delta. V.

César. France, 1936. *Dir.* Marcel Pagnol. 117 min., b/w. Marcel Pagnol. V, LD.

Chagrin et la pitié, La (The Sorrow and the Pity). France, 1971. *Dir.* Marcel Ophuls. 270 min., b/w. Télévision Recontre/ Norddeutscher Rundfunk/ S.S.R. V.

Champ, The. U.S., 1931. *Dir.* King Vidor. 85 min., b/w. Metro-Goldwyn-Mayer. V.

Chang. U.S., 1927. *Dir.* Merian C. Cooper, Ernest B. Schoedsack. 71 min., b/w, silent, Magnascope. Paramount. V, LD.

Chan Is Missing. U.S., 1983. *Dir.* Wayne Wang. 80 min., b/w. Wayne Wang Productions. V.

Chant of Jimmy Blacksmith, The. Australia, 1978. *Dir.* Fred Schepisi. 122 min., Eastmancolor, Panavision. Film House.

Charge of the Light Brigade, The. U.S., 1936. *Dir.* Michael Curtiz. 116 min., b/w. Warner Bros. Errol Flynn. V, LD.

Charme discret de la bourgeoisie, Le (The Discreet Charm of the Bourgeoisie). France, 1972. *Dir.* Luis Buñuel. 105 min., color. Greenwich Films. V, LD.

Cheat, The. U.S., 1915. *Dir.* Cecil B. DeMille. 95 min. (16 f.p.s), b/w, silent. Famous Players Lasky/Paramount.

Chelovek s kinoapparatom (The Man with the Movie Camera). U.S.S.R., 1929. *Dir.* Dziga Vertov.

90 min., b/w, silent. VUFKU.

Chelsea Girls. U.S., 1966. *Dir.* Andy Warhol. 195 min., color and b/w, 2 screens.

Chêne, Le (The Oak). Romania, 1992. *Dir.* Lucian Pintilie. 105 min., color. Parnasse Productions/Scarabée Films/MK2 Productions/La Sept Cinéma/Le Centre de la Cinématographie/Canal Plus/Film Production Studio of the Romanian Ministry of Culture.

Cheyenne Autumn. U.S., 1964. *Dir.* John Ford. 170 min., Technicolor, Panavision 70. Warner Bros./Ford-Smith. V.

Chien andalou, Un ("An Andalusian Dog"). France, 1929. *Dir.* Luis Buñuel. 17 min., b/w, silent. Luis Buñuel-Salvador Dali.

Chienne, La (The Bitch). France, 1931. *Dir.* Jean Renoir. 100 min., b/w. Braunberger-Richebé. V, LD.

Childhood Rivalry in Bali and New Guinea. U.S., 1952. *Dir.* Gregory Bateson, Margaret Mead. 17 min., b/w.

Children at School. Britain, 1937. *Dir.* Basil Wright. 24 min., b/w. Realist Film Unit for British Commercial Gas Association.

Chinatown. U.S., 1974. *Dir.* Roman Polanski. 131 min., Technicolor, Panavision. Paramount/Long Road. V, LD.

Chinoise, La (The Chinese). France, 1967. *Dir.* Jean-Luc Godard. 95 min., color. Production De La Guéville/Parc/Simar/Anouchka/Athos.

Chokoreto to heitai (Chocolate and Soldiers). Japan, 1938. *Dir.* Takeshi Sato. 74 min., b/w. Toho.

Christopher Strong. U.S., 1933. *Dir.* Dorothy Arzner. 77 min., b/w. RKO. V, LD.

Chronik der Anna Magdalena Bach (Chronicle of Anna Magdalena Bach). West Germany, 1967. *Dir.* Jean-Marie Straub, Danièle Huillet. 93 min., b/w. IDI/RAI/Franz Seitz/Kuatorium Junger Deutscher Film/Straub-Huillet/Filmfonds/TelePool.

Chronique d'un été (Chronicle of a Summer). France, 1961. *Dir.* Jean Rouch, Edgar Morin. 90 min., b/w. Argos.

Ciel, la terre, La. (The Sky, the Earth). Vietnam/France, 1965. *Dir.* Joris Ivens. Franco-Vietnamienne.

Circus, The. U.S., 1928. *Dir.* Charles Chaplin. 70 min., b/w, silent. Charles Chaplin Productions. V.

Citizen Kane. U.S., 1941. *Dir.* Orson Welles. 120 min., b/w. RKO/Mercury. V, LD.

City, The. U.S., 1939. *Dir.* Willard Van Dyke, Ralph Steiner. 32 min., b/w. American Institute of Planners.

City Lights. U.S., 1931. *Dir.* Charles Chaplin. 87 min., b/w. United Artists. V.

City of Dim Faces, The. U.S., 1918. *Dir.* George Melford. 63 min., b/w, silent. Famous Players-Lasky.

City of Hope. U.S., 1991. *Dir.* John Sayles. 129 min., color. Esperanza Productions. V.

Cléo de 5 à 7 (Cléo from 5 to 7). France, 1962. *Dir.* Agnès Varda. 90 min., b/w and color. Rome-Paris Films. V.

Cleopatra. U.S., 1917. *Dir.* J. Gordon Edwards. 11 reels, b/w, silent. Fox Film Corp.

Cleopatra. U.S., 1963. *Dir.* Joseph L. Mankiewicz. 243 min., De Luxe. 20th Century-Fox. V, LD.

Clockwork Orange, A. Britain, 1971. *Dir.* Stanley Kubrick. 136 min., color. Warner Bros./Polaris. V.

Close Encounters of the Third Kind. U.S., 1977. *Dir.* Steven Spielberg. 135 min., Metrocolor, Panavision. Columbia/EMI. V, LD.

Cobweb, The. U.S., 1955. *Dir.* Vincente Minnelli. 124 min., Eastmancolor, CinemaScope. Metro-Goldwyn-Mayer. LD.

Cocoanuts, The. U.S., 1929. *Dir.* Joseph Santley, Robert Florey. 96 min., b/w. Paramount Famous Lasky Corp. V, LD.

Color of Money, The. U.S., 1986. *Dir.* Martin Scorsese. 119 min., DuArt Color. Touchstone. V, LD.

Como era gostoso o meu Francês (How Tasty Was My Little Frenchman). Brazil, 1971. *Dir.* Nelson Pereira Dos Santos. 82 min., color. Dos Santos-Barros Productions.

compadre Mendoza, El. Mexico, 1933. *Dir.* Fernando de Fuentes.

Condamné à mort s'est échappé, Un (A Man Escaped). France, 1956. *Dir.* Robert Bresson. 102 min., b/w. GAU/SNE.

Condemned. U.S., 1929. *Dir.* Wesley Ruggles. 86 min., b/w. Samuel Goldwyn.

conformista, Il (The Conformist). Italy, 1970. *Dir.* Bernardo Bertolucci. 115 min., color. Mars/Marianne/Maran. V.

Connection, The. U.S., 1961. *Dir.* Shirley Clarke. 100 min., b/w.

Constans (The Constant Factor). Poland, 1980. *Dir.* Krzysztof Zanussi. 96 min., color. PRF-Zespol Filmowy.

Conversation, The. U.S., 1974. *Dir.* Francis Ford Coppola. 113 min., Technicolor. Paramount/Francis Ford Coppola. V, LD.

Corbeau, Le (The Raven). France, 1943. *Dir.* Henri-Georges Clouzot. 92 min., b/w. L'Atelier Français. V.

Corner in Wheat, A. U.S., 1909. *Dir.* D.W. Griffith. 14 min., b/w, silent. Biograph Co.

Corradino di Svevia (Conrad of Swabia). Italy, 1909. *Dir.* Romolo Bacchini. 12 min., b/w, silent. Vesuvio Films.

Čovek nije tica (Man Is Not a Bird). Yugoslavia, 1966. *Dir.* Dušan Makavejev. 80 min., b/w. Avala Film.

Cría cuervos (Cria!, "Raise Ravens"). Spain, 1976. *Dir.* Carlos Saura. 115 min., color. Elias Querejeta Productions. V.

Crime de M. Lange, Le (The Crime of M. Lange). France, 1935. *Dir.* Jean Renoir. 85 min., b/w. Obéron. V.

Cristo si è fermato a Eboli (Christ Stopped at Eboli). Italy, 1979. *Dir.* Francesco Rosi. 155 min., color. Vides/RAI/Action/Gaumont. V.

Cronaca di un amore (Story of a Love Affair). Italy, 1950. *Dir.* Michelangelo Antonioni. 96 min., b/w. Villani Films.

Crowd, The. U.S., 1928. *Dir.* King Vidor. 98 min., b/w, silent. Metro-Goldwyn-Mayer. V, LD.

Crying Game, The. Britain, 1992. *Dir.* Neil Jordan. 112 min., color. Palace/Channel Four Films.

Człowiek z marmuru (Man of Marble). Poland, 1976. *Dir.* Andrzej Wajda. 165 min., b/w and color. PRF/Zespol. V.

Człowiek z żelaza (Man of Iron). Poland, 1981. *Dir.* Andrzej Wajda. 152 min., b/w and color. PRF/Filmowy.

Dahong denglong gaogao gue (Raise the Red Lantern). Hong Kong, 1991. *Dir.* Zhang Yimou. 125 min., color. Era International/China Film. V.

Da Lu (The Big Road). China, 1934. *Dir.* Sun Yu. 10 reels, b/w, sound effects. Lianhua Studios.

Dames. U.S., 1934. *Dir.* Ray Enright, Busby Berkeley. 90 min., b/w. Warner Bros. V, LD.

Dances with Wolves. U.S., 1991. *Dir.* Kevin Costner. 180 min., DeLuxe, Panavision. Guild/Tig Productions. V, LD.

Dancing Mothers. U.S., 1926. *Dir.* Herbert Brenon. 70 min., b/w, silent. Famous Players-Lasky. V.

Danton. Poland/France, 1982. *Dir.* Andrzej Wajda. 136 min., color. Les Films du Losange/Group X/Gaumont/TF1/SFPC/TM. V, LD.

Daoma Zei (Horse Thief). China, 1986. *Dir.* Tian Zhuangzhuang. 88 min., color. Xi'an Film Studio.

Daughters of the Dust. U.S., 1992. *Dir.* Julie Dash. 114 min., color. Geechee Girls Productions. V

Day the Earth Stood Still, The. U.S., 1951. *Dir.* Robert Wise. 92 min., b/w. 20th Century-Fox. V, LD.

Da Yuebing (The Big Parade). China, 1986. *Dir.* Chen Kaige. 103 min., color. Guangxi Film Studio.

Débarquement du Congrès de Photographie à Lyon, Le (Debarkation of the Photographic Congress Members at Lyon). France, 1895. *Dir.* Louis Lumière. 40 sec., b/w, silent. Société Lumière.

Débuts d'un patineur, Les (Max Learns to Skate). France, 1907. *Dir.* Louis Gasnier. 6 min., b/w, silent. Pathé Frères/Max Linder.

Déclin de l'empire américain, Le (The Decline of the American Empire). Canada, 1986. *Dir.* Denys Arcand. 101 min., color. Corporation Image M &M/National Film Board of Canada/Téléfilm Canada/Société Générale du Cinema du Québec. V.

Deer Hunter, The. U.S., 1978. *Dir.* Michael Cimino. 182 min., Technicolor, Panavision. Universal/EMI. V, LD.

Démolition d'un mur (Demolition of a Wall). France, 1896. *Dir.* Louis Lumière. b/w, silent. Société Lumière.

Dernier tournant, Le (The Last Turning). France, 1939. *Dir.* Pierre Chenal. 90 min., b/w. Gladiator Films.

Dersu Uzala. U.S.S.R./Japan, 1975. *Dir.* Akira Kurosawa. 140 min., color. Mosfilm/Toho. V.

Desert Hearts. U.S., 1985. *Dir.* Donna Deitch. 91 min., color. Desert Hearts Productions. V, LD.

Desperately Seeking Susan. U.S., 1985. *Dir.* Susan Seidelman. 104 min., De Luxe. Orion. V, LD.

Destination Moon. U.S., 1950. *Dir.* Irving Pichel. 91 min., Technicolor. Universal/George Pal. V, LD.

Destination Tokyo. U.S., 1943. *Dir.* Delmer Daves. 135 min., b/w. Warner Bros. V.

Detour. U.S., 1945. *Dir.* Edgar G. Ulmer. 68 min., b/w. PRC. V, LD.

Deus e o diabo na terra do sol (Black God, White Devil). Brazil, 1964. *Dir.* Glauber Rocha. 120 min., b/w. Luiz Augusto Mendes/Copacabana.

Deutschland, bleiche Mutter (Germany, Pale Mother). West Germany, 1980. *Dir.* Helma Sanders-Brahms. 109 min., color. Literarisches Colloquium/WDR.

Deutschland im Herbst (Germany in Autumn). West Germany, 1978. *Dirs.* Alf Brustellin, Alexander Kluge, Maximiliane Mainka, Edgar Reitz, Katja Rupé, Hans Peter Cloos, Volker Schlöndorff, Rainer Werner Fassbinder, Bernhard Sinkel, Beate Mainka-Jellinghaus, Peter Schubert, Heinrich Böll. 134 min., color. Filmverlag der Autoren/Hallelujah/Kairos Film.

Dezertir (The Deserter). U.S.S.R., 1933. *Dir.* Vsevolod Pudovkin. 88 min., b/w. Mezrabpom-film.

Diagonale Sinfonie (Diagonal Symphony). Germany, 1925. *Dir.* Viking Eggeling. 7 min., b/w, silent.

Dial M for Murder. U.S., 1954. *Dir.* Alfred Hitchcock. 105 min., color (originally shot in 3-D). Warner Bros. V, LD.

Diexue Shuang Xiong (The Killer). Hong Kong, 1989. *Dir.* John Woo. 110 min., color. Film Workshop.

Dim Sum—A Little Bit of Heart. U.S., 1985. *Dir.* Wayne Wang. 88 min., color. CIM. V, LD.

Dirty Harry. U.S., 1971. *Dir.* Don Siegel. 103 min., Technicolor, Panavision. Warner Bros./Malpaso. V, LD.

Divide and Conquer. U.S., 1943. *Dir.* Frank Capra, Anatole Litvak. 58 min., b/w. U.S. War Department. V.

Dix-septième parallèle, Le (The Seventeenth Parallel). Vietnam/France, 1968. *Dir.* Joris Ivens. 114 min., b/w. Capi-Films/Argos Films.

Dr. Mabuse, der Spieler (Dr. Mabuse, the Gambler). Germany, 1922. *Dir.* Fritz Lang. Part I, 153 min.; Part II, 112 min., b/w, silent. UFA. V.

Dr. Strangelove, or How I Learned to Stop Worrying and Love the Bomb. Britain, 1963. *Dir.* Stanley Kubrick. 93 min., b/w. Columbia/Stanley Kubrick. V, LD.

Dodesukaden. Japan, 1970. *Dir.* Akira Kurosawa. 140 min., color. Yonki Nokai/Toho. V.

Dog Star Man. U.S., 1961–64. *Dir.* Stan Brakhage.

74 min., color, silent.

dolce vita, La (La Dolce Vita, aka *The Sweet Life).* Italy, 1960. *Dir.* Federico Fellini. 174 min., b/w. Riama/Pathé. V, LD.

Dolgiye provody (The Long Farewell). U.S.S.R., 1971. *Dir.* Kira Muratova.

Dolina miru (The Valley of Peace). Yugoslavia, 1956. *Dir.* France Stiglic. 87 min., b/w. Triglav Film.

Don't Change Your Husband. U.S., 1919. *Dir.* Cecil B. DeMille. 50 min., b/w, silent. Famous Players-Lasky.

Don't Look Back. U.S., 1967. *Dir.* D.A. Pennebaker. 96 min., b/w. Leacock-Pennebaker Productions. V, LD.

Do the Right Thing. U.S., 1989. *Dir.* Spike Lee. 120 min., color. 40 Acres and a Mule Filmworks. V, LD.

Double Indemnity. U.S., 1944. *Dir.* Billy Wilder. 103 min., b/w. Paramount. V, LD.

Down by Law. U.S., 1986. *Dir.* Jim Jarmusch. 107 min., b/w. Black Snake/Grokenberger. V.

Dracula. U.S., 1931. *Dir.* Tod Browning. 64 min., b/w, silent. Universal. V, LD.

Drifters. Britain, 1929. *Dir.* John Grierson. 40 min., b/w. Empire Marketing Board.

Drums Along the Mohawk. U.S., 1939. *Dir.* John Ford. 100 min., Technicolor. 20th Century-Fox. V, LD.

Duck Soup. U.S., 1933. *Dir.* Leo McCarey. 70 min., b/w. Paramount. V.

Duel. U.S., 1971. *Dir.* Steven Spielberg. 90 min., color. Universal. V.

Duminica la ora 6 (Sunday at 6). Romania, 1965. *Dir.* Lucian Pintilie. 75 min., b/w. Buceresti.

Easy Rider. U.S., 1969. *Dir.* Dennis Hopper. 94 min., Technicolor. Columbia/Pando/Raybert. V, LD.

Easy Street. U.S., 1917. *Dir.* Charles Chaplin. 22 min., b/w, silent. Mutual/Charles Chaplin.

Eat a Bowl of Tea. U.S., 1989. *Dir.* Wayne Wang. 102 min., De Luxe color, Panavision. Artificial Eye/American Playhouse Theatre. V, LD.

Ehe der Maria Braun, Die (The Marriage of Maria Braun). West Germany, 1978. *Dir.* Rainer Werner Fassbinder. 119 min., color. Albatros/TrioFilm/WDR/FDA. V.

1860. Italy, 1934. *Dir.* Alessandro Blasetti. 75 min., b/w. Cines.

Eléna et les hommes (Paris Does Strange Things). France, 1956. *Dir.* Jean Renoir. 95 min., color. Franco London/Les Films Gibé/Electra Compania Cinematographica. V.

Elephant Man, The. U.S., 1980. *Dir.* David Lynch. 124 min., b/w, Panavision. EMI/Brooksfilms. V, LD.

Eltávozott nap. (The Girl). Hungary, 1968. *Dir.* Márta Mészáros. 70 min., b/w. Mafilm Productions. V.

Elusive Isabel. U.S., 1916. *Dir.* Stuart Paton. 6 reels, b/w, silent. Bluebird Photoplays, Inc.

Emak Bakia. France, 1927. *Dir.* Man Ray. 17 min., b/w, silent.

Emitai. Senegal, 1971. *Dir.* Ousmane Sembene. 103 min., color. Films Domirêve.

Empire. U.S., 1964. *Dir.* Andy Warhol. 480 min. (16 f.p.s.), b/w, silent.

Empire Strikes Back, The. U.S., 1980. *Dir.* Irvin Kershner. 124 min., Eastmancolor, Panavision. 20th Century-Fox/Lucasfilm. V, LD.

End of World in Our Usual Bed in a Night Full of Rain, The. U.S., 1978. *Dir.* Lina Wertmüller. 104 min., color. Gil Shiva/Liberty/Warner Bros.

Enfants du paradis, Les (Children of Paradise). France, 1945. *Dir.* Marcel Carné. 195 min., b/w. Pathé. V, LD.

En résidence surveillée (Under House Arrest). Senegal, 1981. *Dir.* Paulin Soumanou Vieyra. 102 min., color.

Entertainer, The. Britain, 1960. *Dir.* Tony Richardson. 96 min., b/w. British Lion/Bryanston/Woodfall/Holly. V.

Entr'acte. France, 1924. *Dir.* René Clair. 22 min., b/w, silent. Ballets Suédois.

Eraserhead. U.S., 1976. *Dir.* David Lynch. 89 min., b/w. David Lynch. V.

Erotikon (Bonds That Chafe). Sweden, 1920. *Dir.* Mauritz Stiller. 67 min., b/w, silent. Svensk Filmindustri.

Escamotage d'une dame chez Robert-Houdin (The Vanishing Lady). France, 1896. *Dir.* Georges Méliès. 1 min., b/w, silent.

espíritu de la colmena, El (The Spirit of the Beehive). Spain, 1973. *Dir.* Victor Erice. 98 min., color. Elias Querejeta Productions. V.

E.T. The Extra-Terrestrial. U.S., 1982. *Dir.* Steven Spielberg. 115 min., De Luxe. Universal. V, LD.

ewige Jude, Der (The Eternal Jew). Germany, 1940. *Dir.* Fritz Hippler. Deutsche Film-Herstellungs und Verwertungs GmbH.

Ex-Convict, The. U.S., 1904. *Dir.* Edwin S. Porter. 10 min., b/w, silent. Edison Co.

Exorcist, The. U.S., 1973. *Dir.* William Friedkin. 122 min., Metrocolor. Warner Bros./Hoya. V, LD.

Fad Jal (Come and Work). Senegal, 1979. *Dir.* Safi Faye. 108 min., color.

Fallen Idol, The. Britain, 1948. *Dir.* Carol Reed. 94 min., b/w. British Lion/London Films. V.

Family Viewing. Canada, 1987. *Dir.* Atom Egoyan. 86 min., color. Ego Film Arts/Ontario Film Development/Canada Council/Ontario Arts Council.

Fanny. France, 1932. *Dir.* Marc Allégret. 128 min., b/w. Marcel Pagnol/Braunberger-Richebe. V, LD.

Fantasia. U.S., 1940. *Dir.* Ben Sharpsteen. 135 min., Technicolor. Walt Disney. V, LD.

Fantômas. France, 1913–14. *Dir.* Louis Feuillade. 5-part series, each c. 50 min., b/w, silent. 1. Fantômas; 2. Juve contre Fantômas; 3. La Mort que tue (1913); 4. Fantômas contre Fantômas; 5. Le Faux Magistrat (1914). Gaumont.

Far Country, The. U.S., 1955. *Dir.* Anthony Mann. 97 min., Technicolor. Universal-International. V.

Fast Times at Ridgemont High. U.S., 1982. *Dir.* Amy Heckerling. 92 min., Technicolor. Universal/Refugee. V, LD.

Faust. Germany, 1926. *Dir.* F.W. Murnau. 100 min., b/w, silent. Ufa.

Faustrecht der Freiheit (Fox and His Friends). West Germany, 1974. *Dir.* Rainer Werner Fassbinder. 123 min., color. Tango Film. V.

Feast, The. U.S., 1970. *Dir.* Timothy Asch, with Napoleon Chagnon. 29 min.

Feldzug im Polen (Campaign in Poland). Germany, 1939. *Dir.* Fritz Hippler. 34 min., b/w. Produced by the Third Reich.

Femme mariée, Une (A Married Woman). France, 1964. *Dir.* Jean-Luc Godard. 98 min., b/w. Anouchka/Orsay. V.

Ferris Bueller's Day Off. U.S., 1986. *Dir.* John Hughes. 103 min., Metrocolor, Panavision. Paramount. V, LD.

Feuertaufe (Baptism of Fire). Germany, 1940. *Dir.* Hans Bertram.

Fièvre ("Fever"). France, 1921. *Dir.* Louis Delluc. 40 min., b/w, silent. Alhambra-Film.

Film About a Woman Who. . . . U.S., 1974. *Dir.* Yvonne Rainer. 105 min., b/w.

Finyé (The Wind). Mali, 1982. *Dir.* Souleymane Cissé. 100 min., color. Les Films Cissé.

Fire. Britain, 1902. *Dir.* James Williamson. 5 min., b/w, silent.

Fires Were Started. Britain, 1943. *Dir.* Humphrey Jennings. 63 min., b/w. Crown Film Unit.

Fireworks. U.S., 1947. *Dir.* Kenneth Anger. 15 min., b/w. V.

First Blood. U.S., 1982. *Dir.* Ted Kotcheff. 94 min., Technicolor, Panavision. Carolco. V, LD.

Flame of New Orleans. U.S., 1941. *Dir.* René Clair. 79 min., b/w. Universal.

Flowers and Trees. U.S., 1932. *Dir.* Walt Disney. 7 min., Technicolor. Walt Disney Productions.

Foolish Wives. U.S., 1922. *Dir.* Erich von Stroheim. 140 min., b/w with hand-colored segments, silent.

Universal. V, LD.

Fool There Was, A. U.S., 1915. *Dir.* Frank Powell. 82 min., b/w, silent. Fox Film Corporation.

Footlight Parade. U.S., 1933. *Dir.* Lloyd Bacon, Busby Berkeley. 102 min., b/w. Warner Bros. V, LD.

Forbidden Planet. U.S., 1956. *Dir.* Fred M. Wilcox. 98 min., Eastmancolor, CinemaScope. Metro-Goldwyn-Mayer. V, LD.

Forgerons, Les (The Blacksmiths). France, 1895. *Dir.* Louis Lumière. b/w, silent. Société Lumière.

Fort Apache. U.S., 1948. *Dir.* John Ford. 127 min., b/w. Argosy/RKO. V, LD.

49th Parallel, The. Britain, 1941. *Dir.* Michael Powell. 123 min., b/w. GFD/Ortus. V, LD.

42nd Street. U.S., 1933. *Dir.* Lloyd Bacon, Busby Berkeley. 89 min., b/w. Warner Bros. V, LD.

Four Horsemen of the Apocalypse, The. U.S., 1921. *Dir.* Rex Ingram. 130 min., b/w, silent. Metro.

400 Million, The. U.S., 1939. *Dir.* Joris Ivens and John Ferno. 55 min., b/w. Garrison Films.

Fox Movietone Follies of 1929. U.S., 1929. *Dir.* David Butler, 80 min., b/w and color, Grandeur (70mm widescreen). Fox.

Francisca. Portugal, 1981. *Dir.* Manoel De Oliveira. 166 min., color. V.O. Filme.

Frankenstein. U.S., 1931. *Dir.* James Whale. 71 min., b/w. Universal. V, LD.

Frau im Mond, Die (Woman in the Moon). Germany, 1929. *Dir.* Fritz Lang. 125 min., b/w. silent. UFA. V.

French CanCan. France, 1955. *Dir.* Jean Renoir. 105 min., color. Franco London/Jolly. V.

freudlose Gasse, Die (The Joyless Street). Germany, 1925. *Dir.* G.W. Pabst. 139 min., b/w, silent. Sofar Film. V, LD.

Front Page, The. U.S., 1931. *Dir.* Lewis Milestone. 100 min., b/w. Caddo/United Artists. V.

Fuehrer's Face, Der. U.S., 1943. Technicolor. Walt Disney Co.

Funny Girl. U.S., 1968. *Dir.* William Wyler. 169 min., Technicolor, Panavision 70. Columbia/Rastar. V, LD.

Furong Zhen (Hibiscus Town). China, 1986. *Dir.* Xie Jin. 135 min., color. Shanghai Film Studio/China Film Corporation.

Fury. U.S., 1936. *Dir.* Fritz Lang. 90 min., b/w. Metro-Goldwyn-Mayer. V.

Garden of Allah, The. U.S., 1936. *Dir.* Richard Boleslawski. 80 min., Technicolor. Selznick. V.

Gates of Heaven. U.S., 1978. *Dir.* Errol Morris. 82 min., color. Errol Morris Productions.

Gay Shoe Clerk, The. U.S., 1903. *Dir.* Edwin S. Porter. 1 min., b/w, silent. Edison Co.

General, The. U.S., 1927. *Dir.* Buster Keaton, Clyde Bruckman. 90 min., b/w, silent. Buster Keaton Productions-United Artists. V, LD.

Genou de Claire, Le (Claire's Knee). France, 1970. *Dir.* Eric Rohmer. 106 min., color. Films du Losange. V, LD.

Genroku Chushingura (The Loyal 47 Ronin). Japan, 1941–42. *Dir.* Kenji Mizoguchi. 222 min., b/w. Koa/Shochiku. V.

Gentlemen of the Press. U.S., 1929. *Dir.* Millard Webb. 75 min., b/w. Paramount.

Gentlemen Prefer Blondes. U.S., 1953. *Dir.* Howard Hawks. 91 min., Technicolor. 20th Century-Fox. V, LD.

Germania, anno zero (Germany, Year Zero). Italy, 1947. *Dir.* Roberto Rossellini. 78 min., b/w. Tevere/Sadfilm.

Gertie. U.S., 1914. *Dir.* Winsor McCay. 9 min., b/w.

Gertrud. Denmark, 1964. *Dir.* Carl Th. Dreyer. 115 min., b/w. Palladium/Pathé Contemporary.

Ghare-Baire (The Home and the World). India, 1984. *Dir.* Satyajit Ray. 140 min., color. National Film Development Corporation of India. V.

Ghostbusters. U.S., 1984. *Dir.* Ivan Reitman. 105 min., Metrocolor, Panavision. Columbia/Delphi. V, LD.

Gigi. U.S., 1958. *Dir.* Vincente Minnelli. 119 min., Metrocolor, CinemaScope. Metro-Goldwyn-Mayer. V, LD.

Gilda. U.S., 1946. *Dir.* Charles Vidor. 110 min., b/w. Columbia. V, LD.

Gimme Shelter. U.S., 1970. *Dir.* David and Albert Maysles, Charlotte Zwerin. 96 min., color. Maysles Film Inc. V.

Girl of the Golden West, The. U.S., 1915. *Dir.* Cecil B. DeMille. 50 min., b/w, silent. Jesse L. Lasky Feature Play Co.

Godfather, The. U.S., 1972. *Dir.* Francis Ford Coppola. 175 min., Technicolor. Paramount/Alfran. V, LD.

Godfather Part II, The. U.S., 1974. *Dir.* Francis Ford Coppola. 200 min., Technicolor. Paramount/The Coppola Company. V, LD.

Gold Diggers, The. Britain, 1983. *Dir.* Sally Potter. 89 min., color. British Film Institute.

Gold Diggers of 1933. U.S., 1933. *Dir.* Mervyn LeRoy, Busby Berkeley. 94 min., b/w. Warner Bros. V, LD.

Gold Rush, The. U.S., 1925. *Dir.* Charles Chaplin. 81 min., b/w, silent. Charles Chaplin Productions. V, LD.

Goluboi ekspress (The China Express, aka The Blue Express). U.S.S.R., 1929. *Dir.* Ilya Trauberg. 65 min., b/w, silent. Sovkino.

Gone with the Wind. U.S., 1939. *Dir.* Victor Fleming. 217 min., color. Metro-Goldwyn-Mayer/Selznick. V, LD.

Gonin no sekkohei (Five Scouts). Japan, 1938. *Dir.* Tomotaka Tasaka. 73 min., b/w. Nikkatsu Tamagawa. V.

GoodFellas. U.S., 1990. *Dir.* Martin Scorsese. 146 min., color. Warner Bros. V, LD.

Gösta Berlings saga (The Story of Gösta Berling). Sweden, 1924. *Dir.* Mauritz Stiller. 137 min. (originally in 2 parts, 114 min. and 106 min.), b/w, silent. Svensk Filmindustri. V.

Graduate, The. U.S., 1967. *Dir.* Mike Nichols. 105 min., Technicolor, Panavision. United Artists/Embassy. V, LD.

Grande Illusion, La (Grand Illusion). France, 1937. *Dir.* Jean Renoir. 117 min., b/w. Cinedis. V, LD.

Grandma's Reading Glass. Britain, 1900. *Dir.* George Albert Smith.

Grapes of Wrath, The. U.S., 1940. *Dir.* John Ford. 129 min., b/w. 20th Century-Fox. V, LD.

Great Day in the Morning. U.S., 1955. *Dir.* Jacques Tourneur. 92 min., Technicolor, Superscope. RKO. V.

Great Dictator, The. U.S., 1940. *Dir.* Charles Chaplin. 127 min., b/w. Chaplin/United Artists. V.

Great Expectations. Britain, 1946. *Dir.* David Lean. 118 min., b/w. Rank/Cineguild. V.

Great Meadow, The. U.S., 1931. *Dir.* Charles Brabin. 80 min., b/w, Realife. Metro-Goldwyn-Mayer.

Great Train Robbery, The. U.S., 1903. *Dir.* Edwin S. Porter. 11 min., b/w, silent. Edison Co.

Greed. U.S., 1924. *Dir.* Erich von Stroheim. 150 min., b/w, silent. Metro-Goldwyn-Mayer. V, LD.

Green Berets, The. U.S., 1968. *Dir.* John Wayne, Ray Kellogg. 141 min., Technicolor. Warner Bros./Batjac. V, LD.

Guess Who's Coming to Dinner? U.S., 1967. *Dir.* Stanley Kramer. 112 min., Technicolor. Columbia/Stanley Kramer. V.

Guillaume Tell. France, 1903. Pathé Frères.

Gun Crazy. U.S., 1950. *Dir.* Joseph H. Lewis. 87 min., b/w. King Brothers/Universal-International. V.

Habanera, La. Germany, 1937. *Dir.* Detlef Sierck. 95 min., b/w. Bruno Duday/Ufa.

Hachigatsu-no-Kyoshikyoku (Rhapsody in August). Japan, 1991. *Dir.* Akira Kurosawa. 98 min., color. Kurosawa Productions/Feature Film Enterprise/Shochiku Company, Ltd.

Hair. U.S., 1979. *Dir.* Miloš Forman. 121 min., Technicolor, Panavision. United Artists/CIP. V, LD.

Haizi Wang (King of the Children). China, 1987. *Dir.* Chen Kaige. 107 min., color. Xi'an Film Studio.

Haktou Tsauhan (Song of the Exile). Hong Kong/Taiwan, 1989. *Dir.* Ann Hui. 113 min., color. Tian Heo Films/Xi'an Film Studio/China Film.

Halbblut (Halfbreed). Germany, 1919. *Dir.* Fritz Lang. 58 min., b/w, silent. Decla.

Hallelujah. U.S., 1929. *Dir.* King Vidor. 109 min., b/w. Metro-Goldwyn-Mayer.

Hamlet. Britain, 1948. *Dir.* Laurence Olivier. 142 min., b/w. Rank/Two Cities. V, LD.

Hammett. U.S., 1982. *Dir.* Wim Wenders. 97 min., Technicolor. Orion/Zoetrope. V.

Hangmen Also Die. U.S., 1943. *Dir.* Fritz Lang. 131 min., b/w. United Artists.

Hannah and Her Sisters. U.S., 1986. *Dir.* Woody Allen. 106 min., Technicolor. Orion. V, LD.

Hanoi Martes 13 Diciembre (Hanoi Tuesday the 13th). Cuba, 1967. *Dir.* Santiago Alvarez. 40 min., b/w. ICAIC.

Hans Westmar, Einer von Vielen (Hans Westmar, One of Many). Germany, 1933. *Dir.* Franz Wenzler. Volksdeutsche Film GmbH.

Happy Days. U.S., 1930. *Dir.* Benjamin Stoloff. 86 min., Grandeur (70mm widescreen). Fox.

Happy Mother's Day, A. U.S., 1963. *Dir.* Richard Leacock and Joyce Chopra. 30 min., b/w. Leacock-Pennebaker, Inc.

Harakiri. Germany, 1919. *Dir.* Fritz Lang. 92 min., b/w, silent. Decla-Film Ges.

Hare Force. U.S., 1944. *Dir.* I. Freleng. color. Warner Bros. V.

Heaven's Gate. U.S., 1980. *Dir.* Michael Cimino. 219 min., Technicolor. United Artists/Michael Cimino. V, LD.

Hei ai yuan hun (Wrong Ghosts in an Opium Den). China, 1916. *Dir.* Zhang Sichuan. Huanxian.

Heiress, The. U.S., 1949. *Dir.* William Wyler. 115 min., b/w. Paramount. V.

Hell's Angels. U.S., 1930. *Dir.* Howard Hughes. 119 min., b/w and Multicolor sequence. Caddo.

Hell's Hinges. U.S., 1916. *Dir.* Charles Swickard. 5 reels, b/w, silent. New York Motion Picture Corp.

Henry V. Britain, 1945. *Dir.* Laurence Olivier. 137 min., Technicolor. Rank/Two Cities. V.

Herr Meets Hare. U.S., 1945. *Dir.* I. Freleng. color. Warner Bros. V.

High Noon. U.S., 1952. *Dir.* Fred Zinnemann. 84 min., b/w. Kramer/United Artists. V, LD.

High School. U.S., 1968. *Dir.* Frederick Wiseman. 75 min., b/w. Osti Films.

High Sierra. U.S., 1941. *Dir.* Raoul Walsh. 96 min., b/w. Warner Bros. V, LD.

Himmel über Berlin, Der (Wings of Desire). West Germany/France, 1987. *Dir.* Wim Wenders. 127 min., b/w and color. Road Movies/Argos Films. V, LD.

Hintertreppe, Die (Backstairs). Germany, 1921. *Dir.* Leopold Jessner. 60 min., b/w, silent. Ufa.

Hiroshima, mon amour. France, 1959. *Dir.* Alain Resnais. 91 min., b/w. Argos/Comei/Pathé/Daiei. V.

His Girl Friday. U.S., 1940. *Dir.* Howard Hawks. 92 min., b/w. Columbia. V.

historia oficial, La (The Official Story). Argentina, 1985. *Dir.* Luis Puenzo. 115 min., color. Historias Cinematograficas/Progress Communicatias. V, LD.

Hitlerjunge Quex (Hitler Youth Quex). Germany, 1933. *Dir.* Hans Steinhoff. 102 min., b/w. Ufa.

Hitler's Madman. U.S., 1942. *Dir.* Douglas Sirk. 84 min., b/w. Metro-Goldwyn-Mayer/PRC.

Hollywood Canteen. U.S., 1944. *Dir.* Delmer Daves. 124 min., b/w. Warner Bros. V.

Hollywood or Bust. U.S., 1956. *Dir.* Frank Tashlin. 95 min., Technicolor, Vistavision. Paramount. V.

Home from the Hill. U.S., 1960. *Dir.* Vincente Minnelli. 150 min., Metrocolor, CinemaScope. Metro-Goldwyn-Mayer/Sol C. Siegel. V, LD.

Hong Gaoling (Red Sorghum). China, 1987. *Dir.* Zhang Yimou. 92 min., Eastmancolor. Palace/Xi'an Film Studio. V.

Hongse niangzijun (The Red Detachment of Women). China, 1961. *Dir.* Xie Jin. 139 min., color. Tianma Studios.

hora de estrela, A (Hour of the Star). Brazil, 1985. *Dir.* Suzana Amaral. 96 min., color. Raiz Produçoes Cinematografixas. V.

hora de los hornos, La (The Hour of the Furnaces). Argentina, 1968. *Dir.* Fernando Solanas, Octavio Getino. 260 min., b/w and color. Grupo Cine Liberación/Arger Film.

Hoři, má panenko! (The Fireman's Ball). Czechoslovakia, 1967. *Dir.* Miloš Forman. 73 min., color. Barrandov Studios/Carlo Ponti. V.

Horse Feathers. U.S., 1932. *Dir.* Norman McLeod. 70 min., b/w. Paramount. V, LD.

Hôtel du nord. France, 1938. *Dir.* Marcel Carné. 110 min., b/w. Sedif/Imperial.

Hotel Imperial. U.S., 1927. *Dir.* Mauritz Stiller. 67 min., b/w, silent. Famous Players-Lasky.

House Divided, A. U.S., 1913. *Dir.* Alice Guy Blaché. 13 min., b/w, silent. Solax.

House of Wax. U.S., 1953. *Dir.* André de Toth. 88 min., color, 3-D. Warner Bros.

Housing Problems. Britain, 1935. *Dir.* Arthur Elton, Edgar Anstey. 15 min., b/w. Realist Film Unit for British Commonwealth Gas.

Howards End. Britain, 1992. *Dir.* James Ivory. 142 min., color. Merchant Ivory Productions.

How Green Was My Valley. U.S., 1941. *Dir.* John Ford. 120 min., b/w. 20th Century-Fox. LD.

How the Myth Was Made. U.S., 1978. *Dir.* George Stoney, James Brown. 59 min., color. Stoney Associates.

How to Marry a Millionaire. U.S., 1953. *Dir.* Jean Negulesco. 96 min., Technicolor, CinemaScope. 20th Century-Fox. V, LD.

How Yukong Moved the Mountains. France, 1972–74. A series of 12 films in color, *Dir.* Joris Ivens and Marceline Loridan: *The Drugstore,* 81 min.; *The Oilfields,* 87 min.; *Traditional Handicrafts,* 15 min.; *The Generator Factory,* 129 min.; *A Woman, a Family,* 108 min.; *The Fishing Village,* 102 min.; *An Army Camp,* 57 min.; *Impressions of a City (Shanghai),* 60 min.; *Professor Tchein,* 13 min.; *The Football Incident,* 20 min.; *Rehearsal at the Peking Opera,* 32 min.; *Behind the Scenes at the Peking Circus,* 16 min.

Huang Tudi (Yellow Earth). China, 1984. *Dir.* Chen Kaige. 89 min., color. Guangxi Film Studio.

Hunchback of Notre Dame, The. U.S., 1923. *Dir.* Wallace Worsley. 90 min., b/w, silent. Universal. V, LD.

Hunters, The. U.S., 1958. *Dir.* John Marshall. 73 min.

Hurdes, Las (Land Without Bread). Spain, 1932. *Dir.* Luis Buñuel. 28 min., b/w. Buñuel.

Husbands and Wives. U.S., 1992. *Dir.* Woody Allen. 108 min., color. TriStar Pictures.

Hypothèse du tableau vole, L' (The Hypothesis of the Stolen Painting). France, 1978. *Dir.* Raúl Ruiz. 66 min., b/w. L'Institut National de L'Audiovisuel. V.

Idle Class, The. U.S., 1921. *Dir.* Charles Chaplin. 20 min., b/w, silent. First National.

I Hired a Contract Killer. Finland/Sweden, 1990. *Dir.* Aki Kaurismäki. 79 min., Metrocolor. Electric Pictures/Contemporary/Villealfa/Swedish Film Institute.

Ikiru (To Live). Japan, 1952. *Dir.* Akira Kurosawa. 143 min., b/w. Toho. V, LD.

Illusions. U.S., 1983. *Dir.* Julie Dash. 34 min., b/w.

I Married a Communist (aka The Woman on Pier 13). U.S., 1950. *Dir.* Robert Stevenson. 72 min., b/w. RKO.

I Married a Monster from Outer Space. U.S., 1958. *Dir.* Gene Fowler. 78 min., b/w. Paramount/Gene Fowler Jr. V.

Imitation of Life. U.S., 1934. *Dir.* John M. Stahl. 116 min., b/w. Universal.

Imitation of Life. U.S., 1959. *Dir.* Douglas Sirk. 124

min., Eastmancolor. Universal-International. V.

Im Lauf der Zeit (Kings of the Road). West Germany, 1976. *Dir.* Wim Wenders. 176 min., b/w. Wim Wenders Produktion. V.

Immigrant, The. U.S., 1917. *Dir.* Charles Chaplin. 20 min., b/w, silent. Mutual.

Immoral Mr. Teas, The. U.S., 1959. *Dir.* Russ Meyer. 63 min., Eastmancolor. P.A. De Cenzie/Pad-Ram.

In a Lonely Place. U.S., 1950. *Dir.* Nicholas Ray. 92 min., b/w. Columbia/Santana. V.

Indiana Jones and the Last Crusade. U.S., 1989. *Dir.* Steven Spielberg. 127 min., color. Lucasfilm Ltd. V, LD.

Indiana Jones and the Temple of Doom. U.S., 1984. *Dir.* Steven Spielberg. 118 min., Rank/De Luxe, Panavision. Paramount/Lucasfilm. V, LD.

Indra Sabha. India, 1932.

Industrial Britain. Britain, 1933. *Dir.* John Grierson, Robert Flaherty. 22 min., b/w. E.M.B Film Unit.

Informer, The. U.S., 1935. *Dir.* John Ford. 91 min., b/w. RKO. V, LD.

In the Heat of the Night. U.S., 1967. *Dir.* Norman Jewison. 109 min., De Luxe. United Artists/Mirisch. V, LD.

In the Land of the War Canoes. Canada, 1914. *Dir.* Edward S. Curtis. 6 reels, b/w, silent. Curtis Film Corp.

In the Year of the Pig. U.S., 1969. *Dir.* Emile de Antonio. 101 min., b/w. Emile de Antonio Productions. V (video title: *Vietnam: In the Year of the Pig*).

Intolerance. U.S., 1916. *Dir.* D.W. Griffith. 115 min., b/w, silent. D.W. Griffith. V.

Inundados, Los (Flooded Out). Argentina, 1961. *Dir.* Fernando Birri. 85 min., b/w. America Nuestra.

Invasion of the Body Snatchers. U.S., 1956. *Dir.* Don Siegel. 80 min., b/w, Superscope. Allied Artists/Walter Wanger. V, LD.

In Which We Serve. Britain, 1942. *Dir.* Nöel Coward, David Lean. 114 min., b/w. Rank/Two Cities. V.

Iskindria . . . Leh? (Alexandria . . . Why?). Egypt, 1978. *Dir.* Youssef Chahine. 125 min., color. Misr International Films/Oncic.

It Came from Outer Space. U.S., 1953. *Dir.* Jack Arnold. 80 min., b/w, 3-D. Universal-International. V.

It Happened One Night. U.S., 1934. *Dir.* Frank Capra. 105 min., b/w. Columbia. V, LD.

It's a Wonderful Life. U.S., 1946. *Dir.* Frank Capra. 120 min., b/w. RKO/Liberty. V, LD.

Ivan grozny (Ivan the Terrible). U.S.S.R., 1944–46. *Dir.* Sergei Eisenstein. Part I: 99 min., b/w; Part II: 88 min., b/w and color. Mosfilm. V, LD.

Janitzio. Mexico, 1934. *Dir.* Carlos Navarro.

Jaws. U.S., 1975. *Dir.* Steven Spielberg. 125 min., Technicolor, Panavision. Universal/Zanuck-Brown. V, LD.

Jazz Singer, The. U.S., 1927. *Dir.* Alan Crosland. 88 min., b/w. Warner Bros.. V, LD.

Jean de Florette. France, 1986. *Dir.* Claude Berri. 122 min., color. Renn Productions/Films A2/RAI 2/DD Productions. V, LD.

Jeanne Dielman, 23 Quai du Commerce, 1080 Bruxelles. Belgium, 1975. *Dir.* Chantal Akerman. 225 min., color. Paradise Films/Unité Trois.

Jésus de Montréal (Jesus of Montreal). Canada/France, 1989. *Dir.* Denys Arcand. 120 min., color. Max-Gerard Mital. V, LD.

Jetée, La (The Jetty). France, 1964. *Dir.* Chris Marker. 29 min., b/w.

Jeux interdits, Les (Forbidden Games). France, 1952. *Dir.* René Clément. 84 min., b/w. Robert Dorfmann. V, LD.

JFK. U.S., 1991. *Dir.* Oliver Stone. 188 min., b/w and color. Camelot Productions/Warner Bros./New Regency Films/Canal Plus/Ixtlan. V, LD.

Jigokumon (Gate of Hell). Japan, 1953. *Dir.* Teinosuke Kinugasa. 90 min., color. Daiei. V.

Jinruigaku Nyumon (The Pornographers). Japan, 1966. *Dir.* Shohei Imamura. 128 min., b/w.

Nikkatsu. V.

Joli Mai, Le (The Lovely Month of May). France, 1963. *Dir.* Chris Marker. 190 min., b/w. Sofracima.

Jonas qui aura 25 ans en l'an 2000 (Jonah Who Will Be 25 in the Year 2000). Switzerland, 1975. *Dir.* Alain Tanner. 110 min., color. Cite/SSR/Action/SFP.

Journal d'un curé de campagne (Diary of a Country Priest). France, 1950. *Dir.* Robert Bresson. 120 min., b/w. UGC. V.

Journey to the Center of the Earth. U.S., 1959. *Dir.* Henry Levin. 132 min., De Luxe, CinemaScope. 20th Century-Fox. V.

Jour se lève, Le (Daybreak). France, 1939. *Dir.* Marcel Carné. 95 min., b/w. Vog/Sigma. V.

Juarez. U.S., 1939. *Dir.* William Dieterle. 125 min., b/w. Warner Bros. V.

Judith of Bethulia. U.S., 1913. *Dir.* D.W. Griffith. 42 min., b/w, silent. Biograph.

Ju Dou. China, 1990. *Dir.* Zhang Yimou. 94 min., color. Tokuma Shoten Communications/China Film Corporation. V.

Jud Süss (Jew Süss). Germany, 1940. *Dir.* Veit Harlan. 85 min., b/w. Terra.

Jules et Jim (Jules and Jim). France, 1961. *Dir.* François Truffaut. 105 min., b/w. Films du Carrosse/SEDIF. V, LD.

junge Törless, Der (The Young Törless). West Germany, 1965. *Dir.* Volker Schlöndorff. 85 min., b/w. Franz Seitz/Nouvelles Edition de Film.

jungfrauen Maschine, Die (The Virgin Machine). West Germany, 1988. *Dir.* Monika Treut. 85 min., b/w. V.

Jungle Fever. U.S., 1991. *Dir.* Spike Lee. 132 min., color. Fever Films/40 Acres and a Mule Filmworks. V, LD.

Just Imagine. U.S., 1930. *Dir.* David Butler. 102 min., b/w. Fox.

Juvenile Jungle. U.S., 1958. *Dir.* William Witney. 69 min., b/w. Coronado Productions.

Kaaghaz ke Phool (Paper Flowers). India, 1959. *Dir.* Guru Dutt. 148 min., b/w. Guru Dutt Films Pvt. Ltd.

Kaddu Beykat (Letter from My Village). Senegal, 1975. *Dir.* Safi Faye. 95 min., b/w.

Kagemusha. Japan, 1980. *Dir.* Akira Kurosawa. 181 min., color. Toho/Kurosawa. V.

Kameradschaft ("Comradeship"). Germany, 1931. *Dir.* G.W. Pabst. 92 min., b/w. Nerofilm.

Kamigami no Fukaki Yokubo (The Profound Desire of the Gods). Japan, 1968. *Dir.* Shohei Imamura. 172 min., color, CinemaScope. Imamura Productions/Nikkatsu.

Kanal. Poland, 1957. *Dir.* Andrzej Wajda. 97 min., b/w. Film Polski. V.

Kanchenjungha. India, 1962. *Dir.* Satyajit Ray. 102 min., Eastmancolor. Satyajit Ray Productions.

Keep Your Mouth Shut. Canada, 1944. *Dir.* Norman McLaren. 3 min., b/w. National Film Board.

Kid, The. U.S., 1921. *Dir.* Charles Chaplin. 60 min., b/w, silent. First National. V.

Kid Auto Races at Venice. U.S., 1914. *Dir.* Henry Lehrman. 16 min., b/w, silent. Keystone Film Company.

Killing of a Chinese Bookie, The. U.S., 1976. *Dir.* John Cassavetes. 113 min., color. Faces International.

Kind Hearts and Coronets. Britain, 1949. *Dir.* Robert Hamer. 106 min., b/w. Ealing. V, LD.

Kindergarten Cop. U.S., 1990. *Dir.* Ivan Reitman. 111 min., color. Universal. V, LD.

King of Comedy, The. U.S., 1983. *Dir.* Martin Scorsese. 109 min., Technicolor. 20th Century-Fox/Embassy International. V.

King of Kings, The. U.S., 1927. *Dir.* Cecil B. DeMille. 155 min., b/w, silent. Pathé. V, LD.

Kino-Pravda ("Film-Truth"). U.S.S.R., 1922–25. *Dir.* Dziga Vertov. A newsreel series; more than 20 were produced. b/w, silent. VUFKU.

Kismet. U.S., 1930. *Dir.* John Francis Dillon. 90 min.,

b/w, 65mm. First National/Warner Bros. V, LD.

Kiss, The. U.S., 1929. *Dir.* Jacques Feyder. 64 min., b/w, silent. Metro-Goldwyn-Mayer. V, LD.

Kiss Me Deadly. U.S., 1955. *Dir.* Robert Aldrich. 105 min., b/w. United Artists/Parklane. V.

Kiss Me Kate. U.S., 1953. *Dir.* George Sidney. 111 min., Anscolor 3-D. Metro-Goldwyn-Mayer. V, LD.

Kleptomaniac, The. U.S., 1905. *Dir.* Edwin S. Porter. 10 min., b/w, silent. Edison Co.

Knockout, The. U.S., 1914. *Dir.* Charles Avery. 22 min., b/w, silent. Keystone Film Company.

Komissar (The Commissar). U.S.S.R., 1967. *Dir.* Alexander Askoldov. 108 min., color, CinemaScope. Artificial Eye/Gorky Studios.

Komsomol (Song of Heroes). U.S.S.R., 1932. *Dir.* Joris Ivens. Mezhrabpom Film.

Konets Sankt-Peterburga (The End of St. Petersburg). U.S.S.R., 1927. *Dir.* Vsevolod Pudovkin. 122 min., b/w, silent. Mezhrabpom. V.

Kongbufenzi (The Terrorizer). Taiwan/Hong Kong, 1986. *Dir.* Edward Yang. 109 min., color. ICA/Sunny Overseas Corp./Golden Harvest.

Körkarlen (The Phantom Chariot). Sweden, 1921. *Dir.* Victor Sjöström. 84 min., b/w, silent. Svensk Filmindustri.

Korotkiye vstrechi (Brief Encounters). U.S.S.R., 1967. *Dir.* Kira Muratova. 88 min., b/w. Odessa Feature Film Studio.

Koshikei (Death by Hanging). Japan, 1968. *Dir.* Nagisa Oshima. 117 min., b/w. Sozosha.

Kriemhild's Rache (Kriemhild's Revenge). Germany, 1924. *Dir.* Fritz Lang. Part II of *Die Nibelungen.* 95 min., b/w, silent. Decla-Bioskop. V, LD.

Kurutta ippeiji (Page of Madness). Japan, 1926. *Dir.* Teinosuke Kinugasa. 60 min., b/w. Kinugasa Motion Picture League.

Laberinto de pasiones (Labyrinth of Passions). Spain, 1982. *Dir.* Pedro Almodóvar. 100 min., color. Tesauro/Kaktus. V.

Ladri di biciclette (Bicycle Thieves). Italy, 1948. *Dir.* Vittorio De Sica. 90 min., b/w. PDS/ENIC. V, LD.

Lady from Shanghai, The. U.S., 1948. *Dir.* Orson Welles. 86 min., b/w. Columbia. V, LD.

Lady Windermere's Fan. U.S., 1925. *Dir.* Ernst Lubitsch. 80 min., b/w, silent. Warner Bros.

Lainlian Feng Chen (Dust in the Wind). Taiwan, 1986. *Dir.* Hou Hsiao-Hsien. 107 min., Eastmancolor. ICA/Central Motion Picture Corporation.

Land, The. U.S., 1942. *Dir.* Robert Flaherty. 45 min., b/w. Robert Flaherty Production for the U.S. Department of Agriculture.

Lao Jing (The Old Well). China, 1986. *Dir.* Wu Tianming. 130 min., color. Xi'an Film Studio.

Lásky jedné plavovlásky (Loves of a Blonde). Czechoslovakia, 1965. *Dir.* Miloš Forman. 82 min., b/w. Barrandov Studios. V, LD.

Last Command, The. U.S., 1928. *Dir.* Josef von Sternberg. 100 min., b/w, silent. Paramount. V.

Last of the Mohicans, The. U.S., 1920. *Dir.* Maurice Tourneur, Clarence L. Brown. 60 min., b/w, silent. Maurice Tourneur Productions.

Last Temptation of Christ, The. U.S., 1988. *Dir.* Martin Scorsese. 164 min., color. Universal. V, LD.

Last Wave, The. Australia, 1977. *Dir.* Peter Weir. 106 min., Atlab color. United Artists. V.

Laura. U.S., 1944. *Dir.* Otto Preminger. 88 min., b/w. 20th Century-Fox. V, LD.

Lavender Hill Mob, The. Britain, 1951. *Dir.* Charles Crichton. 78 min., b/w. Ealing. V, LD.

Lawrence of Arabia. Britain, 1962. *Dir.* David Lean. 221 min., Technicolor. United Artists/Scimitar. V, LD.

League of Their Own, A. U.S., 1992. *Dir.* Penny Marshall. 128 min., Technicolor, Panavision. Parkway Productions.

Learning Tree, The. U.S., 1969. *Dir.* Gordon Parks. 106 min., color. Warner Bros./Seven Arts. V.

Lebenszeichen (Signs of Life). West Germany, 1967. *Dir.* Werner Herzog. 90 min., b/w. Werner Herzog

Filmproduktion.

Leningrad Cowboys Go America. Finland/Sweden, 1989. *Dir.* Aki Kaurismäki. 78 min., color. Artificial Eye/Villealfa/Swedish Film Institute/Finnish Film Foundation. V, LD.

Léolo. Canada, 1992. *Dir.* Jean-Claude Lauzon. 105 min., color. Les Productions du Verseau/Flach Film/Le Studio Canal Plus/National Film Board of Canada.

Let There Be Light. U.S., 1946. *Dir.* John Huston. 58 min., b/w. Army Pictorial Service.

Lettre de Sibérie (Letter from Siberia). France, 1958. *Dir.* Chris Marker. 60 min., color. Argos Films.

Letyat zhuravli (The Cranes Are Flying). U.S.S.R., 1957. *Dir.* Mikhail Kalatozov. 94 min., b/w. Mosfilm. V, LD.

letzte Mann, Der (The Last Laugh). Germany, 1924. *Dir.* F.W. Murnau. 73 min., b/w, silent. Ufa. V.

ley del deseo, La (Law of Desire). Spain, 1987. *Dir.* Pedro Almodóvar. 100 min., color. El Deseo/Laurenfilm. V, LD.

Liebe der Jeanne Ney, Die (The Love of Jeanne Ney). Germany, 1927. *Dir.* G.W. Pabst. 120 min., b/w, silent, Ufa.

Life and Death of 9413 — A Hollywood Extra, The. U.S., 1928. *Dir.* Robert Florey, Slavko Vorkapich. 11 min., b/w, silent.

Life Is Cheap . . . But Toilet Paper Is Expensive. Hong Kong/U.S., 1990. *Dir.* Wayne Wang. 89 min., color. Far East Stars.

Life of an American Fireman. U.S., 1902. *Dir.* Edwin S. Porter. 6 min., b/w, silent. Edison Co.

Lifeboat. U.S., 1944. *Dir.* Alfred Hitchcock. 86 min., b/w. 20th Century-Fox. V, LD.

Lights of New York. U.S., 1928. *Dir.* Bryan Foy. 57 min., b/w. Warner Bros.

Lilies of the Field. U.S., 1930. *Dir.* Alexander Korda. 60 min., b/w. First National.

Lilies of the Field. U.S., 1963. *Dir.* Ralph Nelson. 94 min., b/w. United Artists/Rainbow. V.

Lili Marleen. West Germany, 1980. *Dir.* Rainer Werner Fassbinder. 120 min., color. Roxy/CIP/Rialto Film/Bayerische Rundfunk.

Limelight. U.S., 1952. *Dir.* Charles Chaplin. 135 min., b/w. Celebrated/United Artists. V.

Linjia puzi (The Lin Family Shop). China, 1959. *Dir.* Shui Hua. 83 min., color. Beijing Film Studio.

Listen to Britain. Britain, 1943. *Dir.* Humphrey Jennings. 20 min., b/w. British Ministry of Information.

Little American, The. U.S., 1917. *Dir.* Cecil B. DeMille. 6 reels, b/w, silent. Artcraft Film Co./Paramount.

Little Big Man. U.S., 1970. *Dir.* Arthur Penn. 147 min., Technicolor, Panavision. Stockbridge/Hiller/Cinema Center. V, LD.

Little Caesar. U.S., 1930. *Dir.* Mervyn LeRoy. 77 min., b/w. First National Pictures. V, LD.

Little Nemo. U.S., 1911. *Dir.* Winsor McCay. 12 min., b/w and tinted.

Lives of Performers. U.S., 1972. *Dir.* Yvonne Rainer. 90 min., b/w.

Lodger, The. Britain, 1926. *Dir.* Alfred Hitchcock. 84 min., b/w, silent. Gainsborough. V.

Loin du Viet-nam (Far from Vietnam). France, 1967. *Dir.* Alain Resnais, William Klein, Joris Ivens, Agnès Varda, Claude Lelouch, Jean-Luc Godard. 115 min., b/w and color. SLON.

Lola. France, 1961. *Dir.* Jacques Demy. 91 min., b/w. Rome-Paris/Euro-International. V.

Lola. West Germany, 1981. *Dir.* Rainer Werner Fassbinder. 114 min., color. Rialto Film/Trio Film.

Lola Montès. France, 1955. *Dir.* Max Ophuls. 140 min., color. Gamma/Florida/Oska. V, LD.

London Can Take It. Britain, 1940. *Dir.* Harry Watt, Humphrey Jennings. 9 min., b/w. British Ministry of Information.

Lonedale Operator, The. U.S., 1911. *Dir.* D.W. Griffith. 14 min., b/w, silent. Biograph Co.

Loneliness of the Long Distance Runner, The. Britain,

1962. *Dir.* Tony Richardson. 104 min., b/w. British Lion/Bryanston/Woodfall. V, LD.

Lonely Villa, The. U.S., 1909. *Dir.* D.W. Griffith. 11 min., b/w, silent. Biograph Co.

Long Goodbye, The. U.S., 1973. *Dir.* Robert Altman. 111 min., Technicolor, Panavision. United Artists/Lions Gate. V, LD.

Look Back in Anger. Britain, 1959. *Dir.* Tony Richardson. 99 min., b/w. ABP/Woodfall. V.

Looking for Langston. Britain, 1989. *Dir.* Isaac Julien. 44 min., b/w. Sankofa Film Collective. V.

Lost Horizon. U.S., 1937. *Dir.* Frank Capra. 125 min., b/w. Columbia. V, LD.

Louisiana Story. U.S., 1948. *Dir.* Robert Flaherty. 77 min., b/w. Standard Oil Company. V.

Love. U.S., 1927. *Dir.* Edmund Goulding. 82 min., b/w, silent. Metro-Goldwyn-Mayer. V.

Love Light, The. U.S., 1921. *Dir.* Frances Marion. 8 reels, b/w, silent. Mary Pickford Co.

Love Me Tonight. U.S., 1932. *Dir.* Rouben Mamoulian. 104 min., b/w. Paramount.

Love's Young Dream. U.S., 1897. Photographed by W.K.L. Dickson. 2 min., b/w, silent. American Mutoscope and Biograph Co.

Luch smerti (The Death Ray). U.S.S.R., 1925. *Dir.* Lev Kuleshov. 125 min., b/w, silent. Goskino.

Lucía. Cuba, 1968. *Dir.* Humberto Solás. 155 min., b/w. ICAIC.

Luci del varietà (Variety Lights). Italy, 1951. *Dir.* Alberto Lattuada, Federico Fellini. 94 min., b/w. Film Capitolium. V.

M*A*S*H. U.S., 1970. *Dir.* Robert Altman. 116 min., De Luxe, Panavision. 20th Century-Fox/Aspen. V, LD.

M. Germany, 1931. *Dir.* Fritz Lang. 118 min., b/w. Nerofilm. V, LD.

McCabe and Mrs. Miller. U.S., 1971. *Dir.* Robert Altman. 120 min., Technicolor, Panavision. Warner Bros. V, LD.

Maciste alpino. Italy, 1916. *Dir.* Luigi Maggi and Romano Luigi Borgnetto. 101 min., b/w, silent. Itala Film.

Madame de . . . (The Earrings of Madame de. . .). France, 1953. *Dir.* Max Ophuls. 102 min., b/w. Franco London/Indus/Rizzoli. V.

Madame Dubarry. Germany, 1919. *Dir.* Ernst Lubitsch. 85 min., b/w, silent. Union-UFA.

Madame X: Eine absolute Herrscherin (Madame X: An Absolute Ruler). West Germany, 1977. *Dir.* Ulrike Ottinger. 141 min., color. Autoren Film.

Made in U.S.A. France, 1966. *Dir.* Jean-Luc Godard. 85 min., color. Rome-Paris Films/Anouchka/Sepic.

Mad Max. Australia, 1979. *Dir.* George Miller. 100 min., Eastmancolor, Todd-AO 35. Mad Max Pty. V.

Mad Max II (aka The Road Warrior). Australia, 1981. *Dir.* George Miller. 94 min., color. Warner Bros. V, LD.

Mad Max Beyond Thunderdome. Australia, 1985. *Dir.* George Miller. 106 min., color. Warner Bros. V, LD.

Magnificent Ambersons, The. U.S., 1942. *Dir.* Orson Welles. 88 min., b/w. RKO/Mercury. V, LD.

Magnificent Obsession. U.S., 1954. *Dir.* Douglas Sirk. 108 min., Technicolor. Universal. V.

Mail Early. Canada, 1941. *Dir.* Norman McLaren. 2 min., color. National Film Board.

Maîtres fous, Les (The Mad Masters). France, 1955. *Dir.* Jean Rouch. 35 min., color.

Making a Living. U.S., 1914. *Dir.* Henry Lehrman. 11 min., b/w, silent. Keystone Film Company.

Malcolm X. U.S., 1992. *Dir.* Spike Lee. 201 min., b/w and color. 40 Acres and a Mule Productions.

Malenkaya Vera (Little Vera). U.S.S.R., 1988. *Dir.* Vasili Pichul. 134 min., color. Mainline/Gorky Studios. V, LD.

Maltese Falcon, The. U.S., 1941. *Dir.* John Huston. 100 min., b/w. Warner Bros. V, LD.

Man Called Horse, A. U.S., 1970. *Dir.* Elliot Silver-

stein. 114 min., Technicolor, Panavision. Cinema Center/Sanford Howard. V.

Manchurian Candidate, The. U.S., 1962. *Dir.* John Frankenheimer. 126 min., b/w. United Artists/MC. V, LD.

Mandabi (The Money Order). Senegal, 1968. *Dir.* Ousmane Sembene. 90 min., color. Films Domirêve/Comptoir Français du Film.

Manhandled. U.S., 1924. *Dir.* Allan Dwan. 75 min., b/w, silent. Famous Players-Lasky.

Manhatta. U.S., 1921. *Dir.* Paul Strand, Charles Sheeler. 9 min., b/w, silent.

Manhattan. U.S., 1979. *Dir.* Woody Allen. 96 min., b/w., Panavision. United Artists. V, LD.

Man in the White Suit, The. Britain, 1951. *Dir.* Alexander Mackendrick. 81 min., b/w. Ealing. V, LD.

Man of Aran. Britain, 1934. *Dir.* Robert Flaherty. 75 min., b/w. Gainsborough. V.

Man of the West. U.S., 1958. *Dir.* Anthony Mann. 100 min., De Luxe, CinemaScope. United Artists/Ashton. V.

Manon des sources (Manon of the Springs). France, 1986. *Dir.* Claude Berri. 114 min., color. Renn Productions/Films A2/RAI 2/DD Productions. V, LD.

Ma nuit chez Maud (My Night at Maud's). France, 1969. *Dir.* Eric Rohmer. 110 min., b/w. Films du Losange/Films du Carrosse/Films de La Pléiade. V.

Man Who Envied Women, The. U.S., 1985. *Dir.* Yvonne Rainer. 125 min., b/w and color.

Man Who Knew Too Much, The. Britain, 1934. *Dir.* Alfred Hitchcock. 74 min., b/w. Gaumont-British. V, LD.

Man Who Shot Liberty Valance, The. U.S., 1962. *Dir.* John Ford. 122 min., b/w. Paramount/Ford. V, LD.

Marius. France, 1931. *Dir.* Alexander Korda. 125 min., b/w. Marcel Pagnol/Paramount. V.

Mark of Zorro, The. U.S., 1920. *Dir.* Fred Niblo. 83 min., b/w, silent. Douglas Fairbanks Productions. V, LD.

Marriage Circle, The. U.S., 1924. *Dir.* Ernst Lubitsch. 85 min., b/w, silent. Warner Bros. V.

Marseillaise, La. France, 1938. *Dir.* Jean Renoir. 135 min., b/w. CGT. V.

Marusa no Onna (A Taxing Woman). Japan, 1987. *Dir.* Juzo Itami. 127 min., color. Itami Productions/New Century Producers. V, LD.

Mary, Queen of Scots. 1895. Edison Co.

Masculin féminin (Masculine-Feminine). France, 1966. *Dir.* Jean-Luc Godard. 104 min., b/w. Anouchka/Argos/Svensk Filmindustri/Sandrews. V.

Mat' (The Mother). U.S.S.R., 1926. *Dir.* Vsevolod Pudovkin. 90 min., b/w, silent. Mezhrabpom-Russ. V.

Matewan. U.S., 1987. *Dir.* John Sayles. 130 min., DuArt Color. Cinecom International. V, LD.

Matka Joanna od Aniołów (Mother Joan of the Angels). Poland, 1961. *Dir.* Jerzy Kawalerowicz. 108 min., b/w. Film Polski.

Maya (Illusion). India, 1936. *Dir.* Pramathesh Chandra Barua. New Theatres, Ltd.

May Irwin Kiss, The. U.S., 1896. Photographed by William Heise. 1 min., b/w, silent. Edison Co.

Me'Achorei Hasoragim (Beyond the Walls). Israel, 1984. *Dir.* Uri Barbash. 103 min., color. April Films. V.

Mean Streets. U.S., 1973. *Dir.* Martin Scorsese. 110 min., Technicolor. Taplin-Perry-Scorsese. V, LD.

Medium Cool. U.S., 1969. *Dir.* Haskell Wexler. 111 min., Technicolor. Paramount/H & J Pictures. V.

Meet John Doe. U.S., 1941. *Dir.* Frank Capra. 129 min., b/w. Warner Bros. V, LD.

Megalexandros, O (Alexander the Great). Greece, 1980. *Dir.* Theo Angelopoulos. 210 min., color. RAI/ZDF/Angelopoulos Productions.

Meghe Dhaka Tara (The Cloud Capped Star). India, 1960. *Dir.* Ritwik Ghatak. 120 min., b/w. Chitrakalpa.

Még kér a nép (Red Psalm). Hungary, 1972. *Dir.* Miklós Jancsó. 88 min., color. Mafilm.

Memorias del subdesarollo (Memories of Underdevelopment). Cuba, 1968. *Dir.* Tomás Gutiérrez Alea. 104 min., b/w. ICAIC. V.

Memórias do cárcere (Memories of Prison). Brazil, 1984. *Dir.* Nelson Pereira Dos Santos. 187 min., color. Produçoes L.C. Barreto.

Memphis Belle. U.S., 1990. *Dir.* Michael Caton-Jones. 106 min., color. Enigma. V, LD.

Memphis Belle, The. U.S., 1944. *Dir.* William Wyler. 43 min., Technicolor. War Activities Commission.

Ménilmontant. France, 1924. *Dir.* Dmitri Kirsanov. 50 min., b/w, silent. Dmitri Kirsanov Productions.

Menschen am Sonntag (People on Sunday). Germany, 1929. *Dir.* Robert Siodmak, Edgar G. Ulmer. 59 min. (24 f.p.s.), b/w, silent. Filmstudio Germania.

Mephisto. Hungary, 1981. *Dir.* István Szabó. 144 min., Eastmancolor. Mafilm/Manfred Durniok. V.

Mépris, Le (Contempt). France, 1963. *Dir.* Jean-Luc Godard. 103 min., color, Franscope. Rome-Paris Films. V, LD.

Merry Widow, The. U.S., 1934. *Dir.* Ernst Lubitsch. 99 min., b/w. Metro-Goldwyn-Mayer. V.

Meshes of the Afternoon. U.S., 1943. *Dir.* Maya Deren and Alexander Hammid. 14 min., b/w, sound added in 1959.

Mest' Kinematograficheskogo Operatora (The Cameraman's Revenge). U.S.S.R., 1912. *Dir.* Ladislas Starewicz. 12 min., b/w, silent. Khanzhonkov.

Metropolis. Germany, 1926. *Dir.* Fritz Lang. 153 min., b/w, silent. Ufa. V, LD.

Midnight Cowboy. U.S., 1969. *Dir.* John Schlesinger. 113 min., De Luxe. United Artists/Jerome Hellman. V, LD.

Midnight Express. U.S., 1978. *Dir.* Alan Parker. 121 min., Eastmancolor. Columbia/Casablanca. V, LD.

Mighty Joe Young. U.S., 1949. *Dir.* Ernest Schoedsack. 94 min., b/w. RKO. V, LD.

Mildred Pierce. U.S., 1945. *Dir.* Michael Curtiz. 109 min., b/w. Warner Bros. V, LD.

Million, Le (The Million). France, 1931. *Dir.* René Clair. 89 min., b/w. Tobis.

Ministry of Fear. U.S., 1944. *Dir.* Fritz Lang. 84 min., b/w. Paramount.

Miracolo a Milano (Miracle in Milan). Italy, 1950. *Dir.* Vittorio De Sica. 101 min., b/w. ENIC. V, LD.

Mirt sost shi amit (Harvest 3,000 Years). Ethiopia, 1975. *Dir.* Haile Gerima. 138 min., b/w. Haile Gerima.

Misère au Borinage (Misery in Borinage, aka Borinage). Belgium, 1933. *Dir.* Joris Ivens and Henri Storck. 32 min., b/w, originally silent. E.P.I./Club de l'Ecran/Brussels.

Mr. Deeds Goes to Town. U.S., 1936. *Dir.* Frank Capra. 115 min., b/w. Columbia. V.

Mr. Skeffington. U.S., 1944. *Dir.* Vincent Sherman. 126 min., b/w. Warner Bros. V, LD.

Mr. Smith Goes to Washington. U.S., 1939. *Dir.* Frank Capra. 126 min., b/w. Columbia. V, LD.

Moana. U.S., 1926. *Dir.* Robert Flaherty. 85 min., b/w, silent. Famous Players-Lasky. V, LD.

Modern Times. U.S., 1936. *Dir.* Charles Chaplin. 85 min., b/w. United Artists. V.

Monanieba (Repentance). U.S.S.R., 1984/86. *Dir.* Tengiz Abuladze. 150 min., color. Gruziafilm/Georgian State TV. V, LD.

Monkey Business. U.S., 1931. *Dir.* Norman McLeod. 77 min., b/w. Paramount. V, LD.

Mon Oncle (My Uncle). France, 1958. *Dir.* Jacques Tati. 116 min., color. Spectra/Gray/Alterdel/Centaure. V, LD.

Mon Oncle Antoine (My Uncle Antoine). Canada, 1971. *Dir.* Claude Jutra. 110 min., color. National Film Board. V.

Monsieur Ripois (Knave of Hearts, aka Lovers, Happy Lovers). Britain, 1954. *Dir.* René Clément. 103 min., b/w. Transcontinental.

Monsieur Verdoux. U.S., 1947. *Dir.* Charles Chaplin. 122 min., b/w. United Artists. V.

Monterey Pop. U.S., 1968. *Dir.* D.A. Pennebaker. 80 min., color. Leacock-Pennebaker Foundation. V.

Mothlight. U.S., 1963. *Dir.* Stan Brakhage. 4 min., color.

müde Tod, Der (Destiny). Germany, 1921. *Dir.* Fritz Lang. 79 min., b/w, silent. Decla-Bioskop.

Mujeres al borde de un ataque de nervous (Women on the Verge of a Nervous Breakdown). Spain, 1988. *Dir.* Pedro Almodóvar. 98 min., color. El Deseo/Laurenfilm. V, LD.

mulino del Po, Il (The Mill on the Po). Italy, 1949. *Dir.* Alberto Lattuada. 105 min., b/w. Lux Film.

Mumia, El (The Night of Counting the Years). Egypt, 1969. *Dir.* Shadi Abdelsalam. 102 min., color. Egyptian Cinema General Organisation.

Mur, Le (The Wall). France, 1983. *Dir.* Yilmaz Güney. 117 min., color. Güney Productions/MK2 Productions/TF1 Films/Ministère de la Culture. V.

Murder, My Sweet. U.S., 1945. *Dir.* Edward Dmytryk. 92 min., b/w. RKO. V.

Musical Poster #1. Britain, 1940. *Dir.* Len Lye. 3 min., color. British Ministry of Information.

Musketeers of Pig Alley, The. U.S., 1912. *Dir.* D.W. Griffith. 15 min., b/w, silent. Biograph Co.

My Brilliant Career. Australia, 1979. *Dir.* Gillian Armstrong. 98 min., color. New South Wales/GUO/Analysis. V.

My Hustler. U.S., 1965. *Dir.* Andy Warhol. 70 min., b/w.

My Man Godfrey. U.S., 1936. *Dir.* Gregory LaCava. 93 min., b/w. Universal. V.

My Son John. U.S., 1952. *Dir.* Leo McCarey. 122 min., b/w. Paramount/Rainbow.

Mystery Train. U.S., 1989. *Dir.* Jim Jarmusch. 110 min., color. MTI. V, LD.

Naked Spur, The. U.S., 1953. *Dir.* Anthony Mann. 91 min., Technicolor. Metro-Goldwyn-Mayer. V.

Nan fu nan qi (The Difficult Couple). China, 1913. *Dir.* Zhang Shichuan, Zheng Zhenqui. Asia Company.

Naniwa ereji (Naniwa Elegy, aka Osaka Elegy). Japan, 1936. *Dir.* Kenji Mizoguchi. 66 min., b/w. Daiichi. V.

Nanook of the North. U.S., 1922. *Dir.* Robert Flaherty. 75 min., b/w, silent. Revillion Frères. V.

Napoléon. France, 1927. *Dir.* Abel Gance. 270 min., b/w, silent, 3 screens. WESTI/Société Générale de Film. V, LD.

Nashville. U.S., 1975. *Dir.* Robert Altman. 161 min., Metrocolor, Panavision. Paramount/ABC. V, LD.

National Lampoon's Animal House. U.S., 1978. *Dir.* John Landis. 109 min., Technicolor. Universal. V, LD.

nave bianca, La (The White Ship). Italy, 1941. *Dir.* Roberto Rossellini. 77 min., b/w. Scalera/Centro Cinematografico del Ministero della Marina.

Nazis Strike, The. U.S., 1943. *Dir.* Frank Capra, Anatole Litvak. 42 min., b/w. U.S. War Department.

Ned Kelly. Britain, 1970. *Dir.* Tony Richardson. 103 min., Technicolor. United Artists/Woodfall.

Negro Soldier, The. U.S., 1944. *Dir.* Stuart Heisler. 40 min., b/w. U.S. War Department.

Neobychainiye priklucheniya Mistera Vesta v strane bol'shevikov (The Extraordinary Adventures of Mr. West in the Land of the Bolsheviks). U.S.S.R., 1924. *Dir.* Lev Kuleshov. 94 min., b/w, silent. Goskino. V.

Network. U.S., 1976. *Dir.* Sidney Lumet. 121 min., Metrocolor, Panavision. Metro-Goldwyn-Mayer/United Artists. V, LD.

Never the Twain Shall Meet. U.S., 1925. *Dir.* Maurice Tourneur. 80 min., b/w, silent. Cosmopolitan Corp.

New York Hat, The. U.S., 1912. *Dir.* D.W. Griffith. 15 min., b/w, silent. Biograph Co.

Next of Kin. Canada, 1984. *Dir.* Atom Egoyan. 73 min., color. Ego Film Arts. V.

Nibelungen, Die. Germany, 1924. *Dir.* Fritz Lang.

See *Siegfried* (Part I), *Kriemhild's Rache* (Part II).

Nicht Versöhnt oder Es hilft nur Gewalt, wo Gewalt herrscht (Not Reconciled, or Only Violence Helps Where Violence Rules). West Germany, 1965. *Dir.* Jean-Marie Straub, Danièle Huillet. 53 min., b/w. Straub-Huillet.

Night Mail. Britain, 1936. *Dir.* Basil Wright, Harry Watt. 24 min., b/w. GPO Film Unit.

Nihon no yoru to kiri (Night and Fog in Japan). Japan, 1960. *Dir.* Nagisa Oshima. 107 min., color, CinemaScope. Shochiku Co.

Niluohe Nuer (Daughter of the Nile). Taiwan, 1988. *Dir.* Hou Hsiao-hsien. 91 min., color. Fu Film Productions.

Ninotchka. U.S., 1939. *Dir.* Ernst Lubitsch. 111 min., b/w. Metro-Goldwyn-Mayer. V, LD.

Nippon Konchuki (The Insect Woman). Japan, 1963. *Dir.* Shohei Imamura. 123 min., b/w. Nikkatsu Corp. V.

Nobleza gaucha (Gaucho Nobility). Argentina, 1915. *Dir.* Eduardo Martínez de la Pera, Ernesto Gunch and Humberto Cairo.

Noce en Galilée (Wedding in Galilee). Belgium/France, 1987. *Dir.* Michel Khleifi. 116 min., color. Maris/LPA/French Ministry of Culture. V.

Noire de . . ., La (Black Girl). Senegal, 1966. *Dir.* Ousmane Sembene. 80 min., b/w. Domirev Films.

Non c'è pace tra gli ulivi (No Peace under the Olives). Italy, 1950. *Dir.* Giuseppe De Santis. 107 min., b/w. Lux.

North by Northwest. U.S., 1959. *Dir.* Alfred Hitchcock. 136 min., Technicolor, Vistavision. Metro-Goldwyn-Mayer. V, LD.

Nosferatu. Germany, 1922. *Dir.* F.W. Murnau. 72 min., b/w, silent. Prana. V, LD.

Nosferatu—Phantom der Nacht (Nosferatu the Vampire). West Germany, 1979. *Dir.* Werner Herzog. 107 min., color. Werner Herzog Filmproduktion/Gaumount.

Nothing but a Man. U.S., 1965. *Dir.* Michael Roemer. 95 min., b/w. Nothing but a Man Co./Du Art Lab Productions.

notte di San Lorenzo, La (The Night of the Shooting Stars). Italy, 1982. *Dir.* Paolo and Vittorio Taviani. 107 min., color. RAI/Ager Cinematografica. V.

Novecento (1900). Italy/France/Germany, 1976. *Dir.* Bernardo Bertolucci. 175 min. (Part I), 165 min. (Part II), color. PEA/Les Artistes Associés/Artemis. V.

Nóz w Wodzic (Knife in the Water). Poland, 1962. *Dir.* Roman Polanski. 94 min., b/w. ZRF Kamera. V, LD.

Nuit et brouillard (Night and Fog). France, 1955. *Dir.* Alain Resnais. 31 min., b/w and color. Argos/Como/Cocinor. V.

Odd Man Out. Britain, 1947. *Dir.* Carol Reed. 115 min., b/w. GFD/Two Cities. V, LD.

Of Human Bondage. U.S., 1934. *Dir.* John Cromwell. 83 min., b/w. RKO. V, LD.

Oktyabr' (October). U.S.S.R., 1928. *Dir.* Sergei Eisenstein. 164 min., b/w, silent. Sovkino. V, LD.

Oliver Twist. Britain, 1948. *Dir.* David Lean. 116 min., b/w. GFD/Cineguild. V, LD.

Olvidados, Los (The Young and the Damned). Mexico, 1950. *Dir.* Luis Buñuel. 88 min., b/w. Ultramar/Oscar Dancigers.

Olympia. Germany, 1938. *Dir.* Leni Riefenstahl. Part I: Festival of the Nations, 118 min; Part II: *Festival of Beauty*, 107 min., b/w. Tobis. V.

One Flew over the Cuckoo's Nest. U.S., 1975. *Dir.* Miloš Forman. 134 min., De Luxe. United Artists/Fantasy Films. V, LD.

On est au coton. Canada, 1970. *Dir.* Denys Arcand. 159 min., b/w. National Film Board.

Only Angels Have Wings. U.S., 1939. *Dir.* Howard Hawks. 120 min., b/w. Columbia. V.

On the Waterfront. U.S., 1954. *Dir.* Elia Kazan. 108 min., b/w. Columbia. V, LD.

Opening Night. U.S., 1978. *Dir.* John Cassavetes. 144 min., Metrocolor. Faces International.

Ordet ("The Word"). Denmark, 1955. *Dir.* Carl Th. Dreyer. 125 min., b/w. Palladium.

Ordres, Les (Orders). Canada, 1974. *Dir.* Michel Brault. 107 min. b/w and color. Les Productions Prisma.

Örökbefogadás (Adoption). Hungary, 1975. *Dir.* Márta Mészáros. 89 min., b/w. Hunnia. V.

Orphans of the Storm. U.S., 1921. *Dir.* D.W. Griffith. 140 min., b/w, silent. D.W. Griffith, Inc. V, LD.

Ososhiki (The Funeral). Japan, 1984. *Dir.* Juzo Itami. 123 min., color. Itami/N.C.P. V.

Ossessione ("Obsession"). Italy, 1942. *Dir.* Luchino Visconti. 135 min., b/w. Industria Cinematografica Italiana. V.

Ostře sledované vlaky (Closely Watched Trains). Czechoslovakia, 1966. *Dir.* Jiří Menzel. 92 min., color. Ceskoslovensky Film. V, LD.

Out of the Past. U.S., 1947. *Dir.* Jacques Tourneur. 95 min., b/w. RKO. V, LD.

Padenie dinastii Romanovykh (The Fall of the Romanov Dynasty). U.S.S.R., 1927. *Dir.* Esfir Shub. 82 min., b/w, silent. Sovkino/Museum of the Revolution. V.

Padre padrone ("My Father, My Master"). Italy, 1977. *Dir.* Paolo and Vittorio Taviani. 113 min., color. RAI. V.

Painted Lady, The. U.S., 1912. *Dir.* D.W. Griffith. 15 min., b/w, silent. Biograph.

Paisà (Paisan). Italy, 1946. *Dir.* Roberto Rossellini. 115 min., b/w. OFI/Foreign Films Prod./Capitani. V.

Palais des Mille et une Nuits, Le (The Palace of the Arabian Nights). France, 1905. *Dir.* Georges Méliès. 19 min., b/w, silent. Star-Film.

Paramount on Parade. U.S., 1930. *Dir.* Dorothy Arzner. 102 min., b/w and Technicolor segments. Paramount.

Paris nous appartient (Paris Belongs to Us). France, 1961. *Dir.* Jacques Rivette. 140 min., b/w. AJYM/Les Films du Carrosse.

Paris qui dort (The Crazy Ray). France, 1924. *Dir.* René Clair. 40 min., b/w, silent. Films Diamant.

Paris, Texas. West Germany/France, 1984. *Dir.* Wim Wenders. 148 min., color. Road Movies/Argos. V, LD.

Pasazerka (The Passenger). Poland, 1963. *Dir.* Andrzej Munk. 63 min., b/w. WFF Lódz Kadr Unit.

Pasqualino Settebellezze (Seven Beauties). Italy, 1976. *Dir.* Lina Wertmüller. 115 min., color. Medusa Cinematografica. V.

passado e o presente, O (The Past and the Present). Portugal, 1971. *Dir.* Manoel de Oliveira. 115 min., color. Manoel de Oliveira.

Passion de Jeanne d'Arc, La (The Passion of Joan of Arc). France, 1928. *Dir.* Carl Th. Dreyer. 114 min., b/w, silent. Société Générale des Films. V.

Pather Panchali. India, 1955. *Dir.* Satyajit Ray. 122 min., b/w. Government of West Bengal. V.

Patton. U.S., 1970. *Dir.* Franklin Schaffner. 171 min., De Luxe, Dimension 150. 20th Century-Fox. V, LD.

Pay Day. U.S., 1922. *Dir.* Charles Chaplin. 20 min., b/w, silent. First National.

Peeping Tom. Britain, 1960. *Dir.* Michael Powell. 109 min., color. Anglo-Amalgamated. V.

People of the Cumberland. U.S., 1938. *Dir.* Sidney Meyers, Jay Leyda. 21 min., b/w. Frontier Films.

Peppermint frappé. Spain, 1967. *Dir.* Carlos Saura. 94 min., color. Elias Querejeta Productions.

Perfido incanto (Wicked Enchantment). Italy, 1918. *Dir.* Anton Giulio Bragaglia and Riccardo Cassano. 68 min., b/w, silent. Novissima Film.

Perils of Pauline, The. U.S., 1914. Serial.

Permission, La (The Story of a Three-Day Pass). France, 1968. *Dir.* Melvin van Peebles. 87 min., b/w. Opera Productions.

Phantom Lady. U.S., 1944. *Dir.* Robert Siodmak. 81 min., b/w. Universal.

Phantom of the Opera, The. U.S., 1925. *Dir.* Rupert Julian. 100 min., b/w with Technicolor sequences, silent. Universal. Lon Chaney. V, LD.

Photographing a Female Crook. U.S., 1904. Produced by Wallace McCutcheon, photographed by A.E. Weed. 40 sec., b/w, silent. American Mutoscope and Biograph Co.

Physician of the Castle. France, 1908. 5 min., b/w, silent. Pathé Frères. (English title only available).

Pickup on South Street. U.S., 1953. *Dir.* Samuel Fuller. 80 min., b/w. 20th Century-Fox. V.

Picnic at Hanging Rock. Australia, 1975. *Dir.* Peter Weir. 115 min., Eastmancolor. Picnic Productions/Australia Film Corporation. V.

Pie in the Sky. U.S., 1935. *Dir.* Ralph Steiner. 16 min., b/w, silent. Nykino.

Pierrot le fou ("Crazy Pierrot"). France, 1965. *Dir.* Jean-Luc Godard. 110 min., color. Rome-Paris Films/Dino De Laurentiis/Georges De Beauregard. V, LD.

Pilgrim, The. U.S., 1922. *Dir.* Charles Chaplin. 40 min., b/w, silent.

pilota ritorna, Un (A Pilot Returns). Italy, 1942. *Dir.* Roberto Rossellini. 87 min., b/w. ACI.

Pinocchio. U.S., 1940. *Dir.* Ben Sharpsteen, Hamilton Luske. 77 min., Technicolor. Walt Disney. V, LD.

Pirate, The. U.S., 1948. *Dir.* Vincente Minnelli. 101 min., color. Metro-Goldwyn-Mayer.

Plaisir, Le (House of Pleasure). France, 1952. *Dir.* Max Ophuls. 97 min., b/w. Stera/CCFC.

Platoon. U.S., 1986. *Dir.* Oliver Stone. 120 min., CFI color. Hemdale. V, LD.

Playtime. France, 1967. *Dir.* Jacques Tati. 152 min., color. Spectra Films. V.

Plow That Broke the Plains, The. U.S., 1936. *Dir.* Pare Lorentz. 28 min., b/w. Resettlement Administration Film Unit.

Pociag (Night Train). Poland, 1959. *Dir.* Jerzy Kawalerowicz. 100 min., b/w. Kadr Unit/Film Polski.

Pointe Courte, La. France, 1955. *Dir.* Agnès Varda. 85 min., b/w. Tamaris Film.

Point of Order. U.S., 1964. *Dir.* Emile de Antonio. 95 min., b/w. Point Films. V.

Pokolenie (Generation). Poland, 1954. *Dir.* Andrzej Wajda. 85 min., b/w. Film Polski.

Popiol i diament (Ashes and Diamonds). Poland, 1958. *Dir.* Andrzej Wajda. 104 min., b/w. Film Polski. V.

Potomok Chingis-khana (Storm over Asia). U.S.S.R., 1928. *Dir.* Vsevolod Pudovkin. 93 min., b/w, silent. Mezhrabpom. V.

Potted Psalm, The. U.S., 1946. *Dir.* James Broughton and Sidney Peterson. 25 min., b/w.

Power and the Land. U.S., 1940. *Dir.* Joris Ivens. 36 min., b/w. Rural Electrification Administration/U.S. Department of Agriculture.

Po zakonu (By the Law). U.S.S.R., 1926. *Dir.* Lev Kuleshov. 83 min., b/w, silent. Goskino.

Predator. U.S., 1987. *Dir.* John McTiernan. 107 min., De Luxe. 20th Century-Fox/Gordon-Silver-Davis. V, LD.

Prelude to War. U.S., 1943. *Dir.* Frank Capra. 53 min., b/w. U.S. War Department.

Pretty in Pink. U.S., 1986. *Dir.* John Hughes. 96 min., Technicolor. Paramount. V, LD.

Primary. U.S., 1960. Produced by Robert Drew. 54 min., b/w. Time-Life Broadcasting.

Prince of Tides, The. U.S., 1991. *Dir.* Barbra Streisand. 132 min., color. Barwood Films/Longfellow Productions/Columbia. V, LD.

Private Life of Henry VIII, The. Britain, 1933. *Dir.* Alexander Korda. 96 min., b/w. London/United Artists. V, LD.

Prix de Beauté ("Beauty Prize"). France, 1930. *Dir.* Augusto Genina. 109 min., b/w. Sofar. V.

Procès de Jeanne d'Arc (Trial of Joan of Arc). France, 1962. *Dir.* Robert Bresson. 65 min., b/w. Agnès Delaharè.

Psycho. U.S., 1960. *Dir.* Alfred Hitchcock. 109 min., b/w. Paramount. V, LD.

Public Enemy, The. U.S., 1931. *Dir.* William Wellman. 83 min., b/w. Warner Bros. V, LD.

Qiu Ju Da Guansi (The Story of Qiu Ju). China, 1992. *Dir.* Zhang Yimou. 100 min., color. Sil-Metropole Organisation.

Quai des brumes, Les (Port of Shadows). France, 1938. *Dir.* Marcel Carné. 89 min., b/w. Ciné Alliance/Pathé.

Quatre cents coups, Les (The 400 Blows). France, 1959. *Dir.* François Truffaut. 94 min., b/w. Films du Carrosse/SEDIF. V, LD.

Queen Kelly. U.S., produced 1928-29; released 1985. *Dir.* Erich von Stroheim. 100 min., b/w, silent. Joseph P. Kennedy. V, LD.

Quingmei Zhuma (Taipei Story). Taiwan, 1985. *Dir.* Edward Yang.

Quo Vadis?. Italy, 1913. *Dir.* Enrico Guazzoni. 116 min., b/w, silent. Cines Company.

Raging Bull. U.S., 1980. *Dir.* Martin Scorsese. 119 min., b/w and color. United Artists/Chartoff-Winkler. V, LD.

Ragtime. U.S., 1981. *Dir.* Miloš Forman. 155 min., Technicolor. Todd-AO/Ragtime/Sunley. V, LD.

Raiders of the Lost Ark. U.S., 1981. *Dir.* Steven Spielberg. 115 min., Metrocolor, Panavision. Paramount/Lucasfilm. V, LD.

Raja Harishchandra (King Harishchandra). India, 1913. *Dir.* Dadasaheb Phalke. 135 min., b/w, silent. Phalke.

Rambling Rose. U.S., 1991. *Dir.* Martha Coolidge. 112 min., color. Carolco Pictures. V, LD.

Rambo: First Blood Part II. U.S., 1985. *Dir.* George Cosmatos. 92 min., Technicolor. Anabasis Investments NV/Buzz Feitshans. V, LD.

Ran. Japan, 1985. *Dir.* Akira Kurosawa. 162 min., color. Herald Ace/Nippon Herald/Greenwich Films. V, LD.

Rancho Notorious. U.S., 1952. *Dir.* Fritz Lang. 89 min., Technicolor. RKO/Fidelity. V, LD.

Rashomon. Japan, 1950. *Dir.* Akira Kurosawa. 83 min., b/w. Daiei. V, LD.

Razgrom nemetzkikh voisk pod Moskvoi (Defeat of the German Armies near Moscow, aka Moscow Strikes Back). U.S.S.R., 1942. *Editor* Slavko Vorkapich. 55 min., b/w. Central Newsreel Studios.

Real Genius. U.S., 1985. *Dir.* Martha Coolidge. 105 min., color. Tri-Star. V.

Rear Window. U.S., 1954. *Dir.* Alfred Hitchcock. 112 min., Technicolor. Alfred Hitchcock. V, LD.

Rebecca. U.S., 1940. *Dir.* Alfred Hitchcock. 130 min., b/w. Selznick/United Artists. V, LD.

Rebel Without a Cause. U.S., 1955. *Dir.* Nicholas Ray. 111 min., Warnercolor, CinemaScope. Warner Bros. V, LD.

Reconstituirea (Reconstruction). Romania, 1969. *Dir.* Lucien Pintilie.

Red River. U.S., 1948. *Dir.* Howard Hawks. 126 min., b/w. United Artists/Monterey. V, LD.

Red Shoes, The. Britain, 1948. *Dir.* Michael Powell, Emeric Pressburger. 136 min., Technicolor. GFD/The Archers. V, LD.

Règle du jeu, La (Rules of the Game). France, 1939. *Dir.* Jean Renoir. 113 min., b/w. La Nouvelle Edition Française. V, LD.

Reise ins Licht—Despair, Eine (Despair). West Germany, 1977. *Dir.* Rainer Werner Fassbinder. 119 min., color. Bavaria Atelier GmbH.

Rekopis znaleziony w Saragossie (The Saragossa Manuscript). Poland, 1965. *Dir.* Wojciech Has. 175 min., b/w. Kamera Film Unit/Film Polski.

Rendez-vous d'Anna, Les (The Meetings of Anna). Belgium/France/West Germany, 1978. *Dir.* Chantal Akerman. 122 min., color. Hélène Films/Paradise Films/Zweites Deutsches Fernsehen. V.

Repas de bébé (Feeding the Baby). France, 1896. *Dir.* Louis Lumière. b/w, silent. Société Lumière.

Rescued by Rover. Britain, 1905. *Dir.* Cecil Hepworth. 6 min., b/w, silent. Cecil Hepworth.

Retapeur de cervelles, Le (Brains Repaired). France, 1911. *Dir.* Emile Cohl. 5 min., b/w, silent. Pathé.

Return of the Jedi, The. U.S., 1983. *Dir.* Richard Marquand. 132 min., De Luxe, Panavision. 20th Century-Fox/Lucasfilm. V, LD.

Return of the Secaucus Seven. U.S., 1980. *Dir.* John Sayles. 110 min., color. Salsipuedes/Libra. V.

Rhythmus 21. Germany, 1921–24. *Dir.* Hans Richter. 3 min., b/w, silent.

Riddles of the Sphinx. Britain, 1977. *Dir.* Laura Mulvey, Peter Wollen. 92 min., color. BFI.

Rio Bravo. U.S., 1959. *Dir.* Howard Hawks. 141 min., Technicolor. Warner Bros./Armada. V.

Rio Grande. U.S., 1950. *Dir.* John Ford. 105 min., b/w. Republic/Argosy. John Wayne. V.

Riso amaro (Bitter Rice). Italy, 1949. *Dir.* Giuseppe De Santis. 107 min., b/w. Lux/De Laurentiis.

River, The. U.S., 1937. *Dir.* Pare Lorentz. 30 min., b/w. Farm Security Administration.

River, The. India, 1951. *Dir.* Jean Renoir. 87 min., Technicolor. Oriental/International/Theatre Guild. V, LD.

Robe, The. U.S., 1953. *Dir.* Henry Koster. 135 min., Technicolor, CinemaScope. 20th Century-Fox. V, LD.

Robin Hood. U.S., 1922. *Dir.* Allan Dwan. 120 min., b/w, silent. Douglas Fairbanks Pictures.

Rocco e i suoi fratelli (Rocco and His Brothers). Italy, 1960. *Dir.* Luchino Visconti. 180 min., b/w. Titanus/Les Films Marceau. V, LD.

Rocky. U.S., 1976. *Dir.* John G. Avildsen. 119 min., Technicolor. United Artists/Chartoff-Winkler. V, LD.

Roger & Me. U.S., 1989. *Dir.* Michael Moore. 87 min., DuArt color. Warner Bros./Dog Eat Dog Films/Michael Moore. V, LD.

Roma città aperta (Rome, Open City). Italy, 1945. *Dir.* Roberto Rossellini. 101 min., b/w. Minerva/Excelsa. V.

Ronde, La (Rondelay). France, 1950. *Dir.* Max Ophuls. 97 min., b/w. Sacha Gordine. V.

Rosemary's Baby. U.S., 1968. *Dir.* Roman Polanski. 137 min., Technicolor. Paramount/William Castle. V, LD.

Rosita. U.S., 1923. *Dir.* Ernst Lubitsch. 90 min., b/w, silent. Mary Pickford Co.

Roue, La ("The Wheel"). France, 1923. *Dir.* Abel Gance. 144 min. (303 min. restored), b/w, silent. Pathé.

Rough Sea at Dover, A (aka Sea Waves). Britain, 1896. Photographed by Robert W. Paul. 53 sec., b/w, silent.

SA—Mann Brand (S.A. Man Brand). Germany, 1933. *Dir.* Franz Seitz. b/w. Emelka.

Safety Last. U.S., 1923. *Dir.* Fred Newmeyer, Sam Taylor. 70 min., b/w, silent. Hal Roach Studios. V.

Saikaku Ichidai Onna (The Life of Oharu). Japan, 1952. *Dir.* Kenji Mizoguchi. 133 min., b/w. Shin Toho. V.

Salesman. U.S., 1969. *Dir.* Albert and David Maysles, Charlotte Zwerin. 90 min., b/w. Maysles Film Production. V.

Salvation Hunters, The. U.S., 1925. *Dir.* Josef von Sternberg. 66 min., b/w, silent. Academy Photoplays.

Sansho Dayu (Sansho the Bailiff). Japan, 1954. *Dir.* Kenji Mizoguchi. 125 min., b/w. Daiei. V.

Sans soleil (Sunless). France, 1982. *Dir.* Chris Marker. 100 min., color. Argos.

Santa. Mexico, 1932. *Dir.* Antonio Moreno. 81 min., b/w. Compañía Nacional Productora de Películas.

Sarraounia. Burkino Faso, 1986. *Dir.* Med Hondo. 121 min., color. Films Soliel O.

Saturday Night and Sunday Morning. Britain, 1960. *Dir.* Karel Reisz. 89 min., b/w. Bryanston/Woodfall.

Sayat nova (The Color of Pomegranates aka Red Pomegranates). U.S.S.R., 1969. *Dir.* Sergei Paradjanov. 73 min., color. Armenfilm. V.

Scarface. U.S., 1932. *Dir.* Howard Hawks. 90 min., b/w. Hughes/United Artists. V, LD.

Scarface. U.S., 1983. *Dir.* Brian de Palma. 170 min., Technicolor, Panavision. Universal. V, LD.

Scarlet Street. U.S., 1945. *Dir.* Fritz Lang. 96 min., b/w. Universal/Diana. V.

sceicco bianco, Lo (The White Sheik). Italy, 1952. *Dir.* Federico Fellini. 88 min., b/w. Luigi Rovere/PDC/OFI. V.

Scherben (Shattered). Germany, 1921. *Dir.* Lupu Pick. 62 min., b/w, silent, Rex Film.

School Daze. U.S., 1988. *Dir.* Spike Lee. 120 min., color. 40 Acres and a Mule Productions. V.

Sciuscià (Shoeshine). Italy, 1946. *Dir.* Vittorio De Sica. 93 min., b/w. Alta/ENIC. V.

Scorpio Rising. U.S., 1963. *Dir.* Kenneth Anger. 29 min., color. V.

Searchers, The. U.S., 1956. *Dir.* John Ford. 119 min., Technicolor, Vistavision. Warner Bros./C.V. Whitney. V, LD.

Sehnsucht der Veronika Voss, Die (Veronika Voss). West Germany, 1981. *Dir.* Rainer Werner Fassbinder. 104 min., b/w. Maura/Tango Film/Rialto Film/Trio Film/Maran. V.

Senso. Italy, 1954. *Dir.* Luchino Visconti. 115 min., color. Lux. V.

Senza pietà (Without Pity). Italy, 1948. *Dir.* Alberto Lattuada. 94 min., b/w. Lux Films.

Sergeant Rutledge. U.S., 1960. *Dir.* John Ford. 111 min., Technicolor. Warner Bros./John Ford.

Sergeant York. U.S., 1941. *Dir.* Howard Hawks. 134 min., b/w. Warner Bros. V.

Shadows. U.S., 1959. *Dir.* John Cassavetes. 81 min., b/w. Cassavetes/Cassel/Maurice McEndree.

Shaft. U.S., 1971. *Dir.* Gordon Parks. 100 min., Metrocolor. Metro-Goldwyn-Mayer/Shaft Productions. V.

Shang hai zhan zheng (War in Shanghai). China, 1912. Asia Company.

Sheik, The. U.S., 1921. *Dir.* George Melford. 70 min., b/w, silent. Famous Players-Lasky. V.

Shen nu (The Goddess). China, 1934. *Dir.* Wu Yonggang. 9 reels, b/w, silent. Lianhua Studios.

Sherlock, Jr. U.S., 1924. *Dir.* Buster Keaton. 50 min., b/w, silent. Buster Keaton Productions.

She's Gotta Have It. U.S., 1986. *Dir.* Spike Lee. 100 min., b/w and color. A Spike Lee Joint/40 Acres and a Mule Filmworks. V.

Shestaya chast' mira (A Sixth Part of the World). U.S.S.R., 1926. *Dir.* Dziga Vertov. 64 min., b/w, silent.

She Wore a Yellow Ribbon. U.S., 1949. *Dir.* John Ford. 103 min., color. RKO/Argosy. V, LD.

Shichinin no Samurai (Seven Samurai). Japan, 1954. *Dir.* Akira Kurosawa. 200 min., b/w. Toho. V, LD.

Shining, The. U.S., 1980. *Dir.* Stanley Kubrick. 146 min., color. Warner Bros./Stanley Kubrick. V, LD.

Shinjuku dorobo nikki (Diary of a Shinjuku Burglar). Japan, 1969. *Dir.* Nagisa Oshima. 94 min., b/w and color. Sozosha.

Shinju ten no amijima (Double Suicide). Japan, 1969. *Dir.* Masahiro Shinoda. 106 min., b/w. Hyogesha/Nippon Art Theatre Guild. V.

Shoah. France, 1985. *Dir.* Claude Lanzmann. Part I: 274 min., Part II: 292 min., color. Aleph/Historia. V.

Shooting the Chutes. U.S., 1896. Photographed by William Heise. 29 sec., b/w, silent. Edison Co.

Show People. U.S., 1928. *Dir.* King Vidor. 106 min., b/w, music score and sound effects. Metro-Goldwyn-Mayer. V.

Siegfried. Germany, 1924. *Dir.* Fritz Lang. Part I of *Die Nibelungen.* 131 min., b/w, silent. Decla-Bioskop. V, LD.

Simfoniya Donbassa (Enthusiasm). U.S.S.R., 1930. *Dir.* Dziga Vertov. 96 min., b/w. Kiev Film Studio/Ukrainfilm.

Since You Went Away. U.S., 1944. *Dir.* John Cromwell. 158 min., b/w. United Artists/Selznick. V, LD.

Singin' in the Rain. U.S., 1952. *Dir.* Gene Kelly, Stanley Donen. 102 min., color. Metro-Goldwyn-Mayer. V, LD.

Sinking of the Lusitania, The. U.S., 1918. *Dir.* Winsor McCay.

Sixteen Candles. U.S., 1984. *Dir.* John Hughes. 93 min., Technicolor. Universal. V, LD.

Sjunde Inseglet, Det (The Seventh Seal). Sweden, 1957. *Dir.* Ingmar Bergman. 90 min., b/w. Svensk Filmindustri. V, LD.

Skupljaci perja (I Even Met Happy Gypsies). Yugoslavia, 1967. *Dir.* Aleksander Petrovic. 90 min., color. Avala Film.

Sleep. U.S., 1963. *Dir.* Andy Warhol. 360 min. (16 f.p.s), b/w, silent.

Smierc Prezydenta (Death of a President). Poland, 1977. *Dir.* Jerzy Kawalerowicz.

Smithereens. U.S., 1982. *Dir.* Susan Seidelman. 90 min., color. New Line. V, LD.

Smouldering Fires. U.S., 1924. *Dir.* Clarence Brown. 85 min., b/w, silent. Universal.

Smultronstället (Wild Strawberries). Sweden, 1957. *Dir.* Ingmar Bergman. 93 min., b/w. Svensk Filmindustri. V, LD.

Snow White and the Seven Dwarfs. U.S., 1937. *Dir.* David Hand. 82 min., Technicolor. Walt Disney.

Solaris. U.S.S.R., 1972. *Dir.* Andrei Tarkovsky. 165 min., color. Mosfilm/Magna. V.

Soldier Blue. U.S., 1970. *Dir.* Ralph Nelson. 114 min., Technicolor, Panavision. Avco. V.

Sole ("Sun"). Italy, 1929. *Dir.* Alessandro Blasetti. 99 min., b/w, silent. S.A. Augustus.

Soleil Ô (O Sun). Mauritania, 1970. *Dir.* Med Hondo. 105 min., b/w. Shango Productions.

Some Came Running. U.S., 1959. *Dir.* Vincente Minnelli. 136 min., Metrocolor, CinemaScope. Metro-Goldwyn-Mayer/Sol C. Siegel. V, LD.

Some Like It Hot. U.S., 1959. *Dir.* Billy Wilder. 122 min., b/w. United Artists/Mirisch. V, LD.

Sommarnattens Leende (Smiles of a Summer Night). Sweden, 1955. *Dir.* Ingmar Bergman. 105 min., b/w. Svensk Filmindustri. V, LD.

Song of Ceylon. Britain, 1934. *Dir.* Basil Wright. 40 min., b/w. Ceylon Tea Board.

Sortie de l'Usine Lumière à Lyon, La (Workers Leaving the Lumière Factory). France, 1895. *Dir.* Louis Lumière. 40 sec., b/w, silent. Société Lumière.

Sound of Music, The. U.S., 1965. *Dir.* Robert Wise. 172 min., De Luxe. 20th Century-Fox/Argyle. V, LD.

Souriante Madame Beudet, La (The Smiling Madame Beudet). France, 1923. *Dir.* Germaine Dulac. 32 min., b/w, silent. Film d'Art/Vandal/Dulac-Aubert.

Sous les toits de Paris (Under the Roofs of Paris). France, 1930. *Dir.* René Clair. 92 min., b/w. Tobis. V.

Spacehunter: Adventures in the Forbidden Zone. U.S., 1983. *Dir.* Lamont Johnson. 90 min., Metrocolor 3-D. Columbia/Delphi. V, LD.

Spanish Earth, The. U.S., 1937. *Dir.* Joris Ivens. 53 min., b/w. Contemporary Historians Inc.

Sparrows. U.S., 1926. *Dir.* William Beaudine. 90 min., b/w, silent. Pickford Corp. Mary Pickford. V, LD.

Spartaco (Spartacus). Italy, 1913. *Dir.* Giovanni Enrico Vidali. 89 min., b/w, silent. Pasquali e C.

Spartacus. U.S., 1960. *Dir.* Stanley Kubrick. 196 min., color, SuperTechnorama 70. Universal-International/Bryna. V, LD.

Speaking Parts. Canada, 1989. *Dir.* Atom Egoyan. 92 min., color. Ego Film Arts. V, LD.

Spellbound. U.S., 1945. *Dir.* Alfred Hitchcock. 111 min., b/w. United Artists. V, LD.

Spinnen, Die (The Spiders). Germany, 1919–20. *Dir.* Fritz Lang. Part I: *Der Goldene See (The Golden Sea)*, 69 min., b/w, silent; Part II: *Das Brillantenschiff (The Diamond Ship)*, 81 min., b/w, silent. Decla-Film Ges. V, LD.

Stachke (The Strike). U.S.S.R., 1925. *Dir.* Sergei Eisenstein. 82 min., b/w, silent. Goskino. V.

Stagecoach. U.S., 1939. *Dir.* John Ford. 95 min., b/w. United Artists. V, LD.

Star Is Born, A. U.S., 1937. *Dir.* William Wellman. 111 min., b/w. Selznick/United Artists. V, LD.

Staroe i novoe (The Old and the New, aka *The General Line).* U.S.S.R., 1929. *Dir.* Sergei Eisenstein. 90 min., b/w, silent. Sovkino.

Star Trek: The Motion Picture. U.S., 1979. *Dir.* Robert Wise. 132 min., Metrocolor, Panavision. Paramount. V, LD.

Star Wars. U.S., 1977. *Dir.* George Lucas. 121 min., Technicolor, Panavision. 20th Century-Fox/Lucasfilm. V, LD.

Stazione Termini (Indiscretion of an American Wife). Italy/U.S., 1953. *Dir.* Vittorio De Sica. 75 min., b/w. David O. Selznick. V.

Steamboat Willie. U.S., 1928. *Dir.* Ub Iwerks. 8 min., b/w. Disney.

Story of the Kelly Gang, The. Australia, 1906. *Dir.* Charles Tait. 59 min., b/w, silent. J. and N. Tait.

strada, La. Italy, 1954. *Dir.* Federico Fellini. 115 min., b/w. Trans-Lux. V, LD.

Stranger Than Paradise. U.S., 1984. *Dir.* Jim Jarmusch. 95 min., b/w. Goldwyn/ZDF. V, LD.

Struktura krysztalu (The Structure of Crystals). Poland, 1969. *Dir.* Krzysztof Zanussi. 137 min., b/w. Tor Film Unit.

Student von Prag, Der (The Student of Prague). Germany, 1926. *Dir.* Henrik Galeen. 116 min., b/w, silent. H.R. Sokal-Film.

Sugarland Express, The. U.S., 1974. *Dir.* Steven Spielberg. 110 min., Technicolor, Panavision. Universal. V.

Sugata Sanshiro (Sanshiro Sugata). Japan, 1943. *Dir.* Akira Kurosawa. 80 min., b/w. Toho. V.

Sunny Side Up. U.S., 1929. *Dir.* David Butler. 80 min, b/w and Multicolor. Fox. LD.

Sunrise. U.S., 1927. *Dir.* F.W. Murnau. 95 min., b/w, musical score. Fox. V.

Sunset Boulevard. U.S., 1950. *Dir.* Billy Wilder. 110 min., b/w. Paramount. V, LD.

Superman. U.S./Britain, 1978. *Dir.* Richard Donner. 142 min., color, Panavision. Warner Bros./Alexander Salkind. V, LD.

Sweet Sweetback's Bad Asssss Song. U.S., 1971. *Dir.* Melvin Van Peebles. 97 min., color. Van Peebles.

Swing Time. U.S., 1936. *Dir.* George Stevens. 103 min., b/w. RKO. V, LD.

Tampopo. Japan, 1986. *Dir.* Juzo Itami. 117 min., color. Itami Productions/New Century Producers. V, LD.

Tascones lejanos (High Heels). Spain/France, 1991. *Dir.* Pedro Almodóvar. 112 min., color. El Deseo/CiBy 2000. V.

Taxi Driver. U.S., 1976. *Dir.* Martin Scorsese. 114 min., Metrocolor. Columbia/Italo-Judeo. V, LD.

"Teddy" Bears, The. U.S., 1907. *Dir.* Edwin S. Porter. 15 min., b/w, silent. Edison Co.

Temptress, The. U.S., 1926. *Dir.* Mauritz Stiller. 80 min., b/w, silent. Metro-Goldwyn-Mayer.

Ten Commandments, The. U.S., 1923. *Dir.* Cecil B. DeMille. 160 min., b/w, silent. Paramount. V

Teni zabytykh predkov (Shadows of Forgotten Ancestors). U.S.S.R., 1964. *Dir.* Sergei Paradjanov. 100 min., color. Dovzhenko Studio. V.

Terminator, The. U.S., 1984. *Dir.* James Cameron. 108 min., CFI color. Orion/Hemdale/Pacific Western. V, LD.

Terra em transe (Land of Anguish, aka *Earth Entranced).* Brazil, 1967. *Dir.* Glauber Rocha. 115 min., b/w. Ramon Acin. V.

Terra madre ("Mother Earth"). Italy, 1930. *Dir.* Alessandro Blasetti. 90 min., b/w. Cines-Pittaluga.

terra trema, La (The Earth Trembles). Italy, 1948. *Dir.* Luchino Visconti. 160 min., b/w. Universalia.

Tess of the Storm Country. U.S., 1922. *Dir.* John S. Robertson. 143 min., b/w, silent. Mary Pickford Co.

Testament des Dr. Mabuse, Das (The Last Will of Dr. Mabuse). Germany, 1933. *Dir.* Fritz Lang. 122 min., b/w. Nero. V.

tetto, Il (The Roof). Italy, 1956. *Dir.* Vittorio De Sica.

101 min., b/w. Titanus/Les Films Marceau.

Thaïs. Italy, 1917. *Dir.* Anton Giulio Bragaglia and Riccardo Cassano. 70 min., b/w, silent. Novissima Film.

Thelma and Louise. U.S., 1991. *Dir.* Ridley Scott. 128 min., color. Percy Main Productions. V, LD.

Them! U.S., 1954. *Dir.* Gordon Douglas. 94 min., b/w. Warner Bros. V, LD.

They Live by Night. U.S., 1948. *Dir.* Nicholas Ray. 96 min., b/w. RKO. V, LD.

Thief of Bagdad, The. U.S., 1924. *Dir.* Raoul Walsh. 138 min., b/w, silent. Douglas Fairbanks Pictures. V, LD.

Thin Blue Line, The. U.S., 1988. *Dir.* Errol Morris. 101 min., DuArt color. British Film Institute/Third Floor/American Playhouse. V, LD.

Third Man, The. Britain, 1949. *Dir.* Carol Reed. 93 min., b/w. London. V, LD.

Thirteen Most Beautiful Boys, The. U.S., 1965. *Dir.* Andy Warhol. 40 min., b/w, silent.

Thirteen Most Beautiful Women, The. U.S., 1964. *Dir.* Andy Warhol. 40 min., b/w, silent.

39 Steps, The. Britain, 1935. *Dir.* Alfred Hitchcock. 86 min., b/w. Gaumont-British. V, LD.

This Is Cinerama. U.S., 1952. Produced by Thomas-Merian C. Cooper and Robert L. Bendick. 120 min., b/w and color. Thomas-Merian C. Cooper Production.

Three Musketeers, The. U.S., 1921. *Dir.* Fred Niblo. 140 min., b/w, silent. Douglas Fairbanks Pictures/United Artists.

Three-Must-Get-Theres, The. U.S., 1922. *Dir.* Max Linder. 50 min., b/w, silent. Max Linder Productions.

Thriller. Britain, 1979. *Dir.* Sally Potter. 33 min., b/w. Sally Potter/Arts Council of Great Britain.

THX-1138. U.S., 1971. *Dir.* George Lucas. 95 min., Technicolor, CinemaScope. Warner Bros./American Zoetrope. V, LD.

Tianyushan Chuangi (The Legend of Tianyun Mountain). China, 1980. *Dir.* Xie Jin. 127 min., color. Shanghai Film Studio.

Tilai. Burkina Faso/Switzerland/France, 1990. *Dir.* Idrissa Ouedraogo. 81 min., color. Les Films de l'avenir/Waka Films/Rhea Films.

Tillie's Punctured Romance. U.S., 1914. *Dir.* Mack Sennett. 66 min., b/w, silent. Keystone Film Company.

Time Machine, The. U.S., 1960. *Dir.* George Pal. 103 min., Metrocolor. Metro-Goldwyn-Mayer/Galaxy. V, LD.

Tirez sur le pianiste (Shoot the Piano Player). France, 1960. *Dir.* François Truffaut. 80 min., b/w. Films de la Pléiade. V, LD.

Titicut Follies. U.S., 1967. *Dir.* Frederick Wiseman. 85 min., b/w. Bridgewater Film Productions.

To Have and Have Not. U.S., 1944. *Dir.* Howard Hawks. 100 min., b/w. Warner Bros. V, LD.

Tokyo Monogatari (Tokyo Story). Japan, 1953. *Dir.* Yasujiro Ozu. 136 min., b/w. Shochiku. V.

Tokyo Orimpikku (Tokyo Olympiad). Japan, 1965. *Dir.* Kon Ichikawa. 130 min., color. Toho. V, LD.

Tom Jones. Britain, 1963. *Dir.* Tony Richardson. 129 min., Eastmancolor. United Artists/Woodfall. V, LD.

Tongnian Wangshi (The Time to Live and the Time to Die). Taiwan, 1985. *Dir.* Hou Hsiao-hsien. 137 min., color. Central Motion Picture Corporation—Taipei.

Top Hat. U.S., 1935. *Dir.* Mark Sandrich. 101 min., b/w. RKO. V, LD.

Topio stin omlichi (Landscape in the Mist). Greece, 1988. *Dir.* Theo Angelopoulos. 125 min., color. Greek Film Centre/Greek Television/Paradis Film/RAI.

Tora no O o Fumu Otokatachi (The Man Who Tread on the Tiger's Tail). Japan, 1952. *Dir.* Akira Kurosawa. 58 min., b/w. Toho Film.

Touben Nuhai (Boat People). Hong Kong, 1982. *Dir.* Ann Hui. 106 min., color. Bluebird

Movie Enterprises.

Touch of Evil. U.S., 1958. *Dir.* Orson Welles. 95 min., b/w. Universal-International. V, LD.

Trafic (Traffic). France, 1970. *Dir.* Jacques Tati. 96 min., color. Corona/Gibe/Selenia.

Trance and Dance in Bali. U.S., 1952. *Dir.* Gregory Bateson and Margaret Mead. 20 min., b/w.

Traversée de Paris, La (Four Bags Full). France/Italy, 1956. *Dir.* Claude Autant-Lara. 90 min., b/w. Franco-London-Continentale.

Travolti da un insolito destino nell'azzurro mare d'agosto (Swept Away). Italy, 1974. *Dir.* Lina Wertmüller. 120 min., color. Medusa Cinematografica. V, LD.

Tret'ya Meshchanskaya (Bed and Sofa). U.S.S.R., 1927. *Dir.* Abram Room. 115 min., b/w, silent. Sovkino. V.

Triumph des Willens (Triumph of the Will). Germany, 1935. *Dir.* Leni Riefenstahl. 120 min., b/w. NSDAP. V.

Trois Couronnes du matelot, Le (Three Crowns of the Sailor). France, 1982. *Dir.* Raúl Ruiz. 117 min., b/w and color. Société du Cinéma du Panthéon/INA/Antenne 2.

Trouble in Paradise. U.S., 1932. *Dir.* Ernst Lubitsch. 81 min., b/w. Paramount.

Tulitikkutehtaan Tytto (The Match Factory Girl). Finland/Sweden, 1989. *Dir.* Aki Kaurismäki. 70 min., Eastmancolor. Electric Pictures/Swedish Film Institute/Villealfa/Aki Kaurismäki.

Tüzoltó utca 25 (25 Fireman's Street). Hungary, 1973. *Dir.* István Szabó. 97 min., color. Budapest Studio. V.

Tva Manniskor (Two People). Denmark, 1945. *Dir.* Carl Th. Dreyer. 78 min., b/w. Svensk Filmindustri.

20,000 Leagues under the Sea. U.S., 1954. *Dir.* Richard Fleischer. 122 min., Technicolor, CinemaScope. Walt Disney. V, LD.

Twin Peaks: Fire Walk with Me. U.S., 1992. *Dir.* David Lynch. 134 min., color. Twin Peaks Productions. V, LD.

Twins. U.S., 1988. *Dir.* Ivan Reitman. 112 min., color. Universal. V, LD.

2001: A Space Odyssey. Britain, 1968. *Dir.* Stanley Kubrick. 141 min., Metrocolor, Panavision. Metro-Goldwyn-Mayer/Stanley Kubrick. V, LD.

Ugetsu Monogatari (Ugetsu). Japan, 1953. *Dir.* Kenji Mizoguchi. 96 min., b/w. Daiei. V.

Ultimo tango a Parigi (Last Tango in Paris). France/Italy/U.S., 1972. *Dir.* Bernardo Bertolucci. 129 min., Technicolor. Les Artistes Associés/PEA/United Artists. V, LD.

Umarate wa mita keredo (I Was Born, But . . .). Japan, 1932. *Dir.* Yasujiro Ozu. 100 min., b/w, silent. Shochiku/Kamata.

Umberto D.. Italy, 1952. *Dir.* Vittorio De Sica. 89 min., b/w. Dear Films. V, LD.

Uncle Josh at the Moving Picture Show. U.S., 1902. *Dir.* Edwin S. Porter. 2 min., b/w, silent. Edison Co.

Uncle Tom's Cabin. U.S., 1903. *Dir.* Edwin S. Porter. 16 min., b/w, silent. Edison Co.

Underworld. U.S., 1927. *Dir.* Josef von Sternberg. 80 min., b/w, silent. Paramount Famous Lasky Corp.

Unemployment Special. U.S., 1931. Photographed by Robert Del Duca and Leo Seltzer. 7 min., b/w, silent. Film and Photo League.

Unforgiven. U.S., 1992. *Dir.* Clint Eastwood. 130 min., Technicolor, Panavision. Malpaso.

Unsere Afrikariese (Our Trip to Africa). Austria, 1966. *Dir.* Peter Kubelka. 12.5 min., color.

Unsichtbare Gegner (Invisible Adversaries). Austria, 1978. *Dir.* Valie Export. 109 min., color. Valie Export. V.

Untouchables, The. U.S., 1987. *Dir.* Brian DePalma. 119 min., color. Linson/Paramount. V, LD.

uomo della croce, L' (The Man on the Cross). Italy, 1943. *Dir.* Roberto Rossellini. 88 min., b/w. Continentalcine.

Vacances de Monsieur Hulot, Les (Mr. Hulot's Holi-

day). France, 1953. *Dir.* Jacques Tati. 91 min., b/w. Cady/Discina. V, LD.

Valehtelija (The Liar). Finland, 1980. *Dir.* Mika Kaurismäki.

Valley Girl. U.S., 1983. *Dir.* Martha Coolidge. 95 min., color. Atlantic. V, LD.

Valley Town. U.S., 1940. *Dir.* Willard Van Dyke. 35 min., b/w.

Vampires, Les. France, 1915-16. *Dir.* Louis Feuillade. 10-part series, each c. 40 min., b/w, silent. 1. La *Tête coupée* ; 2. *La Bacque qui Tue*; 3. *Le Cryp-togramme*; 4. *Le Spectre*; 5. *L'Evasion du mort*; 6. *Le Yeux qui fascinent*; 7. *Santanas*; 8. *Le Maître de la foudre*; 9. *L'Homme des poisons*; 10. *Les Noces sanglantes.* Gaumont.

Vampyr (Vampire). France/Germany, 1932. *Dir.* Carl Th. Dreyer. 83 min., b/w. Tobis Klangfilm/Carl Dreyer. V.

Variété (Variety, aka *Vaudeville).* Germany, 1925. *Dir.* E.A. Dupont. 104 min., b/w, silent. Ufa.

Variety. U.S., 1983. *Dir.* Bette Gordon. 100 min., color. Horizon. V.

Venice, Florida. U.S., 1981. *Dir.* Errol Morris.

Vertigo. U.S., 1958. *Dir.* Alfred Hitchcock. 128 min., Technicolor, Vistavision. Paramount. V, LD.

V for Victory. Canada, 1941. *Dir.* Norman McLaren. 2 min., color. National Film Board.

Vidas Secas (Barren Lives). Brazil, 1963. *Dir.* Nelson Pereira Dos Santos. 135 min., b/w. Richers/Barreto/Trelles.

Vie de Boheme, La. Finland, 1992. *Dir.* Aki Kaurismäki. 100 min., b/w. Sputnik Oy/Pyramide Productions/Films A2/The Swedish Film Institute/Pandora Film GmbH.

Vie est à nous, La (Life is Ours, aka *People of France).* France, 1936. *Dir.* Jean Renoir, Jean-Paul Le Chanois, Jacques B. Brunius, Jacques Becker. 62 min., b/w. Partie Communiste Français.

Vietnam! Vietnam!. U.S., 1972. *Dir.* Sherman Beck. 58 min., Eastmancolor. United States Information Agency.

Virus kennt keine Moral, Ein (A Virus Knows No Morals). West Germany, 1989. *Dir.* Rosa von Praunheim. 82 min., color. V.

Vivere in pace (To Live in Peace). Italy, 1947. *Dir.* Luigi Zampa. 80 min., b/w. Lux-Pao.

Volga-Volga. U.S.S.R., 1938. *Dir.* Grigori Alexandrov. 102 min., b/w. Mosfilm.

Voyage dans la lune, Le (A Trip to the Moon). France, 1902. *Dir.* Georges Méliès. 11 min., b/w, silent. Star-Film.

Vredens Dag (Day of Wrath). Denmark, 1943. *Dir.* Carl Th. Dreyer. 105 min., b/w. Palladium. V.

Waiting for Fidel. Canada, 1974. *Dir.* Michael Rubbo. 58 min., color. National Film Board.

War Comes to America. U.S., 1945. *Dir.* Anatole Litvak. 67 min., b/w. Army Pictorial Services.

War Game, The. Britain, 1965. *Dir.* Peter Watkins. 50 min., b/w. BBC-TV. V.

War of the Worlds, The. U.S., 1953. *Dir.* Byron Haskin. 85 min., Technicolor. Paramount/George Pal. V.

Watermelon Man. U.S., 1970. *Dir.* Melvin Van Peebles. 100 min., Technicolor. Columbia/Johanna. V, LD.

Wavelength. U.S., 1967. *Dir.* Michael Snow. 45 min., color.

Way Down East. U.S., 1920. *Dir.* D.W. Griffith. 107 min., b/w, silent. D.W. Griffith, Inc. V.

Way of All Flesh, The. U.S., 1927. *Dir.* Victor Fleming. 90 min., b/w, silent. Paramount.

Wedding March, The. U.S., 1928. *Dir.* Erich von Stroheim. 196 min., b/w and Technicolor segments, musical score and sound effects. Paramount/Celebrity. V.

Weekend. France, 1968. *Dir.* Jean-Luc Godard. 105 min., color. Lira/Comacico/Copernic/Ascot Cineraid. V.

West Indies. France, 1979. *Dir.* Med Hondo. 110 min., color.

West Side Story. U.S., 1961. *Dir.* Robert Wise. 155 min., Technicolor, Panavision 70. United Artists. V, LD.

When Worlds Collide. U.S., 1951. *Dir.* Rudolph Maté. 82 min., Technicolor. Paramount. V, LD.

Why Change Your Wife?. U.S., 1920. *Dir.* Cecil B. DeMille. 70 min., b/w, silent. Famous Players-Lasky.

Why Viet-nam. U.S., 1965. Directorate for Armed Forces Information and Education. 25 min., color. U.S. Department of Defense.

Wild and Woolly. U.S., 1917. *Dir.* John Emerson. 67 min., b/w, silent. Douglas Fairbanks Pictures.

Wild at Heart. U.S., 1990. *Dir.* David Lynch. 127 min., color. Polygram/Propaganda Films. V, LD.

Wild Bunch, The. U.S., 1969. *Dir.* Sam Peckinpah. 145 min., color, Panavision 70. Warner Bros./Seven Arts. V, LD.

Will Success Spoil Rock Hunter? U.S., 1957. *Dir.* Frank Tashlin. 95 min., Eastmancolor, Cinema-Scope. 20th Century-Fox.

Winchester 73. U.S., 1950. *Dir.* Anthony Mann. 92 min., b/w. Universal-International. V.

Wind, The. U.S., 1928. *Dir.* Victor Sjöström. 74 min., b/w, silent. Metro-Goldwyn-Mayer. V, LD.

Wings. U.S., 1927. *Dir.* William Wellman. 139 min., b/w and color, silent, Magnascope. Paramount. V, LD.

Wishing Ring, The. U.S., 1914. *Dir.* Maurice Tourneur. 60 min., b/w, silent. World Film Corp.

Wizard of Oz, The. U.S., 1939. *Dir.* Victor Fleming. 100 min., b/w and Technicolor. Metro-Goldwyn-Mayer. V, LD.

Woman Hungry (British title: *The Challenge*). U.S., 1931. *Dir.* Clarence Badger. 65 min., Technicolor. First National.

Woman in the Window, The. U.S., 1944. *Dir.* Fritz Lang. 90 min., b/w. RKO/International.

Woman of Affairs, A. U.S., 1929. *Dir.* Clarence Brown. 90 min., b/w. Metro-Goldwyn-Mayer. V.

Woman of Paris, A. U.S., 1923. *Dir.* Charles Chaplin. 80 min., b/w, silent. United Artists. V.

Woman Under the Influence, A. U.S., 1974. *Dir.* John Cassavetes. 146 min., color. Faces International. V.

Working Girls. U.S., 1986. *Dir.* Lizzie Borden. 90 min., color. Lizzie Borden/Alternate Current. V.

Written on the Wind. U.S., 1956. *Dir.* Douglas Sirk. 99 min., Technicolor. Universal-International. V.

Wutai jiemei (Two Stage Sisters). China, 1964. *Dir.* Xie Jin. 114 min., color. Tianma Film Studio.

Wuthering Heights. U.S., 1939. *Dir.* William Wyler. 103 min., b/w. United Artists/Goldwyn. V, LD.

Wuya yu Maque (Crows and Sparrows). China, 1949. *Dir.* Zheng Junli. 113 min., b/w. Kunlun.

Xala ("The Curse"). Senegal, 1974. *Dir.* Ousmane Sembene. 123 min., color. Films Domirêve/Société Nationale de Cinématographie.

Xiangnü Xiaoxiao (Girl from Hunan). China, 1985. *Dir.* Xie Fei and U Lan. 99 min., color, Cinema-Scope. V.

Yaaba ("Grandmother"). Burkina Faso, 1989. *Dir.* Idressa Ouedraogo. 90 min., color. Arcadia/Les Films de l'avenir/Thelma/Television Suisse Romande/ZDF/La Sept/Centre National de la Cinemagraphic/Department Federal des Affaires Etrangeres/COE.

Yanzhi Kou (Rouge). Hong Kong, 1987. *Dir.* Stanley Kwan. 98 min., color. Golden Way.

Yawar Mallku (Blood of the Condor). Bolivia, 1969. *Dir.* Jorge Sanjines. 74 min., b/w. Britainaman Limitada.

Yeelen (The Light). Mali, 1987. *Dir.* Souleymane Cissé. 106 min., color. Les Films Cissé.

Yellow Menace, The. U.S., 1916. Serial, 16 episodes. Unity Sales Corp.

Yentl. U.S., 1983. *Dir.* Barbra Streisand. 133 min., Technicolor. MGM-UA/Barwood/Ladbroke. V, LD.

Yijiang Chunshui Xiang Dong Liu (A Spring River Flows East). China, 1947. *Dir.* Cai Chusheng, Zheng Junli. 188 min., b/w. Lin Hua Film Co.

Yoidore Tenshi (Drunken Angel). Japan, 1948. *Dir.* Akira Kurosawa. 102 min., b/w. Toho.

Yol (The Way). Turkey/Switzerland, 1982. *Dir.* Serif Gören. 114 min., Fujicolor. Güney Film/Cactus Film/Maran Film/SRG/Antanne 2. V.

You Are on Indian Land. Canada, 1969. *Dir.* George Stoney. 37 min., b/w. National Film Board.

You Can't Take It with You. U.S., 1938. *Dir.* Frank Capra. 126 min., b/w. Columbia. V, LD.

Young Frankenstein. U.S., 1974. *Dir.* Mel Brooks. 108 min., b/w. 20th Century-Fox. V, LD.

Young Mr. Lincoln. U.S., 1939. *Dir.* John Ford. 101 min., b/w. 20th Century-Fox. V, LD.

Young Soul Rebels. Britain, 1991. *Dir.* Isaac Julien. 103 min., color. British Film Institute/Film 4 International/Sankofa Film and Video/La Sept/Kinowelt/Iberoamericana.

You Only Live Once. U.S., 1937. *Dir.* Fritz Lang. 86 min., b/w. United Artists. V.

Z. France, 1968. *Dir.* Constantin Costa-Gavras. 125 min., color. Reggane Films/ONCIC. V, LD.

Zelig. U.S., 1983. *Dir.* Woody Allen. 79 min., b/w and color. Orion. V, LD.

Zemlya (The Earth). U.S.S.R., 1930. *Dir.* Alexander Dovzhenko. 90 min., b/w, silent. VUFKU. V.

Zéro de conduite (Zero for Conduct). France, 1933. *Dir.* Jean Vigo. 45 min., b/w. Gaumont/Franco/Aubert. V.

Zhivoi trup (A Living Corpse). U.S.S.R., 1929. *Dir.* Fyodor Otsep. 108 min. b/w, silent. Prometheus/Mezhrabpomfilm.

Zvenigora. U.S.S.R., 1928. *Dir.* Alexander Dovzhenko. 66 min., b/w, silent. VUFKU.

554

Credits

The author and the publisher would like to thank Debra Lemonds Hannah for her assistance in picture research for the first three chapters of the book.

PHOTOGRAPH AND ILLUSTRATION CREDITS

All numbers refer to figures except where noted.

AB Svensk Filmindustri: 6.8, 6.9, 15.19, 15.21, 15.22; Courtesy of the Academy of Motion Picture Arts and Sciences: 1.25, 3.10, 3.15, 3.16, 3.34, 4.11, 4.12, 5.4, 5.5, 5.18, 5.25; Agence Christophe L.: 6.16, 15.29, 18.4, 19.4; American Museum of the Moving Image: p. 4, 8.18; AP/Wide World Photos: 14.4; Archivio fotografico enciclopedico: 2.33, 2.34, 3.7, 3.31, 3.33, 3.39, 6.12, 6.14, 6.17, 6.22, 6.25, 10.22, 10.24, 10.26, 11.23, 12.21, 12.26, 12.28, 13.4, 13.6, 13.10, 13.11, 13.14, 13.15, 13.17, 13.18, 13.20, 13.21, 13.24, 15.1, 15.2, 15.16, 15.17, 15.30, 15.35, 15.36, 19.2; Asian Cinema Vision: 24.10, 24.11; BBC/Kingston Public Library: 1.16; The Bettmann Archive: 14.5, 14.6; BFI Stills, Posters and Designs: 2.32; B'Hend & Kaufmann Archive: 4.17; John David Biggs, Courtesy of Stoney Assoc.: 11.8; Bildarchiv preussischer kulturbesitz: 10.5; The Billy Rose Theatre Collection, The New York Public Library for the Performing Arts, Astor, Lenox and Tilden Foundations: 5.6; British Film Institute: 1.13, 1.17, 1.20, 1.24, 1.27–29, 1.32, 2.1, 2.8, 2.19, 2.21, 2.30, 2.32, 3.17, 3.21, 3.29, 3.40, 4.3, 4.4, 4.6–4.9, 6.7, 6.8, 7.1, 7.14–17, 7.29, 7.30, 11.9, 11.10, 11.14, 12.14, 12.15, 23.13, 23.27; Brown Brothers: 2.24; Bundesarchiv/Filmarchiv, Berlin: 12.20; © Dick Busher: 4.16; Courtesy Centro Sperimentale di Cinematografia, Cineteca Nazionale, Rome: 10.1, 10.2; Courtesy of Professor Cheng Jihua: 10.12, 10.17; China Film Import & Export Corporation: 24.4–6, 24.8; Cineaste Magazine: 18.17, 18.21; La Cinematheque Française: 1.5, 2.20, 3.2, 3.27, 3.35, 6.15, 6.18, 8.13, 10.25, 11.2, 11.3–5, 17.8, 17.13, 17.23, 17.28, 19.1, 19.5, 19.6, 24.27; Culver Pictures: 2.26; Daiei Co., Ltd.: 15.5, 15.11–13; Dennis Davidson Associates, Inc., Public Relations: 24.14; Deutsches Filmmuseum: 1.2, 1.4, 1.6–9, 1.11, 1.12, 1.14, 1.18, 1.21, 4.15, 6.11, 8.31, 10.6, 11.22, 21.26–28; Courtesy Eastman Kodak Co., Rochester, N. Y.: 5.13; Edison National Historic Site: 1.22, 1.26, 2.11, 2.12, 2.15, 2.17; Courtesy the Estate of Jay Leyda: p. 5, 11.16; Everett Collection: 5.11, 5.24, 5.26, 5.32, 5.34, 8.21, 8.23, 8.24, 9.2, 9.6, 9.11, 9.22, 9.23, 9.30, 9.35, 11.21, 14.3, 14.10, 14.18, 14.20, 14.21, 16.19, 20.1, 20.5, 20.6; Valie Export: 23.14; Filmarchivum Fototarnak tulajdona: 21.10; Finnish Film Foundation: 24.20; Fundacion Cinemateca Argentina: 4.1, 4.2, 13.25; HNA Archive: 21.15; © 1962 Horizon Pictures (GB). All Rights Reserved. Courtesy Columbia Pictures Industries, Inc.: 21.2; Instituto Mexicano de Cinematografia: 10.13, 10.14; International Center for Photography at George Eastman House: 1.19, 2.5, 2.6, 2.10, 2.18, 2.22, 5.38, 5.42, 14.14; International Film Circuit: 24.7; Japan Film Library Council: 2.31, 7.34, 10.10, 12.23, 12.24, 18.24; Kino: 23.18; Kisch/Photofest: 3.8; The Kobal Collection: pg. 9, 3.13, 3.24, 3.28, 4.13, 5.7, 5.12, 5.30, 5.31, 5.35, 6.21, 6.29, 6.30, 7.26, 8.1, 8.11, 8.26–28, 8.30, 9.15, 9.28, 10.4, 10.7, 10.23, 10.29, 11.1, 11.11, 11.18, 11.24, 11.27, 12.9, 12.16, 12.19, 13.1, 13.3, 13.7, 13.22, 13.27, 13.28, 14.12, 14.13, 15.18, 15.33, 16.11, 16.16, 17.10, 17.12, 17.26, 17.29, 17.30, 18.6, 18.7, 18.12, 18.13, 18.22, 19.14, 20.12, 20.14, 20.16, 20.18–21, 20.23, 20.25, 20.26, 20.28, 21.13, 21.18, 21.21, 21.25, 21.29, 22.2, 22.13, 20.14, 22.23, 22.25, 22.27, 23.20, 23.22, 24.1, 24.23, 24.25; Courtesy of Kodak Corporation (Research Laboratories), Rochester, N.Y.: 8.2, 8.3; Library of Congress: 2.4, 2.9; Los Angeles Library: 1.15; © Lucasfilm Ltd: 22.6–7 (photos: Kerry Nordquist), 22.9, 22.37; Magyar Filmintezet: 21.7, 21.8; Courtesy of M-G-M, Turner Entertainment: 9.26; Courtesy of Miramax: 23.28; Museum of Modern Art/Film Stills Archive: p. 8, 2.2, 2.28, 3.26, 3.32, 3.42, 4.10, 4.22, 4.23, 5.16, 5.17, 5.22, 6.2, 6.13, 6.19, 6.28, 6.31, 6.32, 7.2–13, 7.18–25, 7.27, 7.28, 7.31–33, 8.6, 8.29, 9.16, 9.37, 9.38, 10.8, 10.21, 10.27, 10.28, 11.6, 11.12, 11.15, 11.19, 11.20, 11.25, 11.26, 11.29–31, 12.7, 12.8, 12.11, 12.12, 12.19, 12.22, 12.25, 12.27, 15.7, 15.9, 15.10, 15.14, 15.15, 15.23–25, 15.27, 15.28, 16.2, 16.6, 17.4, 17.7, 18.10, 18.16, 18.18–20, 18.23, 18.25, 18.26, 19.2, 19.16–18, 19.20, 21.1, 21.9, 21.12, 21.17, 21.24, 21.30, 22.28, 23.1, 23.2, 23.4, 23.5, 23.7, 23.9, 23.12, 23.21, 24.16; Charles Musser: 1.23, 2.4, 2.9, 2.11, 2.12, 2.15; National Film Archive of India: 15.26, 24.15; National Film Board of Canada: 19.23; New Yorker Films: 24.29, 24.30; Courtesy of Pennebaker Assoc.: 19.7–11; Photo: Umberto Montiroli/Archivio fotografico enciclopedico: 13.29, 21.22; Photo: Richard Todd—Collection Howard Boyle: 20.2; Photo: Mario Tursi/Archivio fotografico enciclopedico: 13.19; Photofest: pp. 6, 7, 10–11, 12–13; 2.7, 2.13, 2.14, 3.6, 3.9, 3.11, 3.14, 3.30, 3.36, 4.18, 5.15, 5.20, 5.21, 5.23, 5.28, 5.37, 5.39, 5.40, 6.1, 6.3–5, 6.20, 6.23, 6.24, 6.26, 6.27, 6.33, 6.34, 8.4, 8.9, 8.12, 8.15, 8.16, 8.20, 8.22, 8.25, 8.32–34, 9.1, 9.3, 9.5, 9.7–10, 9.12–14, 9.17–21, 9.24, 9.25, 9.27, 9.29, 9.31, 9.32, 9.36, 10.3, 10.11, 10.18, 11.28, 12.1–6, 12.10, 12.17, 13.8, 13.9, 13.12, 13.13, 13.16, 13.23, 13.26, 13.30, 14.2, 14.7–9, 14.11, 14.15–17, 14.19, 14.22–32, 15.3, 15.6, 15.7, 15.20, 15.31, 15.32, 16.1, 16.3–5, 16.7–10, 16.12, 16.15, 16.17, 16.18, 16.21–34, 17.1–3, 17.6, 17.9, 17.11, 17.14–17, 17.19–22, 17.24, 17.25, 17.31, 18.1, 18.6, 18.8, 18.9, 18.11, 18.14, 18.15, 18.27, 19.12, 19.13, 19.19, 19.21, 19.22, 20.3, 20.4, 20.7–10, 20.13, 20.15, 20.17, 20.22, 20.24, 20.27, 20.29–31, 21.3, 21.4, 21.6, 21.11, 21.14, 21.19, 21.20, 21.23, 21.25, 22.1, 22.3, 22.4, 22.6, 22.10–12, 22.15–18, 22.20–22, 22.24, 22.26, 22.29–32, 22.34–36, 22.40, 22.41, 23.3, 23.6, 23.8, 23.10, 23.16, 23.17, 23.23–26, 24.3, 24.12, 24.13, 24.17–19, 24.21, 24.22, 24.24, 24.28; Photofest/Jagerts: 20.11, photograph by Maurice Schell: 17.27; Yvonne Rainer: 23.15; Royal FilmArchive, Belgium: 11.17, 23.11; V. Sazmiento: 23.19; Leo Selzter: 11.13; © Sam Shaw: 22.05; Soviet Photo Agency: 11.16; State Historical Society of Wisconsin: 1.30, 3.12, 10.15, 10.16; Stiftung Deutsche Kinemathek: 2.3, 2.27, 3.41; Courtesy of Stoney Assoc.: 11.7; UPI/Bettmann: 15.34; USC Cinema-Television Library: 3.43, 16.20; Jerry Vermilye: 4.14, 10.19, 10.20, 12.2, 13.2, 13.5, 15.4, 16.13, 16.14, 17.5, 17.18, 21.5, 21.16, 24.2; © The Walt Disney Co.: 8.5, 9.33, 9.34, 22.39; Marc Wanamaker/Bison Archives: 2.16, 2.25, 3.18, 3.19, 3.23, 3.25, 3.37, 4.19–21, 5.1–3, 5.8–10, 5.14, 5.19, 5.27, 5.29, 5.36, 8.10, 8.17; Wisconsin Center for Film and Theater Research: pp. 2–3, 2.23, 2.29, 3.1, 3.3, 3.4, 3.20, 3.22, 3.38; From The World Book Encyclopedia: © 1992 World Book, Inc. By permission of the publisher: 8.19; Allen Zindman: 22.38; Zipporah Films, Inc.: 19.15.

FILM CREDITS

5.11, 5.12: *Foolish Wives* Copyright © 1921 by Universal City Studios, Inc. Courtesy of MCA Publishing Rights, a Division of MCA Inc. 5.15: *Greed* © 1924 Turner Entertainment Co. All Rights Reserved. 5.16, 5.17: *Queen Kelly* Kino International Corporation. 5.21: *The Sheik* Copyright © 1928 Renewed 1948 by Paramount Pictures Corporation. All Rights Reserved. Courtesy of Paramount Pictures. 5.23: *The Gold Rush* Chaplin Films © and property of Roy Export Company Establishment. 5.25: Courtesy of Turner Entertainment Co. 5.28: *Smouldering Fires* Copyright © 1928 by Universal City Studios, Inc. Courtesy of MCA Publishing Rights, a Division of MCA, Inc. 5.30, 5.31: *Flesh and the Devil* © 1927 Turner Entertainment Co. All Rights Reserved. 5.33: *The Big Parade* © 1925 Turner Entertainment Co. All Rights Reserved. 5.34: *Phantom of the Opera* 1925, Copyright © by Universal City Studios, Inc. Courtesy of MCA Publishing Rights, a Division of MCA, Inc. 5.37: *Underworld* Copyright © 1927 Renewed 1954 by Paramount Pictures Corporation. All Rights Reserved. Courtesy of Paramount Pictures. 5.38: *Body and Soul* © 1927 Turner Entertainment Co. All Rights Reserved. 5.40: *Moana* Copyright © 1926 Paramount Pictures Corporation. All Rights Reserved. 5.41: *The Crowd* © 1928 Turner Entertainment Co. All Rights Reserved.

6.2: *Dr. Mabuse, der Spieler* © UFA. 6.5: *Der letzte Mann* © Ufa Films, Inc. 6.8: *Gösta Berlings Saga* © AB Svensk Filmindustri. 6.9: *The Phantom Chariot* © AB Svensk Filmindustri. 6.10, 6.11: *Variété* © UFA Films, Inc. (Germany). 6.14: *La Roue* © Pathé. 6.21–6.26: *Metropolis* © Foremco (Germany). 6.27: *Die freudlose Gasse* © UFA Films, Inc. (Germany). 6.29: *Die Liebe der Jeanne Ney* © UFA Films, Inc. (Germany). 6.30: Still from the film *The Lodger* courtesy of The Rank Organisation Plc. 6.31, 6.32: *La Passion de Jeanne d'Arc* © Societe Generale des Films. 6.33, 6.34: *Un Chien andalou* © Les Grands Films Classiques, Paris, France.

7.16: *Fall of the Romanov Dynasty* © 1991 Kino International Corp.

8.5: *Steamboat Willie* © The Walt Disney Company. 8.6: *The Big Trail* © 1930 Twentieth Century-Fox Film Corp. All Rights Reserved. 8.9: *Napoléon* Copyright © 1980 The Images Film Archive, Inc. All rights reserved. 8.10, 8.11: *Wings* Copyright © 1927 Paramount Pictures Corporation. All Rights Reserved. 8.12, 8.13: *Sunrise* © 1927 Twentieth Century-Fox Film Corporation. All Rights Reserved. 8.14: *The Wind* © 1928 Turner Entertainment Co. All Rights Reserved. 8.15: *The Kiss* © 1929 Turner Entertainment Co. All Rights Reserved. 8.16, 18.17: *The Jazz Singer* © 1927 Turner Entertainment Co. All Rights Reserved. 8.20: *Lights of New York* © 1928 Turner Entertainment Co. All Rights Reserved. 8.22: *Anna Christie* © 1930 Turner Entertainment Co. All Rights Reserved. 8.25: *Applause* 1929, Copyright © by Universal City Studios, Inc. Courtesy of MCA Publishing Rights, a Division of MCA, Inc. 8.26–8.28: *Hallelujah!* © 1929 Turner Entertainment Co. All Rights Reserved. 8.29: *Blackmail* British International Pictures & Kartes Video Communications, Dist. 8.30: *The Blue Angel* 1930, UFA (Germany). 8.32, 8.33: *M* © Foremco Pictures Corp. and Nassau Films, Inc.

9.1: *Scarface* Thorn-E.M.I. 9.2: *The Public Enemy* © 1931 Turner Entertainment Co. All Rights Reserved. 9.3: *Dracula* 1931, Copyright © by Universal City Studios, Inc. Courtesy of MCA